Taking a

Gap
Year

Taking a
Gap
Year

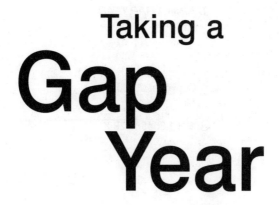

Susan Griffith

**Distributed in the USA by
The Globe Pequot Press, Guilford, Connecticut**

**Published by Vacation Work, 9 Park End Street, Oxford
www.vacationwork.co.uk**

First published 1999
Revised every other year
Fourth edition 2005

TAKING A GAP YEAR
by Susan Griffith

ISBN 1 85458 328 X

Cover design by mccdesign ltd

Text design and typesetting by Brendan Cole

Illustrations by John Taylor

Publicity: Charlie Cutting

Printed and bound in Italy by Legoprint SpA, Trento

Contents

PART I – PREPARATION

PART II – GAP YEAR PLACEMENTS

PART III – COUNTRY BY COUNTRY

Europe

PART IV – APPENDICES

Acknowledgments

This fourth edition of *Taking a Gap Year* would not have been possible without the help of many gap year students, year out organisations and an army of travel informants who have generously shared their information and stories by letter, email, telephone and, in a few cases, down the pub.

Hannah Adcock *(France, Greece)*
Roger Blake *(Australia, New Zealand)*
David Breckenridge *(Tanzania)*
Catharine Carfoot *(Spain)*
Nikki D'Arcy *(Peru)*
Ed Fry *(Australia, Mexico)*
Debra Fuccio *(Italy)*
Claire Gunn *(Swaziland)*
Mike Jarvis *(India)*
Joe Keely *(Tanzania)*
Keith Leishman *(France)*
Naomi Lisney *(China)*
Kathryn Lydon *(Japan)*
Sam Martell *(Australia)*

Lucy Mills *(Ghana)*
Alice Mundy *(Canada)*
Richard New *(Sri Lanka)*
James Nibloe *(Austria)*
Alex Nice *(Russia)*
Joe Philp *(Togo)*
Frances Pountain *(France, Costa Rica)*
Mark Ramsden *(Belize & Guatemala)*
Emily Reardon *(Greece)*
Damien Rickwood *(Belize & Guatemala)*
Tom Saunders *(Costa Rica)*
Katherine Shirtcliffe *(Peru)*
Rebecca Udy *(Italy)*
Kate Wilkins *(France)*

Preface

For a few anxious moments, the introduction of top-up fees made the gap year look wounded, if not dying. The prospect of a huge increase in tuition fees forced many pre-university students to consider putting aside their dreams of taking a year off, in a bid to avoid paying the excess. However the government relented at the eleventh hour and deferred the increase until 2006. Basically anyone reading this book who is going on to higher education will have no choice but to pay top-up fees, whether or not they take a gap year. And whether or not they take a gap year, most students will leave university carrying a great deal of debt. You may decide that it doesn't matter all that much whether you start paying back the debt in, say, 2012 or 2013 (i.e. the year you start earning more than £15,000). Most adults live with long-term debt in the form of a mortgage, and (leaving aside market fluctuations) don't lose or gain much by buying a house this year or next. Similarly, the decision to take a year off before (or after) university will not have significant long-term financial implications. Students along with the many companies that provide packaged gap years can again breathe easily now that the fee situation has sorted itself out.

Young people approaching the end of school or university are uniquely privileged to be able to contemplate taking a year off before going on to the next phase of their lives. It is an opportunity that is unlikely to be repeated. The number of school leavers opting to take a year out continues to rise steadily, reflecting the ongoing democratisation of the gap year. Gap years have acquired so much status and respectability that the British government and UCAS officially endorse them and royal princes opt for them.

Most gap years comprise a medley of activities which complement one another, work and play, earning and spending, challenge and self-indulgence, worthiness and fun. Fortunately the rising popularity of taking a year out has prompted a dramatic increase in the number of programmes and schemes targeted at young people. The path to exciting and memorable gap year experiences whether in Argyll or Argentina (but probably not Argos) may be smoother than you think. The range of choices open to young people these days is astonishing. (If your parents express envy of your gap year, why not give them a copy of our sister volume *Gap Years for Grown-ups* for Christmas?)

This book aims to canvas the possibilities comprehensively, and covers a wealth of both mainstream and obscure options. While browsing through its pages you will find detailed descriptions of the integrated programmes offered by gap year specialist organisations in all the continents of the world. The older I get or, more to the point, the closer my children get to the gap year age, the more impressed I am with the services provided by the scores of charities and companies that can help 18 year olds to arrange exciting and fulfilling experiences as part of a gap year. In these pages you may stumble across never dreamed-of possibilities like a film-making course in New York, apple picking in New Zealand, reef-monitoring in Madagascar, interning in a company in Berlin, teaching in a Tamil school in Sri Lanka, work experience with the BBC or Shakespeare's Globe, ranching in Uruguay, project work with Bedouins, helping at an orphanage in Russia, learning Spanish in Guatemala. The amazing thing is that the vast majority of these opportunities are open to everyone.

In reply to those who still feel some knee-jerk resistance to the idea of 'interrupting' an education to take a year out, I would say that education consists of so much more than book-learning and exam grades. Views of education are changing and nowadays emphasis is placed on educating the 'whole person,' by attaching importance to personal and social as well as intellectual development. This is what a good gap year can achieve so effortlessly. Never mind the dewy-eyed prose about the life-enriching or CV-enhancing experience of taking a gap year, the key benefits are to have a rest from studying, to experience the world of work and travel, and most of all to have fun.

Susan Griffith
Cambridge
July 2005

PART I

Preparation

Introduction

Planning & Preparation

Travel

Introduction

Deciding whether to take a year off and then how to spend it may not be as momentous as some other life decisions like getting married, having babies, choosing or changing careers, but it is as individual. No book or even trusted adviser can make the decision for you. All that outsiders can do is set out the possibilities and see if any of them takes your fancy enough to pursue. Do as much research as possible, let the ideas swill around in your head and see what floats up.

DECIDING TO TAKE A GAP YEAR

For many young people approaching the end of school, the decision about gap years is a difficult and complex one. The first question to ask yourself is does the idea have a strong appeal? If you close your eyes and imagine yourself in the student union bar at university and then transport yourself in your imagination to a Costa Rican rainforest or a Tanzanian village school or an Italian language class, which gives you more of a buzz? Think of the bad bits. Think of yourself sitting in a college library with an essay crisis and then think of yourself swatting mosquitoes and doing some manual job in tropical heat. If the idea of striking off to some remote corner of the world, far away from family and (most likely) friends, gives you the heebie-jeebies, then maybe a gap year is not for you. You can always come back to the idea after college. What you want to avoid is spending a year hanging around waiting for something to turn up (though in some cases this also might be beneficial in sorting yourself out).

There is no doubt that it is easier to stay on the funicular that leads directly from the sixth form to higher education. After all, the majority of school leavers still do just that. Yet the number of people deferring is much higher than it used to be and an increasing number of students from a variety of social backgrounds are at least giving the idea some serious thought. Of course not every school leaver who defers is bound for exotic travels and exciting overseas projects. With the introduction of top-up fees, some students are taking a year off before higher education to work and save to support themselves, although most universities have bursaries and grants for students with financial constraints.

In many circles, taking a gap year is still considered something that only the rich and privileged do; but the explosion in the number of specialist organisations helping students to set up gap years is the result of a democratisation of the concept. Of course there are still plenty of people from top public schools and privileged backgrounds who take gap years (famously both the royal princes) but anybody who is determined and enthusiastic enough can do it.

Widening Access

In April 2005 the Labour government began depositing a lump sum of £250 for all babies born since 2002 to encourage a habit of saving for the future (see page 41). When pressed to identify concrete uses to which the money could be put when it is cashed in at age 18, a structured gap year was mentioned by several MPs, illustrating how far up the agenda the idea of taking a constructive year out between school and university has moved. Speaking on a Radio 4 programme, one MP said that the benefits derived by so many middle class school leavers from taking a gap year abroad could be extended to a broader cross section of the population. It would be disingenuous to claim that taking a gap year is open to all, since clearly anything that costs in the neighbourhood of £2000 or more is not open to all. However in this case the government is putting its money where its mouth is.

The introduction of top-up fees in 2006 will make many young people think hard about the implications of taking a gap year. Students who left school in 2005 and wanted to defer entry until September 2006 were granted a reprieve and will be allowed to pay the current tuition fees of about £1200 a year. Whether or not they take a gap year, those who leave school in 2006 will be required to pay the increased tuition fees of up to £3000 a year at most universities. Students from lower income families will still get the first £1100 of the fees paid for them. As is well known, the fees do not have to be paid back until graduates are earning more than £15,000 a year. Whatever the amount of debt, students will pay back at a fixed rate so that the only variable is the length of time. One positive difference is that upfront fees have been abolished for everyone, which in theory means that there might be more ready cash available for a gap year. The levels of debt with which students will now leave university are so horrendous (typically £20,000+) that to delay the paying back for one more year may strike you as trivial in the scheme of things.

Pros and Cons

Employers have been shown to value gap years. Some company application forms are beginning to include a question about the gap year and possibly to pay more attention to that than to your hobbies. In a report published in the spring of 2005 commissioned by the national volunteering organisation CSV, research showed that of members questioned from the Association of Graduate Recruiters, 100% believed a constructive gap year helps young people to prepare for the workplace. In total 88% thought that a well-structured gap year helped to furnish graduates with skills such as communication skills, decision-making and relationship building. In the words of a recruitment manager at the multinational company Ernst & Young, 'Travel or a year out will not in itself be a positive factor; however if the candidate can demonstrate that he or she has learnt and developed as a result of the experience this would be seen as a strength'.

According to the most recent statistics from UCAS (the Universities & Colleges Admissions Service), a record 28,727 students requested deferred entry, a massive increase of 12% over the previous two years (i.e. the lifetime of this edition). This means that approximately one in 13 university applicants defers a place for a year, a significantly higher percentage than a decade ago. The culture is changing; education is no longer seen as a linear progression without interruption. Yet universities, parents and friends often go on assuming that there is no real alternative and it is all too easy to stay on the loop, especially if none of your friends or contemporaries is planning to take time out. But it is worth stepping back at some point (preferably early on, but not necessarily) and considering alternatives. Fifteen months is a miraculous period of time in which to pursue dreams and create memories. There will of course be opportunities later in life to take a break from routine – after university, between jobs, after having a child, sabbatical leave, after retirement, etc. But the combination of freedom from responsibility and leisure time is much harder to manage later on.

The standard objections raised by the doubting Thomases of the academic and parental world go as follows:

- You'll be a year behind your friends.
- You'll lose the impetus to study (though you may lose that over the four months between A-levels and university anyway).
- You'll be seduced by travel and find it difficult to settle back into a comparatively boring routine on your return.
- You'll be seduced by the things that money can buy if you spend your year out earning

enough money to save and spend and then will find it difficult to contemplate reverting to the poverty of studenthood.

○ You'll be seduced full stop and abandon everything for love.

Your parents will be relieved to learn that the vast majority of gap year students do not lose their way. Some are changed enormously but very few bring grief to their families by cashing in their return ticket to settle in Koh Samui or Goa. The experience of working hard at a local job in order to fund a gap year experience is usually enough to persuade even those who are lukewarm about the benefits of higher education to stay on as a student for a few more years.

Whereas six months of slogging at a local chain store or pizza restaurant usually works wonders as aversion therapy, six months of working in a developing culture can alter your view of what you want to do with your life. For example **Joe Keely's** six months in Tanzania with *GAP Activity Projects* prompted him to change direction completely:

> *Not only did I achieve a fantastic feeling of well being, great friends and great memories from this six months, but I have (excuse the cliché) found myself. Before I left for Tanzania I was going to follow the Electronic and Electrical Engineering line. I have now changed course and wish to become a journalist and have looked into working for Oxfam on completion of University. I wouldn't have dreamt of such a change before I left, a change I am very grateful for now. This GAP year gave me the break and the sense to choose what I really wanted to do in life and to see my life from a different angle. In fact the only problem with the gap year is it makes life back here seem so much more dull.*

Parents worry that a gap year will alter future plans. But of course there are thousands of school leavers with precious few plans to alter and travel might be a catalyst for moving in one direction or another. This was the case with Carisa Fey from Germany who headed off to England when she was 18 and scraped a living in various jobs before travelling to Mexico and South America for an extended period. She eventually returned to Stuttgart and found to her surprise that she enjoyed working in a 'real' job:

> *When I started out I didn't have much of an idea what I wanted to do afterwards. But pretty soon in my travels the idea of studying became more and more attractive. Especially since one can realise one's own abilities and preferences a lot better while on the road. When I was 18 I was absolutely sure I'd never want to work in an office. But now I love my office and my computer. If I studied now it would not be music or history (dreams of the 18 year old) but business or economics (which I always thought extremely boring). Some of my friends' kids say, you see, no need to study or make a proper training. Look at Carisa, she just travelled around the world and came home to land a great job. But I learned things you can't learn in any university, how you get out of any situation yourself, to stand up for yourself, to get along with all kinds of people. And I didn't just sit at the beach. I was working very very hard. And in every job I did, I learned all I could and gave my best. No matter if I waited tables, worked in a factory, did gardening or whatever. You can learn something everywhere. Even if it is just that you are a bloody lucky person because you hate doing nightshifts at the frozen chips factory; for some people that is their life, but you can get out.*

If major doubts remain about what the next step in your life should be, there is nothing better than taking a year out to do something completely different, to give yourself time and space to decide, away from all the pressures of home and school. Students repeatedly say that travelling and/or working abroad really help to focus their minds on what they want to do with their lives.

In **Rachel Thomas's** case, the pros easily outweighed the cons, and she enthusiastically accepted a place teaching in China, again through GAP Activity Projects:

> *I never had any doubts about a gap year as it was something I had planned to do for as long as I can remember. It took longer to convince my parents, but once they recognised my commitment, they supported me wholeheartedly. The gap year provides the ultimate opportunity for independence and to prove yourself. I knew I would be experiencing new places and cultures which appealed to my sense of adventure. I had worked very hard for my A-levels while also working as a part-time waitress and so I was exhausted. I had been under a lot of stress and I wanted a break before returning to studies. I knew I needed to relax and take the chance to step back to assess my future choices. More practically, if I failed to get the grades I needed to do medicine, I also had the option to retake once I returned. I was somewhat worried about homesickness and missing friends, family and boyfriend, and there was the expense to consider, but in the end I didn't need to deliberate very long.*

Jake Lee found that he had lots of motives for wanting to take a gap year:
My parents are pretty liberal and wanted me to see the world. But I had my own reasons. I wanted to break through the middle class bubble that we're all living in back here. I wanted to see how the rest of the world lived. I wanted to do something for myself, gloriously independent of interfering teachers, parents and friends. Most importantly I wanted to grow up.

DECIDING HOW TO SPEND YOUR GAP YEAR

After deciding to take a year out, it is necessary to decide how to divide it up. The options are open-ended but usually involve a combination of working locally to save money, travelling and possibly signing up with an organisation for an expedition or placement overseas. Deciding whether you want to join a project overseas or just travel is crucial.

One advantage of joining a scheme is that it makes you stay put for an extended period instead of drifting from place to place in what can end up giving a superficial view of the countries visited. The great travel writer Dervla Murphy expressed her views on this subject in an essay in *The Traveller's Handbook* published by WEXAS (£14.99):

> *The past decade or so has seen the emergence of another, hybrid category: young-sters who spend a year or more wandering around the world in a holidaymaking spirit, occasionally taking temporary jobs. Some gain enormously from this experi-ence but many seem to cover too much ground too quickly, sampling everywhere and becoming familiar with nowhere. They have been from Alaska to Adelaide, Berlin to Bali, Calcutta to Cuzco, Lhasa to London. They tend to wander in couples or small packs, swapping yarns about the benefits - or otherwise - of staying here, doing that, buying this. They make a considerable impact where they happen to perch for a week or so, often bringing with them standards (sometimes too low) and expectations (sometimes too high) which unsettle their local contemporaries.*
>
> *Of course one rejoices that the young are free to roam as never before, yet such rapid 'round-the-worlding' is, for many, more confusing than enlightening. It would be good if this fashion soon changed, if the young became more discriminating, allowing themselves time to travel seriously in a limited area that they had chosen because of its particular appeal to them, as individuals.*

The chapters that make up this book survey the range of possibilities and provide lots of concrete information to help you decide whether to earn a salary in a high-tech industry in Britain or join an expedition to Patagonia (or both). Details are provided on voluntary work in residential situations in the UK and abroad, work experience, courses and homestays, seasonal jobs like working in ski resorts, au pairing, English teaching, travelling around Europe: all are covered.

In some sixth forms a certain amount of one-upmanship prevails about who can do the most adventurous and exotic trip (though most end up going to Thailand or India where there are whole colonies of gap year students). Paraguay and Outer Mongolia are great if you have a particular interest in those regions but if you would be happier working on an American summer camp or a Scottish sailing school or attending a language school in Barcelona, so be it. It is possibly a mistake to think of the Himalayan gap year as vastly superior to the one spent closer to home. Trekking in Northern Thailand does not neces-sarily trump working in a Swiss ski resort or volunteering to teach gypsy children in Spain. Do not fall into the trap of making plans to impress. Find the route that suits you.

Using a Gap Year Agency

The ambition of many gap year students is simply to travel with a mate. However if you have set your sights on something more concrete like a stint of volunteering or doing work experience or joining an expedition, it will be difficult to fix this up independently. You and your parents may not feel happy about wandering around without any structure. Although some 18 year olds fresh from school have the confidence and maturity to set off without anything set up (perhaps with a working holiday visa for Australia or a return ticket to Lima) most will prefer to enlist the help of a mediating organisation or agency to set up a placement and provide a back-up service if things go wrong.

Assuming you want to do something other than just travel, you must decide whether to throw in your lot with a sending organisation or arrange something independently. Many of the advantages of going on an organised scheme are self-evident but it is worth canvass-ing a few here:

1. Makes the choice available less overwhelming since placement agencies have a finite number of destinations and opportunities.
2. Saves you the time of contacting many organisations abroad and the anxiety of liaising with them assuming they do express interest. Pre-departure orientation will be provided. Even just a briefing booklet can be helpful and reassuring. Agencies are usually in a position to give reliable advice on necessary health precautions, insurance and flights.
3. Back-up is available if you have an accident, become ill or the placement is unacceptable in some way.
4. Reassurance for anxious parents. The agency often provides a conduit of communication between gap year student and family.
5. Placement is normally in groups or pairs, so moral support is always available from gap year or volunteer partners.

The majority of students coming home from a gap year are grateful for the help and back-up given to them by their agency, claiming that they considered the fee they paid well spent. On the other hand, some find that their agency's local rep is not easy to contact and therefore not of much use. Others who end up not needing to make use of the support network begrudge the fee. The fee paid to a sending agency can be viewed as an insurance policy which many students and their parents are more than happy to pay.

You should try to research the company and the project as thoroughly as you can. Guido Encimeras always assumed he would travel in his gap year after his two older brothers had done likewise. He went to Mexico with a specialist gap year agency in the UK whose services left a lot to be desired. He was quite happy with his teaching placement and with the family accommodation he was assigned, but some of the other volunteers were not so lucky. This was the first year the agency had run a programme in that destination and there were lots of teething problems, with little on-the-ground support, especially for the journalism trainees who found themselves working for a horrible expat rag and could do nothing about it. It is always sensible to ask the agency how long a project which interests you has been running. For a list of searching questions to put to a provider, see the introduction to the chapter 'Specialist Gap Year Programmes'.

Of course there are also drawbacks to signing up with an organisation, principally the expense. Orientations and back-up in the field cost money, with some commercial organisations charging more than charitable ones. Up to a point these schemes are inflexible. Naturally you will be expected to commit yourself to a certain length of stay, possibly even 11 or 12 months. A lot can change in that time: you can fall in love, become lonely and homesick, decide that your contribution is pointless.

Only you know whether you have the stamina and initiative to create a constructive gap year without the shelter of an umbrella in the form of a placement organisation. Bear in mind that locally-run NGOs may profess to need your help but may have little experience of dealing with the kinds of problem faced by homesick 18 year olds. Without contact with a like-minded person, you can feel lonely and isolated. On the other hand, some gap year students do arrange their own job/placement, with or without contacts, and find the experience immensely gratifying. Arranging something independently shows great initiative (always something worth boasting about on future CVs) and of course saves the money which would otherwise go to a middle man. This is something which **Rachel Sedley** wishes she had done instead of signing up with a gap organisation to teach in Kathmandu:

> *It's frustrating to see in retrospect how easy it would have been just to come here and present myself to a school. I have met several people from various schools and orphanages far more needy that the one where I'm working who would love English volunteers. Back in England of course I had no idea, so I paid up without questioning. The training course was held in a beautiful stately home with delicious meals and friendly staff, but in retrospect was probably superfluous and extremely expensive.*

The old proverb, 'It is easy to be wise after the event' may be apt here.

Schemes and pre-arranged projects are not for everyone. **Eleanor Padfield** decided to avoid them because she wanted to make her way on her own in the Spanish-speaking world (Salamanca, Bolivia, Chile) away from all her gap year contemporaries. **Emma Hoare** did lots of research on a gap year but couldn't find an approach that suited her at first:

> *For years I had always been saying 'yes, I really want to travel…maybe after A-levels, maybe after my degree, maybe when I retire' and all my friends would go 'yeah, me too, definitely' and all my family, teachers, elders and betters would smile and nod in that way they do when a young person starts talking vaguely about the Big Things, that there is really no fear of them actually doing.*
>
> *On results day I found that I had managed to get four A grades. At some point in all the celebrations I decided that, no, I didn't want to go straight to university. I wanted to go backpacking, see the world, have a spiritual epiphany, etc. To say this did not please my mother, teachers, etc. is an understatement. When I started talking about cancelling my place at York University and reapplying the next year, every adult I knew (except my Dad) was 100% against it. They did have a small point, I suppose. I didn't have any plans, though I had about £1000, not even enough for a ticket to New Zealand as it turned out.*
>
> *So I had about four days before I had to accept or decline my place at York. By the end of the third day, I had been pretty much convinced that it would be a stupid thing to go gallivanting around the world. I went into my local careers advisory centre and was sat down with a pile of leaflets dealing with gap years. Every single one of these dealt with either a structured voluntary course abroad or how to arrange work experience. 'On the road' it wasn't. Then – portentous roll of thunder, sudden bright light – one of the receptionists gave me a book that had just come in, 'Work Your Way Around the World'. No exaggeration, I promise you. I sat there and read it until they closed the centre. Then I went straight to Waterstones and bought a copy. Then I went home and wrote to York University declining my place. Three months later I was off to New Zealand… As you can probably surmise from the gushing tone of this letter, I had an amazing time. I crewed on a yacht, helped with haymaking, went to a sheep-shearers' reunion, did a 12,000ft skydive, saw sperm whales, etc… And now I'm off to start my degree (at Oxford!). I can assure you the transformation is nothing short of miraculous.*

Overcoming Anxiety

Often the hardest step is committing yourself to a decision, i.e. fixing a departure date and

destination. Once you have booked a place on a scheme or bought a ticket and explained to your friends and family that you are off to see the world, the rest seems to fall into place. Inevitably first-time travellers suffer pre-departure anxieties as they contemplate leaving behind the comfortable routines of home. But these are usually much worse in anticipation than in retrospect.

Prepare yourself for a horrid 48 hours after saying good-bye at the airport (tip: don't look back after going through Passport Control). **Jake Lee** who went to Sri Lanka in his gap year puts it rather brutally:

Let me just state for the record. It doesn't matter who you are, but if you are travelling alone to a faraway place for a relatively long time, you will cack yourself on the plane. The excitement you previously had turns to fear, and you are desperate for the plane to turn around. I don't think there is anything you can do about this. Just ride it out. As a Buddhist monk at my school always said, 'There is never anything to worry about - Nothing.' This is true.

Sources of Information

If you happen to come from a school with no tradition of sending students on gap years, you will have to do your own research. Access to the internet makes this task much easier and at the same time more complicated since there is so much information scattered through cyberspace. One obvious starting point is www.gapyear.com set up in 1998 by Tom Griffiths to help people plan gap years and round-the-world trips. Users can chat with other travellers on the message boards, browse 6000 pages of information, find travel mates and access the database of opportunities. This is of course a commercial venture.

The non-profit trade association, the Year Out Group, aims to promote and advise on structured years out. Their website (www.yearoutgroup.org) has links to its 36 member organisations and contains guidelines and questions to ask when comparing year out providers; more information about the Year Out Group can be found in the introduction to the chapter 'Specialist Gap Year Programmes'.

Wherever you look, services and websites target gap year students from the newly launched Gap Year NZ, a 'dedicated guide to taking a gap year in New Zealand' to Travel-tree.co.uk, a website directory that enlightens visitors with opportunities for gap year ideas as well as adventure and educational travel, internships and volunteering opportunities. Many of these are referred to in the appropriate context throughout this book. An additional resource is the magazine *Gaptastic*, published three times a year by the Ink Well Press (info@gaptastic.com); a subscription costs £5.

Springboard is a web-based advisory service for young people aged 16-18 which describes itself as a complete guide to careers, study and gap year opportunities after leaving school (www.springboard.hobsons.co.uk/gapyearsearch.jsp). Anyone who is in the early stages of thinking about a gap year and wants to discuss the educational and career implications with someone might approach Connexions, the Government's advice and guidance service for 13-19 year olds whose brief is to encourage young people not to abandon their schooling prematurely.

An impressively long list of contacts can be found at www.efutures.co.uk/documents/gap_year_database.htm or check www.gapyeardirectory.co.uk. Meanwhile *Jobs Abroad Bulletin* is a useful one-man and one-woman site (www.jobsabroadbulletin.co.uk) which dispenses with pretty graphics to deliver actual job vacancy details each month. E-mail subscriptions to what is billed as an 'online magazine for working abroad and taking a gap year' are free. Also look at www.payaway.co.uk/gap.shtml from the same people.

Gap year fairs are held around the country through the spring and early summer and are generally open to anyone. One series is organised by ISCO/Careerscope; in 2005 they organised fairs in 18 locations. Visiting one gives you the chance to meet in person the representatives of the various organisations as well as real live ex-gappers. These fairs are free to attend, though a larger scale Gap Year Show (www.gapyearshow.com) held at Wembley at the end of June 2005 charged £7 admission on the door. The organisers hope to make this an annual event.

Some schools invite representatives from the companies to visit. **Ed Fry** went along to one of these at his school but wanted more independent advice:

I was given some advice at school as to how I might wish to structure my gap year in terms of travel, work and so on but many of the people that came to speak at school had a commercial slant to their talks which made me slightly dubious of their advice. Teachers were very helpful in terms of advising on countries to visit and things to do. A short course was also offered on how to stay safe in your gap year, but it was an extra cost and basically all common sense.

An independent gap year consultancy *Gap Enterprise* offers private client consultations and school talks for planning a gap year. For a substantial fee, the director John Vessey can save students and their parents the time and effort of researching the vast range of possibilities and will advise on matching specific requirements to a high quality multi-faceted programme; contact details may be found in the 'Directory of Specialist Gap Year Programmes'.

A new company GapProfile has been set up to formalise the gap year by granting a City & Guilds Profile of Achievement to those who can show on paper how their gap year has benefitted their development. This means that people who take a structured gap year have something to show to future employers, though it is not known how widely recognised this documentation is. Registration with this scheme costs £250: GapProfile.co.uk, Thornton Chenie House, 27 Bloomfield Road, Bromley, Kent BR2 9RY (020 8466 8773; info@gapprofile.co.uk).

THE REWARDS

Any number of publications and careers documents list the advantages of taking a gap year which are mostly to do with gaining self-confidence and independence. All of one's education is a movement in this direction. The first time primary school age children are taken camping for a few nights, they are learning to depend on themselves rather than on their parents to keep track of their socks and their pocket money. A gap year abroad moves the individual in the same direction probably at a faster rate than if they had continued straight to university (without passing Goa).

While some of the rewards of taking a gap year may be unpredictable, others are more obvious: the interesting characters and lifestyles you are sure to meet, the appetite to see more of the world that it will engender, the wealth of anecdotes you will collect with which you can regale your grandchildren and photos with which you can bore your friends, learning how to do your own cooking and laundry, a feeling of achievement, an increased

self-reliance and maturity, learning to budget, a better perspective on your own country and your own habits, a good sun tan... the list could continue. **Stephen Psallidas** summed up his views on travelling:

> *Meeting people from all over the world gives you a more tolerant attitude to other nationalities, races, etc. More importantly you learn to tolerate yourself, to learn more about your strengths and weaknesses. While we're on the clichés, you definitely 'find yourself, man'.*

A host of gap travellers have mentioned how much they value their collection of memories and photos. When looking back on your year off, you are not going to remember that it was the year you gained self-confidence or learned how to live within a budget; you will remember being invited to a Buddhist initiation ceremony, learning a few words of Spanish from a Mexican fisherman, your encounter with what might have been a redback spider at a Queensland barbecue or how you nearly missed your plane in Nairobi.

While some young people can make a smooth and sensible transition from school to university, others find their sudden freedom from constraints a temptation to indulge in excesses. **Alice Mundy** had noticed this in others and thought it would do her good to take 2004/5 off before starting a BSc at the University of Swansea:

> *My main reason for taking a gap year before university was hopefully to enter higher education with a bit more maturity and worldly experience. A lot of people I know who went straight into higher education either spent their first year partying too hard because of their new found freedom or went in still feeling stressed from all the seemingly never-ending AS & A level exams. Because they felt that they had never really had time to relax, the work just got too much for them. I knew I was grateful for the opportunity of higher education but also felt I would appreciate a step back from it.*
>
> *Obviously the main worry is being unable to step back into the studying routine again after a year out but, as there is a completely different approach to learning in university, it seemed that the old routines would have to change anyway. I can maybe even see benefit in having time off to wipe the slate clean so you go back into it without relying too heavily on the way you used to learn and are more open to new styles. I did try to keep a certain amount of discipline though and towards the end of my gap year started to read up on some of the textbook material for my course (Biological Sciences and Psychology) to bring the subject matter back to my consciousness again.*

Long-term Benefits

Gap years can change you and change the direction of your life forever. After enjoying her gap year carrying out conservation work in the coral reefs of Tanzania through *Frontier* (see entry in the 'Directory of Specialist Gap Year Programmes') **Emily Jimsor** changed her university course:

> To me the most important part of the experience has been the effect it has had on my career. I became really involved in the conservation side of things while I was in Tanzania, particularly looking at the effects of pollution on coral reefs. I learnt so much from the field staff out there and their enthusiasm really inspired me. When I came home I contacted my university (Portsmouth) and told them I really wanted to study marine biology. The tutors were very understanding and I was able to swap courses. My entire life has changed, all thanks to that one article I read in the local paper about three years ago.

Sometimes travels abroad have a similar impact. After working his way around the world in many low-paid and exploitative jobs, **Ken Smith** decided to specialise in studying employment law. Several gap year students have become so involved with their destination community that they carry on raising funds and sometimes recruiting volunteers to carry on the work. After his gap year in Kenya, **Rob Breare** set up a charity called Harambee Schools Kenya that continues to support the education of village children in the Central Highlands. The repercussions of **Rachel Battilana's** gap year in Africa were quite different. When choosing a fourth year structural engineering project, she was attracted to one which involved re-designing a tent for refugees. She claims that she managed to be accepted onto the project by referring to her gap year in Uganda (and her many family camping holidays) and her tent went on to win a prestigious Science, Engineering and Technology Student of the Year award.

Nearer home, you might come back from a work experience placement or language course on the Continent feeling a part of Europe rather than just English, Scottish, Welsh or Northern Irish. Such experiences will enhance your CV if you ever want to pursue a job with a European dimension. Volunteering in the UK can provide a useful taster of an alternative career especially if you have decided that the world of commerce is not for you and you are considering the caring professions, conservation or development field.

A gap year is often a defining moment in the life of an almost-adult. Mostly the rewards are highly personal. Successful gap years abroad allow you to learn how to relinquish your own customs, desires and expectations. Exposure to a completely different way of viewing and managing time is something that might teach you to resist stress and competition in our own culture. A young participant who went on an expedition to Kenya with the *Borders Exploration Group* felt he had had a revelation about different attitudes to life:

> Most people feel that we are so much better off; we are in money, but in what else? They have lots of fun and laughter, even though their lives are so hard. It's a lesson to all of us.

Learning to find joy and pleasure in simple things like running water or the sunset over the desert is a lesson worth learning. Exposure to new people and cultures teaches you that you can (generally) rely on instinct about whether a stranger is trustworthy or not.

Prolonged exposure to people with different value systems is bound to change your perspective and teach you how subjective one's values and view of society are. Just before taking his final exams at Cambridge, **Matthew Applewhite** reflected on the impact the six months of his gap year spent working at an outback school for Aboriginal people had had on his subsequent development and attitudes. His students in the Northern Territory had drawn pictures, written poems, made friends but hadn't been made to do any exams. He realised that whatever the class of degree he ends up with doesn't matter nearly as much as his certainty that he has acquired an education in the broadest sense; he has made friends, read books, pursued new ideas, indulged his passion for the theatre and generally had a very worthwhile three years at university.

Meeting the challenge of doing something completely different from the norm can

have a positive effect on your personal development too. Like millions of others, **Edward Brown** is from a 'sheltered and safe' middle class background. After graduating, he was determined not to slide into an office job and spotted an advert for CSV (see 'Directory of Volunteering in the UK'). Soon Edward had taken up his placement in London working with young offenders:

London filled me with fear. I thought I would be surrounded by hardened criminals. But I soon realised that the young people I work with are just like everyone else and not at all as I imagined. My role has had a really positive effect. It hasn't been easy and things have been very slow to change and very unpredictable. I'm much more streetwise now. I used to be very shy and now I feel like I am being myself more and more. I wanted to experience some real life. I'm much more tuned into things and am able to communicate to people on loads of different levels. Being a volunteer is a life-changing experience. It helps you to discover who you are and what your strengths and weaknesses are. It has helped to shape my future.

THE RISKS

Of course things can go desperately wrong. Several young women and men who have been on gap year projects have had fatal accidents or worst of all, as in the case of the British backpacker Caroline Stuttle, have been murdered. A much less remote possibility is losing your passport or having your backpack stolen. You may get sick or lonely or fed up. You may make a fool of yourself by allowing yourself to be tricked by a con-man who sells you some fake gems or rips you off in a currency transaction. You may feel desperately homesick for a situation in which you do not have to behave like an adult when you have only had an adolescent's experiences.

While some identify the initial decision to go abroad as the hardest part, others find the inevitable troughs, such as finding yourself alone in a cheap hotel room on your birthday, running out of money faster than anticipated, getting travellers' diarrhoea, more difficult to cope with. But if travelling requires a much greater investment of energy than staying at home, it will reward the effort many times over.

Friends and family are seldom reluctant to offer advice, and normally the perceived risks are far greater than the actual ones. When **Cathleen Graham** from Canada announced that she was bound for rural South Africa with the charity SCORE (see Africa chapter), many came forward to express grave concerns for her safety as a young woman:

> *People's reactions to my choice of destination were determined by what they saw portrayed about South Africa in the media. Of course, people who knew me best knew this was an opportunity that suited me. You really need to develop a strong filter about listening to people's opinions before you go: are they sound and balanced, or more reflecting the person's own fears and anxieties if they were the one going?*

Some gap year travellers undergo a process of disillusionment, which is not a bad thing in itself, since no one wants to live in a world of illusions. You harbour a desire to see some famous monument and find it surrounded by touts or chintzy boutiques. The reality of seeing the Taj Mahal or walking down the Gorge of Samaria in Crete or meeting an Amazonian Indian may be less romantic than you had imagined. (See Alain de Botton's elegant *The Art of Travel* for an in-depth study of the conflict between dreams of travel and the reality.)

Of the thousands of placements that gap year students accept, a few are bound to be disappointing. **Victoria Greaves** describes how what she found on arrival at a farm in France (where she had been taken on as a volunteer assistant during her gap year) failed to match her expectations:

> *Before setting off I made particular efforts to check the reliability of the organisation with the local tourist information office, etc. However when I arrived, the situation was not as I had been led to believe. On arrival I discovered that I was the only person there apart from Monsieur, although he had led me to believe that he lived with his wife and son, and that there would be other volunteers on site. After a 20-hour journey I was put to work immediately mucking out the horses. Monsieur refused to let me phone home. I spent the next day cleaning the buildings and stables which had obviously not been done for some weeks. There was no suitable vegetarian food available although he had promised to make arrangements. At one point I actually found him in my dormitory reading my personal letters and diary. My visit was an extremely traumatic experience which ended after three days, with me being dismissed at 30 minutes notice and my employer dumping me in the nearby town with no travel arrangements and nowhere to stay. It was a totally unsuitable environment for an 18 year old volunteer, especially a female on her own.*

In rare cases, students can be traumatised by what they experience in a gap year. According to the Senior Tutor of a Cambridge college who regularly meets students before and after their gap year, most come back much more changed than the students who have not deferred for a year. Some benefit enormously, but not all. He recalls one in particular who had gone to work in a Romanian orphanage with young children with AIDS. She came back so traumatised that she suffered from nightmares for a long time afterwards. But usually the changes are not so dire. A tutor at St. Anne's College Oxford wrote in the college magazine how offended students are if she fails to recognise them, even though there can be a two-year gap between interview and arrival: 'The problem is that they can have changed in appearance completely, from scrubbed and tidy interview candidate to world-weary international traveller, sans hair but plus several ear or facial rings.'

REASSURANCE FOR PARENTS

The departure of a child from the family home is traumatic enough when they're merely going to university, but is made much more frightening if he or she is travelling to the ends of the earth on a year out adventure. When you were 18, you probably hadn't even heard of, let alone considered visiting, some of the destinations that gap travellers now visit, from Vientiane to Antananarivo, Port Stanley to Sulawesi. The relative cheapness of long-distance flights, the range of gap year providers offering remote destinations and the raised expectations of the new generation account for these heightened travel ambitions. How you as a parent react will have a lot to do with what you did when you were 18. The parents who motorcycled through Afghanistan to India or hitch-hiked round Greece with no money may be more sympathetic than the ones who carried straight through from school to university or a job.

The parental imagination is bound to dwell on the possible disasters (and the actual ones such as the Childers Hostel fire a few years ago). Feelings of helplessness when a child is far away fuel these anxieties. But a calm assessment of the risks will result in a startling realisation, that staying at home is just as risky. Clubbing in a city centre or driving on a British road poses risks, too, though parents don't tend to focus on those. According to an article in *The Times* headed 'Gap year away safer than rock festival at home,' research published in the *Journal of the Royal Society of Medicine* showed that taking part in a structured expedition brought with it less risk of death or injury than attending a music festival in Britain or going to a Scout camp.

As the number of young people taking gap years abroad increases (an estimated 400,000 go backpacking every year), it is inevitable that more accidents will occur. The raised profile of young people travelling abroad on their gap year means that these accidents tend to be widely reported. So if a young man slips down a waterfall in Costa Rica or a British girl is killed by a freak accident with a high voltage cable in Ecuador or a bus carrying overlanding travellers is held up by armed bandits in the Andes, the world hears about it. By the same token some reported tragedies take place in Britain, as in the case of a young woman working at a Plymouth supermarket in her gap year who was murdered by the store manager. But mostly, if an 18 year old dies of a drug overdose or is killed on his bicycle in his hometown, this is not reported nationally.

It is arguable that children nowadays are overprotected and should be given more not less freedom so that from an early age they learn to be street-wise and how to navigate dangers outside the home. Some say that adventures are now too easy. Young people are lulled into a false sense of security by the number of people doing likewise. A trek round Annapurna can be arranged in an instant, but that does not mean that a blizzard won't reduce visibility to nil inside 20 minutes.

Still, a parent will want to take every possible precaution on his or her child's behalf, knowing that all 18 year olds believe themselves immortal. They should check with the Foreign Office on world trouble spots (www.www.fco.gov.uk/travel; 0870 606 0290). They should consider giving their son or daughter a gold-plated travel insurance policy as a birthday present or urge their child not to skimp on insurance. If you have resisted going on e-mail, now is the time to relent, because your child is almost guaranteed to spend time in internet cafés and will be able to let you know that all is well at more frequent intervals than they could if they have to rely on phones. Try not to be too prescriptive about how often your son or daughter contacts you because if they are out of contact for some reason, you will worry unnecessarily. A few causes of tragedy are avoidable, such as in the case of an A-level girl who died of heat stroke and dehydration on an expedition in Borneo. Urging your child to take sensible precautions like dressing modestly in countries where it is expected, not flaunting valuables, not falling prey to smooth-tongued con men, may have some beneficial effect. Those who can't rein in their anxiety might investigate enrolling their progeny on a gap year preparation course (see entries for *Objective Travel Safely, Planet Wise, Safetrek* and *Ultimate Gap Year*).

But really the hard truth is that it is time to let go. Try to give your child lots of credit for their initiative, enterprise and courage and remind yourself daily that they are now grown-up. It is amazing how anxieties vanish once your child has actually left home. As the mother of a son who went to Togo for part of his gap year put it: 'It's curious how my high anxiety lasted for about 24 hours after I waved him off. Since then it's been pretty much uninterrupted envy and bile.'

Any parents considering investing in one of the gap preparation courses might wonder how useful they are. Most of what they try to impart is basic common sense, something that can be in short supply at 18. One of the companies *(Planet Wise)* describes a case in which their training came in handy:

Recently one of our ex-students was on a bus in Ecuador that was held up. He was fine, having been taught that nothing is worth your life, but he had everything he owned taken. Thanks to the fact that he had taken scans of his passport and all other relevant documents which he had emailed to himself, he got a new passport in a record-breaking two days.

Supporting your offspring can be hard work, especially for the hands-on kind of parent. A friend of mine in Canada recently wrote to me about her daughter (aged 17½) in the planning stages of a gap year placement at a school for the deaf in South India starting September 2005:

One of the recent low points was when I was waiting for my daughter and her friend to show up at the travel agent and they came in (late) asking whether they should put money in the parking meter! I tried to remain calm while I suggested they read the instructions and then make an executive decision. I try not to think about all the practical skills they will have to acquire very quickly when they are off on their own. I have got her a fantastic (cheap and very flexible) flight from Halifax to India at the end of August and back from Kuala Lumpur to Toronto at the end of April. I have confirmed all her insurance coverage. I have acquired signing authority on her bank account, I have photocopied all the relevant documents, and I have supplied her with an extra card on my VISA account. She has managed to do much less ... although she is spending a fair bit of time making DVDs for her friends and dreaming about what she will do next summer.

The Beaten Track

A report by an academic was published a few years ago lambasting the negative impact that backpackers have on places where they congregate (Sinai, Kathmandu, Goa, Kho Pha-Ngan, Machu Picchu, etc). The organisation for responsible tourism Tourism Concern (www. tourismconcern.org.uk) is also worried by the number of young people who travel to places they are not really interested in just to meet up with other travellers, to eat, drink and socialise in exactly the way they would at home but without as many inhibitions. There is even a novel about it. For a satirical account of the wrong way to go about being a gap year traveller, read William Sutcliffe's novel *Are You Experienced?* based on his own gap year experiences. In this extract, the anti-hero Dave is being lectured by an old-India hand:

Hippies coming for spiritual enlightenment have been replaced by morons on a pov-erty-tourism adventure holiday. Going to India is no longer an act of rebellion but an act of conformity for ambitious middle-class kids who believe that a trip to the third world shows the kind of initiative which companies are looking for. You come here

TourismConcern

Exploring the World

Being sensitive to these ideas means getting more out of your travels – and giving more back to the people you meet and the places you visit.

● *Learn about the country you're visiting*
Start enjoying your travels before you leave by tapping into as many sources of information as you can.

● *The cost of your holiday*
Think about where your money goes - be fair and realistic about how cheaply you travel. Try and put money into local people's hands; drink local beer or fruit juice rather than imported brands and stay in locally owned accommodation.

Haggle with humour and not aggressively. Pay what something is worth to you and remember how wealthy you are compared to local people.

● *Culture*
Open your mind to new cultures and traditions - it will transform your experience.

Think carefully about what's appropriate in terms of your clothes and the way you behave. You'll earn respect and be more readily welcomed by local people.

Respect local laws and attitudes towards drugs and alcohol that vary in different countries and communities. Think about the impact you could have. *"The effect on the local community of travellers taking drugs when visiting the hilltribes of Thailand can be devastating. People become trapped into selling drugs to travellers and become addicted themselves, especially young people who want to be like the travellers."* Jaranya Daengnoy, REST

● *How big is your footprint? – minimise your environmental impact*
Think about what happens to your rubbish - take biodegradable products and a water filter bottle. Be sensitive to limited resources like water, fuel and electricity.

Help preserve local wildlife and habitats by respecting rules and regulations, such as sticking to footpaths, not standing on coral and not buying products made from endangered plants or animals.

● *Guidebooks*
Use your guidebook as a starting point, not the only source of information. Talk to local people, then discover your own adventure!

● *Photography*
Don't treat people as part of the landscape, they may not want their picture taken. Put yourself in their shoes, ask first and respect their wishes.

The ideas expressed in this code were developed by and for independent travellers. They show what individuals can do to play their part towards Tourism Concern's goal of more ethical and fairly traded tourism. For more information see Tourism Concern's website: www.tourismconcern.org.uk Telephone: +44 (0)20 7133 3330

This TourismConcern initiative is supported by

and cling to each other as if you're on some kind of extended management-bonding exercise in Epping Forest... It's a modern circumcision ritual, a badge of suffering you have to wear to be welcomed into the tribe of Britain's future elite. Your kind of travel is all about low horizons dressed up as open-mindedness. You have no interest in India and no sensitivity for the problems this country is trying to face up to. You treat Indians with a mixture of contempt and suspicion reminiscent of the Victorian colonials. Your presence here in my opinion is offensive and you should all go home to Surrey.

Hard-hitting stuff but worth pondering.

Choosing a culturally sensitive organisation with which to work can prevent this kind of situation from arising, as **Rosie Bywaters** found when she joined an *SPW* health and sanitation project in India:

For the first time, SPW India has partnered Indian volunteers with western volunteers. This makes the projects more easily sustainable and ensures that we are sensitive to the community's needs. I have found it tremendously helpful and enlightening to be working with our six counterpart volunteers. Not only is their knowledge of Tamil a great asset, but they guide and support us in all sorts of way, even with the difficult task of crossing the street without getting run over by a bus, auto-rickshaw or stray cow. My counterpart is called Sasikala. She is the same age as me (21) and has a degree in Nutrition and Dietetics. She calls me her right hand but I feel that it is she who is my right hand, teaching me about her culture and introducing me to a whole new way of being. India is a very special place, impossible to describe, impossible to forget. I cried so much when I had to leave and say goodbye to some amazing friends, but it just makes me all the more sure that I want to go back as soon as I can.

Coming Home

Coming home and experiencing reverse culture shock is a problem for some. Settling back will take time especially if you have not been able to set aside some money for 'The Return'. It can be a wretched feeling after some glorious adventures to find yourself with nothing to start over on. Life at home may seem dull and routine at first, while the outlook of your friends and family can strike you as narrow and limited. If you have been round the world between school and further study, you may find it difficult to bridge the gulf between you and your stay-at-home peers who may feel a little threatened or belittled by your experiences.

Peta Miller came back to the same grey airport she'd left six months before to go to Ghana with a classic case of reverse culture shock:

I had thought it would be relatively easy to slot back into my life seeing friends, socialising and in the end looking for my first proper job. But my soul was true to Ghana. I scrutinised those around me and found the way they behaved rude, selfish and pretentious. They looked sallow, pale and unhealthy as they shuttled back and forth between home and the office, compressed into tube compartments, breathing black air. Nobody smiled or communicated. Train tickets, bars of chocolate, cinema tickets could all be purchased without uttering a word. Even my own friends seemed changed into frivolous consumers intent on image and appearance. There was no colour, no sincerity and no content. People seemed to be wasting the working week doing jobs that made rich men richer so that at the weekends they could go on frenzied shopping trips. From such a perspective the world seemed to have gone mad. Five months later I'm better acclimatised. But the fact remains that Ghanaians smile and laugh more than we do because their pleasures are simpler, more easily and more often fulfilled.

For **Frances Pountain** from Cambridge, the lowest point of her gap year came when she returned home from an exciting summer in Costa Rica to find that all her friends were working and not seeing as much of each other as they had at college. The sudden realisation that everyone is growing up and moving on can make some gappers feel disoriented or lonely. Once you settle into your own job or course or whatever, things will look up.

The restlessness passes, the reverse culture shock wears off soon enough and you will begin to feel reintegrated. Gap year experiences are great conversation openers when you're meeting new people at university. **Simon Rowland** found that of the 16 other first years in his hall of residence at York University, the four who had taken a gap year gravitated to one another and ended up sharing a unit.

As has been noted, what you did in your gap year provides an easy topic of conversation for future interviews so in official contexts you should be prepared to put as positive a spin on it as possible. Any evidence of initiative and organisational abilities will help. If you travel alone you can boast of your independence; if you travel with friends you can claim to have learned about co-operation and team work.

UNIVERSITY APPLICATION

Applying to university is a stressful and complicated business on which your school should offer detailed advice. The worst aspect of it is the uncertainty of outcome. Conditional offers are the bugbear of prospective students because it means it is difficult to make definite plans until you know your A-level results. Of course the specialist placement organisations are used to coping with the problem and can offer support throughout. Many school leavers feel forced to make up their minds about university courses too early. More mature students make better decisions about what they want to study and are statistically less likely to drop out.

Taking a lead from Tony Higgins, former Chief Executive of UCAS who endorsed the Year Out Group, organisations involved in gap year travel always urge students to sort out their university applications before taking off. It is also important to ascertain what line the department or college you're applying to takes on gap years. Brian Heap's book *Degree Course Offers* (£26.99 for the 2006 edition) devotes a line or two to the attitude taken by individual institutions to gap years. The vast majority will be more than tolerant of them, provided you can demonstrate that you will do something constructive with your year out. Perfecting the art of sleeping until 11am and watching morning television may turn out to be good preparation for university, but not according to admissions tutors.

Timing

Wherever possible, students should begin preparations for a gap year well in advance. There are so many plans to make and problems to sort out that the best way to avoid panics and disappointments is not to leave things to the last minute. On the other hand, not all applications are dealt with swiftly. In the November of his last year of high school in Victoria, Canada, **Graham Milner** got excited about a gap year scheme to assist at boarding schools in England, which his school recommended:

The application deadline was the first week of December, and we just got letters to say we were accepted the first week of June. They seemed to put a lot of weight on the interview rather than the written application. Anyway, be prepared to wait.

University application forms have to be submitted to UCAS by January 15th of your A-level year at the latest (earlier for Oxbridge and some courses like medicine). This leaves seven months until exams finish, which may seem plenty of time to decide how to spend your gap year until you realise that some of the schemes are already filling up or that you'll have to raise several thousand pounds in order to join your preferred programme. Similarly, many *Year in Industry* jobs require early application to ensure the chosen company and placement have places left.

Whatever decision is made about your gap year, it is important to keep the university informed. They are unlikely to look favourably on someone asking for deferred entry at the last minute, nor are they likely to permit it.

Pre A-Level Application

The pros and cons of taking a gap year need to be weighed up for a period of time to ensure that the idea has substance and is not just a passing whim. Students need to crystallise their reasons for taking a gap year before speaking to university admissions tutors. It may be beneficial to stress the fact that time spent in the 'real world' will encourage a more mature outlook. Tutors are fully aware of the fact that many students who defer for a year go on to do comparatively better at university. According to a survey carried out on behalf of the Year Out Group, nine out of ten university vice-chancellors agreed that a 'structured year out benefits the personal development of the typical undergraduate'.

However, there is evidence of hostility to deferring entry to certain courses such as maths, engineering and possibly music. Equally, students pursuing a particularly long course such as veterinary studies and architecture may choose not to delay embarking upon the long haul of the course. **Ed Fry** from near Reading divided his gap year in 2004/5 between sailing in Australia, working in London and travelling in Central America. He has no idea if taking a gap year affected his university applications and wasn't sure whether or not to trust the much touted line that Oxbridge and other hard-to-get-into establishments do not discriminate against gap years. Attitudes to the gap year vary from tutor to tutor, subject to subject. The only way of assessing the situation is to speak personally to the individuals involved. Certainly a high proportion of first years in the best universities arrive after a year out, dispelling the anxiety that there is vestigial distrust of people who take a year out. To take just one example of the level of acceptance, Churchill College in Cambridge even has a dedicated Gap Year Adviser and the college website has much useful information (www.chu.cam.ac.uk/admissions/undergraduates/decisions/gap_year/gap_years.shtml).

The received wisdom on the subject of gap years and medical studies is that a year out will be tolerated only if it is spent in some way related to medicine. **Tom Watkins** who hoped to be accepted for medicine disagrees strongly with the claim that medical schools are suspicious of gap years. His impression is that they do not want to accept people straight out of school and would really prefer older students who will have more chance of sticking the course. His plan was to apply after getting his A-level results in August and then to work as a care worker with damaged children (via an agency like the British Nursing Association) until university interviews in the winter (between December and February). After that he was looking into going to Accra, Ghana with *Projects Abroad* to work in a hospital where he hoped to be involved in the setting up of an immunisation programme.

Students need to impress upon the university that they really want to have a place on that particular course and that come hell or high water they will return to take it. Universities have been made uneasy in the past by too many students provisionally accepting courses and then changing their minds. Having a coherent plan and focusing on the potential benefits will make the university realise that you are serious about spending the year in a responsible manner. Questions about gap years often form a large part of an interview and can potentially be impressive.

Once it has been decided that a gap year is the best plan, this needs to be indicated on the UCAS form. To offer a deferred-entry place is then at the university's discretion and they will send their conditions to UCAS, who in turn send this to the student. Provided the student fulfils the requirements, their place is assured for the September following the gap year. If there are any queries about the university application process, UCAS can be contacted on 01242 222444 while information on retakes is available on the UCAS enquiries line 0870 1122211.

Post A-Level Application

If you haven't applied for deferred entry in the upper sixth, then you can apply during your gap year. One advantage of doing it earlier is that you will be able to access the resources of your sixth form advisers. But not everyone's plans work out. In the words of Robert Burns, 'the best-laid schemes of mice and men gang aft agley'. Come results day, some students find that they have not done as well as anticipated and have not met the requirements of their preferred university. Several options are now possible:

1. Contact your first choice university to see if they will take you for the following year.
2. Proceed to early entry in Clearing, bearing in mind that most places gained through Clearing will be for that year and not for the year after. Courses with vacancies are published in the *Independent* and on the UCAS website www.ucas.com. Speed of reaction and decisiveness are essential at this stage because lots of people are competing for remaining places. You must communicate directly with the institutions, which is easier said than done since the phone lines are often jammed in the days following results day. The BBC operates a Student Essentials Helpline in August which includes advice on what to do (including how to break bad news to your parents); check on their website for the number.
3. Plan to retake and reapply to your preferred university.
4. Carry on with your gap year plans and apply again the following year with the same exam results.

If the first choice university will not offer a place, you need to ask yourself some hard questions. Was the original choice of course suitable anyway? Would it be better to apply for something else? If the first course was vocational, it could be worthwhile having a serious chat with the Careers Service to reassess the situation, particularly if the grades fell a long way short. Reapplying post A-level for the following year is straightforward; universities will either make an unconditional offer or reject your application.

Some people choose to have a gap year and some have one thrust upon them. Mark Ramsden fell into the latter category when he discovered in August that he had not met the offers of his first choice universities:
When I got my A-level results I realised I hadn't made it into my first choice, even my second, and after spending the rest of the day fruitlessly on the phone I slowly realised that that wasn't the way I wanted to get to university. A gap year it had to be.

I looked at a lot of different places to take me somewhere different and exciting, where I could really achieve something with my year out. Trekforce Expeditions were organised, enthusiastic and the prospect of living in untouched rainforest in Belize and Guatemala was too perfect. The leaders were truly inspirational, and the sights we saw were indescribable.

If I had reached the grades I needed, I never would have discovered waterfalls, seen howler monkeys in the wild casually walk past just a few feet away, built the finest ranger station in South America, and met some of the most interesting, fun, amazing people in my life. Now I am at university, doing a different course that I know I enjoy far more than the one I didn't get on to. Honestly, I think I learnt as much in two months with Trekforce as I did in the whole of my first year here at university. It was amazing.

Retakes

Another reason you may end up having to take an unplanned gap year is if you decide to retake one or more exams in the winter or spring. Not many schools will allow students to stay on for an extra year to re-sit nor is it really advisable. It would be more beneficial to have different tuition to provide a fresh approach to the subject. Even the keenest student will be reluctant to dredge up and study from the same tired old notes all over again.

Tutorial colleges or crammers cater specifically for students needing to retake. Students will re-sit just the subjects in which they need to boost their grades, thus making them part-time students and leaving lots of time for other pursuits like working and earning, gaining extra skills or doing voluntary work. The downside is that they are extremely expensive. Private colleges charge up to £3500 for each subject and anxious parents have been known to invest £12,000 on improving their son or daughter's overall grades. Students need to be really sure that they are serious about re-sitting and are prepared to put in the hard work to make it worthwhile spending so much.

If you can't find a suitable tutorial college close to home, you may have to consider travelling elsewhere to cram for your re-sits. Students need to be mature and self-disciplined to avoid the temptations that arise when one leaves home for the first time. An alternative is distance study or online learning. The website of the Open Distance Learning Quality Council (www.odlqc.org.uk) has links to accredited providers. Expect to pay at least £350 per A level. When choosing, ask for details of their success rate.

Further information about tutorial colleges can be found from CIFE (Council for Independent Further Education); their website www.thecapability.uk.com/cife has links to their 27 independent sixth-form and tutorial colleges around the country and offers more detailed information about retake courses. For those ambitious to improve in order to get into a highly competitive course, the lists of best results that appear in the national press (especially *The Times*) after results day, may help to choose. Among the best are the ones that sound like old firms of solicitors: Mander Portman Woodward in London, Birmingham and Cambridge (www.mpw.co.uk) and Davies Laing & Dick in London (www.dld.org).

The timetable below may serve as a useful guide to where you should be in your application and arrangement of gap year activities. Ideally, students should be around for Results Day in case results are not as expected so that decisions can be taken. Alternative arrangements may need to be made, although if the entry is deferred there is plenty of time to do this.

TIMETABLE FOR UNIVERSITY APPLICATION

Plan A

Lower Sixth	*Autumn/Spring*	Begin to think about university courses and the possibility of taking a Gap Year
	Spring/Summer	Visit university Open Days. Speak to Admissions tutors about taking Gap Years. Students should try to visit as many universities as possible to get a feel for the place.
Upper Sixth	*Sept-Dec*	Fill in UCAS forms and clearly mark preference for deferred entry. Hand in no later than 15th January (or 15th October for Medicine and Oxbridge applications)
	Oct-Apr	Make plans for Gap Year (apply to placement scheme/s, volunteer organisations, consider travel options, etc.). Earn as much money as possible to fund your Gap Year
	Jan-March	Receive conditional offers from universities
	Around April	Submit final decision for first and second choice university courses
	May/June	Sit A2 Exams
	August	Results Day
		i) Sufficient grades; accept the place and enjoy the Gap Year
		ii) Insufficient grades; implement Plan B

Plan B

Upper Sixth	*Late August*	Phone universities to see if they will still offer a place. Be prepared to stay on the phone for a week. Clearing has been going on since mid-July
		If yes, take the place offered and proceed with original Gap Year plans
		If no, reapply the next year for alternative courses and proceed with original plans
		Find a tutorial college and proceed as below.
	Late Sept	Closing date for Clearing
Gap Year	*Sept-May*	Study at tutorial college and spend spare time working, doing voluntary work, taking a skills course, etc.
	Sept-Dec	Reapply to universities via UCAS (presumably no deferred entry this time)
	Jan-March	Receive offers
	May/June	Resit examinations
	June-Sept	Free time for travelling, work, etc.
	August	Results Day (again)
First Year	*Sept-Oct*	Freshers' Week at university

Planning &
Preparation

Every successful gap year combines periodic flights of fancy with methodical planning; any homework you do ahead of time will benefit you later, if only because it will give you more confidence. Your first task in the planning stages, is to consider some of the programmes and organisations described in this book and to obtain details from the addresses and websites given. If an organisation offers a project that appeals, the next step is to find out whether you are eligible. Usually the hardest part is not being accepted to join but raising enough money to fund it.

FUNDRAISING

For many gap year students, a shortage of money is the main obstacle. The most straightforward way of gathering together some cash for travels is to work locally and save like mad. Many gappers find that their parents are more willing to help them financially if they want to pursue a worthwhile ambition such as spending a month in Spain to learn the language or joining a voluntary scheme in the developing world. Of course many 18 year olds baulk at the idea of accepting hand-outs from parents and a possible compromise is the one arrived at by Alice Mundy whose ski instructor course in Canada cost a cool £6000 before insurance or spending money. To finance her gap year she worked for around 7 months over the year but the majority was covered by a loan from her parents which she will pay back once she is earning enough (possibly as a snowboard instructor in her vacations).

As we have seen, many of the most attractive gap year schemes are expensive (£3000+) so fundraising becomes a major issue for those sixth formers and others who have decided to take a gap year. Others who simply want to travel will also have to save a substantial sum that should include a contingency fund as well as the minimum for airfares and living expenses.

Once you have resolved to meet a particular target, it is surprising how single-mindedly you can pursue it. Most sending agencies provide extensive advice and support on fundraising, and a lot of useful tips and tricks can be found on the web. For example www.gapyear.com carries plenty of information and links to real life examples (click on 'Money'). For example at the time of writing, the site included the detailed fund-raising diary of Tori Oram from Kent who was 'binge-saving' to join a wildlife project in South Africa later in 2005; see the section below for some of her ideas.

If you have signed up for an organised placement, you will probably have been sent a timetable for paying the placement fee in instalments. Estimate how long it will take you to reach your target and stick to the deadline come what may. It might help to break the saving down into smaller amounts, so that you aim to save £X per week. Dedicated savers consider a 70-hour week at a local job quite tolerable (which will have the additional advantage of leaving you too tired to conduct an expensive social life). Bear in mind that saving over a long period, especially from a job which doesn't pay well, can be depressing since you will have to deny yourself all those expensive little treats. **Kitty Hill** is just one of the many gap year students who spent six months working 60-hour weeks and the valuable thing she learned from that experience was that 'it is a million times nicer to be in a job you enjoy than a job you hate but pays a bit better'.

Letter Writing

Some year out organisations provide a template of a letter seeking sponsorship and a list of suggested trusts to try. It helps to include a photo and make the letter succinct. Although time-consuming, hand-written letters are thought to attract more attention than slick computer-generated ones. The more obvious care you have taken, the better your chances of success so, for example, you should try to find out the name and job title of the person to whom your request will be referred, and enclose a letter of endorsement from your head teacher. Be aware that a great many businesses and charities have a policy of not funding individuals.

Zoe Nisbet from Madras College in St. Andrew's published a fundraising diary on www.kayem.co.uk/zoe/projecttrust, recording all the ways she used to reach her target of £3350 to go to Malawi with the Project Trust. In Zoe's case she baked cakes and sold them in the staff room every week. But a few of her many letters to charities and trusts met with a positive response and a donation of £800 from a charitable trust meant that she exceeded her target months before she was due to depart.

In writing a report about her very successful post-university gap year in Ghana, Clare Cooper describes the trepidation she felt at the prospect of undertaking to raise the necessary funds to join an AfricaTrust Networks team:
I accepted the offer (against the better judgement of some friends and family) and, armed with positivity, I began the mammoth task of raising £2500. Already working as a care assistant to cover rent and living costs, I took on two extra jobs in a bar and cinema to begin saving. I wrote literally hundreds of letters to local shops, businesses, schools, charities and churches explaining what I was doing and appealing

for sponsorship. To raise awareness of my fundraising, the local newspaper ran a story on me explaining that I would be working with orphans in West Africa and any help with my fundraising would be much appreciated. I followed up this article by visiting local businesses in person asking them if they had received my letter and if not could I leave them another one. I found that using the local paper and visiting people in person really effective.

Still a fair distance from my financial target I had exactly six weeks left to raise the money or I couldn't go. As I worked in a cinema in a thriving local arts centre I decided to organise a fundraising art exhibition. After a couple of weeks of manic organisation and with the invaluable help of friends, family and local artists we held an exhibition of local arts, craft and textiles. The day was a real success, with lots of visitors and many of the artists selling work. With less than a month to go, I was closer to my financial target, but still not there, and running out of time and ideas. With the priceless help and support from the managers, staff and locals in the bar I worked in we organised an African-themed fundraising day. We had a BBQ, bring-and-buy stall, face painting, children's games, art and craft and traditional story telling followed by an evening of music from a number of local bands, a raffle with great prizes provided by local shops, restaurants and businesses and a fantastic African fire sculpture and fireworks display. As well as raising the rest of the money, the night was a great way of saying thank you and good-bye to all my friends and people who had been fundamental to my fundraising.

Target organisations, companies, schools and clubs with which you or your family have links, or which might have some connection with your project. The skill of fundraising is itself impressive when it appears on a CV. Local businesses are usually inundated with requests for donations and raffle prizes and are unlikely to give cash but some might donate some useful items of equipment. Keep track of all the individuals and businesses that have contributed and be sure to send them a thank you note mentioning your fundraising target and progress and then another letter describing the success of your gap year venture.

If you want to go down the route of applying to trusts and charitable bodies, consult a library copy of the *Directory of Grant Making Trusts* (new edition published each April) or contact the Association of Charitable Foundations (020-7255 4499; www.acf.org.uk) which can offer advice on how to approach grant-giving trusts. Also check the National Charities Database on www.charitiesdirect.com or search www.caritasdata.co.uk. If your gap year is being organised by a registered charity, always include the charity reference number in your letter of request since this may be needed by their accounts department. In fact the policy of a great many grant bodies is not to support individuals and so you may meet mostly with rejections, especially at a time when the financial markets are at a low ebb and investments are giving low returns. (One enterprising fundraiser got his friends and family to sponsor him for every rejection.) To avoid wasting a lot of time, see the list headed 'Do Not Approach These Donors' on the Project Trust website (www.projecttrust. org.uk). Another possible source of useful information is the website www.funderfinder. org.uk/advice_pack.php.

One potential source of benefactors cannot be found in the library or on the internet but in your parents' address book. Kitty Hill hit upon a more painless way to raise money than her 60 hour-a-week job:

For sponsorship I wrote to everyone on my parents' Christmas card list asking them to sponsor me for a day of my trip, at about £30 a day. Then I promised to send them a postcard on that day. I raised about £2500 with this method.

Fundraising Ideas

The ingenuity which sixth-formers have demonstrated in organising money-making events, etc. is impressive. If you happen to recall ideas that worked for Comic Relief, think of ways of adapting these. For example one fundraiser got everybody he knew to sponsor him to stay up a tree for a week. You may choose to shave your head, jump out of an aeroplane, organise a fancy dress pub crawl or a thousand other ways to raise money. Try to organise events that will be fun as well as expensive for your well-wishers. For example if you organise a fund-raising quiz in your local pub, give away a few prizes like glitter nail polish. If you have been sponsored to do a bungy jump or swim a mile, hand out sweets when you go round to collect the pledges. If you are seeking sponsorship from businesses, think of ways in which they might benefit, e.g. promise to wear the company T-shirt in a publicity photo on the top of Kilimanjaro or down the Amazon. Other ideas include holding a sweepstake on a big sporting event, hosting a garden fete with stalls and raffles, charging admission to a ceilidh or a salsa evening. One gap year student who went to Mexico organised a huge fashion show which cost £5000 to put on but raised a massive £11,000.

Among Tori Oram's tireless efforts as described on www.gapyear.com, she organised a karaoke night with the support of her local pub landlord at which she charged £1 per person per song and raised more than £400; she painted children's faces at local events, she had her friends (well used to her tomboy ways) to sponsor her to dress and act all girlie for a day, and most successful of all, she arranged to sit in a bathtub of catfood (donated by Budgens) on the forecourt of a petrol station, a fundraising event which was given coverage in the local papers. Perusing such detailed accounts of raising money could be instructive, since it makes clear how much dogged effort and attention to practical detail is needed. (Her worst problem was how to dispose of the catfood after the event.)

Publicise your plans and your need of funds wherever you can. Local papers and radio stations may be willing to carry details of your planned expedition, which may prompt a few local readers/listeners to support you. Ask family and friends to give cash instead of birthday and Christmas presents. Consider possibilities for organising a fundraising event like a concert or a barn dance, a quiz night, wine tasting or an auction of promises. (If your mum or dad was ever on the PTA ask them for advice but don't expect them to run your campaign for you.)

Sources of Funding

In 2005 the government launched its Child Trust Fund, which might help to finance the gap years of the future. All children born after September 1st 2002 received a lump sum of £250 (or £500 for families with an income of less than £13,480). Family and friends are able to add a further £100 a month to the fund, tax-free. Assuming the government of the day is willing, a further £250/£500 will be deposited in the fund (colloquially known as a baby bond) when the child turns 11. This money can be accessed at age 18 to be used for higher education, driving lessons or, of course, a gap year project, course or trip. (If a family were to invest the full £1200 a year in the CTF account from its launch and if the return on the investment averaged 6%, the lucky child would have a lump sum of £33,000 on his or her 18th birthday.) Further information about the CTF can be seen at www.childtrustfund.gov.uk.

A small percentage of schemes operate as scholarships and bring with them their own funding, e.g. the *Youth for Understanding* Japan exchange. *European Voluntary Service* (see entry in the 'Directory of Specialist Gap Year Programmes') provides full funding for a 6-12 month stint as a volunteer on socially beneficial projects in Europe and beyond.

Some schools (not exclusively fee-paying schools) have odd bursaries and travel scholarships which the careers teachers will be able to tell you about. Various scholarships and grants are available to those who fulfil the necessary requirements. To take just a couple of examples: the Caley Gap Scholarship of up to £1000 is offered by the Royal Caledonian Schools Trust (Unit 75, Wenta Business Park, Colne Way, Watford, Herts. WD21 4ND) to the children of Scottish past or current servicemen and women or people with a Scottish parent living in Greater London on a low income. Applicants must submit a proposal for a worthwhile project abroad which will be of at least six months duration.

The Peter Kirk Memorial Scholarship (c/o Secretary, 17 St. Paul's Rise, Addingham, Ilkley, Yorks. LS29 0QD; mail@kirkfund.org.uk; www.kirkfund.org.uk) funds 10-12 young people aged 18-27 to investigate and write about some aspect of modern Europe. Awards of up to £1500 are made to those carrying out research over 6-12 weeks. The deadline for applications is the end of February, interviews in mid-April. Several school leavers were awarded £1500 in 2005, one to look at traditional summer festivals in Scandinavia, another to investigate why Milan has become the fashion capital of Europe and a third to compare homelessness in different capital cities.

The Winston Churchill Memorial Trust (15 Queen's Gate Terrace, London SW7 5PR; www.wcmt.org.uk) awards about 100 four to eight week travelling fellowships to UK citizens of any age or background who wish to undertake a specific project or study related to their personal interests, job or community. The deadline for applications falls in October. Past winners are listed on the website with their age and topic of study; most are older than school/college leaving age. One young winner looked at the development of the choral tradition; another project took as its theme badminton coaching in New Zealand.

In 2004, STA Travel launched a Year Out Travel Trust to support individuals or small groups joining voluntary projects abroad. In 2005, the grants (usually of £1000) were directed at Tsunami relief projects. For details see the website www.statravel.co.uk/c_yearout/traveltrust.asp.

Sixth formers at one of the 240 independent boys' and coed schools that belong to the Headmasters' and Headmistresses' Conference (HMC) may apply for one of the 30 annual Bulkeley-Evans gap year scholarships worth between £300 and £500. Full details of eligibility can be found on the website www.gapyear-bulkeley-evans-hmc.co.uk or can be requested from the Administrator, A. H. Beadles (Chaff Barn, Downyard, Compton Pauncefoot, Yeovil, Somerset BA22 7EL; tonybeadles@freeuk.com). Applications should be in by the beginning of March.

The London livery companies can be worth investigating. For example the Worshipful Company of Cutlers offers at least three Captain F.G. Boot scholarships per year valued at £500-£1000 depending on the financial need of the successful students. Applicants must be aged 17-25 and planning to spend at least six consecutive months in a foreign country to increase their understanding of the language and culture of that country. The closing date for applications is 12th June; details from the Clerk to the Cutlers' Company, Cutlers' Hall, Warwick Lane, London EC4M 7BR (clerk@cutlerslondon.co.uk).

Archaeology Abroad (www.britarch.ac.uk/archabroad; with an entry in the 'Directory of Volunteering Abroad' below) makes Fieldwork Awards of up to £500 to selected candidates joining an archaeological excavation who must be subscribers to *Archaeology Abroad* (see first-hand account in the chapter on Greece).

Anyone over 18 without access to funds for vocational courses may be eligible to apply for a Career Development Loan. CDLs are bank loans covering up to 80% of the cost of a vocational course lasting less than two years followed by up to a year's practical experience. The Department for Education and Skills (DfES) pays the interest until a month after your course finishes whereupon you must begin repayments at a favourable rate of interest. You may be able to apply a CDL to such diverse courses as TEFL and ski instructor training. Write for details to Freepost, Career Development Loans (0800 585505; www.lifelonglearning.co.uk/cdl).

INSURANCE

Any student heading beyond Europe should have travel insurance. Within Europe private insurance is not absolutely essential because European nationals are eligible for reciprocal emergency health care in the EEA. In 2005 the United Kingdom began to introduce the new Europe-wide European Health Insurance Card (EHIC) to replace the E111. The phasing-in process involves an interim E111 form which will be valid until 31st December 2005. It is possible to apply in advance for the new EHIC by ticking the box on the new

E111 application form (available from post offices). The new card will then be automatically issued when the EHIC is introduced. In the first phase of introduction, the new card will cover health care for short stays and by 2008, the electronic card will take the place of the current E128 and E119 which cover longer stays for job-seekers and students. At present this reciprocal cover is extended only to emergency treatment, so private insurance is also highly recommended, not least to cope with theft.

Outside Europe, a solid travel insurance policy is essential. Research carried out by the Foreign & Commonwealth Office revealed that more than a quarter of young travellers aged 16-34 do not purchase travel insurance, which means that about three million people are taking a serious risk. Most students and backpackers shop around to find the cheapest policy. But if you are going outside the developed world or considering doing any kind of adventure sport, give some thought to what the policy covers, for example look closely at whether the policy will repatriate you or fly out a parent in an emergency. Check the exclusions carefully and the amount of excess you'll have to pay if you claim.

In situations where you might be two days from civilisation, it is imperative that you (or your sending agency) have water-tight insurance. During **Tom Watkins'** expedition with *BSES* to Lesotho, one of the members of the expedition had a fit. He was picked up by helicopter in less than half an hour (and was subsequently fine). At that point Tom was very glad that his expedition organisers had the best insurance policy that money could buy, even though earlier he had felt disappointed that he had not been allowed to go rock-climbing for reasons of insurance.

Most insurance companies offer a standard rate that covers medical emergencies and a premium rate that in addition covers personal baggage, cancellation, etc. Always read the fine print. Sometimes activities like bungy-jumping or scuba diving (now quite commonplace in parts of the world) are excluded. Some travel policies list as one of their exclusions: 'any claims which arise while the Insured is engaged in any manual employment'. If you are not planning to visit North America, the premiums will be much less expensive. Most insurance companies operate 24-hour helplines in the UK which can be dialled from anywhere in the world.

Some companies to consider are listed here with an estimate of their premiums for 12 months of worldwide cover (including the USA). Expect to pay roughly £20-£25 per month for basic cover and £30-£35 for more extensive cover.

Boots Insurance Services, Travel Cover Centre, PO Box 1940, Kings Orchard, 1 Queen St, Bristol BS99 2TT (0845 840 2020; www.bootsinsurance.com). Dedicated Gap Year travel cover which costs £299 for one year. Available to anyone up to 34.

Club Direct, Dominican House, St John's St, Chichester, W Sussex (0800 083 2455; www.clubdirect.com). Work abroad is included provided it does not involve using heavy machinery; £337 for year-long cover including baggage cover.

Columbus Direct, 17 Devonshire Square, London EC2M 4SQ (020-7375 0011; 08450 761030; www.columbusdirect.com). Globetrotter policy (basic medical cover only) costs about £200 for one year. More extensive cover is offered for £312 and £364. In association with www.gapyear.com, has developed a range of specialised policies; see *www.noworriesinsurance.com.*

Coverworks, 47a Barony Road, Nantwich, Cheshire CW5 7PB (08702 862828; www.coverworks.com). Policy specially designed for working holidays. £235 (€325).

Downunder Worldwide Travel Insurance. 3 Spring St, Paddington, London W2 3RA (0800 393908; www.dinsure.com). Backpacker policy starts at £250. Adventurer policy covering adventure sports costs £340.

Endsleigh Insurance, Endsleigh House, Cheltenham, Glos GL50 3NR. Offices in most university towns. Twelve months of cover worldwide costs from £202, £305 for higher cover. Maximum age 35.

gosure.com – 0845 222 0020; www.gosure.com. Worldwide backpacker policy (which doesn't cover lost baggage) for just over £200 to cover 18 months including up to 3 months in North America.

Insure and Go, 0870 901 3674; www.insureandgo.com. £176 (no cover for theft) or £235 worldwide; from £140 for 12 months' very basic cover to Australia/New Zealand only. Allows people who take out its plan to cancel if they do not get the A-level grades required for university.

MRL Insurance, Enterprise House, Station Parade, Chipstead, Surrey CR5 3TE; 0870 876 7677; www.mrlinsurance.co.uk. £210 for backpackers under 35.

Navigator Travel Insurance Services Ltd, 19 Ralli Courts, West Riverside, Manchester M3 5FT (0870 241 0576; www.navigatortravel.co.uk). Covers gap years, working holidays, etc.

Travel Insurance Agency, Suite 2, Percy News, 755B High Road, North Finchley, London N12 8JY (020-8446 5414/5; www.travelinsurers.com) £210/£290.

HEALTH & SAFETY

No matter what country you are heading for, you should obtain the Department of Health leaflet T6 *Health Advice for Travellers.* This leaflet should be available from any post office or doctor's surgery. Alternatively you can request a free copy on the Health Literature Line 08701 555455 or read it online at www.dh.gov.uk, which also has country-by-country details.

If you are planning to include developing countries on your itinerary, you will want to take the necessary health precautions, though this won't be cheap unless you happen to have a well informed GP who doesn't charge much for non-essential injections. Competition among private travel clinics may bring prices down, though this benefits the 'consumer' only in London. At many clinics you will pay between £20 and £40 per vaccine, and more for hepatitis A and B. An added difficulty is that GPs cannot be expected to keep abreast of all the complexities of obscure tropical diseases and malaria prophylaxis for different areas, etc. Many are downright ignorant, though internet access to expert sites has alleviated this problem to some extent.

Pre-eminent among specialist providers are Nomad Travel Clinics which specialise in longhaul travel; the Nomad Travel Stores can be found in Russell Square, Victoria and North London plus Bristol (www.nomadtravel.co.uk) all of which have travel clinics that can offer expert advice. The Hospital for Tropical Diseases (Mortimer Market, Capper St, Tottenham Court Road, London, WC1E 6AU; www.uclh.org) operates an automated information line on 09061 337733 (50p per minute and calls should last 7-8 minutes). To make an appointment ring 020-7388 9600. Consultations are offered at their clinic near Oxford Circus for £15 but if you have your jabs there, the fee is waived. The respected travel agent Trailfinders operates a walk-in Travel Clinic at 194 Kensington High St (020-7983 3999).

MASTA (Moorfield Road, Yeadon, Leeds LS19 7BN; enquiries@masta.org/ www.masta.org) is one of the most authoritative sources of travellers' health information in Britain and maintains a database of the latest information on the prevention of tropical and other diseases. Calls to the Travellers' Health Line (0906 822 4100) are charged at 60p per minute (average cost of call £2). MASTA can provide personalised advice depending on your destinations, which can be either e-mailed or posted to you. Here you can find explanations about protection against malaria, guidelines on what to eat and drink, and how to avoid motion sickness, jet lag and sunburn. MASTA's network of travel clinics administers inoculations and, like their online shop, sells medical kits and other specialist equipment like water purifiers and survival tools. MASTA also co-operates with the Blood Care Foundation, a charity that aims to deliver properly screened blood and sterile transfusion equipment to members in an emergency. If you are going to be spending a lot of time in countries where blood screening is not reliable you should consider carrying a sterile medical kit. Some countries have introduced HIV antibody testing for long-stay foreigners and the certificate may be required to obtain a work or residence visa.

For advice on protecting your sexual health, Marie Stopes International (020-7574 7400; www.mariestopes.org.uk) is helpful; they have published a free guide to traveller's sexual health called the *Back Pocket Guide*. The government's free booklet 'Drugs Abroad' and the National Drugs Helpline (0800 776600) can give information on drugs laws abroad.

It is worth looking at a general guide to travel medicine such as *Bugs, Bites and Bowels* by Dr. Jane Wilson Howarth (Cadogan, £9.99) or *Traveller's Health: How to Stay Healthy Abroad* by Richard Dawood (OUP, £15.99). These books emphasise the necessity of avoiding tap water and recommend ways to purify your drinking water by filtering, boiling or chemical additives (iodine is more reliable than chlorine). MASTA and Nomad market various water purifiers; among the best are the 'Aquapure Traveller' (£40) and the 'Trekker Travel Well' (£65). Tap water throughout Western Europe is safe to drink.

Increasingly, people are seeking advice via the internet; check for example www.fitfor-travel.scot.nhs.uk; www.tmb.ie and www.travelhealth.co.uk. Agropharm (www.Agropharm.co.uk) markets an impressive range of medications and equipment for the prospective traveller to tropical countries. Agropharm is an independent private pharmacy based in Devon and the website conveys country-by-country advice on anti-malarials, etc.

Americans seeking general travel health advice should ring the Center for Disease Control & Prevention Hotline in Atlanta on 404-332-4559; www.cdc.gov/travel.

Malaria is continuing to make a serious comeback in many parts of the world, due to the resistance of certain strains of mosquito to the pesticides and preventative medications which have been so extensively relied upon in the past. You must be particularly careful if travelling to a place where there is falciparum malaria which is potentially fatal. Out of up to 2500 British travellers who return home to the UK with malaria each year, 10 to 20 will die. The two main drugs can be obtained over the counter: Chloroquine and Proguanil (brand name Paludrine). In regions resistant to these drugs, you will have to take both or a third line of defence such as Maloprim or Mefloquine available only on prescription. Because of possible side effects it is important that your doctor be able to vary the level of toxicity to match the risks prevalent in your destination. A newly licensed (and expensive) drug called Malarone is used as an alternative to mefloquine or doxycyline, and is recommended for short trips to highly chloroquine-resistant areas. New drugs are being developed all the time and sometimes there is a time lag before they are licensed in the UK or USA. For example in her gap year in Madagascar, Karen Hedges twice contracted malaria but was quickly treated with an effective drug called Coartem, expensive by local standards, and not yet licensed in the UK.

Unfortunately these prophylactic medications are not foolproof, and even those who have scrupulously swallowed their pills before and after their trip as well as during it have been known to contract the disease. It is therefore essential to take mechanical precautions against mosquitoes. Wearing fine silk clothes discourages bites. If possible, screen the windows and sleep under a permethrin-impregnated mosquito net since the offending mosquitoes feed between dusk and dawn. (Practise putting your mosquito net up before leaving home since some are tricky to assemble.) Some travellers have improvised with some netting intended for prams which takes up virtually no luggage space. If you don't have a net, cover your limbs at nightfall with light-coloured garments, apply insect repellent with the active ingredient DEET and sleep with a fan on to keep the air moving. Try to keep your room free of the insects too by using mosquito coils, vaporisers, etc.

In tropical countries be aware of all the potential risks including the innocuous sounding 'heat exhaustion'. If your body temperature shoots up and you become dehydrated by not drinking enough water, heat exhaustion can lead to heat stroke which can lead to organ failure and death.

Consider taking a first aid course before leaving. The St. John Ambulance (020-7324 4000; www.sja.org.uk) offers a range of Lifesaver and Lifesaver Plus courses. The standard half-day emergency first-aid course costs from £20 (depending on region). Several short courses specialise in preparing young people for potential danger and unpredictable situations abroad; see entries in the 'Directory of Gap Year Safety & Preparation Courses'.

RED TAPE

Passports

A ten-year UK passport costs £42 for 32 pages and £54.50 for 48 pages, and should be processed by the Passport Agency within ten days, though it is safer to allow more time. The one-week fast track application procedures costs £70 and an existing passport can be renewed in person at a passport office, but only if you have made a prior appointment by ringing the Passport Agency on 0870 521 0410 and are willing to pay £89 (£95.50 for 48 pages). Passport office addresses are listed on passport application forms available from main post offices All relevant information can be found on the website www.passports. gov.uk.

Travel Visas

Outside the Schengen Area of Europe in which border controls have been largely abolished, you can't continue in one direction for very long before you are impeded by border guards demanding to see your papers. EU nationals who confine their travels to Europe have little to worry about. Everyone else should do their homework. Post September 11th, immigration and security checks are tighter than ever before and many countries have imposed visa restrictions, particularly on North Americans in retaliation for all the new restrictions the US has implemented. Embassy websites are the best source of information or you can check online information posted by visa agencies. For example Thames Consular Services in London (www.thamesconsular.com) allows you to search visa requirements and costs for UK nationals visiting any country. Addresses for some foreign Consulates and High Commissions in London are listed in Appendix II. Getting visas is a headache anywhere and often an expensive headache, but is usually easier in your home country.

If you are short of time or live a long way from the Embassies in London, private visa agencies like Thames Consular may be of interest. Others include the VisaService, 2 Northdown St, London N1 9BG (020-7833 2709/fax 020-7833 1857; www.visaservice. co.uk) and Global Visas (020-7009 3800; www.globalvisas.com). In addition to the fee charged by the country's embassy, there will be a service charge normally of £30-£35 per visa.

If you intend to cross a great many borders, especially on an overland trip through Africa, ensure that you have all the relevant documentation and that your passport contains as many blank pages as frontiers which you intend to cross. Travellers have been turned back purely because the border guard refused to use a page with another stamp on it.

Work Visas

The free reciprocity of labour within the European Union means that the red tape has been simplified (though not done away with completely). The standard situation among EU countries (plus Norway and Iceland which belong to the European Economic Area or EEA) is that nationals of any EU state have the right to look for work in another member state for up to three months. At the end of that period they should apply to the police or the local authority for a residence permit, showing their passport and job contract. Note that there are transitional controls operating in some of the ten countries that were admitted to the Union in May 2004 (ee section 'Working in Europe' in the chapter *Work Experience* for information about the new member states of the European Union.)

Outside Europe, obtaining permission to work is next to impossible for short periods during a gap year unless you are participating in an organised exchange programme where the red tape is taken care of by your sponsoring organisation. If you come up against bureaucratic obstacles, try to work around it as **Jaime Burnell** did in her gap year:

> *I wanted to find work in South Africa but work permits were too difficult and expensive. Instead, I exchanged au pair work for room and board and enjoyed two months in Durban.*

Student and Youth Hostel Cards

With an International Student Identity Card (ISIC) it is often possible to obtain reduced fares on trains, planes and buses, £1 off each night's stay at a youth hostel in the UK, discounted admission to museums and theatres, and other perks. The ISIC is available to all students in full-time education. There is no age limit though some flight carriers do not apply discounts for students over 31. To obtain a card (which is valid for 15 months from September) you will need to complete the ISIC application form, provide a passport photo, proof of full-time student status (NUS card or official letter) and the fee of £7. Take these to any students' union, local student travel office or send £7.50 to ISIC Mail Order (OPS Hull Ltd, Unit 132, Louis Pearlman Centre, Goulten St, Hull HU3 4DL). When issued with an ISIC, students also receive a handbook containing travel tips, details of national and international discounts and how to get in touch with the ISIC helpline, a special service for travelling students who need advice in an emergency.

Membership in the Youth Hostels Association costs £14 or £7 for the under 18s; contact the YHA at Trevelyan House, Dimple Road, Matlock, Derbyshire DE4 3YH (0870 770 8868; www.yha.org.uk). Seasonal demand abroad can be high, so it is always preferable to book in advance if you know your itinerary. You can pre-book beds over the internet on www.iyhf.org or through individual hostels and national offices listed in the *Hostelling International Guides*: Volume I covers Europe and the Mediterranean, Volume II covers the rest of the world. They can be ordered by ringing Customer Services on the above number or online for £6.50 each including postage.

A growing number of privately-owned hostels is providing lively competition for the International Youth Hostels Federation; check the websites www.hostels.com, www. hostelworld.com or www.hostels.net for a selection worldwide. VIP Backpacker hostel group (www.vipbackpackers.com) includes hundreds of hostels in Australia, New Zealand, South Africa and Europe; a membership card costs £16.

Three hundred hostels are listed in the pocket-sized annually revised *Independent Hostel Guide* from the Backpackers Press, Speedwell House, Upperwood, Matlock Bath, Derbyshire DE4 3PE (tel/fax 01629 580427; sam@backpackerspress.com), at a cost of £4.95 (plus £1 postage); most are in the UK. Hostel details are now available online at www.IndependentHostelGuide.co.uk.

Hostels are a good source of temporary work, often providing a few hours a day of work in return for bed and board. For many travellers, hostels are the key to an excellent holiday. Not only do they provide an affordable place to sleep (typically £10-£20 in the first world, less in developing countries), they provide access to a valuable range of information about what to see, how to get there and who to go with. Additional services are often provided such as bicycle hire or canoeing and trekking trips.

Travel Warnings

The Foreign Office has a Travel Advice Unit which can be contacted on 0870 606 0290; www.fco.gov.uk/travel. This site gives frequently updated and detailed risk assessments of any trouble spots, including civil unrest, terrorism and crime. If you have access to BBC Ceefax look at pages 470 and following. Several years ago the FCO launched a 'Know Before You Go' campaign to raise awareness among backpackers and independent travellers of potential risks and dangers and how to guard against them, principally by having a good insurance policy. The same emphasis can be detected on the FCO site launched in 2005: www.gogapyear.co.uk. According to FCO research younger travellers are twice as likely as the average to get into some kind of trouble abroad.

General advice on minimising the risks of independent travel is contained in the book *World Wise - Your Passport to Safer Travel* published by Thomas Cook in association with the Suzy Lamplugh Trust and the Foreign Office (www.suzylamplugh.org/worldwise; £6.99 plus £2 postage). Arguably its advice is over-cautious, advising travellers never to ride a motorbike or accept an invitation to a private house. Travellers will have to decide for themselves when to follow this advice and when to ignore it.

Taxation

Students who find holiday jobs often have more tax deducted by their employers than they are liable for. If you earn less than the annual tax-free personal allowance (£4895 in 2005/6), you should pay no tax at all. It is a time-consuming and bothersome business to claim back what you've overpaid at the end of the tax year (April 6th). It is better to obtain the relevant form P38(S) from the Inland Revenue before starting work which proves that you are a student doing a vacation job; note that it does not apply to longer-term work even if you are a student.

In theory EU students working in the EU for less than six months are not liable for tax, so students should always show their employers documents to prove their status. In many countries your employer will expect you to clarify your tax position with the local tax office at the beginning of your work period. This can be to your advantage for example in Denmark or Australia where, unless you obtain a tax card, you will be put on a very high emergency rate of tax.

MONEY

The average budget of a travelling student is at least £25 a day though many survive on much less in cheap countries. Whatever the size of your travelling fund, you should give some thought to how and in what form to carry your money. Travellers' cheques are safer than cash, though they cost an extra 1% and banks able to encash them are not always near to hand, even in Europe. The most universally recognised brands are American Express and Visa (Thomas Cook now sells American Express products). It is advisable also to carry cash and a debit or credit card. Sterling is fine for most countries but US dollars or euros are preferred in much of the world such as Latin America, Eastern Europe and Israel. The easiest way to look up the exchange rate of any world currency is to check on the internet (e.g. www.xe.net/ucc) or to look at the Monday edition of the *Financial Times*. A Currency

Conversion Chart is included in Appendix I. The best way to find out where you can change American Express cheques in advance is to log on to www.americanexpress.co.uk/travellerscheques, where the contact details of fee-free exchange partners are listed. For Thomas Cook/MasterCard cheques, go to www.cashmycheques.com.

Hole-in-the-wall cash dispensers can be found in major cities around the world but find out in advance what charge your bank makes for withdrawals from hole-in-the-wall machines abroad. For example the transaction fee for withdrawing foreign currency abroad or paying at point-of-sale with a standard Maestro card is 2.65% in addition to the ordinary exchange rate disadvantage plus cash machine withdrawals cost 2.25% of the sterling transaction up to a maximum £4 (no minimum) and POS fee is 75p. If you are going to be going to remote parts, ask your bank for a list of ATMs in the areas you will visit. Otherwise you can check the ATM locator on www.mastercard.com or http://visa.via.infonow.net/locator/global (where you'll learn where the facility is in Antarctica).

Theft takes many forms, from the highly trained gangs of gypsy children who artfully pick pockets in European railway stations to violent attacks on the streets of American cities. Risks can be reduced by carrying your wealth in several places including a comfortable money belt worn inside your clothing, steering clear of seedy or crowded areas and moderating your intake of alcohol. If you are robbed, you must obtain a police report (often for a fee) to stand any chance of recouping part of your loss from your insurer (assuming the loss of cash is covered in your policy) or from your travellers' cheque company. Always keep a separate record of the cheque numbers you are carrying, so you will know instantly the numbers of the ones that have been taken.

Haggling is a topic of endless fascination among world travellers. Try to avoid boasting about how hard a bargain you are able to drive. Remember that in some countries, the rickshaw driver or temple guide could feed his family that day with the 20p you saved. But spreading largesse randomly is not advisable either. It is not uncommon for children to skip school in order to frequent tourist haunts where they stand a chance of being given a few coins.

Transferring Money

Assuming your account at home remains in credit and you have access to a compatible ATM, it shouldn't be necessary to have money wired to you urgently. If you run out of money abroad, whether through mismanagement, loss or theft and cannot use an ATM, you can contact your bank back home by telephone, fax or online, and ask them to wire money to you. This will be easier if you have set up a telephone or internet bank account before leaving home since they will then have the correct security checks in place to authorise a transfer without having to receive something from you in writing with your signature. You can request that the necessary sum be transferred from your bank to a named bank in the town you are in – something you have to arrange with your own bank, so you know where to pick the money up.

A new service has been launched by MasterCard called Cash2Go (www.cash2go.com). The system provides a pre-paid debit card which can be loaded up before your departure and then reloaded by your parents if necessary. Similarly Visa has a TravelMoney service which works like a phone card; you credit it with cash and then access the money from cash machines worldwide with a PIN number. This is probably the most efficient way of transferring funds abroad, however find out whether your credit card charges a handling fee (typically 1.5%). If both you and your parents have a MasterCard, they could use the MoneySend system to send cash in a crisis.

Western Union offers an international money transfer service whereby cash deposited at one branch can be withdrawn by you from any other branch or agency, which your benefactor need not specify. Western Union agents – there are 90,000 of them in 200 countries – come in all shapes and sizes, e.g. travel agencies, stationers, chemists. Unfortunately it is not well represented outside the developed world. The person sending money to you simply turns up at a Western Union counter counter, pays in the desired sum plus the fee, which is £14 for up to £100 transferred, £21 for £100-200, £37 for £500 and so on. For an extra £7 your benefactor can do this over the phone with a credit card. In the UK, ring 0800-833833 for further details, a list of outlets and a complete rate schedule. The website www.westernunion.com allows you to search for the nearest outlet.

Thomas Cook, American Express and the UK Post Office offer a similar service called Moneygram. Cash deposited at one of their foreign exchange counters is available within ten minutes at the named destination or can be collected up to 45 days later at one of 60,000 co-operating agents in 160 countries. The fee is £12 for sending £100, £18 for up to £200, £24 for up to £300, £46 for between £750 and £1000 and so on. Ring 0800 018 0104 for details or check the Post Office website (www.postoffice.co.uk).

Making Contacts

The importance of knowing people, not necessarily in high places but on the spot, is stressed by many gap year travellers. Some people are lucky enough to have family and friends scattered around the world in positions to offer advice or even accommodation and employment. Others must create their own contacts by exploiting less obvious connections.

Dick Bird, who spent over a year travelling around South America, light-heartedly anticipates how this works:

In Bolivia we hope to start practising another survival technique known as 'having some addresses'. The procedure is quite simple. Before leaving one's country of origin, inform everyone you know from your immediate family to the most casual acquaintance, that you are about to leave for South America. With only a little cajoling they might volunteer the address of somebody they once met on the platform of Clapham Junction or some other tenuous connection who went out to South America to seek their fortunes. You then present your worthy self on the unsuspecting emigré's doorstep and announce that you have been in close and recent communication with their nearest and dearest. Although you won't necessarily be welcomed with open arms, the chances are they will be eager for your company and conversation. Furthermore these contacts are often useful for finding work: doing odd jobs, farming, tutoring people they know, etc.

A number of organised schemes exist whereby you can link up with people willing to offer accommodation for short periods, sometimes in exchange for some help. The international WWOOF scheme operates this way, allowing travellers to stay on organic farms around the world (see entry in chapter on Volunteering). One way of developing contacts is to join a travel club such as the Globetrotters Club (BCM/Roving, London WC1N 3XX; info@globetrotters.co.uk) for £15/€27 a year. The Club has no office and so correspondence addressed to the above box office address is answered by volunteers. Members receive a bi-monthly travel newsletter and a list of members, many of whom are willing to extend hospitality to other globetrotters and possibly to advise them on local employment prospects.

Servas International is an organisation begun by an American Quaker, which runs a worldwide programme of free hospitality exchanges for travellers, to further world peace and understanding. Normally you don't stay with one host for more than a couple of days. To become a Servas traveller or host in the UK, contact Servas Britain, 68 Cadley Road, Collingbourne Ducis, Marlborough, Wilts. SN8 3EB; 020 8444 7778 (www.servasbritain. u-net.com) who can forward your enquiry to your Area Co-ordinator. Before a traveller can be given a list of hosts (which are drawn up every autumn), he or she must pay a fee of £25 (£35 for couples) and be interviewed by a co-ordinator.

Workaway.info is a volunteer programme run by Britons resident in Spain to facilitate contact between gappers and families or businesses that are looking for volunteers. They work by providing a contact list for a modest charge of €15. The site was set up to promote a fair work exchange between budget travellers, language learners or culture seekers and families, individuals or organizations who are looking for help with a range of varied and interesting activities. Five hours of honest work are given each day in exchange for food and accommodation with hosts in varying situations and surroundings. The host list is accessible on-line and potential volunteers contact hosts directly (www.workaway.info).

Other hospitality clubs and exchanges are worth investigating. Women Welcome Women World Wide (88 Easton St, High Wycombe, Bucks. HP11 1LT; tel/fax 01494 465441; www.womenwelcomewomen.org.uk) enables women of different countries to visit one another. There is no set subscription, but the minimum donation requested is £25/$47, which covers the cost of the membership list and three newsletters in which members may publish announcements. There are currently 3,500 members (aged 16-80+) in 70 countries.

Hospitality exchange organisations crop up from time to time. Check out www.hospitalityclub.org (which has a special area for hitch-hikers) in which membership is free. Other possibilities include the Hospitality Exchange, 822 W. Watson St, Lewistown, Montana 59457 (406-538-8770; www.hospex.net) which charges $20 for a year's membership.

WHAT TO TAKE

Packing for travelling as a backpacker will always entail compromises because you will be limited in the amount of clothes and equipment you can take with you. When you're buying a backpack/rucksack in a shop try to place a significant weight in it so you can feel how comfortable it might be to carry on your back, otherwise you'll be misled by lifting something usually filled with foam.

Another important consideration is what you take for sleeping. A tropical quilt might be preferable to a sleeping bag for travel in hot climates. Either you can spread out the quilt as a bed to sleep on or it can be folded to create a lightweight sleeping bag. The other advantage is that it is much lighter to carry and takes up less room in your luggage. Alternatively, it can be wrapped around your shoulders for warmth in an air-conditioned space or on a chilly evening in the mountains. After washing, the quilt dries in 20 minutes. However, it will not provide enough warmth if you're planning to travel at high altitudes. A down vest might be a solution for travelling at altitude and can also double up as a comfortable pillow.

While aiming to travel as lightly as possible, you should consider the advantage of taking certain extra pieces of equipment like comfortable walking boots or a tent if you will have the chance to travel independently. One travelling tip is to carry dental floss, useful not only for your teeth but as strong twine for mending backpacks, hanging up laundry, etc.

In the tropics you must carry water, in order to prevent dehydration. Belts with zips worn under a shirt are very handy for carrying money unobtrusively. A bandana is also advisable in the tropics to mop up sweat or to put round your face in windy desert conditions. Some even have backgammon and chess sets printed on them to provide portable entertainment.

When packing it's best to roll clothes to save space and put the heaviest objects at the bottom of the pack. One bizarre piece of advice passed on by a backpacker is to take a spare set of clothes to your local butcher and ask to have them vacuum-packed, to keep an emergency set of clothes dry and clean. Always carry liquids (like shampoo or iodine for purifying water) inside a plastic bag in case they leak.

If you have plumped for a placement scheme which is sending you to one place for a long period of time like a village school or kibbutz, you might allow yourself the odd (lightweight) luxury, such as a Mini-disk, short-wave radio or jar of peanut butter.

HANDY TRAVEL TIPS FOR BACKPACKERS

- Keep a record of vital travel documents like passport number, driving licence, travellers' cheque serial numbers, insurance policy, tickets, emergency number for cancelling credit cards, etc. Make two copies: stow one away in your luggage and give the other to a friend or relation at home. You can scan and/or email this information to yourself so that in an emergency you can access it from any internet café.
- Make sure your passport will remain valid for at least three months beyond the expected duration of your trip; some countries require six months worth of validity.
- Carry valuable items (like passport, essential medicines and of course money) on your person rather than relegating them to a piece of luggage which might be lost or stolen.
- Only take items you are prepared to lose.
- When deciding on clothes to take, start at your feet and work your way up the body; then try to shed up to half. If you find that you really need some missing item of clothing, you can always buy it en route
- Take waterproof and dustproof luggage.
- Remember to ask permission before taking photographs of individuals or groups. In some cultures it can be insulting.
- Take advantage of the loos in expensive hotels and fast food chains.
- Use the libraries of the British Council which can be found in most capital cities. The luxuries on offer include British newspapers and air-conditioning.
- Take a list of consular addresses in the countries you intend to visit in case of emergency

---

Good maps and guides always enhance one's enjoyment of a trip. Most people you will meet on the road will probably be carrying a *Rough Guide* or a *Travel Survival Kit* from Lonely Planet. These are both excellent series, though try not to become enslaved by their advice and preferences. Rough Guides has a title which could be of interest to gap year students *First Time Around the World*. Even though so much advance information is available over the internet (for example www.travelleronline.co.uk allows you to link to selected extracts of Rough Guides and London Planet publications), nothing can compete with a proper guide book to pore over and take away with you. If you are going to be based in a major city, buy a map ahead of time. Visit the famous travel book shop Stanfords (12-14 Long Acre, Covent Garden, London WC2E 9LP; 020-7836 1321/fax 020-7836 0189) now with branches in Bristol and Manchester, and Daunt Books for Travellers (83 Marylebone High Street, London W1M 4DE; 020-7224 2295) which stocks fiction and travel writing alongside guide books and maps. The Map Shop (15 High St, Upton-on-Severn, Worcestershire WR8 0HJ; 01684 593146/e-mail: Themapshop@btinternet.com) does an extensive mail order business and will send you the relevant catalogue for the part of the world you are intending to visit.

If you are going to a country to learn or improve a language, you might take a good dictionary and a language course at a suitable level, for example the *Quick Take Off In…* series from Oxford University Press which includes 2½ hours of audio with a clear course-book for a modest £12.99 (www.askoxford.com/languages). For more information about language learning, see the chapter below on Courses.

Preparation is half the fun but choose like-minded company before discussing your intended anti-malarial regimen and your water sterilising equipment since you don't want to turn into a pub bore.

What to leave behind

Make sure you leave a record of all-important documents with your parents plus at least four signed passport photos which are needed for university loan applications and by some university admissions departments. Whereas forms can be e-mailed, faxed or posted to you abroad for your attention, it is difficult to arrange for photos to be sent and impossible if you are on a placement teaching at a village school in Tanzania or Nepal.

Depending on your destination, don't take your trendy clothes and trainers. For tropical countries, leave behind anything that isn't made of natural fibres like cotton or silk.

STAYING IN TOUCH

The revolution in communication technology means that you are never far from home. Internet cafés can be found in almost every corner of the world where, for a small fee, you can access your e-mail or check relevant information on the web. The technically minded might wish to take a digital camera in order to be able to send photos home electronically. Many gap year travellers also set up their own websites so that they can share their travelogue.

The easiest way to stay in touch is by e-mail, using free messaging services such as www.hotmail.com or www.yahoo.co.uk. Spending time in travel chatrooms like Lonely Planet's thorntree or www.gapyear.com might turn up gems of little-known travel wisdom or put you on your way to connecting up with a like-minded companion. Rough Guides has launched some reasonably priced travel planner software called intouch (www.rough-guidesintouch.com) which might be worth investigating. Clearly there are advantages to such easy communication, though there are also travellers out there who spend an inordinate amount of time tracking down and inhabiting cybercafés instead of looking around the country and meeting locals in the old-fashioned, strike-up-a-conversation, get-in-and-out-of-scrapes way. Just as the texting generation is finding it harder to cut ties with home knowing that a parent or a school friend is only a few digits away wherever they are, so too travellers who spend too much time online risk failing to look round the destination country in depth. Of course parents will want to hear from you frequently but make sure you don't set up an expectation that will leave them worrying if for some reason you are away from a computer for an extended period.

If you prefer the human voice, don't rely on your mobile phone unless you have specifically bought a tri-band model; most European mobiles do not interface with the US roaming system. Roaming charges for mobiles can cost an arm and a leg. Instead, a plethora of companies in the UK and US sell pre-paid calling cards intended to simplify international phoning. You credit your card account with an amount of your choice (normally starting at £10 or £20), or buy a card for $10 or $20. You are given an access code which can be used from any phone. Lonely Planet, the travel publisher, has an easy-to-use communications card called eKno which offers low cost calls, voice mail and email (www.ekno.lonelyplanet. com). A company called 0044 (www.0044.co.uk) sells foreign sim cards which allow you to take your mobile with you and call at local rates while you're away. For example the price of a sim card for Spain (with up to €22 credit and free Nokia unlocking) costs £30.

For very anxious gappers and/or parents, there is a back-up system on the market called SafetyText (www.safetytext.com/gapyear.shtml) which was launched by the father of the British woman Lucie Blackman who was murdered when she was working as a hostess in Japan. SafetyText is a delayed text messaging system which depends on the user remembering to cancel the text once he or she has arrived safely.

Without any new-fangled technology, it is of course possible to buy phone cards locally to use in pay phones, though be sure you're buying what you need. Nineteen-year-old **Eloise Weddell** was anxious at first about staying with a Mexican family in order to improve her Spanish and naturally wanted to keep in touch with home. The card she bought locally allowed her to make very cheap calls within Cuernavaca but it cost her £7 for a 3-minute call to England. **Lucy Jackson** fared even worse on her first homesick night in a Quito hotel; her phone card didn't work at all, so she paid $17 on the hotel phone for one minute's reassurances from her father.

The humble radio offers a way of keeping in touch with events back home. Access to the World Service can be a comfort. You will need a good short-wave radio with several bands powerful enough to pick up the BBC. 'Dedicated' short-wave receivers which are about the size of a paperback start at £65. Some travellers now can't live without their iPods and tune in to their favourite Podcasts including some BBC radio programmes.

A British Consul can:
- Issue an emergency passport.
- Contact relatives and friends to ask them for help with money or tickets.
- Tell you how to transfer money.
- Cash a sterling cheque worth up to £100 if supported by a valid banker's card.
- As a last resort give you a loan to return to the UK.
- Put you in touch with local lawyers, interpreters or doctors.
- Arrange for next of kin to be told of an accident or death.
- Visit you in case of arrest or imprisonment and arrange for a message to be sent to relatives or friends.
- Give guidance on organisations who can help trace missing persons.
- Speak to the local authorities for you.

But a British Consul cannot:
- Intervene in court cases.
- Get you out of prison.
- Give legal advice or start court proceedings for you.
- Obtain better treatment in hospital or prison than is given to local nationals.
- Investigate a crime.
- Pay your hotel, legal, medical, or any other bills.
- Pay your travel costs, except in rare circumstances.
- Perform work normally done by travel agents, airlines, banks or motoring organisations
- Find you somewhere to live or a job or work permit
- Formally help you if you are a dual national in the country of your second nationality
- A Foreign & Commonwealth Office leaflet 'Backpacking and Independent Travellers' is widely distributed at British airports, etc.

Travel

It would be a pretty sad gap year that didn't include at least some travel. Placement schemes abound which can set you down in near or far destinations and give you a chance to get to know a foreign city or region while working, volunteering or studying there. But of course many people taking a year out will simply decide to spend part of it on holiday, usually near the end after they have had a chance to earn and save some money. If you have a friend who wants to go with you, many happy sessions can be spent in the pub planning the itinerary. If your friends are all disappearing in different directions, do not give up on the idea of going on a trip.

Many gap travellers have found that even if they start off alone, they soon meet like-minded travellers in hostels, trains, cyber-cafés and so on. Some even bump into some-one from their school by chance as happened to Ben Hartley when he was changing buses in outback Australia. People who pluck up the courage to travel on their own often find that it is easier for them to have contact with local people.

One solution to the problem of having no available travel companions is to join a group of like-minded people on an overland expedition. There are distinct advantages to having your travel arrangements organised for you en route. For a start you can hand over most concerns about personal security to someone else. Travelling with an overland company saves time and stress usually expended on things like the bureaucratic snags of border crossings and provides help with food, accommodation, activities and excursions. Taking advantage of such insider knowledge removes all the hassle of solitary independent travel. For example Oasis Overland (www.oasisoverland.co.uk) specialises in adventure travel for young travellers with truck-based overland expeditions in South America, Africa and the Middle East lasting 19 days to 29 weeks. Some trips attract more mature travellers while others (such as their 'Egypt Encompassed' trip) tend to emphasise partying. So it is worth making enquiries before booking.

Most overland companies cater for the backpacking market and keep prices down by providing basic accommodation, often camping, and expecting participants to share the cooking duties. Overland trips include optional adventurous excursions, such as mountain trekking, white water rafting or adrenaline sports. An average trip would cost between £100 and £150 a week plus £40-£50 a week for the food kitty. The longer the trip the lower the weekly cost, for example Oasis Overland trips start at £65 per week plus £30 a week local payment (for food and camping fees) on 29-week trips and go up to around £135 a week for shorter South American trips (see *Directory of Expeditions*).

Specialist Tour Operators

Agencies that specialise in trips for backpackers can be just what a solo gap year traveller needs to overcome a reluctance to strike off into the unknown. Small-group tours can allow you to experience a country at closer range and avoid the beaten path of larger groups. For example Intrepid Travel (76 Upper St, Islington, London N1 0NU; 0800 917 6456; www.intrepidtravel.com) is a leading operator of adventure holidays to Asia, Europe, Middle East, Latin America, Africa and Australasia. The company runs more than 400 trips a year to 35 destinations. Their 'Basix' trips are no-frills small-group trips suitable for first-time backpackers, lasting from a few days in Northern Thailand to 60-day trips around Central America.

Here is a selected list of overland operators whose websites provide detailed information about their trips. The average age on most of these would be 20-30 with a higher ratio of women to men. For more companies, see the directory of tour operators maintained by Overland Expedition Resources (www.go-overland.com). Specialist companies which operate only in one region (e.g. Africa) are mentioned in the relevant chapter later in this book.

Dragoman, Camp Green, Kenton Road, Debenham, Suffolk IP14 6LA (01728 861133; www.dragoman.co.uk).

Encounter – same address as above (0870 499 4478/ fax 01728 861127; www.encounter. co.uk).

Exodus, Grange Mills, 9 Weir Road, London SW12 0NE (www.exodus.co.uk). Africa, Asia and the Americas.

Explore Worldwide Ltd, 1 Frederick St, Aldershot, Hants. GU11 1LQ (01252 760200; www. exploreworldwide.co.uk). Europe's largest adventure tour operator with trips in Europe, Africa, Asia and the Americas.

First 48, Annapurna House, Victoria St, Featherstone, Pontefract, W Yorks. WF7 5EZ (0845 130 4849; www.first48.com).

Guerba Expeditions, Wessex House, 40 Station Road, Westbury, Wilts. BA13 3JN (01373 858956; www.guerba.co.uk). Originally an Africa specialist, now runs trips to other continents.

Imaginative Traveller, 1 Betts Avenue, Martlesham Heath, Suffolk IP5 7RH (0800 316 2717; www.imaginative-traveller.com) runs small group adventures around the globe.

Kumuka Expeditions, 40 Earl's Court Road, London W8 6EJ (020-7937 8855; www. kumuka.co.uk).

Oasis Overland, The Marsh, Henstridge, Somerset BA8 0TF (01963 363400; info@oasisoverland.co.uk). Africa, Middle East, Egypt and Latin America.

The Adventure Company, 15 Turk St, Alton, Hants. GU34 1AG (0870 794 1009; www. adventurecompany.co.uk).

Cost is usually the crucial factor for gap students wondering where to go or how to get there. Those who go through a sending agency will either have their travel arranged for them or be offered plenty of guidance. But for those students who want to organise their own trip independently, here are some travel tips to get started.

AIR TRAVEL

Scheduled airfares as laid down by IATA, the airlines' cartel, are best avoided. They are primarily designed for airline accountants and businessmen on expense accounts. You should be looking at no frills airlines, discounted student tickets, cheap charters and tickets from unpopular carriers (e.g. Garuda instead of Qantas). Air travel within individual countries and continents is not always subject to this choice, though some special deals are available.

High street travel agents and mainstream internet travel agents can offer good deals. But the very lowest fares are still found by doing some careful shopping around on the telephone and internet. Even if you choose not to book online and want the reassurance of dealing with a human being, the web can still be a great source of information about prices and options.

For longhaul flights, especially to Asia, Australasia and more recently Latin America, discounted tickets are available in plenty and there should never be any need to pay the official full fare. The major student travel agency *STA Travel* is one of the best starting places. STA Travel are specialists in student and youth travel offering low cost flights, accommodation, insurance, car hire, round-the-world tickets, overland travel, adventure tours, ski, and gap year travel. STA Travel have about 50 branches in the UK and over 450 worldwide staffed by experienced travellers. STA Travel attend lots of gap year fairs at schools around the country in co-operation with a selection of leading gap year placement organisations. For bookings and enquiries call STA Travel on 0870 160 6070 or log on at www.statravel.co.uk to find fares, check availability, enter competitions, find your nearest branch or book online. It is now possible to book onto a TEFL course or voluntary programme with i-to-i at any STA Travel branch and on to selected other gap year programmes mentioned on the STA Travel website.

The price of round-the-world tickets has not risen too drastically over the past few years, though taxes and fuel surcharges will add at least £100 and up to £180 to basic fares. Check www.roundtheworldflights.com (0870 442 4842) or the RTW section of www. thetravellerslounge.co.uk. RTW fares start at about £800 (London-New York-Sydney-Singapore-London). Some of the cheapest fares involve one or more gaps which you must cover overland. Most are valid for up to a year. An example of a good fare (available through STA) is £843 plus tax for a RTW fare from London to Sydney and Auckland with stopovers in Japan, Singapore and Fiji and on to the USA. The standard RTW stopovers are Singapore/Bangkok, Sydney, Los Angeles and London but there are endless combinations. If you don't want to include North America on your itinerary, you don't need a RTW ticket. An offbeat example of a route downunder uses Emirates and SriLankan Airways to travel via Dubai to Mumbai (Bombay), overland to Trivandrum in Kerala, on to Colombo, Singapore, Sydney (or Melbourne or Perth) then back to London via Dubai for less than £1000.

Other reliable agencies specialising in longhaul travel including for student and budget travellers are:

Trailfinders Ltd, 194 Kensington High St, London W8 7RG (020-7938 3939 longhaul; 0845 050 5940 Europe). Also more than a dozen branches in UK cities plus Dublin and five in Australia.

Marco Polo Travel 24A Park St, Bristol BS1 5JA (0117-929 4123; www.marcopolotravel. co.uk). Discounted airfares worldwide.

Flight Centre – 0870 499 0040; www.flightcentre.co.uk. Many branches in London and around the UK (1200 shops worldwide). Cheap student flights and extra services like working holiday packages.

North South Travel, Moulsham Mill Centre, Parkway, Chelmsford, Essex CM2 7PX (01245

608291). Discount travel agency that donates all its profits to projects in the developing world.

Quest Travel – 0870 444 5552; www.questtravel.com.

Bridge the World – 0870 444 1716; www.bridgetheworld.com.

These agencies offer a wide choice of fares including RTW. When purchasing a discounted fare, you should be aware of whether or not the ticket is refundable, whether the date can be changed and if so at what cost, whether taxes are included, and so on. **Roger Blake** was pleased with the round-the-world ticket he bought from STA for £940 that took in Johannesburg, Australia and South America. But once he embarked he wanted to stay in Africa longer than he had anticipated and wanted to alter the onward flight dates:

> *That is the biggest problem of having an air ticket. I had planned for six months in Africa but I've already spent five months in only three countries. I have been into the British Airways office here in Kampala to try my verbal skills but have been told the 12-month period of validity is non-negotiable. How stupid I was to presume I would get a refund when it states clearly on the back of the ticket that they may be able to offer refunds/credit. A lesson for me and a warning to future world travellers, to check before they buy whether or not the ticket is refundable/extendable.*

Ben Spencer came to a similar conclusion on his gap year when his travel plans changed and he regretted not having studied the fine print of his ticket which indicated that he could change the date but not the route. Having booked a return flight London-Hong Kong and Moscow-London on Lufthansa (for £500 with STA), his plans changed and he decided to extend his stay. When making enquiries in Moscow, the airline claimed that changes could only be done by the travel agent and the travel agent claimed that they could only be made by the airline. So he bought an exceedingly cheap ticket from St. Petersburg to Tallinn & Helsinki and then a new one-way flight Helsinki-London on SAS for £100 (via email with STA in Helsinki). Again, he did not use this ticket because he was hospitalised in Moscow and his insurance company (Columbus) arranged for his return flight (accompanied by a nurse).

Discount agents advertise in London weeklies like *TNT* and *Time Out,* as well as in the travel pages of newspapers like the *Independent*. Phone a few outfits and pick the best price. General websites like www.cheapflights.co.uk, www.travelocity.com and www.opodo.com are good starting points though comparison shopping this way can be time-consuming and frustrating.

If you are spending time in North America through *BUNAC* or *Camp America*, you will have had to book your return ticket before leaving the UK. But if you are in the US without a ticket and need to find a cheap transatlantic or onward flight, the best bet by far is available to people who are flexible about departure dates and destinations and are prepared to travel on a standby basis. The passenger chooses a block of possible dates (up to a five-day 'window') and preferred destinations. One company that tries to match these requirements with empty airline seats at knock-down prices is Air-Tech in New York (212-219-7000; www.airtech.com) which advertises its fares by saying 'if you can beat these prices, start your own damn airline'. The transatlantic fares being advertised at the time of writing were $165 one way from the east coast, $233 from the west coast and $199 from Chicago, all excluding tax, a registration fee of $29 and a FedEx delivery charge of $18+. Note that post September 11th regulations stipulate that US citizens must purchase a return ticket.

EUROPE

Airfares

From the UK to Europe it is often cheaper to fly on one of the no-frills ticketless airlines shuttling between British airports and many European destinations than it is to travel by rail or bus. The explosion of competition on European routes has seen some amazingly low fares, though with increasing publicity about the damage to the environment for which the cheap flight bonanza is partly responsible, these low prices will not last forever. Destinations and even airlines come and go, but you should always start by checking Ryanair and easyjet. No-frills airlines do not take bookings via travel agents so it is necessary to contact them directly, preferably booking over the internet since that invariably saves money, usually £5 per ticket. When comparing prices always factor the tax in which routinely adds £20-£30 to fares and often represents more than 100% of the fare cost. A new website has been launched to help people compare fares: http://cheap0.com.

An unusual way of locating cheap flights is available from Adventurair (PO Box 757, Maidenhead, SL6 7XD; 01293 405777; www.rideguide.com) who produce *The Ride Guide* as a book or CD which gives details of companies operating cargo planes, aircraft deliveries and private planes. Any of these may have seats available for bargain prices. The book costs £15.99 in the UK ($19.99) plus £1.50 postage.

Rail

The Inter Rail ticket is widely available. You must choose how many zones you intend to cover and bear in mind that seat reservations will cost extra; current prices for the under-26s are £159 for 16 days in one zone, £295 for a month's travel in all zones which includes 28 countries. Anyone intending to do some concentrated travelling by train should contact a specialist operator like Rail Europe (08705 848848; www.raileurope.co.uk) or Rail Choice (www.railchoice.co.uk) who sell a large range of European and international rail passes.

Other youth and student discounts can be very useful; for example the *Wochenendticket* (weekend ticket) in Germany is valid for the whole country on Saturdays and Sundays but only on regional trains. It costs €28 for up to five people which means that you can get from the Austrian to the Danish border for less than £4 each.

The Thomas Cook *World Timetable* is the bible for overland travellers outside Europe; within Europe, consult the *European Timetable,* both for £13.99.

Coach

Eurolines is the name given to all the separate national coach services of Europe working together and selling various coach passes. To find out about a straightforward journey from England to the Continent, just book through National Express offices or website (www.nationalexpress.com). Prices start at £49 return for London-Amsterdam. Passengers under the age of 26 are eligible for a 10% discount.

For smaller independent coach operators, check advertisements in London magazines like *TNT*. For example Kingscourt Express (125 Balham High Road, London SW12 9AJ; 020-8673 7500; www.kce.cz) runs daily between London and Prague or Brno; standby fares from £50.

One of the most interesting revolutions in youth travel has been the explosion of backpackers' bus services which are hop-on hop-off coach services following prescribed routes. These can be found in New Zealand, (MagicBus; www.magicbus.co.nz), Australia (Waywardbus.com.au), South Africa (bazbus.com), Turkey (feztravel.com) and of course Europe. For example a month long coach pass on Busabout Europe (258 Vauxhall Bridge

Road, London SW1V 1BS; 020-7950 1661; www.busabout.com) costs £339 for those under 26.

Shared Lifts

The European land mass is one of the most expensive areas of the world to traverse. If your mum is unhappy about the idea of hitching, reassure her that in Europe a network of lift-sharing agencies or 'allostop' makes hitching respectable. The practice is especially widespread in Germany where there are Citynetz offices in all the big cities. For a varying fee (usually £10-£20 plus a share of the petrol) they will try to find a driver going to your chosen destination. An example of a lift advertised in early 2005 was €50 for Amsterdam to Warsaw. They are certainly worth trying if, say, you are signed up for a four-week language course and know some weeks in advance when you want to move on or head home.

Check notice boards in hostels or youth travel bureaux or try websites such as http://europe.bugride.com which publicises long distance rides offered and sought on its site. Here are some details of European agencies:

France: Allostop, 30 rue Pierre Sémard, 75009 Paris (1-53 20 42 42 or 8-25 80 36 66; www.allostop.net or http://pcb.ecritel.fr/allostop/welcome.html). Prices are set according to distance of journey, e.g. €9 for less than 250km, €14 for up to 350km, up to €91 for a journey of 3000km plus a small registration fee on a sliding scale.

Belgium: Taxistop/Eurostop, 28 rue Fossé-aux-Loups, 1000 Brussels (+32 70-22 22 92; fax +32 2-223 22 32). Also has offices in Ghent and Ottignies (www.taxistop.be). The admin fee charged to passengers by Taxistop is 80 cents per 100km (minimum €6.20, maximum €20). In addition passengers pay drivers €2.50 per 100km.

Germany: Citynetz-Mitzfahrzentrale – www.citynetz-mitfahrzentrale.de. Website gives addresses, phone numbers and emails of offices around Germany. Prices are calculated at 6 Euro-cents per kilometre.

NORTH AMERICA

Incredibly, the price of flying across the Atlantic has been steadily decreasing over the past decade. Off-peak student returns to New York start at less than £200 including tax. Competition is fiercest and therefore prices lowest on the main routes between London and New York, Miami and Los Angeles. In many cases, summer fares will be twice as high as winter ones. Cheap one-way fares are also available to eastern seaboard cities like Washington. When comparing fares, always take the taxes into consideration since they now represent about £45-£50.

Outside summer and the Christmas period you should have no problems getting a seat; at peak times, a reliable alternative is to buy a discounted ticket on one of the less fashionable carriers which fly to New York, such as Air India or El Al. A one-year return London-New York on Kuwait Air might start at £250 plus taxes.

The USA and Canada share the longest common frontier in the world, which gives some idea of the potential problems and expense of getting around. You will want to consider Drive-aways (see *United States* chapter) and also bus and air travel which are both cheaper than in Europe. The Greyhound bus pass (Ameripass) is alive and well, and represents a bargain for people who want to cover a lot of ground. Greyhound has no office in the UK but their US and Canada passes can be bought through STA and a few others such as Western Air Travel in Devon (0870 330 1100; www.westernair.co.uk). In 2005, Greyhound (www.greyhound.com) were offering 4, 7, 10, 15, 21, 30, 45 and 60 day passes in the low season to students and under 26s for £78, £98, £121, £140, £168, £186, £210 and £251; high season passes add approximately another 20%. Once you are in the US timetable and fare information is available 24 hours a day on the toll-free number 800-231-2222. Greyhound also offer a Canada Pass which costs £130 for 7 days, £203 for 21 days up to £281 for 60 days (adult fares).

Other forms of transport in the USA are probably more expensive but may have their own attractions, such as the trips run by *Green Tortoise* (494 Broadway, San Francisco, California 94133; 800-867-8647/ www.greentortoise.com) which uses vehicles converted to sleep about 35 people and which make interesting detours and stopovers.

LATIN AMERICA

Two fully-bonded agencies that specialise in travel to and around this area of the world are Journey Latin America (12-13 Heathfield Terrace, Chiswick, London W4 4JE; 020-8747 3108; www.journeylatinamerica.co.uk) and South American Experience (South American Experience Ltd, 47 Causton St, Pimlico, London SW1P 4AT; 020-7976 5511; www.southamericanexperience.co.uk). These consistently offer the lowest fares and the most expertise. Another advantage is that they deal exclusively with Latin America and hence are the best source of up-to-date travel information. One of the best deals at the time of writing was a six-month return to Rio on Air Portugal for £517.

Heavy taxes are levied on international flights within South America: the cheapest way to fly from one capital to another (assuming you have plenty of time) is to take a domestic flight (within, say, Brazil), cross the border by land and then buy another domestic ticket (within, say, Peru). The alternatives include the remnants of a British-built railway system and the ubiquitous bus, both of which are extremely cheap and interesting.

For information on travel in Latin America join *South America Explorers* who maintain clubhouses in Lima, Cusco and Quito. The US office is at 126 Indian Creek Rd, Ithaca, NY 14850 (607-277-0488; www.saexplorers.org) and membership costs $50.

Gap year traveller Ed Fry arrived back in England in June 2005 from Mexico where he had found the business of travelling easier than expected:
In May I came to Central America which has been wonderful. Travelling has been huge fun and I have seen some amazing things. I was worried about the logistics of travelling before I left but I found that travelling around is very easy and with only the smallest amount of Spanish one can get around very easily. Buses and travellers' infrastructure make getting about and staying everywhere relatively easy even in the most obscure locations. We have relied minimally on guidebooks and have instead made much more use of other travellers' advice. Travelling, as far as I can tell, can be as expensive or cheap as one wants it to be. Hostels range from £2-£20 a night and here in southern Mexico you could certainly survive on less than £15 a day. Tours and alcohol drive the cost of travelling up significantly. Budgeting is also quite tricky as one-off experiences such as skydiving can send costs up. It is possible to save a lot of money by cooking for oneself in hostel kitchens and not going on organised tours.

AFRICA

Flights to Cairo are advertised from £150 single, £200 return, while the special offers to Nairobi start from £280 single, £395 return. A specialist agency for Southern Africa is Melhart Travel in Manchester (0161-772 6900; info@melharttravel.com). A 12-month return to Johannesburg on Virgin in the low season was costing about £590 including tax at the time of writing. Another agency to try is the Africa Travel Centre (21 Leigh St, London WC1H 9QX; 0845 450 1520; www.africatravel.co.uk).

As noted above, the overland routes are fraught with difficulties, and so joining a trip with an established overland tour company is a good idea.

ASIA

Most gap year travellers take advantage of the competitive discount flight market from London to Asian destinations. For example the cheapest quoted return price London to Delhi is about £340 includiing tax on Etihad Airways (the airline of the United Arab Emirates). The cheapest carrier to Bangkok is Tarom, the Romanian airline, which has a one-year return for £330 with a stopover in Bucharest. The price of flights to Japan has dropped in the past few years, especially if you are willing to fly on the Russian carrier Aeroflot.

Once you're installed in Asia, travel is highly affordable. The railways of the Indian sub-continent are a fascinating social phenomenon that cost next to nothing provided you are willing to rough it. Throughout Asia, airfares are not expensive, particularly around the discount triangle of Bangkok, Hong Kong and Singapore. The notable exception to the generalisation about cheap public transport in Asia is Japan, where the possibility of hitching compensates for the high cost of living and travelling, as described by **Robert Kerr** who spent last year in Japan on a post-university gap year, teaching English for the big language chain the Nova Group (see Asia chapter).

Considering I hadn't really planned for a holiday I decided to try my hand at hitch-hiking. So I made a few signs for places I wanted to visit and walked along the high-way first thing on Sunday morning. I soon got picked up by a family on their way to Fukuoka, who gave me some good travel tips. From Fukuoka I got another couple of rides all the way to Kagoshima. This is a long journey and took most of the day. After some detours to islands by ferry I hitched into the mountains, where I stumbled upon a mountain guide who led me and one other guy up a steep waterfall to a mountain cabin where we spent the night. In Kagoshima I got a lift with a salary man from Fukuoka, but just as far as Kumamoto. I ended up sleeping in a service station and this morning I took the slow train back to Yamaguchi.

AUSTRALASIA

Per mile, the flight to the Antipodes is cheaper than most. The cheapest fares become available when airline promotions are advertised. Malaysian Airlines often turns out to be the cheapest; for example they were charging £616 including tax at the time of writing. Austravel (0870 166 2020) sells charter flights to Sydney starting at £500 before tax, though these fares allow a maximum stay of only a month.

For ways of minimising the cost of getting round the vast country of Australia, see the section on Travel at the end of the chapter on Australia later in this book.

PART II

Gap Year Placements

Specialist Gap Year Programmes

Expeditions

Work Experience

Volunteering

A Year Off for North Americans

Paid Seasonal Jobs

Au Pairing

Courses

Specialist Gap Year Programmes

Specialist gap year placement organisations can arrange the logistics and save you (and your parents) a great deal of anxiety. They find voluntary and occasionally paid placements, provide orientation and sometimes group travel and, crucially, provide back-up, usually in the form of an in-country representative who can sort out problems. Mediating agencies come in all shapes and sizes. Some are bastions of the establishment with longstanding programmes in a range of countries and links forged over many years with certain schools. Others are more entrepreneurial and are always seeking new projects in developing countries to which they can send paying volunteers.

A plethora of organisations both charitable and commercial offers a wide range of packaged possibilities, from work experience placements in French businesses to teaching in Himalayan schools. This section provides a general description of the programmes run by the major gap year placement agencies. Younger school leavers should be aware that 18 is often quoted as a minimum age, which might exclude them. Further details of programmes mentioned here are (if available) included in the country-by-country chapters, with stories of people who have done placements.

All participants must fund-raise substantial sums which are paid to the mediating agency. In recent years the expectation that parents will finance the year off has declined and most organisations provide much detailed advice on how to obtain sponsorship and raise money. Fees and services differ enormously, so research is essential, preferably well in advance. Generally speaking, the high profile organisations that invest a lot in publicity are considerably more expensive than the more obscure small charities active in just one country. Before committing yourself and your backers to a large financial outlay, you must be sure that your choice of organisation is sound. Researching all the possibilities is time-consuming and sometimes confusing since it can be difficult to compare programmes simply on the basis of their publicity.

The Year Out Group was launched five years ago by 23 founding member organisations. The launch took place in the presence of two MPs including Margaret Hodge, then Minister for Employment and Equal Opportunities, proof that the gap year had moved onto the political agenda. The founding members plus the thirteen organisations that have joined since all have entries in this book (almost all in this chapter) and their entries indicate their membership.

Year Out Group members are working towards models of good practice and seeking to maintain high standards of quality (while at the same time being in competition with one another). The role of the non-profit Year Out Group is to promote and advise on structured years out. Their website contains guidelines and questions to ask when comparing providers, most of which are common sense, e.g. find out whether it is a charity or a profit-making company, look at safety procedures and in-placement support, ask for a breakdown of costs, and so on. The Year Out Group may be contacted at Queensfield, 28 Kings Road, Easterton, Wilts. SN10 4PX (07980 395789; info@yearoutgroup.org/ www. yearoutgroup.org). Note that it cannot intervene in any dispute between member companies and disgruntled clients.

Another source of guidelines on what to investigate when trying to differentiate among gap year providers is the website www.gapyearresearch.org/ethicalvolunteering.htm. Kate Simpson is attached to the University of Newcastle and did a PhD in gap year provision. She has compiled a searching list of questions under the heading 'How to be an ethical volunteer: Picking the worthwhile from the worthless'. A good organisation should be able to tell an applicant exactly what work they will be doing and precise contact details for the overseas project. Assuming you care about such things (and even if you don't beforehand, you probably will after spending some time in a developing country), ask the company what financial contribution they make to the voluntary project and about their ethical tourism policy. Some gap year companies wait until a paying customer has signed up before finding a placement abroad and these are often less satisfactory.

Everybody will tell you that you have to set the wheels in motion about a year before you're ready to go. But in fact lots of people start their gap year with nothing fixed up. It turns out that all those organisations whose literature contains dire warnings of the consequences of procrastination often have last minute vacancies due to cancellations, so it is worth ringing around whenever you decide you want to go for it. In many cases they need you more than you need them.

This chapter sets out the programmes of about 60 leading organisations which are equipped to organise all or part of your gap year for you. The majority is based in the UK though some American organisations welcome all nationalities onto their programmes. For agencies and organisations that target North American school leavers, see the chapter *A Year Off for North Americans*. The organisations listed below specifically target gap year students. Many other organisations listed in the other directories in the chapters on Volunteering, Work Experience, Au Pairing, Courses and also in the country chapters welcome gap year students with open arms but do not specialise in catering for them.

Another consideration is the financial soundness of the company. Not all gap year companies have financial protection for the consumer in the form of an ATOL license and personalised insurance certificates. The 1992 package travel act states that any company that arranges a package (and this is simply two or more elements of travel such as flights, accommodation and transport) should have coverage in place, whether it be a bond, ATOL licence or insurance policy.

Directory of Specialist Gap Year Programmes

ADVENTURE ALTERNATIVE
31 Myrtledene Road, Belfast BT8 6GQ. ☎/fax: 02890 701476. E-mail: office@ adventurealternative.com. Website: www.adventurealternative.com.
Three-month programmes for gap year students (among others) in Kenya and Nepal.
Programme description: Combine 8 weeks of teaching/community work, group activities (e.g. climbing, trekking, rafting, safaris) and independent travel. In Kenya participants teach and work in HIV-education in rural schools. In Nepal, participants help to build village schools, clinics and other projects for the charity Moving Mountains (www. movingmountains.org.uk). Medical electives also available for medical students and doctors in both countries.
Destinations: Rural Kenya and Himalayan Nepal.
Number of placements per year: 32 for Kenya, 60 for Nepal.
Prerequisites: Minimum age 17; average age 22. Hard-working committed enthusiastic gap year students who are not fazed by the hardships of living in a developing country. All nationalities.
Duration and time of placements: 1-3 months.
Costs: 3-month placement costs £1800 plus £650-£700 for flights, insurance and other necessities.
Contact: Gavin Bate, Director; Chris Little or Andy MacDonald, Expedition Co-ordinators.

AFRICA AND ASIA VENTURE
10 Market Place, Devizes, Wiltshire SN10 1HT. ☎01380 729009. Fax: 01380 720060. E-mail: av@aventure.co.uk. Website: www.aventure.co.uk.

Founding member of the Year Out Group. Africa and Asia Venture is an organisation which enables students to gain work experience (unpaid) with youth in Africa, Northern India, Nepal and Mexico.

Programme description: Students are placed in selected rural secondary and primary schools for approximately three months, teaching a variety of subjects and helping with extracurricular activities, especially sports. This is followed by two weeks of backpacking before going on safari to areas of interest and outstanding beauty in the chosen country. Also opportunities to join community and conservation projects.

Destinations: Kenya, Tanzania, Botswana, Uganda, Malawi, India, Nepal and Mexico.

Number of placements per year: 380-420.

Prerequisites: A-level students going on to Further Education or undergraduates considering taking time out can apply. Students must be aged 18 when they join the scheme and enjoy working with young people.

Duration and time of placements: 4/5 months, with departures to Africa in September, January and late April, to Nepal in October or January, and to India in September or April. Also offer 5-week placements in Kenya and Uganda.

Selection procedures and orientation: On application students are invited to an interview to assess suitability. Applications should be submitted as early as possible since places are on a first-come-first-served basis for interview.

Cost: The basic cost is approximately £2700 which covers living allowance, food, accommodation, safari, health and personal effects insurance and an orientation course. Fee does not include airfares, entry visas and extra spending money.

AFRICAN CONSERVATION EXPERIENCE
PO Box 206, Faversham, Kent, ME13 8WZ. ☎0870 241 5816. E-mail: info@ConservationAfrica.net. Website: www.ConservationAfrica.net.
Member of the Year Out Group.

Programme description: Conservation work placements for young people on game reserves in Southern Africa. Tasks may include darting rhino for relocation or elephant for fitting tracking collars. Game capture, tagging, assisting with veterinary work, game counts and monitoring may be part of the work programme. Alien plant control and the re-introduction of indigenous plants is often involved.

Destinations: Southern Africa including South Africa, Botswana and Zimbabwe.

Prerequisites: Must have reasonable physical fitness and be able to cope mentally. Enthusiasm for conservation is most important qualification. Programme may be of special interest to students of environmental, zoological and biological sciences, veterinary science and animal care.

Duration and time of placements: 4-12 weeks throughout the year.

Selection procedures & orientation: Candidates are matched to a suitable project on the information provided on their application form but do have final say on their placement. Optional Open Days are held at various locations in the UK.

Cost: Varies depending on reserve and time of year. Students can expect an average total cost of about £2700 for 4 weeks up to £4000 for 12 weeks, which includes international flights (from London), transfers, accommodation and all meals. Support and advice given on fund-raising.

Contact: Sarah Bishop, Marketing Manager.

AFRICATRUST NETWORKS
Africatrust Chambers, PO Box 551, Portsmouth, Hants. PO5 1ZN. ☎01873 812453. E-mail: info@africatrust.gi. Website: www.africatrust.org.uk or www. africatrust.gi.

Programme description: Ghanaian NGO that works with disadvantaged young people in Africa. Residential placements for pre-university and post-university students, to teach young children, help with disabled, homeless, blind and orphaned children, etc.

Destinations: Ghana (Cape Coast and Kumasi), Cameroon and Morocco.

Prerequisites: Volunteers must be 18-25, in good health and have an EU passport. A-level French is needed for Mali.
Duration and time of placements: 3 and 6 months.
Selection procedures and orientation: Application form available on website. References will be taken up and interviews scheduled in London. Briefing information on health, fundraising and projects are sent. There is a compulsory pre-departure briefing in London for volunteers and their families plus 2-week in-country induction course.
Cost: 3-month programme will be at least £2200 and 6 months will cost £3400. Volunteers are also expected to raise donations, typically £500/£750 which the volunteers as a team distribute themselves in-country. Costs include all travel, food, accommodation, induction courses, mid-visit holiday tour programme and management supervision/review programme.
Contact: David Denison (UK Director).

AFS INTERCULTURAL PROGRAMMES UK
Leeming House, Vicar Lane, Leeds LS2 7JF. ☎0113-242 6136. Fax: 0113-243 0631. E-mail: info-unitedkingdom@afs.org. Website: www.afs.org or www.afsuk. org.
According to its mission statement, AFS is an international, voluntary, non-governmental, non-profit organisation that provides intercultural learning opportunities to help people develop the knowledge, skills and understanding needed to create a more just and peaceful world. AFS currently has 54 member countries.
Programme description: On the International Volunteer Programme, participants spend 6 months in another country, living with a family and volunteering on a local community project. On the Schools Programme, participants spend an academic year in another country, attending a local school and living with a local family. 3-month placements on the Schools Programme can be requested.

Destinations: Argentina, Bolivia, Brazil, Costa Rica, Ecuador, France, Germany, Ghana, Guatemala, Honduras, Hong Kong, Indonesia, Italy, Japan, Mexico, Panama, Paraguay, Peru, Russia, South Africa, Spain, Thailand, USA and Venezuela.

Number of placements per year: AFS tries to place anyone eligible who applies.

Prerequisites: Applicants for the International Volunteer Programme are normally aged 18-29 at the time of departure. Older applicants are welcomed. No particular qualifications or skills are needed but experience of voluntary work or skills in a particular area would enhance the suitability of the applicant. Applicants for the Schools Programme must be aged 15-18 at the time of departure.

Duration and time of placements: 6 months for volunteers, departing January/February and July/August. One academic year for the Schools Programme with departures in August/September.

Selection procedures and orientation: Initial application form must be accompanied by a £10 fee. Selection is conducted at a group event, after which a full application will have to be completed. It is preferred that applications are sent at least six months before the intended departure to give time to raise contribution costs and for the organisation to find a suitable placement. Late applications can be considered. Selection for the Schools Programme is a group activity for applicants and parents. A pre-departure orientation is held for all programmes.

Costs: For the International Volunteer Programme, each participant is requested to raise £3300. Advice and support for fundraising are given. For the Schools Programme, participants are requested to contribute £3950 for a year-long programme and £2950 for a 3-month programme. The money raised covers travel, medical insurance, orientation materials and events, language tuition and emergency support. The host family provides food and accommodation. Some financial assistance may be available for the Schools Programme.

THE ARMY
HQ Recruiting Group, ATRA, Bldg 165, Trenchard Lines, Upavon, Wiltshire SN9 6BE. ☎08457 300111. Website: www.armyofficer.co.uk.

The British Army offers gap year students the opportunity to spend a year in the Army. The Gap Year Commission (formerly called the Short Service Limited Commission), offers the opportunity for students taking a year out to be placed in an Army regiment. There is no obligation after the year has been completed for the student to have any further links with the Army. However those who do wish to use their Gap Year Pass to enter after university may do so. Financial sponsorship may be available through university.

Programme description: A 4-week course is undertaken at Sandhurst before joining the regiment. At first students serve under supervision of an experienced officer, but soon are given their own responsibilities.

Destinations: Virtually anywhere around the world. Previous participants have travelled to the Rockies of Canada, Norway, Hong Kong and Guatemala.

Number of placements per year: Around 30.

Prerequisites: Applicants must have a confirmed place at a UK university with all A-level examinations completed before entry to Sandhurst. Applicants must have been resident in the UK for 5 years and be a British or Commonwealth citizen.

Duration and time of placements: The minimum service is 4 months; maximum is 18 months. Six weeks' notice must be given to terminate a commission.

Selection procedures and orientation: Students must be recommended by their Head Teacher, have reached the age of 17 and 11 months and be less than 24 on the day of commissioning, be accepted by the Corps or Regiment of their choice and have passed an Army Medical Board and the Regular Commissions Board. The most successful candidates are those of high academic ability with a history of leadership at school, such as sports captain or prefect. A taste for active outdoor pursuits and a sense of adventure is of paramount importance. Sandhurst courses are in September so applications must be made early in the upper sixth and certainly by the end of January.

Payment: Gap Year Commission officers are paid at a special rate of £14,728 per year rising to £16,071 after 9 months. Additional allowances, e.g. for uniform, may also be paid.

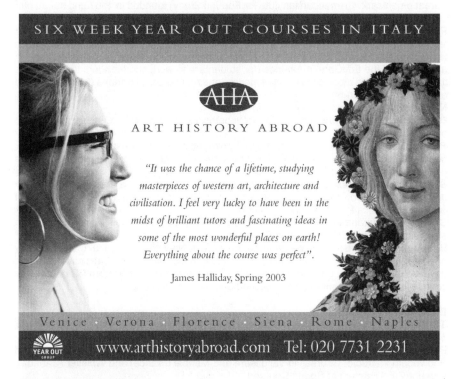

SIX WEEK YEAR OUT COURSES IN ITALY

AHA

ART HISTORY ABROAD

"It was the chance of a lifetime, studying masterpieces of western art, architecture and civilisation. I feel very lucky to have been in the midst of brilliant tutors and fascinating ideas in some of the most wonderful places on earth! Everything about the course was perfect".

James Halliday, Spring 2003

Venice • Verona • Florence • Siena • Rome • Naples

YEAR OUT GROUP   www.arthistoryabroad.com   Tel: 020 7731 2231

ART HISTORY ABROAD
179C New Kings Road, Fulham, London, SW6 4SW. ☎020-7731 2231. Fax: 020-7731 2456. E-mail: info@arthistoryabroad.com. Website: www.arthistory-abroad.com.
Year Out Group founding member. BETA member.
Programme description: Unique programme designed for the Year Out that looks to broaden participants' sense of self as well as cultural and intellectual horizons. Programme includes art, history, architecture, politics, philosophy, economics, music, poetry, theology, literature and classics. 6 weeks of travel throughout Italy including Venice, Verona, Florence, Siena, Naples and Rome plus at least 6 other cities. No classroom work and all tuition is on-site and in groups of no more than 8. From 2006 new two-week summer Contemporary Art course based in London with visits throughout the UK as well as Paris and Amsterdam.
Number of placements per year: 24 per course, 4 times per year.
Duration and time of placement: 6-week course offered 4 times a year (Autumn, Spring, Early Summer and Late Summer) and 2-week courses offered in July/August.
Cost: £5400 for the Autumn, Spring and Early Summer courses including travel to, from and within Italy, hotel accommodation and breakfast throughout, all museum entry, expert tuition in small groups as well as drawing and Italian conversation classes and a private visit to the Vatican Museum. Fees do not include lunch or supper. Price for 2-week Summer courses in Italy is £2050. London-based courses are from £900.
Accommodation: Shared rooms in hotels in the centre of each city visited.

AU PAIR IN AMERICA
37 Queen's Gate, London SW7 5HR. ☎020-7581 7322. Fax: 020-7581 7355. E-mail: info@aupairamerica.co.uk. Website: www.aupairamerica.co.uk
Parent organisation (American Institute for Foreign Study) founded in 1967 and the au pair programme authorised in 1986.

Programme description: Au Pair in America operates the largest and longest established legal childcare programme to the United States. Au pairs are placed with a screened American family for a minimum of 12 months and maximum of 24 months. Other programmes that run alongside are the EduCare in America (for students who work shorter hours to allow more time for studies and receive less pocket money) and Au Pair Extraordinaire (for qualified and experienced childcarers).

Number of placements per year: 4000+.

Duration and time of placements: 12-24 months. Au pairs provide 45 hours of childcare per week.

Prerequisites: All nationalities are eligible provided there is an established interviewer network in their country. Ages 18-26. Must have recent practical childcare experience, hold a full driving licence and be available for 12 months.

Selection procedures and orientation: Applicants must submit a complete application and attend a personal interview with an appointed Au Pair in America interviewer. Contact Au Pair in America for a full colour brochure.

Cost: $600 Programme Fee. Au Pairs who successfully complete their 12 month minimum stay will receive a $400 Completion Payment.

Benefits: 4-day orientation programme held near New York, legal J-1 visa, weekly payment of $139 (approximately £80), $500 study tuition allowance, medical insurance, 2 weeks paid holidays, optional 13th month travel, year-long support from US community counsellor and placement in an established au pair 'cluster group'.

BASE CAMP GROUP
30 Baseline Business Studios, Whitchurch Road, London W11 4AT. ☎020-7243 6222. E-mail: contact@basecampgroup.com. Website: www.basecampgroup.com.
Programme description: Adventure training company founded in 2002 offering Ski and Snowboard Instructor Courses in Val d'Isère and Méribel (France) and Whistler (Canada). See entry in 'Directory of Sports Courses'.

BRITISH COUNCIL ASSISTANTS PROGRAMME
10 Spring Gardens, London SW1A 2BN. ☎020-7389 4596. E-mail: assistants@britishcouncil.org. Website: www.britishcouncil.org/education.
Also in Scotland: The Tun (3rd Floor), 4 Jackson's Entry, Holyrood Road, Edinburgh EH8 5EG; 0131-524 5700.
Northern Ireland: Norwich Union House, 7 Fountain St, Belfast BT1 5EG; 028-9024 8220.
Wales: 28 Park Place, Cardiff CF10 3QE; 029 2039 7346.
The British Council's Education and Training Group manages various programmes for students and young people such as IAESTE and the Leonardo Programme (see chapter on *Work Experience*). General enquiries to the British Council Information Centre (Bridgewater House, 58 Whitworth St, Manchester M1 6BB; 0161-957 7755).

Programme description: *English Language Assistants Programme* for modern language students and recent graduates. Applicants should be aged 20-30 with at least two years of university level education in the language of the destination country.

Destinations: Country-by-country details are available from the British Council (020-7389 4596; assistants@britishcouncil.org/ www.languageassistant.co.uk). Most posts are in France, Germany, Austria, Belgium, Switzerland, China and Latin America.

Duration and time of placements: One academic year, i.e. September or October to May or June, depending on country.

Selection procedures & orientation: Application forms are available from October; the

deadline is 1st December of the year prior to placement.
Cost: None. Monthly stipend paid to assistants, e.g. €900 in France, €700 in Germany. Assistance may be given with accommodation but cost deducted from stipend.

THE BRITISH INSTITUTE OF FLORENCE
Piazza Strozzi 2, 50123 Florence, Italy. ☎ +39 055-2677 8200. Fax: +39 055-2677 8222. E-mail: info@britishinstitute.it. Website: www.britishinstitute.it.
The Institute runs year-round courses in Italian language and Renaissance art history, and also Italian culture, life drawing, opera, film, landscape watercolours and Tuscan cooking. University accredited courses are also available during the year including Italian Cinema.
Programme description: Various events such as lectures, concerts and films are arranged on a weekly basis for students and local people at the Institute's library and cultural centre.
Duration and time of placements: Courses last from 5 days to 3 months and start year round. Summer courses are also available near the Tuscan coast.
Cost: Tuition fees vary according to length and intensity of the course chosen. For example a 1-week Italian Language course costs from €190 (£130) approximately, and a 5-day History of Art course costs from €155 (£105). Accommodation can be arranged in local homes, *pensione* and hotels starting at €22 (£15) a day.
Contact: Tracy Bray, PR & Marketing Manager.

BSES EXPEDITIONS
Royal Geographical Society, 1 Kensington Gore, London SW7 2AR. ☎020-7591 3141. Fax: 020-7591 3140. E-mail: info@bses.org.uk. Website: www.bses.org.uk.
Founding member of the Year Out Group. BSES Expeditions organises overseas expeditions worldwide for 16-20 year olds. See entry in 'Directory of Expeditions'.

BUNAC
16 Bowling Green Lane, London EC1R 0QH. ☎020-7251 3472. Fax: 020-7251 0215. E-mail: enquiries@bunac.org.uk. Website: www.bunac.org.
Founding member of the Year Out Group. BUNAC is a non-profit national student club offering work and travel programmes worldwide. It acts as an aide before and after arrival in the country of travel and acts as a 'security blanket' if situations go wrong whilst the student is abroad.
Programme description: Various work programmes in North America and elsewhere. A large number of students and non-students are placed on summer camps. BUNAC makes it possible for candidates to obtain the necessary visas and publishes its own job directories which help members to fix up short-term jobs before or after arrival.
Destinations: USA, Canada, New Zealand, Australia, South Africa, Ghana, Costa Rica and Peru.
Prerequisites: For Work Canada and Work America students must have documentary evidence that they are returning to a university degree or HND course, or already be a full-time student. Work Australia and New Zealand is open to anyone who is eligible for the working holiday visa (see country chapters).
Duration and time of placements: 9 weeks on summer camps in the US. Participants on the Work America programme must return to a full-time course in the UK in September/October. Other programmes in other countries can last up to two years.
Selection procedures and orientation: Students need to join BUNAC, either through the local club at university or at the time of applying. Applicants must also provide proof of student status, the fee and (if relevant) a job offer. In some cases, an attendance certificate from a BUNAC presentation (held at university campuses) is compulsory.
Cost: £5 BUNAC membership fee, plus programme fee from £67 for employment on summer camps to £1700 for Work New Zealand. First-time Work America participants must purchase BUNAC's travel package (average of £650 includes flight and airport taxes, airport collection and the first night's accommodation). Reductions are available to those applying early. Students cover living costs by working. Compulsory insurance for the summer costs about £124.

CACTUS WORLDWIDE LTD.
4 Clarence House, 30-31 North St, Brighton BN1 1EB. ☎0845 130 4775. Fax: 01273 775868. E-mail: enquiry@cactuslanguage.com. Website: www.cactuslanguage.com.
Provider of language courses and holidays worldwide. In Latin America in conjunction with voluntary placements (see *Directory of Language Courses*) and worldwide with TEFL courses.
Destinations: Guatemala, Costa Rica, Peru, Ecuador, Bolivia, Argentina and Brazil. Language courses in Germany, France, Spain, Italy, Greece, Russia, China and many others. TEFL courses in Spain, Thailand, Australia and more.
Duration and time of placements: Combination language and volunteer programme in Latin America from 5 to 8 weeks, with extensions possible. Language courses from 1 week; TEFL courses usually 4 weeks.
Costs: from £389 for 5 weeks in Guatemala to £999 for 8 weeks in Costa Rica. Costs of language and TEFL courses are clearly searchable on Cactus website.

CALEDONIA LANGUAGES ABROAD
The Clockhouse, 72 Newhaven Road, Edinburgh EH6 5QG. ☎0131-621 7721/2. E-mail: courses@caledonialanguages.co.uk. Website: www.caledonialanguages.co.uk.
Established in 1994.
Programme description: Short and long-term language courses throughout Europe and Latin America suitable for forming the basis of a gap year, for imparting basic language

skills and to supplement travels. Courses available to suit all levels and ages, year round. Volunteer work for those with at least 'intermediate' level language is available in Latin America in ecological, community, conservation and social welfare projects, working and living with local people.

Destinations: Caledonia's partner language schools are in France, Italy, Germany, Spain, Russia, Portugal, Peru, Mexico, Ecuador, Cuba, Bolivia, Chile, Costa Rica, Brazil and Argentina. (see entry in 'Directory of Language Courses').

Duration of courses: Language courses from 2 weeks upwards; volunteer work from 3 weeks upwards.

Selection procedures and orientation: Briefing meetings for volunteers are held during the pre-placement language courses and regular discussion with the language school. Depending on the location, site visits can be organised before the placement. In-country back-up support is given.

Cost: Volunteers must pay for the pre-placement language course in the overseas country plus accommodation and travel. In Peru, 3-week Spanish course plus 3 weeks voluntary work in a children's home plus accommodation throughout costs around £1100. Working with street children in Brazil for 3 months plus 3-week language course plus accommodation costs from £1800. In Ecuador 3-week language course plus 2 months work in a wildlife or cloud forest reserve plus accommodation costs from £1450.

CAMP COUNSELORS USA (CCUSA)

Devon House, 171/177 Great Portland St, London W1W 5PQ. ☎020-7637 0779. Fax: 020-7580 6209. E-mail: info@ccusa.co.uk. Website: www.ccusa.com. Northern office: 27 Woodside Gardens, Musselburgh, Scotland EH21 7LJ (0131-665 5843; 101355.257@compuserve.com). US headquarters of CCUSA are at 2330 Marinship Way, Suite 250, Sausalito, CA 94965, USA.

Programme description: Camp counsellor placement in the US plus Work Experience in the US, Australia, New Zealand and Brazil. Placements on summer camps in Russia and Croatia.

Prerequisites: Ages 18-30 for most programmes.

Duration and time of placements: 9 weeks for camp counsellors, 3-4 months working in the US (between late May and October), 3 or 6 months in Brazil and up to 12 months in Australia and New Zealand.

Cost: Camp Counselors USA fee from £299, Work Experience USA Placement £515, Independent £335; Work Experience Downunder £230. First year counsellors aged 18 earn $675 in pocket money.

CAMPS INTERNATIONAL LIMITED

Unit 1, Kingfisher Park, Headlands Business Park, Salisbury Road, Blashford, Ringwood, Hants. BH24 3NX. ☎01425 485390. Fax: 01425 485398. E-mail: info@campsinternational.com. Website: www.campsinternational.com.

Run gap year safari camps and expeditions in Kenya and Tanzania for 18-24 year olds and 25 years upwards, based in local communities where participants undertake a range of wildlife and community projects.

Destinations: Kenya and Tanzania including national parks and possibility to climb Mount Kenya, Mount Kilimanjaro or to do a scuba diving course.

Duration and time of placements: 2 weeks to 3 months.

Selection procedures and orientation: Must be motivated and enthusiastic.

Costs: Sample price of £1300 for 28-day Gap adventure which includes 20 days of voluntary work assisting rangers, teaching or building; excluding flights and insurance. 3-month programme costs £2600.

Contact: Sarah Webber.

CESA LANGUAGES ABROAD

CESA House, Pennance Road, Lanner, Cornwall TR16 5TQ. ☎01209 211800. Fax:

01209 211830. E-mail: info@cesalanguages.com. Website: www.cesalanguages.com.
Founding member of the Year Out Group. Major provider of language courses in France, Guadeloupe, Spain, Ecuador, Argentina, Chile, Costa Rica, Mexico, Germany, Austria, Italy, Portugal, Greece, Russia, Morocco and Japan. See entry in 'Directory of Courses'.

CHANGING WORLDS
Hodore Farm, Hartfield, East Sussex TN7 4AR. ☎01892 770000. Fax: 0870 990 9665. E-mail: welcome@changingworlds.co.uk. Website: www.changingworlds.co.uk.
Member of the Year Out Group. Aims to provide full cultural immersion through challenging and worthwhile work placements with a safety net if required.
Programme description: A range of gap year placements ranging from voluntary teaching placements in developing countries to paid placements in prestigious hotels.
Destinations: Australia, Canada, Chile, India, Nepal, New Zealand, Romania and Tanzania.
Number of placements per year: 200.
Prerequisites: A-levels or equivalent plus initiative, determination, adaptability and social skills.
Duration and time of placements: from 3 to 6 months. Minimum placement time for Canada is 6 months. Placements begin throughout the year.
Selection procedures and orientation: Interview days held in Surrey every 6-8 weeks. All participants attend a pre-departure briefing; for those going to a developing country, this is a 2-day residential course. Participants are met on arrival in-country and attend orientation with the local representative before proceeding to placement. Local representatives act as support during placement.
Cost: From £1975 for 6 months in Banff, Canada. Prices include return flights but exclude insurance (approximately £200 for 6 months).
Contact: David Gill, Director.

CIEE – see IST Plus Ltd

CORAL CAY CONSERVATION
The Tower, 13th Floor, 125 High Street, Colliers Wood, London SW19 2JG. ☎0870 750 0668. Fax: 0870 750 0667. E-mail: info@coralcay.org. Website: www.coralcay.org
Founding member of the Year Out Group. CCC sends teams of volunteers to survey some of the world's most endangered coral reefs and tropical forests. Volunteers are trained to carry out scientific research which is used to help protect threatened tropical environments.
Programme description: The aim of CCC expeditions is to help gather data for the protection and sustainable use of tropical resources and to provide alternative livelihood opportunities for local communities. CCC also offers intern opportunities at their London Head Office (see *Directory of Work Experience*).
Destinations: Fiji, Honduras, Malaysia and the Philippines.
Number of placements per year: hundreds. Sites vary in the number of volunteers they can accommodate.
Prerequisites: No previous experience is required as full training in marine and terrestrial ecology is provided on-site. Scuba tuition is also provided at no additional cost.
Duration and time of placements: Expeditions depart monthly throughout the year. Minimum stay 2 weeks (no maximum stay).
Selection procedures and orientation: A free information pack is available on request.
Cost: A fortnight's Marine Skills Training costs £700 and surveying starts at £300 per week. Terrestrial training is a one-week course at £350, followed by surveying at £200 per week. A sample 6-week marine project would cost £1800 (£1900 for dive trainees) and a 6-week Terrestrial project would cost £1150. Prices exclude flights and insurance.

Contact: Lauren Beatty, Volunteer Recruitment Co-ordinator.

CROSS-CULTURAL SOLUTIONS
UK Office: Tower Point 44, North Road, Brighton BN1 1YR. ☎0845 458 2781/2. E-mail: infouk@crossculturalsolutions.org. Website: www.crosscultural-solutions.org.
See entry in 'Directory of Volunteering in the UK'.

CSV
Community Service Volunteers, 5th Floor, Scala House, 36 Holloway Circus, Queensway, Birmingham B1 1EQ. ☎0800 374991/0121-643 7690. E-mail: volunteer@csv.org.uk. Website: www.csv.org.uk/fulltimevolunteering.
Founding member of the Year Out Group. CSV is the largest voluntary placement organisation in the UK. It provides voluntary placements to UK/EU nationals resident in the UK and aged over 16 who are committed to volunteering full-time and away from home for up to 12 months in a huge range of social care projects. See entry in 'Directory of Volunteering in the UK'. Other international volunteers can participate provided they apply through one of CSV's international partnerships (details from www.csv.org.uk/ftvol).

THE DANEFORD TRUST
45-47 Blythe Street, London E2 6LN. ☎020-7729 1928. Fax: 020-7729 1928. E-mail: info@danefordtrust.org. Website: www.danefordtrust.org.
Small educational trust which aims to encourage education and work exchanges between young people from inner-city London and young people from Africa, Asia and the Caribbean.
Programme description: Limited number of assistant teacher, youth worker and general worker placements in selected locations worldwide.
Destinations: Bangladesh, Botswana, Namibia, South Africa, Zimbabwe, St Vincent, St Lucia and Jamaica, Nepal and India.
Number of placements per year: 15-20.
Prerequisites: Must be from London, Asia, Africa or the Caribbean.
Duration and time of placement: Minimum 3 months, maximum 1 year. Standard length is 6-9 months.
Selection procedures and orientation: There are monthly briefings and a residential seminar prior to departure. Local supervision provided.
Cost: All costs are raised by the volunteer and Trust in close partnership. No one who is committed gets left behind.
Contact: Anthony Stevens, Trust Co-ordinator.

DEVELOPMENT IN ACTION
Voluntary Services Unit, UCL Union, 25 Gordon St, London WC1H 0AY. ☎07813 395957. E-mail: info@developmentinaction.org. Website: www.developmentinaction.org.
Programme description: Arrange voluntary attachments to various Indian non-governmental organisations for 2 months in summer or 5 months from September. See entry in 'Directory of Volunteering Abroad'.

ECHO COMMUNITIES
56 Ridgeway Road, Bristol BS16 3EA. ☎07971 853927. E-mail: pete@echocommunities.org.uk. Website: www.echocommunities.org.uk/gap-year-projects-mexico/gap-year-projects.html.
Programme description: Community projects in areas of conservation (including turtles), education or child development in Oaxaca; or placements in ecology centres throughout Mexico.
Destinations: Mexico.

Prerequisites: Ages 18-24. No skills or qualifications required.
Duration and time of placements: 3 months. In the ecology programme, volunteers spend up to 1 month at permaculture sites and can move between them on dates to suit their travel plans.
Selection procedures & orientation: Face-to-face interview required for community projects; telephone interview sufficient for ecology projects. Deadline for applications is 4 weeks before departure. One-week orientation on arrival in Mexico.
Cost: £2700 for 3 months on community projects, £300 per extra month. £1500 for one month on ecology project, £250 per extra month. Discounts often advertised on website.
Contact: Pete Masters, UK Director.

ECO AFRICA EXPERIENCE / WORLDWIDE EXPERIENCE
Guardian House, Borough Road, Godalming, Surrey GU7 2AE. ☎01483 860560. Fax: 01483 860391. E-mail: info@WorldwideExperience.com. Website: www. WorldwideExperience.com.
Programme description: Conservation, teaching and sports coaching opportunities for volunteers in South Africa, Kenya, Australia and Scotland. Participants get involved in conservation projects working with Africa's big five (lion, leopard, elephant, rhino, buffalo) as well as marine life such as dolphins, whales, sharks and seals. Other programmes in Africa involve coaching underprivileged children in football, tennis, cricket and rugby. Exposure to the local community's outreach programmes will bring volunteers closer to the many diverse cultures of Southern Africa.
Number of placements per year: 300-450.
Prerequisites: No particular skills needed. All nationalities accepted.
Duration and time of placements: 2-12 weeks. Placements are available all year round (gap year and summer break).
Selection procedures and orientation: Applications accepted year round. Interviews

are informal and can be done by telephone. Open days are arranged throughout the year when Worldwide Experience crew meet potential volunteers. Full medical and personal checklist is supplied during preparation.

Costs: £1450 for a 4-week placement; £3900 for a 12-week placement, inclusive of international flights, meals, accommodation (furnished and comfortable, shared between two) and placement activities. Accommodation is fully furnished and extremely comfortable.

Contact: William Moolman, Marketing Manager.

ECOLOGIA TRUST
The Park, Forres, Moray, Scotland IV36 3TZ. ☎01309 690995. E-mail: gap@ecologia.org.uk. Website: www.ecologia.org.uk.
Programme description: Volunteer programme specifically for gap year students at the Kitezh Children's Community for orphans in western Russia. Russian language is not essential although students of Russian will quickly become fluent. (See entry in 'Directory of Volunteering Abroad' and further details in chapter on Russia.)

EF GAP YEAR
Dudley House, 36-38 Southampton Street, London WC2E 7HF. ☎Freephone 0800 0683385. Fax: 020-7836 7334. E-mail: eflanguages@ef.com. Website: www.ef.com.
Programme description: Range of possibilities such as combining language course with an internship in Nice, or volunteering and community work in Quito with a trip to the Galapagos.
Cost: Sample price £2800 for 3 months in Quito, Ecuador, including accommodation, tuition, and meals.
Accommodation: Host families or student residence.
Other services: EF has its own Travel Service and tailor-made student insurance
Contact: David Burton, Academic Programme Co-ordinator.

EIL: EXPERIMENT IN INTERNATIONAL LIVING
287 Worcester Road, Malvern, Worcs. WR14 1AB. ☎0800 018 4015. Fax: 01684 562212. E-mail: info@eiluk.org. Website: www.eiluk.org.
Focuses on educational and cultural travel and offers a variety of opportunities for young people in their gap year or long vacations. Partner offices in 30 countries.
Programme description: Various programmes include European Voluntary Service (EVS) described below, Farmstays in the USA, volunteer programmes in Argentina, Brazil, Chile, Ecuador, Ghana, Guatemala, India, Ireland, Kenya, Mexico, Morocco, Nepal, Nigeria, South Africa and Thailand. Also homestays worldwide.
Destinations: Africa, Asia, Australasia, Europe, South America and USA.
Duration and time of placements: Varies from 2-week volunteer stay in Latin America to 12 months at EVS host institution on the Continent.
Cost: Costs vary depending upon the type of stay chosen.

EMERSON COLLEGE
Forest Row, East Sussex RH18 5JX. ☎01342 822238. Fax: 01342 826055. E-mail: gapyear@emerson.org.uk. Website: www.emerson.org.uk.
International adult education centre and community based on the work of Rudolf Steiner.
Programme description: Orientation Year specifically designed for gap year students aged 18-24. (See 'Directory of Miscellaneous Courses' for more information.)

ENGLISH SPEAKING UNION
Dartmouth House, 37 Charles St, London W1J 5ED. ☎020-7529 1550. Fax:

020-7495 6108. E-mail: education@esu.org. Website: www.esu.org.
The ESU was founded in 1918 and has played an important role in fostering links between different nationalities. It stresses the importance of the English language as a means of shared communication between different races and cultures.

Programme description: The ESU's Secondary School Exchange Scheme makes it possible for students to spend 6 months or a full academic year (i.e. two or three terms) in one of about 30 participating independent schools in the US and Canada. Opportunities to travel in the school holidays and at the end of the academic year.

Destinations: USA and Canada.

Number of placements per year: Approximately 30 per year.

Prerequisites: A-levels or equivalent, an outgoing personality and past participation in extra-curricular activities. Candidates accepted from both private and state schools.

Duration and time of placement: 6 months from January or 9 months from September.

Selection procedures and orientation: Students are selected for interview on the basis of a submitted application form. Prior to departure there is a lot of contact with the ESU and former scholars. A compulsory pre-departure briefing is held. Students are expected to make their own travel arrangements although an ESU representative or member of the school will meet them at the destination.

Cost: Board and tuition are free as part of the scholarship. Travel and other expenses (insurance, visa and spending money) of approximately £2500 must be met by scholar and his or her family.

Contact: Katherine Plummer, Education Officer.

EUROPEAN VOLUNTARY SERVICE (EVS)
Connect Youth, British Council, 10 Spring Gardens, London SW1A 2BN. ☎020 7389-4030. Fax: 020-7389 4033. E-mail: connectyouth.enquiries@britishcouncil. org. Website: www.connectyouthinternational.com.
Programme description: EVS allows young people (aged 18-25) to volunteer in European countries, engaging in cultural, educational and training opportunities.

Destinations: Europe.

Prerequisites: Applicants must be aged 18-25 and be a legal resident in one of the EU member states (including Norway, Iceland and Liechtenstein). No specific qualifications are needed and language training may be provided.

Duration and time of placements: Standard voluntary service is for 6-12 months. Shorter-term placements are on offer (3 weeks - 6 months) to young people with fewer opportunities.

Selection procedures and orientation: Applicants need to apply through an approved sending organisation (details for volunteers and organisations can be obtained through Connect Youth). For further information on potential placements, see the website: www. europa.eu.int/comm/youth/program/sos/index_en.html. Sending organisations with entries in this book include ICYE, EIL and AFS.

Cost: No cost to volunteers, as the programme is funded through the European YOUTH programme. Pocket money is provided weekly or monthly.

FLYING FISH
25 Union Road, Cowes, Isle of Wight PO31 7TW. ☎0871 250 2500. Fax: 01983 281821. E-mail: mail@flyingfishonline.com. Website: www.flyingfishonline.com.
Member of the Year Out Group. Flying Fish trains water and snowsports staff and arranges employment for sailors, divers, surfers, kitesurfers and windsurfers, skiers and snowboarders. Founded in 1993 it can help young people to fix up a year of travel, training and adventure, or to start a career in the action sports industry.

Programme description: A gap year with Flying Fish starts with a course leading to qualification as a surf, sail, kitesurf or windsurf instructor, yacht skipper, Divemaster or dive instructor, ski or snowboard instructor (see entry in 'Directory of Sports Courses'). After qualifying you can choose a period of work experience or go into a paid job in many locations worldwide, with advice from a Flying Fish careers adviser.

Destinations: Training courses are run at Cowes in the UK, at Sydney and the Whitsunday Islands in Australia, the Bay of Islands in New Zealand, Vassiliki in Greece, Pissouri in Cyprus, Dahab in Egypt and Whistler Mountain in Canada. Jobs are worldwide with main employers located in Australia, the South Pacific, the Caribbean and the Mediterranean.

Number of placements per year: 600.

Duration and time of placements: 1 week to 12 months with start dates year round.

Selection procedures & orientation: Applicants submit an application before training and will be asked to attend job interviews.

Cost: Fees range from £800 to £11,000 but most gap year students choose a programme costing about £3500. Accommodation and airfares are provided, with normal wages during employment.

FRONTIER
50-52 Rivington St, London EC2A 3QP. ☎020-7613 2422. E-mail: info@frontier. ac.uk. Website: www.frontier.ac.uk.

Founding member of the Year Out Group. Frontier is a conservation research and development NGO, working in tropical countries since 1989 dedicated to saving endangered species and protecting tropical forests and reefs. Frontier works in partnership with host-country institutions and communities to address conservation priorities.

Programme description: Frontier offers the opportunity to work in coral reefs, savannas, forests and mangrove areas as part of long-term conservation programmes in far-off destinations. Programmes are established in response to problems; surveys of damaged areas are carried out so that possible solutions can be identified. For example, dynamite fishing in Tanzania was damaging the web of delicate marine life. Frontier volunteers carried out more than 6000 dives, resulting in the establishment of a Marine Park where the marine life is protected.

Destinations: Tanzania, Madagascar, Cambodia, Fiji, the Pacific Isles and Nicaragua.

Number of placements per year: 250+.

Prerequisites: Minimum age 17. No specific qualifications required as training is provided in the field leading to a BTEC Level 3 Advanced Diploma in Tropical Habitat Conservation.

Duration and time of placements: 4, 8, 10 or 20 weeks.

Selection procedures and orientation: Informal information sessions are held on Saturdays and Wednesdays (check website for dates) where interested parties can find out more from past volunteers. After an application has been submitted and a telephone briefing, applicants will hear within a week whether they have been accepted. Prior to the expedition, a briefing weekend is held in the UK.

Cost: Depending on location and duration, international volunteers raise from £1100 for 4 weeks, £1700 for 8 weeks, £2000 for 10 weeks and £3500 for 20 weeks, which covers all individual costs, including a UK weekend briefing, scientific and dive training, travel, visas, food and accommodation but excludes flights and insurance. The organisation helps with fund-raising ideas but the onus is on the individual.

GAP ACTIVITY PROJECTS (GAP) LTD
44 Queen's Road, Reading, RG1 4BB. ☎0118 959 4914. Fax: 0118 957 6634. E-mail: Volunteer@gap.org.uk. Website: www.gap.org.uk.

Founding member of the Year Out Group. GAP Activity Projects is an educational charity more than 30 years experience of sending volunteers to work overseas during their year out. GAP is committed to the principle of service to others and intercultural exchange.

Programme description: Voluntary work placements are organised in various fields, including teaching English as a foreign language, assisting with sport, drama and general activities in schools, care work with the disadvantaged and people with disabilities, outdoor education, environmental, specialist and hospital work.

Destinations: 29 countries worldwide.

Number of placements per year: 2000+.
Prerequisites: Applicants must be aged between 17 and 25.
Duration and time of placements: From 4-12 months (average 6 months).
Selection procedures and orientation: The GAP brochure is published annually in August. After an application is received, an interview will be held, after which the applicant will hear if he or she has been offered a place. There is a group briefing which all applicants are encouraged to attend. Any necessary courses (e.g. TEFL) must be attended before leaving for the destination country or sometimes on arrival.
Cost: Applicants pay a fee, currently £900. All places are subsidised by GAP's own fundraising by over 20%. Additional costs are airfares, insurance and medical costs, but accommodation and food in the destination country are provided. In most cases pocket money will also be paid.

gapadvice.org
12 Hutchings Road, Beaconsfield, Buck. HP9 2BB. ☎07973 548316. E-mail: info@gapadvice.org. Website: www.gapadvice.org.
New independent advisory service for individuals and organisations.
Programme description: gapadvice.org provides independent and unbiased information, research and advice on gap years, for people of all ages.
Contact: Phil Murray, Director.

GAP ENTERPRISE CONSULTANTS
East Manor Barn, Fringford, Oxfordshire OX27 8DG. ☎01869 278346. E-mail: johnvessey@gapenterprise.co.uk. Website: www.gapenterprise.co.uk.
Gap year consultancy.
Programme description: Gap Enterprise Consultants can assist in the planning and support of a structured year out, whether taken as an academic course, skills training, work experience, paid employment, expedition, volunteer placement or ambitious adventure travel.
Destinations: Worldwide. Library of information and computerised database of projects and activities around the world.
Cost: £400 for a consultation consisting of detailed confidential questionnaire, three-hour interview, comprehensive 50-page written report (including client-specific contacts list) and follow-up. A review with recommendations on university application procedure is included, as well as advice on a range of relevant topics such as risk assessment, health and safety, insurance, red tape, cultural orientation and fundraising.
Contact: John Vessey, Director.

GAP GURU
6 Forest Hill, Great Bedwyn, Marlborough, Wilts. SN8 3LP. ☎0870 609 1796. E-mail: info@gapguru.com. Website: www.gapguru.com.
Part of Futuresense Ltd.
Programme description: Specialist in arranging individualised gap year programmes in India, with options to work, travel and volunteer including working in an upmarket hotel group in Kerala as a management trainee, working as a dance instructor in Delhi, volunteering to teach underprivileged children or participate in conservation or media projects. Gap Guru also arranges interesting travel programmes.
Number of placements per year: 150-200.
Destinations: Throughout India.
Prerequisites: All applicants require a minimum of 3 A-levels or equivalent and must be fluent in English. No previous experience needed for some placements; specific work experience on a submitted CV needed for some work placements.
Duration and time of placements: 4 weeks to 12 months.
Selection procedures & orientation: All applicants will undertake an interview either in person or on the telephone. Successful applicants will be given a full pre-departure

briefing and work place orientation in India.

Cost: Programme fees start at £940 for 4 weeks. Work placements are paid placements.

GAP SPORTS
Willow Bank House, 84 Station Road, Marlow, Bucks. SL7 1NX. ☎0870 837 9797. E-mail: info@gapsports.com. Website: www.gapsports.com.

Programme description: Programmes for those who want to play, coach and qualify in sports overseas. Opportunities to join sports (and non-sports) community projects in Africa and Latin America. Also ski/snowboard instructor courses in Canada (see 'Directory of Courses') with guaranteed paid employment. Opportunities to play and train at international football, rugby, golf and cricket academies abroad or become a qualified dive master and work in dive schools worldwide.

Destinations: Ghana, South Africa, Costa Rica, Canada.

Prerequisites: Minimum age 18. No previous experience is needed and volunteers are welcomed from all walks of life.

Duration and time of placements: 5 weeks to 12 months; average is 3 months.

Selection procedures and orientation: Applications should be submitted at least 6 weeks before departure. Interviews not required.

Costs: From £1195 for 5 weeks to £1495-£1695 for 3 months plus £100 for each extra week.

GAPWORK.COM
☎0113-274 0252. E-mail: info@gapwork.com. Website: www.gapwork.com.

Programme description: gapwork is a publisher and provider of gap year and working holiday information. The website provides a range of information on taking a gap year including listings of accommodation providers, employment opportunities and gap year organisations. Gapwork also publish guidebooks on working and travelling and produce a free e-mail newsletter and glossy magazine.

Cost: Work and Travel Guidebooks to Australia, New Zealand, Canada, Europe, and the USA cost £12.99 each but can be bought online for £9.99 at www.gapwork.com.

Contact: Mark Williams.

GAPYEAR.COM
Website: www.gapyear.com.

Largest gap year community in the UK dedicated to helping people plan and prepare for a gap year. The website www.gapyear.com has over 6000 pages of information, details on more than 100 countries and a section to help plan a round-the-world trip (www.gapyear.com/rtw). Users can find travel mates, access a database with thousands of opportunities, and pose questions on the message boards. Gapyear.com also runs gapyearshop.com (specialist gap year travel kit site) and noworriesinsurance.com (specialist gap year insurance).

GAP YEAR NZ
Leeds Innovation Centre, 103 Clarendon Rd, Leeds LS2 9DF. ☎0870 4020 606. Fax: 0870 4020 607. E-mail: info@gapyear-newzealand.co.uk. Website: www. gapyear-newzealand.co.uk.

Gap Year NZ, the sister company to Place Me NZ (see entry in Directory of Work Experience), launched in September 2005 as a dedicated guide to taking a gap year in New Zealand.

Programme description: Live job listings, job search assistance for working holidays including fruit picking, hospitality, catering, clerical and adventure tourism. Web forums plus starter packs for sale and essential services for travellers to New Zealand.

Number of placements per year: Estimated between 300 and 1000.

Destinations: Throughout New Zealand.

Prerequisites: Eligible for NZ working holiday visa (i.e. UK resident aged 18-30 who has

not had the visa before).
Duration and time of placements: 3 months to 2 years.
Selection procedures & orientation: Apply via website or over telephone. Application packs sent out to participants once eligibility has been checked. Applications accepted all year round. Initial accommodation and orientation is provided with starter packs and also job search facility provided within New Zealand. Services such as mailboxes, 24 hour support line and tax assistance can also be purchased.
Cost: Viewing job listings is free. Visa assistance, job search and starter packs from £50 to £300. Wages paid in NZ range from NZ$10 to NZ$17 an hour.
Contact: Chris Challenger, Programme Manager.

GLOBAL ADVENTURES PROJECT
38 Queen's Gate, London SW7 5HR. ☎0800 085 4197 (free phone). E-mail: info@globaladventures.co.uk. Website: www.globaladventures.co.uk.
A division of the American Institute for Foreign Study (AIFS), an educational and cultural exchange organisation founded in 1964, which also oversees Camp America (which is a member of the Year Out Group) and Au Pair in America.
Programme description: 3 to 12-month programme with a choice of work, study and/or volunteer placements in the USA, Brazil, Europe, South Africa, India and Australia/New Zealand. A Round-the-World ticket, included in the programme, allows time for independent travel in between. Any combinations of placements are available up to a maximum of four; each itinerary is tailored to individual requirements.
Destinations: Core destinations are USA (paid work as a camp counsellor), Brazil (conservation volunteer), Europe (language learning in France, Italy, Austria or Spain), South Africa (volunteering in townships plus some cultural study at Stellenbosch University), India (volunteering or paid work) and Australia/New Zealand (paid work).
Prerequisites: Minimum age 18 at time of departure, so suitable for gap year students and people taking a career break.
Duration and time of placements: Each placement lasts 12 weeks (with the exception of Australia/New Zealand which lasts up to 9 months) and departures from UK take place in January, April, June and September.
Selection procedures & orientation: Free one-to-one consultations available for general gap year advice. Applications should be sent at least 12 weeks before departure with £100 fee. Individual interviews arranged to discuss preferences plus a 2-day training weekend before departure.
Cost: From £1745 (12-week placement) to £5295 (for up to four placements and a ten stop a round-the-world ticket).
Contact: Heather Thompson, Director.

GLOBAL CHOICES
Barkat House, 116-118 Finchley Road, London NW3 5HT. ☎020-7433 2501. E-mail: info@globalchoices.co.uk. Website: www.globalchoices.co.uk.
Programme description: Voluntary work, internships, practical training and work experience worldwide.
Destinations: Argentina, Australia, Austria, Brazil, Ghana, Ireland, Nepal, Portugal, South Africa, Spain, UK and USA.
Prerequisites: Majority of programmes open to all over 18.
Duration and time of placements: 2 weeks to 18 months.
Cost: Varies by programme.
Contact: Mr. Giedrius Mazurka.

GLOBAL VISION INTERNATIONAL (GVI)
Amwell Farmhouse, Nomansland, Wheathampstead, St. Albans, Herts. AL4 8EJ. ☎0870 608 8898. Fax: 0870 609 2319. E-mail: info@gvi.co.uk. Website: www.gvi.co.uk.

North American office: PO Box 8124, Delray Beach, FL 33482-8124 (1-888-653-6028/ fax 561-829-8286; info@gviusa.com/ www.gviusa.com).

Programme description: 20+ overseas expeditions and conservation projects in Africa, Latin America and Asia. See relevant chapters for details.

Destinations: South Africa, Namibia, Madagascar, East Africa, Seychelles, Ecuador, Brazil, Mexico, Panama, Guatemala, Costa Rica, Belize, Patagonia, Nepal, Indonesia, Sri Lanka and Thailand.

Number of placements per year: 1000.

Prerequisites: None. Minimum age 18. All nationalities welcome.

Duration and time of placements: 2 weeks to one year.

Selection procedures and orientation: Some projects require a telephone interview; others require only a completed application form.

Cost: from £695 to £2995.

Contact: Chris Ash, Volunteer Co-ordinator.

GREENFORCE GLOBAL CONSERVATION EXPEDITIONS

11-15 Betterton Street, Covent Garden, London WC2H 9BP. ☎020-7470 8888. Fax: 020-379 0801. E-mail: info@greenforce.org. Website: www.greenforce.org.
Member of the Year Out Group. Works with partner organisations such as WWF, UNESCO and Red Cross in self-managed conservation locations.

Programme description: Volunteers work as Fieldwork Assistants, carrying out tasks such as tracking animal movements and studying coral reef species. Choice of land-based or diving projects. In some locations possibility of learning local languages (e.g. Nepali or Masai).

Destinations: Expedition locations on all the tropical continents; current countries of operation are Fiji, Bahamas, Borneo (Kalimantan), Tanzania, Amazonian Ecuador and Nepal.

Prerequisites: No previous experience necessary; no qualifications required. Applicants must be over the age of 18.

Duration and time of placements: 1-6 months, though standard phase is 10 weeks. Departures to all destinations throughout the year.

Selection procedures and orientation: Applicants may attend one of the regular, informal open evenings. A briefing pack is provided, giving information about fund-raising and relevant medical advice, etc. Pre-departure training and BBQ held at Imperial College plus reunion parties held after return to UK.

Cost: From £1400 for short expeditions, £2300 for 10 weeks. Fees cover training, food, accommodation, visas and medical insurance but not flights. PADI dive training costs £200.

Contact: Heidi Reynolds, Volunteer Manager.

GWENDALYNE

c/o Twin Training and Travel Ltd, 2nd Floor, 67-71 Lewisham High St, Lewisham, London SE13 5JX. ☎ +44 (0) 20 8297 3251. Fax: 020-8297 0984. E-mail: info@gwendalyne.com. Website: www.gwendalyne.com.
Gwendalyne is the newly launched Outbound department of Twin Training & Travel offering a range of volunteering and work experience programmes around the world. See entries in the 'Directory of Volunteering Abroad' and the 'Directory of Work Experience Abroad'.

ICYE: INTER-CULTURAL YOUTH EXCHANGE

Latin American House, Kingsgate Place, London NW6 4TA. ☎020-7681 0983. E-mail: info@icye.org.uk. Website: www.icye.org.uk.
Non profit-making charity offering both long-term (6 or 12 months) and short-term (1-12 weeks) volunteering opportunities in many countries (see 'Directory of Volunteering Abroad').

THE INTERNATIONAL ACADEMY plc
St Hilary Court, Copthorne Way, Culverhouse Cross, Cardiff CF5 6ES. ☎02920 672500. Fax: 02920 672510. E-mail: info@theinternationalacademy.com. Website: www.theinternationalacademy.com.
Member of the Year Out Group. Instructor training in skiing, snowboarding, whitewater rafting and diving to help people on a gap year, career break or others become qualified as instructors. See 'Directory of Sports Courses'.

INTERNATIONAL STUDENT EXCHANGE CENTER (ISEC)
89 Fleet Street London EC4Y 1DH. ☎020-7583 9116. Fax: 020-7583 9117. E-mail: isec@btconnect.com. Website: www.isecworld.co.uk.
Programme description: Cultural exchanges with large range of countries in Europe and worldwide, including au pairing, volunteering, paid work, volunteering, etc.
Destinations: Denmark, Finland, France, Germany, Italy, Netherlands, Norway, Sweden, Russia and states of the former Soviet Union, Australia, New Zealand, USA, South Africa, Brazil and Latin America.
Number of placements per year: 200+.
Prerequisites: Majority of programmes open to all over 18. Some have language requirements, some dependent on degree/qualifications (e.g. some teaching programmes).
Duration and time of placements: Mostly 6-12 months though some shorter and longer.
Selection procedures and orientation: Informal telephone interviews often sufficient.
Cost: Varies by programme, from £85 for camp counsellor programme in Russia to £640 for agricultural trainees in USA.
Contact: Patricia Santoriello.

IEPUK LTD
The Old Rectory, Belton, Rutland LE15 9LE. ☎01572 717381. Fax: 01572 717343. E-mail: info@iepuk.com. Website: www.iepuk.com.
Equine staff agency (formerly called Stablemate) with partners in Australia and the USA.
Programme description: Placements in all rural industries including agriculture, horticulture, winery and equine. IEP also assists with organising visas, work permits, placements with the security of back-up from partners or representatives in destination country. In New Zealand adventure trips of up to 6 weeks can be organised as part of the work experience programme.
Destinations: USA, Australia, New Zealand, Canada. Also Europe and within the UK.
Number of placements per year: 300/400.
Prerequisites: Ages 18-30. Minimum one year of practical experience needed though many placements offer additional training. Placements available to graduates and those without formal qualifications but experience. According to IEPUK, If you wear wellies, they can probably find something suitable.
Duration and time of placements: Usually 12 months but variable depending on industry (winery work normally 3-6 months).
Selection procedures and orientation: Interviews and orientation are required for work overseas.
Cost: Participants are asked to budget for about £1800 including airfares.

IST PLUS LTD
Rosedale House, Rosedale Road, Richmond, Surrey TW9 2SZ. ☎020-8939 9057. E-mail: info@istplus.com. Website: www.istplus.com.
Partner agency in UK delivering programmes on behalf of CIEE (Council on International Educational Exchange) which is a member of the Year Out Group.
Programme description: Work, teaching and study abroad programmes for UK students, graduates and young professionals. Programmes include Work & Travel USA, Internship

i-to-i

GET AHEAD – GET A GAP!

STAND OUT FROM THE CROWD WITH I–TO–I

If the gap year bug has bitten, but you want to do more than just bum around on the beach, i-to-i has just the trip for you!

Why you?

With more than 300 (yes, 300!) projects to choose from in 25 countries, i-to-i ventures are a top-tastic way to see the world, make great mates AND improve the lives of others.

Trip tasters:

> Conserve turtles in Costa Rica
> Work with orphans in India*
> Coach sports in Thailand
> Teach English in Ecuador*
> Work with wallabies 'down under'

*TEFL training included

Or choose from around 295 others!

Why i-to-i?

Not that we like to blow our own trumpets, but i-to-i is the largest provider of gap year volunteer placements. Each year we send around 4,000 people to support worthwhile projects overseas, with a further 10,000 training as TEFL (Teaching English as a Foreign Language) tutors.

Our projects last from 1-24 weeks and allow you to make a positive impact on people and cultures – great for a CV or UCAS application!

So if you want to stand out from the 'also rans' who spent their gaps tripping along the tourist trails, simply check out our website or give us a call.

"Going to Costa Rica has, without a doubt, been an amazingly unforgettable experience in my life. Volunteer work is the most rewarding thing in the world and I would recommend a gap year to anyone."

Caroline Wilson, aged 18, community development in Costa Rica.

i-to-i is proud to be a member of the Responsible Tourism Partnership

YEAR OUT GROUP   RYTO   CELDC   INVESTOR IN PEOPLE

Call: 0870 333 2332 quote: GYG2006 | Visit: www.i-to-i.com

USA, Professional Career Training in the USA, Work & Travel Australia, Work & Travel New Zealand, Internship Canada, Teach in China and Teach in Thailand. Also arrange Language Study Abroad programmes in 23 destinations across Europe and Latin America.

i-to-i
Woodside House, 261 Low Lane, Horsforth, Leeds LS18 5NY. Tel: 0870 333 2332. Fax: 0113 205 4619. E-mail: info@i-to-i.com. Website: www.i-to-i.com.
Founding member of the Year Out Group with Investor in People status. i-to-i is a teacher training and volunteer travel organisation.
Programme description: 300 projects in 24 countries including teaching, conservation, community work, building, sports and media placements. Projects are available in Australia, Bolivia, Brazil, China, Costa Rica, Croatia, Dominican Republic, Ecuador, Ghana, Guatemala, Honduras, India, Ireland, Kenya, Mexico, Mongolia, Nepal, Peru, South Africa, Sri Lanka, Tanzania, Thailand, Venezuela and Vietnam. Paid teaching placements are available in South Korea, China and Thailand. i-to-i also organises 20-hour weekend TEFL training courses across the UK and an online version available anywhere in the world. Online and practical weekend packages are available.
Number of placements per year: 4000.
Prerequisites: Native or near-native English speakers are required for teaching placements.
Duration and time of placements: From one week to six months, starting all year round. TEFL courses or voluntary programmes can also be booked through STA Travel.
Selection procedures and orientation: All placements include full pre-departure travel and work briefing, full project inventories, a briefing DVD, comprehensive insurance, round-the-clock emergency support plus in-country staff and an orientation on arrival. All teaching and community development placements include a free i-to-i online TEFL course.
Cost: From £495 (excluding airfares). £195 for TEFL course only. Free taster TEFL course online at www.onlinetefl.com.

JET PROGRAMME
Japan Exchange & Teaching Programme, c/o JET Desk, Japanese Embassy, 101-104 Piccadilly, London W1J 7JT. ☎020-7465 6668/6670. E-mail: info@jet-uk.org. Website: www.jet-uk.org.
Programme description: The Japan Exchange & Teaching (JET) Programme is a Japanese government run scheme to promote international understanding and improve foreign language tuition. UK graduates have the opportunity of working in Japan for a minimum of a year.
Destinations: Throughout Japan.
Number of placements per year: Approximately 400 places are offered to UK candidates.
Prerequisites: Must have a Bachelor's degree in any subject and be under 39 years of age by the time of departure. Neither teaching qualifications nor Japanese language ability is needed for the Assistant Language Teacher (ALT) positions; however the Co-ordinator for International Relations (CIR) role does require Japanese language ability sufficient for everyday working situations.
Duration and time of placements: One-year contracts begin in late July.
Selection procedures and orientation: The application deadline is usually the last Friday in November. Orientations are given at the start of July in London and Edinburgh and in Tokyo upon arrival in Japan.
Cost: None. There is no application fee and return airfares are provided to those who complete their contract. Salary of 3,600,000 yen paid (currently about £18,000-£19,000).

JOHN HALL PRE-UNIVERSITY COURSE
12 Gainsborough Road, Ipswich, Suffolk IP4 2UR. ☎01473 251223. Fax: 01473 288009. E-mail: info@johnhallpre-university.com. Website: www.johnhallvenice.co.uk.

Annual pre-university course on European civilisation specially designed for gap year students, held in London and Venice between January and March. Emphasis is on the visual arts and music. Cost for 1 week in London plus 6 weeks in Venice is £6400 with optional extra periods in Florence and Rome. See 'Directory of Art Courses'.

KIBBUTZ REPRESENTATIVES
16 Accommodation Road, London NW11 8EP. ☎020-8458 9235. Fax: 020-8455 7930. E-mail: enquiries@kibbutz.org.uk. Website: www.kibbutz.org.il.
Programme description: KR represents the Israeli kibbutz movement in the UK and recruits volunteers for kibbutzim on their behalf. The newest programme is 'The New Israeli Experience' which over three months combines a political and cultural introduction to the country, language instruction (Hebrew or English) and volunteering.
Prerequisities: Must be aged 18-40 (or sometimes 50).
Duration and time of placements: Minimum stay is 8 weeks, with departures year round. Maximum stay 6 months.
Selection procedures and orientation: Candidates attend an informal interview in London, and provide a signed medical declaration of fitness. Processing takes 2-3 weeks (summer is the busiest time).
Cost: Package costs about £410 including flights plus compulsory kibbutz insurance.

KWA MADWALA
PO Box 192, Hectorspruit 1330, South Africa. ☎ +27 13-792 4219. Fax: +27 13-792 4534. E-mail: gazebog@mweb.co.za or gm@kwamadwala.co.za. Website: www.kwamadwala.co.za/gap_year.htm. UK representative: Paul Shields (info@kwamadwala.co.uk).
Private game reserve located on the south side of the Kruger National Park in South Africa between Swaziland and Mozambique which offers a range of gap year conservation experiences.
Programme description: Student safari and conservation vacations. Rangers and trackers oversee conservation projects on the longer programmes which may also include microlight game counting, anti-poaching patrols, camping trips to Mozambique, bush survival course, etc. From 2006, interaction with property's domestic elephants will be possible. Accommodation in rustic Kingfisher Camp.
Prerequisities: Minimum age 17.
Duration and time of placements: 84 days (starting 15 May, 15 September, 15 January), 25 days (from mid-April, mid-August and mid-December), 7-day conservation experiences, 6-week practical game ranger training (start dates as for 84-day placement) followed by optional 8-week game ranger field experience
Costs: 84-day programme costs £3455; 25 days costs £1455 and 7 days £490. 6-week game ranger training £2995 and game ranger experience £1495.

LANGUAGE COURSES ABROAD LTD
67 Ashby Road, Loughborough, Leicestershire LE11 3AA. ☎01509 211612. Fax: 01509 260037. E-mail: info@languagesabroad.co.uk. Website: www.languagesabroad.co.uk.
Parent company, Spanish Study Holidays Ltd., is a member of FIYTO (Federation of International Youth Travel Organisations), ALTO (Association of Language Travel Organisations) and GWEA (Global Work Experience Association).
Programme description: In-country language courses in Spanish, French, German, Italian, Portuguese and Russian (see entry in 'Directory of Language Courses') often in conjunction with work experience placements, available in Spain, Latin America, France, Germany and Italy (see entry in 'Directory of Work Experience').
Contact: Mike Cummins, Director.

LAUNCHPAD AUSTRALIA
PO Box 2525, Fitzroy, VIC 3065, Australia. ☎**1300 851 826 (from Australia)** or **+61 3 9419 9147. Fax: +61 3 9445 9375. E-mail: workingholiday@launch padaustralia.com. Website: www.launchpadaustralia.com.**
New company offering range of programmes overseas mainly for travelling Australians, but with a couple of incoming programmes as well.

Programme description: Australians can be placed as nannies in France, UK, USA, Spain, Austria, Germany, Denmark, South Africa, Italy, Netherlands and Australia, as volunteers worldwide and in working holiday programmes in the US and UK. Working holiday makers also placed as nannies in Australia. Working holiday starter packs sold for Australia as well as Canada, France, Italy, Netherlands and the UK. 5-day TESOL courses held in Australia with access to job database. Language courses arranged worldwide. Also half-day gap year advice courses (see 'Directory of Courses: Gap Year Safety & Preparation').

Number of placements per year: 100 and growing.

Destinations: Europe and many other countries for Australian nannies, volunteers, etc. Hospitality placements in the UK. Camp counselling and work experience in the USA for students.

Prerequisites: Australian and New Zealand nannies must have at least 200 hours childcare experience; ages 18-30 (minimum 21 in some countries). Hospitality UK participants must also be Australian or New Zealand citizens eligible for a working holiday visa to the UK and with at least 6 months experience in hospitality (excluding bar tending).

Duration and time of placements: Nannies normally work for one year but 3 months also possible. Volunteer overseas 2-24 weeks. Hospitality UK 1 year.

Cost: For nanny placements A$750-$900 depending on destination. Hospitality UK: $A500 placement fee. Salaries will vary according to position.

Contact: Danielle Ades-Salman, Managing Director.

THE LEAP OVERSEAS LTD
121 High St, Marlborough, Wilts. SN8 1LZ. ☎**01672 519922. Fax: 01672 519944. E-mail: info@theleap.co.uk. Website: www.theleap.co.uk.**
Member of the Year Out Group.

Programme description: Team (up to 12) or solo placements for students (and employees taking career sabbaticals) with overseas voluntary work placements focused on eco-tourism. Placements combine experience of safari camp, conservation and community projects. Volunteers work alongside indigenous people in game parks, jungles and coastal locations.

Destinations: Africa (Kenya, Tanzania, Malawi, Botswana, South Africa, Zambia, Mozambique) and Latin America (Argentina, Guyana, Ecuador, Costa Rica).

Number of placements per year: 130 solo plus 260 team.

Prerequisites: Minimum age 18. Must be committed, enthusiastic and motivated to work in a team and get stuck in. No previous experience needed.

Duration and time of placements: 12, 10 or 6 weeks. Solo placements begin year round; team placements depart January, April, July and September. 'Summer Team Gap' lasts 6 weeks from July.

Selection procedures and orientation: Applicants attend interview or Familiarisation and Selection course for suitability and training/briefing. Induction course carried out in-country on arrival.

Other services: Flights can be arranged through ATOL partner agency STA Travel. Time given for adventure travel e.g. whitewater rafting, kite surfing and scuba diving.

Costs: £1600-£2900 (depending on duration and location) includes selection course, briefing, fundraising guide, food and accommodation, travel insurance, transport, pocket money, project donation and 24-hour support. Price does not include airfares or visas.

Contact: Guy Whitehead, Founder Director.

MADVENTURER

The Old Casino, 1-4 Forth Lane, Newcastle-upon-Tyne NE1 5HX. ☎0845 121 1996. Fax: 0191-269 9490. E-mail: tribe@madventurer.com. Website: www. madventurer.com.

Member of the Year Out Group.

Programme description: With projects and adventures in a dozen destinations lasting between 2 weeks and 6 months, all itineraries can be catered for. While on a project, participants live in a rural village with a group of madventurers while volunteering as a teacher, builder, medic and/or sports coach. A typical 2-month expedition includes 5 weeks of volunteering for a grassroots community project, followed by a 3-week group adventure (trekking, rafting, touring). Projects can be booked in blocks of 5 weeks for a prolonged experience (i.e. 3 projects for a total of 15 weeks).

Destinations: Ghana, Togo, Tanzania, Uganda, Kenya, Peru, Sri Lanka, Thailand, Tonga and Fiji.

Prerequisites: Minimum age 17. No experience is necessary to make a difference.

Duration and time of placements: Projects run in blocks of 5 weeks although there is an option to do 2 weeks. Adventures range from 3 weeks to 88 days. Departure dates available all year round.

Selection procedures and orientation: Volunteers are assigned at least one crew member to lend support and guidance throughout placement. Comprehensive pre-departure information given in UK.

Cost: From £1280 (Africa), £1480 (Latin America and South Pacific) and £1200 (Asia) excluding flights.

Contact: The Tribe at Mad HQ.

MALACA INSTITUTO

Calle Cortada 6, Cerrado de Calderón, 29018 Málaga, Spain. ☎ +34 952-29 3242. Fax: +34 952-29 6316. E-mail: gapyear@malacainstituto.com. Website: www.MalacaInstituto.com.

Programme description: Combination Spanish language course and culture (Hispanic Studies) or combined with work experience placements, dance, cookery and homestays. For further details, see entry in the 'Directory of Language Courses'.

MONDOCHALLENGE

Milton House, Gayton Rd, Milton Malsor, Northampton NN7 3AB. ☎01604 858225. Fax: 01604 859323. E-mail: info@mondochallenge.org. Website: www. mondochallenge.org.

Programme description: Volunteers of all ages including some on their gap year (pre and post university) are sent to villages in Nepal, India, Sri Lanka, Tanzania, Kenya, Gambia, Ecuador and Chile, mainly to teach. Some business development programmes. Fee for 3 months is £1000. (See entry in 'Directory of Volunteering Abroad'.)

NONSTOP SKI & SNOWBOARD
Shakespeare House, 168 Lavender Hill, SW11 5TF. ☎0870 241 8070. Fax 020-7801 6201. E-mail: info@nonstopski.com. Website: www.nonstopski.com.
Member of the Year Out Group.
Programme description: Ski and Snowboard Improvement and Instructor Courses in the Canadian Rockies (see entry in 'Directory of Sports Courses').

OPERATION WALLACEA
Hope House, Old Bolingbroke, Nr Spilsby, Lincolnshire PE23 4EX. ☎01790 763194. Fax: 01790 763825. E-mail: info@opwall.com. Website: www.opwall. com.
Programme description: Scientific research projects in Honduras, Indonesia, Egypt, etc. Wide range of marine and forest projects for students ranging from school groups and gap years to final year dissertations and MSc's.
Destinations: Honduras, Indonesia, Egypt and, from 2006, Cuba and South Africa.
Prerequisites: Minimum age 16. Enthusiasm needed.
Duration and time of placements: 2, 4, 6 or 8 weeks between the beginning of June and the end of September.
Selection procedures and orientation: Telephone interview. No deadlines. Dive training can be given.
Cost: £950 for 2 weeks, £1750 for 4 weeks, £2400 for 6 weeks and £2800 for 8 weeks, exclusive of flights and insurance.
Contact: Pippa Fawcett.

OUTREACH INTERNATIONAL
Bartletts Farm, Hayes Road, Compton Dundon, Somerset TA11 6PF. ☎/fax: 01458 274957. E-mail: gap@outreachinternational.co.uk. Website: www. outreachinternational.co.uk.
Member of the Year Out Group. Outreach International is a specialist organisation with carefully selected projects. There is enough variety to ensure that the interests and skills of individual volunteers can be put to good use.
Programme description: Volunteers participate in local initiatives allowing them to live in communities and work alongside local people. Cambodian placements are with respected international non-government organisations (NGOs). They include working with young landmine and polio victims and children who have become victims of human trafficking. Volunteers might teach English, computer skills and art skills or put on sports activities, providing stimulation to children who often go without. Mexican projects are on the Pacific coast in traditional villages. The projects are with orphans, disabled children, teaching in

local schools or working with giant sea turtles. In Ecuador, volunteers work with street children and also carry out conservation work in the Amazon rainforest.

Destinations: Mexico, Cambodia, Ecuador and the Galapagos Islands.

Number of placements per year: 100 per year; Outreach International knows each volunteer and places him or her in the most appropriate project.

Prerequisites: Most of the projects are ideal for gap year volunteers aged 18-21 and some are ideal for people with some work experience. Ideal for confident young people with a desire to travel, learn a language and offer their help to a worthwhile cause. The projects focus on the most needy sections of the community.

Duration and time of placements: 3+ months.

Selection procedures and orientation: Applicants will be invited to an informal interview within 3 weeks of applying. Volunteers are given a comprehensive briefing and language training. They are also offered a good teacher training course and support with fundraising. In all countries Outreach International employs a full-time co-ordinator who attends to the welfare of individuals.

Cost: £3300 for 3 months includes air tickets, full insurance, language course, in-country support, food, accommodation and all project costs. Additional months are approximately £400 per month. Outreach International rents spacious houses close to the projects or offers volunteers the opportunity of living with a local family. Volunteers live together in an Outreach International house but work in pairs on their project.

Contact: James Chapman, UK Director.

OVERSEAS WORKING HOLIDAYS (OWH)

Level 1, 51 Fife Road, Kingston, Surrey KT1 1SF. ☎ 0845 344 0366 or 020-8547 3664. Fax: 0870 460 4578. E-mail: info@owh.co.uk. Website: www.owh.co.uk.

Programme description: Paid work in hospitality industries of Australia and Canada. Variety of positions available including retail/customer service/guest relations/front desk and bar and catering work. Also offers Work and Play France programme (mainly aimed at Australian working holiday makers) which provides orientation in Paris and assistance with finding accommodation and a casual job. Volunteer placements worldwide also made.

Number of placements per year: 400.

Destinations: Australia and Canada. Other countries for Australians.

Prerequisites: Ages 18-31 for Australia, 18-35 for Canada. No specific qualifications needed. Non-UK citizens must check visa restrictions.

Duration and time of placements: Duration of working holiday visa, i.e. 1 year in Australia, winter or summer seasons in Canada (November-May or March-October).

Selection procedures & orientation: Applications for Australia accepted year round. Interviews for Canada programme are held twice a year, March and late July. Applications close 2 weeks before interviews.

Cost: Choice of programme fee for Australia depending on level of service: £189, £229 or £259. Canada programme fee is £349 and France fee is £259. Volunteer programme fees vary from project to project. Participants earn wages in Australia (up to $20 an hour) and Canada ($7-$12) an hour. Programme fee also includes accommodation assistance, setting up of bank account and SIM card.

Contact: Belinda Ward, Business Leader.

PEAK LEADERS UK Ltd

Mansfield, Strathmiglo, Fife KY14 7QE, Scotland. ☎ 01337 860079. Fax: 01337 868176. E-mail: info@peakleaders.com. Website: www.peakleaders.com.

Member of the Year Out Group.

Gap year ski and snowboard instructor courses in Canada, Argentina, and New Zealand (see *Directory of Ski Training Courses*).

PERSONAL OVERSEAS DEVELOPMENT (POD)

Linden Cottage, The Burgage, Prestbury, Cheltenham, Glos. GL52 3DJ. ☎ 01242

250901. E-mail: info@thepodsite.co.uk. Website: www.thepodsite.co.uk.
Small organisation that aims to provide personal service and to benefit local communities abroad.

Programme description: Flexible Gap Year (and Career Break) programmes in Peru, Thailand, Nepal and Tanzania. English teaching in all destinations, orphanage/care home volunteering in Peru, animal rescue or scuba diving in Thailand.

Destinations: Peru, Thailand, Nepal and Tanzania.

Duration and time of placements: 1-6 months. Standard duration is 3 months, starting throughout the year. Mini-gaps available in the summer after A levels.

Selection procedures & orientation: Written application, reference and phone interview. Depending on programme, volunteers may have to undergo a police check. Training is provided for all programmes including 2 days pre-departure training in the UK for teaching and orphanage projects.

Cost: £1340-£1875 for 3 months in Thailand (depending on project), £1750 in Peru and £2195 in Tanzania.

Contact: Alex Tarrant or Mike.

THE PROJECT TRUST

Hebridean Centre, Ballyhough, Isle of Coll, Argyll PA78 6TE. ☎01879 230444. Fax: 01879 230357. London office: 12 East Passage, London EC1A 7LP. ☎020-7796 1170. Fax: 020-7796 1172. E-mail: info@projecttrust.org.uk. Website: www.projecttrust.org.uk.
Established in 1967. Founding member of the Year Out Group.

Programme description: Voluntary placements specifically for gap year students throughout the developing world. Volunteers can choose to take part in care work, community development and wildlife projects, educational projects or outdoor activity projects, or they can act as English language assistants at schools.

Destinations: Africa (Uganda, Lesotho, Botswana, South Africa, Malawi, Namibia, Mozambique, Mauritania and Morocco), South and Central America (Honduras, Chile, Bolivia, Brazil, Peru, Guyana and the Dominican Republic), Asia and the Middle East (Thailand, China, India, Sri Lanka, Japan, Malaysia, Vietnam and South Korea).

Number of placements per year: Around 200 (80% from state schools).

Prerequisites: Applicants should be between 17 and 19 and be aiming for university.

Duration and time of placements: 12 months from August. Limited number of 8-month placements departing in January, for those needing to attend a university interview in the autumn.

Selection procedures and orientation: In the period between August and March, candidates attend a 4-day course on the Hebridean Isle of Coll where their skills and interests are assessed. About 80% of those who take the selection course are offered a place within a week of leaving Coll. Training courses are held, also on the Isle of Coll, during July to teach skills relevant to the volunteers' work placements as well as country-specific briefings and how to live safely and healthily overseas. Once in the destination country there is always at least one local representative on hand to help volunteers settle in and a full-time Desk Officer for each country based on the Isle of Coll. Both offer support throughout the year including a visit to the volunteers.

Cost: Volunteers are required to raise £3950 for the 12-month programme which includes the costs of selection, training, supervision, debriefing, airfares, medical insurance, board and lodging and a living allowance.

QUEST OVERSEAS

The North West Stables, Borde Hill Estate, Balcombe Road, Haywards Heath, West Sussex RH16 1XP. ☎01444 474744. Fax: 020-8637 7623. E-mail: emailus@questoverseas.com. Website: www.questoverseas.com.
Founding member of the Year Out Group. Quest Overseas specialises in combining worthwhile voluntary work projects and challenging expeditions to Africa and South

America for volunteers of all ages. Since 1996 Quest Overseas participants have raised £750,000 for various charities and NGOs (see chapter on Latin America).

Programme description: The South America programme is split into 3 phases: Phase I – 3-week intensive Spanish or Portuguese language course in Ecuador, Bolivia or Brazil; Phase II – 4-week voluntary work projects, either conservation work in the rainforests of Ecuador or Chile; looking after children in shanty towns in Peru or Brazil; or working in Ambue Ari animal rehabilitation project in Bolivia. Phase III – 6-week expedition covering over 1000km of Peru, Chile and Bolivia including Amazon jungle and Machu Picchu, or throughout Brazil, including surfing, diving and hang gliding over Rio.

The Africa programme is split into 2 phases: Phase I – 6-week voluntary work project, either conservation work in Swaziland or a community development project in Tanzania. Phase II – 6-week expedition through Swaziland, Mozambique, South Africa, Botswana and Zambia.

Destinations: Ecuador, Peru, Chile, Bolivia and Brazil; or Swaziland, Tanzania, Mozambique, South Africa, Botswana and Zambia.

Number of placements per year: 16 students in each team and 12 expeditions per year.

Prerequisites: Volunteers are typically aged 18-30.

Duration and time of placements: 13-week programmes depart throughout January-April, with summer projects and expeditions departing June-August. Flights can be open returns so stays can be extended.

Selection procedures and orientation: Selection is by interview. Preparation and Expedition Skills weekends are organised 3-4 months prior to departure.

Cost: £1560-£4880 (South America) and £1690-£4130 (Africa), excluding return flights (approximately £600), individual insurance (about £150) and personal pocket money for souvenirs and luxuries.

RALEIGH INTERNATIONAL
Raleigh House, 27 Parsons Green Lane, London SW6 4HZ. ☎020-7371 8585. Fax: 020-7371 5852. E-mail: info@raleigh.org.uk. Website: www.raleighinternational.org.

Founding member of the Year Out Group and leading youth development charity which offers young people the chance to take part in challenging environmental, community and adventure projects as part of 4, 7 or 10-week programmes around the world.

Programme description: Choice of project type on 4 or 7-week Explorer programme (environmental, community, adventure) or combination of all three on 10-week Expedition programme. Sample activities include tracking endangered deer in Chile, building a primary school in Namibia or trekking through mountain ranges in Costa Rica. Projects are supported by host country governments and international or local development organisations such as the United Nations Development Programme, SightSavers and World

Vision. These partnerships ensure that the projects are relevant and sustainable.

Destinations: Costa Rica, Nicaragua, Chile, Namibia and Sabah-Borneo.

Prerequisites: Applicants must be aged between 17 and 25, able to understand English, be able to swim and to be enthusiastic, committed and motivated.

Duration and time of placements: 4 or 7 week Explorer programme or 10-week Expedition programme, with the opportunity to travel independently after the expedition. 2 or 3 week Adventures available for people over 21.

Selection procedures and orientation: Programmes are intended to be as widely accessible as possible, so selection is on a self-selection basis. The first step is to attend an Introduction Day, then a briefing day and a training weekend two months before departure. Once in the country, 5 days are spent as orientation.

Cost: 4-week Explorer £1500; 7-week Explorer £2350; 10-week Expedition £2995; prices include food, accommodation, medical insurance and training, but exclude flights (which can be arranged through partner agency Key Travel). Support is provided to achieve the fundraising targets. e.g. Raleigh organise 3 national fundraising events every year.

Contact: Carl Challenger, Venturer Recruitment & Support Team.

ROTARY INTERNATIONAL IN GREAT BRITAIN AND IRELAND (RIBI)
Kinwarton Road, Alcester, Warwickshire B49 6PB. ☎01789 765411. Fax: 01789 765570. E-mail: ye@cavideo.co.uk. Website: www.youthribi.org.

Programme description: One-year international exchanges to promote international understanding and peace through exposure to different cultures. Exchange students stay with families in host country and attend a place of academic or vocational learning.

Number of placements per year: Over 9,000 worldwide (see chapter *A Year Off for North Americans*) but around 20 on Gap Year from UK.

Destinations: Dozens of countries (see website).

Prerequisites: Ages 15-19; average age 18. All nationalities. Students are expected to get involved in the activities of their host Rotary Club.

Duration and time of placements: 10-12 months. Also short-term exchanges in summer of 3-4 weeks.

Costs: Students pay for costs of travel and insurance plus approximately £200 for orientation and sundries. They receive pocket money of £60 per month.

Selection procedures and orientation: Schools normally recommend candidates. Deadline for applications is the end of February. Interviews held in candidate's home with parents. Students should be from the top 10% of their school year in overall achievement. Weekend residential orientation in March and local orientation of half a day prior to leaving. Students receive orientation within one month of arriving in their host country.

SKI LE GAP
220 Wheeler St, Mont Tremblant, Quebec J8E 1V3, Canada. ☎ +001-819-429-6599. E-mail: info@skilegap.com. Website: www.skilegap.com.

Programme description: Ski and Snowboard instructor's programme in Quebec, Canada, designed for gap year students from Britain. See entry in 'Directory of Sports Courses' and further details in chapter on Canada.

SPORT LIVED LTD
The Innovation Centre, 103 Clarendon Road, Leeds LS2 9DF. ☎0870 9503837. E-mail: info@sportlived.co.uk. Website: www.sportlived.co.uk.

Programme description: Gap year company that arranges for young people to play sport in Australia and New Zealand. Matches young people of varying sports abilities with a suitable sports club (some very competitive) and arranges accommodation with like-minded young people. Sports involved are cricket, rugby union, hockey, netball, rugby league, and football in Australia and the first four only in New Zealand.

Destinations: Most of the major cities of Australia and New Zealand.

Prerequisites: Ages 18-27. Various abilities accepted. Suitable for people who want to play for pleasure. For more serious sports men and women Sport Lived can arrange for participants in most cities to become qualified coaches and help in finding coaching work.

Duration and time of placements: Mostly 7 months with varying start dates (which can be flexible).

Selection procedures & orientation: Applicants submit character and sporting references and meet the company for an interview.

Cost: Range of prices depend on level of service. For example basic fee of £500 covers attachment and subscription to suitable club abroad. Top level of service covers 7 months accommodation, an overseas mentor, assistance in finding work and handbook, up to £3695.

Accommodation: Shared houses.

Contact: Ian Dodd.

SPW – STUDENTS PARTNERSHIP WORLDWIDE

2nd Floor, Faith House, Tufton St, London SW1P 3QB. ☎020-7222 0138. Fax: 020-7233 0008. E-mail: spwuk@gn.apc.org. Website: www.spw.org.

Member of the Year Out Group. Young people aged 18-28 are recruited from the UK and Europe, USA and Australia to volunteer and work in partnership with counterparts from Africa and Asia. In pairs or groups they live and work in rural communities for 4-9 months. Their input builds knowledge, skills and self-confidence in young people and begins to change attitudes and behaviour to important health, social and environmental issues amongst young people and communities. All volunteers take part in 4 weeks intensive training which covers health, hygiene, sanitation, nutrition and the environment, with a particular emphasis on HIV transmission as well as cross-cultural awareness, basic development theory and local languages.

Programme description: SPW runs health education and community resource programmes. These programmes tackle youth problems from different perspectives. All placements are in rural villages.

Destinations: India, Nepal, South Africa, Tanzania, Uganda and Zambia.

Number of placements per year: 250 places for European volunteers.

Prerequisites: A-level or equivalent qualifications. Volunteers need to be physically and mentally healthy, hard working, open-minded, enthusiastic and have good communication skills.

Duration and time of placements: 4-9 months with starting dates throughout the year.

Selection procedures and orientation: Applicants should download an application form from the website. Every applicant is required to attend an Information and Selection day in London. This also gives them the opportunity to meet staff and ex-volunteers. Following selection, volunteers are accepted on a first come first served basis, so early application is recommended.

Cost: £3300-£3600 all-inclusive of open return flight, accommodation, basic living allowance, insurance, in-country visa, extensive overseas training and support, UK briefings and general administrative support. SPW is a non-profit making charity, so volunteer fees cover costs only.

SUDAN VOLUNTEER PROGRAMME (SVP)
34 Estelle Road, London NW3 2JY. ☎/fax: 020-7485 8619. E-mail: davidsvp@blueyonder.co.uk.
Programme description: Volunteer teaching programme in Sudan (mainly Khartoum and area). See entry in 'Directory of Volunteering Abroad'.

TEACHING & PROJECTS ABROAD
Aldsworth Parade, Goring, West Sussex BN12 4TX. ☎01903 708300. Fax: 01903 501026. E-mail: info@teaching-abroad.co.uk. Website: www.teaching-abroad.co.uk.
Founding member of the Year Out Group. Company arranges volunteering placements overseas in a range of countries. Also arranges work experience placements in medicine, media and other fields in selected destinations (see 'Directory of Work Experience').
Destinations: Bolivia, Cambodia, Chile, China, Ghana, India, Mexico, Mongolia, Nepal, Peru, Romania, Russia, Senegal, South Africa, Sri Lanka, Swaziland and Thailand. Destinations and programmes can be combined; their 'Grand Gap' combines three or four destinations.
Number of placements per year: 2500.
Prerequisites: Minimum age 17+. Optional UK briefing and TEFL weekend courses before departure.
Duration and time of placements: Very flexible, with departures year round. Placements last 1-12 months.
Selection procedures and orientation: Paid staff in all destinations arrange and vet placements, accommodation and work supervisors. They meet volunteers on arrival and provide a final briefing before the placements.
Cost: Placements are self-funded and the fee charged includes insurance, food, accommodation and overseas support. Three-month placements cost between £895 and £2345, depending on placement, excluding travel costs.

TEMA THEATRE COMPANY LTD
A1 Value Office, 225-229 Church Street, Blackpool, Lancashire, FY1 3PB. ☎01253 299988 or in Ghana +233 24 310 6066. Fax in Ghana: +233 22 413 822. E-mail: Clare@tematema.com. Website: www.tematema.com.
Programme description: Volunteers spend 4 weeks in Ghana teaching drama to children. A production is staged at the end of the placement when the children and volunteers

perform to the local school and community.

Number of placements per year: 36.

Destinations: Ghana (Sakumono or Tema).

Prerequisites: Minimum age 16, average age 19. No formal requirements necessary, other than a passion for the performing arts, especially theatre, plus a strong interest in cultural exchange.

Duration and time of placements: 4 weeks.

Selection procedures & orientation: Application forms can be requested via the website. Deadline is 4 weeks prior to start date.

Cost: £695 excluding flights, visa, insurance, inoculations and food. Price covers the placement itself at the local school, accommodation in an executive home in a gated community, a donation to the school, a donation to the community, pick up and drop off at the airport and 24 hour support in the UK and Ghana.

Contact: Clare Allen, Facilitator.

TRAVELLERS WORLDWIDE

7 Mulberry Close, Ferring, West Sussex BN12 5HY. ☎01903 502595. Fax: 01903 500364. E-mail: info@travellersworldwide.com. Website: www. travellersworldwide.com.

Founder member of the Year Out Group.

Programme description: Teaching conversational English (and other subjects), conservation, language courses, structured work experience and cultural courses (photography, tango, etc.).

Destinations: Argentina, Brazil, Brunei, China, Cuba, Ghana, Guatemala, India, Kenya, Malaysia, Russia, South Africa, Sri Lanka, Ukraine and Zimbabwe.

Number of placements per year: 1000+.

Prerequisites: No formal qualifications required.

Duration and time of placements: From 2 weeks to a year with flexible start dates all year round to suit the volunteer.

Cost: Sample charges for 3 months in Sri Lanka are £1345 and Ukraine £925. Prices include food and accommodation, staff support within the country and transport from airport to school but do not include international travel, visas or insurance. (Travellers can arrange the latter but many volunteers prefer the flexibility of organising their own.)

Contact: Jennifer Muller, Director.

TREKFORCE EXPEDITIONS

Naldred Farm Offices, Borde Hill Lane, Haywards Heath, West Sussex RH16 1XR. ☎01444 474123. E-mail: info@trekforce.org.uk. Website: www.trekforce.org. uk.

Registered charity and founding member of the Year Out Group. Established 1990.

Programme description: Expedition programmes ideal for gap year students focusing on vital conservation, community and scientific projects. Programmes can incorporate a combination of expedition project work, a Spanish language course, teaching in rural communities, trekking, adventure and dive phases.

Destinations: Central America, South America and Southeast Asia. Expeditions last from one month up to five months for those who opt for expedition work, language learning (Spanish) and teaching in rural communities such as the Maya and the Kelabit, or Amerindian villages.

Prerequisites: Minimum age 18. Must be generally fit and healthy.

Duration and time of placements: Programmes last 1, 2, 3, 4 or 5 months, all year round.

Selection procedures & orientation: Interested participants attend an informal introductory session. Briefing day in the UK and in-country training is provided for expedition members.

Cost: Fundraising targets start at £1600 for 4-week project (trekking, adventure and

dive phases also available); £2590 for 2 months, £3275 for 3 months, £3450 for 4-month extended programme in South East Asia; £3900 for 5-month combination programme in Central or South America. Trekforce is a registered charity and fundraising advice is given to all volunteers.
Contact: Trekforce team (info@trekforce.org.uk).

TUTORS WORLDWIDE
38 Dornden Drive, Langton Green, Tunbridge Wells, Kent TN3 0AF. ☎/fax 01892 862943. E-mail: rfinney_tww@compuserve.com. Website: www.tutorsworldwide.org. Also office in New Zealand: Tutors Worldwide, 2/9 Majesty Plc, Half Moon Bay, Auckland 1706 (tel/fax +64 9-534 9999; Mobile +64 21-995 553.
Programme description: School leavers are given the opportunity to work in an overseas school environment as a tutor at either a prep or secondary (high) school in the UK, Australia, New Zealand and South Africa
Destinations: UK, Australia, New Zealand and South Africa.
Prerequisites: Must be students from the list in the line above. Initiative, enthusiasm, adaptability, flexibility, communication, commitment, motivation, reliability and responsibility needed. Many posts involve a lot of sporting activities with children, including coaching and supervision.
Duration and time of placements: One full academic year.
Selection procedures & orientation: Application and referee support forms need to be completed and forwarded. Extensive interview with each applicant to try to get the best match between school overseas and student assistant.
Cost: £40 registration fee. Placement fee of £375 is charged only to candidates who are offered and accept a place overseas. All posts are residential and board and lodging are provided.
Contact: Mr. R. Finney.

UK SAILING ACADEMY
West Cowes, Isle of Wight PO31 7PQ. ☎01983 294941. Fax: 01983 295938. E-mail: info@uksa.org. Website: www.uksa.org.
Programme description: Gap Year Programme up to one year covering range of watersports and work experience in UK and overseas. Approximate cost is £8000. (See entry in 'Directory of Sports & Activity Courses'.

VAE TEACHERS KENYA
Bell Lane Cottage, Pudleston, Nr. Leominster, Herefordshire HR6 0RE. ☎01568 750329. Fax: 01568 750636. E-mail: vaekenya@hotmail.com. Website: www. vaekenya.co.uk. Kenya address: PO Box 246, Gilgil, Kenya.
VAE runs two associated charities: Harambee Schools Kenya providing educational

infrastructure and materials (www.hsk.org.uk) and Langalanga Scholarship Fund providing secondary education to bright children who would not otherwise be able to afford it (www. llsf.org.uk).

Programme description: School leavers or graduates teach in extremely poor rural schools based around the town of Gilgil in Kenya. Volunteers are placed only in schools with a shortage of teachers and resources, and must assume major responsibility as they become integrated and live as part of an African community. VAE is also involved with the local town street children.

Duration and time of placements: Preferred departure time January for 6 months.

Cost: About £3400 including flight, insurance, salary, accommodation, etc.

Contact: Simon C. D. Harris, VAE Director.

VENTURE CO WORLDWIDE
The Ironyard, 64-66 The Market Place, Warwick CV34 4SD. ☎01926 411122. Fax: 01926 411133. E-mail: mail@ventureco-worldwide.com. Website: www. ventureco-worldwide.com.

Hold an ATOL licence. Member of the Year Out Group.

Programme description: Gap Year and Career Gap specialist with programmes that combine language schools, local aid projects and expeditions.

Destinations: *Inca Venture:* Ecuador, Peru, Chile and Bolivia. *Patagonia Venture:* Peru, Bolivia, Chile, Argentina and Tierra del Fuego. *Maya Venture:* Mexico, Guatemala, Belize, Honduras, Nicaragua, Costa Rica and Cuba. *Himalaya Venture:* India and Nepal. *Rift Valley Venture:* Uganda, Kenya and Tanzania. *Indochina Venture* (career gap only): Cambodia, Vietnam, Laos and China. Live Venture reports and dossiers available from website.

Number of placements per year: 275.

Prerequisites: Gap Year 17½-19; Career Gap minimum age 20. Must have motivation, enthusiasm and desire to be part of a Venture team.

Duration and time of placements: Programmes are 4 months long with departures year round. Also shorter VentureGo programmes (1-3 months) in Peru, the Galapagos or East Africa departing July; these trips can be fitted into the long summer vacation.

Selection procedures & orientation: Applicants are invited to attend a 'Workshop' as part of the selection process. Preparation weekends held in UK, and expedition skills training in-country.

Cost: Approximately £4500 including flights and insurance. 4-week VentureGo trips from £2826.

Contacts: Vicky Meikle, Venture Co-ordinator.

See also chapters on Africa, Asia and Latin America.

VOLUNTEER ADVENTURES
915 S. Colorado Blvd, Denver, CO 80246, USA. ☎Toll-free in the US and Canada: 1-888-825-3454. Toll-free in the UK: 0800-028-8051. Tel: 303-785-8889. Fax: 303-777-7246. E-mail: volunteer@volunteeradventures.com. Website: www.volunteeradventures.com.

Programmes offered: Volunteers can choose to work in the areas of Community Development, Conservation or English Teaching in many countries in Africa, Asia and Latin America. Teacher training, language courses, and host families are also available on many projects.

Destinations: Africa (Botswana, Namibia, Zimbabwe), Asia (India), Central America (Costa Rica, Guatemala), and South America (Argentina, Brazil, Chile, Ecuador).

Duration of programmes: Variable. From 1 week to 1 year. Average project length is 3 weeks.

Accommodation: Local host families or volunteer housing.

Other services: TEFL Online training for volunteer teaching projects, language immersion courses, activities and excursions to get to know the local culture.

WORK & TRAVEL COMPANY
45 High St, Tunbridge Wells, Kent TN1 1XL. ☎01892 516164. Fax: 01892 523172. E-mail: info@worktravelcompany.co.uk. Websites: www.worktravelcompany.co.uk.
Specialists in gap years, career breaks (see www.gapyearforgrownups.co.uk) and volunteering abroad. ATOL-bonded with full financial backing.
Programme description: Wide range of volunteer and travel options in 30 countries, including volunteering with wildlife or care projects in Africa, India, Thailand, Australia and Latin America, teaching in Mongolia, China and Latin America, paid work in Australia and New Zealand
Destionations: Australia, New Zealand, South Africa, Namibia, Botswana, Tanzania, Zambia, Kenya, Ghana, Egypt, Israel, India, Nepal, Thailand, Malaysia, Vietnam, Japan, China, Russia, Argentina, Peru, Ecuador, Mexico, Brazil, Costa Rica, Guatemala, Bolivia, USA, Canada, Cuba, Round the World.
Pre-requisites: None, except as limited by visas.
Duration and time of placements: 4 weeks to 12 months. Flexible gap year itineraries can be arranged.
Cost: Varies with programme, from £99 for the cheapest Australia programme to £6000+ for the most expensive round the world Complete Gap Year.

WORLD CHALLENGE EXPEDITIONS
Black Arrow House, 2 Chandos Road, London NW10 6NF. Tel: 020-8728 7200. E-mail: welcome@world-challenge.co.uk. Website: www.world-challenge.co.uk.
Founding member of the Year Out Group.
Programme description: World Challenge Expeditions run four flexible skills development programmes for schools and individuals: TravelSafe (see 'Directory of Gap Year Safety & Preparation Courses'), Team Challenge and First Challenge (see 'Directory of Expeditions') and Leadership Challenge (for groups only). Note that the Gap Challenge programme specifically for gap year students will not run after January 2006.

WORLDWIDE VOLUNTEERING FOR YOUNG PEOPLE
7 North Street Workshops, Stoke sub Hamdon, Somerset TA14 6QR. ☎01935 825588. Fax: 01935 825775. E-mail: worldvol@worldvol.co.uk. Website: www.wwv.org.uk.
Worldwide Volunteering aims to make information about worldwide volunteering programmes in the UK and worldwide more accessible to young people.
Programme description: Maintains a search-and-match database of volunteer opportunities around the world geared particularly to 16-35 year olds. The software matches volunteers' requirements with those of 1200 organisations offering a potential total of 350,000 placements.
Destinations: All over the world.
Prerequisites: These vary from organisation to organisation and will be specified in the database. Anyone can use the database.
Selection procedures and orientation: Once volunteers have found information on the database, they can contact the organisations that interest them using the interactive email and weblinks provided. The database provides a wealth of information about organisations.
Cost: The *Worldwide Volunteering Database* is available for individuals online at www.wwv.org.uk and for subscribers online or by CD-ROM at an annual subscription fee which includes free data update after six months. A one-off payment of £10 entitles you to three searches from your home computer within a 4-week period. Some subscribing schools and careers centres, libraries and volunteer bureaux will allow enquirers to access the information free of charge. A list of these subscribers is found on the WWV website. Note that the print version *Worldwide Volunteering for Young People* (2004 edition) is distributed by How To Books (01476 541080; www.howtobooks.co.uk) for £17.99; a new edition is

due in 2006.
Contact: Jacqueline Dingle.

YEAR IN INDUSTRY
The University of Southampton, Southampton SO17 1BJ. ☎023 8059 7061. E-mail: enquiries@yini.org.uk. Website: www.yini.org.uk.
Founding member of the Year Out Group. Major provider of gap year industrial placements throughout the UK. See entry in 'Directory of Work Experience'.

YEAR OUT DRAMA COMPANY
Stratford-upon-Avon College, Alcester Road, Stratford-upon-Avon, Warks. CV37 9QR. ☎01789 266245. Fax: 01789 267524. E-mail: yearoutdrama@stratford. ac.uk.
Founding member of the Year Out Group. One-year course covers acting, directing, performance, voice work, movement and design. See entry in 'Directory of Courses'.

YOUTH FOR UNDERSTANDING UK
15 Hawthorn Road, Erskine, Renfrewshire PA8 7BT. ☎/fax: 0141-812 5561. E-mail: yfu@holliday123.freeserve.co.uk. Website: www.yfu.org.
Programme description: Scholarship exchange programme funded by government of Japan which grew out of international educational exchanges set up in the US in the 1950s.
Destinations: Japan.
Number of placements per year: 10 for a semester programme.
Prerequisites: 16-18 year olds placed in secondary schools abroad. Must have interest in Japan and be prepared to learn more than just the basics of the language.
Duration and time of placements: 5 months departing in August and returning in January.
Selection procedures and orientation: Applications accepted from October of the year previous up until the deadline at the beginning of June. Two interviews are held in Glasgow or London, one with Programme Co-ordinator, the other in front of a panel including representatives from the Japanese Embassy. Pre-departure preparation orientation and 2 further support orientations whilst in Japan in addition to monthly review calls/meetings with area representative in Japan are included in cost of programme.
Cost: Included in the scholarship is the student's return flight from Heathrow to Japan, board and lodgings whilst in Japan, support before and during stay in Japan. Spending money and insurance not included.
Contact: Lorraine Holliday, National Director.

Also see directories at the end of the chapters on Volunteering, Work Experience, Au Pairing and Courses for other organisations that welcome gap year students (among others).

Expeditions

Adolescence is a good time to discover tales of adventure from the literature of exploration whether it is the casual descriptions of suffering by mountaineers or sailors, classics by Robert Byron or Freya Stark, or more recent classics by Bruce Chatwin, Redmond O'Hanlon or Dervla Murphy. Books can be very influential at a time when life is circumscribed by family and school. Reading a book like the explorer Robin Hanbury-Tenison's *Worlds Apart* can easily inspire a longing to visit the wild and woolly corners of the world instead of joining the annual family holiday to a self-catering cottage in Yorkshire or Tuscany.

It might seem an impossible dream for a 16 or 17 year old with no money and no travel experience beyond a youth hostelling weekend in the Peak District. But a number of organisations cater specifically for gap year students looking for challenging adventures in remote places. These are open to anyone who is mentally and physically fit and who is prepared to raise the fees (typically £2500-£3500). Although the fund-raising target is fairly high, so are the rewards, according to **Hannah Peck** who joined a *BSES* expedition to arctic Svalbard:

> *My reasons for taking a gap year were to travel to a remote environment away from city life to try to regain some direction and inspiration. Now near the end, I feel that my confidence has grown incredibly while I've been here, both socially and physically. In particular I can mix more easily with 'blokes' as having been at an all-girls school I have not had much chance to live and work with them. This should*

make moving on to university a much smoother and more enjoyable experience. I have gained more understanding of my physical strengths and limits and have been pleasantly surprised to see how well I cope under harsh conditions and pleased to see that I can easily keep up with boys. So now I know that being a girl should be of no real consequence for future expeditions. Living here on Svalbard has allowed me to experience the importance of preservation of the wilderness through everyday watching the natural goings on, the weather, wildlife and sea ice, as well as experiencing the silence. I have learnt to be entertained easily and now know the things I rely so much on at home to entertain me are really not that great.

Many bemoan a decline in youth culture, arguing that life at the beginning of the 21st century is too materialistic, too soft and that young people are emerging into adulthood afraid to take risks, not to mention unfit and overweight from years of computer games. There is no equivalent in our culture of the coming-of-age tests and initiation rites to which so many other cultures expose their young people, whether giving them a painful tattoo or sending them into the wilderness to fend alone for a given period. In fact this was going on in Britain as recently as 1933, if Roald Dahl's autobiography *Boy* is to be believed, where he describes the summer after finishing school:

That summer, for the first time in my life, I did not accompany the family to Norway. I somehow felt the need for a special kind of last fling before I became a businessman. So while still at school during my last term, I signed up to spend August with something called the Public Schools' Exploring Society. The leader of this outfit was a man who had gone with Captain Scott on his last expedition to the South Pole, and he was taking a party of senior schoolboys to explore the interior of Newfoundland during the summer holidays. It sounded like fun.

Our ship sailed from Liverpool at the beginning of August and took six days to reach St. John's. There were about 30 boys of my own age on the expedition as well as four experienced adult leaders. But Newfoundland, as I soon found out, was not much of a country. For three weeks we trudged all over that desolate land with enormous loads on our backs. We carried tents and groundsheets and sleeping bags and saucepans and food and axes and everything else one needs in the interior of an unmapped, uninhabitable and inhospitable country. My own load, I know, weighed exactly 114 pounds, and someone else always had to help me hoist the rucksack on to my back. We lived on pemmican and lentils and the 12 of us who went separately on what was called the Long March from the north to the south of the island and back again suffered a good deal from lack of food. I can remember very clearly how we experimented with eating boiled lichen and reindeer moss to supplement our diet. But it was a genuine adventure and I returned home hard and fit and ready for anything.

Significantly this anecdote comes right at the end of *Boy* before he proceeds to the second part of his autobiography called *Going Solo*.

If you feel the need for a similar last fling or would like to show your friends and family what stern stuff you are made of, then a gap year is the perfect time to think about going on an expedition.

After participating on one of the trails through unspoiled places organised by the Wilderness Trust, 18 year old Willem Boshoff reflected:
For me personally, the one single thing which held the most meaning for me, was certainly the fact that my own existence was once more placed in perspective. The wilderness simply indicated once again just how relative and insignificant academic and other values which we consider so important really are. For a change, one is forced to consider again one's place in the whole creation - and that place is surprisingly small!

Helpful Organisations

The *Royal Geographical Society* (1 Kensington Gore, London SW7 2AR) encourages and assists many British expeditions. The Expedition Advisory Centre at the RGS distributes a booklet *Joining an Expedition* (2001, £7.50) which includes about 60 organisations that regularly arrange expeditions. A new edition of *The Expedition Handbook* can be ordered for £16.99. The EAC also hosts a weekend 'Explore' seminar every November on 'Planning a Small Expedition', which covers fundraising and budgeting for expeditions as well as issues of safety and logistics. If you want personal advice on mounting an expedition, you can make an appointment to visit the EAC (020-7591 3030; eac@rgs.org). The Society's historic map room is open to the public daily from 11am to 5pm. The Expedition Advisory Centre has generously put online most of the grant-giving organisations and trusts listed in its publication *Fund-raising and Budgeting for Expeditions.* Although many grants are ring-fenced (e.g. must live within eight miles of Exmouth Town Hall) it is certainly worth checking and applying as widely as possible.

The *Young Explorers' Trust* offers to help groups of students organise their own expedition during their gap year. The organisation was established as a charity nearly 30 years ago to provide for young people participating in exploration, discovery and outdoor activities. YET does not offer pre-arranged expeditions but offers an expert panel of advisors and assessors for expedition plans. It also organises occasional weekend Expedition Leaders' Planning Courses open to everyone for a residential fee of £80 (in Sheffield in 2005). YET also publishes two Codes of Practice for youth expeditions: 'Safe and Responsible Expeditions' and 'Environmental Responsibility for Expeditions'. Some grant aid may be made available to YET-approved expeditions.

Raleigh International (www.raleighinternational.org) is the longest established and most experienced expedition organisation, having run more than 200 three-month expeditions overseas and sent 30,000 volunteers from around the world overseas during its 21 year history. Now offering greater flexibility in their programmes (i.e. a choice of shorter expeditions), they aim to inspire people to reach their full potential through challenging community, environmental and adventure projects as part of an overseas expedition. Trekking through the Andes Mountains in Chile, building schools/clinics in Namibia or collecting scientific data in Costa Rica are examples of projects undertaken in Raleigh International's expedition countries. Applicants attend an introduction day and are asked to fundraise a maximum of £2995 excluding airfares (see entry in 'Directory of Specialist Gap Year Programmes' and mentions in the chapters on Africa, Asia and Latin America).

Tom Saunders wanted a well-organised expedition for his gap year and, after picking up a leaflet, he learned that someone from his school had gone with Raleigh to Costa Rica. He signed up for the same destination and set about fund-raising by being sponsored to walk up the school steps 255 times, equal to the height of Everest, and by writing to local companies and organisations such as the Women's Institute and Round Table. His enthusiasm for the experience is boundless:

> *I chose Raleigh for my gap year because it is a more rounded expedition with different types of projects. With the environmental project you are in a place that you know you are never likely to be again. With the community project you can do something unbelievable and really help people. You think of the smiles from the little kids you have helped and people crying when you leave. The environmental project gives you a totally new experience and I could also do something I loved, which was trekking.*
>
> *One of the things that amazes me is how much people change on expedition, how shy people come out of themselves when they're around lively people. Another thing that surprises me is being able to make such good friends in such a short time. Joining a Raleigh expedition is the most un-monotonous thing you can ever do. Things come and things go. Every moment something new happens. The worst thing about Raleigh is that you have to go to sleep, I wanted to be awake 24 hours a day.*

The British Schools Exploring Society (see entry for *BSES Expeditions* below) organises an impressive range of expeditions which combine exciting research projects and adventurous activities. Expedition members undergo a training weekend outside Sheffield in April so that they can meet the others going on the expedition and can be assessed for fitness. At the weekend there are presentations by the expedition leaders about the various research projects on the expedition and a chance to learn how to use all the new equipment and gain the essential skills required for living in an extreme environment.

School-leavers who have attended schools with a tradition of sending students on expeditions will be at an advantage in tracking down suitable opportunities in their gap year. An expedition forms part of the requirements to gain a Duke of Edinburgh Award. Most people become involved through their local school or youth club though it is possible to enlist through an Open Award Centre. Most take place in the UK (usually the Lake District or Wales) but some go abroad e.g. on canoeing expeditions to Canada. The Duke of Edinburgh's Award Scheme supports personal and social development of young people aged 14-17 and beyond and has links with the main youth expedition organisers. They now cooperate with *Global Adventures* to offer the Award Year Out which involves extensive travels and a choice of wilderness trek e.g. Borneo, Himalayas, Namibia; see www.awardyearout.co.uk or the DofE website www.theaward.org.

Sailing Adventures

Several youth-oriented organisations and charities take young people on character-building sailing expeditions, some on traditional tall ships. Fees vary enormously. The Association of Sea Training Organisations (ASTO) is the umbrella group for sail training organisations in the UK and their website is a useful link to about 30 sail training organisations (www.asto.org.uk). ASTO is based at Unit 10, North Meadow, Royal Clarence Yard, Gosport, Hampshire PO12 1BP, and can grant bursary funding towards the cost of a berth on a tall ship for young people, including disabled trainees. ASTO is affiliated to the international non-profit Sail Training International (5 Mumby Road, Gosport, Hants. PO12 1AA; 023-9258 6367; office@sailtraininginternational.org). See entries below for the *Tall Ships Youth Trust*, *Ocean Youth Trust South* and *Jubilee Sailing Trust*.

Commercial crew agencies match willing sailors with sailing expeditions looking for crew. For example Global Crew Network (23 Old Mill Gardens, Berkhamsted, Herts. HP4 2NZ; 07773 361959 or 01442 389153; info@globalcrewnetwork.com/ www.globalcrewnetwork.com) specialises in crew recruitment for Tall Ships, traditional boats, luxury motor and sailing yachts worldwide. Working holidays and working passages available for beginners and students seeking to gain some sailing experience. Membership costs £35 for 6 months, £45 for 12.

The Tall Ships People (Moorside, South Zeal Village, Okehampton, Devon EX20 2JX; tel/fax 01837 840919; jacci@thetallshipspeople.freeserve.co.uk; www.tallshipspeople.com) co-ordinate crew placement for vessels taking part in the Tall Ships Race (formerly known as the Cutty Sark race). The 2005 race set off from Waterford Ireland bound for Cherbourg, Newcastle and Fredrikstad (Norway) between July 6th and August 9th. More than half the trainees were aged 15-25 and of mixed nationalities; some were using the trip as the residential element of the Duke of Edinburgh Gold Award. The price began at around £700 for one leg. General sailing adventures are also available for those who do not wish to race but to learn to sail, including navigation and standing watch.

Those who want to do some sail training during their gap year but who are short of funds should ask the training organisation whether any financial assistance is available. The Norfolk Boat (Harrisons Farmhouse, East Tuddenham, Dereham, Norfolk NR20 3NF; tel/fax 01603 881121; info@norfolkboat.org.uk) offers financial assistance to East Anglian residents aged 12-24 or disabled people of any age who can't afford but would like to experience the challenge and fun of deep sea sailing with various accredited sailing organisations.

Fundraising

Expeditions tend to be among the most expensive among gap year placements, and some of the targets fixed by the major organisations are truly daunting. See the section on Fundraising in the chapter 'Planning and Preparation' for ideas on how to earn, save and persuade others to give you the necessary funds.

Those with a specialised project might discover that targeted funds are available from trusts and charities. However many, like the Mount Everest Foundation (www.mef.org. uk/mefguide.htm), are earmarked for high level expeditions undertaking first ascents, new routes and scientific research on mountains, which are beyond the capabilities of someone in a gap year.

Relevant companies are sometimes willing to give equipment in lieu of a cheque, though most manufacturers of hiking and camping equipment are inundated with requests. Successful supplicants often present imaginative ways in which they plan to publicise their benefactors' products.

Sponsored Expeditions for Charity

A large and growing number of charities in the UK now offer adventurous group travel to individuals who are prepared to undertake some serious fundraising on their behalf. Household names like Oxfam, the Youth Hostels Association and the Children's Society organise sponsored trips, as do many more obscure good causes. Specialist agent Charity Challenge allows you to select your trip (most of which last no more than a fortnight) and which charity you would like to support. They have an extensive brochure available (7th Floor, Northway House, 1379 High Road, London N20 9LP; 020-8557 0000; www.charitychallenge. com). Participants are asked to raise £2300 (say) for the charity and in return receive a 'free' trip. You are in a far stronger position to ask people for donations if you can say you are supporting the Children's Society/British Heart Fund/Whale Conservation Society or whatever, than if you say you are trying to raise money for a holiday to Morocco/Patagonia/ Borneo. These trips are usually more attractive to older people looking for an interesting way to take a gap than to school-leavers.

DIRECTORY OF EXPEDITIONS

BORDERS EXPLORATION GROUP

c/o Allan S. R. McGee, 3 Burnfoot, Hawick TD9 8ED. ☎01450 376996. E-mail: Bordexpgp@beeb.net. Website: www.borders-exploration-group.org.uk.

Borders Exploration Group is a non-profit making voluntary organisation which organises international and European expeditions for young people living in the Scottish border area.

Programme description: Expeditions are organised every other year and led by teams of volunteer leaders. Most expeditions consist of 4 phases: Community, Adventure, Environmental and Social.

Destinations: Previous expeditions have been to Lesotho, Ecuador, Kenya, Mongolia, India, Peru and (in 2005) Vietnam. These expeditions take place every two years and in between, smaller European expeditions take place, most recently to Romania and the Pyrenees.

Number of placements per expedition: About 35 on a major expedition, 15 on a European trip.

Prerequisites: Must live in Scottish Border catchment area. Minimum age 16. Good humour, stamina and commitment are required as well as the ability to raise the necessary funds through fundraising initiatives.

Duration and time of placements: Major expeditions 5 weeks, European expeditions 3 weeks.

Selection procedures and orientation: Participants are selected during an outdoor adventure day held more than a year before the expedition departure date. Training starts almost immediately and is held over 6 training weekends throughout the year. Basic campcraft, survival, first aid, navigation and team building skills are included in the training.

Cost: International expeditions cost in the region of £1600 and a European expedition around £600. Funds must be secured through fundraising activities.

Contact: Allan S. R. McGee.

BRATHAY EXPLORATION GROUP TRUST LTD
Brathay Hall, Ambleside, Cumbria LA22 0HP. ☎/fax: 01539 433942. E-mail: admin@brathayexploration.org.uk. Website: www.brathayexploration.org.uk. Established 1947.

Programme description: Mounts expeditions and expeditionary courses for young adults. Wide-ranging activities including adventure and environmental awareness.

Destinations: Worldwide, varying from year to year. 2006 expeditions to Tanzania, Malta, Guatemala, India, Norway, the European Alps and a number within the UK.

Number of placements per year: 200.

Prerequisites: Ages 15-24. No qualifications needed. People with disabilities welcome to apply.

Duration and time of placements: 1-5 weeks summer holiday period.

Selection procedures & orientation: Briefing and pre-departure training sessions on outdoor skills and first aid.

Cost: Up to £2000 for a month-long overseas expedition (excluding airfares); less for trips in UK.

Contact: Ron Barrow.

BSES EXPEDITIONS
Royal Geographical Society, 1 Kensington Gore, London SW7 2AR. ☎020-7591 3141. Fax: 020-7591 3140. E-mail: info@bses.org.uk. Website: www.bses.org. uk.
The British Schools Exploring Society is a UK charity which was founded by a member of Scott's Antarctic Expedition. It has provided the opportunity for young people to take part in exploratory expeditions in remote regions since 1932.

Programme description: The expeditions aim to combine living in gruelling and testing conditions with valuable scientific and environmental research. Past expeditions have included climbing a 22,000ft peak in India, investigating the rare spiral aloe plant in Lesotho, scientific field-work through the arctic winter in Eastern Greenland, sea kayaking in Alaska and a year-long expedition in the Arctic. In 2006 there will be a 3-month Gap Year expedition to Svalbard and 4/5-week summer expeditions to Greenland, Peru and the Amazon Rainforest.

Destinations: Worldwide, for example Tanzania, Iceland, Yukon, Alaska, Antarctica, Kenya, Morocco, Sinai, Namibia, Lesotho, Nepal and India. Destinations change from year to year.

Number of placements per year: 180-220.

Prerequisites: Must be aged between 16 and 20 and in a good state of fitness both mental and physical. Candidates are chosen according to their suitability to a particular expedition.

Duration and time of placement: Expedition lengths vary from 4 weeks to 4 months and take place during the summer holidays and throughout the Gap Year.

Selection procedures and orientation: Places are allocated on a first come first served basis on completion of a successful interview. Short-listed applicants will be called for interview in London or a regional office. On accepting the offer of a place, Young Explorers take part in a briefing weekend held prior to their expedition, either in the North of England or at the RGS. Following the expedition an annual gathering is held for a presentation about the experience.

Cost: £2500-£3500. BSES Expeditions offer lots of help and guidance on fundraising. No one showing appropriate commitment and effort in raising the contribution will be denied a place.

CORAL CAY CONSERVATION
The Tower, 13th Floor, 125 High Street, Colliers Wood, London SW19 2JG. ☎0870 750 0668. Fax: 0870 750 0667. E-mail: info@coralcay.org. Website: www.coralcay.org

CCC runs tropical forest and coral reef expeditions in Fiji, Honduras, Malaysia and the Philippines. Volunteers are trained to survey scientifically some of the world's most beautiful yet endangered tropical environments. Details in 'Directory of Specialist Gap Year Programmes'.

DORSET EXPEDITIONARY SOCIETY
Lupins Business Centre, 1-3 Greenhill, Weymouth, Dorset DT4 7SP. ☎/fax: 01305 775599. E-mail: dorsetexp@wdi.co.uk. Website: www.dorsetexp.co.uk.

The Dorset Expeditionary Society promotes adventurous opportunities for young people from throughout the UK. All expedition leaders are volunteers. Expeditions can qualify for two elements of the Duke of Edinburgh Gold Award.

Programme description: Expeditions include trekking, mountain climbing, kayaking, white water rafting, mountain biking and safaris, and experience of other world cultures.

Destinations: Europe, North and South America, Africa, India and Asia, always to wilderness areas off the tourist track.

Prerequisites: Participants must be fit and healthy. Minimum age 15 for some expeditions, 16/18 for others.

Duration and time of placements: 3-5 weeks, usually in the summer holidays.

Selection procedures and orientation: Selection weekend to choose suitable candidates. Training courses for aspiring leaders are organised to gain nationally-recognised qualifications such as Basic Expedition Leaders Award, Mountain First Aid Certificate, Cave Leadership and Mountain Leadership Award.

Cost: £50 for the selection weekend plus expedition costs (roughly £500-£2500). Guidance on fundraising is given.

Contact: Keith Eagleton, Secretary.

FRONTIER
50-52 Rivington St, London EC2A 3QP. ☎020-7613 2422. E-mail: info@frontier. ac.uk. Website: www.frontier.ac.uk.

See 'Directory of Specialist Gap Year Programmes' for details of Frontier's conservation projects in Tanzania, Madagascar, Cambodia, South Pacific and Nicaragua.

GLOBAL VISION INTERNATIONAL (GVI)
Amwell Farmhouse, Nomansland, Wheathampstead, St. Albans, Herts. AL4 8EJ. ☎0870 608 8898. Fax: 0870 609 2319. E-mail: info@gvi.co.uk. Website: www.gvi.co.uk.

Programme description: Since 1998, GVI has been running overseas expeditions and projects in Africa, Latin America and Asia. See relevant chapters for details.

Destinations: South Africa, Namibia, Madagascar, East Africa, Seychelles, Ecuador, Brazil, Mexico, Panama, Guatemala, Costa Rica, Belize, Patagonia, Nepal, Indonesia, Sri Lanka and Thailand.

Number of placements per year: 1000.

Prerequisites: None. Minimum age 18. All nationalities welcome.

Duration and time of placements: 2 weeks to one year.
Selection procedures and orientation: Some projects require a telephone interview; others require only a completed application form.
Cost: From £695 to £2995.
Contact: Chris Ash, Volunteer Co-ordinator.

JUBILEE SAILING TRUST YOUTH LEADERSHIP @ SEA SCHEME
JST, Hazel Road, Woolston, Southampton SO19 7GB. ☎023-8044 9108. Fax: 023-8044 9145. E-mail: info@jst.org.uk. Website: www.jst.org.uk.
Courses offered: Leadership course on a sea voyage to develop communication, leadership and team skills.
Prerequisites: Ages 16-25.
Selection procedures and orientation: By written application; mark form with 'Youth Leadership @ Sea' and enclose short personal statement.
Cost: The JST Youth Leadership @ Sea Scheme offers young people aged 16-25 up to £300 towards the cost of any voyage (prices start from £499).

OASIS OVERLAND
The Marsh, Henstridge, Somerset BA8 0TF. ☎01963 363400. Fax: 01963 363200. E-mail: info@oasisoverland.co.uk. Website: www.oasisoverland.co.uk.
Overland expedition company founded in 1997.
Destinations: South America, Africa, Middle East and Egypt.
Number of placements per expedition: Purpose-built trucks carry up to 24.
Duration: Large choice (see website) between 10 days and 29 weeks.
Cost: From £65 a week plus £30 kitty on longest trips, rising to £135 plus £60 kitty in South America. Sample expedition 105 days Quito to Rio costs £1890 plus US$1250 kitty paid locally.
Contact: Chris Wrede, Director.

OCEAN YOUTH TRUST SOUTH
Spur House, 1, The Spur, Alverstoke, Gosport, Hampshire PO12 2NA. ☎0870 241 2252. Fax: 0870 909 0230. E-mail: office@oytsouth.org. Website: www. oytsouth.org.
Adventure sail training organisation originally formed as Ocean Youth Club over 40 years ago, now operating as 6 separate regions altogether running more than 250 voyages from 40 UK ports every year and giving 3000 young people the chance to sail. Links from above website to OYT North-east, North-west, Scotland, Northern Ireland and East. Each regional group sails one vessel with berths for 12 crew.
Programme description: Short sailing voyages on ocean-going yachts from ports around the coast of the UK.

Destinations: Website posts crew vacancies on forthcoming voyages.
Prerequisites: Ages 12-25 years. Must be able to swim 50 metres. No sailing experience required.
Duration and time of placements: 2-10 days between March and November.
Selection procedures & orientation: By written application.
Cost: Varies according to duration and date, from £300 to £450 for a 6-day voyage. Mates' fees are less if sailing as sea staff. Grants are sometimes available to help with voyage fees.
Contact: David Salmon, General Manager.

OUTWARD BOUND GLOBAL
☎0870 513 4227. E-mail: globalexpeditions@outwardbound-uk.org. Website: www.outwardbound-uk.org/global.
Long-established organisation whose mission is to widen access for young people to experience adventure in the outdoors. Has centres in around 30 countries.
Programme description: International expeditions for individuals and groups.
Destinations: 2005: Sabah (Malaysia), Tatras Mountains (Slovakia), Outinenqua Mountains (South Africa) and Carpathian Mountains (Romania).
Prerequisites: 16-25, sometimes with variations (e.g. 16-20, 16-18 or 18-25).
Duration and time of placements: 2-4 weeks; mostly 3 weeks.
Cost: £2660 for 3 weeks in Sabah and South Africa, £1950 for 3 weeks in Slovakia and Romania.
Contact: Rachel Johnson.

RALEIGH INTERNATIONAL
Raleigh House, 27 Parsons Green Lane, London SW6 4HZ. ☎020-7371 8585. Fax: 020-7371 5852 E-mail: info@raleigh.org.uk. Website: www.raleighinternational.org.
Expeditions for young people aged 17-25 comprise a diverse mix of people including gap year students, graduates and people from the expedition country. The aim is to make a positive contribution to the host countries (Costa Rica, Nicaragua, Chile, Namibia and Sabah-Borneo in Malaysia). Participants take part in adventure, community and environmental projects. See further listings in the 'Directory of Specialist Gap Year Programmes', and in chapters on Africa, Asia and Latin America; the latter includes a first-hand account of a volunteer's experiences in Costa Rica.

SEA-MESTER PROGRAMS
P.O. Box 5477, Sarasota, FL 34277, USA. ☎941-924-6789. Fax: 941-924-6075. E-mail: info@seamester.com. Website: www.seamester.com.
Parent company (Action Quest) has been operating experiential education programmes for youth for over 30 years and Sea-mester programme since 1998.
Programme description: Educational adventure on an 88-ft schooner. Primary academic foci are oceanography, nautical science, communication and leadership skills development. Students undertake research and service projects with local government and private organisations while working toward certification in sailing and scuba diving.
Number of placements per year: About 100.
Destinations: Starts from the British Virgin Islands and travels throughout the Eastern Caribbean visiting up to 20 islands.
Prerequisites: No experience necessary. Minimum age 17 (many students are pre-matriculates). All nationalities.
Duration and time of placements: 80-day voyages during the autumn and spring. Also 40- and 20-day voyages during the summer.
Cost: $14,500 for 80 days, $6950 for 40 days, $4160 for 20 days.
Contact: Jo Meighan, PR and Marketing Manager, ActionQuest, Lifeworks and Sea-mester Programs (jo@actionquest.com).

TALL SHIPS YOUTH TRUST
2A The Hard, Portsmouth, Hants. PO1 3PT. ☎023-9283 2055. Fax: 023-9281 5769. E-mail: info@tallships.org. Website: www.tallships.org.
Youth charity dedicated to the personal development of young people through crewing on its two 60-metre square rigged ships *Prince William* and *Stavros S Niarchos*.
Programme description: Tall Ships adventures and adventure sail training voyages lasting from 1 day to 24 nights take place year round in the waters around the UK and Northern Europe in the summer and around the Canaries, Azores and Caribbean in the winter/spring.
Prerequisites: Minimum age 16 with an upper age limit of 25 on youth voyages, 18-75 for adult voyages.
Selection procedures & orientation: No previous sailing experience needed. Enthusiasm and an ability to work well with others is all that is required.
Cost: About £80 per day (plus flights for voyages abroad). Bursaries may be available.

TANGENT EXPEDITIONS
3 Millbeck, New Hutton, Kendal, Cumbria LA8 0BD. ☎01539 737757. Fax: 01539 737756. E-mail: paul@tangent-expeditions.co.uk. Website: www.tangent-expeditions.co.uk.
Programme description: Mountaineering, climbing and ski-touring expeditions organised mainly for groups. Chance to make first ascents of previously unclimbed but easy grade alpine peaks in the Arctic.
Destinations: Greenland, Spitsbergen and Iceland.
Prerequisites: Minimum age 18. Must have prior winter walking experience and attend a pre-expedition training weekend.
Duration and time of placements: Variable though most are 22 days.
Cost: £2750-£5000.
Contact: Paul Walker, Director.

TREKFORCE EXPEDITIONS
Naldred Farm Offices, Borde Hill Lane, Haywards Heath, West Sussex RH16 1XR. ☎01444 474 123. E-mail: info@trekforce.org.uk. Website: www.trekforce.org.uk.
Registered charity that runs Expedition Programmes that suit gap year students, graduates and career breakers in the rainforests of Central and South America and South East Asia, concentrating on conservation, scientific and community projects. Extended programmes of up to five months offer a combination of conservation project work, teaching in rural communities, trekking, diving and learning languages.

VENTURE CO WORLDWIDE
The Ironyard, 64-66 The Market Place, Warwick CV34 4SD. ☎01926 411122. Fax: 01926 411133. E-mail: mail@ventureco-worldwide.com. Website: www.ventureco-worldwide.com.
Programme description: Gap Year and Career Gap specialist whose 4-month programmes in Latin America, India/Nepal, East Africa and Indochina incorporate an 8 or 9 week expedition through the Andes, Himalayas, Rift Valley and China highlands including the Everest Base Camp Trek. Route planning and day-to-day organisation is done by team members, and leadership roles are shared out (see entry in 'Directory of Specialist Gap Year Programmes').

WILDERNESS FOUNDATION
47-49 Main Road, Broomfield, Chelmsford, Essex CM1 7BU. ☎01245 443073. E-mail: info@wildernessfoundation.org.uk. Website: www.wildernessfoundation.org.uk.

WF-UK is dedicated to preserving wilderness and wild areas worldwide. Its objects are to raise awareness about the value of wilderness, campaign for preservation of areas under threat, and to give direct experience of wild areas through sensitively guided trails and conservation volunteering opportunities (see 'Directory of Volunteering Abroad').

Programme description: Annual trails to remote areas of South Africa, Norway, Kenya and Scotland, using wilderness guides who emphasise the philosophical, spiritual and ecological elements of the wild. Trails have minimum impact on the environment, i.e. all equipment is carried in and out in backpacks and participants sleep under the stars (weather permitting).

Destinations: Norway (Arctic Circle), South Africa, Scotland, Kenya.

Number of placements per expedition: up to 8 per trail group, and up to two groups.

Prerequisites: Must be at least 15.

Duration and time of placements: 5-15 days.

Cost: Sample price £325-£500 depending on length (excluding travel to starting point).

Contact: Jo Roberts, Director.

WIND, SAND & STARS

6 Tyndale Terrace, London N1 2AT. ☎020-7359 7551. Fax: 020-7359 4936. E-mail: office@windsandstars.co.uk. Website: www.windsandstars.co.uk.

In operation for 15 years.

Programme description: Annual Summer Expedition is a 4-week challenge combining project work with the semi-nomadic Bedouin tribes. Opportunities to explore leadership development, remote survival skills and mountain and camel trekking. Projects include environmental work, irrigation schemes, medical work with Bedouin children, archaeological work and painting schools.

Prerequisites: Ages 16-23.

Duration and time of placements: 4 weeks (July-August).

Selection procedures & orientation: Pre-departure training day.

Cost: Approximately £1450 plus return flight.

Contact: Jay Rooney, Marketing Manager.

WORLD CHALLENGE EXPEDITIONS

Black Arrow House, 2 Chandos Road, London NW10 6NF. ☎020-8728 7222. E-mail: welcome@world-challenge.co.uk. Website: www.world-challenge.co.uk.

Parent company of TravelSafe (see 'Directory of Gap Year Safety & Preparation Courses').

Programme description: Two types of expedition: Team Challenge and First Challenge. In a Team Challenge expedition, students plan and lead their own 4 or 6-week expedition, e.g. trekking through the jungles of Borneo and hiking in the Andes. First Challenge offers an introduction to an expedition from 8-14 days attempting to climb North Africa's highest mountain in Morocco or getting involved in project work in Romania.

Destinations: Variety of countries worldwide.

Prerequisites: Team Challenge is the core programme of World Challenge Expeditions. Each expedition lasts one month but is preceded by 15-20 months of planning and preparation.

Duration: 4 weeks between June and September.

XCL LIMITED

Reaseheath, Nantwich, Cheshire CW5 6DF. ☎01270 625825. E-mail: enquiries@xcl.info. Website: www.xcl.info/expeditions.html.

Programme description: Bi-annual expedition to changing destination involves 2 weeks of working alongside indigenous people followed by a week-long adventurous phase.

Destinations: Ethiopia (2006). Past expeditions have been run to Guyana, Uganda, India and Borneo.

Number of placements per expedition: 50.

Prerequisites: 'Ordinary people doing extraordinary things'. Only enthusiasm needed.
Duration and time of placements: 3 weeks.
Selection procedures and orientation: Preparation in UK goes on over the preceding year including 2 residential training weekends which include country and culture orientation, team working, health and safety, project briefings and preparation.
Cost: £2150 in total.
Contact: Dig Woodvine, Director.

YORKSHIRE SCHOOLS EXPLORING SOCIETY
1A Garnett Street, Otley, West Yorkshire, LS21 1AL. ☎/fax: 01943 468049. E-mail: admin@yses.freeserve.co.uk. Website: www.yses.org.uk.
Programme description: Expeditions are organised to wilderness areas, most recently to China, Peru, South America and the Grand Canyon. Young leaders are needed to assist with the expeditions.
Number of placements per year: Around 70/80.
Prerequisites: Students on the expeditions must be in full-time education in Yorkshire (excluding Gap Year students). Leaders can come from anywhere and need not be in full-time education.
Duration and time of placements: 4-5 weeks.
Selection procedures and orientation: Selection weekend held in the Yorkshire Dales where applicants undertake rigorous mental and physical tasks and/or by application form. Good training is given prior to departure, plus help with fundraising. Leaders are required to send a CV. Experience is regarded as just as important as written qualifications. They may also have to attend the selection weekend.
Cost: £1500-£3500.
Contact: Society Administrator.

YOUNG EXPLORERS' TRUST
c/o YET Secretary, Stretton Cottage, Wellow Road, Ollerton, Newark, Notts. NG22 9AX. ☎/fax: 01623 861027. E-mail: ted@theyet.org. Website: www. theyet.org.
The Young Explorers' Trust is the Association of Youth Exploration Societies which advises and assists groups of students who wish to organise their own expedition during their gap year. They organise short courses on how to plan for an expedition.

Work Experience

Any school leaver lucky enough to have some idea of what career he or she is aiming for can try to build into their gap year a component of working in a related field. Work experience considered in its broadest terms applies to any experience of the world of work. A steady stint in even a boring job will enhance your CV and it might also have the salutary effect of reinforcing your desire to get more education so that you won't be consigned forever to the kind of jobs normally available to 18 year olds.

Although UK schools are obliged to organise five or ten-day work experience placements for students in Year 11, a longer period spent working in a particular area gives a much clearer idea of what a job is about and whether it is of interest for your potential future. Even if a work placement is irrelevant to your future plans, it will at least provide a useful introduction to how companies or organisations function.

Work placements are looked upon favourably by university admissions officers; experience of the 'real world' often helps students to develop a more mature outlook on life which enables them to do relatively better at university than their peers who come straight from school. Similarly, employers view students with work experience as more desirable. There is less risk for an employer in choosing someone who has already had some exposure to a particular career, and also less expense in training.

Employers, especially in companies with an international profile, look for employees who have demonstrated that they are open-minded and can adapt to different cultures. One way to impress these employers is with a CV that shows that you have successfully completed a period of work experience abroad. This is particularly impressive if the student uses or learns a foreign language as part of this experience. However, experience in the USA or Australia also tends to be popular and is also viewed favourably by companies.

Nowadays, the demand for many careers often outweighs supply, and exam qualifications no longer seem to be enough to get a job. Work experience can be used as a means of getting a foot in the door with particular companies and occupations. If you are interested in gaining work experience in a competitive field like media, publishing, broadcasting, museology, veterinary science, wildlife conservation, etc. you may find it very difficult to obtain paid work. If you're serious about enhancing your CV or simply getting a taste of what it will be really like, you should be prepared to work on a voluntary basis, which is now standard practice in many professions (for example conservation).

If you foresee yourself working in business, engineering, banking, accountancy or industry after graduation, you may be able to arrange a relevant paid work experience placement in your year between school and university. Not only are you likely to be able to earn and save money but with luck they will like you enough to offer you future vacation jobs or even a permanent career. **Nicky Stead** from West Yorkshire found herself in the unwelcome position of being forced to take a gap year when her A-level results were worse than expected. Undaunted, she decided to work locally before embarking on some world travels (see Australia chapter):

> I had to get a job and decided that to make the best of things I should get a job that was relevant to my preferred career and would look good on my CV as well as raise money for travelling. I got a job inputting mortgage applications for Skipton Building Society for six months, which I really enjoyed. I made so many friends and I loved the business environment. I felt grown up, and it was great. My appraisal was good and they encouraged me to stay.

FINDING A PLACEMENT

Several companies which take students for work placements for a substantial period are listed at the end of this chapter. It is worth visiting the local Connexions office for the names of local companies that might take on students. Students can also write directly to companies enclosing a CV to ask if they offer work placements, though the ratio of replies is likely to be discouraging (let alone favourable ones). The direct approach is more personal and likely to please potential employers, especially if there is a particular aspect of the company which students can say has attracted them.

Much can be achieved by confidently and persistently asking for the chance to help out in your chosen workplace unpaid. **Laura Hitchcock** (from the US) managed to fix up two three-month positions in the field of her career interest by agreeing to pay her own expenses if they would take her on and help her find accommodation in local homes. Her jobs were in the publicity departments of the Ironbridge Gorge Museums (Coach Road, Coalbrookdale, Shropshire TF8 7DQ; education@ironbridge.org.uk) and then in a theatre-arts centre in East Anglia (The Quay at Sudbury, Quay Lane, Sudbury, Suffolk CO10 6AN). Laura discovered that if you were willing to help yourself people could be extremely helpful and encouraging.

Specific Gap Year programmes offered by big companies are generally fiercely competitive. The fortunate few who are successful are usually paid a reasonable salary and many other benefits. The companies offer these schemes in order to attract the best possible candidates to join their companies after university. They tend to make their programmes interesting and varied to impress students. For example, the *Accenture Horizons Gap Year Scheme* is a programme which lasts eight months from September and combines training with paid work experience. Accenture pays £18,500 (pro rata, so equivalent to about £12,400 for the eight months) plus a travel bursary of £1600 on completion of a satisfactory period of work, which leaves plenty of time and money for travelling before university in the autumn. Because of the high rewards, acceptance is very competitive as one contributor to the gapyear.com messageboard describes:

> *I applied for Accenture's gap year scheme and got through the first interview (which was friendly, though they definitely wanted to make sure I had done my research about the company). I was invited back for a further assessment afternoon where there were seven of us. We were split into two groups for a discussion on the most influential people of the 20th century – basically Accenture wanted to see how we worked with other people. I also had another interview which was pretty similar to the first. Although I felt that both these assessments went quite well, I didn't get offered a position. I think I probably just lacked a little bit of confidence compared to some of the others, although it was hard to tell exactly what Accenture was looking for. Basically, this is a tough scheme to get on, but the rewards are good. However, don't be disappointed if, like me, you are rejected! The actual selection process is good experience for job interviews and applications later in life, and on the plus side, I am now going to be spending more of my gap year abroad!*

After the global downturn in business a couple of years ago, household names like Marconi stopped accepting gap year students claiming that 'the current market no longer supports student recruitment'. Yet many schemes are flourishing, including the ones run by *IBM* and *PriceWaterhouse Coopers* (see entries). Many students seeking work experience will entertain more modest ambitions than these gold-plated companies. Agency temping experience in different kinds of office can be a useful stepping stone not only to well-paid holiday work in the future but also to acquiring a broad acquaintance with the working world.

For more leads on work experience placements, check the website of the National Council for Work Experience, an organisation with charitable status whose aim is to promote work experience for students and thereby help the economy. The site www.work-experience.org has a searchable list of opportunities. Also check listings on the national universities careers website www.prospects.ac.uk. The majority of work experience placements are designed for university students and many university careers services have excellent databases of prospective hiring companies.

The Windsor Fellowship offers sponsorship to high-achieving undergraduates (first or second year) from African, African-Caribbean and Asian communities in the UK. The fully-funded two-year leadership programme includes a work placement. The Fellowship can also offer information and advice on work experience (www.windsor-fellowship.org).

Individual universities cater mainly to a local population but can be worth searching; try for example the University of Keele Careers website (www.keele.ac.uk/depts/aa/careers/wkexperience/workexp.htm) and the University of Stirling (www.careers.stir.ac.uk). Shorter placements may be found in the Vacation Trainee sections of the annually revised *Directory of Summer Jobs in Britain* from Vacation Work Publications (£10.99). These shorter placements are suitable for students who wish to spend their year out fitting in more than just work experience.

Robin Campbell graduated from Framlingham College and fixed up a work experience placement for the summer by applying to engineering companies listed on a leaflet put out by the Institution of Civil Engineers. He landed a job with *Sir Robert McAlpine* working on a building project in London's Docklands (which turned out to be in sharp contrast to his later gap year experiences, teaching in Sri Lanka through the Project Trust):

> *Well, here I am, one month since leaving school and I am sitting in my room, in a three storey house, half a mile from the Millennium Dome, working in the London Docklands - not bad! I'm here working on the Excel project for Sir Robert McAlpine for vocational employment during the summer. The Excel (or London International Exhibition Centre) is a huge building, looking similar to Stansted Airport's Termi-*

nal, with the largest roof in Europe, which means a lot of walking. It takes up all of the north side of the Royal Victoria Dock, which is located next to the Millennium Dome...Sir Robert McAlpine are a very high-up construction company, having built in part the Millennium Dome, the good bit of the Millennium Bridge...we could go on! Anyway they are a firm which seems to have a good atmosphere and treats its employees well. More importantly they are very keen to attract the 'next generation' of engineers, which translates to a very attractive set of sponsorship opportunities and graduate placements. That means money, experience and CV building stuff!...
The sense of independence is only just beginning to sink in, I think the thing that hit it all home was driving to the supermarket on the first day, having to set out shopping for the coming week!

Year in Industry

The *Year in Industry* scheme is the largest provider of gap year work placements in the UK. Last year more than 500 students took part in the scheme, gaining skills and experience to enhance their degree course while earning a real salary (typically £8000- £12,000 per annum). Some companies choose to sponsor a student through university or offer vacation work. Around one in four students go on to receive financial support from their company throughout university. Many of the placements are in engineering, science, technology and business, although other opportunities are available. It's a great chance for students to confirm their degree choice and get a feel for the working world before starting university.

Placements generally last for 10-12 months from August/September to mid-July, leaving time at the end for some travelling if desired. The Year in Industry has an affiliation with the expedition company *Madventurer* (see entry in 'Directory of Specialist Gap Year Programmes') whereby students, on successful completion of their YINI placement, get a 20% discount on a Madventurer summer project.

When **Sean Matthews** took a gap year with The Year in Industry, he was placed with Morganite Electrical Carbon Ltd. After going on to graduate from Aston University with a B.Eng. in Electromechanical Engineering, he took his first graduate job with Halcrow Group Ltd Engineering Consultants in July 2004:

The Year in Industry scheme has been hugely instrumental in my career thus far. Based largely on my experience gained from the scheme, I successfully gained two summer placements during my time at University and was sponsored by Morganite to carry out some work part-time for them. I was offered my current job based on my varied and extensive experience (over 18 months at graduation) within engineering. I believe The Year in Industry gives a huge boost that sets students apart from their peers, especially whilst seeking employment.

WORK EXPERIENCE ABROAD

According to the Global Work Experience Association, 'Work Experience is the fastest growing sector in the world of youth travel today.' Established in October 2003, the GWEA has about 100 member organisations actively engaged in arranging international work experience placements. The organisations include language schools providing work experience, youth exchange agencies, training organisations and student travel agencies. GWEA's stated aim is to 'promote work experience programmes for young people throughout the world in order to strengthen cultural and economic ties among nations'. Its website www.gwea.org includes clear links to its members and is a good starting place for anyone interested in fixing up work experience (most of which is unpaid) in Europe. Most mediating organisations charge a substantial fee for their services, normally between €750 and €1500, which may not include living expenses.

Predictably it is easier for students a little further along in their education than their gap year to find a suitable placement. For example the agencies running the internship programme for the USA are looking for university students and recent graduates. Trainee exchange programmes like those run by *CIMO* in Finland and the *Swiss Federal Office for Migration* in Switzerland are also open to those who have completed part of their degree course (see country chapters).

Students and recent graduates in business, management, marketing, accounting, finance, computing, education or economics may be interested in an organisation run by a global student network based in 87 countries. *AIESEC* – a French acronym for the International Association for Students of Economics and Management – has its national office at 29-31 Cowper St, 2nd Floor, London EC2A 4AT (020-7549 1700; national@uk. aiesec.org; www.workabroad.org.uk). It can organise placements in any of its member countries, aimed at giving participants an insight into living and working in another culture. Participants need to contribute only £200.

The *British Council* (10 Spring Gardens, London SW1A 2BN; www.britishcouncil.org/ education) has information about official work schemes and exchanges, many of them aimed at students. *IAESTE* is the abbreviation for the International Association for the Exchange of Students for Technical Experience (iaeste@britishcouncil.org; www.iaeste. org.uk). It provides international course-related vacation training for thousands of university-level students in 80 member countries. Placements are available in engineering, science, agriculture, architecture and related fields. Undergraduates at British universities should apply directly to *IAESTE UK* at the British Council in the autumn term for placements commencing the following summer. The registration form is available on the website www.iaeste.org.uk. Students at universities in other countries should contact their own national IAESTE office through the website www.iaeste.org.The US affiliate is the Association for International Practical Training (AIPT, 10400 Little Patuxent Parkway, Suite 250, Columbia, Maryland 21044-3510; 410-997-3068; www.aipt.org) which can make long and short-term placements of graduates and young professionals as well as college students in related fields.

Often there is a large area of overlap between work experience and volunteering, as **Cathleen Graham** found when she became a volunteer with the SCORE Programme (Sports Coaches Outreach) in South Africa, while pursuing development studies at university in Canada:

An opportunity to gain some work experience overseas was a stepping stone toward my longer-term goals. Living and working locally in another culture, language and country for a year would develop some skills relevant to work areas I was interested in: intercultural communication, development project work, sports development. In terms of disadvantages, some people don't see this kind of opportunity as taking steps toward your future, but rather as sidelining it and I sometimes had to deal with people's judgements. I also had to look ahead to when I came back home and try ahead of time, for my peace of mind anyhow, to define the next steps for me and how I would build on this experience. That was kind of critical, financially anyhow, because you are unlikely to earn much in your year away and you will probably spend some savings.

WORKING IN EUROPE

Legislation has existed for many years guaranteeing the rights of all nationals of the European Union to travel, reside, study and work in any member country. In addition, a number of special exchanges and youth programmes exist to help young Europeans to move easily across borders for short and longer periods. Various schemes have been established by the European Commission to provide financial aid to young people (normally aged 18-25) who wish to study, gain work experience or undertake a joint project with other young people in the EU. Many of these projects cannot be applied for directly by the student, but must be supported by their school, college or university. The best source of information is the Education and Training Group (ETG) at the *British Council*.

The accession of ten countries to the European Union in May 2004 means that the EU now consists of the original 15 member states (Austria, Belgium, Denmark, Finland, France, Germany, Greece, Ireland, Italy, Luxembourg, the Netherlands, Portugal, Spain, Sweden and the United Kingdom) plus Hungary, Poland, the Czech Republic, Slovakia, Slovenia, Estonia, Latvia, Lithuania, Malta and Cyprus. However nationals of these new member states will not necessarily be allowed to work in other member states straightaway. For example Italy, France and Germany (but not the UK) are imposing transitional controls so that it will be up to seven years from accession before full mobility of labour is allowed.

European Employment Service & Exchanges

The computerised, pan-European job information network EURES (EURopean Employment Service) is accessible through Jobcentre Plus offices around the UK and all national employment services in Europe. In the UK, expertise is centred in the International Job Search Advice department of Job Centre Plus (6th Floor, Whitehall II, Whitehall Quay, Leeds LS1 4HR; 0113 307 8090/91; fax 0113 307 8213; international-jobsearch-advice@jobcentreplus.gsi.gov.uk). Throughout Europe hundreds of specially trained EuroAdvisers can advise on vacancies within Europe. It is also possible to access the EURES database online via the EURES portal http://europa.eu.int/eures to see what kinds of vacancies are available in Iceland or Greece.

Euroguidance Centres covering European careers have been set up in all EU member states to provide information on training, education and employment in Europe, mostly to help careers services and their clients. Careers Europe (Onward House, Baptist Place, Bradford BD1 2PS; 01274 829600; www.careerseurope.co.uk) produce the Eurofacts series of International Careers Information, and Exodus, the Careers Europe database of international careers, all of which can be consulted at local Connexions careers offices and Jobcentre Plus in the UK.

The aim of the EU's *Leonardo da Vinci* scheme (see entry) is to improve the quality of vocational training systems and their capacity for innovation. The mobility measure offers opportunities for students and recent graduates to undertake work placements of between 3 and 12 months (for students) or between 2 and 12 months (recent graduates) in one of 31 European countries. It must be noted that applications for Leonardo funding must be submitted by organisations, not individuals.

Unfortunately the long-established gap year programme offered to future engineers in the UK and Europe by the Smallpeice Trust based in Leamington Spa is being discontinued at the end of 2005.

European schemes are reciprocal with many European students coming to Britain. A number of agencies assist European students to arrange internships in Britain where they can improve their English, for example:

Eagle UK, Eagle House, 177 Stourbridge Rd, Halesowen, W Midlands B63 3UD (0121-585 6177; info@eagle-uk.demon.co.uk/ www.eagle-uk.demon.co.uk. Business, hotel and other placements for 1-12 months combined with family stay.

EWEP (European Work Experience Programme), Unit 1, Red Lion Court, Alexandra Rd, Hounslow, Middlesex TW3 1JS (020-8572 2993; www.ewep.com). Charges an admin fee of £265.

LAF Ltd. 101-91 Western Road, Brighton, E Sussex BN1 2NW (01273 746 932; www.laf.uk.com).

Trident Transnational, The Smokehouse, Smokehouse Yard, 44-46 St John St, London EC1M 4DF (020-7014 1420; www.trident-transnational.org). Assists students and recent graduates from Europe to obtain internships and summer holiday jobs in the UK. Work experience placement fee is £235.

Directory of Work Experience in the UK

ACCENTURE HORIZONS SCHOOL SPONSORSHIP SCHEME

60 Queen Victoria St, London EC4N 4TW. ☎0500 100189 (Recruiting helpline). E-mail: ukgraduates@accenture.com. Website: www.accenture.com/ukgraduates.

Programme description: Provides students looking to take a gap year with a combination of training, work experience and the opportunity to travel before going to university. The job involves working alongside high profile clients to deliver Management and IT consultancy solutions. Upon successful completion of the placement, an opportunity is given to do further paid summer vacation work while at university and potentially an offer of a permanent position on graduation.

Destinations: London base, however the work will require travel to client sites across the UK.

Prerequisites: Must be an A-level student currently in the upper sixth year. A strong record of academic achievement is important with good grades in Maths and English at GCSE level and a minimum of 300 UCAS points or 4 B's at Scottish Highers predicted. Candidates should be confident, enthusiastic and mature with excellent communication and team working skills.

Duration and time of placements: 8-month internships from September to April.

Selection procedures & orientation: All applications should be made online at www.accenture.com/ukgraduates. Interviews will be held from the September of the candidate's final year at school. Refer to website for closing date.

Remuneration: Candidates are paid the pro rata equivalent of £18,500 per year, with a possible travel bursary of £1600 awarded at the end of the scheme. Depending on performance, financial sponsorship through university (up to £1500 per year) and the chance to come back and work during summer holidays is extended.

THE ARMY

HQ Recruiting Group, ATRA, Bldg 165, Trenchard Lines, Upavon, Wiltshire SN9 6BE. ☎08457 300111. Website: www.armyofficer.co.uk.

The British Army offers gap year students the opportunity to spend a year in the Army. The Gap Year Commission offers the opportunity for students taking a year out to be placed in an army regiment. There is no obligation after the year has been completed for the student to have any links with the Army. For more information see entry in the 'Directory of Specialist Gap Year Programmes'.

BBC WORK EXPERIENCE PLACEMENTS

www.bbc.co.uk/workexperience.

Programme description: A chance for people to see what the working life of the BBC is like for a few days or up to 4 weeks.

Number of placements: 150+ placement areas from which to choose, based at various UK locations.

Prerequisites: See descriptions online for specific criteria.

Remuneration: none.

Selection procedures and orientation: Deadlines vary according to business area (e.g. Production, Business Management & Support, Journalism). Up to 3 months needed to process applications.

BLACK & VEATCH CONSULTING LTD

Grosvenor House, 69 London Road, Redhill, Surrey RH1 1LQ. ☎01737 774155. Fax: 01737 772767. E-mail: hannahm@bv.com. Website: www.bvl.bv.com.

Civil engineering consultancy recently merged with contracting part of the company. Specialises in water supply, public health and environmental and power engineering.

Programme description: Traineeships and summer positions available.
Number of placements per year: 2 pre-university plus 2-3 undergraduates for summer placements.
Prerequisites: Applicants should have Mathematics and Science A-levels and be applying to read Civil Engineering, Mathematics, Physics or Applied Science at university.
Duration and time of placements: Up to 12 months or 10 weeks for summer.
Selection procedures and orientation: Applications should be sent to the Training Manager by Easter.
Remuneration: Trainees receive around £9000 p.a.

CADOGAN CONSULTANTS LTD
Corunna House, 39 Cadogan St, Glasgow G2 7AB. ☎0141-270 7060. Fax: 0141-270 7061. E-mail: a.jolly@cadoganconsultants.co.uk. Website: www.cadoganconsultants.co.uk.
Independent civil and structural engineering consultancy.
Programme description: Trainees gain first-hand experience of structural and civil engineering. Also accept gap year students looking for Building Services experience.
Number of placements per year: Less than 5.
Prerequisites: Students must be from university or college and studying Civil Engineering or related disciplines.
Selection procedures and orientation: Applicants from abroad will be considered. Applications should be sent by April.
Remuneration: Salary will be discussed at interview.
Contact: Andrew Jolly, Technical Director.

CIVIL SERVICE CAREERS
www.careers.civil-service.gov.uk.
More than 170 departments and executive agencies, employing nearly half a million people make the Civil Service one of the largest employers in the UK. A number of Government Departments and Agencies offer vacation opportunities for students; details are available from Careers Services or Civil Service Careers. Almost all opportunities listed in the booklet 'Work Experience in the Civil Service' are open to graduates and possibly undergraduates in relevant fields and not to school leavers. Students are advised to apply early as most opportunities have deadlines for applications early in the year and by the end of March at the latest.

CORAL CAY CONSERVATION
The Tower, 13th Floor, 125 High Street, Colliers Wood, London SW19 2JG. ☎0870 750 0668. Fax: 0870 750 0667. E-mail: info@coralcay.org. Website: www.coralcay.org
Founding member of the Year Out Group. CCC sends hundreds of volunteers to assist in conserving endangered tropical marine and terrestrial environments in Fiji, Malaysia, Honduras and the Philippines (see 'Directory of Specialist Gap Year Programmes').
Programme description: Opportunities for interns to work at London head office in the Science, Expedition Management and Marketing departments.

CORUS PLACEMENT SCHEME
Ashorne Hill Conference Centre, Leamington Spa, Warks. CV33 9PY. ☎01926 488035. Fax: 01926 488024. E-mail: recruitment@corusgroup.com. Website: www.corusgroupcareers.com.
Number of placements: Corus recruits approximately 100 placement students in to the following fields in the UK: Engineering, Metallurgy & Process Technology, Commercial, Human Resources, Purchasing, RD&T, Product & Market Development, Manufacturing Management, Finance and Logistics. Main locations are in the North East, Midlands and Wales.
Prerequisites: Suitable mainly for undergraduates.

Selection procedures and orientation: Application should be made online via www. corusgroupcareers.com.

Remuneration: About £250 per week. If successful, possibility of receiving sponsorship for following academic year.

DATA CONNECTION LTD
100 Church Street, Enfield, Middlesex EN2 6BQ. ☎020-8366 1177. E-mail: recruit@dataconnection.com. Website: www.dataconnection.com.

Data Connection is one of the few UK companies working at the forefront of communications and networking technology. They develop leading edge software and hardware solutions for major IT and telecommunications companies such as BT, Microsoft and Cisco, as well as Internet service providers and technology start-ups.

Programme description: Vacation work and year-long placements are offered to exceptional pre-university and university students with an interest in the development of complex software. The company provides challenging programming assignments, while offering help and support. Head office in Enfield, North London, and other offices in Edinburgh, Chester, San Francisco and Washington DC.

Prerequisites: Applicants will have all A grades at A-level.

Duration and time of placements: Minimum of 8 weeks over the summer. Early application is advised as vacancies are limited.

Remuneration: A salary of £1100 per month for pre-university students increasing to £1300 a month for university vacation students. Also subsidised accommodation in the company house. Many vacation students go on to join Data Connection as full-time employees, and some receive sponsorship whilst at university.

DAVY'S
59-63 Bermondsey St, London SE1 3XF. ☎020-7407 9670. E-mail: cdt@davy. co.uk. Website: www.davy.co.uk.

Programme description: Work experience placements with both 'on' and 'off' job training for those looking to enter the wine bar business. Training and development courses include Basic Food Hygiene, Introduction to Wine and First Aid.

Number of placements per year: 4.

Prerequisites: Minimum age 18. Should have basic understanding of hospitality, sound spoken English and documented evidence confirming the right to work legally in the UK. Should also possess a strong sense of team spirit and a commitment to providing excellent customer service.

Duration and time of placements: 6-12 months. Some accommodation available.

Selection procedures: Written applications or e-mails quoting reference GAP 0905.

Remuneration: Paid work experience.

Contact: Recruitment Administration Officer.

DELOITTE
Stonecutter Court, 1 Stonecutter Street, London EC4A 4TR. ☎020 7303 7019. Fax: 020 7007 3465. E-mail: hmanthorpe@deloitte.co.uk. Website: www.deloitte. co.uk/scholars.

Programme description: Scholars Scheme offers financial sponsorship and work experience in the financial industry to high calibre students from the start of a gap year through to when they graduate from university.

Number of placements per year: 50-60.

Destinations: Placements offered in a number of regional offices (St Albans, Reading, Bristol, Cambridge, Birmingham, Nottingham, Manchester, Leeds, Edinburgh and Glasgow) as well as London office (on the Strand).

Prerequisites: Good A levels (any subject) with intention to go on to study at a top UK university after their gap year. Must have achieved at least B in GCSE Maths and English language, be predicted 320 UCAS tariff points in first 3 A levels excluding General Studies.

Should have interest in business/finance.

Duration and time of placements: Gap year placements last 30 weeks from the end of August. Successful candidates expected to participate in scheme throughout their university education.

Selection procedures & orientation: Applications open on 1 July (13 months before scheme begins); no closing date since scheme remains open until places are filled with suitable candidates. Applications are made on line from website above.

Remuneration: Salary currently varies between £13,300 and £18,200 pro rata, depending on geographical location. Scholars then receive £1500 travel bursary to spend in the remainder of their gap year. Once at university, they receive £1500 academic bursary each year and return to Deloitte for at least 4 weeks a year in their holidays for further paid work.

Contact: Hana Manthorpe, Scholars Scheme Manager.

EARTHWATCH INSTITUTE (EUROPE)
267 Banbury Road, Oxford OX2 7HT. (01865 31812. Fax: 01865 311383. E-mail: projects@earthwatch.org.uk. Website: www.earthwatch.org/europe.
Earthwatch is an international environmental charity which engages people worldwide in scientific field research and education to promote the understanding and action necessary for a sustainable environment.

Programme description: Various unpaid internship positions are available in the Oxford office (ring or see website for details), offering useful experience to those wishing to enter the charity/environmental sector.

Duration and time of placements: 4-6 months.

Selection procedures & orientation: Internship candidates must submit a CV and are selected subject to interview.

EURA AUDIT UK
Administrative Office, Eva Left House, 1 South Crescent, Ripon, Yorkshire HG4 1SN. ☎01765 690890. Fax: 01765 690296. E-mail: admindept@euraudituk. com. Website: www.euraudituk.com.
One of Yorkshire's largest independent Chartered Certified Accountants with 16 offices from Sheffield to Middlesbrough.

Programme description: The company offers vacation and other traineeships to students including those in their gap year.

Number of placements per year: 4.

Prerequisites: None; should be seriously contemplating accountancy as a career.

Duration and time of placements: Mostly summer but some throughout the year.

Selection procedures and orientation: Written applications.

Remuneration: Wage is £5-£6 per hour, according to age, experience and qualifications.

Contact: Susan Metcalfe, Training Manager.

EUROMONEY INSTITUTIONAL INVESTOR PLC
Nestor House, Playhouse Yard, London EC4 5EX. ☎020-7779 8888. Fax: 020-7779 8842. E-mail: people@euromoneyplc.com. Website: www.euromoneyplc. com.
International publications and events company.

Programme description: No formal scheme but offers work to undergraduates and gap year students with excellent grades. Positions available as researchers, in telesales, administration and data inputting.

Prerequisites: Students of any subject are considered but economics, law and languages are particularly useful.

Remuneration: Varies according to vacancy. No accommodation provided.

Contact: Human Resources Administrator; applications by e-mail only.

GLOBE EDUCATION
International Shakespeare Globe Centre, Globe Education, 21 New Globe Walk, London SE1 9DT. ☎020-7902 1400. Fax: 020-7902 1401. Website: www. shakespeares-globe.org.
Programme description: One year paid gap year student internship to run the 'Lively Action Schools Programme' (the theatre's workshop and lecture programme caters for 45,000 students annually). Shorter unpaid administrative work experience placements in various departments: exhibition, appeals/fundraising and communications. Students will be able to work on special projects and events and act as stewards during the summer.
Number of placements: 1 paid internship, 30 shorter ones.
Duration and time of placements: 12 months from September 1st for internship. 1-2 weeks work experience (or longer if gap year placement) or minimum 3 months unpaid internship.
Remuneration: Stipend paid with 25 days holiday, free access to the majority of Globe Education events and some free theatre tickets. No wage paid for short work experience placements and travel expenses are not covered.
Selection procedures & orientation: Deadline late June. Interviews in July.
Contact: Crispin Hunt.

IBM UK
PO Box 41, North Harbour, Portsmouth PO6 3AU. ☎023 92 564104 (Student Recruitment Hotline) or 023 92 283777. E-mail: student_pgms@uk.ibm.com. Website: www-5.ibm.com/employment/uk.
Programme description: Pre-University Employment scheme for able students in one of several locations around the UK: Portsmouth, Winchester, Basingstoke, Bedfont (near Heathrow), Southbank (London) and Warwick. Work available in various departments such as Finance Operations and Business Controls.
Prerequisites: Good personal, business and technical skills. Predicted A-level results of AAB (with minimum C in GCSE English and Maths). Deadline for applications end of January.
Duration and time of placements: 9-12 months starting in August/September.
Other services: Residential induction course at beginning of year.
Contact: Student Recruitment Officer.

INDEPENDENT TELEVISION
Programme description: A limited number of work experience placements are sometimes available with the regional ITV companies. Vacancies are rarely known in advance and demand constantly outstrips supply.
Prerequisites: Applicants must be students on a recognised course of study at a college or university; their course must lead to the possibility of employment within the television industry (ideally, work experience would be a compulsory part of the course); and the student must be resident in the transmission area of the company offering the attachment, or in some cases, attending a course in that region. However, opportunities occasionally exist for students following computing, librarianship, finance, legal, administrative or management courses.
Duration and time of placements: Placements vary in length from half a day to several weeks or months, depending upon the work available and the candidate's requirements.
Remuneration: Students do not normally receive payment, although possibility that expenses will be paid. Students from sandwich courses who are on long-term attachments may be regarded as short-term employees and paid accordingly.
Selection procedures and orientation: Applications should be sent to the Personnel Department of the applicant's local ITV company. General information on working in media can be obtained from the Sectors Skills Council for the Audio Visual Industries (broadcast, film, video, interactive media and photo imaging) on www.skillset.org. Their careers service, Skillset Careers, offers media careers information, advice and guidance to anyone wanting

to enter or progress in the media industry. Visit www.skillset.org/careers or call one of the free helplines - 08080 300 900 in England or 0808 100 8094 in Scotland.

NATIONAL CENTRE FOR YOUNG PEOPLE WITH EPILEPSY (NCYPE)
St. Piers Lane, Lingfield, Surrey RH7 6PW. ☎01342 832243. Fax: 01342 834639. E-mail: aboyce@ncype.org.uk. Website: www.ncype.org.uk.
Programme description: To support student development by contribution to student's education and social and developmental curriculum, as part of a co-ordinated team.
Number of placements: Up to 5.
Prerequisites: Minimum age 19; suitable for pre-university. Must be legally entitled to work in the UK, obtain enhanced police disclosure and have desire to work with young students.
Duration and time of placements: 1 year minimum (September-July).
Remuneration: £13,548.
Other services: Single hostel accommodation arranged.
Contact: Adrienne Boyce, Recruitment Administrator.

OXFAM
Volunteering Team, Oxfam House, John Smith Drive, Cowley, Oxford OX4 2JY. ☎0870 333 2444. Website: www.oxfam.org.uk/ what_you_can_do/volunteer/ internship.htm.
Programme description: Volunteer Opportunities Scheme in charity/volunteer sector. Successful candidates can make a contribution to Oxfam's work in one of several divisions. Opportunities for specific training if relevant to assigned task, e.g. Influencing People and Time and Staff Management.
Destinations: UK only; most positions are at Oxford headquarters.
Prerequisites: Most candidates are post-university. Some positions can be filled only by people with the right qualifications and experience. Should have basic office and IT skills.
Duration and time of placements: 3-5 days per week for 3-12 months.
Remuneration: Work is unpaid. Lunch and travel expenses paid.

PRICEWATERHOUSECOOPERS
Southwark Towers, 32 London Bridge Street, London SE1 9SY. ☎0808 100 1500 (Student Information Line). E-mail: schoolsteam@uk.pwc.com. Website: www.pwc.com/uk/careers.
World's largest professional services organisation.
Programme description: Gap year students join one of 4 areas: Assurance, Tax, Forensic Services and Actuarial. Gap year students undertake real work with clients and develop skills for the future. Structured induction training programme given at beginning of placement. Vacancies in various offices in the UK (e.g. Bristol, Cambridge, Cardiff). Participants are paid a competitive salary.
Number of placements: 50 per year on the PwC Gap Year programme.
Prerequisites: Skills needed are teamwork, communication, motivation, flexibility, career focus and commercial awareness. Students should have 300 UCAS points (excluding General Studies) in any subjects. Students who require a work permit are not accepted. Applications via website, preferably before end of January when most vacancies are filled.
Duration and time of placements: 7 months, September to March.
Other services: Students have to find their own accommodation, though PwC puts other programme participants in touch with each other. If students perform well on the programme, they will receive a Scholarship of £1500 each year at university and paid work placements during vacations.
Contact: Zoe Gordon (Gap Year Manager) or Louise Heatherson (Gap Year Co-ordinator).

ROLLS-ROYCE PLC
Peoplelink, PO Box 31, Derby DE24 8BJ. ☎01332 244344. E-mail: peoplelink@rolls-royce.com. Website: www.rolls-royce.com/careers.
Programme description: Internships for undergraduates or fresh graduates available for 6-12 months at Rolls-Royce for students in at least their second year of study. Opportunities are available in engineering, finance, purchasing and logistics. Summer internships last 10 weeks in similar departments plus operations management.
Destinations: Several sites around UK but mostly in Bristol and Derby.
Duration and time of placements: 10 weeks to 12 months with various start dates (but usually summer). Deferred placement possible allowing graduates to take a year out after university and come back to an internship.
Remuneration: £15,050 per year (pro rata).

ROYAL OPERA HOUSE EDUCATION
Covent Garden, London WC2E 9DD. ☎020-7212 9410. Fax: 020-7212 9441. E-mail: education@roh.org.uk. Website: http://info.royaloperahouse.org/Education.
Placements offered: Work placements/internships offered across the organisation but predominantly in technical and production areas, e.g. archives, education, music library and publications.
Prerequisites: Minimum age 18. Students should have an interest in ballet, opera or music (though not necessarily performers) with a view to working in arts administration. Former experience in an office environment preferred..
Duration of courses: At mutually agreed start date and period of time.
Other services: 5-day 'Behind-the-Scenes' course in April (see entry in 'Directory of Courses').
Contact: Joanne Allen, Education Secretary/Work Placement Co-ordinator.

SIR ROBERT MCALPINE
Eaton Court, Maylands Avenue, Hemel Hempstead, Herts. HP2 7TR. ☎01442 412910. Website: www.sir-robert-mcalpine.com.
A long-established UK building and civil engineering contractor which is consistently awarded high profile contracts, including the Eden Project.
Programme description: Gap year opportunities based in Hemel Hempstead. Opportunity for candidates to spend some time on a construction site during the latter part of their employment if desired.
Number of placements: 2 gap year student placements in Group Services Office (one in the Civil Tenders Department, the other in the Corporate Development Department).
Prerequisites: Candidates must possess good academic background, basic communication and interpersonal skills. Applicants will, preferably, be planning to start a construction-related degree course in higher education, will be enthusiastic about gaining an insight into careers in construction.
Duration and time of placements: 1 year starting approximately August/September.
Selection procedures and orientation: Applications available from the Human Resources Department or online. Thorough guidance and support provided throughout the year.
Remuneration: Salaried position based in Hemel Hempstead. Working hours are 9.00am-5.30 pm Monday to Friday.
Contact: Peter Miller, Recruitment Manager.

STEP (SHELL TECHNOLOGY ENTERPRISE PROGRAMME)
11-13 Goldsmith Street, Nottingham NG1 5JS. ☎0115 941 5900. Fax: 0115 950 8321. E-mail: enquiries@step.org.uk. Website: www.step.org.uk.
Initiative sponsored primarily by Shell UK and also by the Department of Trade & Industry to match second and penultimate year undergraduates with small and medium-sized businesses and community organisations for work projects.

Programme description: Summer work experience projects and year-long industrial type projects for students to undertake while pursuing degree studies.
Number of projects: Approximately 1,300.
Prerequisites: Must be studying full-time at a UK university in either second or penultimate year. No age restrictions.
Duration and time of placements: 8 weeks over summer; part-time term-time up to 15 hours per week, or 12 months.
Selection procedures and orientation: Application can be made online at www.step.org. uk. Deadline for summer placements falls in the second week of June.
Remuneration: Summer students receive about £180 per week. Average 12-month project pays £12,000. Travelling expenses are paid at the employer's discretion.

TRIDENT TRANSNATIONAL
The Smokehouse, Smokehouse Yard, 44-46 St John St, London EC1M 4DF. ☎020-7014 1420. Fax: 020-7336 8561. E-mail: info.transnational@trid.demon.co.uk. Website: www.trident-transnational.org.
International division of the Trident Trust, an educational charity and organiser of work experience programmes for overseas nationals in the UK.
Programme description: Work experience and working holiday schemes for young people aged 18-35 from the EEA. They send applicants' CVs round relevant companies in the UK. Work placements are accredited with a certificate issued by the University of Cambridge Local Examinations Syndicate.
Duration and time of placements: Work Experience placements last 6 weeks to 12 months starting all year round. Working Holiday placements last 16-52 weeks starting between the beginning of March and end of September.
Selection procedures and orientation: Application should be made at least two months in advance for Work Experience or between October 1st and Feb 28th for Working Holiday. It is occasionally possible to find placements for non-European students who must obtain a TWES permit (Training & Work Experience Scheme) for the UK.
Fees: £235 (work experience); £195 (working holidays).
Contact: Debora de Rooy (debora.derooy@trid.demon.co.uk).

YEAR IN INDUSTRY
The University of Southampton, Southampton SO17 1BJ. ☎023 8059 7061. E-mail: enquiries@yini.org.uk. Website: www.yini.org.uk.
Founding member of the Year Out Group. Major provider of gap year industrial placements throughout the UK.
Programme description: Students are placed in companies where they gain paid work experience of industry relevant to their degree. Participants are encouraged to enter an end-of-year competition with cash prizes.
Number of placements per year: 500+.
Prerequisites: Students should be interested in gaining experience in industry and must be intending to go to university. Most participants are intending to study engineering, science, technology or business, although opportunities are available for other disciplines.
Duration and time of placements: Placements generally last for 10-12 months, from August/September to mid-July.
Selection procedures and orientation: All applicants must be interviewed by the Year in Industry. Participants are also required to attend management training with the Chartered Management Institute.
Remuneration: Minimum recommended salary is £8000-£12,000.

Directory of Work Experience Abroad

AFRICAN CONSERVATION EXPERIENCE
PO Box 206, Faversham, Kent, ME13 8WZ. ☎0870 241 5816. E-mail: info@ConservationAfrica.net. Website: www.ConservationAfrica.net.
Programme description: Conservation work placements for enthusiastic people on game reserves in Southern Africa. See 'Directory of Specialist Gap Year Programmes' and 'Africa' chapter.

AGRIVENTURE
International Agricultural Exchange Association (IAEA), Speedwell Farm Bungalow, Nettle Bank, Wisbech, Cambridgeshire PE14 0SA. Tel/fax: 01945 450999. E-mail: uk@agriventure.com. Website: www.agriventure.com.
Programme description: International agricultural and horticultural work programmes for people aged 18-30.
Destinations: Placements for UK and European participants in the USA, Canada, Australia, New Zealand and Japan.
Prerequisites: Must be aged 18 to 30 with an aptitude for working in agriculture or horticulture.
Duration and time of placements: Placements in the USA and Canada begin in February, April and June and last for 7 or 9 months. Placements for Australia and New Zealand depart throughout the year and last 6-12 months. Placements in Japan begin in April and last 4-12 months. There are also several round-the-world itineraries which depart in the autumn to the southern hemisphere for 6-7 months followed by another 6-7 months in the northern hemisphere.
Selection procedures & orientation: Pre-departure information meeting.
Cost: Participants pay between £2000 and £4100 which includes airline tickets, visas, insurance, orientation seminar, back-up and board and lodging throughout with a host family. Trainees are then paid a realistic wage.

CDS INTERNATIONAL INC
871 United Nations Plaza, 15th floor, New York, NY 10017-1814, USA. ☎(212) 497-3500. Fax: (212) 497-3535. E-mail: info@cdsintl.org. Website: www.cdsintl.org.
CDS International offers practical training placements in the US in a variety of fields including business, engineering and technology; and also overseas practical training internships for American students or recent graduates.
Programme description: CDS arranges various work experience, internships and work-study programmes for Americans in Germany and a number of other countries. For incoming participants to the US, CDS sponsors visa authorisation, arranges internships and provides programme during US stay.
Destinations: Mainly Germany; also Spain, Argentina, Russia and Switzerland. Incoming programme to the US.
Number of placements per year: 2000+.
Prerequisites: The opportunities for internships are limited to young professionals, aged 18-35. Language proficiency required for most programmes, as well as relevant experience and a strong desire to gain international experience.
Duration and time of placements: Internships generally last 3-18 months, although 24-month placements may be available.
Selection procedures and orientation: Qualified applicants are interviewed by telephone. Pre-departure orientation materials are sent and support is provided throughout the programme.
Cost: Programme fee normally $500. Some internships are paid.

C.E.I. (CENTRE d'ECHANGES INTERNATIONAUX)
Club des 4 Vents, 1 rue Gozlin, 75006 Paris, France. ☎ 1-43 29 17 24. Fax: 1-43 29 06 21. E-mail: France@cei4vents.com. Website: www.cei4vents.com.
Programme description: Professional training, academic year abroad and homestays. Work experience in Brittany region.
Prerequisites: Minimum age 17.
Duration and time of placements: 2-4 weeks (or more) year round.
Cost: €750 for 2 weeks; €1000 for 3 weeks, €1250 for 4 weeks including full board accommodation with local family and ongoing back-up.
Other services: C.E.I. offers homestay and residential summer French courses for young people aged 12-18 in Arcachon, Montpellier, Saint Malo and Paris area. Also has residential language courses in Paris at the French school Paris Langues (www.parislangues.com).
Contact: José Luis Ponti, Incoming Programmes Manager.

COLONIAS DE INMERSIÓN AL IDIOMA
Armenia 1973, Departamento 3, 1414 Buenos Aires, Argentina. Correspondence address: Fernando Damián Carro, Colonias de Inmersión al Idioma, Casilla de Correo 044, Sucursal Plaza Italia, 1425 Buenos Aires, Argentina. ☎/fax: +54 (011) 4831 8152. E-mail: info@coloniasdeinmersionalidioma.com. Website: www.coloniasdeinmersionalidioma.com.
Programme description: Cultural exchange in which exchange students and graduates from English-speaking countries study, work and live in Argentina, Chile or Spain. They are placed as language and culture facilitators at schools or language schools while at the same time staying with a family and learning Spanish.
Number of placements per year: 20-40 per semester, 70 total.
Prerequisites: Ages 19-26, average age 22. Must have English mother tongue and been raised in an English-speaking country. Must be communicative, imaginative, fit, team-minded and highly aware of their own culture.
Duration and time of placements: 3-9 months. Start dates in Argentina and Chile: 20th February and 20th July. Start dates in Spain: 10th January and 1st October.
Selection procedures & orientation: Applications online. Application letter, photo and 2 references required. Must be submitted at least 1 month prior to start date. Placements are processed on a first-come-first-served basis. All applicants find a placement if they comply with the requirements.
Cost: Placement fee from US$650. Homestays with full board, Spanish coaching and small stipend given in return. Programme fee includes airport pick-up, orientation on arrival, 4-day intensive TEFL workshop (mandatory for all applicants and optional for those with TEFL Certification) and TEFL assistance throughout. 1-week Spanish Immersion Programme and volunteer work opportunities are optional.
Contact: Fernando Damián Carro, Programme Director.

CULTURAL CUBE LTD
16 Acland Road, Ivybridge, Devon PL21 9UR. ☎ 0870 742 6932. Fax: 0870 742 6935. E-mail: info@culturalcube.co.uk. Website: www.culturalcube.co.uk.
Programme description: Unpaid internships in Armenia, and work experience placements in Australia and the USA.
Prerequisites: Various age limits.
Duration and time of placements: Internships in Armenia last 1-6 months. Flexible durations in Australia starting any time.
Cost: Placement fees excluding travel costs from £230 for shorter placements. Sample costs in Australia £440 for a 6-week placement, £1000 for a 12-month internship. Fee is £1690-£2000 for hospitality internship in the USA lasting 12-18 months, though employers provide free room and board and pay a stipend.
Contact: Tim Swale-Jarman, Director.

EARTHCORPS
6310 NE 74th St, Suite 201E, Seattle, WA 98115. ☎206-322-9296 ext 224. Fax: 206-322-9312. E-mail: mark@earthcorps.org. Website: www.earthcorps. org.
Programme description: 6-month skill-based environmental restoration experience in Seattle. Trail construction, environmental education and invasive plant removal.
Number of placements per year: 20-25 (2 per country).
Prerequisites: All nationalities, so cross-cultural communication skills needed. Ages 20-25. People preferred who have experience of working in the field of environmental restoration.
Duration and time of placements: June-November or February-August.
Selection procedures and orientation: Competitive selection. Applications due by middle of December (for June start) or September (for February start).
Remuneration: All basic needs covered including room and board plus a small stipend. Airfare reimbursement scholarship available that pays 30% of transport costs up to $500.
Contact: Mark Howard, International Co-ordinator.

EcuEVP
Av. 9 de Octubre 1647 y Berlín (PO Box 17-03-1423) Quito, Ecuador. ☎ +593 2-222 6947. Tel/fax: +593 2-255 0898. E-mail: ecuevp2004@yahoo.com. Website: www.ecuevp.com.
Programme description: Internship programme in Ecuador. Unpaid internships in many fields such as journalism and media, medical, business, architecture, human rights and marketing.
Destinations: Throughout Ecuador including Highlands, coastal areas, Amazonia and the Galapagos Islands.
Prerequisites: Good knowledge of Spanish is required. Must be able to adapt to different culture.
Duration of placements: Minimum 2 months, up to 6 months (since foreigners require no visa for stays of less than 6 months). Available any time of year.
Cost: $200 placement fee includes transfer from airport to host family. Language lessons cost $6 an hour (20 hours a week). Sample 3-month package includes 4 weeks language study (80 hours), volunteer arrangement commission, homestay with meals (3 meals a day, 7 days a week) for $1120.
Accommodation: Accommodation with host families costs $12 per day including full board.
Contact: Hendrik Rost, Programme Consultant; Mirian and Patricia Fernández, Programme Directors.

EDUCATION DOWNUNDER
103 The Avenue, Coburg 3058, Melbourne, VIC, Australia. ☎ +61 425 722 417. E-mail: admin@educationdownunder.com.au. Website: www.educationdownunder.com.au.
Programme description: Supervised work or service experience (internships) in Australian working environment for individuals and groups. Non-native speakers of English can improve their English.
Number of placements per year: 300+.
Destinations: Melbourne, Australia.
Prerequisites: Minimum age 18. Internship should be in applicants' field of study and fit in with their intended learning goals. Minimum English language level is 6.5.
Duration and time of placements: 1-12 months. Hours of work vary from 10 to 30 per week over 2 to 5 days.
Selection procedures & orientation: Application form available online (www.educationdownunder.com.au/internship). Placements can be made in as little as 1 week but more usually 1 month. Assistance given with obtaining appropriate visa. Ongoing

back-up provided.
Cost: Internships are unpaid. Internship placement fee is $850 + 10% GST. Internship Orientation fee is $350 + GST (3 days full-time). Homestays or shared accommodation can be arranged at extra cost.
Contact: Patricia Keeley, Managing Director.

ELEP (EXPERIENTIAL LEARNING ECUADORIAN PROGRAMS)
Selva Alegre 1031 y La Isla, Ecuador. ☎ +593 9-940 0851. Fax: +593-9-757 9555. E-mail: info@elep.org or elep@on.net.ec.
Programme description: Internship, Volunteer & Spanish Courses in Ecuador. Unpaid internships in many fields such as media, tourism, computing, environmental science, marketing, engineering and many others.
Destinations: Throughout Ecuador including Highlands, coastal areas, Amazonia and the Galapagos Islands.
Prerequisites: Good knowledge of Spanish is required. Must be able to adapt to different culture.
Duration of placements: 2 weeks to 6 months for volunteer programme. From 8 weeks to 6 months for internships. Available any time of year. No special visa needed for stays of less than 6 months.
Cost: Application fee $100, placement fee $200 includes transfer from airport to host family. Private language lessons cost $6 an hour (20 hours a week). Special offer of 4 weeks of Spanish lessons plus 8 weeks internship (or volunteering) plus accommodation for $1500.
Accommodation: Accommodation with host families in private room costs $91 a week on the mainland, $120 on the Galapagos. 3 meals a day and laundry service included.
Contact: Patricia Parrales (Programme Consultant), Kleber Parrales (Programme Officer), Patricio Fernández (Managing Director).

EUROGROUP
473 rue de la Leysse, BP 429, 73004 Chambéry, France. ☎ +33 479 65 08 06. Fax: +33 479 65 08 11. E-mail: candidatures@eurogroup-vacances.com. Website: www.eurogroup-vacances.com.
Programme description: Work placement programme that places students in 40 hotels and holiday residences in France managed by Eurogroup. Provides professional experience and chance to improve spoken French. Resort placements are available on reception, in the restaurant and in other roles, including customer services and management support.
Number of placements per year: 100+.
Destinations: France including ski resorts, the southern and western coasts and major cities such as Paris and Montpellier. Also some placements in head office in Chambéry in the following departments: Marketing, Human Resources, Legal, Reservations, Planning, Purchasing, Quality and E-commerce.
Prerequisites: Students must be enrolled in a school or university of the EU at the time of applying. Open to gap year as well as year abroad students.
Duration and time of placements: Minimum 2 months in resorts, 4 months in head office. Resort placements are seasonal, normally up to 4 months. Head office positions available for up to 12 months.
Selection procedures & orientation: A good command of French and possibly previous experience in a work environment. Applications accepted year round. All candidates must undergo an interview by telephone, during which their level of French is assessed.
Remuneration: €380 per month if food and accommodation are found independently or €180 per month live-in, usually a shared room in a staff apartment. Ski passes are often provided for those working in ski resorts. Eurogroup has also negotiated favourable rates with various ski shops in resorts for their employees.
Contact: Mme Catherine Oldfield, Work Placement Co-ordinator.

EUROLINGUA
UK Liaison Office, 61 Bollin Drive, Altrincham WA14 5QW. ☎☎/fax: 0161-972 0225. E-mail: info@eurolingua.com. Website: www.eurolingua.com/Work_ Experience.htm. European Corporate Office: Eurolingua Institute sarl, 5 rue Henri Guinier, 34000 Montpellier, France. Tel/fax: +33 467 58 20 17.
International study abroad organisation with locations in many countries worldwide.

Programme description: Paid work experience in the hospitality industry, in UK hotels and French hotels and on Mediterranean holiday camping sites. Free accommodation and meals.

Destinations: France and the UK (for foreigners).

Prerequisites: Minimum age 18. Intermediate level language skills in French (or English for foreigners coming to the UK) needed.

Cost: From €750 according to location and length of stay.

Contact: Barry Haywood, International Director.

EUROPEAN COMMISSION
Bureau des Stages, 200 Rue de la Loi, 1049 Brussels, Belgium. ☎02-299 23 39. E-mail: eac-stages@cec.eu.int. Website: www.cec.org.uk/work/stage.htm.
The scheme is open only to graduates and is administered by the Training Office at the European Commission's General Secretariat in Brussels.

Programme description: Twice a year the Commission organises in-service training periods to give trainees a general idea of the objectives and problems of European integration and provide them with practical knowledge of the workings of Commission departments. Part of the period may be used to prepare a post-graduate thesis or academic paper.

Destinations: Most are in Luxembourg or Brussels.

Number of placements per year: Approximately 600.

Prerequisites: Applicants must have a thorough knowledge of one other EU official language in addition to their mother tongue. The age limit is 30. Applicants must also have completed their degree.

Duration and time of placements: 5 months. Training periods begin on 1st March and 1st October every year.

Selection procedures and orientation: Application forms must be submitted online. Deadlines are August 31st and March 1st. If applicants pass the first selection procedure, it is often helpful to attend informal interviews in Brussels.

Remuneration: Most trainees are paid a grant and their travel expenses.

EXPERIMENT
89 rue de Turbigo, 75003 Paris, France. ☎1-44 54 58 03. Fax: 1-44 54 58 01. E-mail: incoming@experiment-france.org. Website: www.experiment-france.org.
Programme description: Internship Programme in various regions of France. Placements in hotels/restaurants or businesses, e.g. advertising, computing, import/export, etc.

Duration of courses: 2-6 months. Maximum 3 months for non-EU candidates.

Prerequisites: Ages 18-30. Must be able to function at an intermediate level of French. Internship placement fee normally in the range €425-€625.

Remuneration: Hotel/restaurant staff receive monthly stipend of €200. Other businesses pay €150 minimum per month on programmes lasting at least 4 months. Stipends not guaranteed on shorter programmes.

Other services: 20 hours of French classes may be arranged prior to internship. Accommodation can be arranged on request; host family providing half-board costs €220 per week; self-catering in student residence costs €200.

Contact: Anne Blassiau, Director.

FRENCH ENCOUNTERS
63 Fordhouse Road, Bromsgrove, Worcestershire B60 2LU. ☎01527 873645. Fax: 01527 832794. E-mail: admin@frenchencounters.com. Website: www. frenchencounters.com.
Company runs field study trips for 10-13 year olds based in two chateaux in Normandy with British staff who act as guides/couriers/teachers/entertainers/organisers.

Programme description: *Animateurs/animatrices* to work with groups of young people in France. Compulsory 2-week pre-service training includes English Speaking Board's 'Professional Presentation Skills' training and assessment, continuous on-the-job training and French Red Cross *(Croix Rouge)* First Aid Certificate Course.

Prerequisites: A-level French preferred. Minimum age 18. Must be committed enough to work long hours (on-call 24 hours a day) and tackle challenging tasks.

Duration and time of placements: 4 months from beginning or middle of February to mid-June. Applications should be submitted before the end of August for September interviews.

Remuneration: All expenses are paid including reasonable interview expenses, insurance, return travel to France, cost of all training and exam fees and board and lodging. In addition pocket money is paid (£80 in 2005) calculated to be below the taxable threshold. Weekend allowance also paid. Rooms are shared and not en suite. Chateaux are relatively isolated so accommodation normally provides TV and video.

Other services: Experience gives gap year students an opportunity to develop a range of management and business skills and knowledge of the service and tourism industries.

Contact: Patsy Musto, Owner/Director.

GALA SPANISH IN SPAIN
Woodcote House, 8 Leigh Lane, Farnham, Surrey GU9 8HP. ☎/fax: 01252 715319.
Gala offers an information, advisory and placement service for students of Spanish.

Programmes description: Work experience placements following language courses in three cities in Spain.

Prerequisites: Should have at least intermediate level of Spanish (pre-placement language course can be arranged if needed).

Duration and time of placements: 1-3 months during summer. Possibility of placements at other times of the year on request.

Selection procedures: Applications should be submitted by end of February. Later applications (before May 15th) may be surcharged.

Contact: Anne Thomas, Proprietor.

GLOBAL EXPERIENCES
1010 Pendleton St, Alexandria, VA 22314, USA. ☎1-877.GE ABROAD/ 1-877-432-2762. Fax: 703-519-0650. E-mail: admin@globalexperiences.com. Website: www.globalexperiences.com.
Programme description: Professional international internships (especially in Australia and Italy), volunteer abroad programmes, TESOL certification courses, adventure travel and immersion foreign language training. Internships available in Fashion Design, Fashion Merchandising, Graphic Design, Culinary, Marketing, Law/Legal, Architecture, Advertising/Sales, Public Relations, International Business, Information Technology, Web Design, Business Administration, Fine Art/Museum Studies, Finance, Hospitality/Tourism, Hotel/Restaurant Management, Agriculture, etc.

Number of placements per year: 500-600.

Destinations: Italy, Australia, Ecuador, Holland, Costa Rica, Spain, France, New Zealand, Thailand, Vietnam, South Korea, Egypt and China.

Prerequisites: Ages 18-30; suitable for school leavers.

Duration and time of placements: 1 month to 1 year.

Selection procedures & orientation: Applicants must complete an on-line application comprising several brief essays explaining prior professional experience, the motivation behind

Looking for a meaningful and productive year out?

Why not work as an 'animateur' with

French Encounters

the specialists in high level educational and language field trips for schools

Do you want to:
really make a difference?
earn while you learn?
confront exciting challenges and broaden your horizons daily?
develop a variety of essential life and vocational skills?
improve your general communication and presentation skills?
learn to be a guide, courier and entertainer?
perfect your French language skills in France?
use your initiative?
live and work in a château in Normandy?
acquire some practical first aid skills?
work with a great variety of people and as part of a dynamic team?

and, of course, have fun in the process?

What previous animateurs have said of their experience:

"An indication of how much we enjoyed it . . . . we're returning
to the château to get married!" 1999
"The first time I took a group out I was terrified - by the end of the season,
I could cope with anything" 2000
"What a good time we had . . . . we all wish we could do it again" 2002
"Felt valued and gained real experience, often asked for but rarely offered!" 2003
"I couldn't imagine a better way to have spent my GAP year. I'll never forget it.
If future animateurs have half the fun we did, it would still be worth it." 2004
"I'd recommend the experience highly - you'd be hard pushed to find a project as
challenging, as valuable for learning so many skills and acquiring new things.
The trouble is finding something else as good for the rest of the year." 2004
"It surpassed all expectations, season was great and we all made friends for life." 2005
"Recommend it to anyone willing to play hard but work harder. Not only really improved my
French, but gained immensely in historical and cultural knowledge and
acquired an interesting repertoire of alternative jokes!" 2005

Season lasts from mid-February - mid-June
Interested ?
contact: **French Encounters**
63 Fordhouse Road Bromsgrove Worcs B60 2LU
Tel: 01527 873645 Tel/Fax: 01527 832794
email: admin@frenchencounters.com www.frenchencounters.com

their application and prior foreign language skills. The applicant's level of proficiency in the host country's language often determines the duties and the quality of internship that is possible. Rolling admissions. Applications preferred 3 months before proposed start date.

Cost: 95% of the internships are unpaid work experience. All programmes require an application fee, e.g. 2-month programme in Florence costs €3940 and 3 months in Milan €4590 plus $100 application fee. Sample fees in Australia: A$3990 for 4 weeks, A$7990 for 16 weeks. Cost includes accommodation, normally in an apartment.

Contact: Michael Greto, Director of Operations.

GLOBETROTTERS EDUCATION CONSULTING INC
1784 Rosebank Road, Pickering, Ontario L1V 1P6, Canada. ☎416-565-4420. Fax: 905-839-0063. E-mail: laura@globetrotterseducation.ca. Website: www.globetrotterseducation.ca.

Programme description: Experiential programmes give young people the opportunity to live, work (sometimes earn money) and gain practical international experience.

Number of placements per year: 100+.

Destinations: Worldwide. Internships in New Zealand; au pair placements in Italy, Spain and France plus possibly Netherlands; etc.

Prerequisites: Vary depending on programme. Au pair and work/internships often restricted to North Americans, Europeans, Australians and New Zealanders.

Duration and time of placements: 1 week to 1 year. Work placements in Europe (1 week-6 months); work abroad (up to 1 year); internships in New Zealand (6 months with possible extension); au pairing (1-12 months); study programmes (variable).

Selection procedures & orientation: Applications accepted throughout the year, though several months needed to make placements. Varying services such as health insurance and destination services.

Cost: C$300-C$5000.

Contact: Laura Wood, President & Senior Education Consultant.

GLS SPRACHZENTRUM BERLIN
Kolonnenstr. 26, 10829 Berlin, Germany. ☎30-78 00 89/0. Fax: 30-787 41 92. E-mail: germancourses@gls-berlin.com. Website: www.german-courses.com.

Programme description: Minimum 4-week language course followed by an internship lasting 4, 8 or 12 weeks in a company in or near Berlin. Traineeships available in range of fields such as marketing, government and banking. One recent example was at Heinrich-Boell-Stiftung, the foundation of the German Green Party.

Prerequisites: Must be able to express yourself in German and understand everyday conversations. Must also show initiative. Minimum age 18/19.

Cost: Placement fee is €450.

Other services: GLS is a leading centre in Berlin for teaching German as a foreign language and is a founding member of GWEA (Global Work Experience Association).

Contact: Dorothee Robrecht, Director PR & Marketing.

GWENDALYNE
c/o Twin Training and Travel Ltd, 2nd Floor, 67-71 Lewisham High St, Lewisham, London SE13 5JX. ☎ +44 (0) 20 8297 3251. Fax: 020-8297 0984. E-mail: info@gwendalyne.com. Website: www.gwendalyne.com.

Gwendalyne is the newly launched Outbound department of Twin Training & Travel offering a range of work experience and volunteer programmes around the world.

Programme description: Work experience/internship programmes in many countries, sometimes in conjunction with Euro-Academy language course.

Destinations: USA (Career Training), Canada, Brazil, France, Germany, Finland, Spain and Ireland. Work programmes in Australia, New Zealand, South Africa, USA, France, Norway, etc.

Prerequisites: Must meet the age requirements of the relevant visa. Other requirements

vary. Language course may be compulsory before work experience/job placement.

Duration and time of placements: Vary with maximum usually 12 months (according to visa).

Selection procedures & orientation: Enrolment online. Processing time 1-3 months.

Cost: Placement fees normally about £300-£400 excluding courses and accommodation.

Contact: Piero Donat, Global Work Experience Commercial Manager.

IEPUK LTD

The Old Rectory, Belton-in-Rutland, Oakham, Rutland LE15 9LE. ☎01572 717381. Fax: 01572 717343. E-mail: info@iepuk.com. Website: www.iepuk. com.

Programme description: Agricultural, equine, horticultural, landscaping and winemaking work placements. Also acts as a recruitment agency making permanent and relief placements in the equestrian and agricultural industry.

Destinations: Australia, New Zealand, USA, South Africa, Europe and many posts in UK.

Number of placements per year: 300/400.

Prerequisites: Equestrian staff require suitable background. One year of practical experience usually needed though many placements offer additional training. Placements as general farm assistants may not require experience.

Duration and time of placements: Usually one year, but variable.

Selection procedures and orientation: Interviews and orientation are required for work overseas.

Cost: IEP fee is about £1800 including airfares.

INTERNATIONAL STUDENT PLACEMENT CENTRE (ISPC)

Level 8, 32 York Street, Sydney, NSW, 2000. ☎02-9279 0100. Fax: 02 9279 1028. E-mail: info@ispc.com.au. Website: www.ispc.com.au.

Programme description: ISPC offers unpaid professional internships in all fields. Internships are custom designed to suit the applicants' needs in terms of experience and training sought. Most internships are undertaken to gain academic credit with the applicant's university or to enhance the applicant's work experience within their field of studies. Paid internships also available in the hospitality sector (e.g. food and beverage, banqueting, customer service, housekeeping, Kitchen and front desk).

Number of placements per year: 1000.

Destinations: Internships are available in all cities of Australia.

Prerequisites: Minimum age 16; most aged 18-30. Sizeable proportion of applicants are on a gap year and are looking for a taste of the field of studies they are about to undertake at university. School leavers should have relevant academic background or a genuine intention of studying in that field.

Duration and time of placements: Applicants choose the start date and duration. Minimum 1 week.
Cost: Fees for internship placements from $1100 for 1-6 weeks up to $2500 for 52 weeks. Special rate of $1900 for Farm Work & Travel and Paid Hospitality Work.
Other Services: ISPC monitors the internship to ensure quality of training provided by host companies. ISPC also handles university accreditation forms.
Contact: Simon Samaan, Director.

INTERSPEAK
Placements and Homestays, Stretton Lower Hall, Malpas, Cheshire SY14 7HS. ☎01829 250641. Fax: 01829 250596. E-mail: enquiries@interspeak.co.uk. Website: www.interspeak.co.uk.
Since 1981, Interspeak has placed students in homestays and internships.
Programme description: Short and longer term traineeships (unpaid internships/*stages*) in Europe mainly in the fields of marketing, retail, engineering, hotel work and computing. Candidates live with host families. *Mini-stages* lasting 1-2 weeks organised for students aged 16-18.
Destinations: France (Paris, Lille, St. Malo, Limoges), Spain (Madrid) or Germany (Munich, Regensburg). Workplace placements for Europeans in England (London, Manchester, Chester).
Number of placements per year: 300-400.
Prerequisites: Students must be at least 17. Some knowledge of the language required.
Duration and time of placement: 1-24 weeks. Applicants can specify their preferred date of departure.
Selection procedures and orientation: A CV in both English and the destination country's language must be sent, as well as a letter of motivation. This should specify why an Interspeak internship is being requested, what type of placement is preferred, what the student hopes to do during the internship and what relevant course work and experience qualifies them for this placement.
Cost: Agency fee starts at £340 for placements lasting 1-6 months.
Contact: Irene and David Ratcliffe, Owners.

IST PLUS LTD
Rosedale House, Rosedale Road, Richmond, Surrey TW9 2SZ. ☎020-8939 9057. E-mail: info@istplus.com. Website: www.istplus.com.
Partner agency in UK delivering programmes on behalf of CIEE (Council on International Educational Exchange) which is a member of the Year Out Group.
Programme description: Work, teaching and language study abroad programmes including Work & Travel USA, Internship USA and Professional Career Training USA, Work & Travel Australia, Work & Travel New Zealand, Internship Canada, Teach in China and Teach in Thailand.
Destinations: USA, Canada, Australia, New Zealand, China and Thailand.
Prerequisites: Different eligibility requirements for each programme. To work in the USA participants must either be a student, graduate or young professional. To work in Australasia, they must be over 18. To teach in Asia they must be a degree-holder.
Duration and time of placements: Anything from a few weeks up to 18 months. The Work & Travel USA summer programme is open between June and October. Internship USA and Professional Career Training USA can last up to 18 months and runs all year round. Students bound for Australia, New Zealand and Canada can go out for 12 months at any time of year. Five or ten month contracts for Teaching in China start in August or February and for Thailand they begin in May or October.
Selection procedures and orientation: The application deadlines are the end of June for Work and Travel USA; mid-November or early May for Teach in China; and mid-February and mid-July for Thailand. Participants receive seven days of orientation in Shanghai or Bangkok, covering the essentials of TEFL and an introduction to Asia, its culture

and language. Students participating in Work and Travel USA receive a pre-departure orientation.

Cost: Teach in China and Thailand programme fee from £995 plus flights. Participants receive a local wage which allows for a comfortable lifestyle and on completion of ten-month contract have their return flight reimbursed. Work and Travel USA fee starts from £390 which includes first night's accommodation, employment directory and all support services. Other programme fees are listed in application materials, available on request or on the web.

LANGUAGE COURSES ABROAD LTD

67 Ashby Road, Loughborough, Leicestershire LE11 3AA. ☎01509 211612. Fax: 01509 260037. E-mail: info@languagesabroad.co.uk. Website: www.languagesabroad.co.uk.

Spanish Study Holidays Ltd, the parent company, is a member of GWEA (Global Work Experience Association).

Programme description: Work experience placements in range of countries. Any type of work experience can be provided as long as the student has relevant qualifications. A few work placements available in company's own schools.

Destinations: Spain, Latin America, France, Germany and Italy.

Number of placements per year: 100.

Prerequisites: Work placements require at least an intermediate level of the language. Most work placements are preceded by a 4-week in-country language course (see entry in 'Directory of Language Courses').

Duration and time of placements: 4 weeks minimum, normally 8-16 weeks.

Selection procedures and orientation: Applications should be sent at least 8 and preferably 12 weeks in advance. Personal monitor is appointed to oversee work placement.

Costs: Work placements not normally paid, except those in the hotel and catering industry for which students normally receive free board and lodging and sometimes also payment at national minimum wage levels. Fees included on company website.

Contact: Mike Cummins, Director.

LEARN OVERSEAS LTD

47 Greenheys Centre, Pencroft Way, Manchester Science Park, Manchester M15 6JJ. ☎0161-226 5300. Mobile: 0790 3040567. E-mail: office@learnoverseas.co.uk. Website: www.learnoverseas.co.uk.

Programme description: Short work experience placements in India for students applying to medicine and related fields. Mixture of hands-on, observation and work-shadowing in hospitals and clinics in Delhi.

Destinations: Delhi, India

Prerequisites: Ages 16-19. For young people who aspire to study medicine.

Duration and time of placements: 2 weeks with departures between August and April.

Cost: £995 excluding airfares and insurance.

LEONARDO DA VINCI PROGRAMME

c/o British Council, 10 Spring Gardens, London SW1A 2BN. ☎020-7389 4174. Fax: 020-7389 4627. E-mail: leonardo@britishcouncil.org. Website: www.leonardo.org.uk or www.britishcouncil.org/learning-vocationalpartnerships.

The Leonardo da Vinci Programme is funded by the European Union. Application must be made by organisations not individuals.

Programme description: 3-month work placements in Europe. Programme intended to enable participants to acquire professional competencies, improve their foreign language skills and enhance their CV.

Destinations: 31 countries; most recent addition is Turkey.

Prerequisites: Ages 18-35. Must have basic language skills (not needed for all destinations). Applications must be made by a national agency or registered provider, not by individuals.

Duration and time of placements: 3 months.

Cost: Placements are free; only spending money is needed.

MALACA INSTITUTO

Calle Cortada 6, Cerrado de Calderón, 29018 Málaga, Spain. ☎ +34 952-29 3242. Fax: +34 952-29 6316. E-mail: gapyear@malacainstituto.com. Website: www.MalacaInstituto.com.

Programme description: Spanish language course provider that offers unpaid internships to candidates who have attained the necessary level of Spanish. Work experience placements made through ONECO in Seville, a company that provides professional internships in hotels and tourism, architecture and design, business administration, etc. For further details of the Spanish courses, see the entry in the 'Directory of Language Courses'.

M.B. LANGUAGE ASBL

41 rue Henri Bergé, 1030 Brussels, Belgium. ☎ 2-242 27 66. Fax: 2-242 25 36. E-mail: macbaron@chello.be.

Promotes linguistic and cultural exchanges within Europe.

Programme description: Organises work experience abroad for European students aged 16-18.

Destinations: Mainly in Brussels, also Lübeck.

Number of placements per year: 100-200.

Prerequisites: Language skills (French or German), organisation, enthusiasm and self-motivation are needed. Students ought to have studied French or German at school.

Duration and time of placements: 2 weeks or longer if requested throughout the year.

Selection procedures and orientation: A CV is required, but interviews are not essential.

Cost: Work experience fees are €450 for 2 weeks between October and May and €475 in July and August.

Contact: Xavier Mouffe, Manager.

MOSCOW INSTITUTE FOR ADVANCED STUDY (MIFAS)

Lebyazhii Pereulok 8, Building 1, Moscow 119019, Russia. US office: 156 W 56th St, 7th Floor, New York, NY 10019. ☎ 212-245-0461. Fax: 212-489-4829. E-mail: info@mifas.org.

Number of placements: Large number of placements in prestigious organisations like the Gorbachev Foundation and in major companies like American Express.

Prerequisites: For advanced language students or students fluent in Russian. Most internships are filled by students from the US.

Duration and time of placements: Most internships last at least one semester (autumn, spring or summer) and are offered on a part-time basis, 10-15 hours per week.

Accommodation: Homestay or in double occupancy room in a dormitory.

PEOPLE TREE GAP YEAR PLACEMENT

215, 2nd floor, Somdutt Chambers II, 9 Bhikaji Cama Place, 110 066 New Delhi, India. ☎ 011-26174206/ 26193247/ 26163098. Email: peopletree@gapyearini ndia.com or timeless@vsnl.com. Website: www.gapyearinindia.com. London office: Flat 8, 105 Westbourne Terrace, London W2 6QT (020-7402 5576; fax 020-7262 7561).

Programme description: Internship projects cover all spheres of business such as law, business management, software development and fashion design, among others. Tries to match preference and skills of applicants with a suitable company. See entry in 'Directory of Volunteer Placements'.

PIVIAN EXCHANGE
Elbingerstr. 7, 53340 Meckenheim, Germany. ☎ +49 2225-912124. Fax: +49 89-1488-252472. Email: info@pivianexchange.com. Website: www.pivianex-change.com (only in German but soon to be translated into English).

Programme description: Internships can be arranged on Isla Margarita in Venezuela in a professional field (e.g. medicine, economics, law, tourism). Internship programme allows participants to improve their Spanish by completing a language course, and acquire professional skills abroad. Voluntary work following compulsory language course arranged in Argentina, Brazil, Chile and Peru.

Destinations: Venezuela with prospect of introducing unpaid internships, with or without language courses, in other Latin American countries.

Prerequisites: Minimum age 18. Applicants should have at least a medium level of Spanish or Portuguese, which they may acquire during a language course locally. Professional internship positions (not farm stays, etc.) are targeted at people with a higher educational and professional background.

Duration and time of placements: Some programmes as short as 4 weeks though 2 months recommended minimum.

Cost: Students with a professional background may be paid up to US$300 a month, but in the majority of cases they won't be paid anything. For future placement of interns without a language course, a placement fee will be charged. Accommodation will be arranged.

Contact: Philip Schilling, Owner.

PLACEME NZ
Leeds Innovation Centre, 103 Clarendon Rd, Leeds LS2 9DF. ☎ 0870 4020 606. Fax: 0870 4020 607. E-mail: info@placemenz.co.uk. Website: www.placemenz. co.uk.

UK agent for Internship NZ, PO Box 5110, Lambton Quay, Wellington 6005, New Zealand (+64 4-920 7646; fax: +64 4-920 7648; Dianne@internshipnz.org.nz; www.internshipnz. com).

Programme description: Provides work placements in New Zealand for UK students who need to complete a work experience module as part of their course. Can provide for all types of courses.

Number of placements per year: 50.

Destinations: Throughout New Zealand.

Prerequisites: Must be UK resident and currently on a course which requires practical work experience to be undertaken.

Duration and time of placements: 6-12 months.

Selection procedures & orientation: Apply via website or over telephone. CV is then checked for employability by New Zealand office. If eligible, application pack is sent out.

Cost: Programme cost is £660 which includes guaranteed job offer within certain fields, 6-month placement search, assistance and documentation for visa application, pre-depar-ture advice and support on living and working in New Zealand, NZ starter pack and various other services. Participants are paid NZ$10-NZ$17 an hour. 24-hour support line available in New Zealand; drinks evenings for participants are organised.

Contact: Chris Challenger, Programme Manager.

S & S HUMAN RESOURCES DEVELOPMENT
PO Box TN 1501, Teshie-Nungua Estates, Accra, Ghana. ☎ +233-27-740 5512/743 2191; +233-21-719500. E-mail: selitechnologies@yahoo.com.

Limited liability company that arranges paid and unpaid internships in Ghana.

Programme description: Practical training and summer work programmes in businesses and institutions in Ghana. Teaching programme at primary, secondary and tertiary levels.

Destinations: Accra, Kumasi, Cape Coast, Tema, Ho and Takoradi.

Prerequisites: Open to high school students, college students and professionals.

Duration and time of placements: Minimum of 6 weeks starting year round.

Remuneration: Allowance paid by employers rather than full salary. Unpaid positions for volunteers.
Other services: Optional cultural, educational and recreational tours in Ghana and West Africa. Room and board can be arranged on request.
Contact: Senyo T. Dake, Chief Executive.

SPANNOCCHIA FOUNDATION FARM INTERNSHIP PROGRAMME
Tenuta di Spannocchia, 53012 Chiusdino, Siena (SI), Italy. ☎0577-75211. Fax: 0577-752224. E-mail: internships@spannocchia.org. Website: www.spannocchia. ORG.
Programme description: Hands-on internships on a 1,200-acre community organic farm and education centre in the hills of Tuscany, about 30 minutes from Siena. Three-quarters of time is spent working alongside Italian farm staff in the vegetable garden, vineyards, olive groves, forestry operations, etc. Also Spannocchia Guest Services Internship Programme, which accepts two interns per session who work in the guest services operation doing check-in and check-out, setting up breakfast, bottling and labelling products, etc. The rest of the interns' time is devoted to structured courses, particularly in Italian language and culture.
Number of placements: 8 per session, 24 per year.
Prerequisites: All nationalities welcome to apply, although programme and agriturismo attract a mostly American clientele. A very strong interest in manual labour and community living and a positive attitude are essential.
Duration and time of placements: 3-month internships each year in spring, summer and autumn.
Cost: One-time $250 Education Fee plus student membership of Spannocchia Foundation ($25). Interns are responsible for their airfare to Italy plus international health insurance coverage and spending money.
Other services: Accommodation and meals are provided in exchange for the 30 hours per week of farm work.
Contact: Carrie Curtis Sacco, Education Director.

SUBWAY WATERSPORTS
Brick Bay, Roatan, Bay Islands, Honduras, Central America. E-mail: internship@su bwaywatersports.com. Website: www.subwaywatersports.com/Courses/internship. htm.
Programme description: Internship working in a dive shop while training towards a professional PADI Divemaster. (See entry in 'Directory of Sports Courses'.)

TEACHING & PROJECTS ABROAD
Aldsworth Parade, Goring, West Sussex BN12 4TX. ☎01903 708300. Fax: 01903 501026. E-mail: info@teaching-abroad.co.uk. Website: www.teaching-abroad.co.uk.
Teaching & Projects Abroad places fee-paying volunteers in a variety of placements in many countries (see 'Directory of Specialist Gap Year Programmes') and also arranges unpaid work experience.
Programme description: Voluntary work experience opportunities in selected destinations for business, conservation and other fields including archaeology, care, medical, media/journalism and supervised dissertations for degree courses.
Destinations: Include Bolivia, Cambodia, Chile, China, Ghana, India, Mexico, Mongolia, Nepal, Peru, Romania, Russia, Senegal, South Africa, Sri Lanka, Swaziland and Thailand. Destinations and programmes can be combined.
Number of placements: 2500 in total of which 60% are project placements and 40% teaching.
Prerequisites: Minimum age 17+.
Duration and time of placements: Very flexible, with departures year round and varying

lengths of placement.

Cost: Placements are self-funded and the fee charged includes insurance, food, accommodation and overseas support. 3-month placements cost between £895 and £2345, excluding travel costs.

WAIT A LITTLE HORSE SAFARIS (PTY) LTD

African Big Five Horse Safaris, PO Box 126, Ofcolaco 0854, South Africa. ☎ +27-83-273 9788. Fax: +27-83-276 7256. E-mail: safari@waitalittle.co.za or waitalittle@telkomsa.net. Website: www.africanhorsesafari.com.

Programme description: Equine work experience programme. Working as a back-up guide on horse safaris for very experienced riders only (minimum 8 years of daily riding). Opportunity to sit the elementary Field Guide exam in March, June or October if desired. Participants are encouraged to learn about the affinity between research and management of a Private Game Reserve.

Number of placements per year: 2 at a time.

Destinations: Farm in Limpopo Province, South Africa.

Prerequisites: Minimum age 18. Must have a minimum of 8 years of experience of riding every day. Weight limit 80kg. Must be generally fit, as days can be long. Riding ability will be tested before you are allowed to accompany any safari.

Duration and time of placements: 3 months or more.

Selection procedures & orientation: Programme can be booked up as much as 2 years in advance.

Cost: £1450 for 8 weeks, £1650 for 12 weeks.

Accommodation: Individual rooms with a communal bathroom. Meals are taken altogether, with the clients; vegetarians are welcome but will not necessarily be specially catered for.

Contact: Gerti Kusseler, Owner/Director.

Volunteering

The current British government strongly supports the ethos of volunteering and is pouring large sums of money into grand schemes to encourage volunteering at all levels, especially among the young. The Home Office is supporting the celebration of 2005 as the 'Year of the Volunteer.' The newest initiative (2005) is to create a National Community Service Corps consisting of up to one million teenagers doing full-time voluntary work. The Chancellor has indicated that gap-year volunteers could be paid £75 a week. This proposed scheme is partly modelled on the AmeriCorps programme in the US, a kind of 'domestic Peace Corps' as envisioned by President Clinton. American citizens volunteer on a full-time or part-time basis for one year.

Another idea under close scrutiny is to bestow a credit on students who volunteer, including in their gap year, to reduce the costs of university tuition. This is aimed at young people from non-affluent backgrounds who would otherwise find it impossible to justify giving up their time for a worthy cause. For example in Scotland, a new scheme called 'Project Scotland' was introduced in 2005, as a result of investment by the Scottish parliament in encouraging full-time volunteering among young people and students taking a gap year.

The *Millennium Volunteer* scheme is now well-established. It allows 16-24 year olds to get involved with a range of voluntary organisations in their communities or further afield. Young volunteers can log 100 or 200 hours of volunteering with an affiliated organisation in gain points on their Connexions card.

Voluntary work can be not only fulfilling and satisfying in itself but can provide a unique stepping stone to interesting possibilities later on. By participating in a project such as digging wells in a Turkish village, playing football with Ghanaian kids or just helping out at a youth hostel, gap year students have the unique opportunity to live and work in a remote community, and the chance to meet up with young people from many countries. You may be able to improve or acquire a language skill and to learn something of the customs of the society in which you are volunteering. You will also gain practical experience, for instance in the fields of construction, archaeology, museums or social welfare, which will later stand you in good stead when applying for paid work. Less tangible but equally marketable benefits include the acquisition of new skills like problem solving, leadership, relationship building, communication skills and self-development generally. Research based on findings of the recruitment group Reed Executive showed that three-quarters of employers in business prefer applicants with experience of volunteering.

Although this book is devoted largely to canvassing options abroad, do not discount the possibility of spending some of your gap year in the UK doing something worthwhile away from home. A number of such organisations are listed in the UK Directory later in this chapter. Unlike placements abroad, you are unlikely to be out of pocket at the end of an attachment to British organisations which sometimes pay your travel and living expenses and may even pay an allowance of about £30 a week. Note that volunteer organisations taking on people to work with children or vulnerable adults have a statutory obligation to run a police check on new volunteers. Normally it is the responsibility of the organisation rather than the individual to apply to the Criminal Records Bureau (CRB). The standard fee of £28 charged for a CRB disclosure is waived in the case of volunteers. Further details are available from www.crb.gov.uk or on the CRB Information Line 0870 90 90 811.

The Rank Foundation runs a Gap Award Scheme open to volunteers aged 18-24 who are recommended by their school/college or already active in a member charity in the Rank Charities network. Volunteers work in the UK for 6-9 months and receive board and lodging, training, travel and a personal allowance of £40-£45 a week, a bonus on completing the scheme of £600-£1200 plus a Certificate that carries some weight in Youth Work (details from the Rank Foundation, 28 Bridgegate, Hebden Bridge, West Yorks. HX7 8EX; www.rankfoundation.com).

Community Service Volunteers (CSV)

Community Service Volunteers (CSV) guarantee a voluntary placement to anyone aged over 16 who commits him/herself to work full-time away from home for at least four months. As many as 1,300 volunteers throughout the UK receive £30 a week pocket money in addition to accommodation and meals. Details can be obtained from CSV (5th Floor, Scala House, 36 Holloway Circus, Queensway, Birmingham B1 1EQ; 0800 374991; www.csv. org.uk/fulltimevolunteering)

CSV produces oodles of persuasive literature demonstrating how worthwhile a stint as a CSV volunteer can be. Projects are normally with people who need help, such as children with special needs, adults with learning difficulties, teenagers at risk of offending and homeless people. Interestingly, two thirds are women and one third men. CSV is always looking to expand the scheme and would like to see an NHS Corps, Education Corps and Care Corps created to increase opportunities to volunteer in public services.

Elizabeth Moore-Bick volunteered with CSV just after graduating from Cambridge. Studying for a degree in Classics had meant that she had led a fairly rarefied existence and she decided it was time to develop her 'people skills'. Despite initial doubts, she decided to take the plunge and began a placement supporting a woman who had been left paralysed by a car accident 20 years before. Elizabeth and another volunteer provided round-the-clock care:

It took me a lot of time to get used to this kind of role. I was really unsure of myself but felt I owed it to Barbara to see the placement through. Volunteering has certainly been a challenge and of course I doubted my ability at times. I felt like I was taking a real leap in the dark. Looking back over the past few months, I'm really proud of myself and I actually get immense satisfaction through volunteering. I won't pretend it's easy, because it isn't. I've had to do a lot of growing up myself as a CSV. I'm having to make real life decisions and take responsibility for another person. I've had to almost give up a part of myself, which is really hard. The best bit is getting things right. It's the simple things that make me feel like I've really achieved something. I'll never look at a person in a wheelchair in the same way again.

CSV has links with disability services at most British universities and a stint supporting a student might provide a useful initiation as it did for 19 year old **Jo Scluz** who supported three students at Loughborough University for her year between school and university:

After finishing A-levels, I wanted to have a break from study and give something back. Being on placement at a university means that everyone is my own age. I've made so many friends. The other students think it is really great that I get to have all the perks of student life without having to do all the study, but of course I've got that to look forward to next September when I start my geology course. Being a CSV volunteer has been a crash course in university life.

European Voluntary Service (EVS)

Thousands of young people aged 18-25 are eligible to take up fully funded placements lasting six but preferably 12 months in Europe or beyond through the EU-funded EVS programme. Full details are available from Connect Youth at the *British Council* (see entry for European Voluntary Service in the *Directory of Specialist Gap Year Programmes* and also www.europa.eu.int/comm/youth/program/sos/index_en.html).

The programme is generally regarded as excellent though the usual way in is slightly complicated. After making contact with a national agency, you have to find a sending organisation from the list of youth exchange and other participating voluntary organisations supplied by the EVS department. Alternatively, you can ask a group that you already work or volunteer for (e.g. a youth centre, women's refuge, etc.) to become your sending sponsor. When you have found a sending organisation, they will give you a password to the database of host projects across Europe. These are extremely varied, from conference centres to film workshops, orphanages to environmental projects, though all are socially based with the aim of making contacts across Europe and of benefitting the community.

The programme is open to western European nationals of all social and educational backgrounds. In fact young people from disadvantaged situations are especially encouraged. Participants pay nothing to take part. Both the sending and the host organisations receive funding from the European YOUTH programme and the volunteers get their travel costs, insurance, board and lodging, language classes, pocket money, orientation and mid-term programme all provided free. There is also a tutor in each project who is available to help with any difficulties and guide the volunteer.

Volunteering Abroad

Time spent in an Ecuadorian orphanage, an orangutan rehabilitation centre or working with street children in India can be a wonderfully liberating release from the exam struggle, whether at school or university, a welcome break before entering the next fray, the search for a job.

In a past Newsletter of the Daneford Trust, Rosna Mortuza from Tower Hamlets wrote about her decision to leave the tramlines:
I first considered volunteering abroad at an accountancy recruitment fair in my

> *final year at university. Whilst surrounded by the investment bankers, stockbrokers and consultants of the future, I realised that getting into the city was not a journey I wanted to embark on. Instead I found myself referrring to the stories of my peers who had taken gap years in India, South Africa and Cuba, which sounded like exciting, adventurous and romantic experiences that I wanted a taste of too. More importantly, volunteering offered me something challenging without always having to be competitive and under pressure. And the more I planned my trip with the Daneford Trust, the more it apealed to me as something that was going to be in lots of ways unstructured, unpredictable and unassessed.*
>
> *I'm not sure exactly why I chose to volunteer in Bangladesh. It seemed a natural choice in order to make use of being bilingual in Bengali/Sylheti and I felt I would be able to interact on a more comfortable and effective level as a volunteer. On returning, I am aware I have not changed the world or indeed a tiny place called Sylhet. What I'm certain of is that volunteering allows you to extend experiences beyond your own reality, giving a more grounded sense of self and others.*

The spirit to help others may be willing but the cash supplies may be weak. While charities in the UK might be able to cover their volunteers' basic costs, this is almost never the case abroad. We have already seen how expensive specialist gap programmes can be. The organisations listed in this chapter do not specialise in gap year students and the initial outlay of joining one of these organisations will normally be less than for the high profile specialist agencies. As a consequence they may not be so geared up for integrating volunteers as young as 18, which is not normally a problem if the volunteer does not carry unreasonable expectations.

Most voluntary jobs undertaken abroad will leave the volunteer seriously out-of-pocket, which can be disillusioning for those who think that a desire to help the world should be enough. After participating in several prearranged voluntary projects in the United States, **Catherine Brewin** did not resent the fee she had paid to *Involvement Volunteers*:

> *The whole business of paying to do voluntary work is a bit hard to swallow. But having looked into the matter quite a bit, it does seem to be the norm. While it may be a bit unfair (who knows how much profit or loss these voluntary organisations make or how worthy their projects?), most people I've met did seem to feel good about the experience. The group I was with did raise the odd comment about it all, but did not seem unduly concerned. However I should mention that most were around 18 years old and their parents were paying some if not all the costs.*

Sources of Information

The website of Volunteering England (www.volunteering.org.uk) has a listing of UK agencies that send volunteers abroad, as well as disseminating a great deal of other information about volunteering generally.

Worldwide Volunteering for Young People (7 North Street Workshops, Stoke sub Hamdon, Somerset TA14 6QR; 01935 825588; www.wwv.org.uk) has developed an authoritative search-and-match database of volunteering opportunities for 16-35 year olds which is available individually online via website or by subscription (online or CD) for schools, colleges, universities, careers offices, volunteer bureaux, etc.

The revolution in information technology has made it easier for the individual to become acquainted with the amazing range of possibilities. There are some superb websites with a multitude of links to organisations big and small that can make use of volunteers. One of the best website directories is www.traveltree.co.uk that covers gap year ideas and volunteering opportunities worldwide as well as internships, educational travel and related matters.

From Action Without Borders, www.idealist.org is an easily searchable site that will take you to the great monolithic charities like the Peace Corps as well as to small grassroots organisations in Armenia, Tenerife or anywhere else. It lists 43,000 organisations in 165 countries. Another impressive site is one from AVSO, the Association of Voluntary Services Organisations, in Belgium (www.avso.org) which is supported by the European Commission. Although TimeBank is primarily intended to match British volunteers with UK projects, it has developed an online overseas directory (www.timebank.org.uk/givetime/overseas.htm). The Japan-based Go Make a Difference (www.go-mad.org) has links to unusual voluntary projects while www.eVolunteer.co.uk includes small British and international grassroots organisations. The search engine at www.do-it.org is very useful for finding suitable projects in the UK.

The World Service Enquiry of the respected charity Christians Abroad, Bon Marche Centre, Suite 233, 241-251 Ferndale Road, London SW9 8BJ (020-7346 5950/ 0870-770 3274; wse@cabroad.org.uk; www.wse.org.uk) provides information and advice to people of any faith or none who are thinking of working overseas, whether short or long term, voluntary or paid. A frequently updated booklet *The Guide* contains a useful listing of organisations in the UK and overseas, and details how and where to begin a search for work abroad. It can be downloaded in its entirety from the WSE website or posted in exchange for a large s.a.e. with a 60p stamp and £3.

As well as being a web-based resource of voluntary opportunities worldwide, the Brighton-based Workingabroad.com will prepare a personalised report after you complete a detailed request form; the fee is £29/$42 by email, £36/$53 by post: Working Abroad Projects, PO Box 454, Flat 1, Brighton, BN1 3ZS, E. Sussex or WorkingAbroad, 7 rue d'Autan, 11290 Montreal d'Aude, France (tel/fax +33-4-68 26 41 79; Victoria. McNeil@workingabroad.com).

Students with a church affiliation and Christian faith have a broader choice of opportunities since a number of mission societies and charities are looking for young Christians (see the separate listing in this chapter of Religious Organisations). Whereas some religious organisations focus on practical work, such as working with street children, orphans, in schools, building libraries, etc., others are predominantly proselytising, which will appeal only to the very committed. Christian Vocations (St James House, Trinity Road, Dudley, West Midlands DY1 1JB; 0870 745 4825; www.christianvocations.org) publishes a searchable online directory of short-term opportunities with Christian agencies.

Avoiding Problems

Bear in mind that voluntary work, especially in the developing world, can be not only tough and character-building but also disillusioning. Misunderstandings can arise, and promises can be broken just as easily in the context of unpaid work as paid work. If you are in any doubt about an organisation you are considering working for, ask for the names of one or two past volunteers whom you can contact for an informal reference. Any worthy organisation should be happy to oblige.

Carina Strutt's experiences in Central America are uncommon, but worth bearing in mind when considering joining a privately-run project sight unseen. Before going to study in Plymouth, she signed up for an environmental project in Costa Rica where she spent most of her time painting T-shirts for the owners who wanted the task done in time for their holiday in Australia. Worse, they treated the local people with scant respect.

Other organisations are even more sinister. If you see adverts for an international organisation that goes under the names Humana People to People, Tvind or One World, check the website www.tvindalert.com.

Workcamps

Voluntary work in developed countries often takes the form of workcamps which accept unskilled short-term labour. The term 'workcamp' is falling out of favour and is often replaced by 'project'. These short-term projects are an excellent introduction to travelling for 18 to 21 year olds who have never before been away from a family type social structure. Certain projects in the UK are open to 16 and 17 year olds. As part of an established international network of voluntary organisations they are not subject to the irregularities of some privately run projects. As well as providing gap year and other volunteers with the means to live cheaply for two to four weeks in a foreign country, workcamps enable volunteers to become involved in what is usually useful work for the community, to meet people from many different backgrounds and to increase their awareness of other lifestyles, social problems and their responsibility to society.

Within Europe, and to a lesser extent further afield, there is a massive effort to co-ordinate workcamp programmes. This means that the prospective volunteer should apply in the first instance to an organisation in his or her own country (see entries later in this chapter for *International Voluntary Service (IVS), UNA Exchange, Concordia* and *Youth Action for Peace UK*. The vast majority of camps take place in the summer months, and camp details are normally published in March/April with most placements being made in April/May. Understandably, these organisations charge £4-£6 for a printed copy of their international programmes though a great deal of information is available online. It is necessary to pay a registration fee (usually £80-£130 for overseas camps), which includes board and lodging but not travel.

Many projects are environmental and involve the conversion/reconstruction of historic buildings and building community facilities. Interesting projects include building adventure playgrounds for children, renovating an open-air museum in Latvia, organising youth concerts in Armenia, constructing boats for sea-cleaning in Japan, looking after a farm-school in Slovakia during the holidays, helping peasant farmers in central France to stay on their land, excavating a Roman villa in Germany, forest fire spotting in Italy, plus a whole range of schemes with the disabled and elderly, conservation work and the study of social and political issues. It is sometimes possible to move from project to project throughout the summer, particularly in countries such as France or Morocco where the workcamp movement is highly developed.

Archaeology

Taking part in archaeological excavations is another popular form of voluntary work especially among gap year students planning to study a related subject at university. Volunteers are almost always expected to make a contribution towards their board and lodging. Also, you may be asked to bring your own trowel, work clothes, tent, etc. (see entry for *Archaeology Abroad* and the country chapters, especially Israel and France). *Archaeology Abroad* makes Fieldwork Awards of up to £500 to selected subscribers joining an archaeological excavation listed in the Spring or Autumn issues.

For those who are not students of archaeology, the chances of finding a place on an overseas dig will be greatly enhanced by having some digging experience nearer to home. Details of British excavations looking for volunteers are published in *Briefing* which comes out with the magazine *British Archaeology* from the Council for British Archaeology (see UK entry).

Anthony Blake joined a dig sponsored by the University of Reims and warns that 'archaeology is hard work, and applicants must be aware of what working for eight hours in the baking heat means!' Nevertheless Anthony found the company excellent and the opportunity to improve his French welcome.

Conservation

People interested in protecting the environment can often slot into conservation organisations abroad. One enterprising traveller in South Africa looked up the 'green directory' in a local library, contacted a few of the projects listed in the local area and was invited to work at a cheetah reserve near Johannesburg in exchange for accommodation and food.

For a directory of opportunities in this specialised area, consult the 2005 edition of

Green Volunteers: The World Guide to Voluntary Work in Nature Conservation published in Italy and distributed by Vacation Work Publications in Europe (£8.99 plus postage). Related titles from the same publisher are *Working with the Environment* and *Working with Animals*. Also look at the website for Ecovolunteer which is a specialist travel agency that links to wildlife and conservation holidays worldwide (www.ecovolunteer.org.uk).

Global Park Exchanges (www.globalparkexchanges.org) describes itself as an international sourcing agency which provides services to National Parks around the world including matching of volunteers. GPE is based in Italy (Via P. Mascagni 15, 00199 Rome; +39 06-86 01125), however its partner agency in the UK is *Global Visions International* (see entry in 'Directory of Specialist Gap Year Programmes'.

To fix up a short conservation holiday, contact *BTCV* (British Trust for Conservation Volunteers) which runs a programme of UK and international projects in more than 20 countries including Albania, Bulgaria, Slovakia, Iceland, New Zealand, Namibia, Lesotho and Japan (see entries below). Fortnights abroad vary in cost from about £500 to £700.

The international system of working-for-keep on organic farms is another good way of visiting unexplored corners of the world cheaply (see entry for *World Wide Opportunities on Organic Farms/WWOOF*). Of the several thousand WWOOF members in the UK about half are aged 18-25.

Several organisations assist scientific expeditions by supplying fee-paying volunteers, in addition to *Earthwatch* (entry below). For details of scientific expedition organisations which use self-financing volunteers, see entries for *Biosphere Expeditions* (below) and *Coral Cay Conservation, Greenforce, Trekforce Expeditions* and *Frontier* in the 'Directory of Specialist Gap Year Programmes'.

Developing Countries

Commitment, no matter how fervent, is not enough to work for an aid organisation in the developing world. You must be able to offer some kind of useful training or skill. However if you are travelling in underdeveloped countries and take the time to investigate local possibilities, you may discover wildlife projects, children's homes, special schools, etc. in which it will be possible to work voluntarily for a short or longer time. You may simply want to join your new Vietnamese, Sri Lankan or Ecuadorian friends wherever they are working. You may get the chance to trade your assistance for a straw mat and simple meals but more likely the only rewards will be the experience and the camaraderie.

Directory of Volunteering in the UK

L'ARCHE
10 Briggate, Silsden, Keighley, West Yorkshire BD20 9JT. ☎01535 656186. Fax: 01535 656426. E-mail: info@larche.org.uk. Website: www.larche.org.uk.
Programme description: L'Arche is a worldwide network of communities where assistants help people with learning disabilities to live in a congenial atmosphere. The aim is to provide a real home, with spiritual and emotional support.
Destinations: Kent, Liverpool, Inverness, Lambeth, Bognor Regis, Brecon, Edinburgh and Preston.
Number of placements per year: 190-200.
Prerequisites: Assistants need an ability and willingness to live communally and to share life with people with learning disabilities.
Duration and time of placements: Generally 12 months, although shorter and longer stays are sometimes acceptable.
Selection procedures and orientation: Enquirers are sent an information pack along with a searching application form. They are invited to visit the community, meet the members and have an informal interview with house leaders/assistants/co-ordinators. All assistants

work for a probationary period and receive a one-to-one induction with the community leader.
Cost: Assistants must pay their own travel costs and personal insurance. Free board and lodging are provided and a modest allowance is paid.

THE BLACKIE
Great Georges Community Cultural Project, Great George Street, Liverpool L1 5EW. ☎0151-709 5109. Fax: 0151-709 4822. E-mail: staff@theblackie.org. uk.
Long-established community arts venue hosting playschemes, workshops, games, arts and crafts, disabled workshops, etc. set in a former church in inner-city Liverpool.
Programme description: Volunteers are needed to work and play with the children and adults on the schemes. The jobs are shared so that everyone contributes to the cleaning, repairs, administration and playing. Volunteers live in single-sex, shared rooms, with a shared lounge, bathroom and kitchen. Volunteers bring sleeping bags.
Destinations: Inner-city Liverpool.
Number of placements per year: About 100.
Prerequisites: No specific skills or qualifications are required. Minimum age 18.
Duration and time of placements: 4 weeks minimum.
Selection procedures and orientation: A fully detailed letter is required about the person applying.
Cost: Volunteers contribute up to £25 a week for food costs. Accommodation available in annexe.

BRAENDAM FAMILY HOUSE
Thornhill, Stirling, FK8 3QH, Scotland. ☎01786 850259. Fax: 01786 850738. E-mail: braendam.house@care4free.net. Website: www.braendam.org.uk.
Since 1966 this organisation has been offering short holidays for disadvantaged families. Situated in a peaceful environment, the children can play safely and parents can rest.
Programme description: Volunteers are needed to help with the running of the house. They are required to play with the children, drive house vehicles, encourage families to participate in outdoor activities, organise and take part in games, art, crafts and group work and help with domestic duties.
Destinations: Braendam Family House set in seven acres of its own grounds.
Number of placements per year: 7 volunteers at a time.
Prerequisites: Drivers are preferred, as is some experience of children. Volunteers must be enthusiastic but patient.
Duration and time of placements: 6-12 months.
Selection procedures and orientation: 2 references and a police check required (as by law). Telephone interviews are sufficient. Volunteers receive a staff pack and induction training on arrival. Fortnightly training is given.
Cost: £40 is paid towards travel costs and board and lodging are free. Weekly spending money of £32 is paid to each volunteer.
Contact: Brian Guidery, Manager.

BREAK
Davison House, 1 Montague Road, Sheringham, Norfolk NR26 8WN. ☎01263 822161. Fax: 01263 822181. E-mail: office@break-charity.org. Website: www. break-charity.org.
Break was established in 1968 to provide a range of specialist care services for children, adults and families with special needs. This includes holidays, short breaks and respite care at two holiday centres on the North Norfolk coast, day care for adults with learning disabilities, children's homes and a family assessment unit for families in crisis.
Programme description: Volunteers aged 18-25 help at the two holiday centres with the personal care of the guests, including dressing, feeding, toiletting, bathing and getting

about and participate in their recreational programme including trips out to local attractions. Stress is placed on the importance of respecting the dignity of guests and promoting their independence. Volunteer accommodation is provided in the centres with shared common room and bedrooms.

Destinations: At two centres on the Norfolk coast, the Sandcastle at Hunstanton and Rainbow in Sheringham.

Number of placements per year: 30 (maximum 10 at any one time).

Duration and time of placements: 6 weeks to 12 months with flexible start dates.

Selection procedures and orientation: References and police checks required but not interviews. Induction and on-the-job training are given. Volunteers are able to take part in some basic training courses.

Cost: No costs are involved in joining the programme. Free board and lodging and out-of-pocket expenses (currently £45 per week) are provided. Travel costs within the UK are reimbursed.

Contact: Residential Volunteer Co-ordinator.

BTCV

British Trust for Conservation Volunteers, Conservation Centre, Balby Road, Doncaster DN4 0RH. ☎01302 572244. Fax: 01302 310167. E-mail: information@btcv.org.uk. Website: http://shop.btcv.org.uk.

BTCV is a charity established to protect the environment through practical action. With more than 150 offices, thousands of volunteers can take part in a wide range of short environmental projects.

Programme description: Volunteers help with projects such as tree-planting, repairing footpaths and dry stone walls, creating community gardens and recycling materials.

Destinations: England, Scotland, Wales and Northern Ireland. (See *BTCV* entry in 'Directory of Volunteering Abroad' for details of BTCV International Programme).

Number of placements per year: 350+ working holidays a year are organised.

Prerequisites: Energy and enthusiasm needed; no experience necessary.

Duration and time of placements: Mostly 1 week or short weekend breaks.

Selection procedures and orientation: Programmes can be booked on the website or by phone. Full training is given by qualified leaders during the programme.

Cost: All are priced differently depending on whether simple, standard or superior accommodation is offered. Week-long projects cost £70-£130 inclusive of food, accommodation and training in conservation skills.

CATHEDRAL CAMPS

16 Glebe Avenue, Flitwick, Bedfordshire MK45 1HS. ☎01525 716237. E-mail: admin@cathedralcamps.org.uk. Website: www.cathedralcamps.org.uk.

Programme description: Volunteers help to renovate and carry out routine maintenance of parish churches and Cathedrals throughout the UK. Jobs may include cleaning roof voids, conserving marble memorials, washing and painting interior and exterior walls, making detailed records of monuments and helping with gardening activities.

Duration and time of placements: 1 week workcamps, from 6pm Wednesday to noon the following Wednesday July-September.

Selection procedures and orientation: For a volunteer's first camp, a letter of recommendation is required from a Head Teacher, Senior Tutor or a person in a position of authority who is not related to the applicant. All training needed is given on the course.

Cost: Volunteers are asked to contribute £70 towards board and lodging. Many local Education Authorities award grants to Cathedral Camp volunteers. A limited number of bursaries is available to volunteers who would be otherwise unable to afford a camp.

CSV (COMMUNITY SERVICE VOLUNTEERS)

5th Floor, 5th Floor, Scala House, 36 Holloway Circus, Birmingham B1 1EQ. ☎0800 374991/0121-643 7690. E-mail: volunteer@csv.org.uk. Website: www.

csv.org.uk/fulltimevolunteering.
CSV is the largest voluntary placement organisation in the UK. It provides a voluntary placement to those aged 16+ who commit to moving away from home for a minimum of 4 months.
Programme description: CSV volunteers help people throughout Britain in a huge range of social care projects, e.g. working with the homeless, mentoring young offenders, supporting children in special schools or helping the disabled to live independently in their homes, and at the same time learn new skills. CSV volunteers are full-time and live away from home anywhere within Britain.
Number of placements per year: 1300-1500.
Prerequisites: No specific qualifications are needed. Open to UK or EU citizens resident in the UK. Other international volunteers can participate provided they apply through one of CSV's international partnerships (details from www.csv.org/ftvol).
Selection procedures and orientation: Volunteers receive regular supervision and back-up support from their local CSV office.
Cost: CSV volunteers receive £30 per week living allowance; food, accommodation and travel expenses are also provided.

COUNCIL FOR BRITISH ARCHAEOLOGY
St Mary's House, 66 Bootham, York YO30 7BZ. ☎01904 671417. Fax: 01904 671384. E-mail: info@britarch.ac.uk. Website: www.britarch.ac.uk.
The CBA works to promote the study and safeguarding of Britain's historic environment, to provide a forum for archaeological opinion and to improve public knowledge of Britain's past. The magazine *British Archaeology* is produced six times a year and lists archaeological digs to which volunteers can apply. An annual subscription costs £23. Each issue contains an insert,*CBA Briefing,* which gives information about fieldwork projects. Information is also published on the CBA website. Readers should apply directly to the projects listed on the website or in the journal, rather than to the CBA.

EARTHWATCH INSTITUTE (EUROPE)
267 Banbury Road, Oxford OX2 7HT. (☎01865 318838. Fax: 01865 311383. E-mail: projects@earthwatch.org.uk. Website: www.earthwatch.org/europe.
Earthwatch is an international environmental charity which engages people worldwide in scientific field research and education to promote the understanding and action necessary for a sustainable environment.
Programme description: Earthwatch currently supports over 140 research projects in 50 countries, addressing important environmental issues from threatened species to climate change.
Destinations: Volunteer field assistants needed throughout the UK and worldwide (Europe, Africa, Asia, Australasia, the Americas). UK projects include whale and dolphin surveys in the Hebrides and mammal monitoring in Oxfordshire. International projects range from turtle conservation in Malaysia to climate change studies in the Arctic. (Earthwatch also offer internships in their Oxford office, see 'Work Experience' Chapter.)
Duration and time of placements: Projects last between 2 days and 3 weeks and run throughout the year.
Selection procedures: No previous experience necessary. Volunteers must be over 16.
Cost: Earthwatch supporters pay from £2.50 per month. UK projects start at £165, international projects range from £295 to £1975 (excluding travel to the location).

HESSE STUDENT SCHEME
Aldeburgh Festival, Aldeburgh Productions, Snape Maltings Concert Hall, Snape, Saxmundham, Suffolk IP17 1SP. ☎01728 687100. Fax: 01728 687120. E-mail: enquiries@aldeburgh.co.uk. Website: www.aldeburgh.co.uk.
Programme description: Volunteers assist in the day-to-day running of the Aldeburgh Festival of Music and the Arts in June and prepare for the weekly Hesse Students Concert.

Duties include selling programmes, conducting shuttle buses, page turning and assisting Aldeburgh staff. Students are also expected to devise and perform a concert as part of the programme of free events.

Number of placements per year: 2 sets of 10 students are chosen for each half of the Festival.

Prerequisites: Ages 18-25. Must be a music lover, willing to help with the general running of the Aldeburgh Festival and have a cheerful disposition and a professional approach.

Duration and time of placements: One week during the Festival which runs over the middle two weeks in June.

Cost: Volunteers receive bed and breakfast accommodation and tickets to Festival events.

Contact: Carole Bidder (cbidder@aldeburgh.co.uk).

INDEPENDENT LIVING ALTERNATIVES
Trafalgar House, Grenville Place, London NW7 3SA. ☎/fax: 020-8906 9265. E-mail: enquiry@ILAnet.co.uk. Website: www.ILAnet.co.uk.

Volunteers are required to provide support for people with disabilities, to enable them to live independently in their own homes. Placements are suitable for gap year students. The work involves helping clients get dressed, go to the toilet, drive, do the housework, etc. Volunteers receive £63.50 per week plus free accommodation, usually in the London area but also in Cumbria. ILA offers a chance to learn about disability issues and see London at the same time. No qualifications are required, except good English. Vacancies arise all year round.

LOSANG DRAGPA CENTRE
Buddhist College and Meditation Centre, Dobroyd Castle, Pexwood Road, Todmorden, West Yorkshire OL14 7JJ. ☎01706 812247. Fax: 01706 818901. E-mail: info@losangdragpa.com or workingvisits@losangdragpa.com. Website: www. losangdragpa.com.

In return for 35 hours' work per week, volunteers receive good food and accommodation. In the evenings volunteers can participate in meditation classes and on weekends explore the surrounding countryside and villages. Opportunity to enjoy a break and taste life in a Buddhist spiritual community.

MADHYAMAKA BUDDHIST CENTRE
Kilnwick Percy Hall, Pocklington, York YO42 1UF. ☎01759 304832. Fax: 01759 305962. E-mail: info@madhyamaka.org. Website: www.madhyamaka. org.

Buddhist centre housed in Georgian mansion set in 40 acres of parkland.

Programme: Free meditation classes, three vegetarian meals a day and dormitory accommodation given in return for 35 hours of work per week alongside community residents. Work includes decorating, maintenance and gardening.

Prerequisites: No experience necessary.

Contact: Ann Harland, Working Visits Co-ordinator.

MANJUSHRI MAHAYANA BUDDHIST CENTRE
Conishead Priory, Ulverston, Cumbria LA12 9QQ. ☎01229 584029. E-mail: info@manjushri.org. Website: www.manjushri.org.

Working holidays at this residential Buddhist community. 35 hours of work (e.g. cooking, gardening, decorating, office work) per week in exchange for free accommodation. Working guests must contribute £50 for their food (£40 for students.)

MILLENNIUM VOLUNTEERS
Youth Volunteering Team, Room E4C, Department for Education and Skills, Moorfoot, Sheffield S1 4PQ. ☎0800 917 8185. E-mail: millennium.volunteers@dfes.

gsi.gov.uk. **Website: www.millenniumvolunteers.gov.uk or www.mvonline.gov. uk.**
Programme description: UK-wide initiative provides volunteering opportunities for young volunteers in the UK aged 16-24. Volunteers contribute time to a range of voluntary organisations, from their local Citizens Advice Bureau to joining a conservation project organised by BTCV (see entry). Scheme is run in conjunction with CSV (see entry above).
Destinations: Throughout the UK regions.
Number of placements per year: Unlimited.
Prerequisites: Ages 16-24. Useful for enhancing CVs.
Duration and time of placements: Variable.
Cost: Out-of-pocket expenses covered.

THE NATIONAL TRUST
Placement Volunteering, Helis, Kemble Drive, Swindon SN2 2NA. ☎0870 609 5383. E-mail: volunteers@nationaltrust.org.uk. Website: www.nationaltrust.org. uk/volunteers.
Programme description: Volunteer placements for people taking a break from education or work. Opportunities might include working alongside a warden or forester with countryside management, assisting house staff with running and conserving historic buildings, gardening, archaeology, education or promotion.
Destinations: Throughout the UK.
Prerequisites: Minimum age 18. Enthusiasm, common sense and adaptability are as important as experience or qualifications.
Duration and time of placements: 3-12 months, though normal minimum is 6 months. Minimum 21 hours per week.
Selection procedures and orientation: Applications accepted year round.
Cost: No wages. Self-catering accommodation available in most regions.

ROYAL SOCIETY FOR THE PROTECTION OF BIRDS (RSPB)
The Lodge, Sandy, Bedfordshire SG19 2DL. ☎01767 680551. Fax: 01767 692365. E-mail: volunteers@rspb.org.uk. Website: www.rspb.org.uk/volunteer-ing/residential.
Residential Volunteering Scheme operates on 40 sites around the UK and provides participants with the opportunity to gain practical experience of the day-to-day management of an RSPB reserve by living and working on the reserve as a volunteer. The work varies from season to season and from reserve to reserve but can include practical management tasks, work with visitors, survey/monitoring work or habitat management. Ornithological knowledge is less important than a genuine enthusiasm for wildlife conservation, an interest in conservation and a willingness to work as part of a team.
Duration and time of placements: 1-4 weeks (bookings start and finish on Saturdays). Long-term placements available by arrangement.
Prerequisites: Minimum age 16 (18 on some sites). Driving licence useful if over 21.
Cost: Free accommodation provided. Volunteers need to organise and pay for their own travel to and from the reserve, and to provide and cover the cost of their own food during their stay.
Contact: Kate Tycer, Residential Volunteering Development Officer.

SHAD
SHAD Wandsworth, 5 Bedford Hill, London SW12 9ET. ☎020-8675 6095. Fax: 020-8673 2118. E-mail: volunteering@shad.org.uk. Website: www.shad.org.uk.
SHAD (Support and Housing Assistance for people with Disabilities) enables tenants with physical disabilities to live in their own homes. Volunteers are needed to act as the tenants' arms and legs, following their instructions.
Duration and time of placements: Minimum 4 months, maximum 12 months. Work is on

a rota basis: volunteers can expect a minimum of 4 days off a fortnight. A shift system is worked by volunteers allowing plenty of free time to explore London.

Prerequisites: No experience is necessary and support is guaranteed. Opportunity to gain good work experience in a friendly and supportive environment, and to live and work with people from all over the world.

Selection procedures and orientation: Through application form, interview and suitable references. Induction and Safe Manual Handling training is provided.

Remuneration: Volunteers receive an allowance of £60 a week, free accommodation (shared with other volunteers) and expenses. Certificates and references provided on successful completion of a placement.

Contact: Su Connan, Volunteer Manager.

THE SIMON COMMUNITY
PO Box 1187, London NW5 4HW. ☎020-7485 6639. E-mail: info@simoncommunity.org.uk. Website: www.simoncommunity.org.uk.
The Simon Community is a community of homeless people and volunteers. They run two residential projects, an office and conduct outreach via meeting homeless people one-to-one and through 4 weekly soup runs.

Programme description: Workers are first assigned to residential work, and become involved in the varied tasks involved in the running of community.

Destinations: London.

Prerequisites: Minimum age 19.

Duration and time of placements: Preferred minimum time is 9 months.

Cost: None. Volunteers receive free room and board as well as weekly pocket money of £33.

TOC H
The Stable Block, The Firs, High St, Whitchurch, Aylesbury, Bucks HP22 4JU. ☎01296 642020. Fax: 01296 640022. E-mail: info@toch.org.uk. Website: www.toch.org.uk.
Programme description: Toc H organises community projects throughout the UK such as conservation and children's playschemes.

Number of placements per year: Over 500.

Prerequisites: Minimum age 16.

Duration and time of placements: Between 2 and 14 days including weekend projects.

Selection procedures and orientation: Interviews not necessary, only written applications. CRB police check compulsory.

Cost: Standard registration fee is £20.

TREES FOR LIFE
The Park, Findhorn Bay, Forres, Scotland IV36 3TZ. ☎01309 691292. Fax: 01309 691155. E-mail: trees@findhorn.org. Website: www.treesforlife.org.uk.
Programme description: Volunteers needed to restore the native Caledonian Forest in Scotland. Details of different work tasks and locations on website or in brochure.

Destinations: Scottish Highlands.

Prerequisites: No special skills required. Should be fit since projects take place in remote areas accessible by foot.

Duration and time of placements: Work weeks start each Saturday from mid-March to early June and from the beginning of September until the end of October.

Cost: £78 (£44 concessions) includes vegetarian food, accommodation in hostels, bunkhouses or Highland bothies and transport from Inverness.

VITALISE (formerly Winged Fellowship Trust)
12 City Forum, 250 City Road, London, EC1V 8AF. ☎0845-345 1972. Fax: 0845-345 1978. Email: admin@vitalise.org.uk. Website: www.vitalise.org.uk.

Charity that provides essential breaks for disabled people and carers.

Programme description: Volunteers are recruited to help at holiday centres for people with disabilities.

Destinations: Centres in Cornwall, Southampton, Chigwell, Nottingham & Southport.

Prerequisites: Minimum age 16. No experience necessary.

Duration and time of placements: Preferably 1 week between February and January.

Selection procedures and orientation: Trained care staff are always around and induction training and ongoing support are given.

Cost: None. All board, lodging and travel to centres is paid.

Contact: Volunteer Office in Kendal - Tel. 0845-345 1972.

WATERWAY RECOVERY GROUP LTD
PO Box 114, Rickmansworth, Herts. WD3 1ZY. ☎01923 711114. E-mail: enquiries@wrg.org.uk. Website: www.wrg.org.uk.

Programme description: Opportunities for week-long voluntary workcamps (Canal Camps) restoring derelict and abandoned canals in Britain.

Destinations: Camp locations listed on website.

Prerequisites: For ages 17-70. No skills needed.

Duration and time of placements: 1 week camps mostly between April and October.

Cost: £42 per week for board and lodging plus spending money.

WWOOF UK
World Wide Opportunities on Organic Farms, PO Box 2675, Lewes, East Sussex BN7 1RB. ☎01273 476286. E-mail: hello@wwoof.org. Website: www.wwoof. org.

Helps people interested in organic farming to exchange their manual labour for a chance to stay on farms throughout the UK and Ireland. See entry in 'Directory of Volunteering Abroad'.

Directory of Volunteering Abroad

AANG SERIAN ('HOUSE OF PEACE')
P O Box 13732, Arusha, Tanzania. ☎ +255-744-318548 or +255-744-673368. E-mail: aang_serian@hotmail.com. Website: www.aangserian.org.uk.

Programme description: Placements of teaching assistants and qualified teachers in ESL and other subjects at Aang Serian Community School, a newly opened secondary school in the rural Maasai village of Eluwai. Manual workers are sometimes needed seasonally for construction, tree planting and agricultural projects. Placements also available in town of Arusha, e.g. in health, nutrition, environment, appropriate technology, agriculture, veterinary medicine, text book illustration, music and video production, secretarial work and office administration, marketing and fundraising. Volunteers may have possibility of participating in 3-week International Summer School, learning from local people about culture, environment and development issues, and taking part in practical activities such as milking goats, preparing traditional medicines and making bead jewellery.

Number of placements per year: 10-12.

Destinations: Eluwai is in the Monduli District of Tanzania.

Prerequisites: 18 years old accepted provided they are emotionally mature, resourceful and adaptable. Minimum A levels/high school diploma plus ideally one year of higher education. All nationalities accepted.

Duration and time of placements: 2-3 months recommended for short-term volunteers though arrangements are flexible. Ideally 6-12 months from January or July for teachers.

Selection procedures & orientation: Applications can be made online. Orientation given on arrival plus Swahili tuition and optional drum and dance classes.

Cost: Programme fee $350 which includes above plus donation to the school. Volunteers are also asked to cover their living costs, charged at $15 per week in the village and $25 per week in Arusha. Volunteers stay in a 3-bedroom staff house at the school or in homestay in Arusha. Volunteers are also offered reduced rates for wildlife safaris, mountain-climbing expeditions, walking tours, short courses, academic lectures and visits to rural Chagga and Rangi communities, offered by a partner company in Arusha.

Contact: Mrs. Gemma Enolengila, International Liaison.

ACTION FOR CHILDREN IN CONFLICT (AfCiC)
2 Frilford Farms, Hinton Road, Longworth, Oxon. OX13 5EA. ☎01865 821380. Fax: 01865 822150. E-mail: info@actionchildren.org. Website: www.actionchildren.org.

Programme description: Volunteer placements at AfCiC projects in Kenya and Sierra Leone. In Thika, Kenya, volunteers needed to run a school feeding programme for 65+ street children and orphans, to work at a day centre for street children, teaching literacy, maths and life skills including HIV/AIDS awareness, hygiene and communication/ management, to raise awareness of children's rights in conjunction with a Kenyan legal aid group and to run a summer holiday club between July and September. In Sierra Leone, the charity works in Makeni, Lunsar and Freetown on a similar range of projects and including working with girls and young women who were abused (physically, sexually, psychologically) by rebel troops during the civil war.

Number of placements per year: 20.

Destinations: Kenya (Thika, northeast of Nairobi) and Sierra Leone (Freetown plus Makeni and Lunsar in Northern Province).

Prerequisites: Minimum age for summer projects is 18, long-term projects 21. Long term volunteers should preferably be experienced professionals in (for example) social work, counselling, education, medicine, law, marketing, mechanics, plumbing and carpentry.

Duration and time of placements: 3-12 months or 3-week placements in the summer.

Selection procedures & orientation: Applications considered year round. Country directors review CVs and applications sent to UK address followed by an interview.

Cost: £1500-£1800, which includes accommodation, food, airfares and travel insurance.

Contact: Robyn Eastwood, Volunteer Co-ordinator.

AFRICAN LEGACY
46A Ophir Road, Bournemouth, Dorset BH8 8LT. ☎/fax: 01202 554735. E-mail: explore@africanlegacy.info.

Non-profit-making organisation with academic affiliations.

Programme description: Fieldwork adventure holidays in Nigeria with research links to the School of Conservation Sciences, Bournemouth University. To explore and map remote unsurveyed ruins of ancient civilisations, their culture and environment, alongside Nigerian colleagues.

Destinations: Nigeria. Participants choose each day from a list of places where fieldwork is being carried out. Past projects have led to Nigeria's first UNESCO World Heritage Site in the savannah mountains and international publicity for the Queen of Sheba's hidden rainforest kingdom. Previously unsurveyed sites are selected every year from old books, maps and aerial photographs.

Prerequisites: Volunteers join 2-week adventure training course to learn Rapid Survey Technology on-the-job. Candidates must be able to 'wade through undergrowth or plod through soft sand in the hot sun all day and still keep smiling'.

Duration and time of placements: Visits tailored in length, itinerary and content to suit those coming.

Cost: Participants must be self-funding: costs for the first month's in-country training comprise airfare (about £700), visa (£40) and local costs for travel, food and accommodation (£250).Thereafter, posts are mainly at schools where accommodation and basic salaries

usually cover living costs.
Selection procedures and orientation: Enquiries welcomed early, as opportunities need to be planned well in advance.
Contact: Dr. Patrick Darling, Director.

AMERISPAN
PO Box 58129, Philadelphia, PA 19102, USA. ☎800-879-6640. Fax: 215-751-1986. E-mail: info@amerispan.com. Website: www.amerispan.com.
Specialist Spanish-language travel organisation with great expertise in arranging language courses, voluntary placements and internships throughout South and Central America as well as other languages worldwide.
Programme description: Many choices of volunteer placement and internships, all listed on website. Some come with free accommodation. Many set a minimum age for volunteers of 20. A typical programme would be a 2-week language programme followed by a 4-month volunteer placement in health care, education, tourism/marketing or social work.
Cost: Fees start at $1000 for a 2-week course following by a 4-week voluntary placement.

ARCHAEOLOGY ABROAD
31-34 Gordon Square, London WC1H 0PY. Tel: 020-8537 0849. Fax: 020-7383 2572. E-mail: arch.abroad@ucl.ac.uk. Website: www.britarch.ac.uk/archabroad.
Established in 1972 and based at University College London.
Programme description: Provides information about archaeological fieldwork outside the UK in its publication *Archaeology Abroad* published on CD-ROM in spring and autumn volumes each year.
Destinations: Worldwide.
Number of placements per year: 700-1000.
Prerequisites: Archaeological fieldwork involves physical labour and so volunteers need to be fit and healthy. Previous experience useful, though not essential.
Duration and time of placements: From one week.
Selection procedures and orientation: Applications from people with a definite interest in the subject are preferred. Training is generally offered to those with no excavation experience.
Cost: Annual subscription to the magazine costs £20 (£22/€50 in Europe, £24/$65 elsewhere). Fieldwork Awards available to subscribers towards cost of joining excavation projects listed in *Archaeology Abroad*.

ATD FOURTH WORLD
48 Addington Square, London SE5 7LB. ☎020-7703 3231. Fax: 020-7252 4276. E-mail: atd@atd-uk.org. Website: www.atd-uk.org.
ATD (All Together for Dignity) began in Paris in 1957 and has since expanded with branches in 27 countries across five continents working with disadvantaged communities experiencing long-term poverty.
Programme description: Volunteers can join in with street workshops in the most disadvantaged areas in Europe. The aim is to create a festival atmosphere as part of a fight against poverty and social deprivation. Longer attachments undertake projects such as running a street library in Madrid and Guatemala, youth work in Marseille, etc.
Destinations: France, Belgium, Netherlands, Switzerland and Spain in the summer.
Prerequisites: Volunteers must be over 18 and prepared to stay for the duration of the workshops.
Duration and time of placements: 1 and 2 week workshops and summer projects. Also 3, 6, 9 and 12 month placements.
Cost: Weekly contribution for board and lodging required. Travelling is at the volunteers' own expense. Health and accident insurance must also be obtained.

ATLANTIC WHALE FOUNDATION
St. Martins House, 59 St Martins Lane, Covent Garden, London WC2H 4JS. ☎020-7240 5795. Fax: 020-7240 5795. E-mail: edb@whalenation.org. Website: www.whalefoundation.org.uk.

Programme description: Whale and dolphin conservation and research in the Canary Islands of Spain.

Destinations: Tenerife with satellite programmes in La Gomera and El Hierro (Canary Islands).

Prerequisites: Knowledge of European languages is useful. For qualified divers, there is also a marine habitat survey in Tenerife for which a surcharge is payable.

Duration and time of placements: 1-8 weeks from a number of start dates between June and October.

Number of placements per year: 150.

Cost: £75 per week excluding accommodation and meals; tented accommodation available for £10 per week or £25 for bed in a cabin. Special price of £400 for 6 weeks with food and accommodation extra.

Contact: Ed Bentham.

AZAFADY
Studio 7, 1A Beethoven St, London W10 4LG. ☎020-8960 6629. Fax: 020-8962 0126. E-mail: mark@azafady.org. Website: www.madagascar.co.uk.

Registered UK charity and Malagasy NGO.

Programme description: Pioneer Madagascar programme allows volunteers to work with a grassroots organisation tackling deforestation and extreme poverty. Participants gain experience in environmental conservation, sustainable development, health infrastructure and education. Sample projects include bird and lemur monitoring, tree planting and school building.

Destinations: Southeast Madagascar.

Number of placements per year: 10-12 per group, 4 groups per year.

Prerequisites: Enthusiasm, cultural sensitivity and an interest in a future career with not-for-profit organisations. Training given. Volunteers learn basic Malagasy and gather skills relevant to working in the fields of development, conservation and sustainable livelihoods. Minimum age is 18; all ages welcome.

Duration and time of placements: 10 weeks starting in January, April, July and October. Shorter placements available by arrangement. Applications preferably at least 6 months in advance to give ample time to prepare.

Cost: Successful applicants pay for pre-project costs such as flight, insurance and visa and are required to raise a minimum donation of £2000 (different for non-UK applicants) which helps to run the NGO in Madagascar and many of the projects. Applicants are provided with extensive fundraising resources and advice.

Contact: Mark Jacobs, Managing Director.

BIMINI BIOLOGICAL FIELD STATION
9300 SW 99 St, Miami, FL 33176-2050, USA. ☎/fax: 305-274-0628. E-mail: sgruber@rsmas.miami.edu; sharklab@batelnet.bs. Website: www.miami.edu/sharklab.

Shark research station in the Bahamas.

Programme description: Active research on lemon sharks in the field. Studies consist of genetics, behaviour, telemetry-tracking, etc. Volunteers perform all tasks including research, maintenance and cooking.

Duration and time of placements: Minimum 1 month.

Number of placements: About 20 per year (5-7 volunteers at any one time).

Prerequisites: Must speak English, have a biological background and an interest in sharks.

Selection procedures and orientation: Applications via e-mail accepted year round.

Two academic references must be submitted.
Cost: US$575 per month to cover meals and housing on Bimini.
Contact: Prof. Samuel H. Gruber, Director.

BIOSPHERE EXPEDITIONS
Sprat's Water, Nr Carlton Colville, The Broads National Park, Suffolk NR33 8BP. ☎0870 446 0801. Fax: 0870 446 0809. E-mail: info@biosphere-expeditions. org. Website: www.biosphere-expeditions.org.
Programme description: Biosphere Expeditions is a non-profit-making organisation offering hands-on wildlife conservation expeditions to all who seek adventure with a purpose. Volunteers with no research experience assist scientific experts.
Number of placements: 200-300.
Destinations: Worldwide, e.g. 2005 animal monitoring projects included monkeys in the Peruvian Amazon, snow leopards in the Altai Republic of Central Asia, wolves and bears in Slovakia, cheetahs in Namibia, marine mammals in the Azores, coral reefs in Honduras, elephants in Sri Lanka and leopards in Oman.
Duration and time of placements: 11 days to 2 months, starting year round.
Prerequisites: No special skills or fitness required to join and no age limits whatsoever.
Cost: £990-£1250 (excluding flights) for fortnight long trips. Expedition contributions vary depending on the expedition. At least two-thirds of contributions benefit local project directly.
Contact: Michelle Bell, Operations Manager (m.bell@biosphere-expeditions.org).

BLUE VENTURES
52 Avenue Road, London, N6 5DR. ☎020-8341 9819. Fax: 020-8341 4821. E-mail: enquiries@blueventures.org. Website: www.blueventures.org.
Programme description: Field research is carried out in Madagascar by overseas volunteers, who work closely with field research scientists and camp staff. Volunteers learn about the fascinating ecosystems in the area, collect data whilst diving, and work with local communities, schools, NGOs and marine institutes.
Number of placements per year: Up to 12 at one time, with approximately 8 expeditions throughout the year.
Destinations: Andavadoaka, Madagascar.
Prerequisites: Minimum age 18. Must be a competent swimmer, fit enough to pass a diving medical examination, and enthusiastic to work as part of a team in a remote and often challenging environment. Volunteers with previous diving and science backgrounds are welcome, however, this is not essential as all dive training and science training is given on site.
Duration and time of placements: Departures every 6 weeks. Minimum stay 6 weeks, but volunteers welcome to stay for up to 2 expeditions.
Selection procedures & orientation: Rolling admissions. Phone interviews suffice.
Cost: £1780 for non-qualified diver, £1580 for a qualified diver excluding flights, visas and wetsuit.
Contact: Tom Savage, Director.

BTCV
British Trust for Conservation Volunteers, Conservation Centre, Balby Road, Doncaster DN4 ORH. ☎01302 572244. Fax: 01302 310167. E-mail: information@btcv.org.uk. Website: http://shop.btcv.org.uk.
BTCV is a charity established to protect the environment through practical action. There are more than 150 offices within the organisation, allowing over 5000 volunteers to take part in a wide range of environmental projects.
Programme description: Short conservation holidays in 25 countries.
Destinations: International programmes are offered in destinations in Europe, North America, Africa and Asia, including Iceland, Lesotho, Australia and Hungary. (See

'Directory of Volunteering in the UK' for information on BTCV's work in Britain.)
Prerequisites: Energy and enthusiasm only requirements. No experience necessary.
Duration and time of placements: Usually a fortnight but variable.
Selection procedures and orientation: Programmes can be booked on the website or by phone. Full training is given by qualified leaders during the programme. Some international programmes may require a little experience.
Cost: Accommodation, meals and insurance are provided at a cost from £240 per week of international projects.

CACTUS LANGUAGE
4 Clarence House, 30-31 North St, Brighton BN1 1EB. ☎0845 130 4775. Fax: 01273 775868. E-mail: enquiry@cactuslanguage.com. Website: www.cactuslanguage.com or www.volunteers-abroad.com.
Cactus volunteer programmes in Latin America are designed for people who would like to spend some time out helping people whilst experiencing diverse cultures and learning Spanish or Portuguese (see entry in *Directory of Language Courses*).
Programme description: Wide range of social, healthcare, educational or conservation customised and student service placements in Guatemala, Costa Rica, Peru, Ecuador, Bolivia, Argentina and Brazil. Examples include working at a hatchery for Leatherback turtles on Costa Rica's Pacific Coast, helping in an orphanage for girls in Cusco, Peru and a professional internship in Buenos Aires.
Destinations: Guatemala, Costa Rica, Peru, Ecuador, Bolivia, Argentina and Brazil.
Prerequisites: All volunteers take a language course in the destination country to bring their Spanish or Portuguese (Brazil) to the required level before the placement. Minimum age 18 for some projects or higher for others. Specific prerequisites may apply depending on the chosen placement.
Duration and time of placements: Combination language and volunteer programme in Latin America lasts from 5 weeks (for advanced language speakers only) to 8 weeks. Volunteer placement always 4 weeks minimum. Extensions for additional months are possible.
Selection procedures and orientation: Potential volunteers must fill out a registration form (available online) and have an interview before being accepted. All travel needs can be arranged (flights, insurance and visas). Volunteers are looked after by ground operators in the destination country.
Cost: From £389 for 5 weeks in Guatemala to £999 for 8 weeks in Costa Rica. Includes registration and volunteer placement fees, general Spanish or Portuguese language course of 20 lessons per week (length of course depends on your language level and preferences), course materials, host family with meals during language course and volunteer accommodation during volunteer placement.

CAMPHILL COMMUNITIES
The Association of Camphill Communities, Gawain House, 56 Welham Road, Malton, North Yorkshire YO17 9DP. ☎01653 694197. Fax: 01653 600001. E-mail: info@camphill.org.uk. Website: www.camphill.org.uk.
The Camphill movement, founded in 1940 by Dr Karl König, a Viennese paediatrician, encompasses therapeutic communities in 20 countries, e.g. residential special schools, centres providing further education and training for youngsters and therapeutic working communities for adults with learning difficulties.
Programme description: Volunteers or co-workers help to run the communities, often teaching or otherwise supporting those with disabilities, helping with chores, therapy, in the gardens and other work and support activities.
Destinations: 100 communities worldwide.
Number of placements per year: Average of about 10 volunteers are admitted to each centre.
Prerequisites: No specific qualifications are required, although volunteers need to be

enthusiastic, interested in people, approachable and have sufficient grasp of the local language.

Duration and time of placements: Usually around 12 months; 6-12 months in some countries.

Selection procedures and orientation: Prospective volunteers may apply to and request further information directly from the communities. Most offer formal induction and foundation courses geared to the specific tasks.

Cost: None. Short-term volunteers (up to 12 months) are provided with accommodation, food and a modest personal allowance.

CENIT (CENTER FOR THE WORKING GIRL)

Calle Huacho 150 y Jos Peralta, Quito, Ecuador. ☎/fax: +593 2-265 4260. E-mail: contact@cenitecuador.org. Website: www.cenitecuador.org.

Programme description: CENIT relies heavily on volunteers from all over the world to work in projects such as street outreach, early childhood intervention, English classes, a medical clinic and drop-in tutoring centres mainly in south Quito.

Number of placements: 60, usually for short periods, although longer term volunteers are preferred and are able to take on more responsibilities at the project.

Duration and time of placements: Minimum 2 months. Placement depends on the amount of time committed and level of Spanish.

Prerequisites: Most volunteers are aged 18-26, although there are volunteers of all ages. Should be outgoing, self-motivating and (for some projects) willing to work with children who have suffered severe neglect or abuse.

Cost: One time administrative fee $50. Volunteers are responsible for finding (and funding) their own accommodation, though advice on homestays and hostels can be given.

Contact: Sarah Guerette, Director of Volunteer Services.

CENTRO CAMUNO DI STUDI PREISTORICI

Via Marconi 7, 25044 Capo di Ponte, Valcamonica, Brescia, Italy. ☎0364 42091. Fax: 0364 42572. E-mail: info@ccsp.it.; ccspreist@tin.it. Website: www.rockart-ccsp.com; www.ccsp.it.

Programme description: Students can learn about rock art, archaeology and anthropology through apprenticeships and voluntary work. Experience can also be gained concerning how an international research centre is run, how to edit and produce books, how to run conferences and exhibitions and how to carry out an inventory and create a database.

Destinations: Italy and France, Israel, Jordan, China and Australia. Research expeditions take place to Sinai (details on www.harkarkom.com).

Number of placements: 12-15.

Prerequisites: Those with skills in Information Technology, translation, editing, publishing and specific aspects of archaeology, art history and anthropology are preferred. Individuals must be motivated and competent in English, French or Italian.

Duration and time of placements: Up to a year; minimum period is 3 months.

Selection procedures and orientation: Telephone interviews permissible.

Cost: Volunteers must meet their own living costs, but accommodation is available.

CHALLENGES WORLDWIDE

13 Hamilton Place, Edinburgh EH3 5BA. ☎/fax: 0131-332 7372. E-mail: elizab eth@challengesworldwide.com. Website: www.challengesworldwide.com.

Scottish-based international development charity organising 3-6 month placements overseas in locally-run projects which address education, environment, livelihood, health, human rights and culture.

Programme description: Individual placements tailored to the skills and interests of each volunteer.

Destinations: Bangladesh, Belize, Antigua, Ecuador, India, with plans to expand into Tsunami-affected areas during 2005 (check website).

Number of placements per year: 100 (in 2005).
Prerequisites: Minimum age 18. Placements are mostly skill-specific and require some experience of IT/computing, engineering, research, business/finance, marketing/fundraising, law, social care or teaching. However some placements are more general and require only enthusiasm and commitment.
Duration and time of placements: 3-6 months. Rolling recruitment with no group departures.
Selection procedures and orientation: All applicants must attend a one-hour face-to-face interview and briefing and training course in the UK. Placement Leaders act as in-country mentors throughout placement.
Costs: Volunteers must fundraise a minimum contribution of £1950 for 3 months.
Contact: Elizabeth Byrne, Operations Team.

CONCORDIA
Heversham House, 20-22 Boundary Road, Hove, East Sussex BN3 4ET. ☎/fax: 01273 422218. E-mail: info@concordia-iye.org.uk. Website: www.concordia-iye. org.uk.
Small not-for-profit charity committed to international youth exchange since 1943.
Programme description: International volunteer projects worldwide. Projects range from nature conservation, renovation, construction and archaeology to social work including working with adults and children with learning or physical disabilities, children's playschemes, youth work and teaching.
Destinations: Europe, Africa, the Middle East, Southeast Asia and Japan, Latin America and the USA.
Prerequisites: Aged 16-30 and resident in UK. No experience or specific skills needed though enthusiasm is essential.
Duration and time of placements: 2-4 weeks, mainly between June and September. Some longer term placements for 3-12 months available.
Cost: Registration fee approximately £90-£115 plus travel. Board and accommodation are free of charge.
Contact: Helen Bartlett, International Volunteer Co-ordinator.

CROSS-CULTURAL SOLUTIONS
UK Office: Tower Point 44, North Road, Brighton BN1 1YR. ☎0845 458 2781/2. E-mail: infouk@crossculturalsolutions.org. Website: www.crosscultural-solutions.org. See website for US address.
A non-profit international volunteer organisation founded in 1995 and a registered charity in the UK (Number 1106741).
Programme description: Opportunity for participants to work side-by-side with local people, on community-led initiatives. Volunteer programmes are designed to facilitate

hands-on service and cultural exchange with the aim of fostering cultural understanding.
Destinations: Central America, South America, Africa, Asia and Eastern Europe.
Number of placements per year: 2000+.
Prerequisites: No language or specialist skills are necessary. All nationalities welcome. No upper age limit.
Duration and time of placements: 1-12 weeks. Frequent start dates through the year.
Cost: Programme fees start at $2279 (approximately £1250) and cover the costs of lodging, meals and ground transport, plus individual attention and guidance from an experienced Programme Manager, co-ordination of the placement, Perspectives Programming activities, a 24-hour emergency hotline in the US, travel and medical insurance. Airfares not included.

CULTURAL CUBE LTD
16 Acland Road, Ivybridge, Devon PL21 9UR. ☎0870 742 6932. Fax: 0870 742 6935. E-mail: info@culturalcube.co.uk. Website: www.culturalcube.co.uk.
Programme description: Mediates between selected voluntary organisations around the world and potential volunteers. Current projects include summer workcamps and unpaid internships in Armenia, and volunteering and teaching in Ghana. Also arrange work experience in Australia and the USA (see 'Directory of Work Experience').
Prerequisites: Various age limits.
Duration and time of placements: Workcamps last a couple of weeks; internships in Armenia last 1-6 months; placements in Ghana last 1-12 months. (See Africa chapter for further particulars.)
Cost: Placement fees from approximately £230 excluding airfares for shorter placements. Placement fee for Ghana is £375 and an additional £75 per month needed to cover board and lodging.
Contact: Tim Swale-Jarman, Director.

DEVELOPMENT IN ACTION
Voluntary Services Unit, UCL Union, 25 Gordon St, London WC1H 0AY. ☎07813 395957. E-mail: info@developmentinaction.org. Website: www.developmentinaction.org.
Formerly Student Action India.
Programme description: Arrange voluntary attachments to various Indian non-governmental organisations. Grassroots development projects such as teaching children in urban slums, working with women in income generation schemes and working with deaf and blind children.
Destinations: India with projects in New Delhi, Bangalore, Mumbai, Indore, Bhopal, Pondicherry and rural placements.
Prerequisites: Anyone with energy and enthusiasm. No upper age limit.
Duration and time of placements: 2-month summer placements or year-out 5-month placements beginning in September.
Selection procedures and orientation: University recruitment talks/careers fairs take place in January and February (see website). Application deadline around the end of March; interviews held end of April. Pre-departure training over one weekend plus 1 week training on arrival. Sessions led by recently returned volunteers include Hindi training.
Cost: £550 for summer (covers placement, training and accommodation); £1000 for 5 months. Flights, insurance, visa and subsistence costs are extra.
Contact: Claire Bennett, UK Co-ordinator.

EARTHWATCH INSTITUTE (EUROPE)
267 Banbury Road, Oxford OX2 7HT. (01865 318838. Fax: 01865 311383. E-mail: projects@earthwatch.org.uk. Website: www.earthwatch.org/europe.
Earthwatch is an international environmental charity which engages people worldwide in scientific field research and education to promote the understanding and action necessary

for a sustainable environment.

Programme description: Earthwatch currently supports over 140 research projects in 50 countries, addressing important environmental issues from threatened species to climate change.

Destinations: Volunteer field assistants needed throughout the world (Europe, Africa, Asia, Australasia, the Americas). Projects range from turtle conservation in Costa Rica and coral reef monitoring in Jamaica through to rhino tracking in Namibia and climate change studies in the rainforests of Australia. (Earthwatch also offer internships in their Oxford office, see 'Work Experience' Chapter.)

Duration and time of placements: Projects last between 2 days and 3 weeks and run throughout the year.

Selection procedures: No previous experience necessary. Volunteers must be over 16.

Cost: Earthwatch supporters pay from £2.50 per month. UK projects start at £165, international projects range from £295 to £1975 (excluding travel to the location).

ECOLOGIA TRUST
The Park, Forres, Moray, Scotland IV36 3TZ. ☎/fax: 01309 690995. E-mail: gap@ecologia.org.uk. Website: www.ecologia.org.uk.

The Trust promotes creative change in Russia through youth, ecology and education.

Programme description: Volunteer programme ideal for gap year students at the Kitezh Children's Community for orphans in western Russia. (See chapter on Russia for first-hand accounts.)

Destinations: Kaluga, Russia.

Number of placements per year: 15.

Prerequisites: Minimum age 17; most are 17-25. No specific skills needed though any of the following would be useful: some knowledge of Russian, TEFL, experience working with children (sports, arts and crafts, music, drama), building, cooking and gardening. An interest in children and a willingness to participate fully in the life of the community are essential.

Duration and time of placements: 1-3 months; additional months are at the discretion of the Kitezh Council.

Selection procedures and orientation: Introductory questionnaire required to apply. Police check in country of residence required. Extensive preparatory materials are sent including feedback from previous volunteers. Informal orientation given on arrival and ongoing support including email contact with Ecologia Trust and weekly meeting for volunteers.

Cost: 1 month costs £540, 2 months £710 (includes consular visa fee) plus airfare (from £260 depending on time of year) and insurance.

Contact: Liza Hollingshead, Director.

ECO TREK PERU EIRL
Totorapaccha 769, Cusco, Peru. ☎ +51 84-247286. E-mail: info@ecotrekperu. com. Website: www.ecotrekperu.com.
Ecotourism and adventure travel agency.
Programme description: Volunteers teach English in community schools in Peru.
Number of placements per year: 4.
Destinations: Remote Peruvian towns. Often they are very poor but amidst wonderful settings.
Prerequisites: Minimum age normally 25. Must speak Spanish and be adventurous type.
Duration and time of placements: 1-6 months.
Selection procedures & orientation: Rolling admissions based on CV.
Cost: Very little. In many cases the community will provide housing and food is around $4 per day.
Contact: Fiona Cameron, Manager.

EUROPEAN VOLUNTARY SERVICE (EVS)
Connect Youth, British Council, 10 Spring Gardens, London SW1A 2BN. ☎020 7389-4030. Fax: 020-7389 4033. E-mail: connectyouth.enquiries@britishcouncil. org. Website: www.connectyouthinternational.com.
Programme description: EVS gives young people aged 18-25 the opportunity to spend time in a European country (including Eastern Europe) as full-time volunteers on a social project, e.g. working with children with special needs. Volunteers do not have to pay for their placement. Further details in the 'Directory of Specialist Gap Year Programmes'.

FBU (FUNDACION BRETHREN Y UNIDA)
Avenida Granda Centena Or4-290 y Barón de Carondelet, 3° pisa, Casilla 17-03-1487, Quito, Ecuador. ☎/fax: 2-244 0721. E-mail: info@fbu.com.ec. Website: www.fbu.com.ec.
Programme description: Choice of: introduction to Andean organic agriculture at FBU hacienda in Pinchincha; cultural homestays in which participants help host rural families with daily tasks, from milking cows to *mingas* (large group communal work); volunteer teaching in one-room rural schools.
Number of placements: 20 a month.
Destinations: 3 areas of Ecuador: county of Pedro Moncayo in Pichincha, the area of Intag in Imbabura, the community of Columbe in Chimborazo.
Prerequisites: Open mind to become immersed in a new culture; energy and enthusiasm to help. Should have basic level of Spanish (at least intermediate level for teaching programme), though Spanish classes can be arranged at the hacienda.
Duration and time of placements: 1 week minimum; no maximum.
Selection procedures and orientation: Deadline for applications 2 weeks before start date. An orientation document will be sent to facilitate safe arrival.
Cost: $100 for organic agriculture programme, $300 per month for cultural exchange and teaching programme.
Contact: Stuart Franklin, Programme Co-ordinator.

FUNDACION JATUN SACHA
Eugenio de Santillán N34 248 y Maurián, Casilla 17 12 867, Quito, Ecuador. ☎2-432240/2-432246. Fax: 2-453583. E-mail: volunteer@jatunsacha.org. Website: www.jatunsacha.org.
Foundation manages 9 Biological reserves in Ecuador. Jatun Sacha Biological Station is a 2000 hectare tropical rainforest reserve. All reserves protect endangered ecosystems critical to Ecuador, located in all four regions of the country.
Programme description: Volunteers and interns participate in research, education, community service, station maintenance, plant conservation and agroforestry.

Destinations: Amazonian Ecuador.
Number of placements per year: 800 on different projects.
Prerequisites: Minimum age 16 (with parental authorisation); average 23.
Duration and time of placements: Minimum 15 days at 5 reserves and 30 days at Jatun Sacha, year round. Majority stay for 1 month, and some stay 3-6 months.
Cost: $35 application fee plus reserve fees (including lodging and meals) of $395 per month.
Contact: Maria Jose Barragan, Volunteers/Interns Co-ordinator.

GLOBAL ADVENTURES PROJECT
38 Queen's Gate, London SW7 5HR. ☎0800 085 4197 (free phone). E-mail: info@globaladventures.co.uk. Website: www.globaladventures.co.uk.
Programme description: 3 to 12-month programme with a choice of volunteer, study and/or work placements in the USA, Brazil, Europe, South Africa, India and Australia/New Zealand. See 'Directory of Specialist Gap Year Programmes' for details.

GLOBAL VOLUNTEER NETWORK LTD
PO Box 2231, Wellington, New Zealand. ☎ +64 4-569 9080. Fax: +64 8326 7788. E-mail: info@volunteer.org.nz. Website: www.volunteer.org.nz.
Programme description: Volunteers recruited for a variety of educational, environmental and community aid programmes in many countries. Projects include English teaching, care work, environmental work, animal welfare, health and sanitation and cultural homestays.
Destinations: Alaska, China, El Salvador, Ghana, India, Nepal, New Zealand, Philippines, Romania, Russia, South Africa, Thailand, Uganda, Vietnam.
Duration and time of placements: 2 weeks to 12 months depending on the placement. Applications accepted year round.
Prerequisites: Minimum age 18 (average 19–23). No special skills or qualifications needed in most cases. All nationalities placed, although projects in China and Russia accept only Australians, Canadians, Europeans, Irish, British, American and New Zealand.
Cost: US$350 application fee covers administration, marketing and programme information. Programme fees vary but mostly US$500-$600 per month which covers administrative charges, training, accommodation and meals during training and placement, transport for volunteers and supervision.
Contact: Colin Salisbury, Executive Director.

GO DIFFERENTLY LTD
19 West Road, Saffron Walden, Essex CB11 3DS. ☎01799 521950. E-mail: info@godifferently.com. Website: www.godifferently.com.
Programme description: 2 volunteer programmes in Thailand: Elephant Mahout Project and English teaching project. Participants in elephant project learn to ride and care for elephants and about the traditional life of the mahouts. Teaching project involves teaching English to the village children (most of whom don't know any English) while living with a family and helping with household and farm duties.
Number of placements per year: 100.
Destinations: Mahout: Isan (northern Thailand). Teaching: Um-Phang in mountainous Tak province with Karen tribal people.
Prerequisites: Normal level of fitness so that you will be able to do some hiking in a hot climate. Must respect the Thai culture, be open-minded and have a sociable attitude towards the local people.
Duration and time of placements: 1-4 weeks (elephants), 1 week to 6+ months (teaching).
Selection procedures & orientation: Visits can normally be arranged at short notice.
Cost: Average cost for 2 weeks including accommodation and meals but excluding flights is £500 per person which includes homestay accommodation. Part of fees supports sustainable tourism in the villages.
Contact: Nikki Bond, Director.

GoXPLOR

47 Old Main Road; Suite 7a Cowell Park; Hillcrest, 3610; Kwa Zulu Natal; South Africa. ☎ +27 31 765 1818. Fax: +27 31 765 4781. E-mail: wildlife@goxploreafrica.com. Website: www.goxploreafrica.com.
GoXplore combines four youth travel organisations in Africa (including Wild at Heart – see entry below – and Lean on Me).

Programme description: Wildlife and community volunteering in South Africa. Wildlife projects include wildlife rehabilitation centres, monkey sanctuary, reptile parks, wildlife trauma clinics, conservation farm, game farms, cheetah project and lion project. Volunteers participate in for example capturing wounded animals, caring for orphaned animals, feeding animals, preparing enclosures, researching behaviour, counting wildlife at water holes, taking care of injured wildlife and tracking elephants. Community projects serve the local Kwazulu/Natal community as well as other regions in South Africa and countries in Africa via affiliated company Lean on Me.

Number of placements per year: Up to 800.

Destinations: Primarily Kwa Zulu Natal but also Southern and East Africa.

Prerequisites: Volunteers receive all training and orientation after arrival.

Duration and time of placements: Wildlife Programmes vary from 2 weeks to a year; Community Programmes vary from 4 weeks to a year.

Selection procedures & orientation: Applications normally processed within 48 hours.

Cost: Approximate cost of a 4-week stay on the community programme is R8,800-R10,000 (£760-£865). For the Wildlife Program, the range of prices of a 3-month stay would be R30,000-R45,000 (£2600-£3880). Programme fees cover transport, meals, accommodation and a donation to the project, including to AIDS projects.

Contact: Tracie Jones, General Manager.

GREENPEACE

Canonbury Villas, London N1 2PN. ☎ 020-7865 8100. Fax: 020-7865 8200/1. E-mail: info@uk.greenpeace.org. Website: www.greenpeace.org.uk.
Greenpeace has offices around the world and volunteer participation is sometimes welcomed locally. The Public Information Unit at the above address can send a Greenpeace worldwide address list. Greenpeace in the UK regrets that it is unable to offer internships or work experience, nor does it offer sponsorships.

GWENDALYNE

c/o Twin Training and Travel Ltd, 2nd Floor, 67-71 Lewisham High St, Lewisham, London SE13 5JX. ☎ +44 (0) 20 8297 3251. Fax: 020-8297 0984. E-mail: info@gwendalyne.com. Website: www.gwendalyne.com.
Gwendalyne is the newly launched Outbound department of Twin Training & Travel offering a range of volunteering and work experience programmes around the world.

Programme description: Volunteer programme in Peru, Costa Rica, South Africa and Ghana. Other programmes soon to be introduced in Africa and South East Asia. Voluntary projects include conservation in national parks and biological reserves; supporting people in need including orphans and elders; preparation and development of workshops to improve community health, education, sport, technology, etc.; English teaching in rural communities; rehabilitation and integration of young people living on the streets; and promotion and support of small companies.

Destinations: Peru, Costa Rica, South Africa, Ghana and expanding.

Prerequisites: Previous experience needed for some of the projects, e.g. some projects require a basic knowledge of Spanish. Must be enthusiastic and eager to help people.

Duration and time of placements: 2-12 months.

Selection procedures & orientation: Enrolment online. Processing time 1-3 months.

Cost: Sample costs are £690/£890 for Volunteer Peru (for 2/3 months); £420 for Volunteer Costa Rica (for 2-12 months); £950 for Volunteer South Africa (8 weeks plus £100 per extra week), from £380 for Volunteer Ghana.

Accommodation: Varies with programme but usually included (not Costa Rica).
Contact: Piero Donat, Global Work Experience Commercial Manager.

ICEYOM/CAMEROON VISION TRUST/WICO AFRICA

International Centre for Education Youth Orientation and Mobilisation, c/o Cameroon Vision Trust, PO Box 1075, Limbe, South West Province, Republic of Cameroon. ☎ +237 755 4762. E-mail: iceyom@yahoo.co.uk.
Several charities under single leadership. WICO is the Women International Coalition Organisation.
Programme description: Placements for all kinds of voluntary service including hospitality, conservation, community service and fundraising.
Number of volunteers per year: 100.
Destinations: Throughout Africa, especially Cameroon and Nigeria.
Prerequisites: Minimum GCSEs or high school graduation.
Duration and time of placements: Minimum 6 months, maximum 2 years with option to extend.
Selection procedures and orientation: Applications accepted year round.
Cost: £200/$350. Projects normally provide accommodation, holiday schemes, in-country transport and some allowances depending on placement.
Contact: Ms. Rosemary Olive Mbone Enie, Executive Director (Cameroon Vision Trust) & ICEYOM Co-ordinator/WICO Africa President.

ICYE: INTER-CULTURAL YOUTH EXCHANGE

Latin American House, Kingsgate Place, London NW6 4TA. ☎ 020-7681 0983. E-mail: info@icye.org.uk. Website: www.icye.org.uk.
ICYE is a non profit-making charity that offers international exchange and volunteering opportunities in many countries around the world.
Programme description: 3 main volunteering programmes: long-term (6-12 months) or short-term (1-12 weeks) in Africa, Latin America and Asia; European Voluntary Service scheme (see main entry in 'Directory of Specialist Gap Year Programmes'). On the long-term programme, volunteers spend 6 or 12 months abroad with a host family and undertake voluntary work placements with grassroots organisations, for example helping protect street children, assisting people with HIV/AIDS or working on ecological projects. The emphasis of the programme is on both volunteering and cultural interaction. The short-term programme is similar but lasts between one and 12 weeks.
Destinations: Africa (Ghana, Kenya, Morocco, Mozambique, Nigeria, Uganda); Asia (Inida, Japan, Nepal, South Korea, Taiwan, Thailand); Latin America (Bolivia, Brazil, Colombia, Costa Rica, Honduras, Mexico) and throughout Europe.
Number of placements per year: Approximately 100.
Prerequisites: For the long-term programme, applicants must be aged 18-30 and for the

European programme 18-25. The short-term programme is open to all ages.
Duration and time of placements: Year-long placements start in August, with 6-month placements starting in August or January. Short-term opportunities are available all year round.
Selection procedures and orientation: Information and recruitment days are held every month to allow prospective volunteers the chance to learn about the volunteering opportunities and the organisation. Selection is based on an interview which focuses on matching the needs of the volunteer with the opportunities on offer. Orientation for those departing in August on the long-term programme is provided through a pre-departure camp (long weekend) and an induction camp on arrival in country (8-10 days), which includes a 30-hour language course. For the short-term programme a training day is held prior to departure and induction is held on arrival (depending on the project).
Cost: Long-term placements cost approximately £3400 for 12 months (covering flights, visas, insurance, board and lodging for the year, work placement and pocket money) and approximately £2900 for 6 months. The EVS programme is free for European citizens and costs for the short-term programme vary according to duration and country (see website for up-to-date information).
Contact: Catherine Udal, Office Administrator.

INTERACTIVA
1 Avenida Sur #7, Antigua, Guatemala. E-mail: info@interactiva-school.com. Website: www.interactiva-school.com.
Programme description: Range of volunteering opportunities in Guatemalan hospitals, therapy centres, children's homes, day-care centres, etc. preferably for people in the field.
Number of placements per year: 10.
Destinations: Guatemala.
Prerequisites: People with a background in healthcare preferred. Experience working with children or disabled people sufficient. Patience, open-mindedness, adaptability, tolerance, flexibility and enjoyment in learning new things all needed to live and work in Guatemala.
Duration and time of placements: 1-12 months.
Cost: $150 placement fee. Accommodation in families costs $60 a week with 3 meals a day.
Other services: Discounted price at Interactiva Spanish school which specialises in teaching volunteers.
Contact: Amy Orellana, Project Co-ordinator.

INTERNATIONAL SOCIETY FOR ECOLOGY AND CULTURE
PO Box 9475, Berkeley, CA 94709, USA. ☎510-548-4915. Fax: 510-548-4916. UK address: Foxhole, Dartington, Devon TQ9 6EB. E-mail: v.clarke@isec.org.uk. Website: www.isec.org.uk/farmproject.html.
Programme description: Ladakh Farm Project allows volunteers to understand the pressures on rural communities worldwide and ways to strengthen threatened cultures and economies. Participants live with a Ladakhi farming family, help with farm and household work and participate in educational workshops.
Destinations: Ladakh (200 miles and 2 days drive from Kargil in the politically unstable state of Jammu Kashmir).
Prerequisites: Should be in good health to withstand the risks of living and working at high altitude. All nationalities accepted.
Duration and time of placements: 1 month: July, August or possibly September.
Selection procedures & orientation: Programme is oversubscribed so early application recommended.
Cost: £300/$500 for one month.
Contact: Victoria Clarke, Programme Administrator.

IVS - INTERNATIONAL VOLUNTARY SERVICE
Website: www.ivs-gb.org.uk. IVS South: Old Hall, East Bergholt, Colchester CO7 6TQ. ☎01206 298215. E-mail: ivssouth@ivs-gb.org.uk. IVS North: Oxford Place Centre, Oxford Place, Leeds LS1 3AX (0113-246 9900/ fax 0113-246 9910; ivsnorth@ivs-gb.org.uk). IVS Scotland: 7 Upper Bow, Edinburgh EH1 2JN (0131-226 6722/fax 0131-226 6723; scotland@ivs-gb.org.uk).
IVS is the UK branch of SCI (Service Civil International) with links in over 40 countries around the world. IVS is working at a grassroots level to reduce conflict and promote intercultural understanding and co-operation. IVS works to promote a culture of peace and international co-operation by breaking down cultural barriers and prejudices.

Programme description: Programme of projects published each April. Projects bring volunteers together to work on projects such as social projects, dealing with the disabled and disadvantaged in society, environmental and conservation projects including the preservation of heritage to permaculture communities, anti-racist and intercultural projects. Volunteers live and work together, sharing responsibilities for work, cooking and cleaning.

Destinations: In 45 countries throughout the world.

Number of placements per year: About 700 projects are available. Each project group consists of between 6 and 20 volunteers.

Prerequisites: IVS is open to everyone. Volunteers must be over 18 to be placed abroad. No upper age limit. Volunteers with a disability are encouraged to apply, although certain projects will not be accessible for some disabilities.

Duration and time of placements: 2-4 weeks, mainly between June and September.

Selection procedures and orientation: Selection is by application form and motivation statement. IVS runs Preparation Days for volunteers throughout Great Britain.

Cost: In 2005 the cost of registration on workcamps outside the UK was £145 (£120 for students and unwaged) which includes £30/£15 membership of IVS. Fees for UK projects is £95 employed, £50 student/unwaged. Volunteers must make their own travel arrangements. IVS will provide documentation for visas if required.

INVOLVEMENT VOLUNTEERS ASSOC. INC (IVI)
PO Box 218, Port Melbourne, Victoria 3207, Australia. ☎ +61-3-9646 9392. Fax: +61-3-9646 5504. E-mail: ivworldwide@volunteering.org.au. Website: www.volunteering.org.au. German office: IVDE, Volksdorfer Strasse 32, 22081 Hamburg (+49 41269450; ivgermany@volunteering.org.au).
Involvement Volunteers was established in 1988 with the original aim of making volunteering available to young people wanting to assist and learn from volunteer experiences.

Programme description: IVI arranges individual volunteer placements worldwide lasting 2-6 weeks. Projects are concerned with conservation, the environment, animal welfare, social and community service, medicine, education and childcare.

Destinations: Argentina, Australia, Austria, Bangladesh, Brazil, Cambodia, China, East Timor, Ecuador, Egypt, Estonia, Fiji, Finland, France, Germany, Greece, Guatemala, Guinea-Bissau, India, Israel, Italy, Japan, Jordan, Kenya, South Korea, Latvia, Lebanon, Lithuania, Mexico, Mongolia, Nepal, New Zealand, Panama, Peru, Philippines, Poland, Sabah (Malaysia), Samoa, South Africa, Spain, Tanzania, Thailand, Togo, Turkey, Uganda, Ukraine, UK, USA, Venezuela, Vietnam and Zambia.

Prerequisites: Anyone can volunteer, provided they are 18 or older.

Duration and time of placements: 2-6 weeks to one year. A series of projects can be arranged lasting up to one year for a multicultural round-the-world experience.

Cost: Programme fees start at £275/$400. Single placement programme fee is A$710.

Contact: Sonia Morshead, International Volunteer Co-ordinator.

IONIAN SEA RESEARCH CENTRE
Fiskardo's Nautical and Environmental Club, 28084 Fiskardo, Kephalonia, Greece. ☎/fax: +30 26740 41182. E-mail: dolphins@fnec.gr or fnec@otenet.gr. Website: www.fnec.gr.

FNEC is a non-profit-making environmental NGO which runs the Northern Kephalonia Cetacean Observation Project.

Programme description: Volunteers monitor cetacean populations by observing from the coast and from boats, by collecting opportunistic sightings from visitors, promoting awareness of cetaceans among visitors and locals, and carrying out underwater research on seahorses in collaboration with the National Aquarium of Plymouth.

Number of placements per year: 50.

Destinations: Kephalonia, Ionian Islands, Greece.

Prerequisites: All ages. No training needed. Horse patrols organised for people with extensive riding experience. Participants can undertake PADI scuba diving instruction.

Duration and time of placements: 3-week placements; more than one period can be applied for (see website www.fnec.gr/dolphin/availab.htm).

Selection procedures & orientation: Applications can be made online; CVs can be sent by email to dolphins@fnec.gr.

Cost: €550 for each 3-week period, excluding flights and insurance. Cost can include PADI Scuba Diving instruction.

Contact: Stacey Hames, Volunteer Co-ordinator.

IRACAMBI ATLANTIC RAINFOREST RESEARCH AND CONSERVATION CENTER

Fazenda Iracambi, Caixa Postal No 1, Rosário da Limeira, CEP 36878-000, Minas Gerais, Brazil. ☎ +55 32-3721 1436. Fax: +55 32-3722 4909. E-mail: iracambi@iracambi.com. Website: www.iracambi.com.

Conservation organisation based on a working farm, whose mission is to make conservation of the rainforest more attractive than its destruction.

Programme description: Volunteers needed in four areas of research: land use planning, forest restoration, income generating alternatives and community understanding and engagement. Help also needed in centre operations including marketing, fundraising, administration, environmental education and outreach programme, IT/web, GIS and GPS mapping work and working on the trails.

Number of placements per year: 110.

Prerequisites: Any skills or expertise that can help the centre to achieve its aims. Minimum wage 18, average 25.

Duration and time of placements: Minimum 1 month. Normal maximum 6 months because of visa restrictions.

Selection procedures & orientation: Rolling acceptance year round. After receiving application and CV, volunteer's skills are matched with task. Support and advice available throughout stay.

Cost: $350 for first month, $330 for second month, $310 for third and subsequent months. Cost includes full board accommodation in shared housing.

Contact: Sarah Fletcher, Project Co-ordinator.

THE KAREN HILLTRIBES TRUST

Midgley House, Heslington, York YO10 5DX. ☎01904 411891. Fax: 01904 430580. E-mail: enquiries@karenhilltribes.org.uk. Website: www.karenhilltribes. org.uk.

Programme description: Volunteer placements for teaching and also installing water systems in Thailand. Volunteers live with host families, often the village headman.

Destinations: Upland and hill communities of Northwest Thailand.

Number of placements per year: About 20.

Prerequisites: Candidates should be team players, with maturity and a genuine interest in helping the Karen people. No TEFL qualification required.

Duration and time of placements: 6 months or longer, starting October or January.

Selection procedures and orientation: Interviews held in York or London or by phone if necessary. Pre-departure briefings, meetings with past volunteers, training weekend and

continuing support given. Paid manager in Thailand.
Cost: £1500. Advice given on fund-raising and sponsorship (also on website).
Contact: Penelope Worsley, Director.

KIYA SURVIVORS
38 Hove Park Villas, Hove, East Sussex BN3 6HG. ☎01273 721092. Fax: 01273 732875. E-mail: info@kiyasurvivors.org or volunteers@kiyasurvivors.org. Website: www.kiyasurvivors.org.
Programme description: Volunteers work as assistant teachers/therapists, help organise art, drama, sports, music and dance workshops, alongside professionals.
Number of placements per year: 40.
Destinations: 2 projects in Peru: Mama Cocha children's home and Runa Wasi Rehabilitation Centre in Los Organos, Piura or The Rainbow Centre in Urubamba, Cusco.
Prerequisites: No experience needed although Spanish helps with any experience of working with children or adults with learning disabilities. Should be enthusiastic, caring individuals who are able to work alone or as a team using their own initiative.
Duration and time of placements: 2, 3, 4 or 6 month placements.
Selection procedures & orientation: All programmes include a 1-week training programme upon arrival. Spanish course also available. Onsite co-ordinator assists volunteers in writing an individual work plan to ensure they are placed in the correct area.
Cost: £1550-£3500.
Contact: Jan Sampson, UK Co-ordinator (jansarasampson@yahoo.co.uk).

MA'ON SAN SIMON HOME FOR DISABLED PEOPLE
Maa'le Zee'v 9, PO Box 8447, Gonen, Jerusalem 91083, Israel. ☎ +972-2-6792188 or +972-2-6793416. Fax: +972-2-6792188. E-mail: ofra_gur@hotmail.com. Website: none.
Home for disabled adults, located in southwest Jerusalem near the San Simon Greek monastery.
Programme description: Volunteers primarily assist the residents with daily needs by providing physical care and moral support. Activities include helping out of bed, showering, using the toilet, dressing/undressing, and serving food. Volunteers also accompany residents to the supermarket, bank, clinic, hospital, park and outings.
Duration and time of placements: 3 months minimum to 1½ years maximum.
Prerequisites: Previous experience with disabled people preferred but not essential. Medical insurance, certificate of good health and 2 recommendations required.
Remuneration: Pocket money $100 a month in addition to housing, 2 meals a day, laundry and free internet facility.
Contact: Ofra Gur-Ary, Social Worker & Volunteers Co-ordinator.

MONDOCHALLENGE
Milton House, Gayton Rd, Milton Malsor, Northampton NN7 3AB. ☎01604 858225. Fax: 01604 859323. E-mail: info@mondochallenge.org. Website: www. mondochallenge.org.
UK-based organisation sending volunteers to work on community-based teaching and orphanage projects, as well as business development and medical projects in Africa, Asia and South America.
Programme description: Volunteers of all ages including some in their gap year (pre- and post-university) are sent to villages in a number of countries, mainly to teach.
Destinations: Nepal, India (Darjeeling region and Ladakh), Sri Lanka, Tanzania (Arusha, Longido and Pangani regions), Kenya, Gambia, Ecuador and Chile (Monte Grande).
Number of placements per year: 200 including 60 to Tanzania.
Prerequisites: All nationalities accepted. Minimum qualification is A-level or equivalent in subjects to be taught. Must be able to cope with remote posting and to relate to people of other cultures.

Duration and time of placements: 6 weeks to 6 months with start dates throughout the year; average 3 months.
Cost: £1000 for 3 months. Board and lodging in local family homes costs an extra £15 (approximately) per week.
Contact: Anthony Lunch, Director.

NATIONAL MEDITATION CENTER

Rt 10, Box 2523, Jacksonville, TX 75766, USA. ☎903-589-5706. E-mail: nmc@nationalmeditation.org. Website: www.nationalmeditation.org.
Programme description: Volunteer placements in Texas; unpaid volunteer and internship positions, work experience in Thailand and the Philippines, June and December. Preferably for small groups rather than individuals.
Destinations: Texas and Asia, Thailand and Philippines mainly.
Number of placements per year: 100.
Duration and time of placements: 8 weeks in Texas, 2-4 weeks in Asia.
Cost: $850-$3250 excluding airfares.
Contact: Amie Hughes.

ORANGUTAN FOUNDATION

7 Kent Terrace, London, NW1 4RP. ☎020-7724 2912. Fax: 020-7706 2613. E-mail: info@orangutan.org.uk. Website: www.orangutan.org.uk.
Programme description: Volunteers are based in the Tanjung Puting National Park in Kalimantan, Indonesian Borneo. Volunteers spend the majority of their time at Camp Leakey, the historical research site of Dr Biruté Galdikas but may work in other areas of the Park or in the Lamandau Reserve, a new release site for rehabilitated orangutans. Previous projects have included: general infrastructure repairs, trail cutting, constructing guardposts, and orangutan release sites. Volunteers should note that there is no direct work with orangutans.
Number of placements per year: 40-48.
Duration and time of placements: 6 weeks, 3 teams of no more than 12, departing May, June and August. There will be 4 teams in 2006, dates to be confirmed.
Prerequisites: Participants must be at least 18 and be members of the Orangutan Foundation. They must work well in a team, be fit and healthy and adaptable to difficult and demanding conditions.
Selection procedures and orientation: All potential UK volunteers are expected to attend an interview at the Foundation office in London. Phone interviews can be conducted for non-UK applicants. Successful UK applicants are expected to attend a pre-departure briefing day.
Cost: £500, includes all accommodation, food, equipment, materials and transport for the duration of the programme but does not include international and internal travel to the project site.
Contact: Claire Webber, Volunteer Co-ordinator (claire@orangutan.org.uk).

PEOPLE TREE GAP YEAR PLACEMENT

215, 2nd floor, Somdutt Chambers II, 9 Bhikaji Cama Place, 110 066 New Delhi, India. ☎011-26174206/ 26193247/ 26163098. Email; peopletree@gapyearini ndia.com or timeless@vsnl.com. Website: www.gapyearinindia.com. London office: Flat 8, 105 Westbourne Terrace, London W2 6QT (020-7402 5576; fax 020-7262 7561).
Programme description: Volunteers sent to teaching projects and orphanage schools in rural and semi-urban areas. Some schools involve vocational work and farming. Another volunteer project located on an island with no electricity revolves around community development and women's issues. Environmental and conservation projects also available in South and East India, especially to discourage local people from cutting down trees. Placement available on a 'what's on' magazine in New Delhi. Some clients prefer to pursue

an interest such as in yoga, textiles, Ayurveda, languages, sculpture, etc.
Number of placements per year: 300+.
Destinations: India, Nepal and Sri Lanka.
Prerequisites: Only that volunteers can demonstrate an ability to care and a passion for contributing to various initiatives.
Duration and time of placements: 2 weeks to 6 months. Preferred minimum 1 month.
Selection procedures & orientation: Online application. Rolling admission. Fortnightly meeting with a local advisor and 24-hour emergency contact line. Orientation given on arrival in India.
Cost: From $600 for orphanage placement. A part of the placement fee goes to support the projects.
Contact: Sid Tawadey, Project Placement Co-ordinator.

PRETOMA (PROGRAMA RESTAURACIÓN DE TORTUGAS MARINAS)
Apdo. Postal 1203-1100 Tibas, San José, Costa Rica. ☎(506) 241-5227. Fax: (506) 236-6017. E-mail: alexandergaos@tortugamarina.org. Website: www.tortugamarina.org.
Programme description: Sea turtle conservation activities include walking the 4km beach on a nightly basis looking for nesting sea turtles. When found, turtles are measured, tagged and checked. Nests are then placed and protected in the project hatchery. Hatchery duties include monitoring for hatching baby turtles and releasing them into the ocean, as well as post-hatching nest excavations to determine success rates. Plenty of time for relaxation. Opportunities to involve oneself in cultural events and the local school are abundant.
Number of placements per year: 100.
Destinations: Opportunities available at two sites in Costa Rica: Punta Banco and San Miguel.
Prerequisites: All ages and nationalities. Volunteers should be fairly fit for nightly walks and be comfortable in a rustic environment.
Duration and time of placements: 2 weeks to 5 months between mid-July and just before Christmas.
Selection procedures & orientation: Applications accepted on first-come, first served basis.
Cost: $280 for 1 week up to $1430 for 8 weeks including room and board. Homestay accommodation is cheaper ($150 for one week, $920 for 8 weeks). Volunteer payments support the work of the NGO.
Contact: Alexander Gaos, Beach Projects Director.

RIGHT TO PLAY
65 Queen Street West, Thomson Building, Suite 1900, Box 64, Toronto, Ontario M5H 2M5, Canada. ☎416-498-1922. Fax: 416-498-1942. E-mail: recruitment@righttoplay.com. Website: www.righttoplay.com.
International NGO (formerly called Olympic Aid) that is committed to improving the lives of disadvantaged children and their communities through Sport for Development.
Programme description: Teams of volunteer coaches are sent into communities to implement sport and play programme known as 'SportWorks', sometimes combined with health education programme (e.g. to teach the importance of vaccination, HIV/AIDS prevention and physical fitness)
Destinations: Azerbaijan, Benin, Ethiopia, Ghana, Guinea, Kenya, Mali, Mozambique, Sierra Leone, Tanzania, Uganda, Zambia, Pakistan, Thailand.
Prerequisites: Strong passion for sport and community, experience in coaching and leadership development, particularly training of trainers. Looking for volunteers who have previous experience of implementing projects in an international development context.
Duration and time of placements: one-year placements.
Remuneration: RTP pays for training expenses, in-field accommodation and transport, health insurance and vaccination costs up to C$500. Also pays an honorarium of US$8000

for 1 year.
Contact: Don Christie, Recruitment Officer.

RURAL COMMUNITY DEVELOPMENT PROGRAM (RCDP)
Tashindol Marga 95/48 Kalanki-14, Kathmandu (GPO Box 8957), Nepal. ☎977-1-427 8305. Fax: +977-1-428 2994. E-mail: rcdpn@mail.com.np. Website: www.rcdpnepal.org.
Programme description: Himalayan Volunteers programme places volunteers in Nepal in 4 sectors: teaching in a school, orphanage placement, health sector project and conservation project.
Number of placements per year: 350.
Destinations: Nepal (Kathmandu Valley, Pokhara, Chitwan) and more recently India (Delhi and environs).
Prerequisites: All ages; minimum age 18. Volunteers must have good spoken English.
Duration and time of placements: 2 weeks to 5 months. Programme starts on the 9th and 23rd of every month.
Selection procedures & orientation: Applications should arrive at least a month before proposed start.
Cost: $225 registration fee, $300 for 2-week language and cultural immersion programme (including 3-night stay at Royal Chitwan National Park), $150 per month for land costs (room, food, supervision and associated costs throughout), and $190 for seven days Annapurna trek and Pokhara visit.
Contact: Rajan Bajracharya, Country Co-ordinator.

SOFT POWER EDUCATION
PO Box 1346, Jinja, Uganda, East Africa. ☎+256 78 306614. E-mail: admin@softpowereducation.com/ georgiegirl@source.co.ug. Website: www.softpowereducation.com.
British registered non-religious charity to enhance the education facilities for hundreds of Ugandan children.
Programme description: Project to refurbish 20 government primary schools in the region. Work involves assisting with building projects, painting teaching aids in classrooms, assistant teaching, and hosting art & sports workshops.
Number of placements per year: 30 individuals plus 7 groups of organised volunteers from universities/colleges.
Prerequisites: Minimum age 18, no maximum. No qualifications needed. All nationalities accepted. All that is needed is a sense of humour, independence, creativity and initiative. Anyone with experience or skills in building is a bonus.
Duration and time of placements: 1 day to 3 months.
Selection procedures & orientation: Arrival should be arranged at least a couple of months in advance.
Cost: Volunteers must cover their own living and travel expenses as well as a donation to the charity. Recommended amount is £50 a week.
Accommodation: Camping, dorms or living within the local community. Guest houses in Jinja are also an option, but they are located some distance away from the network of schools which means longer travelling times to site.
Contact: Georgie Higginson, Project Manger.

SPORTS COACHES OUTREACH (SCORE)
2nd Floor, Satbel Centre, 2 de Smit Street, Greenpoint (PO Box 4989, Cape Town, 8000), South Africa. ☎21-4183140. Fax: 21-4181549. E-mail: info@score.org.za. Website: www.score.org.za; www.scorefoundation.nl (Dutch website).
In operation since 1991 implementing sports and community development programmes.
Programme description: SCORE is a South African NGO which uses volunteers to teach PE and coach and train children, youth and adults in poor communities in a variety of

sports. Volunteers either live in a programme house or with a local family.

Destinations: Rural and urban locations throughout South Africa: Western Cape, Eastern Cape, Northern Cape, Mpumalanga Province, Limpopo Province and North-West. Some volunteers work in Namibia and Zambia as well.

Number of placements per year: 10.

Prerequisites: Minimum age 20 unless volunteer has specialist background. Volunteers should have skill, experience, enthusiasm, creativity and an ability to adjust to other cultures. Variety of nationalities accepted including British and North American.

Duration and time of placements: Students: 6 or 12 months; graduates: 12 months. Starting in July or January.

Selection procedures & orientation: Applications for January intake should be submitted by 15th September, and for July intake by 15th March.

Cost: Fee of €2500 covers health insurance, room, board, transport within South Africa, orientation and back-up but not international airfares. Airfares are covered for EU citizens. Volunteers receive nominal monthly stipend.

Contact: Jaap Meerhoff, Head of Recruitment and Training, Stichting SCORE (stichting.score@planet.nl).

SUDAN VOLUNTEER PROGRAMME
34 Estelle Road, London NW3 2JY. ☎/fax: 020-7485 8619. E-mail: davidsvp@blueyonder.co.uk.

Programme description: SVP works with gap year students, undergraduates and graduates who are native English speakers and who wish to teach English in Sudan. Teaching tends to be informal in style, with only 4-5 hours of contact a day. Volunteers can plan their own teaching schemes, such as arranging games, dramas, competitions and tests for assessing skills learned by the students.

Destinations: Sudan, mostly in and around Khartoum.

Prerequisites: Minimum age 18. TEFL certificate and knowledge of Arabic are helpful but not obligatory. Volunteers must be in good health and be native English speakers. It is preferred that volunteers have already had experience of travelling in developing countries.

Duration and time of placements: Around 6 months from early September, late December or mid-June.

Selection procedures and orientation: Application forms must be completed and sent with a £5 fee. Two referees are also required. Prior to departure, selection interviews, orientation and briefings take place. Volunteers are required to write a report of their experiences and to advise new volunteers.

Cost: Volunteers must raise the cost of the airfare to Sudan (currently £455 for ticket valid for 12 months) plus £60 (cost of the first 3 months insurance) plus any travel costs to selection interviews and briefings. SVP covers living expenses, accommodation and insurance beyond the initial 3 months.

Contact: David Wolton.

TANZED
80 Edleston Road, Crewe, Cheshire CW2 7HD. ☎01270 509994. E-mail: enquiries@tanzed.org. Website: www.tanzed.org.

Charity that recruits teachers to work alongside Tanzanian teachers in rural government primary schools.

Programme description: The aim is to improve the level of English language teaching by the Tanzanian teachers.

Destinations: Morogoro region of Tanzania.

Number of placements per year: 12-20.

Prerequisites: Teachers and graduates able to commit to 12 months working and living with the local community at grassroots level.

Duration and time of placements: Minimum 1 year; departures in January and

September.
Cost: £2000 to cover airfare, insurance, training in Morogoro and some administrative costs. Volunteer teachers receive living expenses on a local scale.

THAI-EXPERIENCE.ORG
88 Mittaparb Rd, Meaung District, Nongkhai 43000, Thailand. ☎ +66 (0)42 420 903. Mobile: +66 (0)1 934 55 81 or +66 (0)7 222 53 26. E-mail: apply@Thai-Experience.org. Website: www.Thai-Experience.org.
Programme description: Teaching English, computer skills or vocational skills to disadvantaged children and/or adults in Thailand. Maintaining computers.
Number of placements per year: 80.
Destinations: Mainly Northeastern Thailand (Isan province).
Prerequisites: Minimum age 18. Good command of English language. Computer trainers need computer skills, open mind and patience to deal with the different environment. No TEFL certificate needed as volunteers do not replace teachers but assist them, encouraging students to use their English language skills to speak, practise and motivate them to learn more.
Duration and time of placements: 1 week-1 year; typically 2-3 months.
Selection procedures & orientation: Application can be made online. Volunteers can be placed at short notice but 2-3 months advance warning preferred.
Cost: €150 for 1 week, €400 for 1 month, €250 per month if staying 6 months or more. Fees include orientation, pre-arranged accommodation, travels within the project and support before and during the stay.
Contact: Sabine Lindemann, Project Manager.

UNA EXCHANGE
United Nations Association, Temple of Peace, Cathays Park, Cardiff CF10 3AP, Wales. ☎029-2022 3088. Fax: 029-2022 2540. E-mail: info@unaexchange.org. Website: www.unaexchange.org.
Non-political and non-religious organisation which aims to promote international understanding and community development through international voluntary projects.
Programme description: Volunteers from the UK travel overseas to work on short-term projects of benefit to local communities. These include renovation, environmental/conservation, archaeological and cultural projects as well as projects working with refugees, the elderly and people with special needs. The main volunteer programme covers countries in Europe, North America, North Africa and East Asia. The North-South Programme enables volunteers to work in sub-Saharan Africa, Latin America and Southeast Asia.
Destinations: Projects in over 60 countries worldwide including off-the-beaten-track countries like Lithuania, Macedonia, Argentina, South Korea, Mongolia and Namibia.
Prerequisites: Most projects are for volunteers aged 18+ although a few in Europe accept volunteers from 15. Older volunteers also welcome.
Duration and time of placements: Usually 2-3 weeks though longer term volunteering is possible.
Selection procedures and orientation: No formal selection procedure; places allocated on first come first served basis. Volunteers on the North-South Programme are required to participate in a training weekend in Cardiff before applying. Training is available for volunteers on other UNA Exchange programmes.
Cost: £110-£160 registration fee covers food and accommodation. Some projects require additional fees.
Contact: Xenia Davis, Exchanges Co-ordinator.

LA UNION CENTRO LINGUISTICO
1A Avenida Sur No. 21, Antigua, Guatemala. ☎/fax: (502) 7832-7337. E-mail: info@launion.edu.gt. Website: www.launion.edu.gt.

Organisation for sharing Spanish language and Guatemalan culture run by a group of experienced Guatemalan Spanish teachers (see entry in 'Directory of Language Courses').

Programme description: Voluntary placements in a day-care centre (for the children of single impoverished mothers), in a hospital, in a home for elderly people, rebuilding homes and (for longer stays) as assistants in schools.

Number of participants: 100.

Duration of courses: Flexible from 1 or 2 weeks to many months.

Cost: None, though volunteers pay for their accommodation.

Accommodation: Homestays with full board cost $60 a week.

Contact: Juan Carlos Martinez, General Director.

VESL (VOLUNTEERS FOR ENGLISH IN SRI LANKA)
68 Derinton Road, London SW17 8JB. ☎020-8682 3986. E-mail: info@vesl.org. Website: www.vesl.org.

Programme description: VESL is a charity registered in the UK that sends volunteers to work in pairs to run English language summer schools in remote communities in the Southern, Central and North Eastern Provinces of Sri Lanka.

Number of placements per year: Up to 40.

Prerequisites: Minimum age 18, though most volunteers are older. Volunteers should be enthusiastic, motivated and up for a challenge. TEFL experience and some experience overseas are helpful but not a requirement.

Duration and time of placements: Departure mid-July and the placements run for 4½ weeks. Volunteers are free to travel around Sri Lanka after their placement is finished.

Selection procedures & orientation: Applications accepted between November and the deadline at the end of February. All candidates are invited for interviews which normally take place in March.

Cost: £600 includes induction and training day, in-country travel, insurance, visas, food, accommodation and comprehensive back-up and support.

Contact: Tom Harrison, Chair of Trustees.

VILLAGE EDUCATION PROJECT (KILIMANJARO)
Mint Cottage, Prospect Road, Sevenoaks, Kent TN13 3UA. ☎01732 459799/ 743000. E-mail: info@kiliproject.org. Website: www.kiliproject.org.

This organisation was set up in 1994 and is run by an ex-London lawyer, who is one of the few Europeans to be given permission to teach in Tanzanian government primary schools. The Central Ministry of Education and Culture are in full support of the work of the charity.

Programme description: Volunteers teach English as a foreign language in two primary schools in the Marangu area. Class sizes range between 17 and 40 and good textbooks and some teaching aids are available for each class. Extra periods are assigned where volunteers can read with the children or conduct art, sport or other extra-curricular activities.

Destinations: Marangu, Tanzania.

Number of placements per year: 8-12 UK students.

Prerequisites: Good spoken English and an outgoing personality are required. Art/sport/ music skills are an advantage.

Duration and time of placements: 8-9 months, starting in January.

Selection procedures and orientation: On receipt of an application, an interview is arranged. Pre-departure training is given, including preparing for work, using the textbooks and basic Swahili. A project leader in Tanzania meets the students and helps them settle in. Local staff are always on hand to support volunteers.

Cost: £2500 must be paid to the charity. Additional costs include living expenses, medical insurance and initial entry visas (currently £38).

Contact: Katy Allen, Trustee and Project Leader.

VOLUNTEER IN AFRICA

10 Tackie Tawiah Avenue Road, Adabraka, Accra, Ghana. Postal address: PO Box AN 6552, Accra-North, Ghana. ☎ +233-27-7346419. E-mail: ghanaprograms@yahoo.com. Website: www.volunteeringinafrica.org.

Programme description: Volunteer placements in educational, social or environmental projects in Ghana. Educational placements involve assisting in teaching the English language, maths, Christian religion, art and crafts, sports, singing or extracurricular activities at both government and private nursery, primary and junior secondary schools. Social projects include caring for orphans, destitute and abandoned children by assisting in cooking, laundry, bathing, feeding and teaching the children. Environmental preservation work includes assisting in filling seed bags with soil and tree seeds, watering seedlings, digging the ground and planting trees.

Destinations: Various regions of Ghana.

Prerequisites: Minimum secondary school education. Special skills, professional qualifications or previous experience not required. Volunteers should have strong work ethic, ability to work independently or as part of a team, be willing to follow directions, and have good interpersonal skills, flexibility, and a sense of humour. Health placements available to medical students.

Duration and time of placements: 1-12 weeks at any time of year. Work 5-6 hours a day, 4-5 days a week.

Selection procedures & orientation: Minimum 1 week's notice to arrange a placement.

Cost: Most placements cost £377 for 1-4 weeks, £537 for 6 weeks, £697 for 8 weeks, £857 for 10 weeks and £1017 for 12 weeks. Includes private room with host families and all meals, airport pick-ups and supervision. Fees for environmental programme £577 for 1-4 weeks, £827 for 6 weeks, £1077 for 8 weeks, of which just over a third goes to support the project. All fees payable on arrival.

Contact: Rich Aidoo.

VOLUNTEER LATIN AMERICA

PO Box 465, Brighton, East Sussex BN50 9AT. ☎ 01273 606899. E-mail: info @volunteerlatinamerica.com. Website: www.volunteerlatinamerica.com

Volunteer Latin America tries to link international volunteers with hundreds of environmental and humanitarian organisations in Mexico, Central and South America that provide a source of affordable voluntary work and internships.

Programme description: Recruits directly for a sea turtle conservation programme on the Caribbean coast of Costa Rica. Volunteers carry out night patrols and take shifts monitoring the hatchery. Other daytime work may involve beach cleanup and small projects, including initial construction of the hatcheries.

Number of placements per year: 60.

Prerequisites: Students, travellers or anyone interested in hands-on conservation work and data collection with an endangered species. Should be fit and healthy and willing to work in uncomfortable conditions. Some knowledge of Spanish is useful but not essential.

Duration and time of placements: Minimum 1 week during the nesting season for Leatherback turtles (beginning of March to end of July) or for Hawksbill turtles (June to November).

Cost: $7 (£3.70) per day plus £50 ($90) registration fee.

Contact: Stephen Knight, Manager.

VOLUNTEER NEPAL NATIONAL GROUP

Jhaukhel 4, Bhaktapur, Nepal. ☎ 1-661 3724. E-mail: info@volnepal.np.org. Website: www.volnepal.np.org.

Community-based non-profit organisation that co-ordinates local and international work camps to empower community self-help initiatives.

Programme description: Placements for volunteers in schools, colleges and universities.

Volunteers help with sports, music, extracurricular activities, English teaching and other administrative and social welfare work. Also arrange internships in fields of medicine, journalism, etc.

Number of placements per year: 100.

Destinations: Kathmandu Valley near the historic city of Bhaktapur.

Prerequisites: Minimum age 18.

Duration and time of placements: 2 weeks to 5 months, starting January, April, August and November.

Selection procedures and orientation: Application form, CV and references needed.

Cost: $600 includes pre-service training, language instruction, homestay and meals, trekking, rafting, jungle safari and volunteering.

Contact: Anish Neupane, Director.

WILD AT HEART
47 Old Main Rd, Suite 7a, Cowell Park, Hillcrest, Kwa-Zulu Natal, 3610 South Africa. ☎31-765 2947. Fax: 31-765 7245. E-mail: billy@wah.co.za. Website: www.wah.co.za.

Working with wildlife at rehabilitation centres, national parks and private game reserves in Zimbabwe, Botswana, Kenya, Namibia and South Africa.

Programme description: Gap Year programme consists of 24 weeks in 4 different countries (Zimbabwe, Kenya, Namibia and South Africa).

Destinations: Victoria Falls, Namibia, Cape Town and Mount Kilimanjaro.

Prerequisites: Ages 18-35.

Duration and time of placements: Gap Year Programme is 6-9 months. Fruit-picking Volunteer Work Experience programme runs from September to May.

Selection procedures and orientation: All welcome. Orientation is offered at each project on arrival.

Cost: Weekly charge on Gap Year programme is €245, so total for 24 weeks is €5,880. Volunteer fruit-pickers near Cape Town pay US$150 for meals and accommodation in 5-bedroom house near town of Tulbagh.

Contact: Billy Fourie, Director.

THE WILDERNESS FOUNDATION
47-49 Main Road, Broomfield, Chelmsford, Essex CM1 7BU Tel: 01245 443073 Email: info@wildernessfoundation.org.uk. Website: www.wildernessfoundation. org.uk.

Campaigning organisation dedicated to the preservation of wilderness and wild areas.

Programme description: Conservation volunteer work in various parts of South Africa, Scotland and Arctic Norway. Work in South Africa includes collecting scientific data, helping with the general administration and running of a small game reserve, general maintenance and game counts, as well as a mega-reserve programme. Opportunity to join a 5-day wilderness trail (see 'Directory of Expeditions'). Projects in Norway and Scotland involve path clearance, restoration of wildlands, animal and bird counts. Wilderness Trail programme available.

Destinations: South Africa , Finnoy (Arctic Norway) and South Africa.

Number of placements per expedition: Open-ended.

Prerequisites: Must be at least 18. Most programmes open to all except one in Eastern Cape of South Africa where places are reserved for students with scientific interest or in pursuit of career in biology/conservation.

Duration and time of placements: 2 weeks to 3 months. Most placements are from June to September.

Cost: Average £1500 for 3 months excluding airfares.

Contact: Jo Roberts, Director.

WORLDwrite
WORLDwrite Centre, Millfields Lodge, 201 Millfields Road, Hackney, London E5 0AL. ☎020-8985 5435. Fax: 020-8510 0460. E-mail: world.write@btconnect. com. Website: www.worldwrite.org.uk.
WORLDwrite is an education charity which encourages links across the world to champion global equality.

Programme description: WORLDwrite uses documentary film-making as the key medium through which the charity investigates global issues, questions assumptions and puts its ideas across. Charity has film facility and training programme. It organises unique film-based global exchanges, computer and film school appeals for Ghana and conferences and summits on development issues.

Destinations: Ghana.

Prerequisites: No specific skills needed but a passionate commitment to equality for all.

Duration and time of placements: Flexible.

Selection procedures and orientation: Interested people should become acquainted with the work of WORLDwrite. Applications for the 20-week film course can be accessed on website.

Contact: Ceri Dingle, Director.

WWOOF (WORLD WIDE OPPORTUNITIES ON ORGANIC FARMS)
PO Box 2675, Lewes, East Sussex BN7 1RB. ☎01273 476286. E-mail: hello@wwoof.org. Website: www.wwoof.com.
National WWOOF co-ordinators compile a list of their member farmers willing to provide free room and board to volunteers who help out and who are genuinely interested in furthering the aims of the organic movement.

Programme description: Visitors are expected to work around 6 hours per day in return for free accommodation. Visitors have the opportunity to learn all about the organic growing of crops and food.

Destinations offered: Worldwide.

Number of placements per year: Limited to the jobs available and amount of help required by farmers.

Prerequisites: Nothing specific required except must be over 18, prepared to work hard and interested in organic growing and environmental issues.

Duration and time of placements: Anything from a few days upwards.

Selection procedures and orientation: A stamped, addressed envelope needs to be sent to WWOOF for a brochure and application form.

Cost: WWOOF UK membership costs £15 online or £20 if a printed version of the WWOOF Independents Host List is required, i.e. hosts in countries where there is no national WWOOF organisation. Countries which have national WWOOF organisations have to be joined separately (UK, Denmark, Finland, Sweden, Germany, Switzerland, Austria, Italy, Slovenia, Australia, New Zealand, Canada, Ghana, Ivory Coast, Togo, Japan and Korea (some mentioned in country chapters).

YOUTH ACTION FOR PEACE UK (YAPUK)
P.O.Box 43670, London, SE22 0XX. ☎08701 657927. E-mail: action@yap-uk.org. Website: www.yap-uk.org.
Programme description: Worldwide opportunities for unskilled short term voluntary service working with local communities for lasting peace, sustainable development, social justice and protection of the environment.

Destinations: Worldwide coverage (Africa, Asia, Latin America, North America, Europe and the Middle East).

Number of placements per year: 70-100 outgoing.

Prerequisites: Normally none though language skills are required for some countries. Must speak English. Minimum age 18, though there are some teenage camps for students aged 14-17.

Duration and time of placements: Camps normally last 2-4 weeks. Longer stays are available in some countries.

Selection procedures & orientation: List of projects published in April on website. Application forms used for selection. Training compulsory for projects in Africa, Asia, Latin America and Middle East.

Cost: Registration fee of £100 plus membership fee of £10 (unwaged) or £25 (waged). An extra fee of £50 for training weekend for those going to projects in the regions listed above.

Contact: Nigel Watt.

YOUTH FOR DEVELOPMENT PROGRAMME

317 Putney Bridge Road, London SW15 2PN. ☎020-8780 7500. Fax: 020-8780 7300. E-mail: yfd@vso.org.uk. Website: www.vso.org.uk/volunteering/youth.

VSO's Youth for Development (YfD) programme gives young volunteers the opportunity to gain work experience and develop skills in an international setting.

Programme description: VSO's development projects are in the fields of education, HIV and AIDS, disability, health and social well-being, and youth work, and business.

Prerequisites: Participants must be aged 18-25 and living in the UK or Ireland. They must be committed to volunteering by demonstrating that they have at least 12 months volunteering and/or community work experience. They should be interested in longer term involvement in development work, either in the UK or overseas.

Duration and time of placements: 10-12 months.

Selection procedures & orientation: Closing deadline for applications is end of January for departure between August and October. Applicants take part in a competitive assessment process. Selected volunteers are matched to placements developed by VSO programme offices in more than 30 countries. Volunteers also complete a global education project which makes a practical contribution to raising awareness of development issues.

Cost: Volunteers must raise £700 towards their placement.

Contact: YfD Team.

YOUTH WORLD TRAVEL ORGANIZATION (YWTO)

Post Office Box KS 5283, Kumasi, Ghana. ☎ +233-51-44513. Fax: +233-51-44399. E-mail: postmaster@ywtovolunteers.4t.com/ postmaster@ywto.4t.com. Website: www.voluntarywork.tk/ www.ywto.tk.

Programme description: YWTO Voluntary Service offers short-term and long-term voluntary projects in Ghana including teaching, health care, agriculture, web page design, computer training, environmental projects and other social work.

Number of placements per year: 50+.

Prerequisites: Volunteers of all ages and nationalities. Qualifications and skills not needed.

Duration and time of placements: 1-12 months.

Selection procedures & orientation: Applications should be processed at least a month before arrival.

Cost: Programme fee from $300 per month which covers lodging with family, one meal a day, preparatory materials and manuals, administrative expenses, back-up from a team leader and materials for the voluntary projects.

Contact: Afriyie Darkwah Kwame, Executive Director.

Directory of Religious Organisations

BMS WORLD MISSION

PO Box 49, Baptist House, Didcot, Oxon. OX11 8XA. ☎01235 517647. Fax: 01235 517601. E-mail: missionteams@bmsworldmission.org. Website: www.bms-worldmission.org.

Programme description: Action Teams enable young people to spend 6 months living and working alongside BMS missionaries or a partner organisation involved in church work, community development work, basic TEFL teaching, youth and children's work, drama and music outreach.

Destinations: Asia, Europe, Africa, Central and South America.

Number of placements per year: 50.

Prerequisites: Aged between 18 and 25. Must be a committed Christian with support from their local UK church. Health clearance required.

Duration and time of placements: 10 months including 6 months overseas and a 2-month tour of UK churches upon return to share experiences and inspire others for mission. Alternatively, Summer Teams run in July and August for 3-5 weeks (ages 18 upwards) and tailor-made placements for between 3 months and 2 years (graduates only). BMS also has a new year-long programme, 'Extreme Latin America' for 20-27 year olds wanting to serve God in 5 different Latin American countries over the course of 9 months, working with children, churches, and implementing social action projects.

Selection procedures & orientation: Interviews are held over a weekend at BMS International Training Centre in Birmingham. A 1-month period of training and preparation follows. Debriefing is given on return.

Cost: Approximately £3200 for Action Team programme and £800-£1200 for Summer Teams. Cost includes flights, accommodation and living expenses overseas, insurance, visas and training.

Contact: Jo Legg-Bagg, Mission Teams Administrator.

CAREFORCE
35 Elm Road, New Malden, Surrey KT3 3HB. ☎/fax: 020-8942 3331. E-mail: enquiry@careforce.co.uk. Website: www.careforce.co.uk.
Established in 1980, Careforce enables Christians to serve in areas of need in the UK.

Programme description: A year designed for committed Christians in their gap year is spent in the UK working as volunteers with churches and Christian projects amongst vulnerable and needy people.

Number of placements per year: 150.

Prerequisites: Ages 17-30. No specific qualifications are required except commitment to Christianity.

Duration and time of placements: Usually 11/12 months.

Selection procedures and orientation: Interviews are essential, first locally and then at the site of the potential placement. Orientation takes place in the first fortnight of the placement. An induction course for all volunteers is also held within the first month.

Cost: None. All volunteers receive a weekly allowance of £33 per week plus full board and lodging. However, on acceptance, volunteers are asked to raise some financial support to help cover Careforce central costs.

CHURCH MISSION SOCIETY
Partnership House, 157 Waterloo Road, London SE1 8UU. ☎020-7928 8681. Fax: 020-7401 3215. E-mail: info@cms-uk.org. Website: www.cms-uk.org.
Programme description: The 'Encounter' programme is a 3-5 week mission over the summer for 18-30 year olds. Participants have the opportunity to travel with a group of Christians and share in the lives of Christians of another culture. 'Make a Difference UK' is a 6-18 month placement suitable for gap year students in a multicultural inner city area of Britain. Volunteers are placed with a local community-based church and can be involved in anything including youth and children's work, running a café, befriending the homeless, environmental issues or sports and arts projects. The international 'Make a Difference' programme is for people who are 21+ and who may choose to volunteer in a variety of programmes, for example as a youth worker in Georgia, a nursing assistant in Nepal, a hostel warden in Pakistan, teaching in Uganda or working with the deaf and blind in Lebanon.

Destinations: Africa, Asia, Eastern Europe, the Middle East and Britain.

Prerequisites: Volunteers must be British Christians who are involved in their local church, interested in learning about mission and sensitive to other cultures.

Selection procedures and orientation: 'Encounter' participants must attend 2 preparatory weekends and a debriefing on their return. 'Make a Difference' participants must have 2 interviews. Successful candidates attend a 10-day residential training course and attend a debriefing on their return.

Cost: Volunteers must be self-financing, though CMS can advise on fundraising and grants.

Contact: Alexandra Gough, Experience Programmes Team.

CRUSADERS
Kestin House, Crescent Road, Luton, Beds. LU2 0AH. ☎01582 589850. Fax: 01582 721702. E-mail: crusoe@crusaders.org.uk. Website: www.crusaders.org. uk.

This interdenominational Christian organisation was founded nearly 100 years ago and now runs over 400 clubs for young people.

Programme description: Participants in CRUSOE Overseas Challenges work in small close-knit teams dedicated to reaching young people for Christ. Projects may involve painting an orphanage or building a church, working with children in a holiday club or working with street children.

Destinations: Work with youth organisations and ministries worldwide including Europe and in a developing country in South America, Central America, Africa or Asia. Destinations vary from year to year.

Number of placements per year: Approximately 100, working in small teams of 10-12.

Prerequisites: Applicants must be committed Christians, aged 16-20 (14-16 for Euro Crusoe), in good health and prepared to work hard.

Duration and time of placements: 2-4 week placements in summer.

Selection procedures and orientation: Each project begins with an open day/interview, followed by a training weekend in February. Each team arranges an orientation in the UK. There is also a debriefing weekend in September.

Cost: Maximum £1500 for world projects depending on destination, £550 for Europe projects. Applicants are encouraged to raise the money through sponsorship.

Contact: Lyn Ellis, Service and Mentoring Manager.

INTERSERVE
325 Kennington Road, London SE11 4QH. ☎020-7735 8227. Fax: 020-7820 5950. E-mail: ontrack@isewi.org. Website: www.interserveonline.org.uk.

Interserve exists to serve poor and marginalised people, and to help build up the local national church.

Programme description: School leavers and graduates can take part in Interserve's gap year programme which makes individual placements in teaching English, teaching missionary children, work with special needs care, general children's work and administrative support.

Destinations: Asia, the Gulf, the Middle East and North Africa.

Number of placements per year: About 30.

Prerequisites: Applicants must be 18 or over, committed Christians, with a willingness to be flexible and to serve others.

Duration and time of placements: 2-12 months beginning any time of the year. Applications must be made 4-5 months before the intended departure.

Selection procedures and orientation: Interviews are essential, although they are informal. The applicant attends an orientation/training weekend before departure. On-going advice and assistance is available in the country and a debriefing occurs on return home.

Cost: £10 application fee, £300 placement fee, plus £20 per month after 3 months;

placement fee includes selection and screening, medical clearance, orientation and training, debriefing and pastoral care. Additional costs are flights, visa, immunisation, insurance and board and lodging (paid locally).

Contact: Brigitte Testet (brigitte@isewi.org) or Rachel Morton (rachel@isewi.org).

JESUIT VOLUNTEER COMMUNITY
23 New Mount St, Manchester M4 4DE. ☎0161-832 6888. Fax: 0161-832 6958. E-mail: staff@jvc.u-net.com. Website: jesuitvolunteers-uk.org.

Programme description: Full-time volunteering in a range of demanding social projects in the UK e.g. homeless hostels, drug rehabilitation, drop-in centres, victim support. Also run shorter summer programmes.

Destinations: Inner city Liverpool, Manchester, Glasgow and Birmingham.

Prerequisites: Ages 18-35. Must be prepared to work hard and interested in pursuing spirituality in the modern world.

Duration and time of placements: 10 months from beginning of September or shorter summer attachments.

Cost: None. Programme is fully funded. Volunteers are given an allowance equivalent to unemployment benefit (about £55 a week).

Contact: Chris Leigh, JVC Project Co-ordinator.

LATIN LINK STEP & STRIDE PROGRAMMES
175 Tower Bridge Road, London SE1 2AB. ☎020-7939 9000/9014. Fax: 020-7939 9015. E-mail: step.uk@latinlink.org or stride.uk@latinlink.org. Website: www.latinlink.org.

Programme description: STEP: Self-funded team-based programme working on small-scale building projects and church work in Latin America for committed Christians only. Stride: Individual placements in Latin America using participants' specific skills and gifts according to the needs of the Latin American church. Opportunities include school and TEFL teaching, children's work, church work, agricultural and engineering work, project development and prison ministry.

Destinations: Argentina, Bolivia, Brazil, Cuba, Ecuador, Mexico, Peru and Spain.

Number of placements per year: STEP: 150; STRIDE: 25-30.

Prerequisites: Minimum age 17 years for 3-week to 6-month Step Programme; minimum age 18 for 6-month to 2-year Stride programme. Volunteers must have an active Christian faith. Applicants need to be flexible, have initiative and be open to learn. Knowledge of Spanish or Portuguese is not essential but it is a great help. It is suggested that volunteers attend evening classes to prepare for the project.

Duration and time of placements: STEP: Spring projects run from March to July and summer ones during July and August (7 weeks). STRIDE: Orientation in September with departures between then and January.

Cost: STEP: From £1500-£2000 in total; details on application. The cost of the STRIDE programme varies from country to country, but is around £1500 for initial costs followed by £450 per month. As with STEP, the cost includes flights, insurance, training, debriefing, food and accommodation but not language lessons and visa costs.

OASIS TRUST
115 Southwark Bridge Road, London SE1 0AX. ☎020-7450 9000. Fax: 020-7450 9001. E-mail: enquiries@oasistrust.org or globalaction@oasistrust.org. Website: www.oasistrust.org.

In operation since 1985.

Programme description: Practical projects run alongside local Christian groups and churches. Activities include youth and children's work, drama, music and projects with slum-dwellers and AIDS orphans.

Destinations: Brazil, Peru, Romania, Kazakhstan, India, Zimbabwe, Tanzania, Uganda, Mozambique and South Africa.

Number of placements per year: 250.
Prerequisites: Minimum age 18. Applicants should be committed Christians and in sympathy with the aims of the Oasis Trust.
Duration and time of placements: Long-term placements are 5, 7 or 11 months starting in September and April; short-term 6-week projects start in July or 2 weeks throughout the year.
Cost: From £3300 for long-term projects; approximately £1500 for short-term projects.

SALESIAN VOLUNTEERS
Ingersley Road, Bollington, Macclesfield SK10 5RW. ☎01625 575405. E-mail: gill@saviohouse.org.uk. Website: www.saviohouse.org.uk.
Programme description: Gap year scheme for living and working in a Catholic residential community with other volunteers doing hands-on youth work on various projects including youth clubs, retreat centres, outreach and roadshows.
Prerequisites: Ages 18-30.
Duration and time of placements: September to July.
Selection procedures and orientation: Externally accredited leadership training given.
Cost: None. Weekly allowance is paid.
Contact: Gill McCambridge.

SCRIPTURE UNION
207-209 Queensway, Bletchley, Milton Keynes MK2 2EB. ☎01908 856193. Fax: 01908 856012. E-mail: elizabethf@scriptureunion.org.uk. Website: www. scriptureunion.org.uk.
Programme description: Summer teams give children and young people an opportunity to learn about God in a relaxed environment. Volunteers take part through teaching English, playing games, leading craft activities, singing songs and generally having fun. Activities on longer-term placements (6 months to 1 year) vary according to the country of placement. Activities can include teaching life skills in schools, leading outdoor education programmes or camping, or being part of a performing arts team in schools.
Destinations: Summer placements in Hungary, Romania, Slovakia, Bulgaria, Greece and Peru. Longer-term placements (6 months plus) in Peru, France, India, South Africa, Western Australia, Singapore and New Zealand.
Number of placements per year: 35 long-term, 80 short-term.
Prerequisites: Ages 18-30 for longer-term; 18-80 for summer placements. Christian faith essential.
Duration and time of placements: 1-3 weeks in summer, 6+ months longer-term.
Selection procedures and orientation: Interviews are essential. Advice and preparation are given in the UK, including an orientation weekend. Pastoral support is given to participants both overseas and in the UK.
Cost: Flights and living costs vary depending on the country and length of placement. The 1-3 week placement costs between £100 and £300; the 6-month placement costs between £2500 and £3500.
Contact: Elizabeth Fewkes, International Relations.

SOUTH AMERICA MISSION SOCIETY (SAMS)
Allen Gardiner Cottage, Pembury Rd., Tunbridge Wells, Kent TN2 3QU. ☎01892 538647. E-mail: persec@samsgb.org. Website: www.samsgb.org.
Programme description: SAMS is working in various projects run by the Anglican church which has placements for committed Christians who wish to work as self-funding volunteers, particularly in English teaching and work with underprivileged children.
Destinations: Peru, Bolivia, Brazil, Paraguay, Uruguay, Argentina and Chile.
Number of placements per year: 10-12.
Prerequisites: Volunteers must be completely self-funding and must be committed Christians with the backing of their local church. Knowledge of Spanish or Portuguese very useful.

TEARFUND
100 Church Road, Teddington, Middlesex TW11 8QE. ☎020-8943 7777. E-mail: transform@tearfund.org. Website: http://youth.tearfund.org/transform.
Programme description: 2-week to 4-month overseas programme 'Transform Teams' for small teams or shorter summer teams to work mainly with children and the vulnerable. Charity fights against global poverty.
Destinations: Transform teams in 2005 to Kenya, Malawi, Lesotho, Uganda, Thailand, India and Kazakhstan.
Duration and time of placements: 4-month placements start in March or April. Deadline for applications 1st September.
Cost: 4-6 week summer teams cost from £1300-£1700.

TIME FOR GOD
2 Chester House, Pages Lane, Muswell Hill, London N10 1PP. ☎020-8883 1504. Fax: 020-8365 2471. E-mail: recruit@timeforgod.org. Website: www.timeforgod.co.uk.
One of the longest established Christian gap year programmes.
Programme description: Gap year sponsored by 9 Christian denominations. Placements include but are not limited to inner city projects with the homeless and disadvantaged, caring for children with special needs, assisting the ministry team in a Church, children's and youth work, youth retreat centres, drug and alcohol rehabilitation centres and other areas.
Number of placements per year: 150.
Destinations: Ghana, UK and other countries
Prerequisites: Ages 18-25. Must be open and sympathetic to the Christian faith.
Duration and time of placements: 6-12 months from September or January.
Cost: Volunteers must fund-raise £1700 for overseas placements. Fees include orientation and re-entry training, ongoing training and support while in placement, accommodation, food expenses and pocket money.

WORLD EXCHANGE
St Colm's International House, 23 Inverleith Terrace, Edinburgh EH3 5NS. ☎0131-315 4444. Fax: 0131-315 2222. E-mail: we@stcolms.org. Website: www.worldexchange.org.uk.
World Exchange is managed by a number of British Churches and development agencies and draws on the Church's extensive network of international contacts to allow people to work as volunteers in various places around the world.
Programme description: World Exchange sends volunteers to work with community organisations and projects. Work may be in the community, working with apprentices in skilled trades and agriculture, in education related projects or in health projects.
Destinations: Worldwide, including Malawi, Swaziland, India, Pakistan and Lebanon.
Prerequisites: Volunteers must be flexible and adaptable. Minimum age 18. Specific skills sometimes needed.
Duration and time of placements: 6 months for gap year students; otherwise 10-12 months.
Selection procedures and orientation: World Exchange finds suitable placements for individual applicants. It also provides a training and support package.
Cost: Gap volunteers are expected to contribute £2500+ for a six-month placement. Also organise study/workcamps for 4-6 weeks that cost £1500.

WYCLIFFE BIBLE TRANSLATORS
Wycliffe Centre, Horsleys Green, High Wycombe, Bucks. HP14 3XL. ☎01494 682259. Fax: 01494 682300. E-mail: short_termers_uk@wycliffe.org. Website: www.wycliffe.org.uk.
Programme description: Programme with opportunities in linguistics, literacy, IT, home-

schooling, accountancy, design, etc.

Destinations: Worldwide, but mainly Africa and Asia.

Prerequisites: Minimum age 18 for IT and home-schooling. For linguistic work, most applicants are post-university.

Duration and time of placements: Pre-university can be 3-12 months abroad; graduate programme designed as 4-month specialist training period followed by 8 months (or longer) overseas.

Cost: Variable, but normally £400-£450 a month to cover living costs, medical insurance, airfares, etc.

Contact: Hilary Greenwood, Recruitment & Applications Department.

YEAR FOR GOD

Holmsted Manor, Staplefield Road, Cuckfield, West Sussex RH17 5JF. ☎01444 440229. Fax: 01444 450770. E-mail: yfg@holmsted.org.uk. Website: www.holmsted.org.uk.

Gap Year Programme of Youth with a Mission (see next entry) for Christians to devote 12 months to 'radical discipleship' and missions in one of several countries. Locations include Bolivia, Tanzania, India, Malaysia/Indonesia and Europe. Cost is £3000-£4000.

Number of placements per year: 30.

Duration and time of placements: 12 months starting August/September.

Selection procedures and orientation: Enquiry weekends are run for interested applicants in the spring. Interviews are not always required.

Contact: Cherry Smith, YFG Co-ordinator.

YOUTH WITH A MISSION

Highfield Oval, Harpenden, Herts. AL5 4BX. ☎01582 463216. Fax: 01582 463213. E-mail: enquiries@oval.com. Website: www.ywam-england.com.

Founded in 1960, Youth With a Mission is an international, missionary movement of Christians. It currently has more than 11,000 full-time volunteers working in more than 140 countries. 25,000 short-term missionaries sent out each year.

Programme description: Gap Year programmes include life-changing training and outreach that gathers together people from many nations with a desire and commitment to express God's heart to the world. Courses consist of a 3-month lecture phase and 2-3 month outreach. Extensions beyond 6 months working in a variety of ministries depending on location.

Destinations: Urban and youth settings within the UK and globally in the rest of the world, most likely Europe, Malaysia, Indonesia, Philippines, Tanzania, Bolivia, Argentina, India, Far East, Egypt and South Africa.

Number of placements per year: 200.

Prerequisites: Volunteers must be Christian and support the YWAM mission statement. YWAM's motto is 'To Know God and Make him Known'.

Duration and time of placements: 5-12 months starting at various times of the year.

Selection procedures and orientation: Application forms can be downloaded from the website. Interviews are not always required. For some courses, enquiry weekends are run for interested applicants.

Cost: Fees vary from £1700 to £3500 plus outreach expenses.

Contact: Penny Weightman.

A Year Off for North Americans

No tradition has developed in the US or Canada for high school graduates to take a year out before proceeding to university. The expression gap year is almost never used in North America. Americans of course flock to Europe clutching their rail passes and their *Let's Go* guidebooks but they tend to do it merely as summer sightseers. Once they get to university many students find that there is an International Study adviser who encourages them to sign up for a semester or a shorter course abroad (normally in the company of lots of other Americans). But relatively few venture off independently to do an expedition or voluntary placement. Of those that do, many gravitate south to Latin America where there are many language and volunteer programmes geared to American expectations.

Yet a trend has been emerging. It may have started with an article published by the Admissions Office of Harvard University which has had wide circulation entitled 'Time Out or Burn Out for the Next Generation' which argued strenuously for having a break from the intense pressures affecting students trying to get into the top universities. (The article can be read online at http://adm-is.fas.harvard.edu/timeoff.htm). More recently, a special edition of *Newsweek* included an article 'The Lure of the Gap Year' and at a session of New England College Admissions Counselors, one session was on Gap/Interim Years. One of the speakers was Tim Ellis, former director of Global Quest (listed later in this chapter), who called his hand-out 'The Next Thing to Do: Why Deferring College May Make Sense' in which he wrote:

Too many bright, motivated students are heading off to college without a second thought. It doesn't make sense. The typical student, who follows his peers to college because it's 'the next thing to do' faces a risk of aimlessness, burnout, or even drop-out. The more mature, and often more successful, student takes time to discover his or her passion. The U.S. Department of Education reports that more than 30% of college freshmen do not return for their sophomore year. It's a shocking statistic, but the fact is that they were just not clear about WHY they were going. Colleges recognize this problem. Simply put, they know that the student who does something worthwhile between high school and college will likely arrive energized and ready to learn. Colleges seek students who actively choose higher education, rather than just coasting into it like many of their peers.

Parents sometimes worry that if a student steps off the usual track they will lose their momentum. This may be true for a few, but in my forty years of educating teen-agers, my observation is that this is just not the case, particularly for those students who do sit down and make a plan of action. A structured semester or year of travel, volunteering, or work, nearly always inspires a desire to learn more. Parents and students can avoid this uncertainty altogether by deferring entrance for a year... Students can pursue the normal application process in their senior year and then, in May, send a deposit to the college of their choice with a request to defer entrance to the following fall.

Elisabeth Weiskittel is one young American who decided that she did not want to go straight to college:
I was the only person in my graduating high school class to take a gap year or probably even to consider doing it. My friends, after blinking and looking shocked for a minute, thought it was a great idea but, like the adults, shook their heads and said, 'Oh, you'll never be able to go back to finish college.' My family was used to the idea because I had first brought it up in my sophomore year of high school, and they approved wholeheartedly. I knew that I was going to need a break from school, and I've always loved to travel. The only reason not to go was that I would be a year behind my high school classmates, and a year older than my new classmates at college. But I decided that that wasn't so terrible an idea.

I had already applied to college during my senior year of high school, which is the normal time, and had been accepted at several. When I chose one, I included a letter saying that I was planning to take a year off. The college wrote back saying I had permission, and that they would hold my space in the upcoming class the following year. Deciding where to go turned out to be more difficult than deciding to go.

Elisabeth ended up doing courses in Oxford (see introduction to chapter 'Courses') and in Florence plus an internship in Hawaii (see chapters on 'Italy' and 'USA' respectively) and had a very full and productive year out. Although she admits the year was expensive, it wasn't as expensive as a year at college would have been and summarises the way in which she has benefitted:

Now that I am at college, I realise that being a year older than my friends at college is completely unimportant. Most of my friends from high school are graduating col-lege next year, but I am smirking because they have to go look for jobs while I can sit back for another two years and relax. The year also changed my perspective on education, and has made all the studying I do in college seem worthwhile, since I can see where it fits into the world picture. My gap year also gave me the most obvi-ous of benefits, which was a year to relax and let my brain regenerate. The downside of the year occurred during the first few days of each new experience, when I didn't know anybody and was nervous about being in an unfamiliar place where I didn't know what was going to be expected of me. Italy was the worst adjustment because of the language impediment. Another difficult part was when I started college in the fall. Suddenly my movements became restricted again. I couldn't go off on weekend trips or drop everything and go to a museum, because I had reading to do. All things taken together, it was the best year of my life. If I could do it again the only thing I would do differently is to try to make more Italian friends.

Catherine Leopold wasn't too happy with the colleges that had offered her a place and so decided to take a year out. After a stint doing voluntary work in southern England, she did the *John Hall Pre-University Programme* in Italy (see 'Directory of Art Courses') where she found that she was taking the course more seriously than some of the mainly British participants, many of whom were from very privileged backgrounds. Catherine really enjoyed the chance to engage in some of the course's peripheral activities like learning Italian and taking classes in photography, and feels that many other Americans could benefit from taking a year off to mature and expand horizons before going on to university. What some describe as a 13th year programme may be particularly worthwhile for students who are relatively young when they graduate from high school and who might benefit from a structured programme that gives them the space to mature, to learn to manage their time and be independent, and to have a chance to appreciate how sheltered and privileged a background they have had.

Canada has definitely seen an upsurge of interest in taking a year off before university. For example the UK charity *GAP Activity Projects* has a counterpart Gap Canada (www. gapcanada.org) which has recently been expanding its reverse traffic from Canada to the UK as well as India and other countries (entry below). **Graham Milner** from Victoria BC took advantage of this scheme and spent a happy year at a residential school between London and Cambridge. He soon realised his school was not far from Stansted Airport and became an aficionado of cheap European flights with no-frills airlines from Stansted which he could afford even on his modest salary. In order to find a travelling companion, he simply sent a round-robbin email to the other GAP participants from Canada and offered to search out the cheapest flights and accommodation, and as a result he and a young woman GAPper spent a long weekend in Milan not long after they both arrived in England.

Another changing trend is for British gap year organisations to accept more clients from North America. It seems that the increase in competition among the companies, compounded by a decline in the number of British participants due to top-up fees, has prompted many of the British agencies to stop worrying about the reputed litigiousness of Americans and to start not just welcoming but actively recruiting Americans onto their programmes. Several like *i-to-i* and *Teaching & Projects Abroad* have offices in the US.

Of course many Americans taking a gap year do not leave the shores of their country. Some who may be undecided about the next step may join AmeriCorps, the national service programme instituted by President Clinton in 1993 which has been described as a domestic Peace Corps. In exchange for 1700 hours of community service over a 10-month period, AmeriCorps volunteers aged 18-24 receive a $5000 education voucher and a living allowance of $100 or more a week. The Federal Work Study programme is another scheme that encourages a volunteering culture with monetary rewards: financial assistance is given to students in financial need who work in community service positions during term-time or while on holiday, e.g. working with deprived children to raise literacy rates. The Labour government in the UK is attracted to such incentives and is considering introducing a similar scheme in Britain.

Advisory Services

One of the most useful periodicals available to students and adults considering a gap year at any stage of their lives is the bi-monthly magazine *Transitions Abroad,* (PO Box 745, Bennington, VT 05201, USA) which contains practical information on alternatives to mass tourism including ways in which to live, study, work and travel that allow you to get to know your host country. Annual subscriptions (six issues) cost $28 within the US, $32 in Canada and they also maintain a very active website on www.TransitionsAbroad.com.

Companies that maintain databases of opportunities (mostly unpaid) and offer personalised consultations to fee-paying clients (often young people aged 16-25) attempt to match them with a suitable work, volunteer or study placement abroad. Many of the placement organisations to which candidates will be referred offer what are basically volunteer vacations, i.e. two or three week service programmes in developing countries for a substantial fee:

Taking Off - 617-424-1606/ fax 617-344-0481; takingoff@takingoff.net; www.takingoff.net. Provides ongoing personal assistance to those looking for international experiences that include volunteer work, internships and custom-designed situation, but not paying jobs. See website for up-to-date description of services and costs.

Center for Interim Programs LLC, PO Box 195 Nassau St, No 5, Princeton, NJ 08542 (609-683-4300; www.interimprograms.com). Consulting service based in Princeton NJ and Cambridge MA aimed primarily at pre-university and university students looking to arrange a worthwhile experience in the US or abroad that includes room and board, e.g. internships and volunteer work. Database with 5000+ options. Consulting fee from $1900.

LEAPNow, PO Box 1817, Sebastopol, CA 95473 (707-829-1142; www.leapnow.org). Structured programme for Americans aged 17-21 in Central America or India that can count as college credit.

GAP Canada, International House, UBC, 1783 West Mall Vancouver BC V6T 1Z2 (604-822-6110; info@gapcanada.org/ www.gapcanada.org). Gap year placements in UK, Ireland, India, Ghana, Thailand, and Australia (and possibly Fiji in the near future).

Globetrotters Education Consulting Inc, 1784 Rosebank Road, Pickering, Ontario L1V 1P6, Canada (416-565-4420; laura@globetrotterseducation.ca/ www.globetrotterseducation.ca). Experiential and study programmes in Europe, New Zealand and worldwide including internships, work placements and au pairing.

Horizon Cosmopolite, 3011 Notre Dame Ouest, Montreal, Quebec, Canada H4C 1N9 (514-935-8436; www.horizoncosmopolite.com). Database of volunteer work, internships and Spanish immersion in 30 countries around the world. Tries to match clients with suitable placements. Registration fee (C$350-C$495) guarantees placement.

World Wide Volunteer Services (WWVS), PO Box 3242, West End, NJ 07740 (732-571-3210; http://welcome.to/volunteer_services). Individually arranged multi-cultural experiences and internships in a variety of settings around the world. Application fee $50 plus placement fee $100.

The Quaker Information Center (1501 Cherry St, Philadelphia, PA 19102; 215-241-7024; www.quakerinfo.org) collates a great deal of information about volunteering which can be accessed online or by post for a $10 contribution ($12 if outside the US). The information, which is updated sporadically, covers what they aptly call a 'smorgasbord' of opportunities ranging from weekend workcamps through to two-year internships with aid agencies.

KEY NORTH AMERICAN ORGANISATIONS

Of the thousands of organisations large and small throughout North America which are involved with student exchanges and assisting young people to undertake worthwhile projects abroad, here is a small selection of important ones.

Adelante LLC, 601 Taper Drive, Seal Beach, CA 90740; 562-799-9133; info@adelanteabroad.com; www.adelanteabroad.com. Internships, volunteer placements, teaching abroad and semester placements from 1-12 months in Spain (Barcelona, Madrid, Seville and Marbella), France (Pontlevoy, Loire Valley), Costa Rica (San José), Mexico (Oaxaca) and Chile (Vina del Mar/Valparaiso). Prices from $1600 for 1 month in Chile or

Mexico to $4705 and include language classes, housing options and work assignment placement.

AFS International Youth Development, National Service Center, 198 Madison Avenue, 8th Floor, New York, NY 10016; 800-AFS-INFO; http://usa.afs.org. Full intercultural programme lasting 4/6-12 months in 54 countries for volunteers aged 18-29. Most programmes include language training prior to volunteer placement, homestay accommodation and participation in local voluntary projects.

Agriventure, International Agricultural Exchange Association, No. 105, 7710-5th Street SE, Calgary, Alberta T2H 2L9, Canada (403-255-7799; iaea@nucleus.com; www.agriventure.com). Details of the international farm exchange may be found in the chapter 'Work Experience'.

AIPT – Association for International Practical Training, 10400 Little Patuxent Parkway, Suite 250, Columbia, Maryland 21044-3510 (410-997-3069; www.aipt.org or www.iaesteunitedstates.org). Short- and long-term placements in more than 80 countries through the International Association for the Exchange of Students for Technical Experience (IAESTE) available to students in science, engineering, math, agriculture or architecture. Other work exchange schemes with selected countries.

Alliances Abroad, 3 Barton Skwy., Suite 250, 1221 South Mopac Expressway, Austin, TX 78746; 512-457-8062 or 1-888-6-ABROAD; www.allianceabroadgroup.com. Variety of overseas placements including work placements in the UK, France and Australia, teaching in Spain, China and Argentina, and volunteer placements in Ecuador, Costa Rica, Brazil and Peru. Participants pay fees to cover placement, accommodation and emergency insurance, e.g. $850 for summer placement teaching in China, $1090 for up to a year in Spain living with a family and $1600 for 3 months in Argentina.

AmeriSpan PO Box 58129, Philadelphia, PA 19102 or 117 S 17th St, Suite 1401, Philadelphia, PA 19103 (800-879-6640 or 215-751-1100; fax (215) 751-1986; info@amerispan.com; www.amerispan.com). Language training organisation which arranges internships and volunteer placements lasting 2 weeks to 6 months in many Spanish-speaking countries.

Au Pair Canada, 15 Goodacre Close, Red Deer, Alberta, Canada T4P 3A3 (tel/fax 403-343-1418; aupaircanada@shaw.ca). Au pairs to France, Netherlands, Switzerland and Germany.

Bridge Semester - Interlocken, New England College, 26 Bridge St, Henniker, NH 03242; 603-478-3166; jpruyne@nec.edu; www.nec.edu or www.interlocken.org/syp/byp). Bridge Semester Program for high school graduates structured into two 16-week terms to work on strengthening life skills, outdoor adventures and travel.

British American Education Foundation, PO Box 33, Larchmont, NY 10538 (914-834-2064; study@baef.org; www.baef.org). Offers students from North America the opportunity to spend a term or a year in a British boarding school following the normal Sixth Form curriculum. Cost approximately $36,000.

BUNAC USA, PO Box 430, Southbury, CT 06488 (800-462-8622; www.bunac.org). Administer Work in Britain Program which allows full-time college students over the age of 18 to work in Britain for up to six months. BUNAC also operates a number of other programmes for US students and young people including Work in Ireland, Work Australia (up to 4 months), Work New Zealand (up to 12 months), Work Canada, Volunteer South Africa and Volunteer Peru.

CCUSA (Camp Counselors USA), 2330 Marinship Way, Suite 250, Sausalito, CA 94965 (www.ccusa.com). Work Experience programmes in Australia/New Zealand, internships in Brazil and summer camp counsellors in Russia and Croatia.

CDS International Inc, 871 United Nations Plaza, 15th floor, New York, NY 10017-1814 (212-497-3500; info@cdsintl.org). Practical training internships for American students or recent graduates mainly in Germany but also in Spain, Argentina, Russia and Switzerland.

CIEE – Boston: 3 Copley Place, 2nd Floor, Boston, MA 02116 (toll-free 888-268-6245). CIEE-Portland: 7 Custom House Street, 3rd Floor, Portland, ME 04101 (800-407-8839;

207-553-7600/ fax 207-553-7699; www.ciee.org). Work, Volunteer and Teaching programmes in Australia, New Zealand, China, Thailand, etc.

Cross-Cultural Solutions, 2 Clinton Place, New Rochelle, NY 10801 (800-380-4777; www.crossculturalsolutions.org). Volunteer projects to teach English, provide skills training or enhance recreation programmes in village schools in Central America, South America, Africa, Asia and Eastern Europe. The programme fees cover expenses but not airfares: from $2175 for 2 weeks to $4873 for 12 weeks.

Cultural Embrace, 1111 Kingsbury St, Suite D, Austin, TX 78703; 523-428-9089; info@culturalembrace.com/ www.culturalembrace.com). Paying jobs lasting 3-6 months in British pubs for students and people within six months of having been in full-time study. Internships in UK, Australia, Spain and Mexico; volunteer teaching throughout Latin America; culinary and art courses in Italy, and other programmes.

Dynamy, 27 Sever St, Worcester, MA 01609 (508-755-2571; info-email@dynamy.org). Internship year for 30-40 people aged 17-22; Outward Bound expedition, community service and optional college credit. Tuition for 9-month programme is $15,000 plus housing $6000; for one semester fees are half as much. Scholarships are available.

Earthwatch Institute, 3 Clock Tower Place, Suite 100, PO Box 75, Maynard, Massachusetts, 01754-0075, USA. (1-800-776-0188; www.earthwatch.org). Earthwatch is an international environmental charity which engages people worldwide in scientific field research and education to promote the understanding and action necessary for a sustainable environment. Earthwatch recruits over 4,000 volunteers a year to assist scientific field research projects around the world. Prices range from $695 to $3595 excluding travel to the location.

EIL (Experiment in International Living), Kipling Road, P.O. Box 676, Brattleboro, Vermont 05302-0676 (802-257-7751; eil@worldlearning.org; www.usexperiment.org). Programmes lasting 3-5 weeks include some language training.

ELTAP (English Language Teaching Assistant Program), University of Minnesota-Morris, Morris, Minnesota 56267 (320-589-6406; kissockc@mrs.umn.edu; www.eltap. org). Placement programme open to undergraduates, graduate students or as a non-credit certificate option for other adults. Participants sent to 32 countries on all continents for 4-11 weeks throughout the year. $300 placement fee, plus course fee and travel; total cost usually $3500-$4500. Accommodation and board provided by host schools.

Experiential Learning International, PO Box 9282, Denver, CO 80209 (303-321-8278; www.eliabroad.com). Volunteering programmes in Argentina, Ecuador, India, Ghana, Kenya, Mexico, Nepal, Philippines and Poland; plus intern placements in Ecuador, India, Ghana and Nepal. Sample price for 2 weeks of teaching English at Polish summer school is $995, or in the Philippines $495 placement fee plus $50 a week.

Explorations in Travel Inc, 2458 River Road, Guilford, VT 05301 (802-257 0152; www.volunteertravel.com). International volunteers for rainforest conservation, teaching, wildlife rehabilitation, animal rescue and environmental work placements and internships for students and adults in Ecuador, Costa Rica, Belize, Guatemala and Puerto Rico. Placement fees start at around $1000.

Foundation for Sustainable Development, 870 Market St, Suite 231, San Francisco, CA 94102 (tel/fax 415-288-4873; info@fsdinternational.org; www.fsdinternational.org). Short summer and longer term internships for anyone over 18 in the field of development in Argentina, Bolivia, Peru, Ecuador and Nicaragua. Normally volunteers will be expected to converse in Spanish.

Global Citizens Network, 130 N Howell St, St. Paul, MN 55104 (800-644-9292; www.globalcitizens.org). Teams of paying volunteers are sent to rural villages in Kenya, Nepal, Mexico, Guatemala, Peru, Tanzania, Arizona and New Mexico; programme fee is $1250-$1950 plus airfares.

Global Crossroad, 8738 Quarters Lake Road, Baton Rouge, LA 70809 (225-922 7854, fax 225-922 9114; info@globalcrossroad.com; www.globalcrossroad.com). Volunteer teaching and internships in various countries, including Tibet and Mongolia. Paid teaching in Thailand (3-12 months) and China (1-12 months). Placement fees from $699 for China to $2599 for Mongolia.

Global Experiences, 1010 Pendleton St, Alexandria, VA 22314 (1-877-GE-ABROAD or 1-877-432-2762; admin@globalexperiences.com/ www.globalexperiences.com). Offices in Florence (Italy) and Sydney (Australia). Range of internships for young professionals in Italy, Australia and Ecuador. Intensive language course in Italy followed by work placement. Internships may be in graphic design, business, marketing, IT, fashion, etc. (See entry in 'Directory of Work Experience' for sample prices.)

GlobalQuest, One Longfellow Square, Suite 201, Portland ME 04101 (207-879-1722; dcreek@gquest.org/ www.gquest.org). 12-week programme for pre-university gap year students and high school seniors in Thailand including homestay, study of Thai language and culture, environmental issues, etc. Fall semester mainly for gap year students. Semester fees are $14,300. Organisation planning to start up in Ecuador and the Galapagos in 2006 (and would welcome British gap year students); tuition fee $15,500.

Global Routes, 1 Short St, Northampton, MA 01060 (www.globalroutes.org). Offers 12-week voluntary internships to students over 17 who teach English and other subjects in village schools in Kenya, Costa Rica, Ecuador, Ghana and Thailand. Participation fee from $4300 for the summer and $4600 for the spring and autumn (excluding airfares). **Ben Clark** from the US participated in this programme between high school and college:

Previous to my arrival at the Essabba Secondary School in the western provinces, there was no English teacher for the Form 1 students. My school was relatively well off and had most of the appropriate tools needed for learning (text books, notebooks, classrooms, etc.). I was surprised at the ease with which I was inserted into the school as teacher. They simply asked my co-intern and me what subjects we were best at, so I chose to teach English and math. It was a challenge for someone with no experience to manage a class of 37, particularly considering the students' different skill levels. Some of the kids were my age, and it was hard at first to earn the respect and trust of my class. Another problem I encountered was that of corporal punishment. In Kenya, caning is something that a lot of the schools practise as punishment for the students' bad behaviour. If students came in late, failed to do assignments or misbehaved, they were either sent to the Deputy Headmaster or sent out to do manual labour in the field. I chose not to apply these punishments and as a result many of my students did not do the homework that I assigned. The class was also too big for me to go around the room every day and check if each student had done their work. My host family is what I miss most about my time in Kenya.

Global Service Corps, 300 Broadway, Suite 28, San Francisco, CA 94133 (www.globalservicecorps.org). Co-operates with grass-roots organisations in Thailand and Tanzania and sends volunteers and interns for two or three weeks or longer.

Global Visions USA, PO Box 8124, Delray Beach, FL 33482-8124 (1-888-653-6028; www.gviusa.com). UK company that runs over 20 overseas expeditions and conservation projects in Africa, Latin America and Asia. See entry in 'Directory of Specialist Gap Year Programmes'.

Global Volunteers, 375 E Little Canada Road, Little Canada, Minnesota 55117 (651-482-0915/toll-free 800-487-1074; email@globalvolunteers.org; www.globalvolunteers.org). Non-profit voluntary organisation that sends 1500 paying volunteers a year to scores of projects lasting from one to three weeks in Africa, Asia, the Caribbean, the Americas and Europe. Service programmes cost between $500 (for projects in the US) and $2395 excluding airfares, with some student discounts.

Globe Aware, 7232 Fisher Road, Dallas, Texas 75214-1917 (214-823-0083; www.globeaware.org). Short volunteer vacations in Peru, Costa Rica, Brazil, Cuba, Nepal, Thailand and India.

Globetrotters Education Consulting Inc, 1784 Rosebank Road, Pickering, Ontario L1V 1P6, Canada (416-565-4420; laura@globetrotterseducation.ca/ www.globetrotterseducation.ca). Experiential programmes giving young people the opportunity to live, work (sometimes earning) and gain practical international experience in a range of countries.

Programmes include internships and au pairing. Fees from C$300 to C$5000.

Go Global, YMCA International, 5 West 63rd St, 2nd Floor, New York, NY 10023 (212-727-8800 ext 4303; www.ymcagoglobal.org). Progressive volunteer programmes to YMCAs and other organisations around the world. Work normally consists of camping, childcare, sports instruction, health and environmental education, community development or English teaching for 2-12 months. Programmes are available in Africa, the Middle East, Europe, South America, the Pacific, Southeast Asia, Eastern Asia and the Indian Sub-continent. $500 programme fee.

Habitat for Humanity, 121 Habitat St, Americus, GA 31709 (912-924-6935 ext 2489; www.habitat.org). Ecumenical Christian housing ministry building simple decent houses in partnership with low-income families in over 100 countries. Short-term opportunities may be available locally in the communities where Habitat works (see website for locations).

ICADS, Apartado 300-2050 San Pedro Montes de Oca, San José, Costa Rica (506-225 0508; icads@netbox.com; www.icadscr.com). The well regarded programmes of the Institute for Central American Development Studies combine study of the Spanish language and development issues with structured internships in Costa Rica and Nicaragua lasting a semester ($8500) or a summer ($3800).

ICYE: Inter-Cultural Youth Exchange, Fraternitas, United Planet, 11 Arlington Street, Boston MA, 02116 U.S.A (www.unitedplanet.org/www.unitedplanet.org). International exchange organisation that sends volunteers to spend a year abroad with a host family and undertake voluntary work placements, after a one-month orientation including intensive language study. Placements mainly in Bolivia, Brazil, Costa Rica, Honduras, Colombia and Mexico.

Institute for Cultural Ecology, PO Box 991, Hilo, Hawaii 96721 (808-640-2333; www.cultural-ecology.com). Academic internships in Fiji, Thailand and Hawaii working on marine biology projects, environmental advocacy or custom-designed projects in student's major. Projects also in Nepal and New Zealand. 4, 6, 8 or 12 weeks. Sample fees: $1895 for 4 weeks, $3850 for 12 weeks, e.g. reef mapping on the Fiji coast.

InterExchange Inc, 161 Sixth Avenue, New York, NY 10013 (212-924-0446; info@interexchange.org/ www.interexchange.org). Various work programmes including interning in Belgium, the UK and Costa Rica, au pairing in Germany, Netherlands and Spain, working in Australia and volunteering in Peru and South Africa. Fees from $350-$1100.

International Co-operative Education, 15 Spiros Way, Menlo Park, CA 94025 (415-323-4944; www.icemenlo.com). Arranges paid summer work for 2-3 months in England, Germany, Switzerland, Belgium, Singapore, Japan, China, Vietnam, Australia and Argentina. Jobs include retail sales, banking, computer technology, hotels and restaurants, offices, etc.; most require knowledge of relevant language. Placement fee is $700 plus application fee of $250.

International Cultural Adventures, Brunswick, Maine, USA; 888-339-0460; info@ICAdventures.com; www.ICAdventures.com. Cultural, educational and volunteer service experiences in Peru, India (Sikkim) and Nepal. Fees for 6-week summer programmes from $3050 and from $4050 for 12-week extended programmes beginning in March, July and September.

i-to-i, 190 E 9th Avenue, Suite 350, Denver, CO 80203 (800-985-4864; usca@i-to-i.com/ www.i-to-i.com). North American office of British company i-to-i (see 'Directory of Specialist Gap Year Programmes').

Kibbutz Aliya Desk, 633 Third Ave, 21st Floor, New York, 10017 (800-247-7852; kpc@jazo.org.il/ www.kibbutzprogramcenter.org). Volunteer placement service for Israeli kibbutzim, $150 fee.

Living Routes, 79 South Pleasant St, Suite 302, Amherst, MA 01002 (413-259-0025; fax 413-259-1256; info@LivingRoutes.org/ www.LivingRoutes.org). Semester, summer and year-abroad programmes based in eco-villages around the world that help people of all ages gain the knowledge, skills and inspiration to build a sustainable lifestyle. Current programmes in India, Scotland, Australia, Senegal, USA, Mexico and Brazil.

Mountbatten Internship Programme, 50 East 42nd Street, Suite 2000, New York, NY 10017-5405 (www.mountbatten.org). Reciprocal programme places American students in London so that they can acquire practical training in business for 12 months.

NRCSA – National Registration Center for Study Abroad, Box 1393, Milwaukee, WI 53201 (414-278-0631; inquire@nrcsa.com; www.nrcsa.com). Website has links to study and volunteering or career-focussed internship programmes in Latin America plus Spain, France and Germany.

Operation Crossroads Africa Inc, PO Box 5570, New York, NY 10027 (212-289-1949; http://operationcrossroadsafrica.org). 7-week summer projects in Africa; $3500.

Pacific Challenge, PO Box 3151, Eugene, Oregon 97403 (800-655 3513; HQ@pacificchallenge.org; www.pacificchallenge.org). 2-month experiential travel programmes through New Zealand/Australia and Southeast Asia (Thailand, Cambodia, Laos, Vietnam) plus summer programmes in Nepal, Peru and Ukraine. Fees $5200-$6500.

Pacific Village Institute, 4818 43rd Street, #4C, Woodside, NY 11377 (718-786-5426/ fax 940-991-0669; john@pacificvillage.org/ www.pacificvillage.org). PVI offers both summer and semester (fall and spring) small group experiential education programmes in India, China, Vietnam, and Cambodia. 1-3 months for ages 15-22; semester programme designed with gap year students in mind. Programme costs $1880-$8450 including homestays, language lessons, community service projects, etc.

Peace Corps, 1111 20th St NW, Washington, DC 20526 (800-424 8580/ www.peacecorps.gov). Sends volunteers on two-year assignments to 70 countries (see end of this listing).

Projects Abroad, One Davol Square, Providence, RI 02903 (toll-free 888-839-3535; info@projects-abroad.org). US office of British company Teaching & Projects Abroad (see 'Directory of Specialist Gap Year Programmes').

ProWorld Service Corps, PO Box 21121, Billings, MT 59104-1121 (877-733-7378; www.proworldsc.org) offers a range of internships lasting one to six months with aid agencies in Peru, Belize and Mexico. The fee of $1,950 includes Spanish tuition followed by placement with an NGO and lodgings for the first four weeks.

Rotary Youth Exchange, One Rotary Center, 1560 Sherman Ave, Evanston, IL 60201 (847-866-3000; youthexchange@rotaryintl.org; www.rotary.org). Short-term and longer exchanges for 8000 secondary school students aged 15-19 organised through worldwide network of Rotary clubs. Rotary is looking for people who have been involved in their communities and are potentially strong cultural ambassadors.

Schools Without Borders, 115 Cottingham St, Toronto, Ontario M4V 1B9, Canada (514-284-1929; info@schoolswithoutborders.com; www.schoolswithoutborders.com). Registered Canadian charity dedicated to fostering youth leadership through 6-month cross-cultural educational and volunteer programmes in Brazil, Nepal, Kenya and Thailand.

SCI-IVS (Service Civil International-International Voluntary Service), 5474 Walnut Level Road, Crozet, VA 22932 (tel//fax 206-350-6585; info@sci-ivs.org; www.sci-ivs.org).

Travel CUTS, 45 Charles St E, Suite 100, Toronto, Ontario M4Y 1S2, Canadda (416-966-2887; www.swap.ca). Administers the SWAP (Student Work Abroad Program) for Canadian students to the UK, Ireland, France, Germany, Australia, New Zealand, South Africa and Japan.

Visions, PO Box 220, Newport, PA 17074-0220 (717-567-7313; www.visionsservice-eadventures.pa.net). 3 or 4 week 'service adventures' in Dominican Republic, Guadeloupe, Ecuador, Montana, Alaska and Australia. Cost about $4000.

Volunteers for Peace, 1034 Tiffany Road, Belmont, Vermont 05730 (802-259-2759; vfp@vfp.org; www.vfp.org). Annual membership $20. VFP publishes an up-to-date *International Workcamp Directory* with over 2000 listings in 80 countries, available from mid-April. Registration for most programmes is $200.

Where There Be Dragons, PO Box 4651, Boulder, CO 80306-4651 (800-982-9203; www.wheretherebedragons.com). 12-week semester in Asia and Latin America (aimed at 17-22 years olds). Also 6-week summer programmes (for ages 15-19) in Far East, Southeast Asia and Latin America.

Wildlands Studies, 3 Mosswood Circle, Cazadero, CA 95421 (707-621-5665; www. wildlandsstudies.com). Conservation projects lasting 6 weeks in the US (including Alaska and Hawaii), Belize, Thailand, Nepal, etc.

World Endeavors, 2518 29th Avenue South, Minneapolis, MN 55406 (612-729-3400; www.worldendeavours.com). Volunteer, internship and study programmes lasting 2 weeks to 2 months in Costa Rica, Ecuador, Philippines, Thailand, etc.

WISE – Worldwide International Student Exchange, PO Box 1332, Dyersburg, TN 38025 (731-287-9948; wise@wisefoundation.com). Academic year abroad (ages 15-18) in Germany, Austria, Denmark, Japan and Brazil for 5 or 10 months.

WorldTeach Inc., Center for International Development, Harvard University, 79 John F Kennedy Street, Cambridge, MA 02138 (617-495-5527/800-4-TEACH-0; www.worldteach. org). Non-profit organisation that places several hundred paying volunteers as teachers of EFL or ESL in countries which request assistance. Currently, WorldTeach provides college graduates for 6 or 12 months to Costa Rica, Ecuador, China, Namibia, Honduras and the Marshall Islands.

Youth Challenge International, 20 Maud St, Suite 305, Toronto, Ontario M5V 2M5, Canada (416-504-3370; www.yci.org). Teams of volunteers carry out community develop-ment projects lasting from 5 weeks to 3 months in Costa Rica and Guyana.

Youth International (Experience the World) Inc, 232 Wright Avenue, Toronto, Ontario M6R 1L3, Canada (416-438-0152; www.youthinternational.org). One semester pro-grammes to Asia, Africa and Latin America for people 18-25; $7500.

The first organisation that American volunteers think of is the *Peace Corps* (1111 20th St NW, Washington, DC 20526; 800-424 8580/202-692-1800; www.peacecorps.gov) which sends both skilled and unskilled volunteers on two-year assignments to 77 countries.

> **Kristie McComb was posted to Burkina Faso and gradually concluded that the Peace Corps programme places less emphasis on development than on cultural exchange, i.e. sharing American culture with the host country nationals and then sharing the culture of your host country with Americans on your return:**
>
> *The cool thing for Americans is that you don't have to be qualified in anything to be accepted by the Peace Corps. There are many generalist programmes where you can learn what you need to know once you get there through the three-month pre-service training. I would encourage interested parties to be honest about what they can and cannot tolerate since not all volunteers are sent to live in mud huts. In a world changed by terrorism it is comforting to know how much of an active interest the US government takes in the safety and well being of its citizens abroad. However some people might find this stifling and not adventurous enough. How well PC keeps tabs on volunteers in any given country depends on the local PC leadership but, regardless, you are still in a high profile group of well locatable people. Risk reduc-tion is the buzz word in Washington these days.*
>
> *Overall I am happy with my experience though I am often frustrated by the inertia, the corruption and bureaucracy that makes me question whether anything will ever change. But you do gain a lot by (if nothing else) witnessing poverty on a regular basis. You quickly learn to recognise the difference between a problem and an inconvenience and to see how lucky we are as Americans to have some of the 'problems' we have.*

Anyone considering the Peace Corps might look at a website created by a returned volunteer (www.peacecorpsonline.org/crossroads).

LANGUAGE COURSES FOR NORTH AMERICANS

At a time when broad-minded Americans may find themselves wanting to try to dispel accusations of insularity and supremacy, going abroad to learn or improve a foreign language may have special appeal. Classroom learning has its place. But it is axiomatic that the fastest progress will be made when you are forced to use a language in every-day situations both at home and work. Programmes that combine structured study of a language or culture with volunteering are arguably a paradigm of the kind of foreign travel experience that can more than justify taking a year out before proceeding to college. Many organisations both international and local can arrange such placements, often in conjunction with a homestay to maximise exposure to the language.

Using a mediating agency simplifies the process of choosing a language school since they tend to deal with well-established schools and programmes on the ground. These agencies also provide a useful back-up service if something goes wrong. An effective search engine for locating courses is provided by the Institute of International Education on www.iiepassport.org which makes it easy to search by country and programme. Another recommended site is www.worldwide.edu. The magazine *Transitions Abroad* devotes its spring issue to immersion language learning; check their website www.transitionsabroad. com for links to many providers.

Here is a list of language course providers and agents of possible interest to North Americans planning a gap year.

AmeriSpan PO Box 58129, Philadelphia, PA 19102 or 117 S 17th St, Suite 1401, Phila-delphia, PA 19103 (800-879-6640 or 215-751-1100; info@amerispan.com/ www.ameris-pan.com). Language training organisation that started as a Latin America specialist but now offers programmes worldwide learning ten languages.

Bridge-Linguatec – see entry in 'Directory of Language Courses.'

Cactus Language Worldwide – see entry in 'Directory of Language Courses.' Toll-free number from North America: 888-270-3949.

Center for Cultural Interchange, 325 W Huron St, Suite 706, Chicago, IL 60610 (312-955-2544; info@cci-exchange.com/ www.cci-exchange.com). Language courses in Ecua-dor, France, Germany, Mexico, Italy and Spain. Independent homestay programme in 20 countries. High school semester or year abroad in Australia, France, Germany, Ireland, the Netherlands and South Africa.

Cultural Experiences Abroad, 1400 E Southern Ave, Suite B-108, Tempé, AZ 85282 (800-266-4441; info@gowithcea.com/ www.gowithcea.com). Study abroad programmes for college students. Language courses (beginners to advanced) offered through Euro-pean universities.

Eduvacations, 1431 21st St NW, Ste. 302, Washington, DC 20036-6930 (202-857-8384; info@eduvacations.com/ www.eduvacations.com). Travel company specialising in customised language courses combined with sports, art instruction, etc. throughout Europe, Latin America, the Caribbean, Russia, the US, etc.

Language Liaison, PO Box 1772, Pacific Palisades, CA 90272 (800-284-4448; info@languageliaison.com/ www.languageliaison.com). Total immersion language/culture study programmes and leisure learning courses.

Language Link, PO Box 3006, Peoria, IL 61612-3006 (800-552-2051; info@langlink. com/ www.langlink.com). Long-established agency (Director Kay Rafool) which represents dozens of language schools in Spain and Latin America.

The Learning Traveler, Victoria, BC, Canada - 888-364-1411 or 250-748-3297; info@learningtraveller.com/ www.learningtraveler.com. Agent for many language schools worldwide.

Lexia International, 23 South Main Street, Hanover, NH 03755-2048 (800-775-3942; info@lexiaintl.org/ www.lexiaintl.org). Overseas academic programmes, which include intensive language study, civilisation course, research methodology course, academic research project, elective course, internships and community service projects in Argentina, China, Cuba, Czech Republic, England, France, Germany, Hungary, Italy, Poland, South Africa and Thailand.

Lingua Service Worldwide, 5 Prospect St, Suite 4, Huntingdon, NY 11743 (800-394-5327; www.linguaserviceworldwide.com). Represents range of private language schools at all levels.

National Registration Center for Study Abroad, PO Box 1393, Milwaukee, WI 53201 (414-278-0631; info@nrcsa.com/ www.nrsca.com). Full language and culture immersion and other courses offered at 125 language schools and universities in 43 countries. Varying lengths of stay. Gap year students studying at a university may be able to apply the credit to their subsequent university. New website www.teensabroad.com, for summer programmes specifically for adolescents. Summer programmes can be useful for high school students to test in advance if they would enjoy a gap semester or year abroad. Many schools offer an option to participate in volunteer work, career-focused internships or adventure travel programmes.

Talking Traveler, 620 SW 5th Ave, Suite 625, Portland, OR 97204 (503-274-1776 or 800-274-6007; info@talkingtraveler.org/ www.talkingtraveler.org. Full immersion language and culture courses for adults worldwide. Links with schools in various Italian, Spanish, French, German, Mexican and Costa Rican cities.

University Studies Abroad Consortium, Virginia Street Gym 5, University of Nevada, USAC/323, Reno, NV 89557 (775-784-6569; usac@unr.edu/ http://usac.unr.edu). University-accredited courses in Spanish, Basque, Chinese, Danish, French, German, Japanese, Hebrew, Italian, Czech, Thai and Twi languages, plus art history, anthropology, business, communications, literature, history, political science, ecology, environmental studies, education, economics and tourism.

We Study Abroad, 23786 Villena, Mission Veijo, CA 92692 (949-916-1096; travelstudy@yahoo.com/ www.westudyabroad.com). Travel Study Programmes in Spanish, French, Italian and English. Internships, jobs and volunteer projects can sometimes be provided.

Paid Seasonal Jobs

The fastest way to save money is of course to live at home and find a job which pays more than the national minimum wage and has scope for working lots of overtime. Vast numbers of students register with a local temp agency like Blue Arrow and request as many hours as possible or simply find the highest paying job locally that will involve the least expenditure. In addition to allowing you to save for your gap year project, doing a dull unskilled job might have other benefits, as **Alice Mundy** discovered in 2005 when she spent months at a motorway services (because it was a short walk from her home and so required no outlay in petrol) working in the restaurant area, to save for a snowboard instructor's course in Canada:

> *Probably the lowest point of my gap year was working in certain jobs where there were a lot of people who didn't enjoy their jobs and so didn't put much effort in, but at the same time lacked either the resources or the ambition to do anything about changing it. However, on the positive side of that, my gap year has certainly highlighted to me just how lucky I am to have the opportunity of higher education, a privilege that a lot of people in the world don't have. This has definitely encouraged me to make the most of the next three years at university.*

The majority of gappers work locally in the autumn to fund travels or foreign projects after Christmas. If you can manage to do it the other way round, you will probably find it much easier to land a job, as **Ed Fry** did in 2005. He scraped and borrowed to fund a sailing course in Australia between September and January and then returned to London where he found that so many gap year students had taken off, finding a job was very easy.

If the time comes when you can't stand the sight of the same old high street or the same old work mates, and want a complete break while still earning, you might want to consider some of the suggestions in this chapter. Depending on the time of year, you may be able to arrange a short sharp change of routine by, say, working at a Scottish country house hotel over Christmas or going to pick grapes in France or Switzerland in September. The possibilities are so numerous that this chapter can only skim the surface. For much more comprehensive listings of seasonal jobs, look at the annual directories of *Summer Jobs in Britain* and *Summer Jobs Abroad* (price £10.99 each from Vacation Work) and *Work Your Way Around the World 2005* (£12.95).

While opening up an enormous range of possibilities, the internet can be a bewildering place to job-hunt. One of the best specialist recruitment websites is www.seasonworkers. com, a site that has been designed to help people find a summer job, outdoor sports job, gap year project or ski resort job quickly and easily. In 2004 it won in the 'Best Recruitment' category in the Travel and Tourism web awards. Another website that can prove invaluable for job-seeking travellers is the excellent non-commercial free Jobs Abroad Bulletin (www.jobsabroadbulletin.co.uk) which will send a free monthly job listing by email to subscribers. Otherwise try www.gapwork.com (see entry in *Directory of Specialist Gap Year Programmes),* www.anyworkanywhere.com, www.jobmonkey.com (especially for North America), http://jobs.escapeartist.com, www.hotrecruit.com (which has a section on 'Crazy Jobs') and so on. Justjobs4students.co.uk has a section on 'Year Off' jobs. Everywhere you look on the internet potentially useful links can be found. A surprising number of company home pages feature an icon you can click to find out about jobs/recruitment/ careers.

Registration on sites like www.justjobs4students.co.uk is normally free of charge, and will soon see your inbox cluttered up with quite a high proportion of unsuitable jobs. Among the kinds of firm that recruit quite aggressively (possibly because there is such a high turnover) are 'charity fundraising' firms. These are commercial companies hired by mainstream and other charities to raise money on the streets of British cities. Companies like Flow Caritas (www.flowcaritas.co.uk), Dialogue Direct (www.dialoguedirect.co.uk) and Integrity Recruitment (www.integrityrecruitment.com) use worthy sounding lines such as 'championing the search for a better world' in their bid to hire an army of young people to accost passers-by and try to persuade them to sign direct debit donation forms. This activity has been dubbed 'charity mugging' and hence the employees are sometimes referred to as 'chuggers'. A high percentage of those hired are foreign young people on working holiday visas, including 18 year old **David Cox** from Ontario who was hired soon after arriving in London. He was invited to attend a day's training in Oxford before being dispatched to his first location, and looked forward to a chance to see different places:

The last three weeks have been very interesting, but I'm starting to get into the swing of things. So far I've been posted in Brighton, Portsmouth and Newcastle areas and am leaving for Manchester tonight. I love the job but it's literally 7 days a week and can be very stressful so I'm looking forward to time off, I'm going to Norway in 2 weeks.

Working for a local employer abroad is arguably one of the best ways of getting inside a culture, though the kind of job you find will determine the stratum of society which you experience. The student who spends a few weeks picking fruit in Canada will get a very different insight into North American culture from the one who looks after the children of a Texan millionaire. Yet both will have the chance to participate temporarily in the life of a culture and get to know one place well.

Most gap year students looking for holiday jobs abroad will have to depend on the two industries that survive on seasonal labour: tourism and agriculture. School leavers and their parents will probably feel happier with a pre-arranged job, possibly with a British tour operator, but that does limit the choice. Like job-hunting in any context, the competition for seasonal work will be hard to beat unless you are available for interview. If looking for farm work or a berth on a transatlantic yacht, a visit to a village pub frequented by farmers or yachties is worth dozens of speculative applications from home.

The other major fields of paid overseas employment for students are au pairing (see separate chapter) and English teaching (discussed below and also in the relevant country chapters). The more unusual and interesting the job the more competition it will attract. For example it is to be assumed that only a small percentage of applicants for advertised jobs actually gets the chance to work as underwater photographic models in the Caribbean, history co-ordinators for a European tour company or assistants at a museum bookshop in Paris. Rather than try to fill one of these rare but interesting vacancies, you can perhaps invent your own bizarre job, like busking on the bagpipes or delivering croissants to holidaymakers in ski resorts.

TOURISM

Hotels, restaurants, pubs and campsites from Cannes to Canada depend on transient workers. Anyone with some home-town restaurant experience and perhaps some knowledge of a second language should be able to fix up a summer job in a European resort.

If you secure a hotel job without speaking the language of the country and lacking relevant experience, you will probably be placed at the bottom of the pecking order, e.g. in the laundry or washing dishes. Even the job of dish-washer, stereotyped as the most lowly of all jobs with visions of the down and out George Orwell as a *plongeur* washing dishes in a Paris café, should not be dismissed too easily. Simon Canning saved enough money in five months of working as a dish-washer in an Amsterdam office block to fund a trip across Asia. Benjamin Fry spent a highly enjoyable few weeks washing dishes at the Land's End Hotel in Alaska and earned more per hour than he could have in Britain. And **Sean Macnamara** was delighted with his job as dish-washer in a French hotel near Chamonix:

> *After a brief interview I was given the job of dish-washer. The conditions were excellent: a decent monthly wage plus private accommodation and first class meals, including as much wine as I could drink. I earned my keep, though, working six days a week from 8am to 10pm with three hours off each afternoon. I was the only foreigner and was treated kindly by everyone. Indeed I can honestly say I enjoyed myself, but then I was permanently high on the thought of all that money.*

Even if the job is fairly grim, you will probably collect some good anecdotes as **S. C. Firn** did in an upmarket restaurant in Oberstdorf in the Bavarian Alps:

> *I had to peel vegetables, wash dishes, prepare food, clean the kitchen and sometimes serve food. Everything was done at a very fast pace, and was expected to be very professional. One German cook, aged 16, who didn't come up to standard, was punched in the face three times by the owner. On another occasion the assistant chef had a container of hot carrots tipped over his head for having food sent back. During my three months there, all the other British workers left, apart from the chef, but were always replaced by more.*

So if you can't stand the heat...

Applications

The earlier you decide to apply for seasonal hotel work the better are your chances. Hotels in a country such as Switzerland recruit months before the summer season, and it is advisable to write to as many hotel addresses as possible by March, preferably in their own language. A knowledge of more than one language is an immense asset for work in Europe. Those who have a GCSE or A level in German are at a particular advantage since many tourist resorts in Spain, Italy and Greece cater mainly to a German clientele, so they like their staff to be able to communicate. If you have an interest in working in a particular country, get a list of hotels from their tourist office in London and write to the largest ones (e.g. the ones with over 100 rooms). If you know someone going to your chosen country, ask them to bring back local newspapers and check adverts. Do not put too much faith in speculative emails since these are routinely ignored by employers. If you send a postal enquiry, enclose international reply coupons and try to write in the language of the country.

On the other hand you might not be able to plan so far ahead, or you may have no luck with advance applications, so it will be necessary to look for hotel work once you've arrived in a foreign country. All but the most desperate hoteliers are far more willing to consider a candidate who is standing there in the flesh than one who writes a letter out of the blue. One job-seeker recommends showing up bright and early (about 8am) to impress prospective employers. Perseverance is necessary when you're asking door to door at hotels since plenty of rejections are inevitable.

Hotels represent just one aspect of the tourist trade, and many more interesting venues exist for cooking and serving, including luxury yachts, prawn trawlers, holiday ranches, safari camps and ski chalets. People with some training in catering will find it much easier to find a lucrative job abroad than most. Of course, there are opportunities for the unskilled. You might find a job cooking hamburgers in a chain such as McDonalds or Burger King, which can be found from Tel Aviv to Toronto. (Bear in mind that the *Oxford English Dictionary* now includes the coinage 'Mcjob' to refer to any form of dead-end, low-paid employment; yet one in eight Americans will work for Uncle Ronald at some point in their lives.) When applying for jobs which are not seasonal, you should stress that you intend to work for an indefinite period, make a career of fast food catering, etc. In fact staff turnover is usually very high. This will also aid your case when you are obliged to badger them to give you extra hours.

A good way of gaining initial experience is to work for a large organisation with huge staff requirements like *PGL Travel* in Britain and *Village Camps* on the continent. Since they have so many vacancies (most of which pay only pocket money), the chances of being hired for a first season are reasonably good.

Mark Warner is a leading tour operator with Resort Hotels located around the Mediterranean and Aegean, and Chalethotels in top ski resorts in the Alps. They recruit staff to work in Greece, Turkey, Corsica, Sardinia and Italy for the summer season and in Austria, France and Italy for the ski season. Positions are open for chefs, restaurant and bar staff, nursery nurses and children's activity leaders, watersport, tennis and aerobic instructors, pool attendants, customer service and shop staff, ski hosts and many others. Employees are provided with a competitive package including full board, medical insurance, travel expenses, use of watersport and activity facilities (summer) and ski pass, skis and boots (winter). More information can be obtained by ringing 0870 033 0750 or visiting www.markwarner-recruitment.co.uk.

Campsite Couriers

British camping holiday firms (addresses below) hire large numbers of people to remain on one campsite throughout Europe for several months. *Holidaybreak* alone recruits up to 2000 campsite couriers and children's couriers for the self-drive camping brands Eurocamp and Keycamp. The courier's job is to clean the tents and caravans between visitors, greet clients and deal with difficulties (particularly illness or car breakdowns) and introduce clients to the attractions of the area or even arrange and host social functions and amuse the children. All of this will be rewarded with on average £114-£180 a week in addition to free tent accommodation. Many companies offer half-season contracts April to mid-July and mid-July to the end of September.

The massive camping holiday industry generates winter work as well. Brad Agencies Ltd. has a depot in Beaucaire near Avignon that cleans and repairs tents and bedding on behalf of many of the major companies. Staff (who need not speak French though it is an advantage) are needed for the laundry and distribution between September and May. Gite accommodation is provided and a wage negotiated. A driving licence is essential and your own transport helpful. Brad International's UK office is at Abbey Lakes Hall, Orrell Road, Wigan WN5 8QZ (01695 632797; ian.b@bradint.co.uk).

Short bursts of work are available in the spring (about three weeks in May) and autumn (three weeks in September) to teams of people who put up and take down the tents at campsites, known as *montage* and *démontage*. Sometimes the camping tour operators contract out this work to specialist firms like Mark Hammerton Travel (Spelmonden Old Oast, Spelmonden Road, Goudhurst, Kent TN1 1HE; 01580 214000; enquiries@markhammerton.co.uk) who pay their crews about £95 a week in addition to board, lodging and travel expenses.

Some camping holiday and tour operators based in Britain are as follows (with the European countries in which they are active):

Canvas Holidays, VRG Camping Recruitment, East Port House, 12 East Port, Dunfermline, Fife KY12 7JG (01383 629012; www.vrgcampingrecruitment.com). France, Spain, Italy, Austria, Germany, Switzerland, Luxembourg, Holland and Croatia.

Club Cantabrica Holidays Ltd, 146/148 London Road, St. Albans, Herts. AL1 1PQ (01727 866177; www.cantabrica.co.uk). Mobile home tour operator employs couriers on-site in France, Austria, Italy and Spain (Costa Brava).

Eurocamp, Overseas Recruitment Department (Ref TGY/05) – 01606 787525; www.holidaybreakjobs.com. Operate 200 campsites in most European countries. Telephone applications from October. Interviews held in Hartford, Cheshire over the winter. Also trade under Holidaybreak, Hartford Manor, Greenbank Lane, Northwich, Cheshire CW8 1HW (same telephone number).

Holidaybreak, see Eurocamp.

Keycamp Holidays, Overseas Recruitment Department (Ref TGY/05), Hartford Manor, Greenbank Lane, Northwich, CW8 1HW (01606 787525/ www.holidaybreakjobs.com). France, Italy, Spain, Germany.

Siblu Holidays by Haven Europe, Siblu, Human Resources Dept, Bryanston Court, Selden Hill, Hemel Hempstead, HP2 4TN (01442 203970; www.siblu.com). Courier and children's courier staff for France, Spain and Italy.

Solaire Holidays, 1158 Stratford Road, Hall Green, Birmingham B28 8AF (0121-778 5061; www.solaire.co.uk). France, Spain. Postal applications only.

Be warned that an offer of a job may be more tentative than it seems, as Karen Martin describes:

Before we left in May, we had both been interviewed for the job of campsite courier. We got the jobs and signed the contracts, and our rough start date was the 7th of July. They did not make the position clear that an offer 'subject to terms and conditions' means that it is possible that a week before the start date you can be told that there is no longer a job due to lack of customers, which is what happened to us. We really felt let down.

Caroline Nicholls' problems at a campsite in Brittany included frequent power failures, blocked loos and leaking tents, though most of the sites belonging to the established companies are well managed with clean and functioning facilities:

Every time there was a steady downpour, one of the tents developed an indoor lake, due to the unfortunate angle at which we had pitched it. I would appear, mop in hand, with cries of 'I don't understand. This has never happened before.' Working as a courier would be a good grounding for an acting career.

She goes on to say that despite enjoying the company of the client families, she was glad to have the use of a company bicycle to escape the insular life on the campsite every so often. Some companies guarantee one day off-site which is considered essential for maintaining sanity. The companies do vary in the conditions of work and some offer much better support than others. For example a company for which Hannah Start worked ignored her pleas for advice and assistance when one of her clients had appendicitis.

The big companies interview hundreds of candidates and have filled most posts by the end of January. But there is a very high dropout rate (over 50%) and vacancies are filled from a reserve list, so it is worth ringing around the companies as late as April for cancellations. Despite competition, anyone who has studied a European language and has an outgoing personality stands a good chance if he or she applies early and widely enough.

Activity Holidays

Many specialist tour companies employ leaders for their clients, whether children or adults, on walking, cycling, watersports holidays, etc. Any competent sailor, canoeist, diver, climber, rider, etc. should have no difficulty marketing their skills in the UK and abroad. See entries for *Acorn Adventure* and *PGL Travel* for example. Check the website www.adventurejobs.co.uk.

If you would like to do a watersports course with a view to working abroad, see the entries for *Flying Fish* and *UK Sailing Academy* in the 'Directory of Sport & Activity Courses'. They offer training as instructors in windsurfing, diving, dinghy sailing and yachting, followed by a job recruitment service.

Ski Resorts

The season in the European Alps lasts from about Christmas until late April/early May. Between Christmas and the New Year is a terrifically busy time as is the middle two weeks of February during half-term. Because jobs in ski resorts are so popular among the travelling community, wages can be low. So many gap year and older students are (or become) such avid skiers that in their view it is recompense enough to have easy access to the slopes during their time off. One of the best ways to improve your chances of being hired is to do a catering course, some of which specialise in ski chalet cooking (see 'Directory of Cookery Courses').

Specialist ski recruitment websites can be extremely helpful. The superb Natives. co.uk posts current vacancies on behalf of a selection of the major operators and also includes detailed resort descriptions, links to seasonal workers' email addresses. Try also www.seasonworkers.com mentioned above, Free Radicals (www.freeradicals.co.uk), findaskijob.com (part of www.voovs.com) and www.skiconnection.co.uk, all of which describe themselves as one-stop shops for recruitment of winter staff for Europe and North America. The smaller Ski Staff (www.skistaff.co.uk) specialises in placing staff with British ski tour operators in France.

The fifth edition of *Working in Ski Resorts* (Vacation Work, £11.95) contains many addresses of ski companies and details of the job hunt in individual European and North American resorts. In response to the thousands of enquiries about alpine jobs which the Ski Club of Great Britain receives, it distributes *The Alpine Employment Fact Sheet*; send £3 and an s.a.e. to the Ski Club GB, 57-63 Church Rd, Wimbledon SW19 5SB (020-8410 2000; www.skiclub.co.uk).

Either you can try to fix up a job with a British-based ski tour company before you leave (which has more security but lower wages and tends to isolate you in an English-speaking ghetto), or you can look for work on the spot. In the spring preceding the winter season in which you want to work, ask ski tour companies (some of which are listed below) for an application form. Their literature will describe the range of positions they wish to fill. These may vary slightly from company to company but will probably include resort representatives (who may need language skills), chalet staff (who must be able to cook to a high standard), cleaners, odd jobbers and ski guides/instructors. An increasing number of companies are offering nanny and crèche facilities, so this is a further possibility for the suitably qualified.

Here are some of the major ski tour companies in the UK. Some have a limited number of vacancies which they can fill from a list of people who have worked for them during the summer season or have been personally recommended by former employees. So you should not be too disappointed if you are initially unsuccessful.

Inghams Travel & Bladon Lines, 10-18 Putney Hill, London SW15 6AX (020-8780 4400 or 020-8780 8803; www.inghams.co.uk/general_pages/job.html). 450 winter staff including reps, chalet staff, hostess/cleaners, *plongeurs* and maintenance staff for chalets and club hotels in France, Italy, Austria, Switzerland and Finnish Lapland. Perks include free ski pass, ski and boot hire, meals, accommodation and return travel from the UK.

Crystal Holidays, King's Place, Wood St, Kingston-upon-Thames W4 5RT (020-7420 2081; www.shgjobs.co.uk). Part of Thomson Travel Group. 2000 overseas staff in more than 100 ski resorts in Europe and North America (visa required). Resort reps, chalet staff and qualified nannies for France, Austria and Italy.

Esprit Holidays Ltd, 185 Fleet Road, Fleet, Hants. GU51 3BL (01252 618318; recruitment@esprit-holidays.co.uk). Vacancies for resort managers, hotel managers, chalet controllers, resort reps, chalet chefs and host/cooks, chalet and hotel assistants, nannies and snow rangers to work in resorts in France, Austria and Italy.

First Choice/Skibound, 1st Floor, London Road, Crawley, W Sussex RH10 2GX (0870 750 1204; overseas.recruitment@firstchoice.co.uk). 750 winter staff from EU employed in France, Italy, Austria, etc.

NBV Leisure Ltd., PO Box 371, Bromley BR1 2ZJ (0870 220 2148; www.nbvleisure.com/recruitment.html). Catered chalet holidays in France and ski holidays in Austria.

Neilson Overseas, HR Department, Locksview, Brighton Marina, Brighton BN2 5HA (0870 241 2901; skijobs@neilson.com; www.neilson.co.uk/recruitment). Part of Thomas Cook Group. Resorts in Andorra, Austria, Bulgaria, Canada, France and Italy, among others.

PGL Travel Ltd, Ski Department, Alton Court, Penyard Lane, Ross-on-Wye, Herefordshire HR9 5GL (01989 767311; skipersonnel@pgl.co.uk). School group operator with rep and snowboard instructor vacancies for 1-3 weeks during peak school holidays especially February half-term. Reps must be reasonable skiers with knowledge of French, Italian or German.

Powder Byrne, 250 Upper Richmond Road, London SW15 6TG (020-8246 5310; www.powderbyrne.com). Upmarket company operating in Switzerland, France, Austria. Compulsory 1-week training course in Switzerland for full-season staff. Also recruits for Resort programme in Crete, Cyprus, Tunisia, etc.

Simply Ski, Kings House, 12-42 Wood St, Kingston upon Thames W4 5RT (0870 888 0028; www.shgjobs.co.uk). Part of TUI group. Chalet and other staff needed in Austria, France and Switzerland.

Skiworld, 3 Vencourt Place, London W6 9NU (0870 420 5914; recruitment@skiworld.ltd.uk; www.skiworld.ltd.uk). Catered chalet and hotel holidays in France, Austria, Switzerland, Canada and the USA.

Total Holidays, 185 Fleet Road, Fleet, Hampshire GU51 3BL (01252 618 309; recruitment@skitotal.com).

You can find other ski company addresses by consulting ski guide books, magazines and travel agents. Another good idea is to attend the *Daily Mail* Ski Show held each October at Olympia in London where some ski companies hand out job descriptions and applications.

A classic job for the gap year is as a 'chalet girl' (or boy). The number of chalets in the Alps has hugely increased over the past decade or so with the biggest areas of expansion for British holidaymakers being Méribel, Courchevel and Val d'Isère in France, Verbier in Switzerland and St Anton in Austria. Clients in chalets are looked after by a chalet girl or (increasingly) chalet boy. The chalet host does everything (sometimes with an assistant) from cooking first-class meals for the ten or so guests to clearing the snow from the footpath (or delegating that job). She is responsible for keeping the chalet clean, preparing breakfast, packed lunches, tea and dinner, providing ice and advice, and generally keeping everybody happy.

Although this sounds an impossible regimen, many chalet hosts manage to fit in several hours of skiing in the middle of each day. The standards of cookery skills required vary from company to company depending on the degree of luxury (i.e. the price) of the holidays. In most cases, you will have to cook a trial meal for the tour company before being accepted for the job or at least submit detailed menu plans. Average pay for a chalet host starts at about £75 a week, plus perks including accommodation, food and a ski pass. Recruitment of the 1000+ chalet girls needed in Europe gets underway in May so early application is essential.

James Nibloe worked as a chalet host for Thomson Ski and Snowboard in Zell-am-See in Austria a couple of seasons ago. As a trainee chef with a large hotel group, James was always going to be a strong contender and describes the whirlwind nature of his appointment. He contacted several ski companies and favoured Thomson since they allow their cooks more flexibility with menus, etc.:

> We had to attend an assessment day for which we had to take with us a cake we had made. We were given basic literacy and numeracy tests and a kind of theoretical 'Ready Steady Cook' test. The best cake makers were summoned for interview and five days later I was told I had a job. Two days after that I was in Austria for the ten-day induction which took place in Ellmau.

If you wait until you arrive to look for a ski resort job, be prepared for lots of refusals. You will almost certainly have to fund yourself for some weeks before anything crops up (and of course there is no guarantee that anything will). Arrive as early as you can (say early November) so that you can get to know people and let them get to know your face. Apply directly to hotels, equipment rental agencies, tourist offices, etc. If you miss out on landing a job before the season, it could be worth trying again in early January, since workers tend to disappear after the holidays.

If you are already a good skier and interested in qualifying as an instructor, contact BASI, the *British Association of Snowsport Instructors*, or one of the gap year instructor courses such as *Ski Le Gap, Peakleaders* or the *International Academy* (see 'Directory of Sports Courses'). The recent explosion in snowboarding has resulted in an ongoing worldwide shortage of instructors and many new instructing courses in Canada, New Zealand and the Alps.

FARM WORK

Itinerant workers have traditionally travelled hundreds of miles to gather in the fruits of the land, from the tiny blueberry to the mighty watermelon. Living and working in rural areas is often a more authentic way of experiencing another culture than working in the tourist industry. The availability of harvesting work in Europe has been greatly reduced by the large numbers of Slovaks, Poles, Albanians, etc. who have moved into every corner of

Europe trying to earn the money their own struggling economies cannot provide.

To find out which farmers are short of help, check www.pickingjobs.com, which is strongest on the UK and Australia or, if already on the road, ask in the youth hostel, campsite or local café/pub. (According to one experienced traveller, this is great for people who are good at meeting prospective employers in pubs, unlike him who just gets drunk and falls over.) The great advantage of job-hunting in rural areas rather than in cities is that people are more likely to know their neighbours' labour requirements and often are more sympathetic and helpful in their attitudes. **Adam Cook** interrupted a cycling tour of the South of France to look for fruit-picking work:

> *Faced with having to decide between hurrying north to catch up with the cherries and going south to meet the first peaches, I decided to go south. It took ten good days of asking everywhere, cafés, bars, post offices, grocery shops – one of the best places I found to look as the owners very often know who is picking what and where.*

Picking fruit may not be as easy as it sounds. If you are part of a large team you may be expected to work at the same speed as the most experienced picker, which can be both exhausting and discouraging. Having even a little experience can make the whole business more enjoyable, not to mention more financially worthwhile if you are being paid piece work rates. The vast majority of picking jobs are paid piece work (with the notable exception of grape harvests in Europe), though a minimum level of productivity will be expected, particularly if you are being given room and board.

Anyone with a farming background could consider placing an advert in a farmers' journal or small town newspaper in your favoured destination. Something might work, along the lines of: '19 year old Briton taking a year out before university seeks farm work. Willing to exchange labour for board and lodging and chance to get to know the country.' The usual caution must be exercised when considering any replies. If possible, talk to your prospective employer on the telephone and ask them for a reference. Always try to obtain the terms of employment in writing.

Experienced grooms, riding instructors and stable staff may consider registering with an equestrian agency like *World of Experience Equestrian Employment Agency* (52 Kingston Deverill, Warminster, Wilts. BA12 7HF; tel/fax 01985 844102). *IEPUK Ltd,* the rural employment specialist, places suitable applicants in all rural industries including agriculture, horticulture, winemaking and equine and says 'If you wear wellies, we probably do it' (see entry in 'Directory of Specialist Gap Year Programmes'). For people with relevant experience, these agencies have vacancies in dozens of countries in Europe and worldwide which pay between £80 and £300 a week plus free accommodation.

Some European countries have programmes whereby young people spend a month or two assisting on a farm, e.g. Norway and Switzerland (see country chapters). A farming background is not necessary for participating in these schemes, though of course it always helps. The work-for-keep exchange on organic farms known collectively as World Wide Opportunities on Organic Farms (WWOOF) is described in the chapter on Volunteering. **Mike Tunnicliffe** joined WWOOF in New Zealand to avoid work permit hassles and his experience is typical of WWOOFers' in other countries:

> *My second choice of farm was a marvellous experience. For 15 days I earned no money but neither did I spend any, and I enjoyed life on the farm as part of the family. There is a wide variety of WWOOF farms and I thoroughly recommend the scheme to anyone who isn't desperate to earn money.*

TEACHING ENGLISH

The English language is the language which literally millions of people around the world want to learn. There are areas of the world where the boom in English language learning seems to know no bounds, from Ecuador to China, Lithuania to Vietnam. People who are lucky enough to have been born native speakers of English find their skills universally in demand, though it is far easier to land a teaching job in a language school once you have a university degree.

As is obvious by the programme descriptions of the major gap year placement agencies in an earlier chapter, a high percentage of all gap year volunteer placements revolve around teaching English to young children, in secondary schools and to adult learners. Placement organisations like *Teaching Abroad* and *i-to-i* specialise in this field.

One of the best sources of information about the whole topic of English teaching (if I may be permitted to say so) is the 2005 edition of *Teaching English Abroad* by Susan Griffith (Vacation-Work, £12.95) which covers in great detail training courses, recruitment agencies and lists individual language schools around the world.

Your chances of gaining employment in a gap year are much stronger if you have undergone some training, preferably the four-week certificate course (see chapter on Courses for further information).

Job-hunting

Printed advertisements have been largely replaced by the internet, though it is probably still worth checking ads in Tuesday's *Guardian* between February and June. Most advertisers are looking for teachers who have some training or experience but in some cases, a carefully crafted CV and enthusiastic personality are as important as EFL training and experience.

For schools, a website advert offers an easy and instantaneous means of publicising a vacancy to an international audience. People looking for employment can use search engines to look for all pages with references to EFL, English language schools and recruitment. CVs can be e-mailed quickly and cheaply to advertising schools, who can then use e-mail themselves to chase up references. This presupposes a degree of IT awareness which the majority of gap year students are sure to have. The internet has very quickly taken over as the primary means of recruitment.

Arguably it has become a little too easy to advertise and answer job adverts online. At the press of a button, your CV can be clogging up dozens, nay, hundreds of computers. But everywhere you look on the internet, potentially useful links can be found, many of them leading to Dave Sperling's ESL Café (www.eslcafe.com) which so expertly dominates the field that it is hard to see how others can compete (though dozens try). 'Dave' provides a mind-boggling but well-organised amount of material for the future or current teacher including accounts of people's experiences of teaching abroad (but bear in mind that these are the opinions of individuals). It also provides links to specific institutes and language school chains in each country.

Native speaker teachers are nearly always employed to stimulate conversation rather than to teach grammar. Yet a basic knowledge of English grammar is a great asset when pupils come to ask awkward questions. The book *English Grammar in Use* by Raymond Murphy is recommended for its clear explanations and accompanying student exercises.

Most schools practise the direct method (total immersion in English) so not knowing the language shouldn't prevent you from getting a job. Some employers may provide nothing more than a scratched blackboard and will expect you to dive in using the 'chalk and talk' method. If you are very alarmed at this prospect you could ask a sympathetic colleague if you could sit in on a few classes to give you some ideas. Brochures picked up from tourist offices or airlines can be a useful peg on which to hang a lesson. If you're stranded without any ideas, write the lyrics of a pop song on the board and discuss them.

Whatever the kind of teaching you find, things probably won't go as smoothly as you would wish. After a year of teaching English in Italy, **Andrew Spence** had this sensible advice:

Teaching is perhaps the best way there is of experiencing another country but you must be prepared for periods when not all is as it should be. The work is sometimes arduous and frustrating, or it can be very exhilarating. Be prepared to take the very rough with the fairly smooth.

Directory of Paid Seasonal Jobs in the UK

ARDMORE ADVENTURE LTD
Berkshire College, Hall Place, Burchetts Green, Maidenhead, Berkshire SL6 6QR. ☎01628 826699. E-mail: info@theardmoregroup.com. Website: www.theardmoregroup.com.
This organisation runs multi-activity and English language courses for overseas children aged 8-17 at residential centres throughout Britain.
Employment available: Group leaders are required to run a range of sports, drama and art/craft activities. Positions are available for EFL teachers, sports activity leaders, football coaches, lifeguards, overseas work experience placements and more senior posts.
Destinations: Residential centres around the UK.
Prerequisites: Experience with children for group leaders. Applicants aged 20 or over are preferred. Teaching assistants must be native English speakers.
Duration of employment: 2-8 weeks during June, July and August.
Wages: From £50 per week salary is paid for group leaders. Full board accommodation available.
Contact: Oliver Smith, Operations Manager.

BARRACUDAS SUMMER ACTIVITY CAMPS
Bridge House, 27 Bridge St, St Ives, Cambridgeshire PE27 5EH. ☎01480 497533. Fax: 01480 492715. E-mail: jobs@barracudas.co.uk. Website: www. barracudas.co.uk or http://recruitment.barracudas.co.uk.
Children's Multi-Activity Day Camps.
Employment available: Group co-ordinators, activity instructors (fencing, archery, tennis, art, drama, etc.), lifeguards and senior positions are all required to help run the centres.
Destinations: 20 locations in Greater London, Middlesex, Essex, Berkshire, Surrey, Kent, Norfolk and Cambridgeshire.
Number of placements per year: 340 altogether.
Prerequisites: Lifeguards require the RLSS Pool Lifeguard Award. Activity instructors need relevant qualifications for their sport/s. Experience of working with children and fluent English are also necessary.
Duration of employment: 4-6 weeks.
Selection procedures and orientation: Training courses leading to National Governing Body qualifications are organised prior to the camps. Barracudas meet the full cost of these courses, which include accommodation, meals and examination fees for all staff who work a full season.
Wages: Wages between £140 and £180 per week for instructors and group co-ordinators.

CAMBRIDGE PASSENGER CRUISERS
Riverboat Georgina, PO Box 401, Cambridge CB4 3WE. ☎01223 307694. E-mail: info@georgina.co.uk. Website: www.georgina.co.uk.
The *Georgina* is a passenger boat on the River Cam.
Employment available: Crew positions serving food and drink and taking the boat through

the locks.
Number of placements per year: 5-6.
Prerequisites: Minimum age 18; proficient in English. Previous hospitality experience an advantage. Full training given.
Duration of employment: May to September. Part-time work also available through the winter.
Wages: £5 per hour plus tips.
Contact: Nick Bennett, Operations Manager.

CLACHAIG INN
Glencoe, Argyll PH49 4HX, Scotland. ☎01855 811252. E-mail: jobs@glencoescotland.com. Website: www.glencoescotland.com.
Employment available: General assistants, mainly bar work, serving food/drinks, and housework. Also assistant chefs. Website includes detailed jobs section.
Prerequisites: Minimum age 18. Smart and presentable, enthusiastic and able to work well as part of a team. Best suited to those who enjoy outdoor pursuits.
Duration of employment: Minimum 3 months but preference given to those able to work longer. About 40 hours per week, 5 days per week.
Wages: Approx £5 per hour. Chefs earn £5/£6+. Accommodation available in single or twin rooms, some with cooking facilities. Meals are available in hotel for those not self-catering.
Selection procedures and orientation: Phone interviews.
Contact: Guy and Edward Daynes.

CLUB FOR KIDS
Vinalls Business Centre, Neptown Road, Henfield, West Sussex BN5 9DZ. ☎01273 494455. Fax: 01273 494451. E-mail: info@clubforkids.co.uk. Website: www. clubforkids.co.uk.
Non-residential multi-activity holiday clubs for children aged 4-13 years, run on independent school sites in Surrey, West Sussex and Kent, during the summer plus Easter and Christmas holidays.
Employment available: Activity Coaches who plan and deliver the activities (arts & crafts, sports & games, drama & music and so on); and Programme Manager who ensures the smooth running of the programme, motivates staff, overseas health and safety, carries out basic administration, etc.
Number of placements per year: Approximately 40.
Prerequisites: Minimum age 17, though older candidates with some relevant experience preferred. Previous experience working with 4-13 year olds (e.g. sports coach, Brownie leader, youth club assistant, classroom assistant). Qualifications are preferred but not essential (e.g. NVQ or similar in Childcare or Playwork, NNEB, teaching or QTS qualification, NPLQ lifeguard qualification).
Duration of employment: 4-6 weeks in the school summer holidays, 2 weeks in the Easter vacation, or 1 week at Christmas. Hours of work Monday to Friday from 7.45am to 5.30pm.
Selection procedures & orientation: Candidates complete an application pack and may be invited to attend a selection day local to the club where they want to work. They will be assessed on their application forms and practical abilities to plan and run fun activity sessions for children. Training is provided to successful applicants, including a 2-day Paediatric First Aid course.
Wages: From £190 per week for an Activity Coach to £300 a week for an experienced Programme Manager. Accommodation is not available. Uniforms provided.
Contact: Hannah Courtney, Operations Manager.

EF LANGUAGE TRAVEL
EF House, Castle Road, Torquay, Devon TQ1 3BG. ☎01803 297606. Fax: 01803 202941. E-mail: ltrecruitment@ef.com. Website: www.ef.com/ltjobs.

Employment available: Group leaders and teachers are required. Activity organisers are also recruited to plan activity programmes.
Destinations: All around the UK plus Ireland, Central and Southern Europe.
Number of placements per year: 1000 jobs available Europe-wide.
Prerequisites: Activity organisers must have previous organisational experience.
Duration of employment: At least 3 weeks between late May and late August. Staff work flexible hours, 7 days a week.
Wages: Salaries vary depending on region and experience. Both residential and non-residential staff are required.

EXSPORTISE LTD
Cornelius House, 33 Boltro Road, Haywards Heath, West Sussex, RH16 1BP. ☎01444 444 777. Fax: 01444 444 744. E-mail: simon@exsportise.co.uk. Website: www.exsportise.co.uk.
Employment available: Staff for sports holidays: coaching, administration, lifeguarding, nursing, management, held at three centres in southern England.
Number of placements per year: 60-70.
Prerequisites: Sports coaches must be qualified. Lifeguards must hold a current NPLQ.
Duration of employment: 1-8 weeks in July/August.
Wages: Unpaid work experience for those under 19. Qualified staff earn £150-£500 per week.

FACILITIES MANAGEMENT CATERING LTD (FMC)
All England Lawn Tennis & Croquet Club, Church Road, Wimbledon, London SW19 5AE. ☎020-8947 7430. Fax: 020-8944 6362. E-mail: resourcing@fmccatering. co.uk. Website: www.fmccatering.co.uk.
Employment available: Casual bar, waiting, chef, management work at Wimbledon, plus many other prestigious sporting events. 2500 people employed annually.
Destinations: Nationwide with a few opportunities abroad (e.g. for the Paris Air Show).
Prerequisites: Minimum age 18. Good social skills, self-confidence, outgoing personality and ability to use initiative.
Duration of employment: Wimbledon lasts about a fortnight (late June/early July). Other assignments last from 1 day to 6 weeks.
Selection procedures and orientation: Phone interviews sufficient for some jobs.
Wages: Variable. Food and uniform provided. For Wimbledon subsidised accommodation is available in Kingston University halls of residence.
Contact: Alison Gray, Human Resources Manager.

G's MARKETING LTD
Hostel Office, Barway, Ely, Cambs. CB7 5TZ. ☎01353 727245. Fax: 01353 727353. E-mail: recruitment@gs-marketing.com. Website: www.gs-recruitment. com.
Employment available: Packing salad and vegetable crops.
Prerequisites: Must be fit and willing to work hard. Many foreign young people work here.
Duration of employment: Production operatives needed between October and the end of April.
Wages: Piece work rates for picking jobs; from £4.50 hourly wage with overtime from £6.75. Employer claims earnings average £180 per week. Accommodation and evening meal provided on-site.
Contact: Sharon Gudgeon, Recruitment Officer.

HARRODS LTD
Recruitment Centre, 11 Brompton Place, Knightsbridge, London SW1X 7XL. ☎020-7893 8793. Website: www.harrods.com.

Sales staff, clerical staff and selling support staff are required to work October-January and to cover the July sale. Applicants must be a minimum of 18 years old, be eligible to work in the UK, and based within the London region. Fluent English is essential. Minimum period of work is 3 months.

HF HOLIDAYS
Redhills, Penrith, Cumbria CA11 0DT. ☎01768 214528/899988. E-mail: hr@hfholidays.co.uk. Website: www.hfholidays.co.uk/recruitment.
Non-profit making organisation which owns 19 country house hotels based in National Parks for individuals and families on walking and special interest holidays.
Employment available: Walk leaders plus children's activity leaders, assistant managers, general assistants, kitchen porters, assistant chefs and deputy chefs are required.
Destinations: Throughout the UK.
Prerequisites: Experience is not necessary for some positions.
Duration of employment: Jobs are offered for the season lasting from March to November and also at Christmas and New Year.
Selection procedures and orientation: Applications should be made to the Recruitment and Training Department.
Wages: Wages range between £80 and £215 per month plus full board and lodging. Walk leaders receive travel expenses and free room and board.

KIDS KLUB
The Lodge, Finborough Hall, Stowmarket, Suffolk IP14 3EF. ☎01449 742700. Fax: 01449 742701. E-mail: info@kidsklub.co.uk. Website: www.kidsklub. co.uk.
Kids Klub runs activity holidays for children aged 6-17 in 10 centres across England.
Employment available: Activity supervisors, Activity instructors, Arts & Crafts or Dance & Drama Co-ordinators, Lifeguards, EFL teachers and general assistants are required.
Number of jobs: 120 per year.
Prerequisites: No experience for Activity Supervisors, Arts/Crafts/Dance/Drama Co-ordinators or General Assistants as full training is given. Instructors must hold a current National Governing Body award; EFL teachers must hold a TEFL qualification or a PGCE.
Duration of employment: All positions are for 6 days a week. Season runs from January to October with extra staff taken on at Easter and summer. Minimum period of work is 4 weeks.
Selection procedures and orientation: All applicants welcome. An interview with all applicants is required. Applications can be made at any time of the year.
Wages: Salary plus room and board and training opportunities are provided.
Contact: Rob Buckland, Operations Manager.

KING'S CAMPS
The Manor House, Ecclesall Road South, Sheffield, S11 9PS. ☎08700 434495. Fax: 08700 429321. E-mail: recruitment@kingscamps.org. Website: www.king-scamps.org.
Non-residential sports and activity camps for children throughout the UK and also France and Spain.
Employment available: Staff lead and assist children with sports and activity sessions.
Destinations: 30 venues throughout the UK plus children's holiday clubs on French and Spanish campsites.
Number of placements per year: 350.
Prerequisites: Minimum age 17. UK nationality. Experience of working with children, sports coaching or childcare qualifications needed.
Duration and time of placements: 1-2 weeks in Easter vacation and 5 weeks in summer holidays. In Europe the full season lasts 4 months, half season lasts 2½ months.

Selection procedures & orientation: Deadline for applications is July 1st. Interviews are essential but can be conducted by telephone.
Wages: Varies depending on position (see website). UK camps are non-residential so staff should live locally. Camping accommodation provided in Europe.
Contact: Emma Justice or Rebecca Padgett, Recruitment & Training Officers.

KINGSWOOD GROUP
11 Prince of Wales Road, Norwich, Norfolk NR1 1BD. ☎01603 284284. Fax: 01603 284250. E-mail: jobs@kingswood.co.uk. Website: www.kingswood. co.uk.
The Group operates 6 year-round educational activity centres in Staffordshire, Norfolk, the Isle of Wight, Lake District and North Wales. Also the parent company of Beaumont Summer Camps (Jobline 01263 835151).
Employment available: Activity, IT and environment studies instructors, chefs, cooks, catering assistants, drivers and domestic assistants are required to work at the camps.
Prerequisites: Minimum age 19 for group leaders. All applicants must have a keen interest in working with children.
Duration of employment: 3-8 month contracts, 5½-6 days per week.
Selection procedures and orientation: Training for catering assistants, activity/IT/ environmental studies instructors and domestic assistants is provided.
Wages: Sports instructors are paid £250 per month net; environmental instructors are paid £728 per month gross.

OPTIONS TRUST
4 Plantation Way, Whitehill, Bordon, Hants. GU35 9HD. ☎01420 474261. E-mail: hcil@pvm.ndo.co.uk.
Registered charity.
Employment available: This organisation is run by disabled people who require help with washing, dressing, moving around, household tasks and driving about.
Destinations: Mainly the South of England.
Prerequisites: Applicants need to be physically fit, reliable, able and willing to listen and carry out instructions, enjoy a varied routine and have a sense of humour. A driving licence is essential.
Duration of employment: 6 months or more.
Selection procedures and orientation: Once an application form is returned to the Co-ordinator, details will be passed on to members who need staff at this time. The individual employer will then contact the applicant, ask for references, arrange interviews and discuss the possibility of offers.
Wages: Salaries vary among employers. However, in all cases, board and lodging are provided in the home of the employer.
Contact: Mrs. Virginia Mason.

PGL TRAVEL LTD
Alton Court, Penyard Lane, Ross-on-Wye, Herefordshire HR9 5GL. ☎01989 767833. Fax: 01989 768769. E-mail: pglpeople@pgl.co.uk. Website: www.pgl. co.uk/people.
PGL Travel runs activity holidays for children, usually involving lots of outdoor activities.
Employment available: Group leaders, activity instructors, catering staff, support staff, overseas couriers and administrators.
Destinations: Various locations around the UK, France and Spain.
Number of jobs: Over 2500 per year.
Prerequisites: Qualifications are not necessary except in certain activity positions. PGL training is available for most jobs and the company will help candidates obtain the relevant qualifications. Experience of working with children is also helpful.
Duration of employment: The minimum period is usually 6-8 weeks. The centres are

open between February and early October.

Selection procedures and orientation: As soon as an application form is received, a decision will be made as to whether the applicant can be offered a position. Nominated referees will be contacted. If an applicant is only available for the summer, it is better to apply earlier. The earlier a worker is available, the better their chances of being offered employment.

Wages: Workers are paid between £60 and £100 per week on top of free board and lodging.

PORTH TOCYN COUNTRY HOTEL

Abersoch, Pwllheli, Gwynedd LL53 7BU. ☎01758 713303. Fax: 016758 713538. E-mail: bookings@porthtocyn.fsnet.co.uk. Website: www.porth-tocyn-hotel.co.uk.

Employment available: General assistants and assistant cooks (about 14 in total). Owners specify gap year students as possible employees.

Prerequisites: Intelligence and sense of humour required. Cooking experience useful but not required.

Duration and time of placements: Minimum period of work 6 weeks between March and November, e.g. over Easter and outside the university vacations.

Selection procedures & orientation: Applications with s.a.e.

Wages: Above the national minimum wage. Free board and lodging and use of tennis court and swimming pool. Travel expenses paid for staff who come for short stints on the fringes of the season (e.g. at Easter and to cover May bank holidays).

Contact: Mr. and Mrs. Fletcher-Brewer.

YOUTH HOSTELS ASSOCIATION

YHA England & Wales Recruitment Department, PO Box 6030, Matlock, Derbyshire DE4 3XA. ☎01629 592650. E-mail: jobopportunities@yha.org.uk. Website: www.yha.org.uk.

Seasonal assistants are required to help run the YHA's 240 youth hostels in England and Wales.

Employment available: Assistants undertake various duties including catering, cleaning and reception work.

Number of placements per year: Varies (usually about 400).

Prerequisites: Minimum age 18. Experience in one or more of the relevant duties is essential, as are enthusiasm, excellent customer service and a flexible approach to work.

Duration of employment: Work is available for varying periods, though more vacancies occur between Easter and the autumn.

Wages: Basic monthly salary of £807 plus free accommodation. Food can be included if required.

Selection procedures and orientation: All posts are subject to a face-to-face interview at applicant's expense, at the hostel where the vacancy arises. Interviews may be called at short notice. Most recruitment takes place between December and June.

Directory of Paid Seasonal Jobs Abroad

ACORN ADVENTURE LTD

Operations Department, 22 Worcester St, Stourbridge DY8 1AN. ☎0870 121 99 51. Fax: 0870 121 99 81. E-mail: topstaff@acornadventure.co.uk. Website: www.acorn-jobs.co.uk.

Outdoor adventure camping holidays for schools, youth groups and families in Europe and the UK.

Employment available: 300 seasonal work opportunities for activity instructors, catering staff, administrators and drivers between mid-April and September.

Destinations: France (Ardèche), Italy (the Alps) and Spain (Costa Brava), Wales and the Lake District.

Wages: All staff receive an on-site living allowance (minimum £50) plus an end-of-contract bonus and (if applicable) a qualification bonus.

Application procedure: Application enquiries welcome all year round.

Contact: Chris Lloyd, Recruitment Manager.

APPELLATION CONTROLEE

Ulgersmaweg 26C, 9731 BT Groningen, Netherlands. ☎050-549 2434. Fax: 050-549 2428. E-mail: info@apcon.nl. Website: www.apcon.nl.

Employment available: Seasonal picking jobs arranged with farmers.

Destinations: France, England and special projects.

Number of placements per year: 500-1000.

Prerequisites: Minimum age 18. Must be in good health and physical condition. Must have EU passport/identity card or valid working permit.

Duration of employment: 2 weeks to 6 months. Hours of work mainly between 5 and 10 per day depending on weather and amount of ripe fruit, 5 or 6 days per week. Grape-pickers work 7 days a week, 8 hours a day.

Selection procedures and orientation: Interviews not necessary.

Wages: At least national minimum wage or piece work by kilo, normally £25-£40 a day.

Contact: Itziar van Breemen (itziar@buitenreclame.nu).

BRITANNIA SOCCER USA

10281 Frosty Court, Suite 100, Manassas, VA 20109, USA. ☎703-330-2532. Fax: 703-330-6850. Website: www.britanniasoccerusa.com.

Soccer education organisation operating in the USA.

Employment available: Soccer coaching opportunities.

Destinations: Nationwide throughout the USA, including Hawaii, plus the Caribbean.

Number of placements per year: 200 summer coaches plus 50 coaches on 9-month contracts. Recruit specifically in the UK.

Prerequisites: U.E.F.A. coaching qualification, plus coaching and teaching experience needed. Must also have playing background and dynamic personality.

Duration of employment: Variable between June and August for summer positions, March-November for longer contracts.

Selection procedures & orientation: Interviews and coaching sessions held in most UK locations. Full orientation provided on arrival in the USA. J-1 visa can be arranged through BUNAC or H2B visa arranged for 9-month contracts.

Wages: $100-$300 a week. Homestay accommodation and transport provided (including upfront airfares). Apartments provided for 9-month contracts.

CANVAS HOLIDAYS

VRG Camping Recruitment, East Port House, 12 East Port, Dunfermline, Fife KY12 7JG. ☎01383 629012. E-mail: recruitment@vrgcampingrecruitment.com. Website: www.vrgcampingrecruitment.com.

Canvas Holidays offers over 400 seasonal vacancies to work in Europe over the summer season.

Employment available: Various positions including Campsite Courier, Children's Courier and more senior positions over Europe.

Destinations: France, Spain, Italy, Austria, Germany, Switzerland, Luxembourg, Holland and Croatia.

Prerequisites: Minimum age limit of 19 for France and 18 for all other destinations.

Duration of employment: Minimum 2-month fixed-term contract between March and October.

Application procedure: Apply on-line at www.vrgcampingrecruitment.com or call 01383 629012 for an application pack.

Wages: From £110 per week plus accommodation, travel insurance, uniform and return travel.

CLUB CANTABRICA HOLIDAYS LTD
146/148 London Road, St. Albans, Herts. AL1 1PQ. ☎01727 866177. Fax: 01727 843766. Website: www.cantabrica.co.uk.

Employment available: Mobile home tour operator which employs couriers on-site.

Destinations: France, Spain (Costa Brava), Italy and Austria.

Prerequisites: Minimum age 21. Good working knowledge of relevant language an advantage.

Duration of employment: April to November, but peak season positions also available.

Application procedure: Applications before end of December. Interviews held in January/ February.

Wages: From £75-£100 a week plus end-of-season bonus.

R J CORNISH & CO PTY LTD
RMB 2024 Cottons Road, Cobram, Victoria 3644, Australia. ☎ +61 3 5872 2055. Fax: +61 3 5872 1054. E-mail: picking@rjcornish.com. Website: www. rjcornish.com.

Employment available: Casual fruit picking work in the months of January (starting mid to late), February and March. Pickers needed for pears and peaches, also some apples at the end of the above season.

Number of jobs per year: 200+.

Prerequisites: Minimum age 18. Must be prepared to work in hot conditions and to undertake heavy lifting of ladders and bags of fruit. Must have legal right to work in Australia.

Duration of employment: Normal maximum would be 7 weeks; most people work a week or two. Hours of work are normally 7.30am-4pm Sunday to Friday.

Selection procedures and orientation: Applications accepted until December. Interviews not necessary since jobs are mainly fixed up over the internet.

Wages: Piece work rates paid according to how many bins of fruit picked. In 2005 the rate was $33.21 per wooden bin. Barrack-style accommodation meals provided at a weekly cost of $116. (See website for up-to-date information.)

Contact: Doug McKean, Office Manager.

EQUITY TRAVEL
Dukes Lane House, 47 Middle Street, Brighton BN1 1AL. ☎01273 886911. Fax: 01273 203212. E-mail: recruitment@equity.co.uk. Website: www.equity. co.uk/employment.

Employment available: Winter resort staff (reps, ski companions, chalet, bar and housekeeping staff, plongeurs, night porters, handymen, etc.).

Destinations: Austria, France and Italy.

Number of placements per year: 200+.

Prerequisites: EU nationality essential.

Duration of employment: Some jobs start October-December; others last December to May.

Wages: Accommodation, board, ski pass, insurance, uniform and transport to the resort provided.

Selection procedures and orientation: Application form on website. Applications begin to be processed from May onwards. Interview expenses are not reimbursed.

Contact: Carrie Husband, Overseas Recruitment Co-ordinator.

EUROCAMP HOLIDAYS
Overseas Recruitment Department (Ref TGY/05), Hartford Manor, Greenbank Lane, Northwich, CW8 1HW. ☎01606 787525. Website: www.holidaybreak-jobs.com.
Employment available: Family camping tour operator that employs summer season campsite and children's couriers. See entry for *Holidaybreak* below.

FAMILY SKI COMPANY
Bank Chambers, Walwyn Road, Colwall, WR13 6QG. ☎01684 541444 or 540333. Fax: 01684 540203. E-mail: miked@familyski.co.uk. Website: www.familyski.co.uk.
The Family Ski Company specialises in providing catered chalet holidays with flexible childcare.
Employment available: Activity leaders to design a weekly activity timetable for children aged 6 weeks to 12 years.
Destinations: Ski resorts in the French Alps: Les Trois Vallées, Paradiski, and Les Portes du Soleil.
Prerequisites: Experience necessary, qualifications preferred. Staff must be enthusiastic, imaginative and self-motivated. All applicants must have a UK National Insurance number and an EU passport.
Duration and time of placements: Season lasts from late November to late April.
Wages: All meals and accommodation provided plus full season lift pass, ski or snowboard hire, uniform (including ski jacket), return transport from the UK to resort, medical and personal liability insurance provided in addition to a weekly wage, which will be disclosed at the time of interview, and an end-of-season discretionary bonus.
Contact: Mike Duffin.

FOUR WINDS MERISKI

1st Floor, Carpenters Buildings, Carpenters Lane, Cirencester, Gloucestershire GL7 1EE. ☎01285 648518. Fax: 01285 651685. E-mail: sales@meriski.co.uk. Website: www.meriski.co.uk.

Méribel specialist with 12 chalets in this top French resort.

Employment available: Chalet host, chalet chef and nanny vacancies.

Number of placements per year: 45.

Prerequisites: Minimum age 23. Must hold an EU passport. Should be professional nannies or chefs.

Duration of employment: Full winter season from beginning of December to the end of April.

Selection procedures and orientation: Applications accepted from May. Training and management support offered throughout the season.

Wages: Usual ski perks.

Contact: Catherine Whittaker, Sales Manager.

GOAL-LINE SOCCER INC.

PO Box 1642, Corvallis, OR 97339, USA. ☎541-753-5833. Fax: 541-753-0811. E-mail: info@goal-line.com. Website: www.goal-line.com.

Employment available: Qualified football coaches are required to teach football to American children and play exhibition games against local teams. Coaches stay with American families and are able to participate in recreational activities such as golf and water skiing.

Destinations: USA, especially west coast states of Washington and Oregon.

Number of placements per year: 26.

Prerequisites: Coaching certificates from recognised national soccer associations are required. Applicants must be over 21. J-1 visas available through BUNAC.

Duration of employment: 5 weeks, starting at the beginning of July and running to mid-August. Additional weeks may be available.

Selection procedures and orientation: Applicants must commit themselves by mid-March. Interviews are conducted 2-3 times a year in the UK. Prior to coaching, staff receive a 4-day Pre-Camp Orientation at Oregon State University.

Wages: Flights to the USA, the J-1 visa (arranged through BUNAC) and a registration fee of approximately £200 must be paid. Coaches are paid a wage of $300+ per week.

Contact: Tom Rowney, Director.

HOLIDAYBREAK

Overseas Recruitment Department (Ref TGY/05) ☎01606 787525. Website: www.holidaybreakjobs.com.

Employment available: Camping tour operator which employs a large number of campsite couriers and children's couriers in Europe for the self-drive camping brands: Eurocamp and Keycamp.

Destinations: Austria, Belgium, Holland, France, Germany, Italy, Spain, Switzerland and Croatia.

Prerequisites: Minimum age 18. Must have UK or EU nationality. Customer service skills essential.

Duration of employment: Minimum period is April/May to July.

Application procedure: Applications accepted from September/October. Interviews held in Hartford Cheshire between October and April.

Wages: Competitive salary plus tented accommodation, uniform and travel to and from Britain provided.

IAN MEARNS HOLIDAYS

Tannery Yard, Witney St, Burford, Oxon. OX18 4DP. ☎01993 822655. Fax: 01993 822650. E-mail: enquiries@ianmearnsholidays.co.uk.

Tour operator offering self-drive family camping holidays.
Employment available: Campsite reps and montage/demontage assistants.
Destinations: France.
Number of placements per year: About 50.
Prerequisites: Must be healthy and able to work without supervision.
Duration of employment: Minimum 10 weeks between Easter and September. People available to start work at beginning of season especially in demand.
Wages: Wages plus accommodation, insurance, uniform, training and transport.
Selection procedures and orientation: Applications with CV from 1st October. Interviews held in Burford.

JOBS IN THE ALPS
E-mail: info@jobs-in-the-alps.com. Website: www.jobs-in-the-alps.com.
Agency arranges summer and winter jobs in hotels and restaurants in alpine resorts for students with language skills.
Employment available: Waiters, bar staff, kitchen staff, chambermaids, night porters and receptionists for first-class hotels, family hostels, etc. Limited amount of au pair work also available.
Destinations: Switzerland and France.
Number of placements per year: 150.
Prerequisites: Applicants must have a good knowledge of French or German (e.g. A-level) and be EU passport holders. Restaurant or pub work experience preferred.
Duration of employment: Applicants must be prepared to sign a contract for the whole winter season, i.e. December to Easter. Summer contracts more flexible, i.e. 2-4 months between June and September.
Selection procedure and orientation: Initial contact should be made via website. Applications should be submitted by November for the winter, May for the summer. There is an agency fee (if you become a member) of £30 plus £20 per month of the contract up to a maximum of £110. All workers are visited by a representative during the season.
Wages: £500-£700 a month net, working on a local contract and getting paid in local currency. Board and keep are included and most staff benefit from discounts on ski passes.
Contact: Alan Mullins, Proprietor.

KEYCAMP HOLIDAYS
Overseas Recruitment Department (Ref TGY/05), Hartford Manor, Greenbank Lane, Northwich, CW8 1HW. ☎01606 787525. Website: www.holidaybreakjobs. com.
Employment available: Family camping tour operator that employs summer season campsite and children's couriers. See entry for *Holidaybreak* above.
Duration of employment: April-July, July-October or March-October.

KING'S CAMPS
The Manor House, Ecclesall Road South, Sheffield, S11 9PS. ☎08700 434495. Fax: 08700 429321. E-mail: recruitment@kingscamps.org. Website: www.king-scamps.org.
Employment available: Staff lead and assist children with sports and activity sessions.
Destinations: Children's holiday clubs on French and Spanish campsites (as well as non-residential summer activity camps throughout the UK)
Prerequisites: Minimum age 17. UK nationality. Experience of working with children, sports coaching or childcare qualifications needed.
Duration and time of placements: Full season lasts 4 months, half season lasts 2½ months.
Selection procedures & orientation: Deadline for applications is July 1st. Interviews are essential but can be conducted by telephone.

Wages: Varies depending on position (see website). Camping accommodation provided in Europe.
Contact: Emma Justice or Rebecca Padgett, Recruitment & Training Officers.

OVERSEAS WORKING HOLIDAYS

Level 1, 51 Fife Road, Kingston, Surrey KT1 1SF. ☎0845 344 0366 or 020-8547 3664. Fax: 0870 460 4578. E-mail: info@owh.co.uk. Website: www.owh.co.uk.
Programme description: Paid work in hospitality industries of Australia and Canada. Variety of positions available including retail/customer service/guest relations/front desk and bar and catering work. Also offers Work and Play France programme (mainly aimed at Australian working holiday makers). See entry in 'Directory of Specialist Gap Year Programmes'.

PERFECT WAY

Hafnerweg 10, 5200 Brugg, Switzerland. E-mail: info@perfectway.ch or perfectway@bluewin.ch. Website: www.perfectway.ch.
In operation since 1995.
Employment available: Au pair and nanny agency making placements in Swiss, American and other international families in Switzerland.
Destinations: Switzerland.
Number of placements per year: 100-200.
Prerequisites: Ages 18-29. Candidates must have common sense, be honest and have good manners. 2 references required. EU nationals need no seasonal work permits.
Duration of employment: 6-18 months.
Selection procedures & orientation: Some families fly candidates in for interview; otherwise telephone contact.
Wages: At least SFr700 per month plus other perks.
Contact: Karin Schatzmann, Owner (speaks English, German and Swedish).

SIBLU HOLIDAYS BY HAVEN EUROPE

Siblu Human Resources Dept, Bryanston Court, Selden Hill, Hemel Hempstead, Herts. HP2 4TN. ☎01442 203970 (Recruitment hotline). E-mail: mark. young@bourne-leisure.co.uk. Website: www.siblu.com.
Employment available: European holiday parks employing Park Reps, Children's Club Reps, Reception/Bar/Accommodation Team Members, Lifeguards and Entertainers.
Destinations: France, Spain and Italy.
Prerequisites: Minimum age 18. Language skills needed for some roles.
Duration of employment: Various contract lengths between Easter and October.
Wages: Accommodation, insurance, uniform and travel provided.
Contact: Mark Young.

SNOWLINE/VIP

Collingbourne House, 140-142 Wandsworth High St, Wandsworth, London SW18 4JJ. ☎08701 123617 or (for nanny positions) 08701 121323 E-mail: recruitment@snowlineVIP.com. Website: www.snowline.co.uk or www.valdisere. co.uk.
Employment available: Positions available: Chalet host, ski host/driver, concierge/driver and driver/handyman.
Number of placements per year: 140.
Prerequisites: Minimum age 21 for most positions, but 18 for nanny applicants. Chalet hosts need previous catering experience; ski hosts need about 20 weeks of ski experience and a driving licence for 3 years. All staff must be UK residents with a National Insurance number.
Duration of employment: Mid-November to end of April or early May.
Selection procedures and orientation: Online applications welcomed until the beginning

of November which is the deadline. Interviews are essential.
Wages: Details on application. Package includes a full area ski pass, travel to and from the Alps and ski hire if needed.
Contact: Jane Irwin, Personnel Manager; for nanny positions: Rachael Waite (rachael. waite@snowlineVIP.com).

SPECIALIST HOLIDAYS GROUP
King's Place, 12-42 Wood St, Kingston upon Thames, Surrey KT1 1SG. ☎0845 055 0258. E-mail: overseasrecruitment@s-h-g.co.uk. Website: www.shgjobs.co.uk or www.tui-uk.co.uk/jobopps.
The Specialist Holidays Group and TUI UK employ 10,000 staff with 13 leading tour operators including Crystal Holidays (www.crystalholidays.co.uk), Thomson Ski & Lakes (www.thomson-ski.com) and Simply Travel (www.simplytravel.com).
Employment available: Resort representatives, chalet hosts, chalet assistants, catering staff, hotel chefs, hotel assistants, maintenance staff, kitchen/night porters and nannies.
Destinations: Many European, American and Canadian destinations.
Prerequisites: Qualified and unqualified staff are recruited. Flexible and friendly attitude needed plus a good understanding of customer requirements and the ability to work within a busy team. All employees must be aged 18 and over. Overseas reps should be over 21 and able to communicate in Spanish, Portuguese, Italian or French.
Duration of employment: Winter season is November to April; summer season is May to September or sometimes March to November.

TORRENS VALLEY ORCHARDS
Forreston Rd, Gumeracha, South Australia, Australia. ☎ +61 8-8389 1405. Fax: +61 8-8389 1406. E-mail: tvo@hotkey.net.au. Website: www.tvo.com.au.
Large orchard just south of the Barossa Valley wine region which employs steady stream of backpackers. Access to Adelaide via a daily bus (30 minutes, A$5).
Employment available: Range of orchard work including cherry picking and packing (December/January), pear picking and packing (Feb-Sept), tree planting and training, pruning, maintenance and office work.
Number of placements per year: 500, usually about 20 at one time.
Prerequisites: Travellers must be over 18.
Duration of employment: Minimum 2 weeks, up to several months. Normal hours are 8 per day, 5 days per week. During cherry harvest, pickers may work up to 12 hours per day, 7 days a week.
Selection procedures and orientation: Interviews not necessary; most recruitment conducted over internet.
Wages: Normal daily minimum of A$50 (after tax and accommodation deductions). Up to $1000 for key personnel during cherry season. Accommodation in hostel-like conditions. Friendly workers may be invited to join locals in football, fishing, barbecues and parties.
Contact: Tony Hannaford, Owner.

VENUE HOLIDAYS
1 Norwood St, Ashford, Kent TN23 1QU. ☎01233 649950. Fax: 01233 634494. E-mail: info@venueholidays.co.uk. Website: www.venueholidays.co.uk.
Family-run camping tour operator.
Employment available: Campsite reps and other jobs.
Destinations: France, Spain, Italy.
Prerequisites: Must be outgoing, fit and able to work hard in difficult conditions. Minimum age 18. Knowledge of a language useful but not essential.
Duration of employment: Minimum period of work June-August but longer period preferred between March and October.
Wages: £450 per month with accommodation provided.
VILLAGE CAMPS

rue de la Morache, 1260 Nyon, Switzerland. ☎**022-990 9405. Fax: 022-990 9494. E-mail: personnel@villagecamps.ch. Website: www.villagecamps.com.**
Employment available: Counsellors, sports instructors, TEFL teachers and general domestic and administrative staff needed for multi-activity centres and language camps for international children in Europe. Also hire up to 100 ski counsellors and other staff for the winter season in the Swiss Alps.
Number of jobs: 300.
Destinations: Switzerland (Anzère, Leysin), Austria (Zell-am-See), England and France (Ardèche).
Prerequisites: Candidates must have experience of working with children, while instructors must be qualified in canoeing/kayaking, gymnastics, arts and crafts, climbing, tennis, soccer, archery, golf or swimming. Knowledge of any European language or Japanese, Korean, Russian or Arabic is a distinct advantage.
Wages: Staff receive room and board, accident and liability insurance and an expense allowance of €240 a week (plus a ski pass in the winter).
Contact: Rose DeMarco.

WORLDNETUK
Emberton House, 26 Shakespeare Road, Bedford MK40 2ED. ☎**0845 458 1550/1. E-mail: info@worldnetuk.com. Website: www.worldnetuk.com.**
Programme description: Nannies and au pairs placed in ski and summer resorts in Europe and in the USA via the Au Pair in America programme (see 'Directory of Specialist Gap Year Programmes'). Place counsellors on American summer camps and other exchange programmes in the US.
Destinations: USA, France, Corsica, Spain, Balearics, Turkey, Italy, Sardinia, Greece, Austria, Switzerland.
Prerequisites: *Nanny/Childcare Programme USA* – 18-26 year olds with childcare training, NNEB, BTEC National Diploma in Nursery Nursing or NVQ Level III. Full clean driving licence. Departures every month on 12-month programme. Opportunity to travel at end of year.
Au Pair Programme USA – 18-26 year olds with 200 hours childcare/babysitting. Full clean driving licence. Departures every month. Opportunity to travel at end of year.
Ski/Summer Resort Nannies – Applicants must be qualified/experienced in childcare to work either in activity clubs, crèches or with individual families. No age limit. Applicants must be available for either the full summer or ski season (some shorter term placements sometimes available).
Contact: Elizabeth Elder.

Au Pairing

Gap year students who choose to become au pairs are generally looking for an affordable way to improve their knowledge of a country's language and culture. For several generations, female school leavers have been flocking to the Continent, and more recently to the United States and even Australia, attracted by the safe and stable environment which a family placement can provide. When the au pair arrangement works well, it is ideal for young, under-confident and impecunious students who want to work abroad. Occasionally, young men can find live-in jobs, but the number of families and therefore agencies willing to entertain the possibility of having a male au pair is still painfully small.

The terms au pair, mother's help and nanny are often applied rather loosely, since all are primarily live-in jobs concerned with looking after children. Nannies may have some formal training and take full charge of the children. Mother's helps work full-time and undertake general housework and/or cooking as well as childcare. Au pairs are supposed to work for no more than 30 hours a week and are expected to learn a foreign language while living with a family. Although the term au pair is used in the American context, the hours are much longer and there is no language learning element for British au pairs (see chapter on the USA).

One of the great advantages of these live-in positions generally is that they are relatively easy to get (at least for women over 18). After proving to an agency or a family that you are reasonably sensible, you will in the majority of cases be able to find a placement, though it is much easier and quicker in some countries than others, e.g. easy in France, Austria and Italy, but more difficult in Scandinavia and Portugal. Furthermore au pairs can usually benefit from legislation which exempts them from work permit requirements.

> **The minimum age can be a stumbling-block for some school leavers who are not yet 18. The majority of agencies prefer to accept applications only from candidates over 18, as Camilla Preeston discovered:**
> *I had decided even before I had finished school that I would take a year off between school and university, and au pairing seemed like the perfect way to do this. Being seventeen and a half made things much more difficult in the beginning though I sent off endless letters to agencies in Britain and overseas. Most flatly replied that I was too young, though a couple said that they would try anyway. I eventually had success with a foreign agency. The reason they didn't turn me away may have been because the fee they levy is paid upfront before a family is found. By the time they had found me a family in Calais, four months of my year off had already gone by and I was almost ready to give up. I immediately accepted the offer, perhaps a little hastily. However, had I refused it, I might not have found another family willing to accept me due to my age, and it was the first family offer I had received in the four months I had been trying.*

Camilla's youth did not prevent her from coping with what turned out to be a difficult situation in which she was expected to accept a lot of responsibility for the children (including a newborn baby) and the running of the household, while the mother was away for five days and two nights a week.

The standard length of au pair stay is for one academic year, typically September to June. Summer stays can also be arranged to coincide with the school holidays and there is some inevitable turn-over at Christmas when homesick au pairs go home to their families and then decide not to return. The advantage of a summer placement is that the au pair will accompany the family to their holiday destination at the seaside or in the mountains; the disadvantage is that the children will be your responsibility for more hours than they would be if they were at school, and also most language classes will close for the summer. Make enquiries as early as possible, since there is a shortage of summer-only positions.

Anyone interested in finding out about all aspects of live-in childcare should consult *The Au Pair & Nanny's Guide to Working Abroad* (Vacation-Work, £12.95).

PROS AND CONS

The relationship of au pair to family is not like the usual employer/employee relationship; in fact the term au pair means 'on equal terms'. The Home Office information on au pairs in Britain uses the terminology 'host family' rather than 'employer' (see the website of the Immigration & Nationality Directorate, Apollo House, 36 Wellesley Road, Croydon CR0 2AY; enquiry line 0870 606 7766; www.ind.homeoffice.gov.uk (then search `Au Pair'). Therefore the success of the arrangement depends more than usual on whether individuals hit it off, so there is always an element of risk when living in a family of strangers. The Council of Europe guidelines stipulate that au pairs should be aged 18-27 (though these limits are flexible), should be expected to work about five hours a day, five days per week plus a couple of evenings of babysitting, must be given a private room and full board, health insurance, opportunities to learn the language and pocket money. The standard pocket money paid to au pairs in Europe is usually in the neighbourhood of €240-€300 a month, though it can be more, for example in Switzerland.

Once you have arrived in the family, it is important to clarify immediately what your hours and duties will be, which day you will be paid, whether you can expect a rise and how much notice either party must give if they wish to terminate the arrangement. This gets everyone off to a business-like start. But no matter how well-defined your duties are, there are bound to be occasions when your extra services will be taken for granted. It may seem that your time is not your own. So the standard working hours can soon turn into an unofficial string of 14 hour days. Whether you can tolerate this depends entirely on your disposition and on the compensating benefits of the job, e.g. free use of car and telephone, nice kids, good food, lots of sunshine, etc.

Gillian Forsyth's au pairing experience in Bavaria was a great success:

> *I had no official day off or free time but was treated as a member of the family. Wherever they went I went too. I found this much more interesting than being treated as an employee as I really got to know the country and the people. In the evenings I did not have to sit in my room, but chatted with the family. Three years later we still keep in close contact and I have been skiing with them twice since, on an au pair/friend basis.*

If you do not have such a friendly arrangement with your family, you may feel lonely and cut off in a foreign country. Many au pairs make friends at their language classes. Some agencies issue lists of other au pairs in the vicinity.

Most au pairs' duties revolve around the children. For some, taking sole responsibility for a child can be even more alarming than cooking for the first time. You should be prepared to handle a few emergencies (for example sick or lost children) as well as the usual excursions to the park or collecting them from school. The agency questionnaire will ask you in detail what experience you have had with children and whether you are willing to look after infants, etc., so your preferences should be made known early. You must also be prepared to hurt the children's feelings when you leave. **Nicky Parker** left a family in Majorca after just nine weeks and reported, 'I could only feel guilty and sad at the distress caused to the children by yet another in a long line of people whom they had learned to love, leaving them forever.'

APPLYING

Au pair and nanny agencies are never more than referral services. If you have a contract, it will be with the family not the agency, though the agency may facilitate drawing up a contract. Since 2003 agencies in the UK have not been allowed to charge the applicant a fee. Their only chance of making a profit is if their partner agencies abroad are willing to share the fees they collect from the client families employing au pairs. Agencies which at one time sent many British girls abroad are now concentrating almost exclusively on placing foreign girls with paying client families in the UK.

If you are already abroad, check in the local English language newspaper such as the *Athens News* or the *Anglo Portuguese News* in Lisbon, or visit an au pair agency office in the country where you are (addresses provided in country chapters). Other ways of hearing about openings are to check the notice boards at the local English-speaking churches, ask the headteacher of a junior school if she/he knows of any families wanting an au pair or visit a school at the end of the school day and chat with the mothers and au pairs who are there to collect their charges. One tip for finding babysitting jobs in resorts is to introduce yourself to the *portière* or receptionist on the desk of good hotels and ask them to refer guests looking for a babysitter to you, possibly offering 10-15% commission.

The Internet

Cyberspace buzzes with an exchange of information about live-in childcare. Finding agency details is very easy with several clicks of a mouse and some agencies now conduct most of their business on the web. Au pair placement was something that was always done by telephone and correspondence rather than requiring a face-to-face interview, so it is an activity that is very well suited to the web. Among the most popular sites are www.

au-pair-box.com; www.aupairsearch.com (based in South Africa), www.aupairconnect. com/default.asp, www.aupair-world.net (German-based), www.findaupair.com and www. perfectaupair.com. Two internet-based agencies also worth trying are www.au-pair.net which calls itself the free 'No agency Au Pair Service' and the Almondbury Au Pair Agency (www.aupair-agency.com). Both act as international internet databases of au pair and other live-in vacancies. In 2005 Almondbury's site claimed that its database included 9,230 applicants and 689 registered families. Another possibility is the Kent-based Aupair-Select on www.aupair-select.com.

Internet databases like these enable families and applicants to engage in DIY arrangements. Prospective au pairs register their details, including age, nationality, relevant experience and in many cases a photo, to be uploaded onto a website which then becomes accessible to registered families. The families then make contact with suitable au pairs after paying an introduction fee to the web-based agency. Registration is usually free or reasonably priced for the job-seeker.

One problem identified by the traditional agencies is that this method makes it very difficult to carry out any effective screening of either party. On the other hand, the same could be said for sits vac advertising in the conventional way (see below). If relying on the internet it is essential to ascertain exactly the nature of the situation and the expectations of your new employer. Work out in your mind what you will do in the event the arrangement does not work out; if the agency is simply a database-provider, they will be able to offer no back-up.

Jayde Cahir turned to the internet, found an agency, was emailed several families' portfolios from which she was able to make direct contact, and eventually chose a family in Germany. In initial discussions with the host family, she was misled on several counts and found that she was expected to be more a paid companion for the neglected wife than an au pair. Even though she did develop a good relationship with the wife and boy, the husband took against her and unceremoniously dismissed her: *'I left the house within two hours of receiving his note asking me to leave or he would 'throw me out'. So I was left in a foreign country, unable to speak the language with nowhere to live. In most cases, the agencies are there to support you; however mine never returned my phone calls. This ended up being a very expensive experience as I am still owed unpaid wages.'*
Of course this lack of agency back-up is not confined to internet agencies; in-country partner agencies can also be derelict in a crisis.

The old-fashioned way of looking for live-in vacancies was by answering or placing advertisements in *The Lady* magazine (39/40 Bedford St, London WC2E 9ER) published each Tuesday. Most of the major agencies continue to advertise in its pages.

Agencies

Many leading au pair agencies and youth exchange organisations in Europe belong to IAPA, the International Au Pair Association (c/o FIYTO, Bredgade 25H, 1260 Copenhagen K, Denmark), an international body trying to regulate the industry. The IAPA website www. iapa.org has clear links to its member agencies around the world.

Agencies that specialise in one country are mentioned in the country chapters. The following UK au pair and/or nanny agencies all deal with a number of European countries:

Abacus Au Pair Agency, 2 Byron Terrace, Byron St, Hove, E. Sussex BN3 5AY (tel/fax 01273 203803; info@abacusaupairagency.co.uk).

A-One Au Pairs & Nannies, Top Floor, Union House, Union St, Andover, Hampshire SP10 1PA (01264 332500; info@aupairsetc.co.uk). Some outgoing placements but mainly places incoming au pairs in the UK.

The Au Pair Agency, 231 Hale Lane, Edgware, Middlesex HA8 9QF (020-8958 1750; elaine@aupairagency.com). Mainly France, Spain (including Majorca) and Italy.

Au Pair Connections, 39 Tamarisk Road, Wildern Gate, Hedge End, Southampton SO30 4TN (01489 780438; www.aupair-connections.co.uk). France, Spain, Italy.

Childcare International Ltd., Trafalgar House, Grenville Place, London NW7 3SA (020-8906 3116; www.childint.co.uk). Separate divisions for Europe, Canada, Australia and South Africa.

Childcare Solution & Worldnet UK, Emberton House, 26 Shakespeare Road, Bedford MK40 2ED or Avondale House, 63 Sydney Road, Haywards Heath, W Sussex RH16 1QD (0845 458 1550/1; www.worldnetuk.com or www.thechildcaresolution.com). Seasonal nannies placed in European resorts, among other placements.

Edgware & Solihull Au Pair & Nanny Agency, PO Box 147, Radlett, Herts. WD7 8WX (01923 289739; www.the-aupair-shop.com).

International Student Exchange Center, 89 Fleet Street London EC4Y 1DH; 020-7583 9116; fax 020-7583 9117; isecinfo@btconnect.com/ www.isecworld.co.uk/ap.htm. Au pair placements in Denmark, France, Germany, Netherlands, Norway and the USA.

Janet White Agency, 67 Jackson Avenue, Leeds LS8 1NS (0113-266 6507; www.janetwhite.com).

Jolaine Agency, 18 Escot Way, Barnet, Herts. EN5 3AN (020-8449 1334; aupair@jolaine.prestel.co.uk). Placements in France, Italy, Spain and Belgium.

Lucy Locketts & Vanessa Bancroft Nanny Agency, 400 Beacon Road, Wibsey, Bradford, BD6 3DJ (tel/fax 01274 402822; www.Lucylocketts.com).

Nannies Abroad, Abbots Worthy House, Abbots Worthy, Winchester SO21 1DR (01962 882299/fax 01962 881888; www.nanniesabroad.com).

Nanny & Au Pair Connection, 435 Chorley New Road, Horwich, Bolton BL6 6EJ (tel/fax 01204 694422; info@aupairs-nannies.co.uk; www.aupairs-nannies.co.uk). Placements in Belgium, France, Spain, Portugal, Switzerland, Austria, Germany, Greece, Turkey, and USA.

Quick Help Agency Ltd, 307A Finchley Road, London NW3 6EH (020-7794 8666; mailbox@quickhelp.freeserve.co.k/ www.quickhelp.co.uk).

Worldnet UK, see Childcare Solution above.

UK & Overseas Agency Ltd, Vigilant House, 120 Wilton Road, London SW1V 1JZ (020-7808 7898; london@nannys.co.uk; www.nannys.co.uk). Au pairs placed in France, Italy, Spain, Switzerland, Germany, etc.

Courses

After the rigours and stresses of sitting A-levels, many school leavers aspire to spend the following 15 months reading nothing more challenging than *Backpack* by Emily Barr about an obnoxious young Londoner who gradually comes to appreciate the joys of extended travel in Asia (while narrowly escaping murder by a serial killer). But after a decent recovery period has elapsed after exams, the idea of studying something either for fun or with a view to your future at university or in a career may come to seem more bearable. Some universities require preparatory work in a particular subject, for example some art colleges require students to do a foundation course. Whatever course is embarked on, extra qualifications and skills are viewed favourably by universities and potential employers, and students will gain practical knowledge for use at university and in later life.

Several new course providers, principally *Objective Travel Safely, Planetwise, Safetrek* and *Ultimate Gap Year,* have begun offering short preparatory courses for gap year students embarking on expeditions and world travel. See entries under 'Gap Year Preparation Courses' below. Andrew Wilson from *Planet Wise* describes a potentially lethal situation for which his course prepared the clients well:

> *About 18 months ago, we trained a group going off to Belize. On arrival they went to pick up the two 4WDs they had arranged (through Avis) and found one of them to be seriously sub-standard. They were told that there was no alternative but that*

the vehicle would be replaced the next day and so they reluctantly took the vehicle. Before they signed their life away though, they took very thorough photos of all aspects of the vehicle. Halfway through their journey, the rear axle sheared and the vehicle rolled off the road. Thanks to sensible planning, they only had the two team leaders in the 'dodgy' vehicle and all the gear. The two escaped with only bad scrapes thanks to the kit being correctly packed and stopping the vehicle from being squashed too much. On return to the car hire company, they were given short shift and so went straight to the police with the photographs. On return to the shop, they got a much better response!

RANGE OF COURSES

Depending on how you have decided to divide up your gap year, you may find yourself spending a good chunk at the beginning trying to earn money in a less-than-stimulating workplace like a supermarket or chain store. If most of your friends have gone off to university or travelling, you may have the leisure to take a course locally (see section below). This can provide an ideal chance to learn the basics of word processing, get your driving licence, obtain a life-saving qualification or sports instructor certificate, etc.

If you go abroad later in the year with no pre-arranged placement, it is a good idea to take documentary evidence of any qualifications you have earned in case you have the chance to work as an office temp in Sydney, drive a van for a charity in the Balkans or spend a week cooking on a private yacht.

The long established educational consultancy *Gabbitas* offers one-to-one advice on options of interest to gap year students and can also recommend suitable courses in areas such as business, secretarial and computer skills, cookery and catering, as well as foreign language courses in the UK and abroad and American universities. Gabbitas also offers extensive guidance on university entry and careers. Contact Gabbitas Educational Consultants, Carrington House, 126-128 Regent St, London W1 5EE (020-7734 0161; admin@gabbitas.co.uk/ www.gabbitas.co.uk); they charge from £70 for a telephone consultation, £170 for a face-to-face consultation.

The current government is keen to disseminate information about training and education opportunities nationwide. Although many of its initiatives are aimed at adult learners, some may be of use to gap year students including the National Grid For Learning (www.ngfl.gov.uk). The NGFL web portal brings together a vast and growing collection of sites that support education and lifelong learning including a large number of resources for parents and students assembled by the Department for Education & Skills.

Learndirect (0800 100 900; www.learndirect.co.uk) is a government-financed helpline that tries to provide advice and information about any aspect of training courses available in your area plus careers and funding. The helpline is open 9am to 9pm Monday to Friday and 9am to 12 noon on Saturday.

Language Courses

The gap year is an ideal opportunity for students to brush up on a barely-remembered GCSE language or even start from scratch with a new language. Most employers will view this as a very constructive allocation of time, and anyone with competence in another language has an advantage in many job hunts. Even people who are not planning to study modern languages at university should consider the advantages of getting to grips with one of the main European languages. Evening language classes offered by local authorities usually follow the academic year and are aimed at hobby learners. Intensive courses offered privately are much more expensive. If you are really dedicated, consider using a self-study programme with books and tapes, online or broadcast language course, though dedication is required to make progress. Hold out a carrot to yourself of a trip to a country where your target language is spoken. Even if you don't make much headway with the course at home, take it with you since you will have more incentive to learn once you are immersed in a language.

Although many people have been turning to the web to teach them a language, many conventional teach-yourself courses are still on the market, for example from OUP (www. askoxford.com/languages), Berlitz, the BBC, Linguaphone (www.linguaphone.co.uk) and Audioforum (www.audioforum.com). All of them offer deluxe courses with refinements such as interactive videos and of course these cost much more. Linguaphone recommends half an hour of study a day for three months to master the basics of a language.

If you are interested in an obscure language and don't know where to study it, contact the CILT Library (020-7379 5110; www.cilt.org.uk) which has a certain amount of documentation on courses especially in London.

A more enjoyable way of learning a language (and normally a more successful one) is by speaking it with the natives. Numerous British companies represent a range of language schools abroad offering in-country language courses. They are very familiar with differences between schools, qualifications, locations, etc. and what is most suitable for clients. *CESA Languages Abroad, Caledonia Languages Abroad, Cactus Language, Euro-Academy* and *Language Courses Abroad*, among others, all have wide-ranging programmes abroad in Europe and beyond. These agencies also provide a useful back-up service if the course does not fulfil your requirements in any way. In addition to the agencies listed at the beginning of the 'Directory of Language Courses' later in this chapter, see also www.tandem-schools.com, www.worldsbestlanguageschools.com and www.languagesoutthere.com. For agencies in the USA and Canada, see the chapter 'Gap Years for North Americans'.

Of course it is also possible to book a course directly with a language school abroad which is the route that Annabel Iglehart from Edinburgh chose in her post-university gap year:

After completing my university degree, I decided to take a year (or two) out to gain new skills and participate in interesting activities around the world. After working in a variety of jobs at home, I went to Salamanca to do a three-month intensive Spanish language course with Mester. I planned and paid for my course and accommodation directly through Mester and this saved me a lot of money; it was by far the most economical way to organise the trip. The course was fantastic. The classes were fast-paced and the teachers excellent. I lived with a Spanish family for a while and then moved to a flat with other students. I met loads of people with whom I am still in touch.

While learning a language at secondary school, you normally have two or three hours of classes a week which could work out at as little as 80 hours a year. While doing an eight-week intensive course, you might have 240 hours, the equivalent of three years of school instruction plus you will be speaking the language outside the classroom, so progress is normally very quick.

Literally thousands of language schools around the world would like your business, so care needs to be taken in choosing one that suits individual needs. Possible sources of language school addresses on the web are www.languageschoolsguide.com, www.language-learning and http://language.shawguides.com. After considering the obvious factors like price and location when choosing a language school, also try to find out the average age and likely nationalities of your fellow learners, how experienced and qualified the staff are, whether there will be any one-to-one tuition and whether the course concentrates on oral or written skills, whether there are extracurricular activities and excursions included in the fee, and generally as much as you can. One key factor is whether or not a school prepares its students for exams. If they do and you are there only for the fun of it, you may find that lessons are not suitable (and vice versa).

Whereas some language schools run purely recreational courses, others offer some kind of qualification. Some schools are instantly recognised such as the Alliance Française and the Goethe Institute. At the other end of the spectrum, some schools offer nothing more than a certificate outlining the period of study and perhaps the level of language reached or work covered in the course, which may be of limited value if you ever need to show proof of language attainment.

Serious language schools on the continent usually offer the possibility of preparing for one of the internationally recognised exams. In France, the qualification for aspiring language learners is the D.E.L.F. *(Diplôm Elémentaire de Langue Français)* while the Spanish counterpart is the D.E.L.E. *(Diploma de Español como Lengua Extranjera)* both of which are recognised by employers, universities, officialdom, etc. The D.E.L.E is split into three levels: *Certificado Inicial de Español, Diploma Básico de Español* and the *Diploma Superior de Español.* Most schools say that even the Basic Diploma requires at least eight or nine months of study in Spain. A prior knowledge of the language, of course, allows the student to enrol at a higher level and attain the award more quickly. No single qualification in Italy is as dominant as the D.E.L.E. or the D.E.L.F. Typical of Italian exams is C.I.L.S. *(Certificato di Italiano come Lingua Straniera)* which was established by Siena University and is authorised by the Italian Ministry of Foreign Affairs.

Recreational language courses are offered by virtually every school and are preferred by many gap year students. Some programmes are much more structured than others, so students need to look for flexible courses which allow them to progress at their own rate. Many people agree that the fastest way to improve fluency is to have one-to-one lessons, though of course these are more expensive than group classes. Usually a combination of the two works best.

Another factor that can impede progress is if you are in the midst of your compatriots. A class in which many languages are represented is more likely to use the target language rather than slip into English. Even if you get to spend a lot of time in the company of locals, you may be expected to help them improve their English. One wily young woman studying French in Bordeaux during her gap year arrived at a solution to this problem:

> The only real frustration of my time so far has to be coming across French people who wish to improve their English. They respond to your attempt in French with their own attempt in English. However I have developed a cunning solution. I provide them with a quick explanation that I am in fact Icelandic or Russian and we are soon back on track.

Increasingly, major language schools are offering work experience placements to their 'graduates'. Many belong to GWEA (Global Work Experience Association) described in the chapter on Work Experience. Many language courses abroad combine language tuition with cultural and other studies. For instance while learning Spanish in Malaga, for example with the *Malaca Instituto* (see entry), you can also take lessons in dance or cookery or follow the course up with an unpaid internship; while studying Italian in Florence, you can also take drawing classes, and so on. The possibilities are endless. Living with a family is highly recommended especially for beginners since it usually forces you to speak the target language from the beginning.

TEFL Training

In some cases, a preparatory course in Teaching English as a Foreign Language (known as TEFL, pronounced 'teffle') is required by year out placement agencies or individual language schools, whereas in others a willingness to communicate is sufficient.

If you are entertaining the idea of teaching English in your gap year, the best way to outrival the competition and make the job-hunt (not to mention the job itself) easier is to do a TEFL training course of which there is an enormous choice in the UK. Two standard recognised qualifications will improve your range of job options. The best known is the Cambridge Certificate in English Language Teaching to Adults (CELTA) administered and awarded by the University of Cambridge Local Examinations Syndicate (ESOL Examinations, 1 Hills Road, Cambridge CB1 2EU; 01223 553355; esol@ucles.org.uk/ www. cambridgeESOL.org/teaching). The other is the Certificate in TESOL (Teaching English to Speakers of Other Languages) offered by Trinity College *London*, 89 Albert Embankment, London SE1 7TP (020-7820 6100; info@trinitycollege.co.uk/ www.trinitycollege.co.uk). Both are very intensive and expensive, averaging £850-£950. These courses involve at least 100 hours of rigorous training with a practical emphasis (full-time for four weeks or part-time over several months). Most centres expect applicants to have the equivalent of university entrance qualifications, i.e. three GCSEs and two A-levels, but some admit only university graduates.

A list of the 250+ Cambridge Certificate centres both in the UK and abroad offering the CELTA course can be found on the website mentioned or requested from UCLES in exchange for a large s.a.e. Here is a small selection:

Ealing, Hammersmith & West London College, Gliddon Road, London W14 9BL (020-8563 0063; www.wlc.ac.uk). £745.

International House, 106 Piccadilly, London W1J 7NL (020-7518 6999; www.ihlondon. com). Also offer course at IH Newcastle.

Oxford House College, 28 Market Place, Oxford Circus, London W1W 8AW (020-7580 9785; www.oxfordhousecollege.co.uk).

Regent Language Training, 90 Banbury Road, Oxford OX2 6JT (01865 515566; oxford@regent.org.uk). Centres also in London, Brighton and Edinburgh (the latter two offer the Trinity TESOL course); www.regent.org.uk. From £690 + VAT. Possibility of free training if trainee spends summer working for Regent.

St. Giles Educational Trust, 51 Shepherd's Hill, Highgate, London N6 5QP (020-8340 0828; www.tefl-stgiles.com). Also offer course at Brighton school.

Stanton Teacher Training, Stanton House, 167 Queensway, London W2 4SB (020-7221 7259; www.stanton-school.co.uk). £741.

Centres offering the Trinity College Certificate include:

EF English First, 5th Floor, Arthur House, Chorlton St, Manchester M1 3EJ (0161-236 7494; manchester@englishfirst.com).

Golders Green Teacher Training Centre, 11 Golders Green Road, London NW11 8DE (020-8731 0963; www.goldersgreen-college.co.uk). 5-week full-time course £749 plus moderation fee of £90.

Inlingua Teacher Training, Rodney Lodge, Rodney Road, Cheltenham, Glos. GL50 1HX (01242 253171; training@inlingua-cheltenham.co.uk).

The Language Project, 27 Oakfield Road, Clifton, Bristol BS8 2AT (0117-927 3993; www. languageproject.co.uk). £1150. Also offer weekend Introduction to TESOL.

A large number of other centres offer TEFL courses in the UK and abroad which vary in duration and price. Note that taking a TEFL course in a non-English speaking country provides a head start when looking for a job in that country. Among the best known providers are the British Council and International House offering the CELTA in many cities from Madrid to Sydney, but scores of independent providers provide TEFL training courses of varying lengths, including this small selection:

Bridge-Linguatec Language Services, 915 S. Colorado Blvd, Denver, CO 80246, USA (1-888-827-4757 toll-free in North America; 0800-028 8051 toll-free in the UK; tefl-celta@bridgelinguatec.com; www.bridgetefl.com). Bridge-Linguatec is a language training company which offers TEFL teacher certification and job placement programmes in Asia, Europe, and Latin America. Also offers online TEFL course. TEFL training (2-4 weeks) available in Argentina, Brazil, Chile, China, Costa Rica, Czech Republic, Mexico, Peru, Spain, and the USA.

Global Vision International (GVI), Amwell Farmhouse, Nomansland, Wheathampstead,

St. Albans, Herts. AL4 8EJ (0870 608 8898; info@gvi.co.uk/ www.gvi.co.uk). Intensive weekend TEFL courses held monthly at the London School of Economics. Course will enable prospective volunteer teachers to survive in the classroom. £210 non-residential.

International English, PO Box 50, Arundel, West Sussex, BN18 9LQ (01903 889797; info@internationalenglish.co.uk/ www.internationalenglish.co.uk). Short intensive training courses offered in association with the placement agency Teaching & Projects Abroad to prepare teaching volunteers. 2-day and 4-day courses throughout the year. Residential and non-residential options available at a conference centre in Sussex or in University Halls in London. 2-day weekend course from £245; 4-day course £465. Accommodation can be arranged (£275/£555 inclusive).

i-to-i, Woodside House, 261 Low Lane, Horsforth, Leeds LS18 5NY (0870 333 2332; info@i-to-i.com/ www.teflcourses.com). 20-hour weekend TEFL training courses across the UK or a 40-hour online version, accessible anywhere in the world, including a CD-ROM, teaching plans, plus support from a designated TEFL tutor. An 80-hour combined weekend and online TEFL course is available, which also includes a 20-hour online grammar awareness module. From £195. A free taster TEFL course online at www.onlinetefl.com. 'TEFL Experience' courses, which include practical work experience in Brazil, Costa Rica, Ecuador, India, Mexico or Thailand are also available through i-to-i. (See entry in 'Directory of Specialist Gap Year Programmes').

Teaching Abroad, Aldsworth Parade, Goring, West Sussex BN12 4TX (01903 708300; www.teaching-abroad.co.uk). TEFL taster course and volunteer preparation in association with International English (see above).

TEFL International, 38/53-55 Moo 1, Klaeng, Muang Rayong 21160 (+66 38-652280; info@teflint.com; http://teflinternational.com). 130-hour+ certificate course offered in Thailand and many other countries including England, France, New Zealand, Egypt and China. US$1590 (includes private accommodation).

After finishing A levels, **Sam James** and **Sophie Ellison** from Yorkshire decided to spend their gap year in Barcelona if possible. They both signed up to do the Trinity Certificate in TESOL course at Oxford House in their destination city, deciding that this would give them the introduction they needed, and it worked (see *Spain* chapter).

IT and Business Skills Courses

Colleges of Further Education and private colleges offer a wealth of courses that many Gap Year students might choose to pursue, possibly with a view to earning money quickly for a planned placement or expedition later in the year. IT and Business skills courses can prove very useful for finding well-paid temporary work before and during university. Many vocational courses attract government grants for students and the college should be able to tell you whether funding is available and how to apply.

The British Accreditation Council for Independent Further and Higher Education or BAC (020-7224 5474; www.the-bac.org) accredits around 200 private colleges in the UK. Many of these offer Business and IT courses, while others specialise in subjects such as hospitality management and cookery, which may be useful to those wishing to spend part of their gap year working for a tour company or in a ski resort. Note that many of BAC's accredited colleges specialise in tutoring students from abroad (e.g. for A-levels) and not all of the colleges run short courss. The BAC website includes links to the colleges' own websites with details of the courses on offer.

A variety of qualifications can be gained to impress future employers. A range of general and specialist certificates and diplomas are offered by OCR (combination of the Oxford & Cambridge exam board with Royal Society of Arts), City & Guilds/Pitman and LCCI (London Chamber of Commerce and Industry).

The basic qualifications are:

BTEC (Business and Technology Education Council) (www.edexcel.org.uk) run courses in media studies, graphic design, health studies, public services, etc. as well as IT.

Oxford Cambridge & RSA (www.ocr.org.uk) specialise in secretarial and administrative qualifications.

London Chamber of Commerce & Industry (www.lccieb.org.uk) grants a Diploma in Secretarial Administration and a Private Secretary's Diploma.

Pitman (www.pitmanqualifications.com) now part of City & Guilds. Has long offered secretarial skills courses such as IT, business studies and office administration.

Information on courses in London can be obtained from the *Floodlight* directories produced by the Association of London Government and sold by newsagents and bookshops (www.floodlight.co.uk). *Part-time Floodlight in London* appears in early July (price £3.95 including postage); *Summertime Floodlight* is published before Easter and *Full-time Floodlight* comes out in the early autumn.

Outdoor Pursuits and Sports Courses

A recognised qualification in any sport will make it very easy to pick up work later in your gap year and find enjoyable holiday jobs throughout your university career. Skilled sportsmen and women can often find gainful employment in their area of expertise whether instructing tennis locally or joining a scheme to coach soccer in the USA or South Africa (see country chapters). Numerous multi-activity centres in Britain and Europe recruit staff to lead and instruct and offer their own pre-season training, sometimes free of charge.

A structured way of acquiring skills and qualifications during your sporting gap year is to participate in the Duke of Edinburgh Award scheme (described in the chapter on Expeditions). This can lead to a qualification in a variety of activity and sporting areas, including expedition skills.

A life-saving qualification allows you to work as a lifeguard, though there are different qualifications for pool and beach lifeguarding. Relevant courses leading to these qualifications are offered by the Swimming Teachers' Association (01922 645097; www.sta.co.uk) which recommends the National Aquatic Rescue Standard (NaRS) group of qualifications and by the Royal Life Saving Society (01789 773994; www.lifesavers.org.uk) which recommends the National Pool Lifeguard Qualification (NPLQ) and the National Beach Lifeguard Qualification (NBLQ) for individuals wishing to work as professional lifeguards.

Further afield, diving instructors work at Red Sea resorts, mountain leaders are hired to guide groups in the Himalayas, trainee parachutists find work packing parachutes in the US and Competent Crew get positions on ocean-going yachts. The best starting place for acquiring the necessary training and certification is the governing body of the sport that interests you which will be able to point you towards instructors' courses in the UK and beyond. For example see entries for the *British Association of Snowsport Instructors* which offers a 10-week course aimed specifically at gap year students, and the *Royal Yachting Association* below. Others include the British Canoe Union (0115 982 1100; www.bcu.org.uk), the British Mountaineering Council (0870 010 4878; www.thebmc.co.uk) and the British Horse Society (0870 120 2244; www.bhs.org.uk). The Mountain Leader Training Board for England (MLTE; www.mltb.org) offers certificates at different levels e.g. Walking Group Leader and the Single Pitch Award, some of which are offered by the Edale Youth Hostel (01433 670302; edale@yha.org.uk). The Bremex Trust puts on reasonably priced short winter skills and mountaineering courses in Aviemore and the Lake District (0870 240 8057; www.bremex.org.uk).

Many companies and youth training organisations run expedition and related courses at varying levels. For example a selection of youth hostels located in appropriate places offer weekend courses in various outdoor pursuits, typically costing £125. You can start gently with an Introduction to Bushcraft weekend where you learn basic survival skills from TV survival expert Ray Mears; details of their range of courses from Woodlore Ltd (PO Box 3, Etchingham, East Sussex TN19 7ZE; 01580 819668; www.raymears.com)

with weekend prices starting at £250. Then you might graduate to a climbing course in the Welsh mountains, for instance at the Plas y Brenin National Mountain Centre (Capel Curig, Gwynedd; 01690 720214; www.pyb.co.uk); a 5-day residential course will cost £430. The most ambitious courses are run by companies like Jagged Globe based in Sheffield (www.jagged-globe.com) which runs ice climbing and other courses in Scotland, the Alps and Canada.

Many multi-activity youth holiday companies run their own training programmes for leaders and instructors, normally to work a summer season in their network of camps and holiday schemes in the UK and abroad. For example Junior Choice Adventures offer training over two or three weeks leading to seasonal employment with them (www.travel-class.co.uk). The cost of training is from £350 but this may be reimbursed on successful completion of a contract.

There are global shortages of qualified instructors in several sports including watersports and snowboarding. The International Academy provides professional instructor training courses for all standards in sports ranging from skiing and snowboarding to diving and mountain biking. The courses run from 4 to 12 weeks and are based at some of the top locations in the world, including Whistler, Lake Louise, Mammoth and Seychelles. See the next section and also the entry below for *Water by Nature* for rafting courses abroad which lead to guide qualifications.

Ski Training

The past five years have seen a remarkable increase in the number of programmes specially tailored to avid or just aspiring skiers and snowboarders taking a year out who want to improve their skiing or to train as instructors. For instance the major focus of **Alice Mundy's** year out was an 11-week course in the Canadian Rockies (January to April 2005) to become a snowboard instructor with *Nonstop Ski & Snowboard*:

> *I decided on a course of this kind as I felt it combined one of my passions with a globally recognised qualification which would open up the future possibility of travelling around the world whilst being able to make a living. The course was expensive – just over £6000 (covering flights and transfers, accommodation, weekday breakfast and evening meals, full season lift pass, 20 hours a week coaching, CASI Level 1 exam fee and selected weekend trips and activities) plus £200 dangerous sports insurance and £2000-£3000 spending money. So, it didn't come cheap for something that could be arranged on an individual basis (sorting out your own flights and accommodation and then entering for your instructor exams off your own bat). But by doing that you would miss out on the high-level 5-days-a-week coaching, which was the overwhelming advantage of this course for me. You receive invaluable preparation for the instructor examinations and the world of work as a snow sports instructor so, if it is your aim to use the qualification at some point in the future, the cost of the course is definitely justified. Also, it provided exactly the right balance that a lot of people my age were looking for – plenty of independence and the experience of living away from home but enough aspects already taken care of and organised for you not to be totally terrified of having to make all the arrangements by yourself on your first big trip away.*

Many companies arrange these courses in a number of locations worldwide, mainly in Canada and more recently in New Zealand, but also in Europe and Patagonia. So far instructor training has not been generally available in the USA to non-Americans. The providers normally claim that they can accommodate beginner skiers, though the majority (like Alice) have been on regular ski holidays for some years. There was no one on Alice's course who had never skied before and in her view it would defy logic for someone who had never even tried a sport to want to become an instructor in it. On the other hand a number of gap year skiers simply want to improve rather than qualify as an instructor. The pass rate for Level 1 in Alice's case was 100%, which indicates that it is an achievable goal even for those with minimal skiing experience.

Those who want to arrange to spend a whole season in a ski resort without joining one of these elite programmes can book accommodation through an operator that specialises in long-stay ski and snowboard holidays like *Mountain Life, Planet Subzero* (see entries) or Seasonaires ('Derwood', Todds Green, Stevenage, Herts. SG1 2JE; 0870 068 4545; www.seasonaires.com) who have properties in a large number of resorts from Morzine in the French Alps to Mammoth in California.

Cookery Courses

The days of the finishing school are nearly over, although apparently after the ITV programme *Ladette to Lady* was aired in 2005, a number of young women enquired at Eggleston Hall (where filming took place) about etiquette and deportment training on their gap year! However a practical cookery course can prove immensely useful in finding temporary employment both at home and abroad. (It can also put you in a class of your own when you come to share a house with friends at university.) A catering certificate opens up many appealing employment options in ski resorts, private villas or private yachts. For further information on this subject, consult *The Good Cook's Guide to Working Worldwide* by Katherine Parry (Vacation Work, £11.95). The recruitment website www.voovs.com has a useful listing of cookery courses; click on 'Jobseekers – Cookery Courses'.

The private courses are expensive, but some students (and their parents) decide to splash out in order to acquire an instantly recognised qualification such as *Cordon Bleu* or *Tante Marie*. Most further education colleges in the UK offer catering courses with NVQ (National Vocational Qualification) or C&G awards though generally speaking these are not attended by students planning to go on to university. A Basic Food Hygiene Certificate can be acquired in half a day or even online (course with voovs.com costs £45 + VAT) and is useful for picking up casual work in restaurants to help fund your gap year.

Creative Arts Courses

While the vast majority of school leavers have no fixed idea what they want to pursue, a few may already have developed a leaning towards one of the creative arts or another vocation. Some do an art foundation course in their gap year purely for pleasure rather than as a springboard for applying to art college. Some may want to pursue a creative interest in their gap year before heading to university, though more usually this kind of course is taken post-university. For example the *London College of Fashion* (entry below) runs summer courses in London. You might take the opportunity to build up a portfolio of photographs perhaps with a view to entering a competition like the one run by *The Times* (www.timesonline.co.uk/youngphotographer). Budding actors might consider auditioning for the National Youth Theatre (443-445 Holloway Road, London N7 6LW; 0845 603 9063; www.nyt.org.uk). Workshop auditions (both acting and technical) are held around the country during the spring half-term or at weekends following the end-of-January deadline for applications.

A gap year can provide a useful space in which to pursue one of the creative arts, as reported by Kirsty on the gapyear.com message board:

> I spent my gap year doing an art foundation course. My friends were trying to persuade me to go travelling with them, and I felt a bit square staying in England, but I had always wanted to study art. I was good at art at school, but got on really badly with the teacher. I got a place at Camberwell Art School and managed to take out a career development loan to fund it. My parents eventually agreed that it was some-

244 Taking a Gap Year

thing worthwhile and they agreed to help support me. I rented a room in a shared house that I found through the newspaper. The course was fantastic - I discovered that sculpture is my thing - and I had a really good time in London. I have now decided to go on to do a fine art degree, rather than English as I planned. I'm so pleased I didn't bow to peer pressure and go off travelling.

For the artistically inclined, the idea of going abroad to paint, sculpt or weave is very romantic. The once charming and very artistic town of San Miguel Allende in Mexico has recently attracted a great many rich Americans who have built ostentatious mansions. Sometimes the best known institutes are the most commercial. One option recommended by a recent visitor is the small art school Bellas Artes where many courses are taught in Spanish and classes attract both Mexicans and Americans.

The boom in interest in media studies show no signs of abating, and many of those school leavers think of themselves as up-and-coming film makers. The idea of making a film while travelling abroad is very appealing, though even the most naïve 18 year old will have worked out that it will be next to impossible to make such a venture a commercial success. Although **Hannah Adcock** was post-university when she braved this field and was already involved with a theatre company, her experiences are instructive. She and some friends out of university had set up a semi-professional production company with a strong theatrical background, specialising in Greek tragedy and Shakespeare. They then turned their hands to film making and set up Outlook Productions which decided to make a film in Greece during the summer of 2004. Plans for making a film adaptation of Shakespeare's *Twelfth Night* had been discussed over a long period but it wasn't until the director and producer visited the Greek island of Patmos that they realised Patmos *was* the Illyria of their dreams (the magical island where the action in *Twelfth Night* takes place). The island was so perfect that even one of *Twelfth Night's* more inconsequential lines took on a deeper meaning, "prithee foolish Greek, depart from me"!

Director of Photography and 'Wardrobe Mistress' Hannah Adcock describes the ins and out of organising one of the most enterprising and glamorous working holidays imaginable:
The company felt confident that they could sell the film, either to digital TV channels, educational institutions, even to a distributor, because Twelfth Night is a well known play, school children have to study it, and everyone will be so glad it is not Kenneth Branagh that they might just go out and buy it. The company failed to extract funding from organisations such as the Arts Council but it did attract private investors: people who had come to theatrical shows, liked what they saw and believed in the company. It is a really good idea if you are a theatre/production company to keep a mailing list of people who appreciate your work. However, private investment only goes so far when you are making a digital feature film. Paying wages was out of the question so cast and crew were invited to 'profit share'. This way all cast and crew rise or fall on the success or failure of the production, which is a huge risk but a good incentive to work hard!

The whole project took more than three years from idea to wrap. This included such necessary phases as location searching, formulating a shooting script, attracting finance, finding cast, crew and equipment, researching markets and organising post-production. The company let cast and crew make their own accommodation arrangements. This was fine but actors who are asked to work at 6am and have forgotten their breakfast will be difficult. The company also underestimated certain logistical difficulties, for example how to transport costumes and how much will this cost. The key seems to be a painful attention to detail.

The Director notified island officials about filming plans but they never replied. As long as the company didn't obstruct the public or tell them to move, red tape wasn't an issue. Once you have researched and then bought suitable equipment don't forget that it can (and will) break down. If possible have contingency plans since if you are miles from anywhere this is difficult. We had a dead mic for a week and will have to fall back on post production dubbing for some close-ups/medium close-ups.

It is important that you all have legally binding contracts and an agreed procedure for expenses, even if you are working with friends. The company learnt this the hard way and has unforeseen expenses claims. The company has tried to ensure that there will be enough money for a professional editing company to sharpen the rough cut. If you want to sell the film as 'professional' you need great sound and picture quality, together with slick editing.

In conclusion this is a great way to get into a tough sector (and not just by making the tea). You should get respect for initiative, but this is not a guaranteed money spinner.

Study Programmes

Socrates-Erasmus grants are available for students following a course of higher education in the UK who wish to study part of their course (between 3 and 12 months) in one of 30 European countries. All UK universities and many other UK institutions of Higher Education are involved with Socrates-Erasmus student mobility programmes, and it is possible to study with Erasmus in every subject area from Agriculture to Nursing. The Erasmus programme is administered by the UK Socrates-Erasmus Council (Rothford, Giles Lane, Canterbury, Kent CT2 7LR; 01227 762712; www.erasmus.ac.uk). The official European Union website with full details is at http://europa.eu.int/comm/education/erasmus.html. Note that for some courses, knowledge of a foreign language may be required whereas other courses may be taught entirely in English.

An Erasmus grant covers tuition fees at the host university and provides a contribution towards the extra costs which arise from studying abroad, but it does not cover all living expenses. Anyone interested in taking part in the Erasmus programme should consult *Experience Erasmus*, a copy of which may be obtained from ISCO Careerscope Publications (01276 21188; www.isco.org.uk) for £15.95.

Conclusion

While some students spend part of their year out cramming to improve their A-level grades, others are in the fortunate position to be able to sign up for courses at these same colleges just for fun, as was the case with **Elisabeth Weiskittel** from the United States:

I decided to begin my gap year in Oxford, England. I chose it because I had been before and loved it there, and because I spoke the language and had family friends, which would make the initial transition easier. When I realised I couldn't get a visa to work, I went with my alternative plan, which was to enroll in one or two classes somewhere. After doing some research on the internet with my family, we sent away for a few brochures and eventually settled on the Oxford Tutorial College (12 King Edward Street, Oxford OX1 4HT; tel 01865 793333/ www.oxtutor.co.uk). The college gave me a letter saying I had enrolled and that my fees were paid in full, which I had to show at Immigration to get me into the country. I enrolled in two classes: Shakespeare and the History of Art. I went to my classes, but very little reading was required and minimal simple assignments. I spent most of my time sightseeing and spending time with the friends I made. There's a 24 hour bus service between Oxford and London, and so I spent many days in London. I also spent weekends in Dublin and Paris. I had an internship with the Museum of Modern Art in Oxford, which the Oxford Tutorial College had arranged for me. I went in one afternoon a week and helped in the archives. It was very low-key and enjoyable. The whole time in Oxford was wonderful.

Italy attracts more than its fair share of gap year students wanting to broaden their minds and learn more about art and architecture, following in the footsteps of the privileged English men and women who took the Grand Tour of the Continent two hundred years ago. But there is more to be studied during a gap year than Renaissance art and architecture. The courses listed in this chapter and others mentioned throughout the book might never have occurred to you but might inspire you to try something different, from studying photography or folk culture in Greece to learning practical conservation skills while studying Spanish in Guatemala, from a course in Thai massage to the care of wildlife in South Africa.

DIRECTORIES OF COURSES

Language Courses

The following entries represent a tiny proportion of language schools worldwide. Of key interest are the first 22 entries which are for companies, the majority in the UK, which represent a selection of language schools. Using an agency simplifies the selection process. Schools and agencies of interest to North Americans are listed in the chapter *A Year Off for North Americans*.

AMERISPAN
PO Box 58129, Philadelphia, PA 19102-8129, USA. ☎800-879-6640 or 215-751-1100. Fax: 215-751-1986. E-mail: info@amerispan.com. Website: www.amerispan.com.
Specialist Spanish-language travel organisation with great expertise in arranging language courses, voluntary placements and internships throughout South and Central America.
Courses offered: Wealth of options throughout South and Central America. Also offers other languages in other countries, e.g. French in Montreal and Quebec, French in Nice and Paris, German in Frankfurt, Italian in Florence plus Chinese, Japanese, Arabic, Russian and Thai.
Accommodation: mostly homestays.
Other services: Unpaid volunteer placements in Costa Rica, Bolivia, Brazil, Chile, Mexico, Guatemala, Ecuador, Argentina and Peru (see entry in 'Directory of Volunteering Abroad').

BRIDGE-LINGUATEC LANGUAGE LANGUAGE STUDY ABROAD
915 S. Colorado Blvd., Denver, CO 80246, USA. ☎Toll-free in the US and Canada: 800-724-4210. Toll-free in the UK: 0800-028-8051. Also 303-777-7783 ext. 850. Fax: 303-777-7246. E-mail: studylanguages@bridgelinguatec. com. Website: www.bridgeabroad.com.

Bridge-Linguatec is a language training company with culture immersion programmes in Europe and Latin America.

Courses offered: Spanish, French, German, Italian and Portuguese. Group, private, and combination group/private classes available. Courses include activities and excursions to help students get to know the local culture, as well as comfortable host family accommodation.

Destinations: Argentina, Brazil, Bolivia, Chile, Costa Rica, Ecuador, France, Germany, Guatemala, Italy, Mexico, Panama, Peru, and Spain.

Duration of courses: Minimum 1 week. Classes start every Monday year-round.

Accommodation: Local host families, apart-hotels, student residences.

Other Services: Activities and excursions, special language and culture courses such as Business Spanish, French Cuisine, Roman Archaeology and Brazilian Dance.

CACTUS LANGUAGE
No 4 Clarence House, 30-31 North St, Brighton BN1 1EB. ☎0845 130 4775. Fax: 01273 775868. E-mail: enquiry@cactuslanguage.com. Website: www. cactuslanguage.com.

Courses offered: Spanish (Spain and Latin America), French, Italian, Chinese, Russian, Japanese, Portuguese (Portugal and Brazil), German (Germany and Austria), Arabic, Basque, Czech and Turkish. Combined language learning with activity holidays (surfing, dance, skiing, music, cookery, etc.), volunteer placements (see entry), group dance holidays, etc. Evening language courses in the UK also available.

Duration of courses: from 1 hour to 1 year.

Qualifications offered: D.E.L.E. preparation offered in Spain, D.E.L.F. offered in France, Goethe exams in Germany and Austria; Cambridge, IELTS in UK and worldwide.

Cost: Sample prices: 1-week General Course (20 lessons) in Hamburg £69, 2-week Individual Course (20 lessons per week) in Antigua, Guatemala including host family and all meals £289.

Accommodation: Choice of full-board host family, half-board host family, bed and breakfast, student residence, budget hotels, luxury hotels and private/shared apartments.

CALEDONIA LANGUAGES ABROAD
The Clockhouse, 72 Newhaven Road, Edinburgh EH6 5QG. ☎0131-621 7721/2. E-mail: courses@caledonialanguages.co.uk. Website: www.caledonialanguages. co.uk.

Caledonia was established in 1994 and offers language courses in Europe and Latin America suitable for those thinking of travelling abroad during their Gap Year and who are looking for a quick beginner's course to give the basics needed whilst travelling or to consolidate language skills. Courses allow students to study in Europe or Central America, stay with a local family, get to know the local accent and idioms, and absorb local cultural life.

Courses offered: Language courses for general interest, exam revision, language and culture. These can often be combined with special interest courses such as walking, cooking, diving and skiing. There are also opportunities to participate in volunteer work programmes in Latin America (see entry in 'Directory of Specialist Gap Year Programmes'). Two or more language programmes can be taken consecutively in different countries to give a long term Gap Year trip.

Duration of courses: Classes for all levels for a minimum of one week, starting throughout the year, and lasting up to a year.

Cost: 2-week programme of French plus surfing in Nice would cost from £815 including accommodation. 6-week Spanish course plus accommodation in Malaga from £980.

Accommodation: Students can stay with local host families or in residential accommodation, although Caledonia recommends the former.

CESA LANGUAGES ABROAD
CESA House, Pennance Road, Lanner, Cornwall TR16 5TQ. ☎01209 211800. Fax: 01209 211830. E-mail: info@cesalanguages.com. Website: www.cesalanguages.com.

Founding member of Year Out Group (www.yearoutgroup.org).

Courses offered: Beginner, intermediate and advanced courses in French (Cannes, Nice, Montpellier, Tours, Bordeaux, Paris or, for a more exotic option, Guadeloupe), Spanish (Seville, Nerja, Salamanca, Malaga or Madrid in Spain, plus Argentina, Chile, Mexico, Costa Rica or Ecuador), German (Berlin, Lindau, Munich, Cologne or Vienna in Austria), Italian (Florence, Rome, San Giovanni, Sorrento, Siena and Viareggio), Portuguese, Japanese, Russian, Greek and Arabic (in Morocco).

Duration of courses: 1-24 weeks with possibility of studying in more than one location during a year-out programme. At least one start date per month year round.

Qualifications offered: D.E.L.E. preparation offered in Spain; D.E.L.F., Alliance Francaise and CCIP exams in France; T.R.K.I. exams in Russia. Full range of Goethe exams offered in Germany and Austria.

Cost: Languages for Life 16-week course in Seville or Madrid costs from £3018 including college residence accommodation and 20 hours tuition per week. A 12-week course with college residence accommodation in Nice costs £2268.

Accommodation: Options include student apartments or residences, on-campus accommodation, host families, sole-occupancy apartments and hotels.

CHALLENGE EDUCATIONAL SERVICES
101 Lorna Road, Hove, East Sussex BN3 3EL. ☎01273 220261. Fax: 01273 220376. E-mail: enquiries@challengeuk.com. Website: www.challengeuk.com.

Courses offered: French language courses in private language schools and Universities throughout France. Courses can be for any age and ability, in preparation for examinations or purely recreational. Junior programmes are offered in the summer (and Easter) which combine language tuition with sports, cultural and social activities. In addition to the short courses, Challenge offer a specially designed Gap Year opportunity which consists of studying at a French *Lycée* for a term or full academic year. This programme requires a high level of French.

Duration of courses: From one week to a full academic year.

Qualifications offered: Students may study towards the D.E.L.F. or D.A.L.F.; University courses may offer the opportunity to sit the *Certificat* or *Diplôme de Langue Francaise*.

Cost: Academic Year at a French University would cost at least £7000 including residential accommodation.

DON QUIJOTE
2-4 Stoneleigh Park Road, Epsom, Surrey KT19 0QT. ☎020-8786 8081. Fax: 020-8786 8086. E-mail: uk@donquijote.org. Website: www.donquijote.org.

Courses offered: Intensive (20 lessons a week) and Super Intensive (30 lessons a week) courses for all levels throughout Spain: Barcelona, Granada, Madrid, Malaga, Puerto de La Cruz (Tenerife), Salamanca, Seville, Valencia, Cusco (Peru) and Guanajuato (Mexico). Also available is 'Spanish for Life' (12 weeks and longer) and in Cusco and Guanajuato a 'Spanish Study and Volunteer Programme'.

Duration of courses: 1-40 weeks.

Qualifications: Students will receive a Don Quijote certificate of attendance and level attained at the end of the course.

Cost: From £426 for 2 weeks intensive course and single room lodging in a self-catering student flat. Spanish for Life courses start at £1984 for 12 weeks including student flat

accommodation.

Accommodation: Homestay, residence and flats.

Follow-up: Specialised courses available including a 'Spanish and Paid Jobs in Spain' programme. Private tuition is available at all schools.

EF INTERNATIONAL LANGUAGE SCHOOLS
Dudley House, 36-38 Southampton Street, London WC2E 7HF. ☎Freephone 0800 0683385. Fax: 020-7836 7334. E-mail: eflanguages@ef.com. Website: www.ef.com.

Courses offered: Foreign language courses at privately owned and EF schools in France, Germany, Italy, Spain, Ecuador, China and Russia.

Duration of courses: 2-52 weeks, beginning every week. Special discounted 6- and 9-month academic year programmes. On all courses there are special interest classes in literature, history, business and culture.

Qualifications offered: DELE (Spain), DELF, DALF, (France), ZDF (Germany), CLIS (Italy).

Cost: Depending on the destination, £370-£880 for a 2-week period. This price includes accommodation, tuition, course material and meals.

Accommodation: Host families or student residence.

Other services: EF has its own Travel Service and tailor-made student insurance.

Contact: David Burton, Academic Programme Co-ordinator.

EIL CULTURAL & EDUCATIONAL TRAVEL
287 Worcester Road, Malvern, Worcestershire, WR14 1AB. ☎0800 018 4015. Fax: 01684 562212. E-mail: info@eiluk.org. Website: www.eiluk.org.

Non-profit cultural and educational organisation, offers short-term homestay programmes in up to 30 countries (see entry in 'Directory of Specialist Gap Year Programmes').

EURO-ACADEMY LTD
67-71 Lewisham High St, London SE13 5JX. ☎020-8297 0505. Fax: 020-8297 0984. E-mail: euroacademy@twinuk.com. Website: www.euroacademy.co.uk.

Courses offered: French, Italian, German, Portuguese, Spanish, Russian and Greek. Opportunities for homestays, individual tuition, vacation courses, intensive courses (for students wishing to make considerable progress in a short time), and long-term courses specially aimed at gap year students. Also arrange work experience in France and Germany (see 'Directory of Work Experience').

Duration of courses: 1-12 weeks.

Qualifications offered: Some destinations offer the chance to prepare for the D.E.L.F./D.A.L.F./D.E.L.E. exam (France and Spain) and Paris Chamber of Commerce certificate; also Kleine Deutsche and Sprachdiplom can be obtained in Germany.

Accommodation: Private homes, student residences or shared apartments.

EUROCENTRES UK
56 Eccleston Square, London SW1V 1PQ. ☎020-7834 4155. Fax: 020-7834 1866. E-mail: vic-info@eurocentres.com. Website: www.eurocentres.com. ☎020-7834 4155. Fax: 020-7834 1866.

Courses offered: German in Cologne; Spanish in Madrid, Barcelona or Valencia; French in Paris, Amboise or La Rochelle (France) or Lausanne (Switzerland); Italian in Florence; Russian in Moscow or St. Petersburg; or Japanese in Kanazawa.

Accommodation: With families or in hotels.

EUROLINGUA
61 Bollin Drive, Altrincham WA14 5QW. ☎/fax: 0161-972 0225. E-mail: info@eurolingua.com. Website: www.eurolingua.com.

Courses offered: Language training worldwide (9 languages in 35 countries) as well

as paid work experience (see entry) and TESOL/TEFL Teacher Training in the UK and France.
Duration of courses: 1-12 weeks.
Cost: Standard fees throughout Europe: one-to-one tuition while living in tutor's home for a week with full board and excursions costs from €850 depending on the number of tuition hours. Year round Group Courses cost €248 per week with special inclusive Summer School Programmes.
Accommodation: Host family homestays, studio apartment or hotel. Approximate prices are from €168 per week half-board (private room, breakfast and evening meal).
Contact: Barry Haywood, International Director.

GALA SPANISH IN SPAIN
Woodcote House, 8 Leigh Lane, Farnham, Surrey GU9 8HP. ☎/fax: 01252 715319.
Operating since 1993 and run by an ex-Director of Studies of a Spanish language school, Gala offers an information, advisory and placement service for students of any level from age 16.
Programmes offered in a number of Spanish cities: Homestays, with or without Spanish language courses. Also offer internships (see *Directory of Work Experience*).
Language courses: From 2 weeks to 9 months duration.
Cost: A minimum placement fee of £25 is required. Cost of course and accommodation varies according to location and time of year. Sample prices of intensive course plus family stay with half-board would be €1100-€1400 for 4 weeks, €3000-€3800 for 12 weeks; or with self-catering accommodation in shared flats €900-€1300 for 4 weeks, €2300-€3700 for 12 weeks.
Accommodation: With families or in student self-catering accommodation. Courses also offered in South America. Arrangements can also be made for 16/17 year olds to spend one or more terms in a senior Spanish school in Madrid while living with a family.
Contact: Anne Thomas, Proprietor.

IALC (INTERNATIONAL ASSOCIATION OF LANGUAGE CENTRES)
Lombard House, 12/17 Upper Bridge St, Canterbury CT1 2NF. ☎01227 769007. Fax: 01227 769014. E-mail: info@ialc.org. Website: www.ialc.org.
Language school association that accredits private language schools, with 91 members in 21 countries.
Courses offered: Hundreds of programmes in nine languages worldwide, ranging from short general language courses to specialised courses combining language with culture, cookery, dance, art, sport, etc. Some IALC schools offer work experience, au pair programmes and volunteering.
Accommodation: Most schools offer a choice of family stay, hall of residence, guesthouse or flat-share.
Application procedures: Canterbury office is not a booking office. Contact details for member schools appear on the IALC website.
Contact: Rebecca Willis or Jan Capper.

IST PLUS LTD
Rosedale House, Rosedale Road, Richmond, Surrey TW9 2SZ. ☎020-8939 9057. E-mail: info@istplus.com. Website: www.istplus.com/language.htm.
Courses offered: Courses at partner language schools in France, Spain, Italy, Germany and Latin America, aimed at gap year students, undergraduates and young professionals.
Duration of courses: Standard and intensive courses are offered for 2-36 weeks throughout the year. Applications should be submitted at least one month before start date.
Accommodation: Self-catering apartment, student residence or host family with bed and breakfast.

KOLUMBUS LANGUAGE TOURS
Wagnerstrasse 4, 52134 Herzogenrath, Germany. ☎ +49 2234-6019933. Fax: +49 2234-6019934. E-mail: info@languageschools-abroad.com. Website: www. languageschools-abroad.com.
Courses offered: Vacation, regular and intensive language courses in Italy, Spain, France and England. Also offer internships in combination with language courses.
Duration of courses: Minimum 1 or 2 weeks (starting every Monday), to long-term exam preparation.
Qualifications offered: Recreational, business language or exam preparation leading to recognised qualifications.
Cost: From €129.
Accommodation: Host family, shared flats, apartments, hotel or hostel.
Contact: Christopher Thebing.

LANACOS
64 London Road, Dunton Green, Sevenoaks, Kent TN13 2UG. ☎ 01732 462309. E-mail: languages@lanacos.com. Website: www.lanacos.com.
Language agency run by linguists.
Courses offered: Language courses in more than 200 locations: Spanish in many Spanish and Latin American cities; French in Paris, Nice, Annecy, Savoie Bordeaux, St. Malo, Brittany, Belgium and Montréal; German in Salzburg, Berlin, Münich, Tyrol Münster, Cologne, Bavaria and Hamburg; Italian in Rome, Florence, Milan, Tuscany, Siena, Sicily, Orvieto, Rimini and Pisa; Portuguese in Lisbon, Porto, Faro and Brazil; Greek in Athens, Crete and Thessaloniki; and Japanese in Tokyo and Osaka.
Duration of courses: 2+ weeks.
Cost: From £394 for a fortnight in Granada to £2433 for 12-week academic course in Paris.
Accommodation: Homestays with full or half board, B&Bs, single or shared apartments.
Contact: Martin Pickett, Director.

LANGUAGE COURSES ABROAD LTD
67 Ashby Road, Loughborough, Leicestershire LE11 3AA. ☎ 01509 211612. Fax: 01509 260037. E-mail: info@languagesabroad.co.uk. Website: www.languagesabroad.co.uk.
Parent company, Spanish Study Holidays Ltd., is a member of FIYTO (Federation of International Youth Travel Organisations) and ALTO (Association of Language Travel Organisations).
Programme description: In-country language courses in Spanish, French, German, Italian, Portuguese and Russian, sometimes in preparation for work experience placements (see entry in 'Directory of Work Experience').
Prerequisites: Minimum age 16 or 18, average age 18-26.
Duration and time of placements: 1-40 weeks.
Accommodation: Shared self-catering student apartments, private studio apartments, host families, student residences or hotels.

LINGULAND LANGUAGE STUDIES
Alfred-Herrhausen-Str. 44, 58455, Witten, Germany. ☎ +49 2302 915 270. E-mail: maria.castro@linguland.com/ welcome@linguland.com. Website: www.linguland.com.
Courses offered: Spanish, French, Italian, Portuguese and German language courses in 45 cities in 17 countries for every language level.
Minimum age: 17/18, average 25.
Duration of courses: 1 week to 1 year. Special starting dates for absolute beginners and exam preparation courses (D.E.L.E., D.E.L.F., D.S.H., etc). Monday start dates for students with previous experience.

Cost: From €88 for 15 lessons in one week of Spanish (Santiago, Chile). From budget to executive prices.
Accommodation: Host family (preferred), shared flat, studio or student residence.
Contact: Maria Castro, General Manager.

OISE INTENSIVE LANGUAGE SCHOOLS
Binsey Lane, Oxford OX2 0EY. ☎01865 258333. E-mail: info@oise.com. Website: www.oise.com.
One of Europe's leading language training organisations.
Courses offered: Small class tuition of French in Paris, German in Heidelberg and Spanish in Madrid. Gap year courses offered leading to recognised qualifications.
Duration of courses: Various. From 1 week to 1 year.
Cost: From £515 per week for 2-week course, including accommodation
Accommodation: Single room in family home with half board or (in Paris) bed and breakfast.

S.I.B.S. LTD
Beech House, Commercial Road, Uffculme, Devon EX15 3EB. ☎01884 841330. Fax: 01884 841377. E-mail: trish@sibs.co.uk. Website: www.sibs.co.uk.
Language consultancy which arranges language courses abroad for clients.
Courses offered: For business and pleasure in France, Italy, Germany, Austria, Portugal, Japan, Spain, Greece, Russia, Argentina, Ecuador and Mexico.
Cost: From £200 per week including accommodation.
Other services: Variety of courses and locations can be combined with cultural subjects, work experience, etc.
Contact: Patricia Cooper, Director.

VIS A VIS
2-4 Stoneleigh Park Road, Epsom KT19 0QT. ☎020-8786 8021. Fax: 020-8786 8086. E-mail: info@visavis.org. Website: www.visavis.org.
Courses offered: Courses for all levels in French at schools in France (Paris, Annecy, Antibes, Montpellier, Nice, Royan and Vichy), Belgium (Brussels) and Canada (Montréal). Many activities and excursions available in all locations.
Duration of courses: From 1 week.
Cost: Prices start at about £500 (2005) for a 2-week course (20 lessons a week) plus single room half-board accommodation with a family in Annecy.
Qualifications: Some courses prepare students for official language diplomas, such as the D.E.L.F. and the more advanced level (D.A.L.F.). These can be worked towards at the student's own pace.
Accommodation: Student flats and halls of residence are available for those wishing to

mingle with other students. Host families also accommodate students which allows the student an insight into French culture.

Language Schools Abroad

ACADEMIA HISPANO AMERICANA
Mesones 4, 37700 San Miguel de Allende, 37700, GTO, Mexico. ☎ +52 415-152 0349/152 4349. Fax: +52 415-152 2333. E-mail: info@ahaspeakspanish. com. Website: www.ahaspeakspanish.com.
Established 1959.
Courses offered: Intensive Spanish programme and Mexican history, literature and sociology.
Duration of courses: twelve 4-week sessions per school year. 35 hours of lessons and activities per week.
Qualifications offered: Diploma in Spanish as a second language, accredited by the Mexican Ministry of Education in the state of Guanajuato. 7 semester units of credit are offered per session.
Cost: 4-week session $580, 3 weeks $530, 2 weeks $430, 1 week $215. One-to-one tuition costs $700 for 2 weeks (5 hours per day) or $14 per hour.
Accommodation: Homestays: $23 per person per night for a single room and $18 for a shared room plus 3 meals a day. Mexican cooking classes also available.
Contact: Paulina Hawkins, Director.

ACCADEMIA DEL GIGLIO
Via Ghibellina 116, 50122 Florence, Italy. ☎/fax: 055-230 2467. E-mail: info@adg.it. Website: www.adg.it or www.italyhometuition.com.
Courses offered: Italian courses for foreigners plus art and art history courses (see below). Intensive classes or one-to-one tuition.
Duration of courses: 1, 2, 4, 8, 12 or more weeks. 4 hours of classes a day, more on one-to-one programme.
Qualifications offered: Students sit a written exam at the end of each month to determine whether they are ready to move to the next level. Language certificates available.
Cost: 1-week intensive course costs €145, 8 weeks costs €810. Enrolment fee of €41.
Accommodation: All kinds of accommodation can be arranged from single room in a family for €28 a day half-board to €750 for 4 weeks in a self-catering flat sharing kitchen and other facilities. School located in a peaceful area of the city centre.
Other services: Visits and social activities included in the price.
Contact: Lorenzo Capanni, Assistant Director.

ACCADEMIA ITALIANA
Piazza Pitti 15, 50125 Florence, Italy. ☎055-284616. Fax: 055-284486. E-mail: modaita@tin.it. Website: www.accademiaitaliana.com.
Courses offered: Italian language and culture courses, drawing and painting, textile design, fashion design, interior design and graphic arts. Language courses can be taken alongside other courses.
Duration of courses: Monthly (except December) or by the semester, beginning in September or January. Month long courses involve 40 or 80 hours of tuition.
Qualifications offered: Students are awarded diplomas for completion of basic, intermediate and advanced level courses.
Cost: Enrolment fee €80 plus €270 for 40 hours tuition, €450 for 80 hours. Individual tuition is roughly double.
Accommodation: Housing can be arranged in apartments shared with other students or in families, residences, hotels or pensions. Prices of a double room in a shared apartment start at €350 a month each. Average price is €50-€100 per day for bed and breakfast.

ALLIANCE FRANCAISE
101 Boulevard Raspail, 75270 Paris Cedex 06, France. ☎1-42 84 90 00. Fax: 1-42 84 91 00. E-mail: info@alliancefr.org. Website: www.alliancefr.org.
Alliance Française has 1000 language centres in 129 countries, including in the UK (see next entry), where students can study French in their own country.
Courses offered in Paris: French language courses at 5 levels with a choice of shared or individual classes at the school in Paris. Students have the chance to study general French or specialised French, e.g. French for tourism, hotel work or secretarial.
Duration of courses: From 2 weeks onwards. Session consists of 16 days of instruction over one month, 4 hours of lessons a day.
Qualifications: Various French diplomas can be awarded including Paris Chamber of Commerce & Industry and the Ministry of National Education. Normally test can be sat after 128 hours (i.e. two sessions).
Cost: 16-day intensive session (as above) costs €610 plus annual enrolment fee of €55.
Accommodation: Provided on demand in student residence or in studios.

ALLIANCE FRANCAISE DE LONDRES
1 Dorset Square, London NW1 6PU. ☎020-7723 6439. E-mail: info@alliancefrancaise.org.uk. Website: www.alliancefrancaise.org.uk.
Courses offered: French language courses for all levels. Daytime, evening or Saturday courses. Short intensive courses, summer courses and revision courses available.
Duration of courses: 2-12 weeks; 2½-15 hours per week throughout the year.
Qualifications offered: Course certificates, preparation for D.E.L.F./D.A.L.F. and Paris Chamber of Commerce examinations.
Accommodation: None available.

ALPHA SPRACHINSTITUT AUSTRIA
Schwartzenbergplatz 16/ Canovagasse 5, 1010 Vienna, Austria. ☎ +43 1-503 69 69. Fax: +43 1-503 69 69-14. E-mail: info@alpha.at. Website: www.alpha.at.
Courses offered: German as a foreign language.
Duration of courses: 2 weeks to one year; intensive or evening courses.
Qualifications offered: Institute is an examination centre for German Language Diploma of the Goethe Institute, Austrian Language Diploma (OESD) and the European Language Certificate. German intensive courses follow Goethe Institute system to highest level diploma (on behalf of Ludwig Maximilians University Munich). Also offer exams in Business German.
Cost: From €470 for 4 weeks (3 hours of tuition each morning), €1290 for 3 months.
Accommodation: Private families, apartments, student hostels.

ANGLO-GERMAN INSTITUTE STUTTGART
Friedrich Strasse 35, 70174 Stuttgart, Germany. ☎/fax: +49 711-60 18 76 50. E-mail: deutsch@anglo-german.com. Website: www.anglo-german.com.
Courses offered: Standard German courses with 20 lessons per week in central Stuttgart. Summer courses plus activities every afternoon and one-to-one tuition offered July and August. Evening courses with 4 lessons per week available year round.
Duration of courses: 2-60 weeks. Students can start any week after a placement test; absolute beginner courses start every month.
Minimum age: 16, average age 20-25.
Qualifications offered: Examination preparation courses with 4 lessons per week; starting dates on request. 6 levels from Elementary 1, 2 and 3 to Intermediate 1, 2 and 3. Students can work towards *Zertifikat Deutsch* after Elementary 3 course and *Zentrale Mittelstufenprüfung* after Intermediate 2 or 3.
Cost: €330 for 2 weeks; €120 per additional week. Longterm students (minimum 20 weeks) pay just over €100 a week. Summer courses are approximately 20% more to cover programme or activities and excursions.

Accommodation: Homestay in host family costs €155 per week with breakfast or €205 with half-board. Student residences cost €25-€30 per night.
Contact: Ms. Christine Hebe, Head of the German Department.

ATHENS CENTRE
48 Archimidous St, 116 36 Athens, Greece. ☎210-701 2268. Fax 210-701 8603. E-mail: info@athenscentre.gr. Website: www.athenscentre.gr.
Courses offered: Modern Greek.
Duration of courses: 3, 4, 7 or 10 weeks throughout the year.
Qualifications offered: Serious courses with certificate given at end.
Accommodation: Hotels, pensions, apartment sub-lets and studios but no homestays.
Cost: From €600 for 2-week course plus accommodation in efficiency apartment.

ATRIUM
Istituto di Lingua e Cultura Italiana, Piazza Papa Giovanni XXIII, 3, 61043, Cagli (PU), Italy. ☎/fax: 0721 790321. E-mail: atrium@istitutoatrium.com. Website: www.istitutoatrium.com.
Courses offered: Italian language courses.
Duration of courses: Monthly sessions year-round. Courses range from 2 weeks to 12 months.
Qualifications offered: Possible CILS examination.
Cost: €255 for 1 week, €510 for 4-week standard course. Private lessons cost €30.
Accommodation: Homestay, apartments, hotels, bed and breakfasts, etc. The latter charges from €200 per week.

AURIGA SERVIZI
Corso Umberto I, 342 bis, 65016 Montesilvano (Pescara), Italy. ☎/fax: +39 85 834620. E-mail: aurigaservizi@tiscali.it.
School of languages recognised by Italian bodies and accredited by Università per Stranieri di Siena, Trinity College London and LCCIEB.
Courses offered: Italian language courses. Also language agency sends Italian juniors and teenagers abroad to learn English, French, German or Spanish.
Duration of courses: 1-12 weeks.
Qualifications offered: DITALS (Università per Stranieri di Siena). Also recreational Italian courses.
Cost: From €350.
Accommodation: Host family, student residence, shared flat, private flat, B&B or hotel.
Contact: Ms. Gabriella Perfetti, Trainer & Language Consultant.

THE BRITISH INSTITUTE OF FLORENCE
Piazza Strozzi 2, 50123 Florence, Italy. ☎ +39 055-2677 8200. Fax: +39 055-2677 8222. E-mail: info@britishinstitute.it. Website: www.britishinstitute.it.
Courses offered: Language tuition among many other courses (see entry in 'Specialist Gap Year Programmes'). Special arrangements regarding length of course, number of hours and course content can be made. Short A-level overview course given at Easter.
Duration of courses: 5 days to 3 months.
Cost: Tuition fees vary according to length and intensity of the course chosen. For example a 1-week Italian Language course costs from €190 (£130) approximately, and a 5-day History of Art course costs from €155 (£105).
Accommodation: Can be arranged in local homes, *pensione* and hotels starting at €22 (£15) a day.
Contact: Tracy Bray, PR & Marketing Manager.

BWS GERMANLINGUA
Bayerstr. 13, D-80335 Munich, Germany. ☎89-59 98 92 00. Fax: 89-59 98 92

Dee Powell taking aim on Camp America

Sail training Sydney style with Flying Fish

MondoChallenge volunteer Ranj Makhni teaching IT to Buddhist monks in Sri Lanka

Sarah volunteering with Global Adventures Project in South Africa

Help change lives in Romania with Changing Worlds

New Zealand afloat with Changing Worlds

Master the slopes with Flying Fish

Flying high in New Zealand with the International Academy

MondoChallenge volunteer Claudia Bicen teaching crafts to youngsters in Tanzania

Take it to the edge in Mammoth with the International Academy

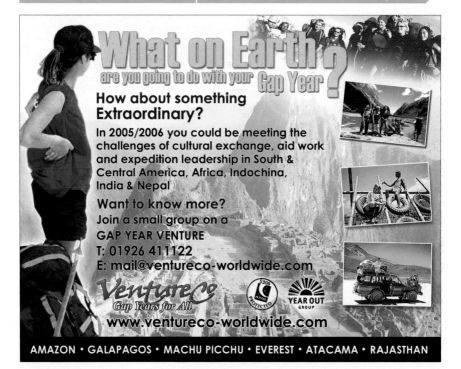

01. E-mail: info@bws-germanlingua.de. Website: www.bws-germanlingua.de.
Courses offered: German language courses in Munich or Berlin, standard (20 lessons per week), intensive (25 lessons) or one-to-one.
Duration of courses: 2-48 weeks. Minimum 1 week for a tailor-made course. Can join on any Monday (unless total beginner).
Cost: €390 for 2 weeks to €6,560 for 48 weeks. Prices higher for intensive courses (from €450) and one-to-one (€340 for 1 week with 10 lessons).
Accommodation: With a German family (€140 per week); in a flat shared with students (€120 per week) or in a studio apartment (€180).
Contact: Florian Meierhofer, Proprietor.

CALES (CENTER FOR ARABIC LANGUAGES AND EASTERN STUDIES)
PO Box 29107, Azzumar St, Sana'a, Yemen. ☎ +967-1-292090. ☎/fax: +967-1-281700. E-mail: cales@ust.edu or cales@y.net.ye. Website: www.y.net. ye/cales.
Courses offered: Arabic language and Yemeni culture for foreigners at centre in heart of Old Sana'a next to the *souk* (market).
Duration of courses: Short courses by the month or full academic year.
Qualifications offered: University credit may be available.
Cost: 80 hours per month (4 hours a day, 5 days a week) costs $360 for shared tuition, $580 for private lessons.
Accommodation: $100 per month for a single room, $75 in a shared room.
Contact: Jameel, Director.

CAMPUS AUSTRIA
Wiener Internationale Hochschulkurse, Universität Wien, Ebendorferstrasse 10, A-1010 Vienna. ☎01-4277 24102. E-mail: info@campus-austria.at. Website: www.campus-austria.at.
Courses offered: Huge range of German language courses offered by 16 language schools throughout Austria, all described in brochure and website of Campus Austria. Some courses lead to Goethe Institut qualifications or the Austrian Diploma for German as a Foreign Language (OESD).
Duration of courses: Normally two or more weeks, year round with choice of holiday courses and youth programmes.
Cost: Prices vary, but approximately €400 per fortnight excluding accommodation.

CIAL CENTRO DE LINGUAS
Av. da República, 41-8°E, 1050-187, Lisbon, Portugal. ☎ +351-21-794 04 48. Fax: +351-21-796 07 83. E-mail: portuguese@cial.pt. Website: www.cial. pt. Also in the Algarve: Rua Almeida Garrett, 44 r/c, 8000-206 Faro, Portugal. ☎ +351-289-807 611. Fax: 289-803 154. E-mail: algarve@cial.pt.
Courses offered: Full Portuguese language and culture course in six stages, with 60 hours of language tuition for every stage.
Duration of courses: 4 weeks for each course, with new courses every month.
Qualifications: Possibility of qualifying for the Diploma of Portuguese as a Foreign Language.
Cost: 4-week course will cost €850.
Accommodation: With families in individual rooms with breakfast included.
Contact: Dr. Alexandra Borges de Sousa, Director of Studies.

CIS (CENTRO DE INTERCAMBIO SOLIDARIDAD)
Mélida Anaya Montes Language School, Boulevard Universitario No. 4, Colonia El Roble, San Salvador, El Salvador. ☎/fax: +503 2-226-2623. E-mail: cis@netcomsa.com. Website: www.cis-elsalvador.org.
Courses offered: Spanish classes and political-cultural programme. English teaching

volunteer opportunities also available.

Duration of courses: Classes start every Monday. Any number of weeks can be booked. Volunteers must commit to teaching for a 9-week English cycle.

Qualifications offered: Recreational courses.

Cost: US$100 per week for 4 hours of morning classes plus one-time $25 application fee and $12.50 for first 4 weeks. $40 per week for afternoon political-cultural programme, plus admin fee of $12.50 per week for first 4 weeks, plus $25 one-time application fee. Volunteers receive a half-price discount on Spanish classes. Volunteers must also pay a one-time programme fee of $100.

Accommodation: Homestays with breakfast and dinner cost $70 a week. Alternatives in guest houses or shared flats can be arranged.

Contact: Rachel Sniadajewski.

CLIC INTERNATIONAL HOUSE
C/ Albareca 19, 41001 Seville, Spain. ☎095-450 21 31. Fax: 095-456 16 96. E-mail: clic@clic.es. Website: www.clic.es.

Courses offered: Spanish intensive courses year round. Junior programme during summer.

Duration of courses: Minimum 2 weeks.

Qualifications offered: Recreational.

Cost: From €290 for a fortnight (tuition only).

Accommodation: Choice of sharing flat with young Spaniards, CLIC IH halls of residence, living with Spanish family or living independently in flats.

COLLEGIUM PALATINUM
CH-1854 Leysin, Switzerland. ☎024-493 03 03. Fax: 024-493 03 00. E-mail: acs-schiller-cp@bluewin.ch. Website: www.american-college.com.

Part of Schiller International University, The American College of Switzerland.

Courses offered: Language courses combined with sport or recreational activities. Opportunity to study a university level course for 3 hours a week.

Duration of courses: Monday-Friday during the academic year (September-December and January-June).

Qualifications offered: Courses are recreational but certificates of attendance and attainment may be awarded. College credits are awarded for completion of the combination course.

Cost: SFr400 per week (1-8 weeks), SFr375 per week (9-15 weeks) and SFr350 per week (16+ weeks). Obligatory activities fee at SFr60 per week. Room and board SFr530 per person per week in a single room or SFr360 per person in a double. Cost of acquiring a Swiss residency permit and medical insurance must be borne by student.

Accommodation: In student residence.

DEUTSCH-INSTITUT TIROL
Am Sandhügel 2, 6370 Kitzbühel, Austria. ☎53-56 712 74. Fax: 53-56 723 63. E-mail: dit@kitz.netwing.at. Website: www.gap-year.at.

Courses offered: German language combined with ski and snowboard instruction specially designed for gap year students. (See 'Directory of Sports Courses').

DID DEUTSCH-INSTITUT
Hauptstrasse 26, 63811 Stockstadt am Main, Germany. ☎6027 41770. Fax: 6027 417741/42. E-mail: office@did.de. Website: www.did.de.

Courses offered: Short and long-term intensive German language courses year round in Berlin, Frankfurt and Munich. Summer programmes in many more cities throughout Germany. Tuition in small classes or on individual basis.

Duration of courses: Long-term courses last 8-48 weeks in Berlin, Munich, Wiesbaden and Frankfurt. Shorter courses available.

Qualifications offered: Diploma examinations at the end of each course level, under supervision of the German Language Society, Wiesbaden.

Accommodation: Choice of homestays with German families; guesthouses and apartments also available.

Other services: Internships are also offered.

ECO-ESCUELA DE ESPANOL & BIO-ITZA

c/o Tikal Connection Tour Operator, Calle 15 de Septiembre, Ciudad Flores, Petén 17001, Guatemala. ☎/fax: (502) 7926-4981. E-mail: info@tikalcnx.com. Website: www.tikalcnx.com.

Courses offered: Students learn Spanish in Guatemala's Petén region. Students accepted at all levels. All lessons are one-to-one with a certified teacher. Intense individual attention focuses on reading, writing, conversation and comprehension skills. In addition to personal language training, interested students are encouraged to participate in daily conservation and community development projects organised by the school, such as developing an interpretive nature trail, environmental education and restoration of public schools and libraries. Opportunities for knowledge exchange with local naturalists, midwives, chicle harvesters, etc. who can teach about traditional cooking and local recipes.

Duration of courses: Courses are offered at weekly intervals, starting every Monday throughout the year. Students may stay as long as they wish.

Cost: $175 per week including 20 hours of private Spanish instruction, lodging with a local famiily for 7 days and 3 meals a day. Advance booking requested.

Accommodation: Students stay with a host family within walking distance of the school. Accommodation is modest but comfortable. Students generally have their own rooms but share a bathroom and shower with the family.

Contact: Manuel Villamar.

ELFCA - Institut d'Enseignement de la Langue Française sur la Cote d'Azur

66 avenue de Toulon, 83400 Hyères, France. ☎04-94 65 03 31. Fax: 04-94 65 81 22. E-mail: elfca@elfca.com. Website: www.elfca.com.

Courses offered: Total immersion French language courses.

Duration of courses: 1-24 weeks.

Qualifications offered: Long-term courses lead to Alliance Française diploma. ELFCA is an exam centre for the Alliance Française and the TEF (Test d'Evaluation de Français).

Cost: From €200 per week for long-term courses.

Accommodation: Homestay accommodation, apartment or hotel.

Contact: Colette Samwells, Director.

EL SALVADOR SPANISH SCHOOLS

Calle E Pol. N #2 Urbanización El Milagro, Santa Ana, El Salvador. ☎ +503 850-9293. USA: 413-374-0159. E-mail: Info@Salvaspan.com. Website: www. salvaspan.com.

Courses offered: Intensive group and individual Spanish language classes, full-immersion homestays with Salvadorean families, excursions to local attractions. One-to-one courses, tutoring, flexible scheduling. Salsa dance classes also available. Year-long Spanish courses available that can include a customised syllabus and chance to study at any of five locations.

Duration of courses: 20 hours per week. Semester and winter/summer session courses available, flexible scheduling.

Cost: $150 per week for 20hrs/5days Spanish course. $100 homestay with family. $60 for 2-3 excursions per week to Mayan ruins, museums, markets, etc. Airport pickup also available for $60.

Accommodation: Family homestays include breakfast and dinner, private room and bath. Help can also be given in arranging hotel or rental accommodation. Classes are offered at the Surfer's Inn and other surf camps near La Libertad.

Contact: Prof. Nelson Pacheco Martinez, Programme Director.

EN FAMILLE OVERSEAS
La Maison Jaune, avenue du Stade, 34210 Siran, France. ☎/fax +33 4-68 91 49 90. Tel (UK): 01206 546741. E-mail: marylou.toms@wanadoo.fr. Website: www.enfamilleoverseas.co.uk.
Arranges homestays in France with or without language tuition. Also in Germany, Italy and Spain.

LA ESCUELA DE IDIOMAS D'AMORE
PO Box PO 67-6350, Quepos, Costa Rica. ☎/fax: (506) 777-1143. E-mail: info@escueladamore.com. Website: www.escueladamore.com. US contact addresses: 2812 Horseshoe Bend, Hartland, WI 53029 (tel/fax 262-367-8598) and 4150 Arch Drive, Suite 216, Studio City, CA 91604 (tel/fax 310-435-9897).
Founded in 1992. Original beach school and campus in Costa Rica.
Courses offered: Intensive Spanish immersion for anyone over 18. Located near Manuel Antonio Beach and National Park with on-campus butterfly farm.
Duration of courses: 2, 3, or 4 weeks or more, Monday to Friday.
Cost: Courses with homestay cost $980 for 2 weeks, $1325 for 3 weeks and $1690 for 4 weeks.
Contact: David D'Amore, Director.

EXPERIMENT
89 rue de Turbigo, 75003 Paris, France. ☎ 1-44 54 58 03. Fax: 1-44 54 58 01. E-mail: incoming@experiment-france.org. Website: www.experiment-france.org.
Courses offered: Serious language courses offered at universities (e.g. universities of Nantes, Poitiers and Angers). Also internships.
Duration of courses: Summer courses, 1 semester or 1 academic year.
Cost: From €6,650 per semester including B&B accommodation.
Accommodation: Private rooms in student residences or with host families.
Contact: Anne Blassiau, Director.

FOREIGN STUDENT SERVICE
Oranje Nassaulaan 5, 1075 AH, Amsterdam, Netherlands. ☎020-671 5915. Fax: 020-676 0555. E-mail: info@foreignstudents.nl. Website: www.foreignstudents.nl.
Organisation for foreign students in the Netherlands distributes a booklet *Non-University Dutch Language Courses in the Netherlands* (price €5). Many courses lead to NT2 exams (Nederlands als tweede taal).

GLS SPRACHENZENTRUM BERLIN
Kolonnenstr. 26, 10829 Berlin, Germany. ☎ 30-78 00 89/0. Fax: 30-787 41 92. E-mail: germancourses@gls-berlin.com. Website: www.german-courses.com.
Courses offered: Language courses offered year round at all levels, starting every Monday. Central location near Brandenburg Gate and New Reichstag.
Duration of courses: 20, 30 or 40 lessons per week for any number of weeks. International mix in classes of about 8.
Cost: Sample price for 2 weeks German language course with 20 weekly lessons, activity programme and self-catering single room is €637.
Accommodation: Shared apartments, bed and breakfast, host family or budget hotels available through accommodation service. Single rooms on adult courses; double or multi-bedded for junior summer programmes.
Other services: Extended sightseeing programme in and around Berlin. GLS runs an internship programme combining a language course of at least 4 weeks with a work experience placement in a Berlin-based company (seee *Directory of Work Experience*).

Contact: Dorothee Robrecht, Director of Marketing.

GOETHE INSTITUT
Headquarters in Munich, Germany. Website: www.goethe.de. UK address: 50 Princes Gate, London SW7 2PH; 020-7596 4000. E-mail: german@london.goethe. org. Website: www.goethe.de/london.
Courses offered: German language at all levels in dozens of locations in Germany and worldwide. All course details and institute addresses are on website. Summer courses offered in four locations including Heidelberg and Lake Constance.
Duration of courses: Variable.
Qualifications offered: The Goethe Institut administers its own language exams at all levels, e.g. the ZdaF, KDS and GDS.

IMAC
Instituto Mexico-Americano de Cultura, A.C., Bi-Cultural Courses, Donato Guerra No. 180, Col. Centro. Guadalajara, Jalisco, C.P. 44100 Mexico. ☎33-3613 1080. Fax: 33-3613 4621. E-mail: spanish-imac@imac-ac.edu.mx. Website: www. spanish-school.com.mx.
Member of GWEA (Global Work Experience Association).
Courses offered: Spanish to students from around the world. Group classes and private tutoring.
Duration of courses: Minimum 1 week. New classes start every week so flexible start dates.
Qualifications offered: Transferable credits for US schools and colleges.
Cost: 4 hours of tuition a day costs $194 per week, $517 for 4 weeks. Private lessons cost $100 a week for 1 hour a day. Discounts offered for longer stays. Free unlimited internet, e-mail and multimedia lab.
Accommodation: Homestay programme costs $98 per week, including 3 meals a day. Hotel accommodation available at a discounted rate.
Contact: Mario Shuttleworth.

INSTITUTO CHAC-MOOL
Privada de la Pradera 108, Colonia Pradera, Cuernavaca, Morelos, Mexico. ☎ +52 777-317 1163 or US phone 530-622-4262. E-mail: spanish@chac-mool.com. Website: www.chac-mool.com.
Courses offered: Spanish immersion classes. Courses offered at 10 levels. When a student's ability falls between 2 levels, one-to-one instruction can be arranged to bring the student up to the higher level. Extracurricular activities such as Mexican cooking and Latin dance lessons included free of charge, weekend excursions offered for a small fee.
Duration of courses: 1-26 weeks. Classes begin each Monday year round.
Qualifications offered: Certificate of completion.
Cost: $199 per week; slightly higher June-August. Discounts for enrolling for 5 weeks or longer. $100 life-time registration fee required. (Mention *Taking a Gap Year* for a tuition discount.)
Accommodation: With Mexican families; $18-$25 per day. Private guest houses begin at $16 a day.
Contact: Sherry Howell, Representative.

INSTITUTO INTERNACIONAL EUSKALDUNA
PO Box 195545, San Juan, Puerto Rico 00919-5545. ☎787-281-8013. Fax: 787-274-8291. E-mail: study@spanishinpuertorico.com. Website: www.spanishin-puertorico.com.
Courses offered: Spanish (and English).
Duration of courses: Starts every Monday. Flexible duration. Recommended minimum 1 month. Long-stay course lasts 3 semesters. Minimum age 18. Average age 34.

Qualifications offered: University credit given by certain US universities.
Accommodation: Homestay with local family, half-board or just lodging.
Other services: Arrangement possible whereby students give English classes in exchange for Spanish so that accommodation would be only expense. Extracurricular activities offered.
Contact: Sacha Delgado, Director.

INTERCULTURA LANGUAGE & CULTURAL CENTRE
PO Box 1952-3000, Heredia, Costa Rica. ☎(506) 260-8480. **Fax: (506) 260-9243. E-mail: info@interculturacostarica.com. Website: www.interculturacostarica.com.**
Courses offered: Spanish language, literature and culture, Latin dance, cooking, music and lectures on feminism, indigenous peoples, ecology, intercultural communication and Costa Rican customs. Language courses are eligible for US college accreditation. Intensive Spanish courses in colonial town of Heredia or at the beach in Playa Sámara.
Duration of courses: 1 week to 1 year. Average duration is 1-2 months.
Cost: US$1165 per month including all classes and homestay with breakfast and dinner.
Other services: Intercultura often hosts students between secondary school and university for up to a year. Voluntary work can be arranged if requested.
Contact: Laura Ellington, Director.

INTER-SEJOURS
179 rue de Courcelles, 75017 Paris, France. ☎ +33 1-47 63 06 81. **Fax: +33 1-40 54 89 41. E-mail: marie.inter-sejours@libertysurf.fr. Website: http://asso.intersejours.free.fr.**
Courses offered: Language courses as part of a homestay in Paris (and French students placed abroad, as au pairs in the USA, Australia, etc., in hotel jobs in the UK and Spain, in internships in Ireland, etc.).
Duration of courses: Minimum 1 week up to 34 weeks, with starting dates at specific times throughout the year.
Qualifications offered: Opportunity to work towards the D.E.L.F. examination and the *Certificat Pratique de Français.*
Cost: Examples of price in Paris: 30 lessons in 2 weeks would cost €610. A standard course with 20 lessons over 2 weeks costs €440.
Accommodation: Accommodation and breakfast with a host family costs €160 per week either in Paris or the suburbs. Same arrangement with half board would cost €175. Prices including breakfast from €219 per week.
Contact: Marie-Helene Pierrot, Director.

IXBALANQUE SPANISH SCHOOL IN HONDURAS
Copán Ruinas, Honduras, Central America. ☎504 651 4432. **Fax: 504 651 4432. E-mail: ixbalanquehn@yahoo.com. Website: www.ixbalanque.com.**
Mayan culture reached its highest point at Copán Ruinas.
Courses offered: Spanish courses followed by option of volunteering in the Copán community. Language courses emphasise cultural topics, e.g. the archaeology and anthropology of the region. Weekly excursion to places of local interest (included in fee).
Duration of courses: 4 weeks (flexible). Classes start every Monday. 4 hours of classes a day, 5 days a week.
Cost: $220 for 1 week, $420 for 2, $600 for 3, $760 for 4 inclusive.
Accommodation: Homestay including 3 meals a day.
Contact: Edgar Duarte, Marketing Manager.

KOINE
Via Pandolfini 27, 50122 Florence, Italy. ☎055-213881. **Fax: 055-216949. E-mail: info@koinecenter.com. Website: www.koinecenter.com.**

Courses offered: Italian language for foreigners offered year round in Florence, Lucca and Bologna, and from spring through autumn at schools in Cortona and Orbetello.
Duration of courses: 1 week to 6 months.
Qualifications: Certificate C.I.L.S. from Siena University.
Cost: €545 for a month's tuition (20 hours a week) plus €410 for a month's basic accommodation without use of kitchen. 2-week homestay from €255, 3 weeks for €340.
Accommodation: With an Italian family.

LIDEN & DENZ LANGUAGE CENTRES
St. Petersburg and Moscow, Central Booking Office, Transportny per. 11, 191119 St. Petersburg, Russia. ☎ +7 812 325 2241/812 572 1040. Fax: +7 812 325 1284. Also: Grusinski per. 3-181, Ground floor, 123056 Moscow, Russian Federation. Tel/Fax: +7 095 254 49 91. E-mail: lidenz@lidenz.ru. Website: www. lidenz.ru or www.russiancourses.com.
Courses offered: Russian language offered at all levels from leisure course to crash course, plus academic year courses.
Duration of courses: Minimum 1 week with choice of 20 hours (standard) or 25 (intensive). One-to-one lessons available with choice of frequency (15, 20, 30 or 40 hours a week). Fixed duration of academic year courses are 24, 36 or 48 weeks.
Qualifications offered: All students receive a graded certificate (in Russian) at the end of their stay, indicating course type, course dates, numbers of lessons and level achieved. Liden & Denz in St.Petersburg and Moscow is an official preparation centre for the state exam T.R.K.I. (Russian as a Foreign Language).
Cost: Standard course costs €205-€250 per week depending on overall duration. Surcharges apply in peak season.
Accommodation: Homestay in single room with half board is the most popular option, at a cost of €125 per week. Shared flats, etc. also offered.
Contact: Julia Patasheva (St. Petersburg) or Elena Dovzhikova (Moscow), International Relations.

MALACA INSTITUTO
Calle Cortada 6, Cerrado de Calderón, 29018 Málaga, Spain. ☎ +34 952-29 3242. Fax: +34 952-29 6316. E-mail: gapyear@malacainstituto.com. Website: www.MalacaInstituto.com.
Students at Malaca Instituto from all over the world create a cosmopolitan environment and a culturally enriching experience. The Instituto is inspected by and meets the quality criteria of the Instituto Cervantes, CEELE, EAQUALS and IALC.
Courses offered: A variety of Spanish language and culture classes are offered, from standard beginner to preparation for university entrance. Gap-year students normally take courses of between 16 and 36 weeks. Hispanic Studies programme is especially suitable. In addition, a range of courses short and long includes Spanish + Dance, Spanish + Cookery, Spanish + Internships, as well as General Intensive Spanish, Summer Courses and one-to-one tuition.
Duration of courses: Hispanic Studies Term I – 16 weeks; Term II – 20 weeks.
Qualifications offered: Students can work towards the D.E.L.E. examinations or Spanish university entrance if their level of language is suitably advanced.
Cost: €65 registration fee for all courses. 2-week intensive course would cost €348; 14-week D.E.L.E. examination preparation would costs €2001 including lessons, materials required, introductory party, a tour of Malaga, Flamenco and Salsa lessons, use of swimming pool and accident insurance. Additional costs are airfare, accommodation, excursions, medical insurance and external examination fees. 2 weeks of accommodation costs from €336 with host family on a half-board basis, and €21 a night (shared) at Club Hispanico.
Accommodation: All types with single and twin rooms.

MESTER SPANISH COURSES

Vázquez Coronado 5, 37002 Salamanca, Spain. ☎923-21 38 35. Fax: 923-21 38 41. E-mail: mester@mester.com. Website: www.mester.com.

Courses offered: Spanish at all levels offered in Granada, Malaga, Salamanca, Seville and Tenerife and on specific dates in Barcelona, Leon, Madrid and Valencia. Courses also arranged in Cuba.

Duration of courses: 1-40 weeks starting every Monday. 40-week Academic Year course includes language classes (including business Spanish) and Spanish culture. Participants need not know much Spanish before starting in September.

Qualifications offered: Some courses are recreational; others lead to D.E.L.E. and Certificate of Business Spanish (exam fees extra).

Cost: From €141 (for a no-frills week-long course of two lessons of conversation and two of grammar); €3314 for an academic year (nearly 900 lessons).

Accommodation: Full range including homestays, student flats, university residences and (in Granada and Salamanca only) independent apartments. Tenerife accommodation is in flats and residential complex 12 minutes from two beaches.

MOSCOW INSTITUTE FOR ADVANCED STUDY

Lebyazhii Pereulok 8, Building 1, Moscow, Russia 119019. US office: 156 W 56th St, 7th Floor, New York, NY 10019. ☎212-245-0461. Fax: 212-489-4829. E-mail: info@mifas.org.

Courses offered: Intensive Russian language courses, history, literature, political science, art and culture. Internships also organised (see 'Directory of Work Experience').

Duration of courses: 2 months in summer, 3½ months in autumn and spring semesters.

Cost: $6800-$7800 all-inclusive (excluding airfares) in autumn and spring, $4500 in summer.

Accommodation: Dormitory or homestay.

Contact: Johanna Brownell, Administrative Director.

OIDEAS GAEL
Foras Cultuir Uladh, Gleann Cholm Cille, Co Donegal, Ireland. ☎073-30248. Fax: 073-30348. E-mail: oifig@Oideas-Gael.com. Website: www.Oideas-Gael.com.
Courses offered: Irish language lessons at all learning levels. Separate cultural activity courses offered bilingually in Irish and English in (for example) Celtic pottery, set dancing, landscape and culture, marine painting, archaeology, hill walking and folklore, flute and whistle playing and Bodhrán playing.
Duration of courses: Mostly 1 week. 2 weeks recommended for language courses.
Qualifications offered: Recreational only.
Cost: Average £160. Cultural courses cost £190.
Accommodation: Choice of host family, bed & breakfast, self-catering (€95 in shared house) and on-campus accommodation.

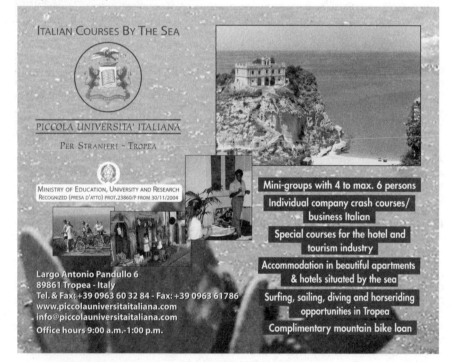

ITALIAN COURSES BY THE SEA

PICCOLA UNIVERSITA' ITALIANA

PER STRANIERI - TROPEA

MINISTRY OF EDUCATION, UNIVERSITY AND RESEARCH
RECOGNIZED (PRESA D'ATTO) PROT.23860/P FROM 30/11/2004

Largo Antonio Pandullo 6
89861 Tropea - Italy
Tel. & Fax: +39 0963 60 32 84 - Fax: +39 0963 61786
www.piccolauniversitaitaliana.com
info@piccolauniversitaitaliana.com
Office hours 9:00 a.m.-1:00 p.m.

Mini-groups with 4 to max. 6 persons

Individual company crash courses/ business Italian

Special courses for the hotel and tourism industry

Accommodation in beautiful apartments & hotels situated by the sea

Surfing, sailing, diving and horseriding opportunities in Tropea

Complimentary mountain bike loan

PICCOLA UNIVERSITÀ ITALIANA
Largo Antonio Pandullo 6, 89861 Tropea, Italy. ☎0963 603284. Fax: 0963 61786. E-mail: info@piccolauniversitaitaliana.com. Website: www.piccolauniversitaitaliana.com.
Courses offered: Italian language courses; special courses for the hotel and tourism industry; individual crash courses in business Italian; Italian for fashion and style. Courses are given to small groups of a maximum of 4-6 students.
Duration of courses: Usually 1-8 weeks, but it is possible to stay longer. Courses begin every Monday year round.
Qualifications offered: Opportunity to work towards the C.I.L.S. examination.
Cost: 8-week conversation course costs €670; 8-week main course costs €1205; 8-week intensive course costs €2387. 10% discount on all course fees from November to March.

Registration fee of €100 includes transfer from and to the airport/train station at Lamezia Terme or 2 excursions of the weekly cultural programme.

Accommodation: Accommodation is extra at €950 for 8 weeks in a single room (shared flat) or €1365 in a single room apartment. Generally holiday flats in the centre of Tropea, with a sea or mountain view. Flats usually have one, two or three rooms, kitchen and terrace or balcony.

Other activities: Piccola Università Italiana (at the same address) offers surfing, sailing, diving, tennis and horse riding. The school offers excursion programmes in Calabria and Sicily. Further courses available in watercolour painting, history of art and cookery.

THE PROBA INTERNATIONAL EDUCATIONAL CENTRE

PO Box 109, Lappeenranta, Fin 53101, Finland. ☎ +007-812-234 5024. Fax: +007-812-346 0086. E-mail: info@studyrussian.spb.ru. Website: www.studyrussian.spb.ru.

Courses offered: Russian language courses, courses at teachers' homes, Study & Work and volunteer programmes in St. Petersburg, Russia. Cultural programme including a weekly excursion or theatre visit.

Duration of courses: From 2 weeks (20 lessons per week) in groups of 4. Semester-long courses also available, 5 months from September, January or May. Language course followed by 4 or 8 weeks volunteering in hospitals, kindergartens, summer camps or teaching English in schools.

Qualifications offered: An examination can be taken at the end of the semester course and there is the possibility of obtaining a Diploma in the Russian language.

Cost: 4-week course followed by 4 weeks of volunteering costs €2050; 8-week course followed by 8 weeks volunteering costs €2850. Semester course costs from €5000. Cost includes half-board accommodation and visa support but not airfares.

Accommodation: Single room in a Russian host family home near the city centre or at least close to an underground station. Possible alternatives in a hotel or hostel (on request).

Contact: Mr. Slava Oguretchnikov, Director General.

RUTA DEL SOL SPANISH SCHOOL

9 de Octubre # N21-157 & Ramón Roca, Santa Teresita Building, 3rd Floor 7N, Quito, Ecuador; postal address PO Box 17-02-5228, Quito, Ecuador. ☎/fax: +593-2 2-56 29 56. E-mail: rutadelsol33@hotmail.com. Website: www.rutasolacademy.com.

Courses offered: Spanish and Quechua language courses held in Quito, in the jungle (www.rutasolacademy.com/jungleclasses.html) and by the coast (www.rutasolacademy.com/coast.html).

Duration of courses: 12-week Spanish course, 10-week Quechua course.

Qualifications offered: Recreational courses for travellers plus others are in preparation for the D.E.L.E. exams (Diploma de Español como Lengua Extranjera) at all levels.

Cost: One-to-one lessons cost $6 for Spanish, $10 for Quechua.

Accommodation: Homestay with Ecuadorian families costs $14 a day.

Other services: Teaches Andean culture and has a gallery of naïf Ecuadorian art. Can arrange travel to the Galapagos Islands or the Amazon jungle.

Contact: Guiovana Camino (Director) and Jorge Tasiguano.

SIN FRONTERAS SPANISH COURSES & HOSTEL

Calle Huala 12307, Esquina Quilpo, San Carlos de Bariloche, Argentina. ☎ +54-2944-461824. E-mail: aprendalo_ya@hotmail.com. Website: www.spanishsinfronteras.tk.

Courses offered: Spanish Language and Latin American Culture, tailored to meet requirements of individuals. For example they offer a 4-day survival course, designed to teach the basics for travelling around Latin America.

Duration of courses: Most students stay at least 2 weeks, studying about 3 hours a day. Flexible starting dates.

Cost: $5 per hour for individual tuition, $4 for group tuition (up to 3 students).

Accommodation: Self-catering with choice of single or double rooms. Laundry service and use of mountain bikes included free of charge.

Contact: Rosana Biondo, Academic Director.

UNIL COURS DE VACANCES

BFSH2, University of Lausanne, CH-1015 Dorigny, Switzerland. ☎ +41 21-692 30 90. Fax: +41 21-692 30 85. E-mail: CoursDeVacances@cvac.unil.ch. Website: www.unil.ch/cvac/page 5651_fr.html (in English).

Courses offered: French for all levels from elementary.

Duration of courses: Intensive 6-week courses for beginners between July and September. Minimum 3 weeks; maximum 12 weeks.

Qualifications offered: Courses are serious but no diploma at the end, only an *attestation*.

Cost: SFr550 (€359) per 3 weeks, SFr1200 (€783.50) for 6 weeks.

Accommodation: List of suitable accommodation given on website or can be fixed up via tourist office (www.lausanne-tourisme.ch/hotels-logements).

LA UNION CENTRO LINGUISTICO

1A Avenida Sur No. 21, Antigua, Guatemala. ☎/fax: (502) 7832-7337. E-mail: info@launion.edu.gt. Website: www.launion.edu.gt.

Organisation for sharing Spanish language and Guatemalan culture run by a group of experienced Guatemalan Spanish teachers.

Courses offered: One-to-one lessons; teacher rotation for variety. Placements can be made on voluntary projects after study (see entry).

Duration of courses: Flexible.

Cost: 4 hours of morning tuition for 5 days costs $95; 25 hours for $105; 30 hours for $115; and 35 hours for $125. Afternoon sessions cost less, e.g. 20 hours for $70; 25 hours for $80.

Accommodation: Homestays cost $60 a week; guesthouse accommodation $70-$80 per week.

Contact: Juan Carlos Martinez, General Director.

VIA HISPANA

Presidente Luis Saenz Peña 277 3°6, Buenos Aires, Argentina. ☎ +54 11-4893 2765. Fax: +54 11-4381 5963. E-mail: info@viahispana.com. **Website: www. viahispana.com.**

Courses offered: General Spanish, Intensive Spanish, Spanish with Tango, Sports, Wine or Cooking, Tango, Latin American Culture: history, art, economics, social movements, cookery, celebrities, etc. Full programme offered at five different schools around the country (Salta, Mendoza, Bariloche and Ushuaia as well as BA).

Duration of courses: 1 week to 1 year.

Cost: $120-$300 per week depending on choice.

Accommodation: Host families: single room with breakfast, or breakfast and dinner. Shared flats also an option.

Other services: Volunteer and internship programmes available.

Contact: Vanina Gigante, Director.

Art, Design, Drama & Film Courses

Art & Design

ACCADEMIA DEL GIGLIO
Lingue Arte Cultura, Via Ghibellina 116, 50122 Florence, Italy. ☎/fax: 055-230 2467. E-mail: info@adg.it. Website:www.adg.it.
Courses offered: Art and art history courses in addition to Italian language courses described above. Fresco workshop available over 4 weeks.
Duration of courses: Mainly one or two week courses with 14 hours of tuition per week.
Cost: 1-week art course costs €180, 2 weeks costs €340, 12 weeks costs €1710. Enrolment fee of €41.
Accommodation: All kinds of accommodation can be arranged from single room in a family for €28 a day half-board to €750 for 4 weeks in a self-catering flat sharing kitchen and other facilities.
Other services: Visits and social activities included in the price.
Contact: Lorenzo Capanni, Assistant Director.

ART HISTORY ABROAD
179C New Kings Road, Fulham, London, SW6 4SW. ☎020-7731 2231. Fax: 020-7731 2456. E-mail: info@arthistoryabroad.com. Website: www.arthistory-abroad.com.
Year Out Group founding member. BETA member.
Programme description: Unique programme designed for the Year Out that looks to broaden participants' sense of self as well as cultural and intellectual horizons. Programme includes art, history, architecture, politics, philosophy, economics, music, poetry, theology, literature and classics. 6 weeks of travel throughout Italy including Venice, Verona, Florence, Siena, Naples and Rome plus at least 6 other cities. No classroom work and all tuition is on-site and in groups of no more than 8. From 2006 new two-week summer Contemporary Art course based in London with visits throughout the UK as well as Paris and Amsterdam.
Number of placements per year: 24 per course, 4 times per year.
Duration and time of placement: 6-week course offered 4 times a year (Autumn, Spring, Early Summer and Late Summer) and 2-week courses offered in July/August.
Cost: £5400 for the Autumn, Spring and Early Summer courses including travel to, from and within Italy, hotel accommodation and breakfast throughout, all museum entry, expert tuition in small groups as well as drawing and Italian conversation classes and a private visit to the Vatican Museum. Fees do not include lunch or supper. Price for 2-week Summer courses in Italy is £2050. London-based courses are from £900.
Accommodation: Shared rooms in hotels in the centre of each city visited.

THE ART INSTITUTE OF FLORENCE LDM
Via Dell' Alloro 14R, 50123 Florence, Italy. ☎055-283142. Fax: 055-289514. E-mail: arte@lorenzodemedici.it. Website: http://artinstituteflorence.lorenzode-medici.it.
Courses offered: Graphic arts, painting and drawing, printmaking, photography, sculpture, ceramics and fine art restoration. All classes conducted in English.
Duration of courses: 1 month in summer, semester or year long.
Qualifications offered: Certificate programme.

THE ART SCHOOL – ART UNDER ONE ROOF
Via Pandolfini 46R, 50122 Florence, Italy. ☎/fax: 055-247 8867. E-mail: arte1@arteurope.it. Website: www.arteuropa.org.

School located a 5-minute walk from the Ponte Vecchio in the centre of Florence in a 14th century palazzo.
Courses offered: Core areas are painting and drawing, figurative sculpture, boutique and interior design, fresco and decorative techniques, ceramics and other electives.
Duration of courses: 13-14 weeks in a semester. Also 2-semester Academic Year Foundation Programme suitable for post-A level candidates.
Accommodation: Single or shared rooms with use of kitchen facilities.
Other services: Italian conversation classes also offered. Other electives include art history. Studio art summer courses held in Paris.

CAMBRIDGE SCHOOL OF ART AND DESIGN
Round Church Street, Cambridge CB5 8AD. ☎01223 314431. Fax: 01223 467773. E-mail: enquiries@catscollege.com. Website: www.cambridgeartschool. com.
Pre-university study programmes in art, design and media.
Courses offered: Art foundation course and portfolio courses. Subject options include painting and drawing, sculpture, art of architecture, ceramics, metal work, fashion, textiles, graphics and illustration, photography and video. Also offer drama courses (see separate entry below for CATS).
Duration of courses: One year for the foundation course and minimum one term for the portfolio courses.
Qualifications offered: The art foundation course offers a diploma on completion.
Cost: Approx £3830 per term.
Accommodation: Hostels, family or self-catering.

CENTRAL ST MARTINS COLLEGE OF ART AND DESIGN
Southampton Row, London WC1B 4AP. ☎020-7514 7023. Fax: 020-7514 7016. E-mail:info@csm.arts.ac.uk.. Website: www.csm.arts.ac.uk.
Courses offered: Fashion Folio, Graphic Design Portfolio Course and a wide range of evening, weekend and vacation courses. Summer school courses are also run July-September.
Qualifications offered: None; most courses are suitable for post-university gap students. Drawing for Portfolio Preparation open to those under 18.
Accommodation: Halls of residence near the college are available for summer courses.

JOHN HALL PRE-UNIVERSITY COURSE
12 Gainsborough Road, Ipswich, Suffolk IP4 2UR. ☎01473 251223. Fax: 01473 288009. E-mail: info@johnhallpre-university.com. Website: www.johnhallvenice. co.uk.
Courses offered: A pre-university course covering art, art history, architecture, music, opera, literature, history and world cinema. Introductory week in London including the museum and commercial art world is followed by six weeks in Venice where daily lectures and visits (including a private visit to San Marco) are combined with practical classes in life-drawing and photography, with optional Italian classes and visits to Padova, Ravenna and Palladian villas in the Veneto. The extensions of a week in Florence and five days in Rome continue the study of history, art, music and architecture on-site and include private visits to the Uffizi, the Accademia, the Keats Shelley Museum, the Vatican and Sistine Chapel.
Duration of courses: 1 week London, 6 weeks Venice. Extensions: 1 week Florence, 5 days Rome. Offered annually from late January.
Qualifications: Interest and enthusiasm.
Cost: 1 week London and 6 weeks Venice: £6400; Florence £875, Rome £830. Travel to and from Italy, entrances, accommodation including breakfast and dinner in Italy, are included in fees. Accommodation in London not included.
Contact: Clare Augarde, Secretary.

LONDON COLLEGE OF FASHION
20 John Princes St, London W1G 0BJ. ☎020-7514 7566. Fax: 020-7514 7490.
E-mail: shortcourses@fashion.arts.ac.uk. Website: www.fashion.arts.ac.uk.
Courses offered: Intensive short evening and day courses in all fashion-related subjects.
Duration of courses: 3-5 days or 4-10 weeks. Courses commence October, January and May. Summer School June-August.
Qualifications offered: Certificate of Attendance.
Cost: Prices range from £99 to £2500.
Other services: Help can be given finding accommodation.
Contact: Short Course Office.

STEVE OUTRAM TRAVEL PHOTOGRAPHY WORKSHOPS
D.Katsifarakis Street, Galatas, Chania 73100, Crete, Greece. ☎/fax: +30 28210-32201. E-mail: mail@steveoutram.com. Website: www.steveoutram.com.
Courses offered: Photo Workshops held annually in Western Crete, Lesbos and Zanzibar. Maximum 8 people (of mixed ability).
Duration of courses: 9-14 days.
Cost: US$2152 per person, excluding travel.
Accommodation: Renovated hotels with character.

STUDIO ART CENTERS INTERNATIONAL (SACI)
Palazzo dei Cartelloni, Via Sant'Antonino 11, Florence 50123, Italy. ☎ +39 055-289948. E-mail: info@saci-florence.org. Website: www.saci-florence.org.
Courses offered: Studio art, art history, architecture, design, art conservation and Italian cultural studies. Courses offered in 40 different studio and academic disciplines.

Duration of courses: Semester courses are from September to December and/or January to April. Late Spring/Summer courses are run May-June and/or June-July.

Qualifications offered: SACI is a complete accredited programme for serious students. Programmes include Semester/Year Abroad, 2-year Diploma, MFA/MA, Post-Baccalaureate Certificate and Summer Studies.

Cost: Tuition is from $3500 for 4-5 weeks late Spring and Summer plus $1200-$1400 for housing. Semester tuition fees are from $9675 plus $3500 for housing.

Accommodation: Furnished apartments throughout Florence.

Contact: SACI Co-ordinator at saci@iie.org.

Dance, Drama & Film

CAMBRIDGE ARTS & SCIENCES (CATS)
Round Church Street, Cambridge CB5 8AD. ☎01223 314431. Fax: 01223 467773. E-mail: drama@catscollege.com. Website: www.cambridgeartschool. com/courses/drama.html.
Pre-university study programmes in art, design and media.

Courses offered: Cambridge School of Visual & Performing Arts runs a one-year Drama Foundation programme, in association with RADA, to provide students with training and experience in the field of acting and theatre production.

Duration of courses: One academic year.

Qualifications offered: The course aims to help students to attain entry to drama degree programmes at university.

Cost: Approx £3830 per term.

Accommodation: Hostels, family or self-catering.

GREEK DANCES THEATRE
8 Scholiou Street, Plaka, 105 58 Athens, Greece. ☎210-324 4395. Fax: 210-324 6921. E-mail: mail@grdance.org. Website: www.grdance.org.
Courses offered: Short courses for foreigners in Greek folk dance and folk culture in conjunction with evening performances in outdoor theatre near the Acropolis.

Duration of courses: 1 week between May and September. 4 hours of instruction every afternoon.

Cost: €110. Volunteers must fund their own stay in Athens.

Contact: Adamantia Angeli.

LONDON ACADEMY OF PERFORMING ARTS
Saint Matthew's Church, St Petersburgh Place, London W2 4LA. ☎020-7727 0220. Fax: 020-7727 0330. E-mail: admin@lapadrama.com. Website: www. lapadrama.com
Courses offered: Summer School for Shakespearean Acting. Course is for amateurs or professionals who wish to update their Shakespearean skills.

Duration of courses: 4 weeks.

Prerequisites: Minimum age 17, no upper age limit.

Cost: £850.

Accommodation: None is provided.

Follow-up: Possibility of further training on one-year Postgraduate Classical Acting course.

Contact: Brian Parsonage Kelly, Administrative Director.

MALACA INSTITUTO
Calle Cortada 6, Cerrado de Calderón, 29018 Málaga, Spain. ☎ +34 952-29 3242. Fax: +34 952-29 6316. E-mail: gapyear@malacainstituto.com. Website: www.MalacaInstituto.com.

Courses offered: Dance with Spanish language course. For further details of the Spanish language courses, see entry in the 'Directory of Language Courses'.
Duration of courses: 2 or 4 weeks, 20 lessons Spanish plus 10 lessons in Salsa or Sevillanas per week.
Cost: €530 for 2 weeks, €1045 for 4 weeks plus registration fee of €65.

NEW YORK FILM ACADEMY
100 E 17th St, New York, NY 10003, USA. ☎212-674-4300. Fax: 212-477-1414. E-mail: film@nyfa.com. Website: www.nyfa.com.
Courses offered: Film-making including writing, producing, directing and editing film in New York, London (King's College) and Universal Studios (LA). Acting for Film, Screenwriting, 3D Animation and Production are also available.
Duration of courses: One year course starting in July, March, July or September. Short 1, 4, 6 and 8-week courses also available.
Cost: $27,500 tuition for full year course, and about $4000 extra for film, processing and production expenses.

ROYAL OPERA HOUSE EDUCATION
Covent Garden, London WC2E 9DD. ☎020-7212 9410. Fax: 020-7212 9441. E-mail: education@roh.org.uk. Website: http://info.royaloperahouse.org/Education.
Courses offered: 'Behind-the-Scenes' course at the Royal Opera House, primarily for 18-22 year olds.
Number of placements per year: 40.
Duration of courses: 5 days in March, offered annually.
Qualifications offered: Purely recreational.
Other services: Course is residential. Accommodation within walking distance. Work placements also offered (see entry in 'Directory of Work Experience').
Contact: ROH Education.

THE SCHOOL OF THE SCIENCE OF ACTING
67-83 Seven Sisters Road, London N7 6BU. ☎020-7272 0027. Fax: 020-7272 0026. E-mail: find@scienceofacting.org.uk. Website: www.scienceofacting.org. uk.
Courses offered: 1 year Acting course. The aim of the course is for the students to understand the basic laws of good acting and to become competent professionals. Students study the syllabus through lessons in theory and a series of assessed exercises. In addition students have classes in the study of Voice, Movement, Dance and other subjects including histories of Art, Music, Psychology and Philosophy. Students take part in the Directing students' exercises, exam days and the Edinburgh Festival. This accumulated knowledge and experience lead to the presentation of two end-of-course plays.
Duration of courses: 1 year of 4 11-week terms.
Qualifications: Certificate of merit issued by the school.
Cost: Average £2475 per term.
Accommodation: Not provided but help given with finding it.

WORLDwrite
WORLDwrite Centre, Millfields Lodge, 201 Millfields Road, Hackney, London E5 0AL. ☎020-8985 5435. Fax: 020-8510 0460. E-mail: world.write@btconnect. com. Website: www.worldwrite.org.uk.
Courses offered: WORLDwrite is an education charity that uses documentary film-making as a medium for investigating global issues. Charity has film facility and training programme. It organises unique film-based global exchanges with Ghana, computer and film school appeals, and conferences and summits on development issues.

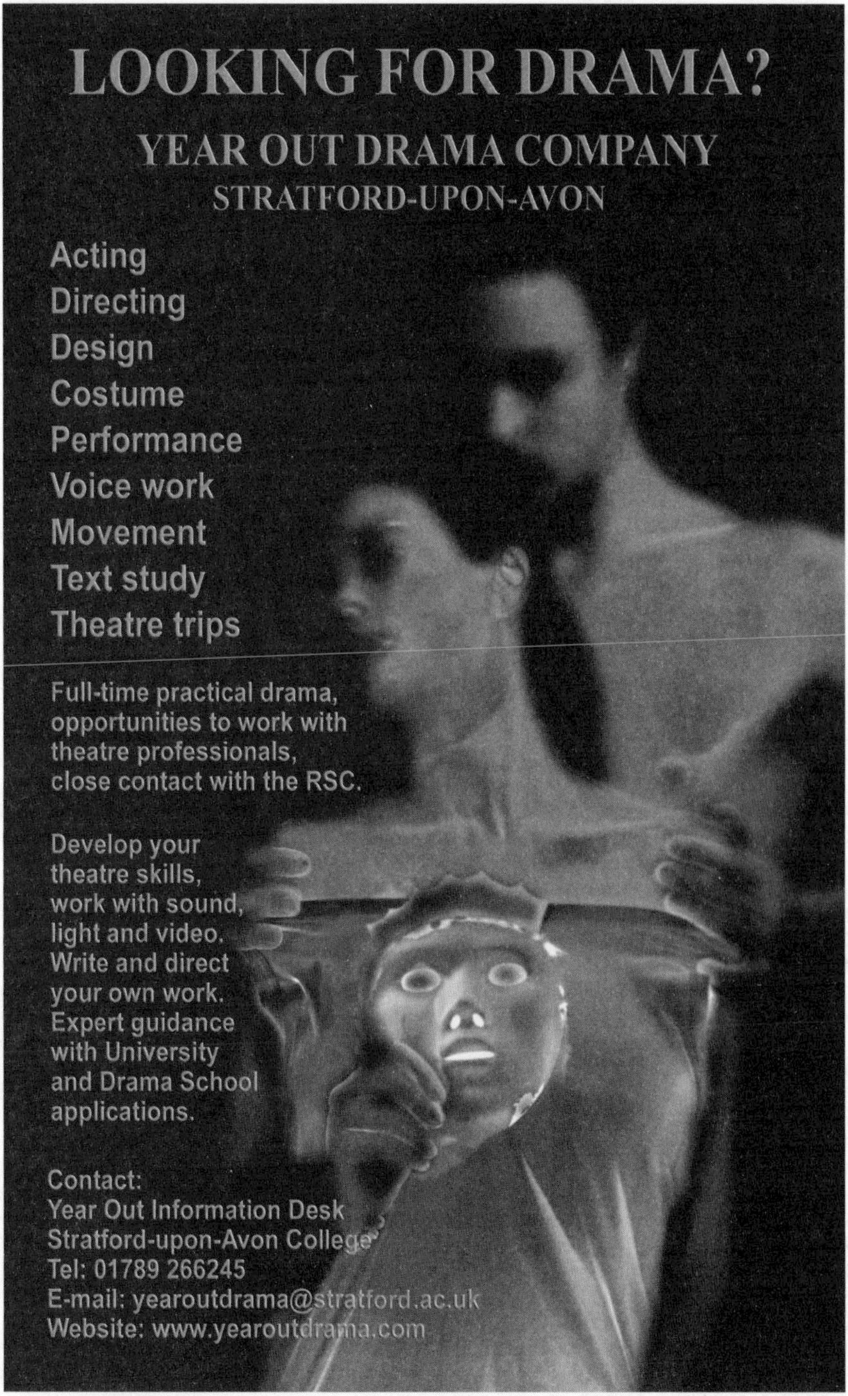
LOOKING FOR DRAMA?
YEAR OUT DRAMA COMPANY
STRATFORD-UPON-AVON
Acting
Directing
Design
Costume
Performance
Voice work
Movement
Text study
Theatre trips
Full-time practical drama, opportunities to work with theatre professionals, close contact with the RSC.
Develop your theatre skills, work with sound, light and video. Write and direct your own work. Expert guidance with University and Drama School applications.
Contact:
Year Out Information Desk
Stratford-upon-Avon College
Tel: 01789 266245
E-mail: yearoutdrama@stratford.ac.uk
Website: www.yearoutdrama.com

Duration of courses: 20 weeks.
Prerequisites: Interested people should become acquainted with the work of WORLDwrite.
Contact: Ceri Dingle, Director.

YEAR OUT DRAMA COMPANY
Stratford-upon-Avon College, Alcester Road, Stratford-upon-Avon, Warks. CV37 9QR. ☎01789 266245. Fax: 01789 267524. E-mail: yearoutdrama@stratford. ac.uk.
Founding member of Year Out Group.
Courses offered: Challenging, intensive, practical Drama course specific to Gap Year students. Led by experts in professionally equipped performance spaces. Students benefit from working with theatre professionals on varying disciplines including Acting Techniques, Voice, Movement, Directing, Text Study and Performance. Students perform annually at the Edinburgh Fringe Festival.
Duration of courses: September to July, split into three terms.
Cost: £4300 for the year which includes all production costs, travel and tickets for frequent theatre trips. Accommodation costs are extra.
Accommodation: Students can live in halls of residence, with landladies or in shared houses.
Follow-up: Students are given help with auditions and UCAS applications. The Company has strong support from The Royal Shakespeare Company and other working professionals.

Business Skills Courses

CAVENDISH COLLEGE
35-37 Alfred Place, London WC1E 7DP. ☎020-7580 6043. Fax: 020-7255 1591. E-mail: learn@cavendish.ac.uk. Website: www.cavendish.ac.uk.
Member of British Accreditation Council.
Courses offered: Business Studies and Secretarial training as well as range of vocational courses including fashion design, interior design, animation, video production, marketing, advertising, travel and tourism and hotel management.
Duration of courses: Majority are 6 or 9 month foundation courses.
Cost: Prices given on website.
Qualifications offered: Cavendish Diploma.
Follow-up: Suitable background for going on to foundation academic and vocational courses for university entrance.

GSC BUSINESS & SECRETARIAL COLLEGE
17 Chapel St, Guildford, Surrey GU1 3UL. ☎01483 564885. Fax: 01483 5347777. E-mail: mail@g-s-c.co.uk. Website: www.g-s-c.co.uk.
Member of BAC.
Courses offered: Full-time, part-time and one-day courses in Computing & Information Technology, Business & Administration, Legal Secretaries, Business Administration and Shorthand. Online learning courses also available.
Duration of courses: Flexible start dates on many courses.
Other services: Students can take French or German as well.

KUDOS TRAINING LIMITED
Suite 10, The Sanctuary, 23 Oakhill Grove, Surbiton, Surrey KT6 6DU. ☎020-8288 8766. Fax: 020-8288 8764. E-mail: enquiry@kudostraining.org. Website: www.kudostraining.demon.co.uk.

Courses offered: One-term full-time intensive course leading to Private Secretary's Diploma or Executive Secretary's Diploma which are professional qualifications of the London Chamber of Commerce & Industry (Educational Development International). Subjects include Business Administration, Communication for Business, Principles and Practice of Management, Audio/Touch Typing. Subject to demand, Pitmans shorthand is also offered.

Qualifications offered: LCCI as above.

Accommodation: Can be arranged; accommodation always provided during weekend intensive courses and examination periods.

Follow-up: Further courses can be taken at the school or by distance learning.

Contact: Mrs. Elaine Howard, Principal.

OXFORD BUSINESS COLLEGE
Kings Mead House, Oxpens Road, Oxford OX1 1RX. ☎01865 791908. Fax: 01865 245059. E-mail: enquiries@oxfordbusinesscollege.co.uk. Website: www. oxfordbusinesscollege.co.uk.

Courses offered: Career Skills courses which include a paid work placement, combining training and experience. Business qualifications for employment or for university entrance.

Duration of courses: Intensive course is 3 months (2 months computer training, 1 month work placement) or 9 months (6 months PA training followed by 3-month paid work placement).

Qualifications offered: Chartered Institute of Marketing (CIM), etc.

Accommodation: Shared houses near college are available through the Accommodation Office. Host family accommodation can be arranged if preferred.

Follow-up: Many courses include optional work placement arranged by the college recruitment service which allows students to earn for college or travel funds as part of their course. Also encourage graduates to apply for the Mountbatten Internship Programme in New York (see USA chapter).

OXFORD MEDIA AND BUSINESS SCHOOL
Rose Place, Oxford OX1 1SB. ☎01865 240963. Fax: 01865 242783. E-mail: courses@oxfordbusiness.co.uk. Website: www.oxfordbusiness.co.uk.

Courses offered: 6 or 12-week Gap Year 'Life Skills' course is a total immersion in taught and practised IT skills designed to help students earn higher wages during their Gap Year. Intensive tuition in Microsoft IT and communication skills; essential project work to tight deadlines simulates a temping assignment in terms of prioritising, time management, working in teams, and production quality; all of these are part of the Course Assessment. The school also offers Business Studies, Marketing, Fashion Studies and Career Start courses.

Duration of courses: 6 or 12 week Gap Course starting September and January. Range of year-long courses also available.

Qualifications offered: ABE (Association of Business Executives) Diploma, CIM (Chartered Institute of Marketing) Stage I & II (Professional Level), ECDL.

Cost: 6-week Gap Year course is £1100, 12 weeks is £1970.

Accommodation: Shared houses within walking or cycling distance or host families in the locality.

Follow-up: Specialist in-house recruitment service. Students can also be matched with an international student at the sister school of English for language exchange.

QUEEN'S BUSINESS & SECRETARIAL COLLEGE
24 Queensberry Place, London SW7 2DS. ☎020-7589 8583. E-mail: info@qbsc. ac.uk. Website: www.qbsc.ac.uk.

Courses offered: Short modular courses of 1-6 weeks cover specific IT and Business Skills. Intensive IT and Business Skills, Executive and Personal Assistant, Marketing, PR

and Advertising with IT and Business Skills courses.
Duration of courses: 1, 2 or 3 12-week terms, starting September, January or April.
Qualifications offered: OCR, LCCI and City & Guilds examinations.
Cost: From £2750 for 1 term course. Short courses: 1 week £225; 4 weeks £795; 6 weeks £1095.
Accommodation: The College does not provide accommodation.
Follow-up: Career Preparation and job search skills are an important part of each course. The College has a strong relationship with a number of London recruitment agencies and is constantly approached by companies looking for well-trained staff. Work experience is an integral part of the 2 and 3 term courses and students on the shorter courses can be assisted in finding placements.
Contact: Corinne Bickford/Lucy Napper.

ST JAMES'S & LUCIE CLAYTON COLLEGE
4 Wetherby Gardens, London SW5 0JN. ☎020-7373 3852. Fax: 020-7370 3303. E-mail: information@sjlccollege.co.uk. Website: www.tftltd.co.uk/sjlc.
Member of the Year Out Group.
Course description: Most popular course for gap year students is the One Term Pre/Post University Course. 12-week course provides a platform from which students acquire the essential skills and confidence required to gain competitive temping rates. In addition to the core skills of keyboarding, IT and Teeline Shorthand, the course includes seminars in a range of personal development areas including assertiveness, interview techniques and self-defence. Also offers an introduction to marketing, public relations, a hands-on creative advertising course, etc.
Duration of courses: 12 weeks (one term) most suitable for gap students but many other shorter options from 2 weeks, including keyboarding and IT courses. Term courses start in September, January, April and July. Short courses start every Monday throughout the year.
Qualifications offered: CIPD Certificates in Personnel Practice, Training Practice and Management.
Cost: £180 + VAT for one week keyboard course up to £2700 + VAT for a 12-week one-term course.
Follow-up: Free career service, CV advice and interview techniques. Work experience forms an integral part of the longer courses. Many students at the end of their training are placed directly by associated recruitment consultancy.

Cookery Courses

ASHBURTON COOKERY SCHOOL

76 East St, Ashburton, Devon TQ13 7AX. ☎01364 652784. Fax: 01364 653825. E-mail: info@ashburtoncookeryschool.co.uk. Website: www.ashburton-cookeryschool.co.uk.

Courses offered: Specialist and diploma cookery courses of varying durations. 1-day courses cover choice of Bakery, Italian, French, Moorish, Thai, Express Dinner Parties, etc. 2-day courses cover for example Chef Skills, Beginners, Italian, Thai or Vegetarian. 5-day 'Pressure Cooks' course originally designed for chalet hosts and boat crew. Also 4-week Basic Cookery Diploma course.

Duration of courses: 1, 2 or 5 days; 4 weeks.

Prerequisites: Minimum age 16 for Beginners 5-day course, 18 for all others.

Qualifications offered: 4-week course designed to mirror NVQ2/3 standards. Successful students on the 5-Day and Diploma courses receive school's own certificate backed up with a skills assessment. Assistance can be given with gaining employment.

Cost: £115 for 1-day course; £249 for 2-day course; £535-£565 for 5-day course; £1995 for 4-week Basic Cookery Diploma.

Accommodation: B&B rooms available within the school charged at £49 per night for a single, £65 for a double; discounts for those staying 5 or more nights.

Contact: Derryck Strachan, Marketing Director.

THE AVENUE COOKERY SCHOOL

74 Chartfield Avenue, Putney, London SW15 6HQ. ☎020-8788 3025. E-mail: info@theavenuecourses.com. Website: www.theavenuecourses.com.

Courses offered: 'The Really Useful Course' is an intensive cookery course to enable students to get jobs in ski chalets, on boats or with families. Also offer evening classes over 6 weeks. This course includes preparing a three-course meal for four which will be taken home and all students will have the opportunity to dine together on food they have prepared in class.

Duration of courses: 1-2 week course offered regularly during the autumn and summer months. Evening courses throughout the year.

Qualifications offered: Certificated First Aid. Graduates of the Really Useful Course take away a useful pack with all the basic equipment required to enable them to cook in any situation.

Cost: 1-week course £565. 2-week course £980. Evening classes £50.

Accommodation: Fully residential if required. £120 per week including dinner and breakfast.

Contact: Mary Forde, Director.

BALLYMALOE COOKERY SCHOOL

Shanagarry, Midelton, Co. Cork, Ireland. ☎21-46 46 785. Fax: 21-46 46 909. E-mail: enquiries@ballymaloe-cookery-school.ie. Website: www.cookingisfun.ie.

Situated on organic farm by the coast with access to excellent ingredients.

Courses offered: 12-week Certificate in Cookery course. Range of short courses also offered.

Duration of courses: Certificate course starting January, April and September. Short courses given between April and July, including two 1-week introductory courses in July.

Qualifications offered: Students who pass written and practical exams at end of course are awarded the Ballymaloe Cookery School Certificates of Food and Wine.

Cost: €8,375 for Certificate course excluding accommodation. 1-day courses cost €195, 2½-day course €455 and 5-day Intro course €755.

Accommodation: Self-catering student accommodation in converted farm cottages costs €95 per week in twin room and €115 in single (2006 prices). Nightly charges for short courses are €25 shared, €32 single.

COOKERY AT THE GRANGE
The Grange, Whatley, Frome, Somerset BA11 3JU. ☎/fax: 01373 836579. E-mail: info@cookeryatthegrange.co.uk. Website: www.cookeryatthegrange.co.uk.
Courses offered: An intensive, hands-on cookery course.
Duration of courses: 4 weeks, offered 9 times per year.
Qualifications offered: Basic Food Hygiene Certificate. A certificate of attendance is also given and a letter of recommendation can be written for future employers, on request.
Cost: £2520-£2940.
Accommodation: Mainly twin rooms, with the majority being en suite, although some single rooms are available for a supplementary payment. Accommodation has a Games Room with a snooker/pool table, plasma TV with Sky, DVD & VHS, CD player, plus large gardens, boules, badminton, croquet and a tennis court.
Follow-up: The course equips students for working in ski chalets, on yachts, in shooting/fishing lodges, working for outside catering companies, cooking for families at home or abroad and for a host of other cooking opportunities.
Contact: Jane & William Averill.

LE CORDON BLEU CULINARY INSTITUTE
114 Marylebone Lane, London W1V 2HH. ☎020-7935 3503. Fax: 020-7935 7621. E-mail: london@cordonbleu.net. Website: www.cordonbleu.net.
Institute has branch in Paris and many other cities; total of 26 institutes in 15 countries.
Courses offered: Le Cordon Bleu Basic Cuisine Certificate course covers both basic and complex recipes, from traditional meals to vegetarian and ethnic recipes.
Duration of courses: 10 weeks. Many shorter full-time and part-time courses.
Cost: £4427.
Accommodation: A list of accommodation agencies, hostels and hotels is available from the Admissions office. They are selected according to proximity to the school.
Follow-up: Le Cordon Bleu has strong links with some of the top ski companies, many of whom recruit directly from the school. The course is ideal for those wishing to work on yachts or find employment during their Gap Year or school and university holidays.

EDINBURGH SCHOOL OF FOOD & WINE
The Coach House, Newliston, Edinburgh EH29 9EB. ☎00 44 (0)131-333 5001. E-mail: info@esfw.com. Website: www.esfw.com.
Courses offered: Practical hands-on cookery - 6 months, 3 months, 4 months, 2 weeks, 1 week and 1 day. Food Handlers Certificate Course for Environmental Health Institute of Scotland, Wine & Spirit Education Trust Certificate Course for Intermediate and Advanced levels, Courses for Chalet, Yacht and Castle cooks, Bar Skills, Flower Arranging, Table Service, Business Start Up and Team Building.
Qualifications offered: Edinburgh School of Food & Wine Diploma & Certificate.
Cost: £95 for 1 day, £395 for 1 week; £2000 for 4 weeks; £8500 for 6 months.
Accommodation: Assistance always offered.
Follow-up: The School works closely with ski companies, agencies and restaurants offering opportunities in the UK and abroad.

FOOD OF COURSE COOKERY SCHOOL
Middle Farm House, Sutton, Shepton Mallet, Somerset BA4 6QF. ☎01749 860116. Fax: 01749 860441. E-mail: louise.hutton@foodofcourse.co.uk. Website: www.foodofcourse.co.uk.
Lou Hutton was the principal teacher at The Grange and now runs her own cookery school. She has extensive experience running chalets as well as her own catering business.
Courses offered: 4-week Foundation Cookery Course is ideal for gap year students who want to work in chalets, lodges and galleys, or simply to broaden their culinary expertise.

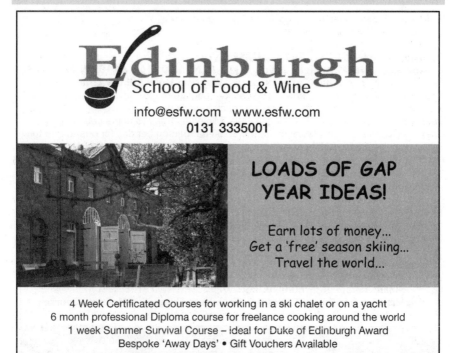
The school is based in a family home and offers individual attention whilst students gain confidence and develop their skills.This intensive hands-on course covers classic and modern methods of cookery, budgeting and menu-planning. Students can take the Basic Food Hygiene Course and examination whilst on the course. Wine tasting, guest cooks and visits to local markets are organised throughout the course. For the experienced cook the 5-day intensive New Food Course introduces new tastes and timesaving recipes.
Cost: 4-week Foundation Course £2650: 5-day New Food Course £790. Included in the costs are all meals, accommodation and equipment. A comprehensive recipe file is provided, together with useful food charts and tips. Single room supplement £50 per week.
Accommodation: In twin guest rooms with en-suite bathrooms and comfortable student sitting room with TV/DVD.
Follow-up: Graduates of the course can be put in touch with ski companies and employment agencies.
Contact: Lou Hutton, Principal.

GABLES SCHOOL OF COOKERY
Bristol Road, Falfield, Glos. GL12 8DF. ☎01454 260444. E-mail: fran. winston@virgin.net. Website: www.thegablesschoolofcookery.com.
Specialists in training chalet hosts and yacht cooks.
Courses offered: 4-week cookery courses ideal for working in chalets or on yachts as well as providing lifelong cookery skills.
Duration of courses: 4 weeks available year round.
Prerequisites: Minimum age 17; average ages 18-50.
Qualifications offered: School certificate equivalent to NVQ 2/3.
Cost: £2395 inclusive.
Accommodation: 3-star accommodation in twin rooms with en-suite bathrooms.

Follow-up: School aims to find positions for all graduates.
Contact: Fran Winston, Principal.

KILBURY MANOR COOKERY COURSES
Colston Road, Buckfastleigh, Devon TQ11 0LN. ☎01364 644079. Fax: 01364 644059. E-mail: suzanne@kilbury.co.uk. Website: www.kilbury.co.uk.
Courses offered: Tailor-made courses for beginners to advanced, amateurs or professionals. An intensive, hands-on approach to cooking.
Duration of courses: To suit 1-3 individuals. Minimum 1 day (6 hours cooking).
Cost: Residential or non-residential terms. £190 per person per day for one-to-one tuition (£220 including B&B); £130 per person for two people (£160 including B&B).
Accommodation: In one of three bedrooms at the Manor Farmhouse where the courses are held, with en suite and colour television.
Contact: Suzanne Lewis.

LEITHS SCHOOL OF FOOD AND WINE
21 St. Albans Grove, London W8 5BP. ☎020-7229 0177. Fax: 020-7937 5257. E-mail: info@leiths.com. Website: www.leiths.com.
Courses offered: Basic Certificate in Practical Cookery, designed for Gap Year students and suitable for anyone wishing to assist in chalets, villas and lodges. Longer alternative course offered: Beginners' Certificate in Food and Wine. Both courses comprise demonstrations and practical cooking, including meat, fish and vegetable preparation, pastries, puddings and sauces.
Duration of courses: Basic Certificate lasts for 4 weeks full-time in September. Beginners' Certificate 10 weeks October-December.
Qualifications offered: Basic Certificate in practical cookery. Beginners' Certificate in Food and Wine.
Cost: 4 weeks £2160 for the course, plus extra fees of around £150 for various extras such as cookery books, clothing and an equipment wallet. 10 weeks £4800 plus extras.
Follow-up: The company also runs Leiths List, an agency for cooks, which helps to place ex-students in suitable careers.

MALACA INSTITUTO
Calle Cortada 6, Cerrado de Calderón, 29018 Málaga, Spain. ☎ +34 952-29 3242. Fax: +34 952-29 6316. E-mail: gapyear@malacainstituto.com. Website: www.MalacaInstituto.com.
Courses offered: Recreational cookery with Spanish language course. For further details of the Spanish language courses, see entry in the 'Directory of Language Courses'.
Duration of courses: 2 weeks.
Cost: €689 for 2 weeks plus registration fee of €65.

THE MANOR SCHOOL OF FINE CUISINE
Old Melton Road, Widmerpool, Nottinghamshire NG12 5QL. ☎/fax: 01949 81371.
Courses offered: Cookery courses covering basics and more advanced creative skills suitable for those embarking on a career in the culinary profession.
Duration of courses: 5-day Beginners' Foundation Course and 4-week Certificate Course, Monday to Friday.
Qualifications offered: A graded certificate on successful completion.
Cost: Beginners' course costs £525 residential, £450 non-residential. Certificate course costs £2350 with accommodation, £2000 without.
Accommodation: Students stay in the 17th Century Manor, site of the cookery school.
Follow-up: A letter of recommendation may be issued for future employment. Skills learned are ideal for careers in chalet cooking, yachts, directors' dining rooms, outside catering, hotels and shooting lodges.

MIRANDA HALL – CHALET COOKS
Old School, Hambleton, Oakham, Rutland LE15 8TJ. ☎01572 723576. E-mail: miranda_hall@btinternet.com. Website: http://uk.geocities.com/miranda_hall@btinternet.com/chaletcookscourse.
Courses offered: Chalet cooks courses. Candidates should be preferably over 21. Every menu has a built-in vegetarian version for speed and ease. Instruction given on coping with varied diets, crisis management and a course on wine in addition to high altitude cake recipes, canapés and interesting breakfasts that every chalet cook needs. Students are given the chance to cook a three-course meal and cakes every day.
Duration of courses: 5 days, Monday to Friday, offered last two weeks of October and possibly November.
Qualifications offered: Certificate recognised by more than 30 chalet companies with which owner is in touch.
Cost: £495 inclusive of accommodation.
Accommodation: Fully residential (Manor House, Hambleton).
Contact: Miranda Hall, School Owner/Lecturer.

THE MURRAY SCHOOL OF COOKERY
Glenbervie House, Holt Pound, Farnham, Surrey GU10 4LE. ☎/fax: 01420 23049. E-mail: KMPMMSC@aol.com. Website: www.cookeryschool.net.
Courses offered: Cookery certificate courses.
Duration of courses: Certificate course lasts 4 weeks; Chalet Chef course lasts 1 week. Held in January, March, July and September. For dates of future courses refer to website.
Qualifications offered: The Certificate Course is accredited by major ski chalet operators, yacht catering agencies and by major companies offering retraining schemes. The Chalet Chef course is approved by major ski holiday operators.
Cost: £1500 for a 4-week course. Chalet chef course costs £395.
Accommodation: Local bed and breakfasts are available at £25 per night.
Follow-up: The courses are designed for people wanting to work in ski chalets or on yachts for those interested in catering to a high standard for small groups.
Contact: P. Murray.

NATIVES.CO.UK
39-40 Putney High St, London SW15 1FP. ☎08700 463355. Fax: 08700 626362. E-mail: info@natives.co.uk. Website: www.natives.co.uk/skijobs/cookery.
UK's leading website for finding jobs in ski and summer resorts.
Courses offered: Cookery courses offered at a girls' school in Surrey or in Rutland. Practical cookery courses designed for winter staff and taught by seasonal workers who

know what the job involves and can share hands-on experience.

Duration of courses: 5 days, with starting dates between May and October (see website).

Prerequisites: Minimum age 21.

Qualifications offered: Course is recognised through the industry. Participants receive Recipe and Alpine Cooking Advice Manual.

Cost: £399 including 4 nights' accommodation.

Other services: Also conduct half-day job workshops (cost £12.95) once a month April-September for ski resort work.

Follow-up: Guaranteed job through natives.co.uk for those who pass.

THE ORCHARDS SCHOOL OF COOKERY

The Orchards, Salford Priors, Nr Evesham, Worcestershire WR11 8UU. ☎/fax: 01789 490 259. E-mail: Isabel@orchardscookery.co.uk. Website: www.orchardscookery.co.uk.

No 4 in Waitrose Food Illustrated 'Best Cookery Schools in Europe'.

Courses offered: Chalet Cooks and recruitment, Off to University, Designer Dinners for Beginners.

Duration of courses: 5 days to 2 weeks, year round.

Qualifications offered: Certificate on completion of the course which is well recognised in the chalet industry. Access Organisation for the Gold Duke of Edinburgh's Award so participants can be awarded a certificate on behalf of the Scheme.

Cost: Chalet Cooks (5 days) £550, (2 weeks) £1050. Off to University (5 days) £520. Designer Dinners (5 days) £550 including accommodation.

Accommodation: Students live in the farmhouse and adjacent cottage.

Contact: Isabel Bomford, Partner.

ROSIE DAVIES

Penny's Mill, Nunney, Frome, Somerset BA11 4NP. ☎01373 836210. Fax: 01373 836018. E-mail: info@rosiedavies.co.uk. Website: www.rosiedavies.co.uk.

Courses offered: A cookery course beginning with essential skills and basic techniques but moving on to more complex aspects. Part of the course will include the specialist skills needed to cook in a chalet or on board a yacht.

Duration of courses: 4 weeks.

Qualifications offered: Certificate of completion and a Basic Hygiene Certificate.

Cost: £2700 including accommodation.

Accommodation: Twin bedded rooms with toilet/shower room and sitting area with TV/video.

Follow-up: Ideal for becoming chalet hosts and yacht cooks.

TANTE MARIE SCHOOL OF COOKERY

Woodham House, Carlton Road, Woking, Surrey GU21 4HF. ☎01483 726957. Fax: 01483 724173. E-mail: info@tantemarie.co.uk. Website: www.tantemarie.co.uk.

UK's largest independent cookery school, accredited by the BAC and member of the Year Out Group.

Courses offered: Variety of practical courses suitable for gap year students. Cordon Bleu Certificate course (11 weeks) offers a formal qualification useful for students who wish to work in ski chalets and on yachts as well as gaining temporary employment during university vacations. The Essential Skills course (4 weeks) is a good foundation though there is no formal qualification. Beginners Course lasts 1 or 2 weeks and is a basic introduction to cookery.

Duration of courses: Essential Skills course offered in July, September, October, January and April; Cordon Bleu Certificate course begins September, January and April. Beginners

course offered in mid-July.

Qualifications offered: Internationally recognised qualifications including Cordon Bleu Diploma and Certificate. Certificate of attendance for other courses.

Cost: £2245 for Essential Skills, £4750 for Certificate Course and £495 for 1-week Beginners or £865 for 2-week Beginners. Prices are inclusive of chef's whites (where applicable), knives, personalised recipe folder, all ingredients and lunch each day.

Accommodation: With homestay families arranged via the school

Follow-up: Certificate courses are excellent for short-term employment during vacations. Essential Skills course recognised by many ski operators. Tante Marie offers employment advice and has good industry contacts.

Contact: Gill Hurst.

LA VIEILLE FORGE

4 Rue de Burguet, Berlou, 34360 Herault, France. ☎ 4-67 89 48 63. E-mail: holidays@lavieilleforge.com. Website: www.lavieilleforge.com/chalet_courses.

Courses offered: Chalet cookery courses aimed at keen amateurs who want to work for the ski season. Course offered in the Languedoc region of France. Classes for up to 3 participants.

Duration of courses: 4 days Monday-Thursday between August and November.

Cost: €675 inclusive of all meals, accommodation and return flight from Montpellier, Carcasonne or Nimes.

Accommodation: Own guest house.

Contact: John McFetridge (01333 451793), Director of Winter Adventure Company, 53 High Street, Crail, Fife KY10 3RA (www.winteradventure.co.uk).

Ski Training

BAHARA SKI INSTRUCTOR TRAINING PROGRAMME

49 Highway 73, Springfield, Canterbury, South Island, New Zealand. ☎ +64 3-318 7960. E-mail: info@bahara.co.nz. Website: www.bahara.co.nz.

Courses offered: 10-week Ski Instructor Training Programme. 10 weeks personal training in the Craigieburn Range, New Zealand (45 minutes from Christchurch). Privately run course for just 6 people at a time means that the course can adjust to the needs of individual trainees.

Duration of courses: 10 weeks from July to October.

Qualifications offered: NZSIA (New Zealand Ski Instructors Alliance) Stage 1 Exam (exam included in course). Written reference from the ski school director will be useful when applying for jobs.

Cost: From about £4500 (excluding ski equipment and flights).

Accommodation: In home of the course providers with all meals provided.
Contact: Jason and Beth Collins, Course Providers.

BASE CAMP GROUP
Unit 30, Baseline Business Studios, Whitchurch Road, London W11 4AT. ☎020-7243 6222. E-mail: contact@basecampgroup.com. Website: www.basecampgroup. com.
Programme description: Ski and Snowboard Instructor courses in the Alps and Rockies to improve all round ability and gain a recognised European or North American ski or snowboard instructor's qualification. Chance to improve skiing and riding (off-piste, freestyle, racing, etc.). Courses include Avalanche courses, First Aid courses, Ski/Snowboard Tuning Clinics, French lessons, weekend trips and social events. Assistance can be given in finding work after the course. Addition to Whistler course from 2005/6: one day a week from which participants choose to work on their chosen speciality whether freestyle, racing or off-piste overseen by a sponsored freestyle competitor.
Destinations: Val d'Isère (France), Méribel (France) and Whistler (Canada).
Duration and time of placements: 4 and 11-week instructor courses from beginning of January. Also 10-week part-time ski instructor course in Val d'Isère for people interested in achieving the BASI qualification, normally for slightly older age group.
Number of placements per year: Up to 200.
Prerequisites: Many clients are spending their first winter in the mountains and are new to the industry. Several Freestyle and Freeskiing camps are run for more experienced skiers.
Costs: £5745-£6395 excluding insurance for 11-week programmes; £2795-£3195 for 4-week programmes. Includes accommodation throughout.
Accommodation: Whistler accommodation in 7-8 bedded chalets is located a short walk from the centre of Whistler village and the lifts. Other accommodation mostly in four-person flats.
Contact: Max Shepherd, Marketing Director.

BRITISH ASSOCIATION OF SNOWSPORT INSTRUCTORS (BASI)
Glenmore, Aviemore, Inverness-shire PH22 1QU. ☎01479 861717. Gap hot-line: 01479 861402. Fax: 01479 861718. E-mail: gap@basi.org.uk. Website: www.basi.org.uk.
BASI runs training and grading courses throughout the year in five disciplines: Alpine Skiing, Snowboarding, Telemark, Nordic and Adaptive. BASI also publishes the *BASI News* in which job adverts for ski and snowboard instructors appear.
Gap courses offered: BASI Gap Year course offered over 10 weeks leading to the first level ski or snowboard instructor's qualification. Courses take place from January to March in Europe (e.g. Zermatt, Courchevel, Andorra) and the USA (New Hampshire and Colorado).
Prerequisites: Minimum age 17. Must demonstrate confidence in parallel skiing at pre-selection in the UK.
Cost: £5500-£6300.
Contact: Nigel McConachie, Gap Programme Manager.

CANADIAN ASSOCIATION OF SNOWBOARD INSTRUCTORS (CASI)
60 Canning Crescent, Cambridge, Ontario N1T 1X2, Canada. ☎519-624-6593. Fax: 519-624-6594. E-mail: info@casi-acms.com. Website: www.casi-acms.com.
Courses offered: Levels 1 - 4 Snowboard Instructor; Basic Freestyle Coach; Basic Race Coach.
Duration of courses: Level 1 Instructor and Basic Coach - 3 days; Level 2 Instructor - 4 days; Level 3 Instructor - 5 days; Level 4 Instructor - 7 days.
Qualifications offered: All CASI courses are certification courses.
Cost: Level 1 Instructor and Basic Coach - C$300; Level 2 Instructor - C$375; Level 3

Instructor - C$475; Level 4 Instructor - C$675.
Contact: Dan Genge, Executive Director & CEO.

DEUTSCH-INSTITUT TIROL
Am Sandhügel 2, 6370 Kitzbühel, Austria. ☎53-56 712 74. Fax: 53-56 723 63. E-mail: dit@kitz.netwing.at. Website: www.gap-year.at.
Courses offered: German language combined with ski and snowboard instruction specially designed for gap year students.
Duration of courses: 12 weeks from end of September to just before Christmas. Course includes 8 weeks intensive German tuition at DIT in Kitzbühel interspersed with 8 3-day weekends skiing/snowboarding on the glacier at Kaprun. Also 7-day trip to Eastern Europe.
Qualifications offered: Preparation for Austrian ski/snowboard instructor exams.
Cost: €8000 (£5500) inclusive of everything except travel to Kitzbühel and insurance.
Accommodation: Half-board accommodation in Kitzbühel; full board in Kaprun.

GAP SNOWSPORTS
Willow Bank House, 84 Station Road, Marlow, Bucks. SL7 1NX. ☎0870 837 9797. E-mail: team@gapsnowsports.com. Website: www.gapski.com.
Programme description: Ski/snowboard instructor courses and adventure training in Canada and professional sports development programmes at international golf, rugby, cricket, football and scuba academies in South Africa. (Also sports coaching placements in Africa and Latin America; see 'Directory of Specialist Gap Year Programes'.)
Destinations: Mont Tremblant, Canada (skiing/snowboarding); South Africa (sports academies).
Prerequisites: Minimum age 18. No previous experience needed; instruction available at beginners and advanced levels.
Duration and time of placements: 10 weeks from early January or short course is 6 weeks from early January or early February.
Costs: From £5580 for 10 weeks, £3480 for short course; flights and insurance are extra.
Contact: James Burton, Director.

MOUNTAIN LIFE
62 Farleigh Road, Addlestone, Surrey KT15 3HR. ☎0845 838 2269. E-mail: contact@mountain-life.co.uk. Website: www.mountain-life.co.uk.
Services offered: Seasonal accommodation arranged from 1-6 months in the Canadian ski resort of Whistler BC. Once in the resort, company helps clients to organise instructor exams, heli-skiing, etc.
Duration: 1-6 months from November-April.

Prerequisites: Minimum age 18 (subject to acceptance); average age 25.
Cost: £650 or £725 for one month (standard or superior). Price drops with longer stays so that monthly charge for those staying 6 months is £400/£475.
Accommodation: Varies from Superior (large chalets, hot tubs, broadband internet, weekly cleaning) to Standard (comfortable houses for those on a budget).
Contact: Andy Tennison, Director.

NEW ZEALAND SNOWSPORTS COLLEGE LTD.
5 Colcord Pl, Methven, New Zealand. Fax: +64 3-302 8697. E-mail: info@snowsportscollege.co.nz. Website: www.snowsportscollege.co.nz.
Courses offered: Ski instructor training and snowboard instructor training. All training is run by a current New Zealand NZSIA Examiner.
Duration of courses: 4 weeks or 10 weeks between July and October.
Qualifications offered: NZSIA Stage 1.
Cost: From NZ$10,000.
Accommodation: Single, twin/double and quad share available at the Snowden Lodge in Methven.
Contact: Marc Davies, Director.

NONSTOP SKI & SNOWBOARD
Shakespeare House, 168 Lavender Hill, London SW11 5TF. ☎0870 241 8070. Fax 020-7801 6201. E-mail: info@nonstopski.com. Website: www.nonstopski. com.
Courses offered: Ski and Snowboard Improvement and Instructor Courses in Banff, Fernie and Red Mountain in the Canadian Rockies. British Columbia. Training in mountain safety, avalanche awareness. Winter survival skills, first aid and ski and snowboard maintenance. Evening classes in French, Spanish, TEFL and cookery can also be taken.
Number of participants: 40-60 on 11-week course, 30-40 on 3-week course.
Duration of courses: 3-week course from late December to mid-January. 6-week course from late December to early February. 11-week programme runs from mid-January to early April.
Prerequisites: Minimum age 18 (about half of participants are gappers).
Qualifications offered: Internationally recognised CSIA (Canadian Ski Instructor Alliance) and CASI (Canadian Association of Snowboard Instructors). Also CAA (Canadian Avalanche Association) Recreational Avalanche 1 certificate and St. John's Ambulance Basic first aid certificate. Freestyle and race coach qualifications can also be obtained.
Cost: £2950 for 3-week course, £4350 for 6-week course and £5850 for 11-week course; prices include flights, accommodation, most meals, lift pass and all tuition. Long course also includes weekend trips.
Accommodation: Twin rooms in hostels, hotels or houses depending on resort.
Other services: Work experience may be arranged with local ski school and contacts with other ski schools for instructing jobs.
Contact: Melissa Taylor, Director.

NZ SNOWBOARD TRAINING
PO Box 846, Queenstown, New Zealand. ☎ +64 21 258 6259 or +64 21 232 5708. E-mail: info@nzsnowboardtraining.com. Website: www.nzsnowboardtrain-ing.com.
Courses offered: Snowboard Instructor Courses in Queenstown, New Zealand. Trainers are NZSIA examiners and highly qualified coaches.
Duration of courses: 10 weeks (July-September) or 5 weeks (August-September).
Qualifications offered: Participants train towards the New Zealand Snowsports Alliance Certificate of Snowboard Instruction and Stage One Instructors Qualification, which are internationally recognised teaching qualifications.
Cost: NZ$12,500 for 10 weeks, NZ$9500 for 5 weeks. Early booking discounts available.

Fee all inclusive including 3-mountain season pass, mountain transport and extras like a bungy jump.
Accommodation: Self-contained apartments in the heart of Queenstown.
Contact: David Poussard or Matt Phare, Course Directors.

PEAK LEADERS UK LTD
Mansfield, Strathmiglo, Fife KY14 7QE, Scotland. ☎01337 860079. Fax: 01337 868176. E-mail: info@peakleaders.com. Website: www.peakleaders.com.
Courses offered: Gap year Ski and Snowboard instructor courses in Canada, Argentina and New Zealand. Course includes structured programmes of mountain safety, first aid, avalanche awareness and leadership. Courses held in Whistler and in the Canadian Rockies, Bariloche in Patagonia and Queenstown, New Zealand.
Duration of courses: 4 Snowsport courses per year lasting up to 11 weeks: July–September in the southern hemisphere, January-March in the northern hemisphere.
Qualifications offered: 5 internationally recognised qualifications: instructor, leader, mountain safety and avalanche awareness. Some courses offer a level 2 award in Team Leading, validated by the Institute of Leadership & Management (www.i-l-m.com).
Cost: £5850 inclusive for 10-11 weeks.
Other services: On winter courses, extras offered like skidoo driving, backcountry training, Spanish and French language, field trips to Argentine Patagonia and Chile. Work experience and advice on job opportunities worldwide.
Contact: David Hughes, Director.

PLANET SUBZERO LTD
26 Woodsyre, London SE26 6SS. ☎ + 33 (0) 679 178 578. Fax: + 33 (0) 479 07 12 11. E-mail: info@planetsubzero.com. Website: www.planetsubzero.com.
Services offered: Long stay and seasonal accommodation in top quality chalets and apartments throughout the European Alps and North America.
Destinations: Resorts include Méribel, Chamonix, Courchevel, Les Arcs, Whistler, Banff, Les 2 Alps, etc.
Duration: 1-6 months.
Prerequisites: Minimum age 18 (number of under-18s limited per property).
Cost: From £600 a month.
Accommodation: Properties are fully equipped including free internet access. Local hosts available.
Contact: Steph Lightfoot, Director.

PRO RIDE SNOWBOARD CAMPS
PO Box 1351, Whistler, BC, V0N 1B0 Canada. ☎604-935-2115. Fax: 604-938-0176. E-mail: snowboard@pro-ride.com. Website: www.pro-ride.com.
Courses offered: Freeride, freestyle and snowboard instructor training. Opportunity to ride with professionally sponsored pro riders and Olympic level coaches. Courses cater for the intermediate to advanced rider.
Duration of courses: 5 days to 12 weeks. Flexible start dates.
Qualifications offered: Both recreational courses and snowboard instructor training to work towards achieving Canadian Association of Snowboard Instructor certification.
Cost: Training starts at C$725.
Accommodation: Twin share in bright clean houses and condos in Whistler.
Contact: Anthony Crute, Director.

ROOKIE ACADEMY
PO BOX 402, Wanaka, New Zealand. ☎ +64 3-443 5100. Fax: +64 3-443 6006. E-mail: info@rookieacademy.com. Website: www.rookieacademy.com.
Courses offered: Ski and snowboard instructor courses.
Duration of courses: 13, 8 and 5 week courses.

Qualifications offered: All courses include an internationally recognised ski or snowboard instructor exam. Only company in New Zealand to offer British and Canadian instructor qualifications in conjunction with the New Zealand qualifications.
Cost: NZ$16,800 for 13 weeks, NZ$1080 for 8 weeks and NZ$8500 for 5 weeks.
Accommodation: Shared apartment style, fully furnished includes cleaning and linen service.
Contact: Garett Shore, Director.

THE SKI & SNOWBOARD INSTRUCTOR TRAINING CO.
PO Box 791, Queenstown, New Zealand. ☎ +64 21-341 214/5. Fax: +64 3-442 5460. E-mail: info@skiinstructortraining.co.nz/ info@snowboardinstructortraining.co.nz. Website: www.skiinstructortraining.co.nz or www.snowboardinstructortraining.co.nz.
Courses offered: Keen skiers and boarders are trained to develop and achieve their Ski & Snowboard Instructor Qualification in Queenstown, New Zealand. Course also exposes candidates to freestyle, freeride and race influences and includes an Avalanche Awareness course, First Aid course or Off-piste Awareness course, and a Heli-Ski/Board day.
Duration of courses: 11 weeks from 29th June to 9th September or 6 weeks from 1st August.
Pre-requisites: Ski trainees should be able to ski a red/black run in control, with confidence so that there is a realistic chance of achieving the NZSIA Stage 1. Snowboarders should be able to ride blue runs on and off trail, linking turns consistently and riding with confidence.
Qualifications offered: NZSIA Stage One Exam (after both courses).
Cost: From NZ$11,500 for 11-week course and NZ$9000 for 6-week course, inclusive of accommodation, whole-season lift pass, and transport between Queenstown and the mountain. Prices for lift pass rise the later the course is booked.
Accommodation: 6 or 11 weeks of accommodation at Pinewood Lodge in central Queenstown; price based on 2 people sharing a triple/quadruple room.
Contact: Gavin McAuliffe or Colin Tanner, Founding Partners.

SKI-EXP-AIR
770 Colonel Jones, Ste. Foy, Québec GIX 3K9, Canada. ☎418-654-9071. Mob: 418 520 6669. UK info: Jake Simpson 078 00 552098 or David Haines 07835 793737. E-mail: info@ski-exp-air.com. Website: www.ski-exp-air.com.
Courses offered: Ski-Exp-Air is a ski and snowboard school located at Mont Ste Anne near Québec City serving an international clientele.
Duration of courses: 3 months.
Cost: £6650 for Ski-Exp-Air; discounts for early booking (before July 1st).
Accommodation: College campus lodgings with private rooms. All meals included.
Contact: Luc Fournier, Director.

SKI LE GAP
220 Wheeler St, Mont Tremblant, Quebec J8E 1V3, Canada. ☎ +001-819-429-6599 or freephone from England 0800 328 0345. Fax: +001-819-425-7074. E-mail: info@skilegap. Website: www.skilegap.com.
Programme description: Ski and Snowboard instructor's programme operating since 1994 specifically designed for gap year students from Britain. The course combines ski/snowboard instruction with French conversation lessons plus other activities such as igloo-building, dogsledding, extreme snowshoeing, and trips to Montreal, Quebec City and Ottawa.
Destinations: Quebec, Canada.
Number of placements per year: 200.
Prerequisites: All nationalities. Must be passionate about skiing, but all levels of ability

accepted from beginners to expert.

Duration and time of placements: 3-month and 1-month placements from November.

Selection procedures and orientation: Places are reserved on a first-come, first-served basis so early reservations are advised.

Cost: £6650 (including tax) for 2006 for 3-month course. Price includes return London-Montreal airfare but not medical insurance or ski equipment. £2900 for 1-month course excluding flights.

Contact: Amelia Puddifer, Programme Director.

SNOWSKOOL LTD
Woodlands, The Straight Mile, Romsey, Hampshire, SO51 9BA. ☎01794 36 76 36. E-mail: team@snowskool.co.uk. Website: www.snowskool.co.uk.

Programme description: Ski & Snowboard Instructor training courses between January and March at Sunshine Village, Banff (Canada) and between August and September in New Zealand. PoloSkool in Argentina (www.poloskool.co.uk) including intensive polo training and Spanish lessons near Buenos Aires between January and March; and divermaster training with ScubaSkool in Belize (www.scubaskool.co.uk) are due to begin operations in 2006.

Number of placements per year: 40+ in Canada, 20 in New Zealand.

Destinations: Banff (Canada) and New Zealand.

Prerequisites: Minimum age 17, average age 24. Officially no minimum qualifications required, but applicants with some experience of the sport preferred, so they are sure they want to spend a prolonged time in the sport of their choice.

Duration and time of placements: 11 weeks in Canada, 6 weeks in New Zealand.

Selection procedures & orientation: Most courses are filled 10 weeks before start date when fees are due.

Cost: £5450 for Banff (2006) all inclusive of flights, etc.; approx £6000 for New Zealand, includes guaranteed job at Sunshine Village for following season, flights to Canada and working Visa. Estimated price for PoloSkool (10 weeks) is £5000 and ScubaSkool (8 weeks) £5250.

Contact: Philip Purdie, Director.

WARREN SMITH SKI ACADEMY
Chalet Zapreskie, 1936 Verbier, Switzerland. 01525 374757 in the UK; ☎ +41 79-359 6566 in Switzerland. Fax: +41 27-771 4247. E-mail: warrensmith@snowsportsynergy.com. Website: www.warrensmith-skiacademy.com.

Courses offered: Gap year Ski Instructor courses.

Duration of courses: 9 weeks (7th January to 11th March).

Prerequisites: Minimum age 16; average age 30.

Qualifications offered: BASI qualifications.

Cost: £6449.

Accommodation: Half board, excellent food, en suite, near lift station.

Contact: Warren Smith, Director.

Sport & Activity Courses

DIVE INDEEP CO. LTD.
162/8 Moo 2 Bophut, Koh Samui, Suratthani 84320, Thailand. ☎ +66 772 30155. Fax: +66 772 30157. E-mail: info@diveindeep.com. Website: www.diveindeep.com.

Long-established dive shop in the most popular beach of Koh Samui Island.

Courses offered: PADI Scuba Diving Courses from beginner through Dive Master.

Duration of courses: Courses offered on a revolving schedule and can start any day.

Speedboats go out to the area's best dive sites every day.

Qualifications offered: PADI Divemaster Certification can be used to find jobs all over the world.

Cost: PADI Scuba Diver 7500 Thai Baht, PADI Open Water Diver B12,750, PADI Advanced Open Water Diver B11,000, PADI Rescue Diver B9000, Emergency First Responder B4000, PADI Divemaster B26,000.

Accommodation: Not included in price but can be arranged in conveniently located apartments for B4500-B9000 rent per month.

Contact: Anna Khamsamran, Owner/Manager.

FLYING FISH
25 Union Road, Cowes, Isle of Wight PO31 7TW. ☎0871 250 2500. Fax: 01983 281821. E-mail: mail@flyingfishonline.com. Website: www.flyingfishonline.com.

Flying Fish trains water and snowsports staff and arranges employment for sailors, divers, surfers, kitesurfers and windsurfers, skiers and snowboarders (see programme details in 'Directory of Specialist Gap Year Programmes').

Courses offered: Professional Dive Training, International Yacht Training and Sail and Board Sports Instructor training programmes. There is a specially organised modular scheme for Gap Year students offering training followed by work experience and a period of employment in Australia or Greece. Recently added kitesurf and surf courses in Australia and ski and snowboard instructor courses at Whistler in Canada.

Destinations: Training takes place at Cowes on the Isle of Wight (UK), at Sydney and the Whitsunday Islands in Australia, the Bay of Islands in New Zealand, Vassiliki in Greece, Pissouri in Cyprus, Dahab in Egypt and Whistler Mountain in Canada. Jobs are worldwide with main employers located in Australia, the South Pacific, the Caribbean and the Mediterranean.

Duration of courses: Courses last from 2 weeks to 4 months. Courses come with a 'professional' option where trainees take part in a period of work experience as an instructor.

Qualifications offered: Flying Fish courses lead to qualifications from the Royal Yachting Association (RYA), Professional Association of Dive Instructors (PADI), the Yachting Australia Federation (YA), Surfing Australia (SA), International Kiteboarding Organisation (IKO), Canadian Ski Instructors Alliance (CSIA), and the Canadian Association of Snowboard Instructors (CASI).

Cost: Prices range from £810 for a 2-week Red Sea milebuilder in Egypt to an 18-week Yachtmaster Professional Traineeship in Sydney for £10,880.

Accommodation: Self-catering apartments. Varies according to course and destination but always provided.

Follow-up: Possibility of employment following qualification. Placements in the Mediterranean, the Caribbean and Australia. Qualifications gained can be used after the year out in holiday periods to gain extra cash.

THE INTERNATIONAL ACADEMY
St Hilary Court, Copthorne Way, Culverhouse Cross, Cardiff CF5 6ES. ☎02920 672500. Fax: 02920 672510. E-mail: info@theinternationalacademy.com. Website: www.theinternationalacademy.com.

Courses offered: Instructor training in outdoor activities that lead to internationally recognised qualifications. All training in line with governing bodies. Locations worldwide. Outdoor pursuits include skiing, snowboarding and diving. Courses allow people to turn their hobbies into a career or make the most of their Gap Year while training in exotic places like Whistler (British Columbia, Canada), Sunshine Coast (Queensland, Australia) and the Seychelles.

Duration of courses: 4-12 weeks.

Cost: £3350-£7950. Sample 12-week course with ski instruction and accommodation and

board costs between £6350 and £6950 in Mammoth and Lake Tahoe (California), Stowe (Vermont) and Whistler, Lake Louise and Tremblant (Canada).
Contact: Cath Lewis, Operations Director.

ITIME EXPERIENCE LTD
105 Ladbroke Grove, London W11 1PG. ☎0845 355 1183. E-mail: info@itimeexperience.com. Website: www.itimeexperience.com.
Company founded in 2005.
Courses offered: Surfing, windsurfing and kitesurfing courses out of Margarita (Venezuela) and the Dominican Republic in the Caribbean. Optional Spanish courses also available.
Duration of courses: 2-12 weeks.
Number of placements per year: Maximum of 350.
Destinations: El Yaque on the island of Margarita is located off the coast of Venezuela and is currently home to the windsurfing freestyle world champion. Cabarete in the Dominican Republic (in the north of the Caribbean) is a world-class kitesurfing destination which hosts world cup events and surfing competitions.
Prerequisites: Minimum age 18; maximum is according to fitness level. Average age anticipated to be 24.
Selection procedures & orientation: Applications preferred at least 6 weeks in advance of course.
Cost: Windsurfing in Margarita costs £1750 for 4 weeks, £2350 for 6 weeks and £3400 for 10 weeks. Kitesurfing in Dominican Republic costs £1050 for 2 weeks, £1850 for 4 weeks, £2750 for 6 weeks, etc. 4-week surfing course in DR costs £900. Prices include standard accommodation plus breakfast and evening meal. Elite accommodation also available. Optional Spanish course costs £200-£400 depending on duration.
Contact: Mark Perry, Director.

OUTWARD BOUND
Hackthorpe Hall, Hackthorpe, Penrith, Cumbria CA10 2HX. ☎01931 740000. E-mail: enquiries@outwardbound-uk.org. Website: www.outwardbound-uk.org.
Courses offered: Outdoor multi-activity courses at three centres in UK (Aberdovey in Wales, Loch Eil in Scotland and Ullswater in the Lake District) plus many abroad. Activities include mountaineering, canoeing, rock climbing, abseiling and in-grounds activities such as zip wire, trapeze and high ropes courses. See entry for *Outward Bound Global* in 'Directory of Expeditions'.
Duration of courses: 1-3 weeks.
Qualifications offered: Recreational or possibility of NVQ key skills.
Cost: Financial assistance available.
Accommodation: Shared, single-sex rooms. There is usually at least one night away from the centre.

PERFORMANCE YACHTING SAILING SCHOOL
Mayflower International Marina, Ocean Quay, Richmond Walk, Plymouth, Devon PL1 4LS. ☎01752 565023. Fax: 01752 569256. E-mail: info@performanceyachting. co.uk. Website: www.performanceyachting.co.uk.
Courses offered: RYA sailing courses from beginner to Yachtmaster Ocean commercial endorsement. 14-week Fast Track course from beginner to Yachtmaster offshore attracts some gap year students. Some courses involve sailing in the Canary Islands.
Duration of courses: 5 days to 16 weeks. Courses run all year round. Fast Track starts January, May and September, with some flexibility.
Qualifications offered: All courses lead to RYA certification.
Cost: £400 for 5-day course, £7500 for the Fast Track Course.
Accommodation Onboard for all practical courses. For Theory courses accommodation is at a nearby B & B.
Contact: Carole Newman, Director.

PLAS MENAI

The National Watersports Centre, Caernarfon, Gwynedd, Wales. ☎01248 **670964. Fax: 01248 673939. E-mail: info@plasmenai.co.uk. Website: www. plasmenai.co.uk.**

Courses offered: Professional Watersports Instructor Training, Professional Yachtmaster and work experience programme.

Duration of courses: 12, 17 and 26 weeks.

Qualifications offered: Professional yacht skipper, watersports instructor or mountain leader training. All courses lead to national governing body qualifications which allow graduates to become multi-qualified and teach a range of outdoor activities such as dinghy sailing, kayaking, climbing, cruising and windsurfing. Other job opportunities include yacht deliveries, professional race crew and expedition leaders.

Cost: from £4300 including full-board and accommodation in single rooms in shared house.

Follow-up: Graduates go on to teach at centres across the UK, abroad or to join a paid work experience programme.

Contact: Suzanne Creasey, Marketing Manager.

ROYAL YACHTING ASSOCIATION

RYA House, Ensign Way, Hamble, Southampton SO31 4YA. ☎023 8060 4100. **E-mail: info@rya.org.uk. Website: www.rya.org.uk.**

The RYA is the governing body for sailing and motor boating in the UK. It's the best starting place for any information about courses at every level for sailing or power boating.

Courses offered: First level is Competent Crew (5-day training) plus other advanced certificates.

Follow-up: Distribute a leaflet 'Careers in Sailing' and a list of crew registers in Britain.

Cost: £300-£400+ for 5-day course.

SUBWAY WATERSPORTS

Brick Bay, Roatan, Bay Islands, Honduras, Central America. E-mail: internship@su bwaywatersports.com. Website: www.subwaywatersports.com/Courses/internship. htm.

Programme description: Internship working in a dive shop while training towards a professional PADI Divemaster. Chance to learn about customer service and how to run a small business focusing on adventure in a resort atmosphere. Good introduction to life in the dive industry.

Number of placements per year: Average 30 per year (maximum 6 per month).

Destinations: Roatan is a tropical island in the Caribbean.

Prerequisites: Minimum 20 years. Open Water diving certification recommended. Must be friendly, fun, motivated and a water-lover. Must be in good physical shape.

Duration and time of placements: 4-8 weeks.

Cost: $990/£650 for 4 weeks; $1400/£900 for 6 weeks; $1700/£1100 for 8 weeks. Prices include instruction, diving, accommodation, lunches and airport pick-up. Prices do not include PADI certification cards or insurance.

Accommodation: Room in hotel or cabin, shared with another intern.

Contact: Patrick & Gillian Zingg, Owners.

UK SAILING ACADEMY

West Cowes, Isle of Wight PO31 7PQ. ☎01983 294941. **Fax: 01983 295938. E-mail: info@uksa.org. Website: www.uksa.org.**

Courses offered: Gap Year Programme up to 12 months includes water sport training and work experience in the UK and abroad (Australia). Also offer instructor training in Windsurf, Dinghy, Kayak and Kitesurf; Professional Crew and Skipper training courses and 2-week Jump Start or Mile Building course for less experienced sailors.

Duration of courses: Gap Year programme lasts up to 1 year. Other courses last 12-17 weeks.

Qualifications offered: Beginners to Watersports Instructor/Yachtmaster.

Cost: £8000 for Gap Year Course, £4795 for Instructor training, £8950 for Professional Crew & Skipper training, and £875 (Jump Start, 2 weeks in UK).

Accommodation: Shared with 2 or 3 others.

Other services: On-site careers service to help with job placement. 500 companies use UKSA for recruitment.

WATER BY NATURE RAFTING JOURNEY LTD

The Trainers Office, Windy Hollow, Sheepdrove, Lambourne, Berkshire RG17 7XA. ☎01488 72293. All enquiries and correspondence through Hamish McMaster on 07887645 233. Fax: 01488 71311. E-mail: raft@waterbynature.com. Website: www.waterbynature.com.

Courses offered: Whitewater raft and kayak guide training in Morocco and Turkey. Trainee raft guides will be taught to kayak on rivers up to Grade 3. Prospective river guides can also join 2-week course in June on the Coruh River in Northeastern Turkey where they can achieve BCU qualifications, leading to a chance to guide in other destinations around the world. (www.waterbynature.com/turkey_rafting/guide_course.html).

Duration of courses: 2 months in each country. 2 weeks for short course in Turkey in June.

Prerequisites: Very suitable for gap year. Affinity with whitewater useful. Should have driving licence because may be expected to drive vehicles. All nationalities accepted provided they can obtain visas for relevant countries.

Cost: £1495 for 2-trip course in either Morocco or Turkey (excluding flights, insurance and spending money). A full season in Morocco or Turkey (maximum 4 trips) would be £2495 including a kayak or rafting course. Both seasons including all land transport and food en route: £3495.

Selection procedures & orientation: Deadline for applications for a handful of places falls in mid-January.

Contact: Hamish McMaster, Managing Director.

Gap Year Safety & Preparation

LAUNCHPAD AUSTRALIA

PO Box 2525, Fitzroy, VIC 306, Australia. ☎1300 851 826 (from Australia) or +61 3 9419 9147. Fax: +61 3 9445 9375. E-mail: workingholiday@launchpad australia.com. Website: www.launchpadaustralia.com.

Courses offered: Gap Year and Travel Advice Courses run in Sydney and Melbourne. The half-day course is designed for first-time travellers and those going on a gap year, with topics such as Responsible Travel, Working Holidays, Studying Abroad, Volunteering, Travel Safety and more.

Duration of courses: 2½ hours.

Cost: A$55.

Contact: Danielle Ades-Salman, Managing Director.

OBJECTIVE TRAVEL SAFELY LTD

Bragborough Lodge Farm, Braunston, Daventry, Northants NN11 7HA. ☎01788 899029. Fax: 01788 891259. E-mail: office@objectiveteam.com. Website: www. objectivegapsafety.com.

Courses offered: One-day pre-gap year preparation and safety awareness training. Course covers situation awareness, crime prevention, security advice, kit and equipment, safe food and water, dealing with corrupt officials, travel safety, legal and etiquette

concerns, emergency first aid, and handling extreme situations such as kidnapping and environmental dangers.
Number of participants: 800 since company was established in 2002.
Duration of courses: Course runs most weeks, usually Tuesdays or Wednesdays in London. Private courses and bespoke courses for schools are available.
Cost: £150 for an individual attending a course in London or Edinburgh.
Special features: The company runs safety training courses for travellers ranging from gap year travellers to journalists covering conflict zones. (Objective trained Ewan McGregor and Charlie Boorman prior to their Long Way Round motorbike expedition to Mongolia.) At the end of the day's training, a separate briefing for female travellers is held.

PLANET WISE
10 Swan Street, Eynsham, Oxfordshire, OX29 4HU. ☎0870 2000 220. E-mail: info@PlanetWise.net. Website: www.PlanetWise.net.
Courses offered: Travel safety and awareness courses. Courses teach students what they need to know to go travelling (what to take, how to take it, how to look after it) and encourage participants to take responsibility for themselves, by going through a variety of scenarios (e.g. how to get out of a burning building; what to do if drugs are planted on you).
Duration of courses: 1 and 3-day courses scheduled every month and more frequently as required.
Qualifications offered: 3-day course includes a first aid package which allows students to gain the 'appointed person' first aid certificate.
Cost: 3-day course £445. 1-day course £160. Group discounts available.
Accommodation: Courses located in hostels where accommodation and meals are included.
Contact: Andrew Wilson, Head of Gap Year Courses.

SAFETREK
East Culme, Cullompton, Devon EX15 1NX. ☎/fax: 01884 839704. E-mail: info@safetrek.co.uk. Website: www.safetrek.co.uk.
Courses offered: Travel preparation and awareness for Gap Year and University students. Also skills for life.
Duration of courses: One-day course run in Exeter or Bristol once a week or by appointment.
Cost: £140.
Contact: John Cummings, Director of Training.

ULTIMATE GAP YEAR
5 Beaumont Crescent, London W14 9LX. ☎020-7386 9101. E-mail: info@ultimategapyear.co.uk. Website: www.ultimategapyear.co.uk.
Courses offered: One-day travel safety awareness courses. Suitable for people (mainly aged 16-23) travelling independently or with gap organisations.
Duration of courses: Occasional Fridays. See website for dates.
Cost: £140.
Contact: Alex Cormack, Managing Director.

WORLD CHALLENGE EXPEDITIONS
Black Arrow House, 2 Chandos Road, London NW10 6NF. Tel: 020-8728 7200. E-mail: welcome@world-challenge.co.uk. Website: www.world-challenge.co.uk.
Courses offered: TravelSafe is a three-day gap year survival course based in the Leadership and Development Centre in Buxton, Derbyshire.
Prerequisites: None
Duration and time of placements: 3 days, 2 nights. Courses run throughout the year.
Cost: £225 all inclusive.

Miscellaneous Courses

ACHILL ARCHAEOLOGICAL FIELD SCHOOL
Achill Folklife Centre, Dooagh, Achill Island, Co. Mayo, Ireland. ☎98-43564. Fax: 98-43595. E-mail: achill-Info@achill-fieldschool.com. Website: www.achill-fieldschool.com.
Courses offered: Introduction to Irish archaeology, ceramics in archaeology, doing local history and landscape archaeology.
Duration of courses: 1, 2, 4 and 6-week modules between March and October each year.
Qualifications offered: Academic credit and/or Certificate available.
Cost: €595/$695 for 1 week, €1000/$1250 for 2 weeks, €1900/$2500 for 4 weeks, €3250/$4000 for 6 weeks. Prices include academic credit from the National University of Ireland at Galway. Special rates available for gropu and semester bookings.
Accommodation: Modern self-catering houses and apartments. Everything supplied except food.
Contact: Theresa McDonald.

CONSTANCE SPRY LTD
Moor Park House, Moor Park Lane, Farnham, Surrey GU10 1QP. ☎01252 734477. Fax: 01252 712011. E-mail: info@constancespry.com. Website: www.constancespry.com.
Courses offered: Flower arranging, floristry, hospitality and catering courses.
Duration of courses: 1 day to 20 weeks.
Qualifications offered: Professional courses lead to qualifications; the diploma course in Floristry Management is accredited by Middlesex University.
Cost: From £88 for a workshop to £12,278 (including accommodation and VAT).
Accommodation: Provided in single and double bedrooms with washbasins and shared bathrooms.
Contact: Bruce & Martine Frost.

DUNHAM INSTITUTE
Avenida Zaragoza 23, Chiapa de Corzo, Chiapas, Mexico. ☎ +961 61 61498. E-mail: academic-coordinator@dunhaminstitute.com. Website: www.dunhaminstitute.com.
Courses offered: TEFL Certification as well as Spanish courses and language exchange.
Duration of courses: 4 weeks to 5 months. Minimum commitment 8 weeks if tutoring local students or 5 months if teaching in schools.
Prerequisites: Minimum age 17; average age 23.
Qualifications offered: TEFL certification ideal for gap year students who can use it later in their year off.
Cost: 4-week TEFL course costs $1300. For English teaching volunteers, salary, housing and vacation times are negotiable depending on experience.
Accommodation: Free homestay with local families.
Other Services: Students may volunteer to teach English classes or tutor local students in exchange for Spanish classes.
Contact: Joanna Robinson, Director.

EMERSON COLLEGE
Forest Row, East Sussex RH18 5JX. ☎01342 822238. Fax: 01342 826055. E-mail: gapyear@emerson.org.uk. Website: www.emerson.org.uk.
International adult education centre and community based on the work of Rudolf Steiner.
Courses offered: The Orientation Year is a gap year programme specifically designed for

18-24 year olds and gives the opportunity to spend a 6-9 week volunteer placement abroad in the second term. The course focuses on historical and contemporary cultural issues, group dynamics and the community and self development. Practical activities include drawing, painting, sculpture, drama, music, pottery, metal work, weaving, environmental work and building. Career development activities will be offered throughout the year. Other courses at the Emerson College are run in Waldorf teaching training, puppetry, storytelling and creative writing, sculpture and organic agriculture.
Duration of courses: Mid-September to mid-June.
Qualifications offered: Certificate of Completion (some universities will evaluate for credit; enquire for more details).
Cost: £4500 for tuition and trips, £3446 for accommodation and meals (meals optional; self-catering available) plus £300-£700 during overseas placement.
Accommodation: Single room accommodation on campus is available for half the students. The rest live with host families in the village of Forest Row.
Contact: Ethan Friedman.

ICA-NEDERLAND (INSTITUTE OF CULTURAL AFFAIRS)

Minahassastraat 1, 1094 RS Amsterdam, Netherlands. ☎020 - 468 50 42. E-mail: icaned@xs4all.nl or info@icanederland.nl. Website: www.icanederland.nl (soon to be available in English).

ICA Netherlands are an autonomous office of ICA World (www.ica-international. org), a non-profit organisation whose mission is to spread community development through participation, enabling people to solve their own problems at grassroots level through taking action. ICA:UK had a similar programme until 2005.
Courses offered: Volunteer Programme is run once a year to prepare people for work in a developing country. Topics covered are project cycles, how to write a project proposal, the basics of TESOL, personal health and hygiene in a developing country, etc. Course mostly conducted in English (especially TESOL component). Participants then have option of joining a project from the ICA database.
Duration of courses: 2 weeks followed by minimum commitment overseas of 6 months.
Prerequisites: Minimum age 21.
Cost: About £1000 including board and lodging in Amsterdam.
Follow-up: Volunteer placements generally include board and lodging.
Contact: Michaela Wouters, ICA Office Co-ordinator.

ITTO - INTERNATIONAL TEACHER TRAINING ORGANIZATION

Madero 469, Guadalajara, Jalisco 44100, Mexico. ☎(52) 33-3658-3224/ 33-3614-3800 or toll-free from UK 0800-404 9800; from USA & Canada 1-866-514-7479. Fax : (52) 33-3614-2462. E-mail: info@teflcertificatecourses.com. Website: www.teflcertificatecourses.com.

Courses offered: TEFL Certification.
Duration of courses: 4 weeks, 140-hour programme, starting every month of the year.
Prerequisites: Minimum age 21. No maximum.
Cost: $1400.
Accommodation: Choice of homestay, Mexican posada or hotel.
Follow up: ITTO guarantees TEFL paid job placement in Mexico for trainees who successfully complete the course. Can also provide secure and trustworthy employment contacts for many other countries and lifelong TEFL job guidance.
Contact: Mr. Jacobo Vallejo, Student Services Co-ordinator.

JST YOUTH LEADERSHIP @ SEA SCHEME

Jubilee Sailing Trust, Hazel Road, Woolston, Southampton SO19 7GB. ☎023-8044 9108. Fax: 023-8044 9145. E-mail: info@jst.org.uk. Website: www.jst. org.uk.

For more information about the Jubilee Sailing Trust, see entry in 'Directory of

Expeditions'.

Courses offered: Leadership course on a sea voyage to develop communication, leadership and team skills.

Prerequisites: Ages 16-25.

Selection procedures and orientation: By written application; mark form with 'Youth Leadership @ Sea' and enclose short personal statement.

Cost: The JST Youth Leadership @ Sea Scheme offers young people aged 16-25 up to £300 towards the cost of any voyage (prices start from £499).

OPERATION NEW WORLD LTD

4 Eccleston Square, London SW1V 1NP. ☎020-7931 8177. E-mail: anne@opnewworld.co.uk. Website: www.opnewworld.co.uk.

Educational charity providing self-help programmes for unemployed young people.

Courses offered: Personal development and environmental studies for unemployed people aged 20-25.

Duration of courses: Weekend training in outdoor skills, followed by studies abroad where trainees can put their new skills into practice. Recent destinations have been the Parc Naturel Regional on the coast of Corsica and on remote Swedish islands.

Cost: None.

Contact: Anne Leonard, Director.

OXFORD TUTORIAL COLLEGE

Oxford Advanced Studies Program, 12 King Edward St, Oxford OX1 4HT. ☎01865 793333. Fax: 01865 793233. E-mail: info@otc.ac.uk. Website: www. oasp.ac.uk or www.otc.ac.uk.

Courses offered: One, two or three term pre-university courses in most academic subjects. See website for details.

Duration of courses: 14-week terms starting September, January and April.

Qualifications offered: All students receive grades and a transcript, and those who wish may opt to study for A level examinations. Most students use this course as a stepping-stone to a place at a good US college or British university.

Cost: £2280 for one subject in first term, £1980 for second term, £1520 for third term.

Accommodation: Single study rooms in host family, with breakfast and evening meal, or self-catering in small hall of residence for some full-year students. Accommodation is at an additional cost.

Contact: Charles Duncan, Senior Tutor.

PACIFIC VILLAGE INSTITUTE

4818 43rd Street, #4C, Woodside, NY 11377. ☎718-786-5426. Fax: 940-991-0669. E-mail: john@pacificvillage.org. Website: www.pacificvillage.org.

Programme description: Introduction to Eastern cultures through a combination of language lessons, community service projects, homestays, and travel off the beaten path. PVI offers both summer and semester small group experiential education programmes in Asia. Semester programme designed with gap year students in mind.

Number of placements per year: Up to 14 per group.

Destinations: India, China, Vietnam, and Cambodia.

Prerequisites: Ages 15-22 (average age 19).

Duration and time of placements: 4-6 weeks in summer or 3-month semester programmes in autumn or spring.

Cost: $1880-$8450 including tuition, homestays, language lessons, community service projects, etc. Financial aid available for qualifying candidates.

Contact: John Eastman, Co-Founder.

PASSAGE: PROJECT FOR INTERNATIONAL EDUCATION

GPO 8974, CPC 373, Kathmandu, Nepal. ☎ +977 1-4434602. In the USA

toll-free: 866-840-9197. E-mail: programs@passageproject.org. Website: www. passageproject.org.

Programme description: Non-profit organisation that arranges cross-cultural experiential education and cultural immersion programmes. Programmes include home stay with a local family, language study and the option of an internship or volunteering.

Number of placements per year: 12 students on semester programmes, 8 students on summer programme.

Destinations: Nepal, Tibet, Darjeeling, Ladakh and Kerala in India.

Prerequisites: Ages 18-22/24. No qualifications needed but participants should be sensitive to others' beliefs and cultures.

Duration and time of placements: 7-12 weeks fall and spring semesters, 8-weeks in winter, 6 weeks in summer.

Selection procedures & orientation: Application and medical forms to be submitted to programs@passageproject.org to be processed by Nepal office. Deposit of $500 and signed waiver form to be sent to US office (2440 North 56th St, Phoenix, Arizona 85008). Application deadlines are normally two months before the program begins.

Cost: $4050-$5825 depending on semester programme; $3555-$3755 for summer programme, inclusive of everything except international airfares. Homestay and lodge accommodation provided throughout.

Contact: Vidhea Shrestha, Director of Programmes.

VISITOZ
Springbrook Farm, MS 188, Goomeri, 4601 Queensland, Australia. ☎07-4168 6106. Fax: 07-4168 6155. E-mail: info@visitoz.org. Website: www.visitoz.org. UK Contacts: Will and Julia Taunton-Burnet, Visitoz UK, 49 Hurst Lane, Oxford OX2 9PR; ☎01865 861516; Mobiles 07966 528644 or 07771 992352; will@visitoz.org.

Courses offered: Training in all aspects of working on a rural property or in rural hospitality with guaranteed work afterwards. Instruction in tractor driving, horse riding, sheep and cattle work, fencing and chainsaw work OR bar and kitchen work, waitressing and hospitality work, drive-in bottle shop, roadhouse and housekeeping work.

Duration of courses: 5 days followed by a series of jobs up to 3 months long throughout rural Australia.

Cost: A$1680 (approx £650).

Other services: Offers all successful candidates with working holiday visas the chance to fill one of 300 vacancies with some of the 950+ employers all over Australia who pay a minimum $300 per week after tax plus free board and accommodation. (Youth wages apply in some cases for those under 20 years of age.) Higher wages are available for top quality tractor drivers, chefs and cooks.

Contact: Robyn and Adam Thrupp in Australia; Will and Julia Taunton-Burnet in UK.

PART III

Gap Year Opportunities listed by Country

Europe

Worldwide

EUROPE

Benelux

Netherlands

The Dutch language is studied by so few students at university that the Netherlands does not attract very many gap year students. However for those who want to experience the country's liberal traditions of tolerance, longer term stays are better than just a brief sightseeing trip to Amsterdam.

Most Dutch people speak excellent English so a knowledge of Dutch is generally not essential for voluntary or seasonal work. The Netherlands has one of the lowest rates of unemployment in Europe (4.6%) so unskilled paid work is available. It may be worth spending a few months working to save for further travels. The Dutch have some of the most progressive laws in the world to minimise exploitation of workers. The minimum wages are very good for those over 23 but are less for younger workers.

Au Pairing

Since Dutch is not a language which attracts a large number of students, au pairing in the Netherlands is not well known; however there is an established programme for those interested and able to stay at least six months. Working conditions are favourable in that pocket money of €250-€340 is paid per month in addition to health insurance costs. The main agencies are reputed to offer solid back-up, guidance on contacting fellow au pairs and advice on local courses. The agency with the largest incoming au pair programme is *Travel Active* (PO Box 107, 5800 Venray; 0478-551900; aupair@travelactive.nl) which places au pairs aged 18-30 as well as sending Dutch young people abroad on various work exchanges. The programme costs €600 for 12 months.

Jill Weseman was very pleased with her au pair placement in a village of just 500 people 30km from Groningen:

> *After graduation I accepted an au pairing position in Holland, mainly because there is no prior language requirement here. I really lucked out and ended up with a family who has been great to me. Though the situation sounds difficult at best – four children aged 1½, 3, 5 and 7, one day off a week and a rather remote location in the very north of Holland – I have benefitted a great deal. The social life is surprisingly good for such a rural area.*

Two other agencies are located in the Hague: Au Pair Agency Mondial, PO Box 17123, 2581 AK The Hague (www.aupair-agency.nl) and the House o Orange Au Pairs, Oostduinlaan 115, 2596 JJ The Hague (www.house-o-orange.nl). For others see the website for the Dutch Au Pair Association NAPO (Nederlandse Au Pair Organisatie; www.napoweb.nl).

Voluntary Work

If you are in the Netherlands you might make enquiries of the Dutch workcamps organisation *SIW Internationale Vrijwilligersprojekten* (Willemstraat 7, 3511 RJ Utrecht; 030-231 7721;

www.siw.nl); otherwise apply through affiliated workcamp organisations at home, e.g. IVS and UNA Exchange (see 'Directory of Volunteering Abroad'). Archaeological and building restoration camps are arranged by *NJBG (Nederlandse Jeugdbond voor Geschiedenis,* Prins Willem Alexanderhof 5, 2595 BE Den Haag; fax 070-335 2536; www.njbg.nl) whose website includes a small section in English.

Working on Boats

A little known opportunity for people who can communicate in German or Dutch is to work on one of the 250 *Platbodems,* traditional sailing boats that cruise the waters of Ijsselmeer and Waddensea off the north coast of the Netherlands in spring, summer and autumn. They cater mainly to school groups and are staffed by a skipper and one mate *(maat)* one of whose jobs is to offer simple instruction to the guests, though he or she must also help the skipper on watch, carry out repairs and so on. Even without any background in sailing, Felix Fernandez was offered ten jobs after adding his CV to the databank *(vacature bank)* of job-seekers and ended up working on the two-masted ship *Citore*. The company that owns *Citore* is Hanzestad Compagnie, Bataviahaven 1, Postbus 300, 8200 AH Lelystad, Netherlands (0320-292100; www.hanzestad.com in Dutch only).

Opportunities for Paid Work

The *Centra voor Werk en Inkomen or CWI* (the Dutch equivalent of Jobcentres formerly known as *Arbeidsbureau*) may be a useful source of paid employment. **Neil Datta** decided he wanted to spend part of his gap year in the Netherlands before applying to study medicine. He simply enquired at his local Jobcentre which passed on details of a heavy labouring job registered through EURES, the Europe-wide employment service. Although the work itself was unexciting, he greatly enjoyed being based in small-town Holland especially during the winter carnival in February (comparable to Mardi Gras). Furthermore he was able to save enough money to fund a big trip to Southeast Asia afterwards.

Both in cities and the country, many employers turn to private employment agencies *(uitzendbureaux* – pronounced 'outzend') for temporary workers. Therefore they can be a very useful source of temporary work in Holland. They proliferate in large towns, for example there are about 250 in Amsterdam alone, though not all will accept non-Dutch-speaking applicants. *Uitzendbureaux* deal only with jobs lasting less than six months. Most of the work on their books will be unskilled work such as stocking warehouse shelves, factory or agricultural work, etc. Among the largest *uitzendbureaux* are Randstad with about 300 branches (www.randstad.nl), Unique (www.uniquemls.com), Manpower (www.manpower.nl), Creyf's Interim and Tempo Team.

The largest employer of seasonal work is the bulb industry, and Dutch agriculture generally employs thousands of short-term helpers. The European Employment Service (EURES) looks beyond Dutch borders to recruit EU young people to fill hundreds of seasonal jobs in the agricultural and horticultural industries, with jobs available in greenhouses, flower and tree nurseries, bulbs packing houses, strawberry farms and so on. Hordes of young travellers descend on the bulb-producing area between Leiden and Haarlem without a pre-arranged job; it is easier to find openings in the early spring and through the autumn than in high summer. Traditionally, itinerant workers congregate on big campsites, where the seasonal regulars will advise newcomers. Excellent earnings are possible with employers who offer a lot of overtime (paid at a premium rate). But the work is hard and boring and the area attracts hardened long-term travellers looking to save money for further travels.

In this richly agricultural land, other opportunities present themselves for students looking for outdoor work. The area around Roermond (about 50km southeast of Eindhoven and north of Maastricht in the province of Limburg) is populated by asparagus growers and other farmers who need people to harvest their crops of strawberries, potatoes and vegetables, especially in the spring. Elsewhere, the area of Westland between Rotterdam, the Hook of Holland and Den Haag is well known for tomato production; the whole region is a honeycomb of greenhouses.

Dutch hotels and other tourist establishments occasionally employ foreigners, especially those with a knowledge of more than one European language. A few tour operators like *Holidaybreak* employ British young people as staff at their camps for the summer season. In **Adam Skuse's** year off before university, he almost succeeded in finding hotel work but not quite:

> *One very useful resource I found was the website www.visitholland.com, where I got a list of hotels and then systematically emailed them all asking for a job. Most had no vacancies, a couple told me to call them when I was in Amsterdam, and one actually arranged an interview with me. But even the knockbacks were pleasant. Quite a few offered to buy me a drink anyway. Alas, I never managed to find the hotel in time, ran out of funds and am now back in Blighty. I had plans for my gap year, but just ended up sitting around on the dole.*

This is exactly what this book is meant to help you prevent.

Those setting their sights higher than work in hotels or campsites, fields or greenhouses, may find it difficult to find work without fluent Dutch. Urban Dutch people have such a high degree of competence in English after they finish their schooling that there is not much of a market for EFL teaching.

Courses & Information

For general information about studying in the Netherlands, contact the *Foreign Student Service* (FSS), Oranje Nassaulaan 5, 1075 AH Amsterdam; www.foreignstudents.nl) for their publications including *Non-University Dutch Language Courses in the Netherlands*. Nuffic (the Netherlands Organization for International Co-operation in Higher Education) publishes *Study in the Netherlands*, a comprehensive catalogue in English of courses available, mostly for post-graduates, which can be requested by writing to Nuffic at PO Box 29777, 2502 LT The Hague (www.nuffic.nl). English is used as the medium of instruction on a variety of courses in the Netherlands.

Regulations

If you intend to stay in the Netherlands for more than three months, the first step is to acquire a sticker in your passport from the local aliens police (*Vreemdelingenpolitie*) or Town Hall, normally over-the-counter. They will expect you to provide a local address. The passport should then be taken to the local tax office to apply for a *sofinummer* (social/ fiscal number). To turn the initial sticker into a residence permit *(Verblijfsvergunning* or *verblijfskaart)* after three months, you will have to show a genuine work contract or letter of employment from an employer (not an agency) and pay a fee. The contract will have to show that the legal minimum wage and holiday pay are being paid and the proper tax and deductions are being made.

Information on working and living in the Netherlands is available on the Dutch Embassy website (www.netherlands-embassy.org.uk/econfaq_eng.htm) and no longer in booklet form. The Consular Department in London (38 Hyde Park Gate, SW7 5DP) has information regarding rules for aliens and how to apply for visas and residence permits, also on its website (www.netherlands-embassy.org.uk/consul_eng.htm).

Belgium

Belgium's proximity to Britain and its distinctive culture make it worth considering for a gap year experience. Its population of just over 10 million can be broadly divided between the French-speaking people of Wallonia in the south (about 42% of the total population) and those who speak Flemish (which is almost identical to Dutch) in the north.

Work Experience

The large number of multinational companies, attracted by the headquarters of the European Union in Brussels, have a constant and fluctuating demand for bilingual office workers. High flyers who would like to work for the European Commission as administrators, translators, secretaries, etc. must compete in open competitions held at regular intervals; the European Commission (see entry in 'Directory of Work Experience Abroad') can send application forms. The Commission runs a five-month *stagiaire* programme whereby graduates from member countries take up short-term training positions mostly in Brussels. Applications must be postmarked not later than 31st August for positions starting in March and 1st March for positions starting in October. They should be addressed to the Traineeships Office, Directorate General for Education & Culture, European Commission, 200 Rue de la Loi, 1049 Brussels, Belgium (02-295 39 93).

One company which arranges work experience placements for students of French or German is M.B. Language asbl (41 rue Henri Bergé, 1030 Brussels, Belgium; 02-242 27 66; macbaron@chello.be). Most linguistic and cultural exchanges last two weeks though longer ones may be possible. The programme is designed for European students aged 16-18 heading into the upper sixth. The placement fee is €450 or €475 depending on the time of year (more expensive in summer).

People who live in the south-east of England can make use of EURES Crossborder HNFK based at South Kent College (Maison Dieu Road, Dover CT16 1DH; 01304 244356) which assists people looking for jobs in the Western Belgian provinces of West-Vlaanderen and Hainaut. Two bilingual Euro-Advisers can put job-seekers in touch with network partners on the continent and can also give advice and information about living and working conditions.

Look for opportunities as a seasonal guide with one of the coach tour companies which run tours of scenic and historic Belgium. Venture Abroad (Rayburn House, Parcel Terrace, Derby DE1 1LY; www.ventureabroad.co.uk) employs reps, including students with a background in scouting or guiding, for its programme in Belgium.

For more casual opportunities, the best way to find out about short-term general work is to visit a branch of the Belgian employment service in any town. A special division called T-Interim specialises in placing people in temporary mostly unskilled jobs. They may also be able to help students who have done an office skills course at the beginning of their gap year to find well-paid temporary office jobs, provided they can function in French.

Americans can apply through Interexchange in New York (www.interexchange.org) to be placed in an internship in Belgium. Applicants over 18 with a working knowledge of French or Dutch can be placed in companies or organisations for between one and three months. The programme fee is $750 and the application deadline is late April.

Au Pairing

Anyone who wishes to be an au pair in Belgium will find it much harder than it used to be. The government has brought in stringent requirements that families pay a very high wage for only 20 hours of work: €400 a month for au pairs from the EU, €450 for non-EU au pairs. These changes have forced several Belgian agencies to cancel their incoming programme, though Stufam (Vierwindenlaan 7, 1780 Wemmel; 02-460 33 95; aupair.

stufam@pi.be) and the Catholic organisation Services de la Jeunesse Feminine (29 rue Faider, 1050 Brussels; 02-539 35 14; or rue de Dave, 174, 5100 Namur; 081-30 91 35) still make placements inside Belgium.

Voluntary Work

The Flemish association of young environmentalists called *Natuur 2000* (Bervoetstraat 33, 2000 Antwerp; 03-231 26 04; www.natuur2000.be) organises summer conservation workcamps open to all nationalities. The sizeable registration fee covers accommodation, food, insurance and local transport. Those interested in participating in residential archaeological digs for three weeks in July should contact *Archeolo-j* (Avenue Paul Terlinden 23, 1330 Rixensart; 02-653 8268/fax 02-673 40 85; www.skene.be). There is a charge for membership in the Society and camp expenses are €372 for 15 days.

Courses & Information

A few UK-based language course agencies send candidates to Belgium to learn French including *Vis-à-Vis*. A number of language schools advertise in the English language weekly magazine *The Bulletin*. Its address is 1038 Chaussée de Waterloo, 1180 Brussels (02-373 99 09); the magazine is published on Thursdays and can be bought from newsstands. *Newcomer* is a bi-annual publication (available from the above address for €3) which is aimed at new arrivals in Belgium and carries useful sections called 'Getting to Grips with the Red Tape' and 'Job-Seekers' Guide'.

The Federation Infor Jeunes Wallonie-Bruxelles is a non-profit making organisation which co-ordinates 12 youth information offices in French-speaking Belgium. The Brussels branch is at rue Van Artevelde 155, 1000 Brussels; 02-514 41 11). These can give advice on work as well as leisure, youth rights, accommodation, etc. Their headquarters are in Namur (081-71 15 90) though much of their information is published on their website www. inforjeunes.be. A related organisation (rue Haute 88, 1000 Brussels) also with a useful site is www.bruxelles-j.be. Among Infor Jeunes' services, they operate holiday job placement offices (Service Job Vacances) between March and September.

Luxembourg

If Belgium is sometimes neglected, Luxembourg is completely by-passed. Yet it is an independent country with a low rate of unemployment, and a number of useful facilities for foreign students. The national employment service *(Administration de l'Emploi)* or ADEM at 10 rue Bender, L-1229 Luxembourg (352-478 53 00; www.etat.lu/ADEM/adem. htm) operates a *Service Vacances* for students looking for summer jobs in warehouses, restaurants, etc. To find out about possibilities, you must visit this office in person, although EU nationals looking for long-term jobs may receive some assistance from EURES counsellors. The *Centre Information Jeunes* (CIJ), 26 Place de la Gare/Galerie Kons, 1616 Luxembourg (26 29 32 00; www.cij.lu) also runs a holiday job service between January and August for students from the EU. The student minimum wage as of 2005 is €6.65 an hour or €1150 a month.

With a total population of 463,000, job opportunities are understandably limited, but they do exist especially in the tourist industry. Even the Embassy in London at 27 Wilton Crescent, London SW1X 8SD (020-7235 6961) maintains that 'seasonal jobs are often to be found in the hotels of the Grand Duchy of Luxembourg' and will send a list of the 250+ hotels in exchange for an A4 envelope and a 50p stamp. Wages are fairly good in this sector, often about £500 per month after room and board.

Opportunities for gap year work experience may be available since many multinational companies are based in Luxembourg, some of whom may regard a knowledge of fluent English in addition to a local language as an advantage. Addresses of potential employers can be obtained from the Luxembourg Embassy who on receipt of an s.a.e. will send lists of British and American firms, as well as of the largest local companies.

Prolinguis runs summer language courses for teenagers near Arlon though its offices are in Belgium (228 Place de l'Eglise, 6717 Thiaumont, Belgium; 063-22 04 62; www. prolinguis.be).

France

Near destinations have been somewhat eclipsed in recent years by the more exotic far-flung gap year destinations like Peru and Ghana, but there is still plenty of glamour to be found in good old France. Your ambition may be to get to know Paris, to spend the winter in a French ski resort, to live with a provincial family as an au pair or a paying guest or simply to improve your schoolboy/girl French by conversing with the natives. All are worthy aims for occupying part of your gap year.

Sources of Information

The *Agence National pour l'Emploi* or ANPE is the national employment service of France, with dozens of offices in Paris and 600 others throughout the country. Their website www. anpe.fr carries lots of recruitment information (in French only). According to the site, it is looking to recruit a colossal 35,000 harvesters a year, e.g. 9000 grape-pickers for Bordeaux, 6000 apple pickers for Limousin and so on, 3000 for Tarn and so on. Other vacancies are also recorded on the regional sites (see www.anpe.fr/contacts for links by *département*). For example the ANPE in Narbonne (ANPE, BP 802, 29 rue Mazzini, 11108 Narbonne Cedex) has seasonal hotel vacancies from May to September.

One of the 32 regional offices of the *Centres d'Information Jeunesse* (CIJ) may be of use to the newly arrived gap year traveller. They can advise on cheap accommodation, local jobs, the legal rights of temporary workers, etc. The main Paris branch is CIDJ *(Centre d'Information et de Documentation Jeunesse)* whose foyer notice board is a useful starting place for the job or accommodation seeker in Paris. It can also provide booklets and leaflets for varying fees on such subjects as seasonal agricultural work, possibilities for work in the summer or winter, and the regulations that affect foreign students in France. Check the site www.cidj-librairie.com for a complete list which includes a recent publication *Etrangers en France: Vos Droits* for €22. CIDJ may be visited at 101 Quai Branly, 75740 Paris Cedex 15 (01-44 49 12 00; www.cidj.com). In order to find out about actual vacancies you must visit the CIDJ offices in person, preferably first thing in the morning. Employers notify centres of their temporary vacancies; some offices just display the details on notice boards, while others operate a more formal system in co-operation with the local ANPE (e.g., CIDJ in Paris registers about 10,000 summer jobs).

COURSES & HOMESTAYS

A good transition between the A-level classroom and a holiday or job in France is an intensive French language course in Britain (see entry for *Alliance Français* in London or try the Institut Français attached to the French Embassy, 14 Cromwell Place, London SW7 2JR). An even better one would be a French course abroad (see listings later in this chapter).

The British Council manages several student exchanges with France including the

Charles de Gaulle Bursary Trust which bequeaths up to £1000 on 17-19 year olds who submit an impressive proposal of what project they want to pursue or study for up to a month. For details, contact the Council's Belfast office on 028 9024 8220 ext 241 and plan to apply by the end of January.

Hundreds of British students do an exchange year in Paris. For example more than 1000 British students participate in the Erasmus European student exchange, though this scheme is open to undergraduates not school leavers. Several hundred more attach themselves to the *British Institute* in Paris (11 rue de Constantine, 75340 Paris Cedex 07), and of course the *Sorbonne* is a magnet for students wanting to take language and civilisation courses.

For a range of standard language courses, look at the brochure from *Vis-à-Vis* which specialises in French language courses. It offers two-week courses in Paris starting at just over £350 (20 hours a week tuition) and in Annecy for about £220. *EIL* in Malvern also arranges homestay, language courses and high school placements in France (see entries for its French counterpart *Experiment Paris* in the 'Directory of Work Experience' and the 'Directory of Language Courses'). On the Schools Programme offered by *AFS Intercultural Programmes UK* (Leeming House, Vicar Lane, Leeds LS2 7JF; 0113-242 6136; info-unitedkingdom@afs.org) students aged 15-18 spend an academic year or term living with a French family and attending the local school.

During her gap year, **Lucinda Capel** was as pleased with the extracurricular activities on the course in Bordeaux which *CESA* fixed up for her as she was with the lessons:

Day to day life in Bordeaux is definitely a fun experience. There is something to satisfy everyone in this city: pubs, bars and night clubs (with DJs from London sometimes). Then there are the museums, historic architecture, vineyard visits, wine tastings, go-karting and trips to the cinema and theatre.

I came over to Bordeaux to work on my French. I'm writing this half way through the 12-week course and I am glad to say it's a case of, so far, so very, very good. Everybody I have met has been really amazed at just how quickly they have picked the language up, even the beginners. The combination of the lessons in the morning and meals with the French family in the evening provide you with a total immersion in the French language and culture that allows you to learn continuously without even being aware of it. The classes are streamed according to ability but it is very flexible. During the first few days, you may move classes until you are comfortable with the pace.

One problem is the food served up nightly by my host family. It is simply too good and I have had to join a gym. Gym life in Bordeaux is a cultural experience in its own right. Having done it, I don't recommend it unless you wish to be outshone by the femme Bordelaise who, whilst being twice your age, are superbly flexible. You need a strong sense of self to survive that ordeal.

Obviously the gym and the DJs didn't provide too many distractions since she passed all four units of her D.E.L.F. exam.

A rough estimate of how much a 20-hour course will cost per week would be €220-€260 plus a further €150-€170 to stay with a host family. Obviously prices are higher in Paris. The prestigious *Alliance Française* offers four hours a day over 16 days in a month for €610. Another major provider is the Eurolingua Institute (5 rue Henri Guinier, 34000 Montpellier; www.eurolingua.com/French_in_Montpellier.htm) which also arranges paid work placements in hotels and on holiday camping sites during the summer. Bookings can be made through their UK office (tel/fax 0161-972 0225; info@eurolingua.com).

Some language schools double as au pair agencies such as *Inter-Séjours* and *Institut Euro'Provence,* 69 rue de Rome, 13001 Marseille; euro.provence@wanadoo.fr) which makes a language course much more affordable. A cheap way to have a base in France from which to improve your knowledge of the language is to participate in a work exchange, for example the one offered by the Centre International d'Antibes, a French language school on the Côte d'Azur. Summer volunteers do administrative or domestic work in exchange for board and lodging and/or French tuition. Details of the scheme are available from CIA, 38 boulevard d'Aguillon, 06600 Antibes (04-92 90 71 70; admin@cia-france.com).

For listings of 200 language schools, see *The Complete Guide to Learning French in France: From Short Study Holidays to Gap Year Breaks* from Summersdale Publishers (£899).

WORK EXPERIENCE

Work experience placements are referred to as *stages* in France and are widely available through a number of organisations. British students enrolled in courses in France who are interested in gaining work experience might find the local CROUS office helpful. The Centres Régional des Oeuvres Universitaires et Scolaires operate a service which has links with local employers; in Paris the office is at 39 avenue Georges Bernanos (www.crous-paris.fr).

Gwendalyne (67-71 Lewisham High St, London SE13 5JX; 020-8297 3251; info@gwendalyne.com) has an Internship France programme for which French-speaking university students are eligible and a Work France programme open to anyone over 18 willing to work in an unskilled job in the hospitality industry. The programme fees are respectively £300 and £500 which guarantees placement but does not include accommodation. The £500 fee includes a choice of two weeks of French classes or a fortnight's hostel accommodation.

Horizon HPL (Signet House, 49/51 Farringdon Road, London EC1M 3JP; 020-7404 9192; horizonhpl.london@btinternet.com; http://horizon1.club.fr/index.htm) is an Anglo-French training organisation which offers packages lasting between three and 12 months combining language tuition and live-in hotel work placements and company placements all over France. The wages are on a trainee scale, from £50 per week plus accommodation, while the package fee starts at £240. Candidates can choose to prepare for Sorbonne University exams. Horizon's office in France is at 22-26 rue du Sergent Bauchat, 75012 Paris (01-40 01 07 07; www.horizonhpl.com).

The major language school France Langue, with centres in Paris and Nice, arranges for its trainees to work in hotels; see www.france-langue.fr/en/specialized_programs/hotel_and_tourism_industry_french.php.

A small company run by a French woman called Boost your French (4 Heol Maesglas, Ysbyty Ystwyth, Ystrad Meurig SY25 6DY; tel/fax 01974 282 563; catherine@boostyourfrench.co.uk) sends Britons on both paid and unpaid work placements in France lasting from two weeks to a whole year. A gap year student recounts her experience on the website www.boostyourfrench.co.uk:

> *I had just passed my A-levels and wanted to earn some money during the summer, but I also wanted to have an interesting time and learn more French. So I decided to look for a job in France. I was not successful in my search until I came across Catherine's web site. She offered me a job as a shop assistant on the coast near Bordeaux. I had a fantastic time, making lots of friends, I earned money and definitely learned more French. Now, I am in my first year at university and I intend to go back to work in France next summer.*

The long established Club des 4 Vents (1 rue Gozlin, 75006 Paris; france@cei4vents.com) has a variety of workplace openings for young people over 17 who have an intermediate standard of French (see Work Experience entry for C.E.I.).

PAID OPPORTUNITIES FOR YEAR OUT STUDENTS

The best areas to look for work in the tourist industry of France are the Alps for the winter season, December-April, and the Côte d'Azur for the summer season, June-September, though jobs exist throughout the country. The least stressful course of action is to fix up work ahead of time with a UK campsite or holiday company in summer or ski company in winter. For example First Choice (1st Floor, London Road, Crawley, W Sussex RH10 2GX; 0870 750 1204; overseas.recruitment@firstchoice.co.uk; www.firstchoice4jobs. com) hires hundreds of reps (resort, transfer, children's) over the age of 18 to work in hotels and chalets in the Alps and Normandy. Staff must have EU nationality but need not have relevant experience.

One important feature of working for a French employer in France is that you should be paid at least the *SMIC (salaire minimum interprofessionel de croissance)* or national minimum wage. There are slightly different rates for seasonal agricultural work and full-time employees; at present the basic SMIC is €7.61 per hour gross or €1,154.27 per month based on a working week of 35 hours. These are adjusted annually to take account of inflation.

With a deferred place to read French and Spanish at university, **Frances Pountain** knew that she wanted to spend part of her gap year in a French-speaking environment. Based on previous trips to France, she and a friend decided to head for Montpellier, not least because they were able to get a £15 flight with Ryanair in February (but spent nearly ten times that on an eight-month insurance policy with Endsleigh). They arrived cold, with nothing pre-arranged:

> *At first we worked solely on improving our French and having some fun. But after a few months we found jobs with a newspaper and leaflet distributing agency called Adrexo (www.adrexo.fr). We found this job by looking in local publications "34" and "Top Hebdo" (www.petites-annonces.fr). The job of distributing publicity was fairly easy and still allowed time to enjoy being in Montpellier.*
>
> *Going to France was exciting yet had lots of very trying times at the beginning since we hadn't arranged anything before going. With hindsight I would have probably tried to set up either a work placement/job or a language course ahead of time, as sometimes we didn't feel we had much direction there. Yet I feel my gap year has been very rewarding. Going to live in France has helped my French no end.*

Campsites and Holiday Centres

British camping tour operators hire an army of language students to staff their network of campsites throughout France. These companies offer holidaymakers a complete package providing pre-assembled tents and a campsite courier to look after any problems that arise. Since this kind of holiday appeals to families, people who can organise children's activities are especially in demand. In addition to the Europe-wide companies like *Eurocamp* and *Canvas* (see 'Directory of Paid Seasonal Jobs'), the following all take on campsite reps/ couriers and other seasonal staff for France:

Carisma Holidays, Bethel House, Heronsgate, Chorleywood, Herts. WD3 5BB (01923 284235; personnel@carisma.co.uk).

Fleur Holidays, 4 All Hallows Road, Bispham, Blackpool FY2 0AS (01253 593333; employment@fleur-holidays.com).

French Life/Camping Life, Unit 2, Rawdon Park Industrial Estate, Green Lane, Rawdon, Leeds LS19 6RW (0870 197 6541; overseasemployment@frenchlife.co.uk).

Ian Mearns Holidays, Tannery Yard, Witney St, Burford, Oxon. OX18 4DP (01993 822655; enquiries@ianmearnsholidays.co.uk). People able to start work by Easter especially in demand.

Select France, Fiveacres, Murcott, Kidlington, Oxford OX5 2RE (01865 331350;

jobs@selectfrance.co.uk).

Venue Holidays, 1 Norwood St, Ashford, Kent TN23 1QU (01233 629950; www. venueholidays.co.uk). Website carries job information.

The best time to start looking for summer season jobs from England is between September and February. In most cases candidates are expected to have at least A-level standard French, though some companies claim that a knowledge of French is merely 'preferred'. It is amazing how far a good dictionary and a knack for making polite noises in French can get you. Many impose a minimum age of 21.

The massive camping holiday industry generates winter work as well. Brad Agencies Ltd. has a depot in Beaucaire near Avignon that cleans and repairs tents and bedding on behalf of many of the major companies. Staff (who need not speak French though it is an advantage) are needed for the laundry and distribution between September and May. Gite accommodation is provided and a wage negotiated. A driving licence is essential and your own transport helpful. Brad International's UK office is at Abbey Lakes Hall, Orrell Road, Wigan WN5 8QZ (01695 632797; ian.b@bradint.co.uk).

Short bursts of work are available in the spring (about three weeks in May) and autumn (three weeks in September) to teams of people who put up and take down the tents at campsites, known as *montage* and *démontage*. Sometimes the camping tour operators contract out this work to specialist firms like Mark Hammerton Travel (Spelmonden Old Oast, Spelmonden Road, Goudhurst, Kent TN1 1HE; 01580 214000; enquiries@markhammerton.co.uk) who pay their crews nearly £95 a week in addition to board, lodging and travel expenses.

Outdoor activity centres are another major employer of summer staff, both general domestic staff and sports instructors. Try the companies mentioned in the introductory section 'Working in Tourism' such as *Acorn Adventure* and *PGL*.

One of the most interesting and varied opportunities is offered by the specialist independent company *French Encounters* (see entry in 'Directory of Work Experience'). They hire gap year students with a knowledge of French for the period February to June. Staff work with groups of British children on field study holidays based at chateaux in rural Normandy, after undergoing a fortnight's intensive training in presentation skills, first aid and the French language.

Eighteen-year-old Kate Wilkins, an *animatrice* in 2005, summarised the benefits with enthusiasm:
I wanted to live and work independently in France, Since I am about to go and study this language for four years at university, and I had hardly ever been to France, I wanted to get a real flavour of French life and culture as well as of course reinforcing and improving my fluency. I also loved the idea of working in an educational environment and being a role model for children. I loved doing the guided walks around places (especially Rouen) and the commentary for Paris – felt it was an opportunity to be adaptable to group decisions, think on the spot and I really enjoyed showing my knowledge of the area and telling stories to the children. Briefings/games with the children were a valuable lesson in presentation skills and keeping your audience captive. Living in such a beautiful location was fantastic. I feel as though I have matured in terms of inner self-confidence and the ability to lose my inhibitions. I've made friends for life, including the directors.

For work in an unusual activity holiday, contact Bombard Balloon Adventures, Chateau de LaBorde, 21200 Beaune (03-80 26 63 30; www.bombardsociety.com/jobs) who hire hot-air balloon ground crew for the summer season May to October. The job requires excellent physical fitness and strength, a cheerful personality, clean-cut appearance and year-old clean driving licence.

Ski Resorts

France is the best of all countries in Europe for finding jobs in ski resorts, mainly because it is the number one country for British skiers, 200,000 of whom go there every year. The main problem is the shortage of worker accommodation; unless you find a live-in job you will have to pay nearly holiday prices or find a friend willing to rent out his or her sofa. If trying to fix up a job from Britain, *Jobs in the Alps* recruits young people with a very good knowledge of French to work in ski resorts.

Another agency is UK Overseas Handling (UKOH, PO Box 2791, London W1A 5JU; 020-7629 3064; vacancies@ukoh.co.uk) which provides seasonal and annual staff to the French tour operator Eurogroup which owns hotels, restaurant and chalets in ski and beach resorts in France (and the rest of Europe). Applicants must be EU-passport holders. Three excellent recruitment websites are www.natives.co.uk, www.seasonworkers.com and www.freeradicals.co.uk which match job-seekers with alpine and other vacancies.

If you attempt to find work in a ski resort on your own, success is far from guaranteed and competition for work is increasing. Val d'Isère attracts as many as 500 ski bums every November/December, many of whom hang around bars or the ANPE (Jobcentre) for days in the hope that work will come their way. If looking for work in Val, try Radio Val which broadcasts from next door to the tourist office. Job vacancies are announced in the morning (mostly babysitting and kitchen portering) and then posted in French outside the studio. The earlier you try for these, the better your chances.

Writing in the *Ink Pellet* (an arts magazine for teachers), Nico Stanford described a success story:

> I'd finished my A-levels and was determined to take a gap year with a snowboard and loads of snow. My parents went on at me to 'go through a tour operator and do washing up' or something equally dull. When I got to France in late November with no job, two flatmates, 20 loo rolls and enough savings for ski pass and flat but no food, it was snowing, so we immediately set about the important business of getting out onto the slopes. The job hunting was intermittent and unsuccessful and, as money ran out, I could almost here the 'I told you so' from my father.
>
> About a month after we arrived, with desperation setting in, I went to a local bar and was told about a job going at the local radio station translating and reading the weather in English, so French was essential. Off I went, feeling very grateful for my French A-level, and the guys at the station were so desperate (the girl had quit suddenly after less than a month) that they hired me on the spot at pretty good pay… I went on to have a wonderful time which was financed by a fascinating hands-on experience in the media and I feel ready to cope with and enjoy university life to the full in October.

Having accommodation provided by your employer is a very valuable perk. The UK company *Planet Subzero* (26 Woodsyre, London SE26 6SS; 07905 097 087; info@planetsubzero. com) rents out affordable accommodation to young skiers and snowboarders for the whole season, some of whom take lessons, others work and others just ski. They have properties in Les Arcs, Tignes, Val d'Isère, Chamonix, Méribel and Val Thorens (though limit the number of 21 year olds in their properties).

Yachts

A few months on the Riviera would be hard for someone taking a gap year to fund unless some means of earning money could be found. Yachts may provide the answer. It is not impossible to penetrate the world of yacht owners and skippers in glamorous resorts like Antibes and St Tropez. It is essential to start looking early, preferably the beginning of March, since by late April most of the jobs have been filled. Boats frequently take on people as day workers first and then employ them as crew for the charter season if they like them. Deckhands on charter yachts are paid a weekly wage, usually around £100 which can sometimes be doubled with tips from big-rollers. The charter season ends in late September (convenient if you're returning to university) when many yachts begin organising their crew for the trip to the West Indies.

Kevin Gorringe headed for the south of France in June with the intention of finding work on a private yacht. His destination was Antibes, where so many British congregate, and he began frequenting likely meeting places like the Gaffe Bar and the Irish bar. The main crewing agencies in Antibes are housed in the same building, viz. La Galerie du Port, 8 boulevard d'Aguillon, 06600 Antibes. Long established agencies in La Galerie du Port include Peter Insull's Crew Agency (04-93 34 64 64/fax 04-93 34 21 22; crew@insull.com) and the Blue Water Yacht Crew Agency (04-93 34 34 13/fax 04-93 34 28 89; crew@bluewateryachting.com). Competition will be fierce, so doggedness together with charm and a good measure of luck will be needed for success. Look tidy and neat, be polite and when you get a job work hard. The first job is the hardest to get, but once you get in with the community of yachties, people will help you move onto other boats.

Grape-Picking

Although the French tourist industry offers many seasonal jobs, there are even more in agriculture especially the grape harvest. Farmers almost always provide some sort of accommodation, but this can vary from a rough and ready dormitory to a comfortable room in his own house. Obviously it is easier for the owner of a small vineyard with a handful of workers to provide decent accommodation than for the owner of a chateau who may have over a 100 workers to consider. Food is normally provided, but again this can vary from the barely adequate to the sublime: one picker can write that 'the food was better than that in a 5-star hotel, so we bought flowers for the cook at the end of the harvest', while another may complain of instant mashed potatoes or of having to depend on whatever he or she can manage to buy and prepare. When both food and accommodation are provided there is normally a deduction of one or two hours' pay from each day's wage.

The work itself will consist either of picking or portering. Picking involves bending to get the grapes from a vine that may be only three and a half feet tall, and filling a pannier which you drag along behind you. The panniers full of grapes are emptied into an *hotte,* a large basket weighing up to 100lb which the porters carry to a trailer.

The first few days as a *cueilleur/cueilleuse* or *coupeur* (picker) are the worst, as you adjust to the stooping posture and begin to use muscles you never knew you had. The job of porter is sought after, since it does not require the constant bending and is less boring because you move around the vineyard.

The demand for pickers in all regions is highly unpredictable. Whereas there is usually a glut of pickers looking for work at the beginning of the harvest (early to mid-September), there is sometimes a shortage later on in the month. Harvests differ dramatically from year to year; a late spring frost can wreak havoc. The element of uncertainty makes it very difficult for farmers to make any fixed commitment in advance.

The best plan is to find out whether the local ANPE (Jobcentre) knows of likely vacancies (www.ANPE.fr). For example the ANPE in Orange (282 Allée Auvergne Roussillon, 84106 Orange Cedex; 4-90 51 64 23) recruits pickers for Chateauneuf-du-Pape. The Dutch agency *Appellation Controlée* (see entry in 'Directory of Paid Seasonal Jobs') can arrange a job for a fee of €99.

Work on Farms

Although the *vendange* may produce the highest concentration of seasonal work, there are tremendous opportunities for participating in other harvests and with far less competition for the available work. France is an overwhelmingly rural country. One additional way of finding harvesting work is to ask at the fruit and vegetable markets where farmers gather daily to watch their farming co-operative sell their produce at the height of the season.

> **Through the European agency Appellation Controlée mentioned above, Karen Martin and Paul Ansell found work castrating maize in the Loire Valley:**
> *While we were in Amsterdam we looked on the internet and found a Dutch agency (www.apcon.nl) who mediate between workers and farmers in England and France. They charged a fee and got us work doing maize castration on a farm where two people had dropped out (God bless 'em). We made our way by hitching from Angers and were greeted by the farmer Bernard and his wife Merielle with lovely cherry wine. They speak little English but it was not an obstacle. You camp on the farm for a pound a day and have good facilities.*

The proprietors cooked barbecues for them, washed clothes and were generally very hospitable and Karen and Paul were delighted to be invited back soon afterwards for a month's apple picking which allowed them to save £1000 between them. Karen thinks that they were among the first non-French workers here but the farmer expressed interest in hosting more foreign young people at this farm which is about 20 miles east of Angers; contact Earl le Chêne du Mensonge, Hye, Bernard, Porteau, 49350 Les Rosiers sur Loire; 02-41 51 90 27.

English Teaching

A more realistic possibility than finding employment with a language school is to offset the high cost of living in Paris by doing some tutoring which sometimes shades into au pairing. Language exchanges for room and board are commonplace in Paris and are usually arranged through advertisements (in the places described below in the section on Paris) or by word of mouth. **Kathryn Kleypas** studied the notice board at the American Church to good effect:

> *I contacted a family from the notice board and was invited to come over to their home for an interview and to meet the three children to whom I would be teaching English every day. I was not asked if I had any teaching experience, yet was offered the position which involved 18 hours of English teaching/conversation in exchange for room, board and pocket money. My family took me with them to the seaside near Bordeaux in July and to their castle near Limoges during August.*

University students and recent graduates who would like to spend a year as an English language *assistant* in a French primary or secondary school should contact the British Council at assistants@britishcouncil.org. Altogether they place about 1000 students aged 20-30 to work 12 hours a week. *Assistants* are paid about €900 gross a month.

Occasionally pre-university students are accepted in this capacity. For example an education authority in the Vendée offers a 'Gap Year for Francophiles' in French primary schools or acting as an assistant in the local lycée. The only requirements are that you be aged 18-25, have an A-level in French and have some experience of living in France. In exchange for 20 hours of teaching a week between the end of September and the end of May, you receive free board and lodging with a local family and a monthly allowance of €177 (after national insurance contributions). Details are available from the Syndicat Mixte Montaigu-Rocheservière, 35 avenue Villebois Mareuil, 85607 Montaigu Cedex (02-51 46 45 45/fax 02-51 46 45 40; www.explomr.com/english).

AU PAIRING

Au pairing has always been a favoured way for young women in their gap year to improve their French and, increasingly, for young men too. The pocket money for au pairs in France is linked to the minimum wage (SMIC) and is currently €65-€75 per 30-hour week. Most British agencies with an outgoing programme deal with France (see list in introductory chapter on Au Pairing) but applying directly through a French agency is commonplace. The most established agencies are members of UFAAP, the Union Francaise des Associations Au Pair, an umbrella group set up in 1999, based at present at Euro Pair Services listed below. Their member agencies are included on their website www.ufaap.org. While some agencies charge nothing, others do charge a registration fee which can be steep (€160+). Here are some agencies to contact:

Apitu, 38 rue Traversière, 75012 Paris (01-44 87 01 42; info@apitu.com).

Association Familles & Jeunesse, 4 rue Masséna, 06000 Nice (04-93 82 28 22; info@afj-aupair.org; www.afj-aupair.org). Places more than 300 au pair girls and boys, mainly in the South of France plus the French Riviera and Corsica.

Association Mary Poppins, 4 place de la Fontaine, 38120 St Egreve (Grenoble); (04-76 75 57 33; mary.poppins@wanadoo.fr; http://assoc.wanadoo.fr/marypoppins.aupair).

Euro Pair Services, 13 rue Vavin, 75006 Paris (01-43 29 80 01; europairservices@wanadoo. fr).

France Au Pair - Eurojobs, 6 Allée des Saules, BP 29, 17420 Saint Palais sur Mer (05-46 23 99 88; contact@eurojob.fr; www.eurojob.fr).

Institut Euro'Provence, 69 rue de Rome, 13001 Marseille (04-91 33 90 60; euro. provence@wanadoo.fr; http://perso.wanadoo.fr/euro.provence). Language school and au pair agency in south of France.

Inter-Séjours, 179 rue de Courcelles, 75017 Paris (+33 1-47 63 06 81; http://asso. intersejours.free.fr).

Oliver Twist Association, 07 rue Léon Morin, 33600 Pessac (05-57 26 93 26; oliver. twist@wanadoo.fr).

Ouest Au Pair, 68 Blvd des Belges, 44300 Nantes (02-51 89 96 75; ouest.au.pair@tiscali.fr).

Soames Paris Nannies, 64 rue Anatole France, 92300 Levallois-Perret (01-47 30 44 04; soames.parisnannies@wanadoo.fr).

By law, families are supposed to make social security payments to the local URSSAF office on the au pair's behalf, though not all do and you might want to enquire about this when applying. Au pairs in or near Paris should receive the *carte orange* (monthly travel pass) which is worth about €50.

Quite a few foreigners are too hasty in arranging what seems at the outset a cushy number and only gradually realise how little they enjoy the company of children and how isolated they are if their family lives in the suburbs (as most do). Unless you actively like small children, it might be better to look for a free room in exchange for minimal babysitting (e.g. 12 hours a week). **Matt Tomlinson** went into his au pair job with his eyes open:

> I'd heard too many horror stories from overworked and underpaid au pair friends to be careless, so chose quite carefully from the people who replied to my notice on the upstairs notice board of the British Church (just off the rue de Faubourg St Honoré). My employers were really laid back, in their mid-20s so more like living with an older brother and sister. The little boy was just over two whilst the little girl was three months old, and they were both completely adorable. On the whole it was great fun. Baking chocolate brownies, playing football and finger-painting may not be everybody's idea of a good time but there are certainly worse ways to earn a living (and learn French at the same time).

VOLUNTARY WORK

France has as wide a range of opportunities for voluntary work as any European country, and anyone who is prepared to exchange work for subsidised board and lodging should consider joining a voluntary project. The majority of short-term projects last two or three weeks during the summer and cost between €8 and €18 a day. Many gap students join one of these to learn basic French and make French contacts as well as to have fun. All workcamp associations in Britain can arrange for you to join camps in France (see 'Directory of Volunteering Abroad').

Archaeology

A great many archaeological digs and building restoration projects are carried out each year. Every May the Ministry of Culture (Direction de l'Architecture et du Patrimoine, Sous-Direction de l'Archéologie, 4 rue d'Aboukir, 75002 Paris; 01-40 15 77 81) publishes a national list of summer excavations throughout France requiring up to 5000 volunteers which can be consulted on its website (www.culture.gouv.fr/fouilles). Most *départements* have *Services Archéologiques* which organise digs. Without relevant experience you will probably be given only menial jobs but many like to share in the satisfaction of seeing progress made.

Anthony Blake describes the dig he joined which the History Department of the University of Le Mans runs every summer:

Archaeology is hard work. Applicants must be aware of what working 8.30am-noon and 2-6.30pm in baking heat means! That said, I thoroughly enjoyed the working holiday: excellent company (75% French so fine opportunity to practise French), weekends free after noon on Saturday, good lunches in SNCF canteen, evening meals more haphazard as prepared by fellow diggers. Accommodation simple but adequate.

Unskilled volunteers are charged a small contribution for their board and lodging. For example every July M. Louis Roussel (28 rue du Bourg, 21000 Dijon; malain_gam@hotmail.com) takes 20 volunteers to work on a Gallo-Roman site outside Dijon; volunteers contribute a modest €15 per week. Further north the Service Archéologique of the Musée de la Chartreuse (191 rue St-Albin, 59500 Douai; 03-27 71 38 90; archeologie@douaisis-agglo.com) carries out summer digs on a Mérovingian abbey and mediaeval town. The registration fee here is €22.87.

Conservation

France takes the preservation of its heritage *(patrimoine)* very seriously and there are numerous groups both local and national engaged in restoring churches, windmills, forts and other historic monuments. Many are set up to accept foreign volunteers, though they tend to charge more than archaeological digs:

APARE/GEC, Association pour la Participation et l'Action Régionale, 25 Boulevard Paul Pors, 84800 L'Isle sur la Sorgue (04-90 85 51 15; www.apare-gec.org). An umbrella organisation that runs volunteer workcamps at historic sites in Provence (plus a few in Morocco and Lebanon). Cost of €91 for 2 weeks, €124 for 3 weeks.

Chantier Histoire et Architecture Médiévale (CHAM), 5-7 rue Guilleminot, Paris 75014 (01-43 35 15 51; www.cham.asso.fr). Paris-based organisation that runs volunteer projects to protect historic buildings, not just in mainland France but in farflung places including Réunion Island (a *département* of France in the Indian Ocean near Mauritius) and in Africa. The address of the delegation in La Réunion is 25 rue Mahé, La Mare, 97438 Sainte Marie, Ile de la Réunion (02-62 53 27 98; CHAM-REUNION@wanadoo.fr). See the CHAM website (which is in English) for details.

Club du Vieux Manoir, Ancienne Abbaye du Moncel, 60700 Pontpoint (03-44 72 33 98; www.clubduvieuxmanoir.free.fr). 15-day summer workcamp to restore ancient monuments. Board and lodging cost €14 per day.

REMPART, 1 rue des Guillemites, 75004 Paris (01-42 71 96 55; www.rempart.com). Similar to the National Trust in Britain, in charge of endangered monuments throughout France. Most projects charge €7 per day plus €40 for membership and insurance. Registration must be done by post.

La Sabranenque, Centre International, rue de la Tour de l'Oume, 30290 Saint Victor la Coste (04-66 50 05 05; www.sabranenque.com). $630-$710 per fortnight. US applicants should contact Jacqueline Simon, 124 Bondcroft Drive, Buffalo, NY 14226 (716-836-8698).

UNAREC (Etudes et Chantiers), Délégué International, 3 rue des Petits Gras, 63000 Clermont-Ferrand (04-73 31 98 04; www.unarec.org). Hundreds of international volunteers for short-term conservation projects and longer-term professional training. €115 fee includes accommodation and insurance for 2-3 week workcamps.

Try to be patient if the project you choose turns out to have its drawbacks, since these organisations depend on voluntary leaders as well as participants. Judy Greene volunteered to work with a conservation organisation and felt herself to be 'personally victimised by the lack of organisation and leadership' or more specifically by one unpleasantly racist individual on her project. Tolerance may be called for, especially if your fellow volunteers lack it.

PARIS

Like all major cities in the developed world, Paris presents thousands of ways to earn your keep, while being difficult to afford from day to day. Unless you are very lucky, you will have to arrive with some money with which to support yourself while you look around.

Expatriate grapevines all over Paris should prove helpful for finding work and accommodation. Many people find their jobs as well as accommodation through one of the city's many notice boards *(panneaux).* The one in the foyer of the CIDJ near the *métro* stop Bir-Hakeim has already been mentioned as being good for student-type jobs such as extras in movies, but sometimes there are adverts for full-time jobs or *soutien scolaire en Anglais* (English tutor). It is worth arriving early to check for new notices.

The other mecca for job and flat-hunters is the American Church at 65 Quai d'Orsay (01-40 62 05 00; *métro* Invalides). Official notices are posted on various notice boards inside and out; the cork board in the basement is a free board where anybody can stick up a notice. Obviously it is necessary to consult the notices in person; they are not available by phoning the church or on the internet.

Although the notice board at the *Alliance Française* is for the use of registered students of French, you may be able to persuade a student to look at the adverts for you, many of which are exchanges of room for some babysitting and/or teaching. The notice board is in the annex around the corner at 34 rue de Fleurus.

Arguably the most eccentric bookshop in Europe is Shakespeare and Company at 37 rue de la Bûcherie in the fifth *arrondissement* (on the south side of the Seine). It has a notice board and is also useful as a place to chat to other expats about work and accommodation. The shop operates as a writer's guesthouse. If you are prepared to write a short account of yourself and pitch in with a few chores you can stay free for a limited period, assuming there is space. The elderly American expat owner George Whitman still hosts weekly Sunday open house for aspiring *literati* and also hires English-speaking staff to clean, run errands and work behind the till.

Hannah Adcock describes herself as a 'rather solemn' eighteen year old when she read *Work Your Way Around the World* and found out about this opportunity:
Soon after, I found myself living at this hippy Parisien bookstore with a view of

> *Notre Dame, a treat of inedible pancakes to look forward to and orders to clean the floor using newspaper and cold water. Kids staying at Shakespeare's do most of the jobs for free. You'll only get a paid job if (a) the owner really likes you, (b) you went to a university like Cambridge or Harvard and (c) you're really cute. The room overlooking Notre Dame is lovely but when I was there it smelt foul and a highly evolved species of bed bug lurked, as big as rats (ok – exaggeration). Shakespeare's is brilliant, but working there has its 'interesting' aspects!*

Most expat places like WH Smith's Bookshop near the Place de la Concorde and the Virgin Megastore on the Champs Elysées distribute the free bilingual newsletter *France-USA Contacts* or *FUSAC* (www.fusac.org) which comes out every other Wednesday. It comprises mainly classified adverts which are best followed up on the day the paper appears. An advert under the heading 'Work Wanted in France' costs US$24 for 20 words, and can be emailed to franceusa@aol.com.

Disneyland Paris

The enormous complex of Disneyland Paris, 30km east of Paris at Marne-la-Vallée, employs about 12,000 people in high season both on long-term and seasonal contracts. Seasonal positions from March or May to September are open to EU nationals. The minimum period covers the high season from the end of June to the end of August.

'Cast members' (Disneyspeak for employees) must all be over 18, have a conversational level of French and preferably a third European language. The majority of jobs are in food and beverage, housekeeping, merchandising and custodial departments, though one of the best(?) jobs is as a Disney character. Further details are available from Service du Recrutement-Casting, Disneyland Paris, BP 110, 77777 Marne-la-Vallée Cedex 4 (www. disneylandparis.com/uk/employment). For all jobs the well-scrubbed look is required (though they do now tolerate neatly trimmed facial hair), and of course they are looking for the usual friendly, cheerful and outgoing personalities. The monthly gross starting wage is €1,103 from which deductions are made for social security (about €160). Staff accommodation costs €230 per month and a contribution is made to travel expenses on completion of a contract.

> **Keith Leishman from Dundee was a cast member two summers ago:**
> *Getting the job was initially quite frustrating. I first sent a letter to the company around November. After another couple of letters and e-mails without reply, I was just about giving up hope. Finally around March I received notification of an interview in Edinburgh and was offered the job. After that you are pretty much left to your own devices and simply expected to turn up at Disney the day before your contract begins. (This was rather a shock to me after working for Eurocamp the year before who provided transport to France and some preparatory material beforehand.)*
> *I was employed on the ticketing side of operations. I had to wear a Prince Charming costume and supervise the entrance of guests to the Park, stamping their hands for readmission. This meant standing for the whole shift in what were often scorching conditions. This was very beneficial for my French as people would ask a whole range of weird and wonderful questions.*
> *The staff apartments were comfortable enough and equipped with kitchens, though I did not cook much due to the cheapness and accessibility of Disney canteens. I could eat well for 3 or 4 euros a day. Another of the main advantages of working at Disneyland is the mixture of nationalities. The sheer number of young people from all over the world means there are always lots of parties and barbecues in the residences. On days off I usually went into Paris which is only 40 minutes away on the train. I stayed for two months of the peak summer season and found it quite hard to keep up the Disney smile when I was hot and tired. The*

> job is demanding because you are creating an illusion. All the same I would urge anybody with an interest in people and a desire to improve their French to try the experience.

Germany

Students who have studied German at school and may intend to pursue those studies in higher education should consider spending at least part of their gap year in Germany, either doing a language course or a work experience placement, as an au pair or a volunteer. Even if you are not planning to specialise in modern languages, German can be combined with many commercial and other subjects to make you ultimately very employable. The economic powerhouse of Europe can absorb a great many foreign students in various capacities. Despite the current high level of unemployment, it is possible to arrange paid work experience independently, though easier with the help of a mediating organisation, teacher or contact.

The stereotype of the obsessively efficient and hard-working German is found by many gap year students to have a basis in truth but is not the whole truth. Institutionally, Germany can be inflexible and rule-bound, but individual Germans can be helpful and humorous.

Placement Organisations

GAP Activity Projects offer a variety of placements in Germany lasting 6-12 months departing September, January and February, with some date flexibility. Most positions are voluntary and in the field of caring, e.g. working in hospitals, schools for children with disabilities and residential homes for the elderly. Normally accommodation and pocket money are provided which means that the outlay for this programme is less than for most others, i.e. about £1000.

EIL (287 Worcester Road, Malvern, Worcs. WR14 1AB; 0800 018 4015; www.eiluk. org) arranges homestay, language courses and high school placements in Germany.

It is possible to use the Federal Employment Service from outside Germany. The *Zentralstelle für Arbeitsvermittlung* (Central Placement Office) has an international department *(Auslandsabteilung)* for dealing with applications from German-speaking people abroad. Details and application forms are available from ZAV, Villemombler Str. 76, 53123 Bonn (0228-713-1330; fax 0228-713 270 1037; Bonn-ZAV.Info-auslaensiche-studenten@arbeitsagentur.de). All applications from abroad are handled by this office. The Zentralstelle has a special department which finds summer jobs for students of any nationality, because this is felt to be mutually beneficial to employers and employees alike. Students who wish to participate in this scheme should contact ZAV before December. Students must be at least 18 years old, have a good command of German and be available to work for at least two months. Work is available in hotels and restaurants, as chamber staff and kitchen helpers, in industrial cleaning and in agriculture. The Zentralstelle assigns jobs centrally, according to employers' demands and the level of the candidate's spoken German. For example those with fluent German may be found service jobs while those without will be given jobs such as chambermaids or dishwashers. If you decline the first job offered by ZAV, you cannot be sure that they will offer another.

The IJAB (International Youth Exchange) in Bonn has a EuroDesk which administers European student exchanges (Heussallee 30, 53170 Bonn; 0228-95 06 208; www. eurodesk.de). The website www.prabo.de, available in English, describes itself as the leading free internship database for companies, students and anyone else who is looking for an internship in Germany. If you can read German fluently, try the job search sites arbeitsplaza.de and jobware.de.

The Happy Hands working holiday scheme places language and gap year students from the UK and the old EU countries in the field of rural tourism. Participants are given weekly pocket money of €51 and full board and lodging with families on farms or in country hotels. In return they look after children and/or horses and farm animals or take up serving and kitchen duties. The preferred stay is three to six months though a two-month commitment is also allowed; details available from Working Holidays in Germany, c/o Anne von Gleichen, Römerberg 8, 60311 Frankfurt; 069-293733; Anne.Gleichen@t-online.de; www. workingholidays.de. A fee of €180 must be paid after the placement is agreed and two weeks before it starts.

Internships for American students and graduates up to the age of 30 who can function in German are available in business, finance, engineering or technical fields through CDS International Inc. (871 United Nations Plaza, 15th Floor, New York, NY 10017-1814; 212-497-3502; www.cdsintl.org). If appropriate, the first month can be spent at an intensive language course in Cologne, after which participants undertake a paid or unpaid internship which they have secured previously with the help of CDS's partner agency InWEnt (Internationale Weiterbildung und Entwicklung gGmbH) with offices in Bonn and Cologne (www.inwent.org). The summer programme is open only to enrolled students (whose placement must be less than six months) whereas graduates are permitted to stay up to 12 months, extendable to 18. The average monthly compensation is €500, which will cover living expenses. The CDS programme fee is $700 and the deadline for the summer programme is mid-December.

Seasonal Work

As well as trying the Zentralstelle beforehand, you can try to fix up a summer job ahead of time by sending off speculative applications. This worked for **Dean Fisher,** an engineering apprentice who decided to take a break from what was turning out to be a discouraging job hunt at home. He went to wash dishes in Berchtesgaden on the Austrian border:

> I spent 2½ months working in a very orderly and efficient kitchen on the top of a mountain in the Kehlsteinhaus (Eagle's Nest) with the most amazing view I've ever seen. I actually enjoyed the work even though it was hard going. I met loads of good people and learned a lot of German.

Get hotel addresses from tourist office brochures or the web.

Recommended areas to try for a summer job are the Bavarian Alps (along the border with Austria), the shores of Lake Constance, the Bohmer Wald (along the Czech border), the Black Forest (in south-west Germany), and the seaside resorts along the Baltic and North Seas. One employer on the Baltic coast hires a number of foreign students as general assistants, food and beverage staff, child-carers and sports instructors at a coastal campsite/golf and holiday park. The hours are long and you must be able to speak German but the wages are good. Apply in the spring to Riechey Freizeitanlagan GmbH, 23769 Wulfen/Fehmarn (04371 862815; www.wulfenerhals.de/ENGLISCH/jobs.shtml).

Although few British tour companies operate in Germany, ski jobs can be found on-the-spot in resorts like Garmisch-Partenkirchen (which also has hotels and services for the American Army) on the Austrian border 50 miles southeast of Munich, and the spa resort of Oberstdorf in the mountains south of Kempten.

An international conference centre in the Harz Mountains employs young Europeans both short term (for the duration of a conference) or longer (up to one year) as domestic staff, looking after children and as conference assistants. Contact Internationales Haus Sonnenberg, Clausthalerstr. 11, 37444 St Andreasberg (www.sonnenberg-international. de).

Work Experience

Work placements can be organised in a wide range of sectors including tourism, trade, telecommunications, marketing and banking, depending on timing and availability. Most internships are organised in conjunction with an intensive language course. Normally an upper intermediate level of language ability is required for work experience to be successful. Most are unpaid or are rewarded only with a subsistence wage. Board and lodging will generally be provided only in the tourism sector.

DID-Deutsch Institute is a major language course provider (see 'Course Directory') which can also arrange two to six month internships following their language courses in Berlin, Frankfurt, Munich and Wiesbaden; the processing fee for an unskilled work placement is €350 while a qualified internship placement will cost €450 in addition to the preceding language course (e.g. €1,665 for 8 weeks). Similarly *GLS (Global Language Services)* combines a minimum 4-week language course with an internship in a Berlin-based company of 4, 8 or 12 weeks. Host companies want their trainees to speak German to at least an intermediate level.

Astur GmbH (Sturmiusstrasse 2, 36037 Fulda; 661-92802-0; info@astur-gmbh.de; www.astur-gmbh.de/work_1.html) organises linguistic stays in about 50 cities and towns around Germany with work experience placements lasting four to ten weeks or more for EU nationals only. An excellent standard of German is required to work in a German company, normally in industry, sales, marketing, administration, accountancy, tourism, law, translation or computers. Astur also arrange hotel experience placements for which candidates need an intermediate standard of German after a compulsory pre-placement language course. The Astur fee includes homestay accommodation starting at €1150 for four weeks.

Gwendalyne tries to match a student's area of interest with an unpaid work placement in a companies in Berlin and other major cities. Unless they are fluent in German, participants must do a 4-week German course (from £490) and also pay the placement fee of £315. Ten weeks of self-catering homestay accommodation would cost a further £690.

Interspeak (Stretton Lower Hall, Stretton, Malpas, Cheshire SY14 7HS; 01829 250641/ www.interspeak.co.uk) can arrange short and longer term traineeships (internships or *stages*) for students in hotels and offices. These unpaid placements last 1-24 weeks and include full board accommodation; the agency's registration fee is £80 and the placement fee is £340.

The Brussels-based linguistic and cultural exchange agency M.B. Language Asbl (41 rue Henri Bergé, 1030 Brussels, Belgium; 2-242 27 66/ macbaron@chello.be) arranges short placements in Lübeck for students aged 16-18 studying German; the placement fee for a two week summer placement and homestay is €475.

Graduates with a background in economics or business who can speak German have a reasonable chance of finding teaching work in a German city, since most of the demand comes from companies. A TEFL Certificate has less clout than relevant experience when looking for freelance English teaching work. University students and recent graduates who would like to spend a year as an English language assistant in a German secondary school should contact the Education & Training Group of the British Council at assistants@britishcouncil.org or www.languageassistant.co.uk. Altogether they place about 500 students aged 20-30 to work 12 hours a week. *Assistants* are paid about €700 a month. A few boarding schools in rural Germany employ gap year students aged 18-20 as helpers (junior assistants). These posts (only 8-10 per year) are normally reserved for students who apply through the *British Council* (10 Spring Gardens, London SW1A 2BN). To be eligible you must have A-level or equivalent German. You will receive free board and lodging and an allowance of at least €170 per month.

A list of opportunities to live and work in Germany can be found in the Jobs section of the British Council-hosted British German Youth portal The Voyage (www.the-voyage. com). Among the listings are work experience placements, au pairing and voluntary work. They suggest links (among others) to Eurostage (www.eurostage.org/de/accueiluk.htm).

School leavers with a particular field of interest can try to pursue it in their gap year in Germany. For example **Robin Lloyd** from Hampshire had always been interested in car design. With an A-level in German and a place at Bristol University to do a German and engineering degree, he wrote to a number of motor car manufacturers in Germany only to be told that he was too young and that they accepted only students already embarked on a university-level engineering degree. The one exception was BMW in Munich which runs a scheme for young trainees and who provided Robin with a pleasant flat on his own and enough wages to support himself in Munich for nine months. Although he found the formal protocol of German industry a little hard to swallow, he greatly enjoyed Munich and quickly developed a social life based on the city's Irish pubs. If you intend to look for a placement with a company, take evidence of any qualifications and some good references *(zeugnisse)* which are essential in Germany.

Philip Oltermann organised two work placements for himself, both in the German media, helped by the fact that he was born and had spent time living in Hamburg, where both the magazines were located:

I had read both magazines before when in Hamburg and got their addresses from the Yellow Pages. I phoned them up about a year before I started my year off and asked about the possibility of doing a work experience, then wrote an application soon after. They were both relatively small publications, one of them a sort of free city-mag with a focus on local politics and culture, the other the local Hamburg section of Germany's most alternative (and poorest) newspaper. This however turned out to be a big bonus in both cases, as I got to do a lot of independent work, i.e. doing research, taking pictures, writing larger articles and reviews, instead of just making coffee, as it seems to be the custom at bigger publishers.

Au Pairing

Most UK au pair agencies have partner organisations in Germany which make family placements. Some, like the Bloomsbury Bureau (Rokeby House, 86-90 Lambs Conduit St, London WC1N 3LX; 020-7430 2280; fax 020-7430 2325; bloomsburo@aol.com; www.bloomsburyaupairs.co.uk), specialise in Germany. Au pairs must have some knowledge of German and experience of childcare and those from outside the European Union must be aged 18-24.

Among the longest established agencies is the non-profit Roman Catholic agency IN VIA with 42 branches throughout Germany (Karlstrasse 40, Postfach 420, 79004 Freiburg (0761-200206; au-pair-invia@caritas.de; www.aupair-invia.de). Its Protestant counterpart is affiliated to the YWCA: Verein für Internationale Jugendarbeit (Goetheallee 10, 53225 Bonn; 0228-698952; www.vij-Deutschland.de). VIJ has 23 offices in Germany and places both male and female au pairs for a preferred minimum stay of one year, though six months can be considered.

With the deregulation of employment and recruitment agencies that took place in Germany several years ago, dozens of private agents have popped up all over Germany, many of them members of the German Aupair Society (www.au-pair-society.org) which carries contact details for its nearly 50 members. Commercial au pair agencies do not charge a placement fee to incoming au pairs.

Au-Pair Vermittlung, AMS Anna-Maria Schlegel, Postfach 5166, 79018 Freiburg (0761-70 76 917; info@aupair-ams.de; www.aupair-ams.de). Information in English on website.

Au Pair Interconnection, Staufenstr. 17, 86899 Landsberg am Lech (08191-941378; www.aupair-interconnection.de).

MultiKultur AuPair Service, Von-Werth-Str.48-50, 50670 Köln (0221-921 30 40; www.aupair.com). Places international au pairs throughout Germany.

Perfect Partners Au Pair Agency, Am Sonnenhügel 2, 97450 Arnstein (09363-994291;

www.perfect-partners.de).

The minimum monthly pocket money for an au pair in Germany has been pegged at €210 a month for a long time, though a proposal to raise it to €280 is awaiting ratification by German states. Some families offer to pay for a monthly travel pass or even cover your fare home if you have stayed for the promised period of nine months, typically up to €150. In return they will expect hard work which usually involves more housework than au pairs normally do.

VOLUNTARY WORK

Countless opportunities exist throughout the vast nation of Germany for undertaking voluntary work whether in environmental protection or in community service. The green movement in Germany is very strong and many organisations concentrate their efforts on arranging projects to protect the environment or preserve old buildings.

All the major workcamp organisations send people of all ages on short-term projects mostly in the summer. It is also possible to apply direct to an indigenous voluntary organisation such as:

As usual workcamps organisations in Germany normally recruit through national partners:

IJGD, Kasernenstrasse 48, 53113 Bonn (0228-22 80 00; www.ijgd.de). Scores of camps in Germany (fee about €100). British applications accepted by Concordia and UNA Exchange.

Internationale Begegnung in Gemeinschaftsdiensten (IBG), Schlosserstrasse 28, 70180 Stuttgart (0711-649 11 28/ www.workcamps.com). Publish a booklet in English of their projects in both eastern and western Germany.

Mountain Forest Project (Bergwald Projekt e.V.), Hauptstr. 24, 7014 Trin, Switzerland (081-630 4145; www.bergwaldprojekt.ch). One-week forest conservation projects in the alpine regions of southern Germany. Basic knowledge of German is useful since the foresters conduct the camps in German. Hut accommodation, food and insurance are provided free though participants must pay an annual membership fee of SFr60/€40.

Norddeutsche Jugend im Internationalen Gemeinschaftsdient (NIG), Am Gerberbruch 13A, 18055 Rostock (0381-492 2914; www.campline.de). Range of environmental and social projects in northeastern Germany.

Pro International, Bahnhofstr. 26A, 35037 Marburg/Lahn (06421-65277; www.pro-international.de). Social projects published in English (booklet and website). Application fee €65.

Vereinigung Junger Freiwilliger (VJF), Hans-Otto-Str. 7, 10407 Berlin (030-428 506 03; office@vjf.de). Camps take place in the former East Germany. Registration fee for applicants who apply directly is €220-€250.

There are some longer term possibilities as well. Internationaler Bund (IB, Burgstrasse 106, 60389 Frankfurt am Main; www.Internationaler-Bund.de) takes on young people for a period of six or twelve months in various social institutions such as hospitals, kindergartens, homes for the elderly or disabled people. In some German states, young people may also work on ecological projects. Volunteers are paid pocket money plus full board and accommodation. Their literature is published in English but their website is only in German.

COURSES AND HOMESTAYS

The main language provider is the government-funded *Goethe Institut* which has centres in London, Manchester, York and Glasgow as well as in nearly 20 German cities and towns. A list of addresses in Germany with full course details offered by each one is available from the website www.goethe.de or from the Goethe Institut in London (50 Princes Gate, London SW7 2PH; 020-7596 4000; german@london.goethe.org). The Goethe Institut administers language exams at all levels, leading to internationally recognised certificates such as the ZdaF, KDS and GDS. **Rosanne Curling** decided to spend eight weeks in the first part of her gap year learning German at the Goethe Institut in Dresden. The cost for the intensive course plus self-catering accommodation was £1300.

> *Although I had learnt German to GCSE level, I soon discovered that I could read and write much better than I could listen and speak, which meant that initially communication proved difficult. However I soon became accustomed to the 'Sachische' dialect and was able to differentiate the words, even if I could not understand them. It also took time to become accustomed to having lessons conducted entirely in German, as opposed to in England, where at least the grammar was explained in English. However in a class combining an Egyptian, a Japanese, a Ukrainian, a Pole, an American, a Cantonese and me, the only language common to all was German. This was a huge advantage of this course: the chance to meet a whole range of personalities from around the world and make great friends from a Venezuelan opera singer to an Italian voluntary worker.*
>
> *As well as enjoying the facilities of Dresden – the parkland, musical culture, hockey club – its location and Germany's fantastic public transport system allowed for many weekend excursions to Berlin, Prague, Leipzig and Weimar. On one trip I visited Buchenwald Concentration Camp which brought home the horrors of war in a way that sitting in a history class simply could not.*

All the major language course agencies like *CESA, EF, Caledonia* and *Euro Academy* run extensive programmes in Germany. Among the most popular destinations for year-out language students are Munich, Heidelberg and Freiberg, though less picturesque places will be cheaper. It might be worth noting that the purest German is spoken in the north, but even if you are living in Bavaria where there is a pronounced accent, the teaching will be of standard German.

BWS Germanlingua, GLS and *DID (Deutsch in Deutschland)* in the 'Directory of Language Courses' offer a selection of language courses. In some cases these can be followed by *stages* (internships) for those who achieve a satisfactory level of German. The average cost for a full-time two-week course is normally around €400 for tuition alone, €600-€650 with accommodation. Dialogue Sprachinstitut, Tonnelet 55, 4900 Spa, Belgium (+32 87-793010; info@dialogue.com/ www.dialogue.com) specialises in one-to-one tuition in Meersburg on Lake Constance with the possibility of a *stage* (internship) afterwards for those who achieve a satisfactory level of German. Fees for 18-22 year olds are from €1950 for one very intensive week (Monday-Friday) consisting of four one-to-one lessons each day and a homestay in a total immersion environment.

One of the great educational institutions of Germany is the *Volkshochschulen (VHS)* or folk high schools which can be found in nearly every town of the republic. In addition to offering 'German for Foreigners', it offers a range of evening classes in drama, handicrafts, sport and so on, all at subsidised prices. Most bookshops sell the prospectus of courses available for terms beginning in September and January. **Emma Colgan** was delighted with the *Volkshochschule* which she attended in Hamburg twice a week and also enjoyed the international make-up of the classes:

> *Our class resembled a United Nations meeting... Naturally the lessons were conducted in German and helped me to maintain my written German. At the end of the course in May, I sat the Mittelstufe Prüfung II as set by the Goethe Institut and passed with 'gut'. Unfortunately nobody seems to have heard of this exam in England.*

Nevertheless Emma was pleased with her achievement, since the *Volkshochschulen* courses are primarily designed for enjoyment.

The German Academic Exchange Service *(Deutscher Akademischer Austausch Dienst* or DAAD) with headquarters in Bonn has offices in London (34 Belgrave Square

London SW1X 8QB; 020-7235 1736; http://london.daad.de) and New York (871 United Nations Plaza, New York, NY 10017; 212-758-3223; fax 212-755-5780; daadny@daad. org/ www.daad.org). It assists people enrolled full-time at an institute of higher education to study or do research in Germany, and also has information about more general German courses. Every year the New York office produces a funding catalogue 'Grants for Study and Research in Germany'.

Greece

A generation ago, Greece was probably as popular a destination for student travellers between school and university as Australia or Thailand is now, but mass tourism has been moving away from Greece. Although many young people do want to spend time relaxing on a Greek island, fewer consider longer-term possibilities in Greece during their gap year. Anyone planning to read classics or archaeology at university will be attracted to the great sites of Greek antiquity as well as to the beautiful scenery and climate, friendly and carefree people, memorable wine and food. Anyone interested in picking up casual work to support a long stay should consult the book *Work Your Way Around the World* which has detailed information about finding work in resorts, on harvests, etc.

AU PAIRING & TEACHING

Living with a Greek family is one of the best ways of organising an extended stay. Yet au pairing hours tend to be longer in Greece than elsewhere, partly because there is no expectation that a gap year student will need time off to study the language. The Nine Muses Agency accepts applications from young Europeans and American women for au pair positions and can also place candidates after arrival in Athens. Hotel positions are also sometimes available. Contact the agency at PO Box 76080, 171 10 Nea Smyrni, (El. Venizelou 4b, 171 21 Nea Smyrni), Athens; 210-931 6588; www.ninemuses.gr). The owner Kalliope Raekou prides herself on her after-placement service, meeting regularly with au pairs at coffee afternoons. There is no fee to au pairs. Among her satisfied au pairs is Riitta Koivula from Finland who, from an unsatisfactory situation on Kos, moved with Popy Raekou's help to a much better one in Athens:

> I started my work as an au pair on Kos when I was 19. At first I was so excited about my new family and the new place since I had never been to Greece before and I loved the sun and the beach. I lived in a small village called Pili where almost no one spoke English. But soon I got tired of the village because winter came, tourists left and it wasn't so warm to spend time on the beach any more. I also got tired of the family. The three little girls didn't speak English and they were very lively. The work-ing hours were also terrible: 8 to 12 in the morning and then 4 to 10 in the evening every day except Sundays. I was very homesick on Kos and decided I wanted things to change. So I went to Athens in November and was soon given a new family. I fell in love with Athens and its people right away. My new family was the best and we are still very close. I met other au pairs and one Finnish au pair became my best friend. I learned so many things, even to read and write and speak Greek because we took Greek lessons during the spring with Popy. I have many happy memories of Athens and friends who are still dear to me.

Thousands of private language schools called *frontisteria* are scattered throughout Greece creating a huge demand for native English speaker teachers. Unfortunately for gap year students, all but the dodgiest schools will expect to see a university degree (which is a government requirement for a teacher's licence). The basic gross hourly wage is currently about €6 gross. Earnings can be increased substantially by compulsory bonuses at Christmas and Easter and holiday pay at the end of the contract.

University graduates who fancy the idea of taking a gap year teaching English in Greece after graduation should be aware that agencies exist to match graduates with 10-month vacant posts. Interviews are carried out in Greece and the UK during the summer for contracts starting in September. These agencies are looking for people with at least a BA and normally a TEFL certificate (depending on the client *frontisterion's* requirements). The following undertake to match EU nationals with *frontisteria* and do not charge teachers a fee:

Anglo-Hellenic Teacher Recruitment, PO Box 263, 201 00 Corinth (tel/fax 27410-53511; jobs@anglo-hellenic.com/ www.anglo-hellenic.com). Dozens of posts in wide choice of locations for university graduates from the UK, preferably with a CELTA or Trinity TESOL.

Cambridge Teachers Recruitment, 17 Metron St, New Philadelphia, 143 42 Athens (/fax 210-258 5155). Interviews conducted in UK in summer by Andrew MacLeod-Smith (macleod_smith_andrew@hotmail.com). One of the largest agencies, placing 75 teachers per year in vetted schools. Applicants must have a degree and in most cases a TEFL Certificate, a friendly personality and conscientious attitude.

After completing a PhD in classics at Cambridge but before landing a job, **Jamie Masters** decided to go to Crete to teach English and play music for a year. He arrived in Heraklion in October, when it was too late to register with agencies:

I advertised (in Greek) in the Cretan newspapers, no joy. I lowered my sights and started knocking on doors of frontisteria. I was put onto some guy who ran an English-language bookshop and went to see him. Turned out he was some kind of lynchpin in the frontisterion business and in fact I got my first job through him. Simultaneously I went to something which roughly translates as the 'Council for owners of frontisteria' and was given a list of schools which were looking for people. The list, it turned out, was pretty much out of date. But I had insisted on leaving my name with the Council (they certainly didn't offer) and that's how I found my second job

OTHER GAP YEAR OPPORTUNITIES

Seasonal Work

The Sani Beach Holiday Resort on the Halkidiki peninsula near Thessaloniki (www.saniresort.gr) employs a large number of hospitality industry trainees aged 18-20 for a minimum of five months on what they describe as a 'training wage' of €16-€18 per eight-hour shift (63077 Kassandra, Halkidiki; 23740-99447; groutsou@saniresort.gr).

Seasonal jobs can be arranged from the UK, preferably by contacting the tour operators in February or March. *Mark Warner* (08700 330750/60; www.markwarner-recruitment.co.uk) run several resort hotels in Greece which require British staff who are paid anything from £50 per week depending on the position in addition to full board and accommodation, use of watersport facilities and flights. Other possibilities are Olympic Holidays (1 Torrington Park, Finchley, London N12 8NN; 0870 499 6742; www.olympicholidays.co.uk) who are always on the lookout for outgoing EU nationals over 20; the Christian tour operator Mastersun Holidays (Thames House, 63-67 Kingston Road, New Malden, Surrey KT3 3PB; www.mastersun.co.uk) which employs about 100 summer staff for Greece; and Pavilion Tours (Lynnem House, 1 Victoria Way, Burgess Hill, West Sussex RH15 9NF; 0870 241 0425; www.paviliontours.com) which need watersports instructors for children.

Tour operators seem to be more interested in finding the right attitude rather than experience when recruiting reps, as Debbie Harrison discovered:

Last summer I worked as a holiday rep on the island of Kos. I was introduced to the tour operator by an English friend who had worked for them before. Despite the fact that I had no qualifications or relevant experience, had never been to Greece and had never even been on a package holiday, I was offered a job on the island I wanted immediately at the end of my interview. Perhaps this had something to do with the fact that it was mid-March, less than a month before training began and they obviously still had positions to fill. However tour operators do hire reps as late as May or June to help out with the extra workload of high season. Six or seven months is a long time to stay in one place. One of the reasons I stuck it out to the end was so I'd get my £100 deposit refunded. As a rep my wages were about £300 per month on top of accommodation. The youngest full-time rep was an 18 year old who had just finished a college course in Tourism, and at the other end of the scale, one of my colleagues was 28 and had resigned from her position at an advertising agency to work in the sun for a bit.

Another possibility is Sunsail International (The Port House, Port Solent, Portsmouth, Hants. PO6 4TH; 02392 222308; www.sunsail.com) who look to recruit staff over the age of 19. Sailing Holidays Ltd (105 Mount Pleasant Road, London NW10 3EH; 020-8459 8787; www.sailingholidays.com) look to hire flotilla skippers and hostesses, boat builders and marine engineers for their upmarket holiday programme in the Greek and Dalmatian islands. The specialist tour operator Setsail Holidays (PO Box 5524, Sudbury, Suffolk CO10 2ED; 01787 310445; boats@setsail.co.uk) recruits a similar range of staff for the six-month season in the eastern Med.

The internet is bound to turn up further possibilities.The monthly electronic jobs listing *Jobs Abroad Bulletin* (www.jobsabroadbulletin.co.uk) carries a sprinkling of vacancies in Greece, most recently by Naxos Camping (zorosia@otenet.gr), Hotel Coral in Roda, Corfu (coralhot@otenet.gr), No Limits Watersports Centre on the north coast of Crete (thoma3@otenet.gr) and the British-style Flying Pig pub in Piraeus (flying_pig_pub@yahoo.com). As always, young people, especially young women, considering a job overseas found over the internet, should go cautiously and should ask to be put in touch with one or two previous student workers before accepting.

It is also possible to show up and shop around for a job, but don't expect anything to happen quickly. Young women are far more likely to be hired by a bar or restaurant than chaps. Many gap year travellers stop a while in one place and swap some labour for free hostel accommodation. They enjoy the hostel atmosphere and the camaraderie among hostel workers, and regard the job as a useful stop-gap while travel plans are formulated, often based on the advice of fellow travellers. Those who stick at it for any length of time may find themselves 'promoted' to reception; in this business a fortnight might qualify you for the honour of being a long-term employee. The work is easy-come, easy-go, and is seldom secure even when you want it to be.

A great many hostels offer the same wage and perks to people who will spend a few hours a day cleaning. Consolas Travel near Omonia Square (100 Eolou St, 105 64 Athens; 210-324 1751; consolas@hol.gr; www.consolas.gr) is a travel agency that may be able to offer work in hostels, etc. in Athens and the islands of Paros and Gavdos.

The 1000-bedded Pink Palace on Corfu has been described by one reader as a cross between a Club Med for backpackers and an American summer camp, though it is to be assumed that neither Club Med nor children's camps are plagued with brawls and noisy drunkenness. The hostel employs an army of foreign workers as bartenders, cooks, receptionists, etc. (26610-53103; root@pink-palace.ker.forthnet.gr; www.thepinkpalace.com/employment.asp). Also on Corfu, the Sunrock Resort takes on young people under 25 for at least a month to work in exchange for room and board but no wages (Sunrock, Pelekas Beach, Sinarades, Corfu 490084; work@sunrockresort.com).

It is sometimes worth checking the Situations Vacant column of the English daily *Athens News* (9 Christou Lada, 102 37 Athens; an-classified@dolnet.gr). You can check the classified ads on the internet (www.athensnews.gr).

Another interesting possibility for people over 18 is at the holistic holiday centre on the island of Skyros in the northern Aegean. A number of 'work scholars' help with cleaning, bar work and domestic and maintenance duties in exchange for full board and accommodation and £40 a week. The minimum stay is three months from April or July. The main perk is that workers are allowed to participate in the multitude of courses and workshops on offer including windsurfing, music, theatre and yoga. Details are available from *Skyros*, 92 Prince of Wales Road, London NW5 3NE (020-7267 4424; www.skyros.com).

Conservation and Archaeology

Conservation Volunteers Greece (Veranzerou 15, 106 77 Athens; 210-382 5506; marina@cvgpeep.gr; www.cvgpeep.gr) is a non-profit organisation promoting intercultural exchanges and nature and heritage conservation. Projects include work in protected landscapes, conservation of traditional buildings and work on archaeological sites. Applications should be sent to a partner workcamp organisation in your country (e.g. UNA Exchange in the UK). The participation fee for people applying directly is €120 for two or three weeks (possible extra fee for special cultural camps).

Volunteers can become involved in monitoring the whale population from the coast of Kephalonia (see entry for the *Ionian Sea Research Centre* in the 'Directory of Voluntary Organisations'). On another Ionian island, Zakinthos, a project to protect sea turtles actively uses volunteer helpers. Archelon is the Sea Turtle Protection Society of Greece (Solomou 57, 104 32 Athens; tel/fax 210-523 1342; stps@archelon.gr; www.archelon. gr) which carries out research and conservation on the loggerhead turtle on Zakynthos, Crete and the Peloponnese. A free campsite is provided for those who stay at least a month; volunteers will need at least €15 a day for food plus pay a registration fee of €100. MEDASSET (Mediterranean Association to Save the Sea Turtles), 1c Licavitou Str, 106 72 Athens (210-361 3572; medasset@medasset.org; www.euroturtle.org/medasset) offers volunteers free accommodation in central Athens in exchange for working for a minimum of three weeks in the office providing administrative back-up for a sea turtle rescue project in Zakinthos and elsewhere in the eastern Mediterranean.

Bears are even more threatened than marine turtles. Arcturos accepts short-term volunteers at its bear protection centre. The office is at Victor Hugo 3, 546 25 Thessaloniki (2310-55 59 20; arcturos@arcturos.gr) whereas the Arcturos Environmental Centre is in the northwest corner of Greece (530 75 Aetos, Prefecture of Florina; 23860-41500, aec@arcturos.gr).

Voluntary Action for Youth (Athinas 13, Agia Varvara, Athens 123 51; 210-561 0728; www.youthcamp.gr) organises summer workcamps lasting 2-3 weeks in both Greece and Cyprus. Camp details are released mid-March. The participation fee is €130 which covers free accommodation and meals for the camp.

Nineteen year old **Giles Standing** became a subscriber to *Archaeology Abroad* at the beginning of his gap year and won one of their Fieldwork Awards to participate in a research dig on the Peloponnese and wrote an account of his experiences for the *Archaeology Abroad Bulletin*:

> On this particular dig, we were lucky enough to be staying and working in a beautiful rural part of Greece, deep in the heartland of the Peloponnesian countryside with its towering hills and ancient olive groves. We worked there Monday to Friday each week, with weekends left free for relaxing or taking trips to other archaeological sites. After years of being interested in ancient sites, it was an incredible experience for me to see Corinth, Delphi and the Acropolis at close quarters. I will not forget the first time I glimpsed the main body of the Parthenon through the massive columns of the Propylaia, truly a remarkable and humbling experience.

I was working on a farm track which was cut in half, running parallel to a field of lemons and another of grapes. We were investigating a target detected last year with GPR. Unfortunately the equipment was incorrectly calibrated and it became clear that this could not possibly be a Classical Greek site as the objects were far too close to the present-day surface level. Digging on the exposed road was surprisingly tough with the hottest part of the day reaching well into the 90s/30s on a daily basis. We worked roughly a seven-hour day with afternoons off to recuperate and we would meet later for dinner at a taverna on the beach.

Giles was the only Briton among Americans, all of whom had paid a large sum to join. The current costs are €800 per week for at least two weeks; further details are on www.helike. org. Note that *Archaeology Abroad* has distributed about a dozen Fieldwork Awards over the past two years, one in April 2005 to a gap year student joining a dig in Israel, but mostly to archaeology undergraduates and graduates.

Courses

Enjoyable as it is to master the Greek alphabet and learn simple greetings with which to befriend the locals, not many gap year students want to make a formal study of modern Greek. Any that do should enquire about courses in Athens, Thessaloniki and Crete such as those lasting between two and ten weeks offered by the *Athens Centre* (see entry in 'Directory of Language Courses') which charge from €300 for a two-week course and the same again for a studio apartment.

Emily Reardon decided she would like to spend February 2005 in Greece, since she had been studying Greek in New York City. She contacted a couple of language agencies and did her own research on the internet (checking past clients' feedback online) and chose the *Athens Centre*. Emily loved everything about Athens and Greece. She adored the Athens Center, her coursework, classmates, the staff, the set-up and the accommodation they offered (small, clean, Ikea-furnished studio/efficiency apartments shared between two). Her classmates were interesting and diverse in age and origins (USA and England in the majority but also France, Sweden and Turkey). The group planned things like eating out and travelling to one of the islands together, yet Emily felt safe and did explore on her own as well. She cannot wait to go back and feels that the Athens Centre is a wonderful place to study the language.

An alternative to the Athens Centre is DIKEMES (the International Centre for Hellenic and Mediterranean Studies in Athens, 5 Plateia Stadiou, 116 35 Athens; www.dikemes.gr) which offers semester and summer courses in Athens, in the history and culture of Greece as well as intensive courses in modern Greek. As well as operating in Athens, it offers summer courses from a secondary location on the island of Paros. This Centre is linked with the US organisation College Year in Athens (www.cyathens.org) but accepts other nationalities for some courses.

The Aegean Center for the Fine Arts (Paros 84400, Greece; 22840-23 287; studyart@aegeancenter.org) has been offering fine arts courses to individuals in small groups for almost 40 years at its centre on the Cycladic island of Paros. Students can create their individual curriculum with the help of artists-in-residence choosing from among the visual arts (photography, print making, painting and drawing) and literary arts (creative writing, literature, voice). One student said that she felt as though she had spent a whole semester on a film set rather than real life. The 14-week session from early March costs from €7,500; tuition fees can be reduced on the Work-Study programme.

Anyone interested in Greek folk culture might wish to contact the *Greek Dances Theatre* (8 Scholiou Street, Plaka, 105 58 Athens; 210-324 4395; www.grdance.org) which runs short courses and workshops on traditional dance and theatre over the summer. The organisation puts on a series of summer performances at the outdoor theatre on Philopappou Hill in Athens and takes on about ten unpaid foreign student volunteers to help look after the large costume collection and assist at performances.

Purely recreational courses in painting and photography can also be found. *Steve Outram's* travel photography courses in western Crete (see entry) are aimed more at photographers wanting to learn enough to take saleable photos. Unfortunately such courses tend to be expensive, e.g. more than $2000 for one week.

Italy

Italy has always been a favourite destination for young people wanting to expand their cultural horizons. In the 18th century, the Grand Tour of Europe, which was considered to be an essential part of the education of young men of good breeding or fortune, was centred on Italy; and generations of educated people journeyed between the great artistic centres of Venice, Florence and Rome. Although their modern-day equivalents are seldom accompanied by a private tutor, many now do enrol in courses which will help them to appreciate the art and civilisation of ancient Rome and Renaissance Italy.

Italy is still a remarkably welcoming country and Italians are capable of breathtaking generosity and hospitality, with no expectation of anything in return. Some first-time visitors mistakenly expect Italy to be poor and backward in some respects but instead they find the most cultivated and sophisticated people in the world, not to mention the best-dressed.

SPECIALIST GAP YEAR PROGRAMMES

Two exclusive cultural programmes in Italy maintain the tradition of the Grand Tour and are still aimed at young people of fortune since they are expensive. *Art History Abroad* and the *John Hall Pre-University Interim Course* both provide a superb introduction to European art and culture on their courses. Both are aimed at school leavers who may be planning to go on to university to study art history or who may just have an independent interest in Western history and civilisation.

John Hall offers courses in Italy for non-specialists on European civilisation, especially the visual arts and music, including architecture, conservation, opera, design, literature and Italian cinema. Practical options include Italian language, drawing, painting and photography. The spring course consists of an introductory week in London followed by six weeks in Venice where accommodation, meals, lectures, visits and classes are included in the price of £6400, with optional extra periods in Florence and Rome. Recent positive feedback from a course participant identifies as a highlight 'the chance to combine large doses of business and pleasure'.

Writing in the Easter 2005 issue of the *Old Sennockian* (the Newsletter of Sevenoaks School) **Johanna Walker** describes the ambitious range of the course:

> *Dr. Samuel Johnson once commented 'A man who has never been to Italy is always conscious of inferiority'. Although this attitude might not quite be at the forefront of a student's mind when it comes to planning the gap year, I can now see what Johnson was getting at. Having spent February and March 2004 on the John Hall Pre-University Course based in Venice, Florence and Rome, my appreciation of the fine arts and their relationship with culture is exceeded only by my desire to gloat to friends and family of my experiences on the Course. These have included notoriously privileged private visits to St. Mark's in Venice, the Accademia and Uffizi in Florence and finally a three-hour visit to the Vatican Museum including the Sistine Chapel.*

The Course was not, however, simply gallery visits. It included lectures from leading academics, day excursions into surrounding towns and elective photography and art classes taught by professionals, as well as Italian classes. The eight weeks spent in Italy offer students remarkable preparation for university life regardless of where their academic interests may ultimately land. The traditional idea of the Grand Tour is still very much alive and flourishing, which would certainly appease Dr. Johnson.

Art History Abroad offers four six-week programmes in the autumn (October-December), spring (January-March), early summer (April-May) and late summer (late August-September) plus three two-week courses in July-August. Their six-week programme involves travel throughout Italy, with all tuition on-site and not in classrooms, so that students are introduced to a broad spectrum of Italian life.

There are two options for the two-week courses with travel and education from Venice to Florence and then Rome, or a Classics-based course from Sicily to Naples, the Amalfi Coast and finally Rome. **Rebecca Udy** participated in the Art History Abroad Gap Course and clearly enjoyed escaping from the classroom between school and taking up a place to read English at Durham University:

Our tutors made the trip. They were absolutely passionate about what they taught, and went to every length possible to make it interesting and fun. It was so refreshing and exhilarating to meet people who had such a love for the arts; if we stopped in a queue, leather-bound notebooks were whipped out of their pockets, stuffed full of hand-written quotes and poetry which they read to us while we waited... If we went out in the evening, our tutors came with us; they took us to restaurants tucked round back streets, where they knew the owners, to little cafés where they knew a particularly good cup of coffee could be had. They became our friends, always up for a laugh and just as much a member of the group as any of us. Some were lecturers at London galleries, others had recently graduated. All had backgrounds in art history, loved what they were doing and were eager to share their enthusiasm. We were always taught in front of the painting or building we were discussing, which made the art come alive. We walked everywhere, or caught boats (Venice) or buses (the other cities), and began to catch our tutors' contagious fervour for their subject, and their sense of humour. We laughed so much.

The *British Institute of Florence* has developed a varied and interesting programme suitable for gap year students. The Institute runs year round courses in Italian language and Renaissance art history, and also Italian culture, life drawing, opera, landscape watercolours and Tuscan cooking. University accredited courses are also available during the year including Italian Cinema. Courses at the British Institute of Florence (www.britishinstitute.it) can combine language tuition with other subjects such as life drawing, opera and cookery, while accommodation is with selected families or in student flats. The Institute accepts other nationalities as well as British.

American students might also be interested in the study abroad semester and foundation year programmes offered by *Art Under One Roof* or the *Studio Art Centers International* both in Florence and both with entries in the 'Directory of Art Courses'. The Aegean Center for the Fine Arts based in Greece (Paros 84400, Greece; 284-23 287; studyart@aegeancenter.org) has been offering autumn courses in fine arts for many years at its centre in the Tuscan city of Pistoia before moving on to Paros (see chapter on Greece). Students study and practise the visual arts of their choice and are taken on excursions to Venice and Rome. The inclusive cost is €8000 for 14 weeks from early September; see www.aegeancenter.org for details.

COURSES & HOMESTAYS

Italian is one of the easiest and most satisfying languages to learn, especially if you already have some knowledge of a Latin-based language. Many courses combine Italian language lessons with art history, cuisine, etc. For example *Accademia Italiana* in Florence offers courses in design (fashion, furniture, graphic, textile, etc.) with language, while Linguadue (Corso Buenos Aires 43, 20124 Milan; 02-2951 9972; info@linguadue.com) and Linguaviva (Via Fiume 17, 50123 Florence; 055-28 00 16; info@linguaviva.it) offer a range of courses on Italian culture and language plus organise internships. The *Accademia del Giglio* in Florence offers Italian courses for foreigners plus art and art history courses.

Caledonia Languages Abroad offers a wide range of courses throughout the country, with schools in the main cities like Florence and Rome and in smaller lively university cities like Siena and Pisa.

An excellent source of Italian language, art and cookery school listings is the website www.it-schools.com. The Italian Embassy in London also provides a useful list at www.italyemb.org/Languagecourses.htm. The US site www.iiepassport.org also has many leads. Serious courses often work towards the *Certificazione di Italiano come Lingua Straniera* (C.I.L.S.) exam of the University of Siena and authorised by the Italian Ministry of Foreign Affairs which is divided into four levels. A further qualification from the Università per Stranieri di Siena is the DITALS.

For Italian language schools in the 'Directory of Language Courses', see entries for the *Koinè Center*, *Accademia del Giglio* and *Accademia Italiana* all in Florence,*Piccola Università Italiana* in Tropea on the western side of Italy's toe, *Atrium* in Cagli and *Auriga Servizi* in Pescara. Others to try include Il Sillabo (Via Alberti 31, 52027 San Giovanni Valdarno (AR); 055-912 3238; www.sillabo.it), most of whose clients are older, and the Accademia Britannica Toscana in Arezzo (Vicolo Pietro da Cortona 10, 52100 Arezzo; 0575.21366; www.etr.it/accademia_britannica). In Sicily Linguaviva's courses are delivered by the Mediterranean Center for Arts and Sciences (Palazzo Ardizzone, Via Roma 124, 96100 Syracuse; www.mediterraneancentre.it) which also puts on some classy summer courses e.g. a two-week course in ancient Greek costs €800 including accommodation.

An average starting price for one week's intensive study of Italian would be €175-€225 and €500 for four weeks. Accommodation in one of the major cities would cost a further €500+ a month bed and breakfast with a host family. Needless to say, courses in central Florence or Venice will be more costly than ones in more obscure towns.

On the Schools Programme offered by *AFS Intercultural Programmes UK* (Leeming House, Vicar Lane, Leeds LS2 7JF; 0113-242 6136; info-unitedkingdom@afs.org) students aged 15-18 spend an academic year or term living with an Italian family and attending the local school.

TEACHING

Hundreds of English language schools around Italy employ native English speakers though the majority are not suitable for gap year students unless they have acquired a qualification in Teaching English as a Foreign Language. But some do manage to find openings, despite their lack of a TEFL certificate. After P. Penn left his selling job, he went to Turin to find TEFL work and he succeeded without any experience whatsoever. But this is certainly the exception. Natalia de Cuba's experience is more typical: she could not persuade any of the language schools in the northern town of Rovereto where she was based to hire her without qualifications. So she decided to enrol in the Cambridge Certificate course run by International House in Rome (Viale Manzoni 22, 00185 Rome). She found the month-long course strenuous but not terribly difficult, and worth the fee (which now stands at €1500 plus €450 for accommodation). Job offers come into IH from all over Italy and no one seems to have a problem getting a job immediately after the course.

Several Italian-based chains of language schools might be worth a try. Recruitment is normally carried out by the individual schools, but the administrative offices or main websites should be able to provide a list of addresses. The British Schools Group (www.britishschool.com) has 70 member schools while the British Institutes (www.britishinstitutes.org) group has nearly 200 member schools. Oxford Schools hire up to 30 teachers for their 15 schools in northeast Italy (Via S. Pertini 14, 30035 Mirano, Venice; 041-570 23 55; www.oxforditalia.it).

As in other European countries, summer camps for unaccompanied young people usually offer English as well as a range of sports. The organisation called A.C.L.E. Summer & City Camps (Via Roma 54, 18038 San Remo, Liguria; tel/fax 0184-506070; www.acle.org) advertises heavily in the UK for more than 150 young people with a genuine interest in children who must be 'fun-loving, energetic and have high moral standards' to teach English and organise activities including drama for two, four or more weeks. The promised wage is €170-€190 per week plus board, lodging, insurance and travel between camps within Italy. However summer staff must enrol in a compulsory three or four-day introductory TEFL course for which €170-€190 is deducted from earned wages.

A less well known organisation also based in San Remo might be worth comparing: Lingue Senza Frontiere, Corso Inglesi 172, 18038 Sanremo (info@linguesenzafrontiere.org). They promise to pay their tutors €1750 plus board and lodging for eight weeks work in their English immersion summer camps. Another company that hires native English speakers to work at summer language camps is Smile (Via Vignolese 454, 41100 Modena; tel/fax 059-363868). The period of work is just three weeks from late August.

Holiday Animators & Entertainers

Various agencies recruit musicians, singers, DJs and entertainers for summer jobs around Italy. Italian companies would be unlikely to hire anyone unless they spoke more than just English. Here are a handful of companies that hire on quite a major scale:

R.I.S.I.C.O. srl, Via del Portonaccio 1, 47100 Forlì (FC) (0543 26199; www.risicoweb.it). Offers services for the tourist industry, mainly entertainers. The most important qualifications in candidates (who must be between 18 and 35) are availability, professionalism, kindness and creativity.

Planet srl, Animazione e Spettacolo, Via Circonvallazione Occidentale n° 102, 47900 Rimini (RN) (0541 787597; fax 0541 786159; www.planetvillager.com). This company recruits hundreds of staff not only in Italy but on recruiting trips to Belgium, Switzerland and the Czech Republic.

Anderson Animatore, Via Tevere 44, 00198 Rome (fax 06-884 4664; animazione@andersonclub.it). Employs more than 100 staff for tour operators and holiday villages.

Darwin srl, Turismo e Spettacolo, Piazza del Pesce 1, 50122, Florence (055 292114; darwinstaff@yahoo.it; www.darwinstaff.com). Large numbers of staff needed, e.g. 150 mini club animators to arrange children's holiday programme plus hostesses, DJs, musicians, etc.

Equipe Smile srl, Via Fioravanti 5/F, 40129 Bologna (051-370774; www.equipesmile.com). 150 animateurs/entertainers for Italian resorts in for example Lake Garda and Sardinia.

Rossodisera srl, Via M. Pagano 9, 71100 Foggia (tel/fax 0881-709951; www.rossodiseraanimazione).

Associazione Nazionale Animatori, Via Sicilia, 166/B, 00187 Rome (06-678 16 47; www.ilportaledegliartisti.it/ana.htm).

AU PAIRING

Summer-only positions are readily available. Most Italian families in the class which can afford live-in childcare go to holiday homes by the sea or in the mountains during the summer and at other holiday times which did not prove as idyllic as it sounds for **Jacqueline Edwards**:

> *My first job as an au pair in Italy was with a family who were staying in the middle of nowhere with their extended family. It was a total nightmare for me. I could just about say hello in Italian and couldn't understand a word of what was going on. After three weeks I was fed up, homesick and ready to jump on the next plane to England. But a few days later we moved back to town (Modena) and from then on things improved dramatically. I was able to go out and meet other au pairs and nannies at the park, etc. and we all socialised together. I ended up learning Italian quite well, making lots of friends (partly through my language school, which was free) and visiting most of the Italian cities. The only part that I didn't like in that job was going away with the family to their holiday houses for skiing, etc. You end up working twice your usual hours for the same pay, have no social life as you don't have any friends there, can't go skiing as you are minding the baby and then they tell you to cheer up because you're on holiday.*

The average weekly pocket money for au pairs is in the range €60-€70 and for mother's helps €500-€800 a month. Wages are slightly higher in the north of Italy than central and southern parts of the country because the cost of living is higher. The demand for nannies and mothers' helps able to work 40+ hours is especially strong since a high percentage of families in Italy have two working parents.

Most staff at Italian agencies speak English and welcome applications from British au pairs. Make sure first that you won't be liable to pay a hefty registration fee. Try any of the following:

ARCE (Attivita Relazioni Culturali con l'Estero), Via XX Settembre 20/124 16121 Genoa (010-583020; fax 010-583092; www.arceaupair.it). Long established agency which makes placements throughout the country.

Au Pair International, Via S. Stefano 32, 40125 Bologna (051-267575/238320; www.aupair-international.com). Member of IAPA. No placement fee.

Au Pairs Recruitment, Via Gaeta 22, 10133 Turin (annaparavia@paravia.it).

Euroma, Viale B Buozzi 19 AA, int 3, 00197 Roma (06-806 92 130). €130 fee.

Euro-Placements Italy srl, Via Felica Cavallotti 15, 20122 Milan (02-760 18 357; www.euro-placements.com).

Intermediate SNC, Via Bramante 13, 00153 Rome (06-57 47 444; www.intermediateonline.com). Intermediate has its own language school in the Aventino district of Rome.

PAID OPPORTUNITIES FOR GAP STUDENTS

Working in Italy is something of a hit and miss situation and if you can't speak a word of Italian, you will be at a distinct disadvantage. Contacts are even more important in Italy than in other countries. Louise Rollett, for example, first went out as a paying guest to a town near Bologna with *EIL* and then extended her stay on a work-for-keep basis as an English tutor. Dustie Hickey went for treatment to a doctor in Milan who immediately offered to pay her to tutor his children in English.

You are not expected to speak Italian if you work for a British tour operator; in fact German is probably more sought after than Italian because of the high number of German tourists in Italy. Try any of the major campsite tour companies like *Canvas, Holidaybreak, Eurosites, Keycamp* or *Siblu Holidays by Haven Europe* who are looking primarily for people over 18 with customer service skills. The smaller Venue Holidays (1 Norwood St, Ashford, Kent TN23 1QU; www.venueholidays.co.uk) employs summer season reps at campsites on the Venetian Riviera, Lake Garda and in Tuscany.

Winter Resorts

Crystal Holidays, part of the Thomson Travel Group (King's Place, Wood St, Kingston-upon-Thames W4 5RT; 020-7420 2081; www.shgjobs.co.uk) hire resort reps and chalet staff for work in the Italian Alps as well as staff for summer holidays. The Ski Department of PGL Travel Ltd (Alton Court, Penyard Lane, Ross-on-Wye, Herefordshire HR9 5GL) offers some jobs as ski reps, leaders and ski/snowboard instructors to fully qualified skiers, especially for short periods during half-term and Easter holidays.

If you haven't fixed up a job with a UK tour operator, job openings can be found on-the-spot in the winter resorts of the Alps, Dolomites and Apennines. Many are part-time and not very well paid, but provide time for skiing and in many cases a free pass to the ski-lifts for the season. During her gap year before going to Nottingham University, Jaime Burnell from Hungerford was not very thrilled with her job with a British ski tour operator near Trento:

> *The initial honeymoon period of thinking I was extremely clever for getting work with a British tour company ended quickly when I was hit with the bombshell that I was to be put in the smallest resort on the programme. Quite frankly the work is only bearable when the nightlife and skiing are great so working in a resort where the nightlife was non-existent and the clients were therefore miserable, is it really surprising that two 18 year olds were unhappy and decided to quit? The whole skiing scene relies on the fun you have outside work. No fun at night, then all you have is a boring life which just happens to be in a ski resort.*

Things looked up enormously when she travelled independently to Sauze d'Oulx to look for work:

> *I cannot recommend enough winter work in Sauze d'Oulx. I arrived on the 14th of January. Everyone tells you that the turnover is high but that is an understatement. Going out every night you couldn't be sure who would be behind the bar that day.*

Jaime goes on to offer one more nugget of information which proves once and for all that blondes really do have more fun:

> *The best investment you can make in Italy is a bottle of blonde hair dye. My tips tripled.*

Other Jobs in Tourism

As throughout the world, backpackers' haunts like hostels and campsites often employ travellers for short periods. While planning her escape route from a less-than-satisfactory summer au pairing job in Naples, Jacqueline Edwards asked in the Sorrento youth hostel about job possibilities and a few weeks later moved in to take over breakfast duties in exchange for free bed and breakfast.

By making use of www.hostels.com Debra Fuccio from the US had little difficulty pre-arranging a hostel job:
Never in a million years did I think that watching MTV would be part of my daily life in Rome. The hostel I was working at was Hostel Casanova (Via Ottorino Lazzarini, 12, 00136 Rome; 06-397 45228; hostelcasanova@yahoo.com). I was working 7 days a week (I was a bit scared about running out of money since this was the first leg of the trip). The shifts would alternate from evening to morning every day: one day doing the morning shift when the hostel was cleaned and the next day the evening shift. As well as getting to stay there for free, they paid me and my co-worker €20 per day in cash which was really nice. Rome was so cheap (from a San Francisco point of view) and with great weather, it was easy to save. I came to

Italy with $700 cash and a plane ticket, I left with about $600 and a plane ticket to England and Ireland, having been there about 5 weeks total.

VOLUNTARY WORK

Many Italian organisations arrange summer work projects which are as disparate as selling recyclable materials to finance development projects in the Third World to restoring old convents or preventing forest fires. An intercultural exchange organisation with a website in English and a far-reaching long-term incoming programme is AFSAI (Viale dei Colli, Portugensi 345 B2, 00151 Rome; 06-537 0332; www.afsai.it).

Here is a selection of voluntary organisations that run working holidays. In some cases, it will be necessary to apply through a partner organisation in your home country:

Abruzzo, Lazio and Molise National Park, c/o National Parks Office, Viale Santa Lucia, 67032 Pescasseroli (AQ) (0863-91131; info@parcoabruzzo.it). Volunteers carry out research and protection of flora and fauna in remote locations. Further details are available by contacting the local park offices in Pescasseroli (0863-911 3242) or Villetta Barrea (0864-89102; fax 0864-89132).

AGAPE, Centro Ecumenico, 10060 Prali (Torino) (0121-807514; www.agapecentroecumenico.org). Volunteers help run this ecumenical conference centre in the Alps, about 80 miles from Turin. Stays usually last 3-5 weeks.

CTS, Dipartimento per la Conservazione della Natura, Via A. Vesalio 6, 00161 Rome (06-4411 1476; www.cts.it).

Emmaus Italia, Campi di Lavoro, Via Mellana 55, 12012 Boves (CN) (tel/fax 0171-387834; www.cuneo.net/emmaus/giovanni/index.htm). Workcamps to collect, sort and sell second hand equipment to raise funds for social and community projects worldwide.

LIPU, Lega Italiana Protezione Uccelli, 0521-273043; www.lipu.it). Long-established environmental and bird conservation association which publishes a catalogue of summer projects at its bird reserves *(oasi)* throughout Italy. Volunteer camps cost approximately €150 per week.

La Sabranenque, Centre International, rue de la Tour de l'Oume, 30290 Saint Victor la Coste, France (04-66 50 05 05; www.sabranenque.com). French-based organisation uses voluntary labour to restore village and monuments in Altamura (inland from Bari in Southern Italy). The cost of participation is $630 for two weeks in July.

WWF Italia, Servizio Campi, Via Po 25/C, 00198 Rome (06-844971; www.wwf.it/ENG/holiday/listcamps.asp). A few environmental conservation camps, though the emphasis is on holidays. Sample 9-day fire-watching camps in Sicily cost €233.

Volunteers can also join archaeological camps. The national organisation Gruppi Archeologici d'Italia is the umbrella group for regional archaeological units that co-ordinate 2-week digs (Via Baldo degli Ubaldi 168, 00165 Rome; tel/fax 06-3937 6711; segreteriagai@infinito.it; www.gruppiarcheologici.org) Paying volunteers may join these digs (e.g. €350).

Malta

Although small in area (30km by 15km), Malta has much of interest. The student and youth travel organisation NSTS (220 St Paul St, Valletta VLT 07; 246628/www.nsts.org) markets English courses in conjunction with sports holidays for young tourists to Malta. NSTS run weekly vacation courses from June to August, which might take on a water sports enthusiast on a work-for-keep basis.

The Malta Youth Hostels Association (17 Triq Tal-Borg, Pawla PLA 06; +356 2169 3957; myha@keyworld.net) can put unpaid volunteers aged between 16 and 30 to work for three hours a day over a short period. A longer commitment of full-time work over 6, 9 or 12 months is open to EU national aged 18-25 who will receive free accommodation and meals. Jobs to be done include administration, decorating, building, etc.

Russia & Eastern Europe

While Russia has been wrestling with its political and economic demons, the more stable Central European states of Hungary, Poland, the Czech Republic and Slovakia have steadily moved towards the west to the point where they have been accepted into the European Union as of May 2004 along with Slovenia, Estonia, Latvia and Lithuania (with a possibility of Romania and Bulgaria joining in a few years time). However there are reciprocal transitional controls on the free movement of labour and in most cases very high rates of unemployment.

During the heady days immediately after the various Communist governments fell (when gap year students were aged about three), thousands of young Westerners flocked to Prague, Budapest and Kraków. Many of them supported themselves for short and longer periods by teaching English to a population which clamoured for access to English-language media and culture. Things have settled down now and there has been a mild backlash in some quarters against what has been seen as a selling out to the West, especially in the major capitals which have been swarming with foreigners (especially Americans) since 1990.

ENGLISH TEACHING

Several English-teaching schemes are described in this chapter suitable for a gap before or after university. Most participants will be sent to small provincial towns and industrial cities rather than to the glamorous capitals. In Russia, the Baltic states of Latvia, Lithuania and Estonia and the other states of the old Soviet Union, the English teaching situation is more fluid. Native speakers can still arrange some kind of teaching, often on a private basis, but with no guarantee of earning a living wage from it.

Placement Organisations

While commercial EFL recruitment agencies are involved with filling vacancies in Eastern Europe with certificate-holding teachers, educational charities and year out placement organisations send volunteer teachers, in ever decreasing numbers as those countries train their own English teachers. For example *Teaching & Projects Abroad* sends TEFL volunteers to Russia and Romania. A Teaching Abroad package of up to three months teaching in Moscow or St Petersburg costs £1445 (without travel) or £1345 in Brasov, Romania. They also offer work experience in various fields, e.g. conservation, journalism and archaeology.

With *Travellers* (7 Mulberry Close, Ferring, West Sussex BN12 5HY; tel/fax 01903 502595; www.travellersworldwide.com), paying volunteers teach conversational English in Russia and the Ukraine. Work experience placements are available in both countries, in journalism, law, medical care and veterinary medicine. Prices start at £925 for 3 months teaching in Kiev (excluding international travel).

Services for Open Learning or *SOL* (2 Bridge Chambers, The Strand, Barnstaple, Devon EX31 1HB; 01271 327319/fax 01271 376650; info@sol.org.uk; www.sol.org.uk) is a non-profit-making organisation which annually recruits about 30 graduates with a recognised TEFL Certificate to teach in schools in the state sector in most Eastern and Central European countries, especially Hungary and Romania. Contracts with individual schools are mostly for a complete academic year September to June.

Language Link (21 Harrington Road, London SW7 3EU; 020-7225 1065; www.languagelink.co.uk) is a TEFL training and recruitment agency that places post A-level (and older) students in one-year teaching positions in Russia after they complete a four-week

Cambridge Certificate in TEFL.

The youth exchange company *CCUSA* runs a Summer Camp Russia Programme whereby teacher/counsellors are placed on youth camps in Russia lasting four or eight weeks between mid-June and mid-August. Participants must be between the ages of 18 and 35, have experience working with children and/or abroad, and have an interest in learning about the Russian language and culture. Camps are widely scattered from Lake Baikal in Siberia to the shores of the Black Sea. The programme fee of £795 includes round-trip travel from London to Moscow, visa, travel insurance, orientations on arrival and room and board. In the UK contact CCUSA at Devon House, 171/177 Great Portland St, London W1W 5PQ (020-7637 0779; www.ccusa.com) or in the US: 2330 Marinship Way, Suite 250, Sausalito, CA 94965 (800-449-3872). Since 2003, CCUSA have been running a new venture in Croatia, a language camp for European teenagers for which English-speaking counsellors are needed; details from www.campcalifornia.com.

APASS UK North is the Anglo-Polish Universities Teaching Project which supplies native-speaker tutors to summer language camps and schools. The programme invites young volunteers over 16 (with parental permission) as well as older volunteers to spend July and/or August in Poland. Furnished accommodation and food are provided for three weeks teaching (2½ hours of English conversation and instruction per day) and there is one week allocated for a tour of Poland. All expenses and pocket money are paid by the Polish host. An information pack about the programme including placement fee can be requested by sending an s.a.e. (45p stamp) and £3 postal order to APASS, UK North, 93 Victoria Road, Leeds LS6 1DR; fax 020-7498 7608 (they have no website). Reports have been received that details of these summer placements are finalised not long before departure, so be prepared to endure some suspense.

Some gap year students are enterprising enough to arrange teaching jobs with indigenous organisations like one of the following:

Akademie J.A. Komenskeho, Trziste 20, Mala Strana, 118 43 Prague 1 (02-5753 1232; www.akademie.cz). Many posts in 50 adult education centres and schools throughout the Czech Republic where British native speakers (including gap year students) are employed. Monthly net wage is 8,000 crowns.

English School of Communication Skills/ESCS, Personnel Department, ul. Walowa 2, 33-100 Tarnów (607-616-605; personnel@escs.pl; www.escs.pl) which hires 100 EFL teachers for five language schools in southern Poland and summer language camps at the Polish seaside. Pay at ESCS is 2200 zloties a month. Candidates with no TEFL training are obliged to take a pre-term methodology course plus ESCS offers its own three-week TEFL training course in September.

International Exchange Center, 20 Kalku St, LV-1050 Riga, Latvia (+371 2-722 8228; fax +371 2-783 0257; info@iec.lv) recruits young people with a TEFL qualification for summer language camps in Russia as well as Ukraine, Belarus and a few in Latvia. It offers between 20 and 40 hours of teaching in return for a salary equivalent to local rates or free board and lodging. The application fee is $150. Further information is available through the partner agency in the UK: International Student Exchange Center (89 Fleet St, London EC4Y 1DH; 020-7583 9116; fax 020-7583 9117; www. isecworld.co.uk).

Svezhy Veter Travel Agency, PO Box 2040, 426000 Izhevsk, Russia (tel/fax 3412-450037; sv@sv-agency.udm.ru/ www.sv-agency.udm.ru). Native speakers needed to teach evening course (15 hours a week) at Secondary School No. 27 in Izhevsk in exchange for homestay with meals and visa support (which costs $34-$132 depending on how far in advance you apply). Registration fee is €148.

Koober Grob from Chicago was impressed with this arrangement she'd tracked down on the internet, and found lots of scope for initiative:
I corresponded with Vladimir Bykov (the teacher I would eventually work with) for seven months before I went to Izhevsk. The students and I would discuss

> *various topics such as domestic violence, cooking, nature, war or even manure and chocolate-covered ants. There was never any pretence in any of the classes. Eventually I started a theatre club for teenagers at a local school and then accompanied a six–week school trip around Siberia helping students individually with their English. The students were all so motivated, respectful and friendly. I only spent $600 for the three-month period that I was in Russia since Russia is very inexpensive and my students and friends paid for most of my expenses.*

Year-out students often end up providing conversational English practice for the older classes in secondary schools, which means they are teaching people nearly the same age as they are, as happened to **Trudie Darch** who spent a year teaching in Hungary through GAP:

> *I had been there three weeks and with very little notice I was told that I'd be teaching on my own for one whole week. This was the scariest thing that had happened so far. Virtually unprepared, I walked into a classroom full of 18 year olds (I was 19) and had to teach. The first lesson was not very good and I had some difficulties getting them to listen to me. It was hard to get over the fact that these were my students not people who were supposed to be my friends. However I overcame this and learnt that to be a more professional teacher, I had to distance myself from trying to be their friend. The school was basic, the food was interesting (pasta and icing sugar was one I hated) and my accommodation left a lot to be desired. But even the bad things I wouldn't swap because they taught me a lot.*

Obviously the experience was not too off-putting since on her return she went off to Lancaster University to start a teaching course.

Helen Fagan did not have to work to gain her pupils' respect in her GAP placement in a remote Hungarian village:

> *Arriving at the children's home where I was to teach is one of my most treasured and vivid memories. As we pulled up outside this very grand old building, the young-est boy from my group met me with a bunch of flowers and a kiss. As I proceeded down the stairs, all 50 children were holding small bunches of flowers which they presented to me individually with a kiss, a traditional Hungarian welcome. The low point of my placement in Hungary was definitely the day I had to leave.*

COURSES & HOMESTAYS

Ironically the study of Russian has been in sharp decline since Russia abandoned Communism and decided to throw in its lot with western capitalism. Compared to the heady 1960s, few schools and universities offer Russian. However there is still a contingent that want to be able to communicate in the language of Tolstoy, undaunted by reports of escalating crime.

The big language agencies like *Caledonia, CESA, EF* and *Euro-Academy* all offer Russian courses in Russia, particularly St Petersburg. The London office of the *Society for Co-operation in Russian and Soviet Studies* (320 Brixton Road, London SW9 6AB; 020-7274 2282; www.scrss.org.uk) can arrange courses and homestays lasting as long as you like. Sample courses include a four-week summer course in Moscow for £595 including accommodation but excluding meals and airfares, and a 'Russian at Home' programme whereby you live in your tutor's home and receive 15 hours of individual tuition a week; the weekly price is £550. Look also at the programmes offered by the Finnish-based *Proba International Education Centre* and the *Moscow Institute for Advanced Study* or MIFAS (entries in 'Directory of Language Courses'). Proba offers a combined language study with voluntary work, one month each for €2050 or two months for €2850. MIFAS arranges post-language course internships with high level companies and organisations, provided the applicant has reached a high enough standard of spoken Russian.

Eighteen year old **Kathryn Emmett** wanted to gain a good basis in Russian and really wanted to get to know the country, so she booked a ten-week course in St Petersburg through *CESA Languages Abroad* with which she was delighted:

> *I was really impressed with how much Russian I could learn in 2½ months. I certainly got to see the many faces of Russia just by going out for a drink and shopping. It was the normal things that made it unforgettable like going to a kiosk to buy a beer. The excursions were a good way of getting to know other students as well as going to places a bit further afield that at the beginning I didn't have the courage to do alone.*
>
> *The teaching staff were brilliant. I still don't know how they got me from absolute beginner who panicked at the utterance of any Russian word to being quite comfortable with the language. I'd tell everyone to go to Russia as long as they don't mind giving up a few creature comforts (like baked beans).*

Kathryn reports that many a friendship with her fellow students blossomed over the topic of food.

VOLUNTARY WORK

The vast region of Eastern Europe is a hive of workcamp activity during the summer, so if a short-term group voluntary project appeals to you at all, contact the main UK workcamp organisations listed in the 'Directory of Volunteering Abroad', all of which have partners in Eastern Europe. In many cases the projects are a pretext for bringing together young people from East and West in an effort to dismantle prejudice on both sides. Often discussion sessions and excursions are a major part of the three- or four-week workcamps and some volunteers have been surprised to find that their experiences are more like a holiday, with very little work expected. The people of Eastern Europe are repeatedly praised for their generosity and hospitality.

Some preparation is recommended by all the recruiting organisations and participants are encouraged to get some workcamp experience closer to home first and to attend orientations. The registration fee is normally higher than for Western Europe, say £130-£150. Projects vary from excavating the ancient capital of Bulgaria to organising sport for gypsy children in Slovenia. There is also a high proportion of much-needed environmental workcamps.

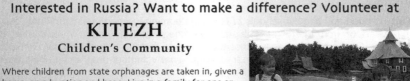

Many international voluntary schemes are particularly active in the region including the fully funded *European Voluntary Service* and its agencies like *Inter Cultural Youth Exchange (ICYE)* whose 'Eastlink' programme this year sent volunteers aged 18-25 to Latvia, Estonia, Poland and the Russian Federation from January to August; the volunteers incur no expense.

Kitezh Children's Community for orphans in Kaluga, 300km south of Moscow, has close links with the *Ecologia Trust* in Scotland (see entry in 'Directory of Volunteering Abroad'). The Trust specifically recruits students in their gap year to spend on average two months at Kitezh and provides extensive preparatory information, down to profiles of the resident children. The joining fee is £540 for one month, £710 for two months, including visa fee but not airfares to Moscow.

Many recent volunteers have found Kitezh a friendly, welcoming and relaxing place to spend some time, among them Alex Nice, now a student (of Russian and German) at Cambridge:

If it weren't for the minibuses, you could almost imagine you'd wandered into the world of Hans Christian Anderson. It's particularly beautiful in winter, when the snow sparkles on the roofs of the log houses, and the birch forests seem to glow in the moonlight. But Kitezh's fairytale quality lies deeper than just its wooden houses and picturesque setting. There really is something almost miraculous about what is being achieved in this small village in the middle of the Russian countryside.

Kitezh is a special and unique place. It is not simply a therapeutic centre for children; it is also an attempt to create a new form of community living. If you want to volunteer in Kitezh you must embrace everything that makes it different from the outside world. Community living can be demanding: you cannot simply work in Kitezh; you have to live in it and be a part of the community. The more you involve yourself in the community, the more you'll get out of it. All of Kitezh's houses are open to everyone at any time and Russians have a sense of active hospitality which is quite alien to most foreigners. Kitezh is held together by a spirit of friendship and openness that very quickly communicated itself to me and helped me to feel at home within a few days.

The actual work you do in Kitezh really depends on you. Teaching English is probably the most important skill you can bring to the community, though there is plenty of opportunity to help with manual labour or in the kitchen if that appeals more. I found myself doing all kinds of things: chopping wood, organising birthday parties, translating texts, helping to direct the New Year musical, even giving an interview for Russian television! It's really up to you. Friends were often surprised that I didn't get bored living for three months in a village of sixty people. The truth is I don't think I've ever been busier in my life.

Romania

The orphanages and special schools of Romania continue to need voluntary input more than 16 years on from the fall of Ceausescu who neglected the needs of his citizens so abominably. Of the many charities that were formed to help the children of Romania, the Nightingales Children's Project operates a full-time volunteer programme. Volunteers spend from one to three months working at an orphanage in Cernavoda, 80km from the Black Sea resort of Constanta. Volunteers work with the children, some of whom are disabled and have special needs, some with the HIV virus. Accommodation is shared with eight volunteers in a flat; volunteers contribute £2.50 a day to cover their rent and food. For further information contact the director on info@nightingaleschildrensproject.co.uk (www. nightingaleschildrensproject.co.uk).

British-Romanian Connections, PO Box 86, Birkenhead, Merseyside CH41 8FU (tel/ fax 0151-512 3355; brc@pascu-tulbure.freeserve.co.uk) operates summer language camps in Romania as well as English clubs year round in Piatra-Neamt. Native speakers are welcome at camps but language clubs are looking for teachers with a TEFL qualification (minimum stay three months).

Writing in her college magazine, Emma Hoskison reminisced about her time spent with the orphans of southeast Romania:

During my Gap Year I spent the summer working for the Nightingales in Romania. Every day we went to the state-run orphanage and spent the morning and evening with our 'salons', groups of about 8 children of varying ages from 6 months to 10 years who had been neglected or abandoned due to some physical disability or financial reason (few of them were truly orphans). Many of the children did not speak and social interactions were minimal, so we used activities and games to stimulate their speech and learning. The charity provided many exciting toys and resources for the children. I tried hand printing once and they seemed more interested in throwing the paint around the room and over me! After every session, all the toys were locked away to prevent the nurses taking them home, such is the poverty there. Several children had mobility problems, so much time was spent walking around the grounds or in the playground; the swings were a great favourite with some. The time I spent in Romania was extremely challenging both emotionally and physically, yet it was the most rewarding experience of my Gap Year. I met some amazing people who have devoted years of their lives to the children's welfare and I often think of how my little friends are growing up, picturing their smiley faces.

Although conditions are much better than they were in the early years, the work can still be emotionally very draining. One gap year student who spent time in a Romanian orphanage suffered recurring nightmares for a long time after going on to university at Cambridge.

In the lead-up to summer 2005, DAD International UK Romania (+40 726 265523; www.dad.ro) was advertising for volunteers (e.g. on the website www.justjobs4students. co.uk) to teach English informally at three summer camps located in Transylvania, Moldavia and on the Black Sea Coast. The three or four week camp sessions begin mid-June, early and late July and mid-August. The scheme bestows full board and accommodation, transfers, travel insurance, a Romanian phrasebook and excursions in exchange for working with the children up to six hours a day. Expect to pay about £370 for the return flight plus admin fee. Writing in the King's College London student newspaper *Roar* in March 2005, a recent volunteer wrote enthusiastically about the DAD scheme:

Despite wanting to, I had been advised not to take a gap year after my A levels and so I was determined to make up for this missed opportunity by doing something productive during my first summer break. It just goes to show that, as long as you make the most of the holidays, you don't need a whole year to experience other cultures. The Romanians I met were tremendously hospitable and gracious and the children were extremely compassionate and affectionate. The 15 kids I taught were articulate and well behaved, their level of English comprehension was phenomenal and they were exceptionally cute. Teaching the children at Bacau camp was an absolute pleasure and privilege.

TRAVEL

The Trans-Siberia rail journey persists in capturing the imagination of adventurous travellers. Note that booking this journey through an agent can more than double the price. On Ben Spencer's gap year, he and his friends started in China and decided to buy the various legs of the journey locally which meant that they got from Beijing to Moscow for £200 each. They greatly enjoyed being the only foreigners out of hundreds of friendly Russians (one of whom came to their rescue when Ben's friend left his wallet containing

$400 in the toilet and it was returned to him). They disembarked a couple of times, i.e. in Ulaan Bator, Mongolia for five days, Irkutsk for five days and Ekaterinburg for two days, so that the longest single stretch was 51 hours.

A recommended specialist for independent travel in Russia is Findhorn EcoTravels, 66 The Park, Forres, Morayshire IV36 3TZ (tel/fax 01309 690995; travel@ecologia.org.uk). They can also arrange homestays.

Scandinavia

Not every gap year traveller wants to hit the trail to the tropics. The Scandinavian countries of Denmark, Sweden, Finland, Norway and Iceland exercise their own fascination and can be visited as part of an Inter-rail tour of Europe or separately. Economy fares are available from DFDS Scandinavian Seaways (www.dfdsseaways.co.uk) on their ferry routes from Harwich or Newcastle to Denmark and Sweden.

One way of getting away from the notoriously high cost of living and of travel in this region is to join one of the organised schemes described in this chapter, for example working on a Norwegian farm or on a Swedish commune. Alternatively you can try to find work on your own, though this will be a challenge.

The demand for English-speaking au pairs is not vast but remains steady, especially in Denmark, where a certain number of young women over 18 are placed with families for 10-12 months. The au pair placement activities of the Danish exchange agency Exis were taken over in 2004 by Au Pairs International, Sixtusvej 15, 2300 Copenhagen S (+45 32-841002; info@aupairsinternational.dk). It makes placements in Denmark, Norway, Iceland and Sweden as well as worldwide. Weekly pocket money varies, but some families pay around €100.

Another possibility is the Scandinavian Au-Pair Service Center (scandinavian@aupair. se; www.aupair.se) whose website provides contact names, phone numbers and email addresses for its representatives in Helsingborg (Sweden), Oslo and Hamar (Norway) and Aalborg (Denmark) among others.

Americans should make contact with the American-Scandinavian Foundation (Exchange Division, 58 Park Avenue, New York, NY 10016; 212-879-9779/fax 212-249-3444; trainscan@amscan.org; www.amscan.org) which places about 30 American trainees aged 21-30 each summer in the fields of engineering, chemistry, computer science and business in Scandinavia, primarily Finland and Sweden. (It also has an English teaching programme in Finland.) Work experience assignments usually last 8 to 12 weeks in the summer, though longer placements are also possible. Trainees are paid the going wage but accommodation is not paid for. The ASF can also help 'self-placed trainees', i.e. those who have fixed up their own job or traineeship in a Scandinavian country, to obtain a work permit.

Denmark

Denmark has the highest average wage of any EU country (90 Danish kroner equivalent to £8/€12) and a reasonable rate of unemployment (6.1%). Work exists on farms and in factories, offices and hotels: the main problem is persuading an employer to take you on in preference to a Danish speaker. New arrivals in Copenhagen should take advantage of the youth information centre Use It, Rädhusstraede 13, 1466 Copenhagen K (33 73 06 20; www.useit.dk). Their primary function is to help young visitors make the most of their stay but they may have facilities and advice to help the job-seeker, for example they can tell you where busking is permitted and how to register for a social security number. It may be possible to consult files, newspapers and *fagboden* (Yellow Pages) in their office and to check their notice board for lift-shares (there is no jobs board).

Copenhagen, the commercial and industrial centre of the country, is by far the best place to look for work. It is also the centre of the tourist industry, so in summer it is worth looking for jobs door to door in hotels, restaurants and the Tivoli Amusement Park. Among the largest employers of casual staff in Denmark are newspaper distribution companies. To get a job as an *omdeler* or 'paper boy/girl', contact A/S Bladkompagniet (Islevdalvej 205, 2610 Rødovre; 70 20 72 25; bladkompagniet@bladkompagniet.dk) or check the *Yellow Pages* under the heading 'Aviser Distriktsblade' for other companies. Another big hiring company is the morning paper *Morgenavisen Jyllands-Posten*. They employ 4000 people on weekdays and 5000 on Sundays to deliver all their papers before 6.30am (8am on weekends). Ring 80 81 80 82 or email avisbud@jp.dk for details; their website www2. jp.dk/avisbud/eng/index.htm is in English.

Another possibility is to contact WWOOF Denmark (VHH) to obtain a list of their 30 or so member farmers, most of whom speak English. In return for three or four hours of work per day, you get free food and lodging. Always phone, email or write before arriving. The list can be obtained only after sending €10/£5/US$10 to Inga Nielsen, Asenvej 35, 9881 Bindslev (98 93 86 07; info@wwoof.dk/ www.wwoof.dk).

Many young Europeans end up picking strawberries in Denmark in the summer, although the strength of the pound against the kroner means that potential earnings are not as high as they once were. Pickers get paid between 5.40kr and 7.25kr per kilo and can expect to pick not more than 5 kilos an hour when they start out. Applications are invited from EU nationals before June 1st ready for a 12th or 26th June start date. Most employers expect you to bring your own tent and cooking equipment but do not charge for camping. The island of Fyn has been recommended for fruit-picking work, especially the area around Faaborg. But Samsø is where most pickers head in June. The website www.samsobaer.dk is a central resource for six Samsø farms including *Else Lysgaard & Ingvar Jørgensen*, Alstrup 2, 8305 Samsø (86 59 03 45; fax 86 59 03 46; else-ingvar@samso.com; www.else-ingvar.dk).

Finland

Finland offers about 1800 short-term paid training opportunities to foreign students every year. The International Trainee Exchange programme in Finland is administered by CIMO, the Centre for International Mobility (PO Box 343, 00531 Helsinki, Finland; +358 1080 6767; http://finland.cimo.fi); their website is in English. British students and graduates who want on-the-job training in their field (agriculture, tourism, teaching, etc.) lasting between one and 18 months should apply directly to CIMO. Short-term training takes place between May and September. Applications for summer positions must be in to CIMO by the middle of February.

The University of Helsinki Language Centre offers Finnish courses for foreigners who are not enrolled as students at the University; for details of summer and termly courses, contact Language Services, PO Box 4, 00014 00014 Helsinki (+358-9-191 23234; www. helsinki.fi/kksc/language.services/eng). Finnish courses for foreigners are also available from the Open University of the University of Helsinki (www.avoin.helsinki.fi) and the Helsinki Summer University (www.kesayliopistohki.fi).

Norway

Atlantis Youth Exchange at Rådhusgt 4, 0151 Oslo, Norway (tel/fax +47 22 47 71 79; atlantis@atlantis.no/ www.atlantis.no) runs an excellent 'Working Guest Programme' which allows people aged between 18 and 30 of any nationality to spend two to six months in rural Norway (Americans and other non-Europeans may stay for no more than three months). The only requirement is that they speak English. In addition to the farming programme open to all volunteers, placements in family-run tourist accommodation are available to European nationals.

Farm guests receive full board and lodging plus pocket money of at least NOK825 a week (£70) for a maximum of 35 hours of work. The idea is that you participate in the daily life, both work and leisure, of the family: haymaking, weeding, milking, animal-tending, berry-picking, painting, house-cleaning, babysitting, etc. A wardrobe of old rugged clothes and wellington boots is recommended.

After receiving the official application form you must send off a reference, two smiling photos, a medical certificate confirming that you are in good health and a substantial registration fee which varies according to country of origin and mediating agency (and which therefore does not appear on the Atlantis website). British applicants are asked to apply through *Gwendalyne,* whose fee is set at £300 for two months, £500 for six months; and Americans through InterExchange (161 6th Avenue, New York, NY 10013; 212-924 0446; www.interexchange.org). Atlantis will try to take into account individual preferences of location and placement. There are about 400 places (for all nationalities), so try to apply at least four months before your desired date of arrival. If they are unable to place you, all but NOK250 will be refunded.

Robert Olsen enjoyed his farm stay so much that he went back to the same family another summer:

> *The work consisted of picking fruit and weeds (the fruit tasted better). The working day started at 8am and continued till 4pm, when we stopped for the main meal of the day. After that we were free to swim in the sea, borrow a bike to go into town or whatever. I was made to feel very much at home in somebody else's home. The farmer and his daughter were members of a folk dance music band, which was great to listen to. Now and then they entrusted me to look after the house while they went off to play at festivals. Such holidays as these are perhaps the most economical and most memorable possible.*

Atlantis also runs a programme for 200 incoming au pairs who must be aged 18-30 and willing to stay at least six months but preferably 8-12 months. The first step is to write to Atlantis or check the information on its website www.atlantis.no. Atlantis charges a sizeable registration fee, a quarter of which is non-refundable if the placement doesn't go ahead. The majority of families are in and around Oslo, Bergen or the other cities in southern Norway, although applicants are invited to indicate a preference of north, south, east or west on their initial application. Virtually all employers will be able to communicate in English.

The pocket money for au pairs in Norway is at least NOK3000 per month which sounds generous until you realise that it could be taxed at 25%-30% (depending on the region), leaving a net amount of NOK1,800-NOK2,200. Atlantis can advise on possibilities for minimising tax by obtaining a *frikort* which entitles you to a personal allowance of NOK30,100. Au pairs are also given a travel card worth NOK400 a month.

Anyone interested in learning Norwegian should find out about the International Summer School offered at the University of Oslo (www.uio.no/iss).

Sweden

Unfortunately Sweden has no equivalent of CIMO or Atlantis. However several agencies do make au pair placements in Sweden (see introduction to this chapter). Swedish language courses are available at the Uppsala International Summer School (www.uiss.org).

WWOOF is now represented in Sweden: Teleskopsg. 2 Lgh 6,5, 41518 Götebord (Jesper_Lagerman@spray.se). In order to obtain the list of 28 WWOOF farms you must send SEK50/€5/$7.

Stiftelsen Stjärnsund (Bruksallén 16, 77071 Stjärnsund; 225-80001/fax 80301; fridhempost@hotmail.com; www.frid.nu) is located amongst the forests, lakes and hills of central Sweden. Founded in 1984, the community aims to encourage personal, social and spiritual development in an ecologically sustainable environment. It operates an international working guest programme throughout the year, but is at its busiest between May and September when most of the community's courses are offered. First-time working guests pay SEK500 (£36) for their first week of work and if the arrangement suits both sides it can be continued with a negotiable contribution according to hours worked and length of stay. Enquiries should be made well in advance of a proposed summer visit.

Iceland

The private employment agency Ninukot (Skeggjastadir 861, Hvolsvöllur; +354 487 8576; ninukot@islandia.is; www.ninukot.is) originally specialised in agricultural and horticultural jobs throughout Iceland but has branched out to offer jobs in babysitting, fisheries, gardening, horse training and tourism as well. Their welcoming website is in English and holds out the prospect of an easy-to-arrange working holiday in Iceland. Rural jobs are normally in picking and packing plants in the south and west of the country, but can also be with riding stables or on holiday farms between May and September. There is still enough demand from employers in the fish processing industry and from foreign job-seekers to justify the involvement of this agency. Provided you are prepared to stay at least six months in an Icelandic town or village, the agency will try to find a job in a fish factory. The minimum pay promised is a handsome €1400 a month gross with the possibility of earning overtime wages. The employer always provides accommodation. The Ninukot Employment Agency also fills vacancies for live-in childcarers who are promised a minimum of €1150 a month gross, with a deduction of €18 a day for room and board. After completing six months, the family pays for one way airfare to Iceland and after 12 months return, an arrangement that pertains to some other employers too.

Exit-IS is a leading exchange agency in Iceland, the only agency certified to bring foreign au pairs to Iceland for six to twelve months. The Au Pair in Iceland programme accepts au pairs aged 18-25 for periods of 9-12 months starting in August/September or for 6, 8 or 12 months from January. (Details from (Bankastraeti 10, 101 Reykjavik, Iceland; 562 2362/fax 562 9662; info@exit.is; www.exit.is). Families undertake to reimburse half the cost of your flights if you stay 6-9 months and all your travel expenses if you stay 9-12 months. The rate of weekly pocket money in Iceland can be as high as kr9,500 (£80) for a 30-hour week. The partner agency in Iceland promises close supervision, opportunities to meet other au pairs and hiking and riding trips offered at a discount.

Spain & Portugal

SPAIN

At the beginning of the 21st century, the popularity of Spanish studies continues to increase in Britain and beyond. It is possible to take short intensive courses in all the major Spanish cities, and bear in mind that it is also possible (and usually cheaper) to study Spanish in Latin America.

Spain has never lost its pre-eminent position as a favourite destination for British holidaymakers, and gap year students are no exception. Many book themselves on cheap packages to the Canaries, Ibiza and the Balearic Islands or any of the Costas as a good place to unwind after exams or after rigorous travels in developing countries. With an explosion in cheap and flexible flights from various UK airports with no-frills airlines like easyJet and MyTravelLite from Birmingham, it is now possible to fly very easily to one of many Spanish cities. However the cost of living is relatively high and opportunities for picking up a job to fund further travels are not very numerous.

The demand for native speakers of English to teach remains strong, but unqualified and inexperienced 18 year olds will have difficulty finding a position during the academic year (with exceptions; see below). They might have more luck at summer language camps. It is always worth checking the English language press in Spanish resorts and cities for the sits vac columns which sometimes carry adverts for live-in babysitters, bar staff, etc. If you can arrange to visit the Spanish coast in March before most of the budget travellers arrive, you should have a chance of fixing up a job for the season. The resorts then go dead until late May when the season gets properly underway and there may be jobs available.

Courses and Homestays

Two UK language course agencies which specialise in Spain are *Don Quijote* (2-4 Stoneleigh Park Road, Epsom, Surrey KT19 0QT; 020-8786 8081; www.donquijote.org) and *Gala Spanish in Spain* (Woodcote House, 8 Leigh Lane, Farnham, Surrey GU9 8HP; tel/fax 01252 715319). All the major agencies like *CESA, Caledonia, Languages Abroad* and *Lanacos* are active in Spain. For a major language school in Malaga that offers a range of Spanish courses at all levels as well as combination courses with dance, cookery, internships, homestays, etc., see the entry for *Malaca Instituto*.

Longer courses will work out cheaper per week. It normally saves money (but not time) to book directly with the school in Spain, as **Annabel Iglehart** from Castle Douglas in Scotland did with Mester (see 'Directory of Language Courses':

I completed my University degree last July and am taking a year (or two) out to gain new skills and participate in interesting activities around the world. I didn't take a year out before I went to University and because of this I think that I am making the most of my opportunities now. As soon as my exams finished I got straight down to organising my year out. I worked for two months in a variety of jobs in Edinburgh and then went to Salamanca, Spain to do a three-month intensive Spanish language course with Mester. The course was fantastic. The classes were fast paced and the teachers excellent. I met loads of people who I am still in touch with now, the social events organised by the school being a lot of fun and there was something for everyone. I lived with a Spanish family for a while and then moved to a flat with other students, something I had arranged before I headed out there. Mester is a company in Spain that provides excellent courses in Spanish, for any number of weeks and in a variety of cities in Spain. I'm afraid I cannot remember exactly how much it cost but it was roughly £1300 for three months. I had an intensive course (five hours of tuition a day), stayed for three weeks with a Spanish family and the rest in a self-catering flat. The costs are calculated according to the type of course (there are many to choose from) and the class of accommodation. The schools seem to be a lot less busy in winter time (when I was there, September to December) and so this can mean that classes are smaller, but not always. Classes are never more than ten people I am told.

Lynn Thomas chose an intensive 12-week course in Malaga, booked through CESA:

I picked CESA out of a book and handed over a lot of money. It could easily have been a disaster, but it was one of the best experiences of my life. I did not just learn Spanish; I learned a lot about life in Spain and made friends in more countries than I care to list, friendships that will continue.

Living with a family usually forces you to speak more Spanish from the beginning. Homestays can often lead to longer-lasting friendships and subsequent exchanges arranged on a private basis.

A client of Gala Spanish in Spain, **Paul Emmett,** was pleased at how much progress in Spanish he was able to make during his five months at *CLIC* in Seville (see entry in 'Directory of Language Courses'). Having done no formal Spanish before arriving, he passed the D.E.L.E. Basico and, on the strength of that, was allowed to do Spanish as a subsidiary subject in his first year at the University of Birmingham. Paul was pleased to discover that his standard of Spanish was better than many of the students on the Honours course.

The youth exchange organisation *Relaciones Culturales Internacionales* at Calle Ferraz 82, 28008 Madrid (91-541 71 03; spain@clubrci.es) places native English speakers (who must join the Club for €16) with families who want to practise their English in exchange for providing room and board; they also arrange voluntary work for English assistants on summer language/sports camps.

The non-profit Instituto Cervantes (www.cervantes.es) is the largest worldwide Spanish teaching organisation, with headquarters in Madrid and a network of centres around the world (comparable to the Alliance Francaise for French). It also has centres in London (102 Eaton Square, SW1W 9AN; 020-7235 0359) and Manchester. For language institutes in Spain, check the 'Directory of Language Courses' for the *Málaca Instituto* (Calle Cortada 6, 29018 Málaga), *CLIC International House* in Seville and *Mester* throughout Spain.

Most language schools prepare interested students for the D.E.L.E. Spanish language exams. For further information on courses, contact the library of the Cervantes Institute mentioned above or check the website www.quality-courses.com. Note that the online listing of Spanish courses on the website of Canning House (home of the prestigious educational organisation for the Spanish and Portuguese speaking world, the Hispanic and Luso Brazilian Council) has not been updated very recently, though this may improve when they launch their new website (Canning House, 2 Belgrave Square, London SW1X 8PJ; 020-7235 2303; www.canninghouse.com).

Of course many other things can be studied in Spain apart from language. Learning some of the traditional dances is the aim of some gap year travellers who have the chance to learn Sevillanas, Malagueras, the Pasadoble or even the very difficult Flamenco.

Anyone interested in learning to sail or participating in a tall ships voyage in this part of the Mediterranean should request the brochure from the *Jubilee Sailing Trust* or the *Tall Ships Youth Trust,* youth charities that run adventure sail training voyages, most of which last one to two weeks. Between November and May, square riggers sail around the Spanish islands of the Canaries off the northwest coast of Africa and also to the Azores (the Portuguese islands in the middle of the Atlantic Ocean). See entries in the 'Directory of Expeditions'.

Opportunities for Paid Work

Year out students have successfully found (or created) their own jobs in highly imaginative ways. One of the most striking examples is a 19-year-old student who wrote to the address on a Spanish wine label and was astonished to be invited to act as a guide around their winery for the summer. **Tommy Karske** returned home 'knowing a lot about wine and believing that anything is possible'.

Many yachts are moored along the Costa del Sol and all along the south coast. It might be possible to get work cleaning, painting or even guarding these luxury craft. There are also crewing possibilities for those with no time constraints and outgoing personalities.

Year-round resorts like Tenerife, Gran Canaria, Lanzarote and Ibiza afford a range of casual work as bar staff, DJs, beach party ticket sellers, timeshare salesmen, etc. A good starting point for finding out about seasonal job vacancies in Ibiza and elsewhere is the website of the Queen Victoria Pub in Santa Eulalia (www.ibizaqueenvictoria.com) which posts jobs and accommodation both on its site and on the pub notice board which anyone can drop by and consult (though it is more polite to buy a drink after consulting the board). As of 2005 it has a new jobs section and accommodation section for both workers and tourists. The Queen Vic itself employs a large number of European fun-seekers as well.

A more conventional form of employment is with a British tour company such as *Canvas Holidays, Eurocamp* or *Keycamp Holidays* (see 'Directory of Paid Seasonal Jobs'). *Siblu Holidays by Haven Europe* needs Spanish-speaking couriers and children's staff to work at mobile home and tent parks from early May to the end of September.

Acorn Adventure (22 Worcester St, Stourbridge, West Midlands DY8 1AN; 01384 446057; www.acorn-jobs.co.uk) hires seasonal staff for their watersports and multi activity centres on the Costa Brava. RYA qualified windsurfing and sailing instructors, BCU qualified kayak instructors and SPSA qualified climbing instructors are especially in demand, for the season April/May to September.

Some language schools can arrange work experience placements (mostly unwaged) in Spanish firms; see entries for *Don Quijote, Gwendalyne* (affiliated to Euro-Academy), *Euro-Practice, Gala Spanish in Spain, Interspeak* and *Language Courses Abroad* in the 'Directory of Work Experience'. ONECO Global Training in Seville is a member of the Global Work Experience Association and can fix up unpaid internships in many fields; its website www.oneco.org gives extensive details of the kind of positions available and also the reasonably priced language courses if offers. Refer also to the list of au pair agencies below, some of which arrange internships. The Californian company Adelante LLC (601 Taper Drive, Seal Beach, CA 90740; 562-799-9133; www.adelantespain.com) places interns in Barcelona, Madrid, Marbella and Seville.

English Teaching

The great cities of Madrid and Barcelona act as magnets to thousands of hopeful teachers. Opportunities for untrained native speakers of English have all but disappeared in respectable language academies. However some determined students have obtained a TEFL Certificate at the beginning of their gap year and gone on to teach.

> **After A levels, Sam James and his girlfriend Sophie Ellison headed off to Barcelona to do the four-week Trinity Certificate course which they found demanding but passed. Then they did the rounds of the language schools:**
> *Though tedious, this did work and we doubt we would have found work any other way. Job availability didn't seem that high in Barcelona when we were looking in October and we both accepted our only job offers. (Our age may have put off some employers.) Most schools seem to have recruited in September, so October was a bit of a lean month. I got my job by covering a class at two hours notice for a teacher who had called in sick. When this teacher decided to leave Barcelona, I was interviewed and offered her classes on a permanent basis. I got the job permanently about a fortnight after handing out CVs. Sophie was asked to her first interview after about three weeks of job-hunting. She was selected but then had to wait for several more weeks while her contract was finalised.*
> *The conventional wisdom says that the beginning of summer is the worst time to travel out to Spain to look for work since schools will be closed and their owners unobtainable. However Sam James handed round his CV again in May (when his hours were cut) and was given some encouragement. He thinks that because so few teachers look for work just six weeks before the end of the academic year, employers are sometimes in need of replacements. With so many no-frills cheap flights on the market, it might be worth a gamble.*

Sam James had to teach a variety of age groups in Barcelona during his gap year and, despite the problems, ended up enjoying it:

> *The children I taught were fairly unruly and noisy. The teenagers were, as ever, pretty uninterested in learning, though if one struck on something they enjoyed they*

would work much better. Activities based on the lyrics of songs seemed to be good. They had a tendency to select answers at random in multiple choice exercises. On the other hand they were only ever loud rather than very rude or disobedient. The young children (8-12) were harder work. They tended to understand selectively, acting confused if they didn't like an instruction. Part of the problem was that the class was far too long (three hours) for children of that age and their concentration and behaviour tended to tail off as the time passed.

Sam James blamed his lack of job security and bitty hours on Barcelona's popularity, 'the result of the great supply of willing teachers here keeping working conditions down and making it hard to exert any leverage on an employer when one is so easily replaced.' For this reason other towns may answer your requirements better. There are language academies all along the north coast and a door-to-door job hunt in September might pay off. This is the time when tourists are departing so accommodation may be available at a reasonable rent on a nine-month lease.

Without a TEFL qualification, the best chance of a teaching job in Spain would be on a summer language camp. Some pay a reasonable wage; others provide little more than free board and accommodation. **Glen Williams** describes his summer job at a summer language camp in Izarra in the Basque Country:

The children learned English for three hours in the morning with one half hour break (but not for the teacher on morning snack duty trying to fight off the hordes from ripping apart the bocadillos). Then we had another three or four hours of duties ranging from sports and/or arts to shop/bank duty. For many of us, inexperienced with dealing with groups of kids, there were a few problems of discipline.

Try for example TECS Summer Camps in Andalucia which recruit camp support staff and monitors for at least a month, plus assistant camp monitors and activity teachers for two months; details at www.tecs.es/employment. They have several appointed interviewers including one based in Birmingham.

It is also possible to arrange an informal exchange of English conversation for a free week in Spain. Englishtown is a unique programme whereby a holiday village in Spain (between Madrid and Barcelona) is 'stocked' with native English speakers and Spanish clients who want to improve their English. The English native-speaking volunteers participate alongside the Spanish adults in an intensive week of activities, sports, games and group dynamics and, in exchange for making English conversation, receive free room and board. All they have to do is cover the travel expenses to Madrid and then agree to chat and exchange stories. Participants come from all over the world and the average age is 40. More information is available from Vaughan Systems (Eduardo Dato 3, 1ª planta, 28010 Madrid, Spain; +34 91-591 4840; www.vaughanvillage.com).

Catharine Carfoot went on what amounts to a classic working holiday at the Vaughan Village in the summer of 2004:
Back in June I took part in an English Language immersion programme in Spain. They want native English speakers (any flavour, although in practice North Americans predominate) to go and talk a lot of English to Spaniards. All people have to do is get themselves to Madrid in time for the pick-up (by the way the cheapest option for getting to Madrid is to fly with Ryanair to Valladolid and then take a bus from there). At the end of the week, you will be delivered back to Madrid, unless you have extraordinary stamina and can manage two (or more) continuous weeks in the programme. It isn't a way to make money, but of course people can and do make friends and contacts both with the other 'Anglos' and with the Spaniards. It's also a week off worrying about food, drink and where to sleep.

Au Pairing

Au pair links between Spanish agencies and those in the rest of Europe have been increasing partly because Spanish is gaining popularity as a modern foreign language. Young people can often arrange to stay with Spanish families without having to do much domestic or childcare duties by agreeing to help with English tuition. In addition to the British au pair agencies making placements throughout Europe (listed in the introductory chapter on Au Pairing), you may deal directly with established Spanish agencies. The pocket money for au pairs at present is €55-€65 a week.

If you deal directly with a Spanish agency, you may have to pay a placement fee:

ABB Au Pair Family Service, Via Alemania 2, 5°A, 07003 Palma de Mallorca (971-752027; abbaupair@telefonica.net).

Babel Idiomas, Calle Larios 4, 2°, 29005 Malaga (952-608487; boelo@babelidiomas. com/ www.babelidiomas.com). Au pairs must stay minimum of 3 months and have intermediate Spanish.

B.E.S.T., Calle Solano 11, 3°C, Pozuelo de Alarcón, 28223 Madrid (www.bestprograms. org). Au pair placements for Americans and Europeans; fee $970 for 3 months. B.E.S.T. also organises internship and work-study programmes for varying fees, e.g. €1370 for a 2-month internship in Seville or €1615 for a 3-month internship in Barcelona including a one-month language course.

Centros Europeos Galve, Calle Principe 12-6°A, 28012 Madrid (91-532 7230; centros-principe@telefonica.net). Mainly places au pairs in the Madrid, Valencia, Alicante and Pamplona areas.

Easy Way Association, C/ Gran Via 80, Planta 10, oficina 1017, 28013 Madrid (91-548 8679; www.easywayspain.com). Also makes hotel and restaurant placements.

Experiment Spain, Fernández de los Rios 108, 1° izda, 28015 Madrid (91-549 3368; eilspain@retemail.es).

GIC Educational Consultants, Centro Comercial Arenal, Avda. del Pla 126, 2.22, 03730 Jávea (Alicante); 096-646 20 15 (ecsl@telefonica.net; http://bancocreativo.com/ trabajos/gic/Guests.htm). Au pair placements and live-in language tutors on the Costa Blanca (registration fee €180). Minimum stay for latter is 2 weeks.

Instituto Hemingway de Español, Bailén 5, 2°dcha, Bilbao 48003 (94-416 7901; www. institutohemingway.com). Accepts most nationalities. Also places interns in local companies, volunteers and English teachers.

Interclass, C/ Bori y Fontestá 14, 6° 4°, 08021 Barcelona (93-414 2921; www.interclass. es).

NuevasLenguas, Avda. Eduardo Dato 23, Local Interior, 41018 Seville; moreinfo@nuevaslenguas.com. Free placement of au pairs with families in Andalucia (Seville, Granada, Cadiz, Huelva, etc.). Bonuses for staying longer than 6 months.

Voluntary Work

Sunseed Trust, an arid land recovery trust, has a remote research centre in southeast Spain where new ways are explored of reclaiming deserts. The centre is run by both full-time volunteers (minimum five weeks) and working visitors who stay two to five weeks and spend half the day working. Weekly charges for part-time volunteers are £65-£118 according to season and for full-time volunteers £49-£70; students and those on unemployment benefit get a discount. Typical work for volunteers might involve germination procedures, forestry trials, hydroponic growing, organic gardening, designing and building solar ovens and stills, and building and maintenance. Living conditions are basic and the cooking is vegetarian. Occasionally workers with a relevant qualification in appropriate technology, etc. are needed who are paid a small stipend. The address of the centre is Apdo. 9, 04270 Sorbas, Almeria (tel/fax 950-525770; www.sunseed.org.uk).

The Atlantic Whale Foundation (St. Martin's House, 59 St Martins Lane, Covent Garden, London WC2H 4JS; www.whalefoundation.org.uk) runs hands-on whale and dolphin conservation and research projects in the Canary Islands, on which volunteers are expected to contribute $160-$250 per fortnight.

The co-ordinating workcamp organisations recruit for environmental and other projects in Spain. The co-ordinating workcamp organisation in Spain is the government-run *Instituto de la Juventud* (José Ortega y Gasset 71, 28006 Madrid; fax 91-309 30 66; svi@mtas.es) which oversees scores of camps every year.

PORTUGAL

Portugal is seen by gap year students mainly as a place in which to relax and have fun rather than spend a large part of their gap year. There is a long and vigorous tradition of British people settling in Portugal, and the links between the two countries are strong so, with luck, you might be able to chase up a contact to provide initial accommodation and orientation. If you want to extend your stay, ask members of the expatriate community for help and advice. A good idea is to scan the advertisements in the English language press or place an ad yourself. The long-established English-language weekly *Anglo-Portuguese News* (Apartado 113, 2766-902 Estoril; 21-466 1551; apn@mail.telepac.pt) carries job adverts.

If your chosen language is Portuguese, one of the best known language schools is *CIAL Centro de Linguas* in Lisbon which offers a well-structured series of courses, normally 15 hours a week for four weeks. Students are billeted in family homes both in Lisbon and Faro. The UK agency *Global Choices* (see 'Directory of Specialist Gap Year Programmes') places people who know or are willing to learn Portuguese in country house and city hotels. The training attachments last two to six months following the compulsory language course included in the fee of £650.

According to some British backpackers, all you need for a working holiday is to fly to Faro with a tent and hitch a lift to Albufeira where any number of bars and restaurants might hire you for the season. Wages are not high, but accommodation is cheap. If you are aiming a little higher and know some Portuguese, it would be worth contacting the British-Portuguese Chamber of Commerce (*Camara de Comércio Luso-Britanica*) in Lisbon (Rua da Estrela 8, 1200-669 Lisbon; 21-394 2020; www.bilateral.biz).

Switzerland & Austria

SWITZERLAND

Every winter a small army of gap year students migrates to the Alps to spend the winter season working and skiing at a Swiss or Austrian ski resort. One of the disadvantages of spending any time in Switzerland is the very high cost of living. But of course this goes with high wages which can be earned by people willing to work hard in hotels in the summer season as well as the winter.

Switzerland is not a member of the European Union. However a bilateral agreement with the European Union has been concluded and the main obstacles to free movement of persons were removed in 2004. The abolition of the category of seasonal worker has been abolished. Now the system is more in line with the rest of Europe so that EU job-seekers can enter Switzerland for up to three months (extendable) to look for work. If they succeed they must show a contract of employment to the authorities and are then eligible for a short-term residence permit (valid for up to one year and renewable). From 2007,

Switzerland aims to allow the unfettered movement of workers.

The Swiss are very *korrect* in regulating employment and foreigner workers (including au pairs) will have many deductions made from their earnings. Students staying longer than four weeks must obtain Swiss medical insurance unless they can prove that their cover is as extensive as the Swiss. Few students head for Switzerland to study French or German though it is possible (see entries for *UNIL Vacation Courses* at the University of Lausanne and *Collegium Palatinum* in the 'Directory of Language Courses'). While it is true that many Swiss and Austrian people speak a dialect of German, language schools teach *Hoch Deutsch*. Austria in particular has been trying to build up its German language tourism and is worth considering (see below).

Work Experience

Trainee exchanges between Switzerland and a number of non-EU countries including the US continue. Permits for temporary trainee placements *(stagiaires)* can be obtained from the Swiss Federal Office for Migration, Emigration and Trainees, Quellenweg 15, 3003 Bern (031-322 42 02; swiss.emigration@bfm.admin.ch; www.swissemigration.ch/elias/en/index.html (in English). The website provides a list of co-operating partner organisations, e.g. AIPT in the USA (www.aipt.org). Guidance may be given to applicants on how to find an employer, though the programme is for individuals who can find a suitable position independently. The trainee position arranged must be in the vocational field of the applicant, who must be aged 18-30.

The Swiss Farmers' Union runs a programme for trainees in agriculture from Europe, North America, Brazil, the Antipodes, South Africa and Japan. Participants who want to work for 3 to 12 months must have professional training in agriculture or horticulture, or at least three years' practical experience or relevant training and be able to speak some English, French or German. Further details are available from Agroimpuls, c/o Farmers' Union, Laustrasse 10, 5201 Brugg, Switzerland (056-462 51 44; www.agroimpuls.ch).

Paid Work in the Tourist Industry

Provided you have a reasonable CV and a knowledge of languages (preferably German), a speculative job hunt in advance is worthwhile. The Swiss Hotel Association has a department called Hoteljob which runs a placement scheme (in the German-speaking part of Switzerland only) for registered EU students from the age of 18 who are willing to spend three to four months doing an unskilled job in a Swiss hotel or restaurant between June and September. Excellent knowledge of the German language is essential (and information on the website is only in German). Individual vacancies with contact details are posted on the website; for example in February 2005 there were 235 vacancies being advertised. Member hotels issue a standard contract on which salary and deductions are carefully itemised. From the gross salary of SFr2,790 in subsidised mountain areas or SFr3,100 in the rest of Switzerland, the basic deduction for board and lodging (for any job) is SFr900 and a further 12-15% is taken off for taxes and insurance. Tips for waiting staff can bring net earnings back up to the gross. Application forms are available from the Swiss Hotel Association, Monbijoustrasse 130, 3001 Bern (+41 31-370 43 33/fax +41 31-370 43 34; hoteljob.be@swisshotels.ch; www.hoteljob.ch). The deadline for applications is 20th April.

The *Jobs in the Alps Agency* (see entry in 'Directory of Paid Seasonal Jobs') places waiters, waitresses, chamber staff, kitchen assistants and porters in Swiss hotels, cafés and restaurants in Swiss resorts, 200 in winter, 150 in summer. Wages will be higher if you work for a Swiss employer than if you are hired by a British tour operator.

Swiss hotels are very efficient and tend to be impersonal, since you will be one in an endless stream of seasonal workers from many countries. The very intense attitude to work among the Swiss means that hours are long (often longer than stipulated in the contract): a typical working week would consist of at least five nine-hour days working split shifts. Whether humble or palatial, the Swiss hotel or restaurant in which you find a job will probably insist on very high standards of cleanliness and productivity.

Most ski tour operators mount big operations in Switzerland, such as Mark Warner, Ski Total and Crystal Holidays (see introduction to chapter 'Paid Seasonal Jobs'). A Swiss specialist is On-the-Piste Holidays (2 Oldfield Court, Cranes Park Crescent, Surbiton KT5 8AW; recruit@otp.co.uk) which operates in Anzère, Nendaz, Villars and Zermatt. The main disadvantage of being hired by a UK company is that the wages will be on a British scale rather than on the much more lucrative Swiss one. A company that recruits ski instructors for children and other staff is Viamonde, Chalet Bruttin, Case Postale 1102, 1972 Anzère (personnel@viamonde.com).

The *Warren Smith Academy* (see entry) runs ski instructor courses in Verbier, as does Altitude Futures (71 Claramount Road, Heanor, Derbyshire DE75 7HS; or Case Postale 55, 1936 Verbier; +41 27 771-6006; www.altitude-futures.com).

Most people go out and fix up their jobs in person, sometimes with the help of the tourist office. In some resorts the tourist office keeps a list of job-seekers which local hoteliers and other employers can consult when they need to, usually well in advance of the start of the season. The most promising time to introduce yourself to potential employers is April/May for the summer and early September for the winter. November is a bad time to arrive since most of the hotels are closed, the owners away on holiday and most have already promised winter season jobs to people they know from previous seasons or ones who approached them at the end of the summer season.

Sometimes it is necessary to escape the competition from all the other gap year and other job-seekers by moving away from the large ski stations. Joseph Tame's surprising tip is to go up as high as possible in the mountains. After being told by virtually every hotel in Grindelwald in mid-September that they had already hired their winter season staff, he despaired and decided to waste his last SFr40 on a trip up the rack railway. At the top he approached the only hotel and couldn't believe it when they asked him when he could start. Although at 18 he had never worked in a hotel before, they were willing to take him on as a trainee waiter, give him full bed and board plus £850 a month. At first he found the job a little boring since there were few guests apart from Japanese groups on whirlwind European tours. But things changed at Christmas and New Year when he had to work three shifts a day, which was rewarded in the end by an increase in pay.

Summer Camps

The Swiss organisation *Village Camps* advertises widely its desire to recruit staff for their multi-activity centres and language camps for children in Anzère and Leysin. They also hire up to 100 ski counsellors and other staff for the winter season. Jobs are available for EFL teachers, sports instructors and general domestic staff. For jobs with Village Camps, room and board are provided as well as accident and liability insurance and an allowance which amounts to pocket money. An application pack is available from Village Camps, rue de la Morache, 1260 Nyon (022-990 9405/fax 022-990 9494; personnel@villagecamps. ch).

Another possible employer is the Haut-Lac International Centre (1669 Les Sciernes; 026-928 4200; info@haut-lac.com) which employs teachers and monitors of any nationality for both their summer and winter camps for teenagers.

Work on Farms

Young Europeans who are interested in experiencing rural Switzerland may wish to do a stint on a Swiss farm. The *Landdienst* is the Central Office for Voluntary Farm Work which is located at Mühlegasse 13 (Postfach 728), 8025 Zürich (1-261 44 88/fax 1-261

44 32; admin@landdienst.ch). It fixes up farm placements for a minimum of three weeks for young people from Western Europe who know some German or French. Last year about 600 foreign young people were placed through the Landdienst. Workers are called 'volunteers' and can work for up to two months without a work permit. They must pay a registration fee of SFr50.

In addition to the good farm food and comfortable bed, you will be paid at least SFr20 per day worked. Necessary qualifications for participating in this scheme are that you be between 18 and 25 and that you have a basic grounding in French or German. On these small Swiss farms, English is rarely spoken and many farmers speak a dialect which some find incomprehensible.

Most places in German-speaking Switzerland are available from the beginning of March to the end of October and in the French part from March to June and mid-August to the end of October, though there are a few places in the winter too. Each canton has a farm placement representative who liaises with the Zürich headquarters.

The hours are long, the work is hard and much depends on the volunteer's relationship with the family. Most people who have worked on a Swiss farm report that they are treated like one of the family, which means both that they are up by 6am or 7am and working till 9pm alongside the farmer and that they are invited to accompany the family on any excursions, such as the weekly visit to the market to sell the farm-produced cheeses.

WWOOF Switzerland (Postfach 59, 8124 Maur) keeps a constantly updated list of farmers around the country, currently 45. To obtain the list you must join WWOOF at a cost of SFr20/£10/$20/€15 in cash. Details are available on WWOOF's web-site www.wwoof. org/switzerland. Volunteers must apply with a photocopy of their passport and an accompanying letter stating why they want to become unpaid volunteers.

> **Joseph Tame made use of the WWOOF website to fix up a place on a farm in the spring:**
> *I can honestly say that it has been an absolutely fantastic experience. The hours could be thought fairly long by some (perhaps 35 per week) considering there is no money involved, but I absolutely love the chance to work outside in this land that reminds me so much of the final setting in 'The Hobbit.' From our farm your eyes take you down the hillside, over the meadows covered in flowers, down to the vast Lake Luzern below and over to the huge snow-capped mountain Pilatus. It really is paradise here. The family have been so kind, and as I put my heart into learning all that I can about the farm they are only too happy to treat me with generosity. I really feel a part of the family.*

Au Pairs

For those interested in a domestic position with a Swiss family there are rules laid down by each Swiss canton, so there are variations. Now that European citizens no longer require a work permit, the au pair system has become more relaxed. However the agencies still work to the old requirements and place females between the ages of 17 and 29 (minimum 18 in Geneva) for at least 12 and up to 18 months. Families in most places are required to pay half the language school fees for six months and half the compulsory health insurance.

Au pairs in Switzerland work for a maximum of 30 hours per week, plus babysitting once or twice a week. The monthly salary varies among cantons but the normal minimum is SFr700-800. In addition, the au pair gets a four or five week paid holiday plus SFr18-20 for days off (to cover food). Au pairs are liable to pay tax and contributions which can mean a deduction of up to a fifth of their wages.

A specialist agency in the UK is Petite Pumpkin Au Pair Agency (45 Nelson St, Buckingham MK18 1BT; 01280 824745; www.petitepumpkin.co.uk) which cooperates with an agency in Geneva and sends au pairs to Switzerland. Pro Filia is a long-established Catholic au pair agency with about 15 branches including 32 Av de Rumine, 1005 Lausanne (021-323 77 66) for French-speaking Switzerland, and Beckenhofstr. 16, 8035 Zürich (01-363 55 00; www.profilia.ch) for the German part. The agency registration fee is SFr30-35 plus a further SFr100-150 to be paid within a month of taking up the placement.

Independent au pair placement agencies include Sunshine Au Pair Agency, 15,Vy des Crêts, 1295 Mies (tel/fax 022-755 20 81; www.au-pair-sunshine.ch); Swissaupair Agence de Placement Au Pair, Quai Maria Belgia 8, 1800 Vevey (tel/fax 021 921 28 47; www.swissaupair.ch) and *Perfect Way* (see entry in 'Paid Work Directory') which vets all families and distributes a list of other au pairs and their contact details.

Voluntary Work

Mountain Forest Project (Bergwald Projekt e.V.), Hauptstr. 24, 7014 Trin, Switzerland (081-630 4145; www.bergwaldprojekt.ch) runs one-week forest conservation projects in the alpine regions of Switzerland and southern Germany. A basic knowledge of German is useful since the foresters conduct the camps in German. Hut accommodation, food and insurance are provided free, though participants must pay an annual membership fee of SFr60/€40. MFP publishes its literature and website in English and is welcoming to foreign volunteers who know some German:

> People from overseas travelling in Europe will surely enjoy a week's workcamp with MFP in Switzerland, Germany or Austria. You will learn a lot about alpine forests and nature in general.

AUSTRIA

Like its alpine neighbour, Austria offers a great deal of seasonal employment to gap year students hoping to save some money and do some skiing. Some knowledge of German will be necessary for most jobs apart from those with UK tour operators. There is no shortage of hotels to which you can apply either for the summer or the winter season. The largest concentration is in the Tyrol though there are also many in the Vorarlberg region in western Austria. The main winter resorts to try are St Anton, Kitzbühel, Mayrhofen, St. Johann-im-Pongau which is a popular destination for British holidaymakers creating a demand for English-speaking staff. Wages in hotels and restaurants are lower than in Switzerland, though still reasonable.

The *Deutsch Institut Tirol* in Kitzbühel (www.gap-year.at) offers 12-week German language course combined with ski and snowboard instruction specially designed for gap year students (see entry in 'Directory of Courses'). If you want to improve your chances of finding work in a ski resort, you could consider joining the two-week 'Learn German and Get a Seasonal Job in the Snow' course at Club Habitat in Kirchberg/Kitzbühel in the Austrian Tyrol. Details are available from Club Habitat Ski Chalet, Kohlgrub 9, 6365 Kirchberg; 05357 2254; info@clubhabitat.at; www.clubhabitat.at). The course takes place from the last week of November and costs from £250 which includes bed and breakfast accommodation and two hours of tuition a day. In fact Kirchberg is such a popular tourist destination that it might be worth job-hunting there in winter or summer.

After spending the first part of her gap year doing a German language course in Dresden, **Rosie Curling** decided she needed to consolidate her new skills by working in a German-speaking environment. She chose to head for Lech in Austria, where she had a friend, and within 24 hours of arriving she had a job as a commis waitress:

> It would be fair to say that my five months in Austria were a rollercoaster ride of emotions. For the first three weeks I was lonely and homesick, finding the work tough, relations with my colleagues a strain and communication difficult. However

after the Christmas period, I began to make friends and enjoy the wonderful skiing and to realise that the work was a means to an end, namely to have some serious fun. Again I was experiencing a new lifestyle, incredibly relaxed, where the major responsibility of the day was deciding where to ski and then where to après ski. Life assumed an idyllic routine. Get up at 8.50am, be the first on the slopes, ski till 11am, work the lunch shift, a couple more hours skiing, a bit more work in the evening, before hitting the night scene. Despite (or possibly because of) all this it was also an incredibly constructive period. For a start I saved £2500 (to fund a Trans-Siberian railway trip). My German is now almost fluent, although I speak an Austrian dialect; my skiing has improved from a Grade 4/5 to 3a, but most importantly I have made some life-long friends, mainly Austrians and Swedes.

Because Austria is a very popular destination for British skiers, jobs abound with UK tour operators, though most are looking for staff over 21. One possibility for both seasons is First Choice Holidays (London Road, Crawley, West Sussex RH10 9GX; 01293 588585; skijobs@firstchoice.co.uk; www.firstchoice4jobs.co.uk) which hires hundreds of people to work in hotels and resorts in Austria; no qualifications are required because staff are given in-house training, but you must be available to stay for the whole season from May to September. Equity Travel (01273 886911; www.equity.co.uk/employment) recruit chefs, housekeeping and waiting staff, handymen, night porters, plongeurs and bar staff (EU nationality essential) for its sizeable operation in the Austrian Alps. Tall Stories (Brassey House, New Zealand Avenue, Walton on Thames, Surrey KT12 1QD; 01932 252970; www.tallstories.co.uk/jobs.shtm) also require resort staff in Austria, among other countries.

One of the more unusual casual jobs in Austria was described on a post card from **Fionna Rutledge** written during her gap year:

I thought you might be interested in my summer job in Vienna. I spent two months working for a classical music concert company (Strauss). There are loads of these in Vienna and most of them employ students. I was paid on commission and spent the day dressed up in Mozart costume in the main Vienna tourist spots. Hard work, but a great opportunity to meet people. You have to sell the concert tickets to complete strangers. I earned about £1300 in six weeks. All you need to do is approach the 'Mozarts' on the street and ask them to introduce you to their boss.

Summer Work

Two organisations that run summer language camps are the similarly named English for Children (Weichselweb 4, 1220 Vienna; 01-958 1972; www.englishforchildren.com) and English for Kids (Postgasse 11/19, 1010 Vienna; 01-667 45 79; www.e4kids.co.at) both of which are looking for young monitors and English teachers with experience of working with children and preferably some TEFL background.

The organisation Young Austria, Ferienhöfe GmbH, Alpenstrasse 108a, A-5020 Salzburg; 0662-62 58 59-0) run summer camps *(Osterreichisches Ferienwerk)* that employ about 30 teachers and monitors to work at summer language and sports camps near Salzburg. For about three or four hours of each day of the two-week camp, 10 to 17 year old children receive English tuition from teachers (who must have teaching experience). Monitors organise the outdoor programme and help the teachers with the social programme as well as with the lessons. Teachers receive about €240 per fortnight and monitors receive €160 in their first year. Application forms are available from December and should be submitted to gudrun.doringer@youngaustria.at by mid-March.

For information about WWOOF Austria, contact Hildegard Gottlieb, Einödhofweg 48, 8042 Graz (tel/fax 0316-464951; wwoof.welcome@telering.at; www.wwoof.welcome.at.tf). Membership costs €20/$25 per year plus two IRCs which entitles you to the list of around 160 Austrian organic farmers looking for work-for-keep volunteer helpers.

Jakob Steixner, a native of Doren in the Vorarlberg region of Austria, thinks that it should be possible to find work on a mountain farm. The best time to ask around for work is March, well ahead of the season which lasts from June till early September:

There is one sort of job available to everybody who doesn't mind working long hours in agriculture in Austria and Switzerland (and probably everywhere along the Alps). It's working temporarily on livestock farms in the mountains. It can be quite interesting not only because it involves so many different activities but also you're outside a lot of the time, often in extraordinarily beautiful surroundings. Pay is by the day and might seem very little by European standards (around £20-£30 in my area, but more if you get deeper into the mountains). But you can save a lot as there is nowhere to spend the money and you get free food and accommodation. Depending on your bosses you might have to work quite long hours though, sometimes searching for lost cattle for hours in the pouring rain or hail, 5000ft above sea level, or repairing fences when it's snowing in the middle of July. But that can be quite hilarious when you think about it later.

Au Pairs

Austria has a well-developed tradition of au pair placement and several well-established and respectable agencies place hundreds of au pairs in Austria each year. Most of the families live in Vienna and Salzburg. The main agency is the Catholic-affiliated Auslands-Sozialdienst, Au-Pair Vermittlung, Johannesgasse 16/1, 1010 Vienna (01-512 7941; www.volunteer.at/aupair/f-contact.htm) which is accustomed to dealing with direct applications from abroad for au pair placements lasting an academic year. Most agencies charge an upfront registration fee of €100-€150. The minimum weekly pocket money is about €60 a week. The Austrian employment service posts a useful list of agencies at www.ams.or.at/neu/tirol/1889.htm including:

Au Pair Austria, Vermittlungs-agentur, Mariahilfer Strasse 99/2/37, 1060 Vienna (tel/fax 01-920 38 42; www.aupairaustria.com). Registration fee of €30 plus completion fee of €70.

AuPair4You, Hasnerstrasse 31/22, 1160 Vienna (01/990 15 74; www.au-pair4you.at).

Au-pair Corner, Josef Buchinger Strasse 3, 3100 St. Pölten (02742/25 85 36; www.au-pair-corner.at).

Language Courses and Homestays

Deutsch in Graz (Kalchberggasse 10, A-8010 Graz; 316-833 900/ www.dig.co.at) can arrange homestays with language courses in Graz and suburbs. The organisation *Campus Austria* at the University of Vienna comprises 16 language schools all providing German language training. Some courses lead to Goethe Institute qualifications while others lead to the OESD (Austrian Diploma for German as a Foreign Language). Campus Austria publishes a clear pamphlet of the courses on offer and prices, with contact details of its 16 member schools. One of the schools, the ActiLingua Academy (Gloriettegasse 8, A-1130 Vienna; 1-877 67 01/ www.actilingua.com) offers some interesting courses including German and Music (in co-operation with the Conservatorium) and German combined with work experience in the Austrian tourism industry for between one and twelve months. Most job opportunities are in Vienna, Salzburg or alpine resorts.

The Austrian Embassy (28 Rutland Gate, London SW7 1PQ; 020-7584 8653; www.bmaa.gv.at) can provide information about language courses in Austria in addition to the ones listed in the 'Directory of Courses'.

WORLDWIDE

Africa

2005 has been named by Prime Minister Tony Blair as the 'Year of Africa' as he, along with Bob Geldof, spearheaded a vigorous campaign to double international aid and provide debt relief to the continent. Stories from Africa have been highlighted in the media as never before, piquing the interest of many young people who may not have considered spending part of their gap year in a Ghanaian orphanage, coaching kids' football in Malawi, caring for cheetahs in South Africa or joining an overland expedition in East Africa. Many organisations large and small can assist in setting up a placement in Africa, whether a stint of voluntary teaching in a village school, an attachment to a scientific expedition or on a safari.

Conditions can be very tough and many gap students teaching or working in rural Africa find themselves struggling to cope, whether with the loneliness of life in a rural West African village or with the hassle experienced by women in Muslim North Africa. A certain amount of deprivation is almost inevitable; for example volunteers can seldom afford to shop in the pricey expatriate stores and so will have to be content with the local diet, typically a staple cereal such as millet usually made into a kind of stodgy porridge, plus some cooked greens, tinned fish or meat and fruit. Typically the housing will not have running water or electricity which means that showers consist of a bucket and cup, and toilets are just a hole in the ground. Local customs can come as a shock, for example being treated with something akin to reverence, even though you may feel yourself to be just a naïve school leaver. But the rewards can also be tremendous and any efforts you put in are bound to be appreciated. When **Amelia Cook** started out teaching in a Ghanaian primary school she was bowled over (not just figuratively) by the curiosity of her class:

> *Even our first shaky classes using ideas from out own schools were met with great enthusiasm. Once my class of 45 teenage boys (plus many others who had sneaked in at the back) literally knocked me over in their enthusiasm to see what was in my bag of props for that day's lesson.*

In the end she was glad that she had chosen a small organisation (*AfricaTrust Networks*) which fulfilled her ambition to be of real benefit to the community and not just on an exotic holiday.

Regional crises also flare up, making volunteering potentially risky. For example programmes in Zimbabwe have been all but decimated by political strife and economic disintegration. Try to research in advance any local issues that may be causing concern. Until 2005, Togo was a reasonable prospect (see first hand account below) but is now off-limits because of civil unrest. News coverage of the Sudan is invariably about the crisis in the Darfur region; however following the Comprehensive Peace Agreement signed early in 2005, there is greatly increased potential for development. Sudan is welcoming, safe and friendly, and the long-established Sudan Volunteer Programme (SVP) has stepped up its efforts to recruit native English-speaking volunteers (including gap year students from summer 2005) to teach English and assist in the effort to restore the use of English as the second official language of Sudan.

The Foreign & Commonwealth Office regularly updates its travel advice for every country in the world and includes risk assessments of current trouble spots. You can contact the Travel Advice Unit by phone on 0870 606 0290 or check their website www. fco.gov.uk/travel.

Often the most useful preparation is to talk to someone who has survived and enjoyed a similar placement in the recent past. It is amazing how many volunteers are glad that they gave up their material privileges for a time and lived like the locals. Some even go on to make a career in development work. One year-out student **Rachel Attree** summed up her experience of teaching in East Africa:

Going to Tanzania has to have been the scariest thing I have done, ever. But as the saying goes, 'Nothing ventured, nothing gained' and this really was the case. Out of a scary daunting experience blossomed a wonderfully rewarding and enriching gift that will stay with me for life. That is not to say that I didn't have any rough times because I did and that was one of the benefits of my trip, learning to cope by yourself with no parents to turn to for support. All in all I have learnt so much about myself and other people and feel that my gap year has let me into a secret that only a special few will ever get to know.

Action against the spread of HIV/AIDS in sub-Saharan Africa is a matter of the utmost urgency and a number of agencies are tackling the issue head on, including the well respected charity SPW (Students Partnership Worldwide). Several years ago **Juliet Austin** joined SPW after finishing her degree at Sussex University:

The biggest challenge is how to change a continent's sexual practices. The task is enormous. However through SPW I discovered that one answer lies with young people educating other young people, an approach known as peer education. I was recruited to work alongside a counterpart Zimbabwean volunteer and together we used participatory and non-formal methods to promote the development of life skills and positive lifestyles with regard to adolescent sexual and reproductive health. We used drama, role-play, discussion groups, debates, poetry writing and recital, poster design, music and dance. Living and working with people from both my own country and Zimbabwe was an incredible experience and so much fun. What struck me most about my stay was the enthusiasm of the local people, coupled with their overwhelming friendliness and support for what we as volunteers were trying to achieve. I have never had a more fun and rewarding experience.

SENDING AGENCIES

In addition to SPW which sends volunteers to Tanzania, Uganda, South Africa and Zambia, the main year-out agencies are all active on the African continent: *GAP Activity Projects* with placements in South Africa, Malawi, Tanzania and Ghana; *Project Trust* with Namibia, South Africa, Lesotho, Uganda, Botswana, Malawi, Mozambique, Mauritania and Morocco as destinations, *Travellers* to Ghana, Kenya, South Africa and Zimbabwe; *Global Adventures Project* in South Africa; and *i-to-i* which sends voluntary English teachers to Ghana and Kenya, has community work and conservation placements in South Africa and Kenya and also sends media and advertising volunteers to Ghana,

The following organisations also recruit gap year volunteers for Africa, mostly for work in schools and community projects. Most have entries in the 'Directory of Specialist Gap Year Programmes' in the first part of this book. Usually a local allowance or pocket money is paid and housing is provided.

Adventure Alternative, 31 Myrtledene Road, Belfast BT8 6GQ (tel/fax 02890 701476; office@adventurealternative.com/ www.adventurealternative.com). Three-month programmes for gap year students (among others) in Kenya combining 8 weeks of teaching/ community work plus climbing, trekking, rafting, safaris and independent travel. Participants teach and work in HIV-education in rural schools and have their own house to live in and manage.

Africa & Asia Venture, 10 Market Place, Devizes, Wilts. SN10 1HT (01380 729009/fax

01380 720060; av@aventure.co.uk/ www.aventure.co.uk). Places British school leavers as assistant teachers in primary and secondary schools in Kenya, Uganda, Tanzania, Botswana and Malawi, normally for one term. Programme includes in-country orientation course, insurance, allowances paid during work attachment and organised safari at end of four months. The 2005/6 participation fee is about £2700 plus airfares.

AfricaTrust Networks, Africatrust Chambers, PO Box 551, Portsmouth, Hants. PO5 1ZN (01873 812453; info@africatrust.gi/ www.africatrust.gi) have three or six month residential programmes in Ghana (Cape Coast and Kumasi), Morocco and Cameroon for gap year students and others aged 18-25, to work with needy children and adults.

AFS Intercultural Programmes UK, Leeming House, Vicar Lane, Leeds LS2 7JF (0845 458 2101; info-unitedkingdom@afs.org/ www.afsuk.org). Participants can go to Ghana or South Africa to join community service programmes for six months, e.g. working on health, welfare or human rights projects. Volunteers contribute £3300.

Azafady, Studio 7, 1A Beethoven St, London W10 4LG (020-8960 6629; www.madagascar.co.uk). 10-week Pioneer Madagascar programme allows volunteers to work on a grassroots level trying to combat deforestation and extreme poverty in Madagascar. Fundraising target is £2000 excluding flights.

Blue Ventures, 52 Avenue Road, London N6 5DR (www.blueventures.org). Volunteers are needed for at least six weeks to carry out marine research, coral reef conservation and day-to-day management of field camps in South Western Madagascar. Fee for 6 weeks is £1780 for non-divers; £1580 for PADI divers. Blue Ventures has also in the past co-ordinated marine projects in Tanzania, South Africa and the Comoros Islands.

BUNAC, 16 Bowling Green Lane, London EC1R 0QH (020-7251 3472; www.bunac.org). Work South Africa (up to 12 months), Volunteer South Africa (2 months) and Volunteer Ghana (3-6 months) programmes. University undergraduates or recent graduates aged 18-30 can have BUNAC's back-up for the duration of their South African working holiday for £350 plus visa fee of £33, travel and insurance. BUNAC also co-operates with Ghana's SYTO (Student & Youth Travel Organisation) to arrange for gappers, students and recent graduates to join three to six month volunteer community service projects in Ghana.

Camps International Ltd, Unit 1, Kingfisher Park, Headlands Business Park, Salisbury Road, Blashford, Ringwood, Hants. BH24 3NX (01425 485390; www.campsinternational.com). Gap year and career gap safari camps and expeditions in Kenya and Tanzania, where participants undertake a range of wildlife and community projects lasting 2 weeks to 3 months. 28-day Gap adventure costs from £1300.

Cultural Cube, 16 Acland Rd, Ivybridge, Devon PO21 9UR (www.culturalcube.co.uk). Go Ghana programme in Ghana with variety of placements in orphanages, conservation projects, charities and rural schools. Normal minimum stay is 2 months; minimum for teachers (who should have some relevant experience) is one 3-month term starting January, May or September. Volunteers contribute £75 a month for food and accommodation plus £375 placement fee.

Daneford Trust, 45-47 Blythe St, London E2 6LN (tel/fax 020-7729 1928; info@danefordtrust.org.uk). Youth education charity that sends students and school leavers resident in London (only) to Namibia, Botswana, South Africa and Zimbabwe for a minimum of 3 but preferably 6-9 months. Volunteers must raise at least £2000 towards costs for a 3-4 month placement and £4000 for 6-9 months, with help from the Trust.

EIL, 287 Worcester Road, Malvern, Worcs. WR14 1AB (0800 018 4015; www.eiluk.org). Run community service and volunteer programmes in Ghana. Prices depend on length of visit.

GAP SPORTS, Willow Bank House, 84 Station Road, Marlow, Bucks. SL7 1NX (0870 837 9797; www.gapsports.com). Football, rugby, cricket, basketball, hockey, netball, tennis and boxing coaching placements in Ghana and South Africa lasting from 5 weeks to 3+ months. Other placements relate to teaching, art and design, media, sports psychology, physiotherapy and medicine; cost £1495-£1695 for three months.

Lucy Mills captures the rewards and frustrations she experienced as a football coach in Ghana with GAP SPORTS:

There are so many life-changing experiences available for gappers that I had great fun researching options for my gap year. I wanted not only to travel, but to adapt and live in a totally different culture. Having always played sports, I thought the football coaching placements in Ghana sounded different. Being outdoors in the sunshine all day, interacting with another culture through sports, it sounded amazing. Initially I had minor worries that a girl football coach would not be respected, but as soon as I got there, this illusion was proven very wrong. I was based at a football academy along with other gap year volunteers in Nungua, a poor part of the capital. The training pitch was a dusty, bumpy patch of land surrounded by waste, sewage and wooden huts. Taxis and goats casually made their way across the pitch during matches. Rubber tyres elbowing out of the ground acted as the spectators' seats.

Facilities at training were painfully limited; no cones, no bibs, no nets... I co-ordinated training sessions with thirty or so boys with merely a few torn, deflated balls and a whistle. Many of the boys played in bare feet and without T-shirts, but their passion for the game outshone their restricting poverty. Training is serious and tough. Attitudes towards sport are tremendously dedicated, unlike the beer-fuelled Sunday League teams in England. The weather was extremely hot so I coached early in the morning and in the evening to avoid the midday sun, but I got used to the weather. During the day I went home to snooze, sunbathe, chill or read on the balcony, looked round markets or went to the beach.

When I came back from Ghana I set up a charity scheme to collect old or unused football strips from family, friends, schools, local pub teams, professional football teams and friends at uni. I have collected hundreds of strips. Leeds United donated 50 shirts and shorts and hundreds of new Nike socks for example, and I fundraised £200 to buy balls, cones and bibs. I am going out to Ghana for three weeks over Easter to give the equipment to the teams I coached last year. I've even been granted free excess baggage from FlyJet for all my kitbags.

Global Adventures Project, 38 Queen's Gate, London SW7 5HR (0800 085 4197; www.globaladventures.co.uk). 3-month placements in South Africa for over 18's teaching English, Maths and sports in the Kayamandi township outside Stellenbosch, working with abandoned and terminally ill children and building houses in the township. Includes orientation, accommodation and enrolment at Stellenbosch University allowing full use of facilities, 2 hours of lectures a week on the History and Political Changes in South Africa. Prices start from £1995 plus airfare and meals. **Jennifer McGhee** is a recent participant:

I have been terrified, elated, shocked and stunned. This cocktail of emotions only manages to scratch the surface of how it feels to be fully immersed in the South African way of life in which I have experienced adventure, discovery, personal growth, and the harsh reality of day-to-day life in the townships.

Global Vision International (GVI), Amwell Farmhouse, Nomansland, Wheathampstead, St. Albans, Herts. AL4 8EJ (0870 608 8898; info@gvi.co.uk/ www.gvi.co.uk). Placements from 1-12 months. South Africa, Namibia and East Africa: wildlife research at Edeni Game Reserve in South Africa and courses in field guiding. Teaching and community development projects in East Africa and elephant research in Namibia. Prices vary from £1420 for a 4-week field guide course to £2450 for a 10-week wildlife research expedition. Also Seychelles Marine Expedition: prices start at £1650 for 5 weeks, including scuba diving equipment, training and accommodation.

Health Action Promotion Association (HAPA), PO Box 24, Bakewell, Derbyshire DE45 1YP (www.volunteerafrica.org). UK charity set up by Simon Headington which works with village projects in the Singida Region of Tanzania. Volunteers may join the project for four, seven or ten weeks for fees (respectively) of £950, £1330 and £1710, a large proportion of which is given as a donation to the host programme. Other vacancies in Africa with various charities and aid agencies are posted on this same site.

The Leap Overseas Ltd, 121 High St, Marlborough, Wilts. SN8 1LZ (01672 519922; www.theleap.co.uk). 12, 10 or 6 week voluntary placements in the field of eco-tourism in game parks and conservation zones in Kenya, Tanzania, Malawi, Botswana, Mozambique, South Africa and Zambia. £1600-£2900 excluding travel.

Madventurer, The Old Casino, 1-4 Forth Lane, Newcastle-upon-Tyne NE1 5HX (0845 121 1996; tribe@madventurer.com/ www.madventurer.com). Development travel organisation that arranges expeditions from anywhere from 2 to 15 weeks to Tanzania, Togo, Uganda and Kenya (as well as Latin America) that combine voluntary work and adventure travel. The summer fee for 8 weeks is from £1880.

MondoChallenge, Milton House, Gayton Rd, Milton Malsor, Northampton NN7 3AB (01604 858225; info@mondochallenge.org). Volunteer teachers including year-out students are sent to projects in 3 African countries. Tanzania (60 volunteers): locations include Longido (teaching in a Maasai village), Arusha (helping in an orphanage, teaching in primary or secondary school near Mt Meru) and Pangani on the coast, teaching adults and children. New programme planned in the Pane Mountains. The Business Development programme in Arusha involves micro-finance and training for small firms. Gambia: teaching in small village near the coast south of Banjul and business development in partnership with the Foresty Department. Kenya: new programme in the Maasai Mara area around Bomet, teaching in secondary schools with accommodation on-site.

> **David Breckenridge, a volunteer for MondoChallenge in 2004, found that he condensed wonderful experiences into the time he spent in Tanzania:**
> *It was the must fulfilling ten weeks of my life. I went into the project with a fairly open mind with intentions of trying, seeing or doing anything. What I didn't expect was to touch as many lives as I did, or to have mine touched by so many amazing people. I have kept contact with many of the people I met through MondoChallenge – local villagers at my project, other volunteers and the office support team– and hope for it to continue. Every week seemed like a month while I was there, in the sense that every day I felt I accomplished, learned and experienced more than I would in an entire week anywhere else.*

Operation Wallacea, Hope House, Old Bolingbroke, Nr Spilsby, Lincolnshire PE23 4EX (01790 763194; info@opwall.com). Marine and forest research projects in Egypt and (from 2006) South Africa.

Quest Overseas, The North West Stables, Borde Hill Estate, Balcombe Road, Haywards Heath, West Sussex RH16 1XP (01444 474744; emailus@questoverseas.com/ www.questoverseas.com). 12-week Africa programme with departures from January to April. 6-week voluntary conservation work in Swaziland or a community development project in Tanzania followed by a 6-week expedition through Mozambique, Botswana and Zambia. £4130 excluding flights and insurance. It was contact with the wildlife at Mbuluzi Game Reserve that proved the highlight for **Claire Gunn** who joined a Quest trip to Swaziland in 2005:

> *I've been sitting here trying to write a list of my best and worst moments from the past three months, which is harder than I originally thought. I'm onto my second page of best moments, but my worst moments page is still empty. I have absolutely loved every moment of the past three months. I couldn't have asked to spend my Gap Year with a better group of people or in a better place. The African pace of life suited me fine and was something I really needed after quite a difficult few years. The experience of living and working in Shewula was a great introduction to Africa and very rewarding when we finished at the environmental education centre. Mbuluzi Game reserve was my highlight of the project phase.*

Reefdoctor.org Ltd, 14 Charlwood Terrace, Putney, London SW15 1NZ (07866 250740; www.reefdoctor.org). New hands-on conservation programme for enthusiastic volunteers to become research assistants for 2-3 months in Madagascar. Based in Ifaty fishing village, volunteers help to survey the coral reef in the Bay of Ranobe. Non-divers can teach in the local school. Fee (2005) is £1100 a month.

Sudan Volunteer Programme, 34 Estelle Road, London NW3 2JY (tel/fax 020-7485 8619; davidsvp@blueyonder.co.uk). Needs volunteers to teach English in Sudan for 6 months or longer starting in early September, late December or 3 months from mid-June. Gap year students are now welcome to apply along with undergraduates and graduates; TEFL certificate and knowledge of Arabic are not required. Volunteers pay for their airfare (from £455) plus initial insurance (£60). Local host institutions pay for living expenses in Sudan; most are in the Khartoum area.

TackleAfrica, Estate Office. Pitt Hall Farm, Ramsdell, Basingstoke, Hampshire RG26 5RJ (01256 851144; www.tackleafrica.org) organises 6-week football tours around Africa which fee-paying volunteers may join (approximately £2500). Destination countries in 2005 are Malawi, Ethiopia and Uganda. Matches and tournaments are organised in collaboration with local NGOs and charities, which then mount HIV/AIDS awareness events on the back of the sporting event.

TANZED, 80 Edleston Road, Crewe, Cheshire CW2 7HD (01270 509994; enquiries@tanzed.org/ www.tanzed.org). Charity that recruits graduates to teach in rural government primary schools in the Morogoro region of Tanzania for one year. Fundraising target £2000 to cover airfare, visas, insurance, training and partial administrative costs.

Trade Aid Tanzania, Burgate Court, Burgate, Fordingbridge, Hants. SP6 1LX (01425 657774; info@tradeaiduk.org; www.tradeaiduk.org). Recruits both gap year volunteers (minimum age 17½) and professionals to work at schools and eco-tourism projects in and around Mikindani in southern Tanzania. Typical cost for 5½ months is £1500.

Travellers, 7 Mulberry Cottage, Ferring, W Sussex BN12 5HY (01903 502595; www.travellersworldwide.com). Teaching placements (English, French, drama, etc.) in Ghana, Kenya, South Africa and Zimbabwe. Conservation volunteering placements (with elephants, seahorses, lions, whales, dolphins, sharks and crocodiles) in South Africa and Kenya. Work experience in law, journalism, TV, veterinary medicine, etc. available in Ghana and South Africa. Placements start at £1095 for one month teaching in Kenya (including food and accommodation but not flights).

VAE Teachers Kenya, Bell Lane Cottage, Pudleston, Nr. Leominster, Herefordshire HR6 0RE (01568 750329; fax 01568 750636; www.vaekenya.co.uk). 6-month gap year placements from January teaching in rural schools in the central highlands of Kenya. Inclusive fee £3400.

A past volunteer with VAE is **Robert Breare** who tells his story on the *Gap Enterprise Consultants* website (www.gapenterprise.co.uk):

I thought I had it sorted: eighteen, House Captain, A-Levels under my belt, a place at Oxford and four months wages to travel on. In Kenya Njoroge thought that he had it sorted: eighteen, primary school exams finished, hands and feet calloused by a lifetime in the fields, but already in debt for his first two children's school fees. Njoroge became a good friend as I taught his children for six months in my year off, cramming eight children to a desk around a torn section of exercise book. Forty perpetually grinning children, driven by a desire to learn, were undeterred by wind driving through the crumbling mud walls...

Robert returned to university and set about raising £30,000 to help build a new school for the 600 children in that community in the Central Highlands of Kenya and went on to co-found the charity Harambee Schools Kenya (www.hsk.org.uk).

Venture Co, The Ironyard, 64-66 The Market Place, Warwick CV34 4SD (01926 411122/fax 01926 411133; mail@ventureco-worldwide.com/ www.ventureco-worldwide.com). Their Rift Valley Venture includes time spent at a Swahili language school on the banks of the River Nile in Uganda. The group do two aid projects: one in Tanzania working with disadvantaged youngsters south of Lake Victoria, and the other in the foothills of Kilimanjaro helping to conserve the ebony tree. The two-month expedition takes place in the Great Rift Valley and includes a camel trek, climbing Mt Kenya, the Mountains of the Moon and Kilimanjaro, a safari across the Serengeti and ends on the island of Zanzibar.

Village Education Project (Kilimanjaro), Mint Cottage, Prospect Road, Sevenoaks, Kent TN13 3UA (01732 459799; www.kiliproject.org). Gap year programme which sends 8-12 British students each year to help teach EFL and other subjects in village primary schools in Tanzania for 8-9 months from January. Fee is £2500.

WORLDwrite, Millfields Lodge, 201 Millfields Road, London E5 0AL (tel 020-8985 5435; world.write@btconnect.com; www.worldwrite.org.uk). International educational charity that uses documentary film making to investigate global issues. WorldWrite is affiliated with a film academy in Accra, Ghana (www.screenartsghana.org) which takes on occasional foreign volunteers to help organise and market the project; details from Kwame Agyapong (Academy of Screen Arts), PMB L13, University Post Office, Legon, Accra, Ghana (+233 2-508583; kwamiyep@africaonline.com.gh).

Joe Philp from Oxford had always planned to take a gap year, as a welcome breather between A levels and the long academic haul he envisioned for himself afterwards:

Because he had enjoyed French at A level, Joe wanted to find a placement in French-speaking Africa and quickly narrowed the destinations down to Togo (which unfortunately in 2005 has become 'No-go,' as the country has become seriously destabilised after the death of President Gnassingbe Eyadema in February 2005).

With a deferred offer to read history at Cambridge, Joe set about saving money to pay for the trip. His placement with Teaching & Projects Abroad was in the Togolese capital of Lomé in a local secondary school where he was to teach English. When faced with a very large class of children of many ages, he taught them songs and explained the lyrics, everything from 'Baa Baa Black Sheep' to Beatles songs. He noticed that gospel songs were very popular (so it might be worth expanding your repertoire before leaving). With the materials he had been advised to take, he devised games, for example to teach the children to put words in correct sentence order by rearranging cards stuck to the board with Blutac. Joe and his fellow volunteer (from the US) were innovative enough to have the children compose haikus and do other creative projects. They took some of the best examples of the pupils' work, mounted it on a large board and presented it to the school before their departure at the end of June, a gesture that was warmly appreciated.

He was happy with his accommodation with a family who had several grown-up sons living at home from whom he learned some Ewe (the main language of Togo), though French was the main means of communication. On a few occasions Joe used Ewe in the classroom which caused a near riot ('White man speak our language') and he was not sure that the teachers at the school approved of this. They ate mainly Togolese food (mashed yams, goat stew) occasionally supplemented with more familiar salads and chips. The situation of the few volunteers in Togo was in contrast to the group in Accra, the enormous sprawling capital of Ghana, where there was far more of a volunteers' scene. The Ghana volunteers swam in the pools of international hotels and went out on the town in herds. The much smaller cohort of volunteers in Lomé meant that each one had to show more initiative. At one point there were just four TPA volunteers which might have been daunting if any problems had arisen. The local rep did not make his presence felt much, although he did host 'palu parties' whenever someone recovered from malaria (palu is French for malaria). Despite taking a barrelful of drugs, Joe caught the disease more than once. Malaria is so commonplace that no one makes too much of a fuss.

He is next off to Colombia with a friend who spent his gap year in South America and invited him to attend the family wedding of a friend in Cartagena, much to the horror of his parents who have of course looked at the FCO travel advisory (which in Joe's opinion should be taken with a tablespoon of salt).

Courses and Work Experience

A few of the main language course organisers can arrange Arabic courses in Morocco, for example *Amerispan* and *CESA*; the latter offers beginner and more advanced courses for three or six weeks starting at £455. **Jill Cavanagh** was very happy with the Arabic course that CESA arranged for her in Fez:

> My aim was to gain a basic grounding in Arabic and to learn about Morocco and Islam from being exposed to the culture. I left feeling I had a strong beginning in conversational Arabic. The family I stayed with were very welcoming and supportive. I was invited to join in many family activities and was always offered help with homework, etc. Plus I was fed wonderfully. The downsides are far outweighed by the good aspects of life here. The men aren't that big a deal. Yeah, they hassle you a bit, but you quickly learn how to deal with this, and even though it doesn't go away, you get used to it.

Other courses of possible interest to year-out students revolve around music and dance. For example it is possible to study drumming, for example at the Academy of Music & Art in Kokrobite not far from Accra in Ghana or on the Senegalese island of Ile de Goree. *African Legacy* (in the Directory of Volunteering) runs trips for paying volunteers to study and preserve the archaeology, ecology, wildlife and cultural landscapes of Nigeria.

An interesting three-week cross-cultural trip is run from the US to Senegal every summer by Intercultural Dimensions (PO Box 391437, Cambridge, MA 02139-0015; www. interculturaldimensions.org). Participants can improve their conversational French while working alongside Senegalese people. Arrangements can be made to extend the stay for volunteer work, field work or internships to study dance, musical instruments, the Madinka language, etc.

Opportunities to do paid work are very limited in Africa although Ghana has a long tradition of welcoming foreign students to participate in its educational and commercial life.

Workcamps

Short-term workcamps operate in many African countries, mainly to assist with rural development, for example installing water supplies or to assist with social welfare, e.g. working in homes for disabled or underprivileged children. You have to finance your own travel and pay a registration fee to cover food and lodging for the three to six week duration of the camp. To find out about the range of workcamps in Africa, it is a good idea to consult the international list of projects from a sending organisation in your own country, e.g. *International Voluntary Service, UNA Exchange* or VFP in the US (www.vfp.org).

If you want to arrange a place on an African workcamp before leaving home, you may have to prove to an international organisation that you have enough relevant experience. The workcamp movement is particularly well developed in North Africa especially Morocco which has a number of regional organisations creating green spaces, building communal facilities, etc. If you decide to try to join a project once you are in an African capital like Nairobi, Accra or Freetown, it should not be hard to track down a co-ordinating office. Ask at the YMCA or in prominent churches.

Organisations in the US

From the US, try any of these voluntary organisations for short or long-term projects in Africa:

Cross-Cultural Solutions, 2 Clinton Place, New Rochelle, NY 10801 (800-380-4777; www. crossculturalsolutions.org). Volunteer vacations in villages in Ghana and Tanzania to teach English, provide skills training or enhance recreation programmes in village schools. The programme fees cover expenses but not airfares: from $2175 for 2 weeks to $4873 for 12 weeks.

Operation Crossroads Africa, Inc, PO Box 5570, New York, NY 10027 (212-289-1949; http://operationcrossroadsafrica.org). Runs 7-week summer projects in rural Africa staffed by self-financing volunteers from the U.S. and Canada. Inclusive cost is $3500. The deadline for applications is 1st February.

United Children's Fund, PO Box 20341, Boulder, CO 80308-3341 (800-615-5229; www. unchildren.org). East Africa aid organisation which places volunteers in Ugandan clinics, schools, farms, etc. for short periods or 6 months. Fees from $820 for 1 week to $6750 for 6 months, excluding airfares.

Visions in Action, 2710 Ontario Rd., NW, Washington, DC 20009 (202-625-7402; www. visionsinaction.org). 6 and 12 month volunteer positions in Uganda, Zimbabwe, Burkina Faso, South Africa, and Tanzania plus short-term opportunities in Tanzania. Volunteers must have a degree or relevant work experience to fill positions in human rights, journalism, micro-enterprise, social work, health, environment and research. Participation fees from $3400 for summer in Tanzania to $6700 for 12 months in South Africa.

World Camp for Kids, 367 Paul Presnell Road, Sugar Grove, NC 28679 (919-967-3303; worldcampforkids@hotmail.com/ www.worldcampforkids.org). Address in Malawi: Box 1866; Lilongwe (+265-991-1377). Volunteers mainly get involved in HIV/AIDS education in Malawi, departing January-February and June-August for 5 or 10 weeks ($2300 or $2800 participation fee).

WorldTeach Inc, Center for International Development, Harvard University, 79 John F Kennedy Street, Cambridge, MA 02138 (617-495-5527/800-4-TEACH-0; info@worldteach.org/ www.worldteach.org). Non-profit organisation that recruits volunteers to teach English for up to 12 months from late December in Namibia (fee $5990) or for the summer ($3990). Minimum age 18 for summer programmes. Longer term volunteers must complete 25 hours of ESL teaching before departure.

YMCA International, 5 West 63rd St, 2nd Floor, New York, NY 10023 (212-727-8800 ext 4303; www.ymcaglobal.org). Places volunteers for 2-12 months in Ghana and Gambia to work in education, youth work and computing. The programme fee is $500.

GRASSROOTS VOLUNTARY ORGANISATIONS

Parts of Africa are still very reliant on aid agencies, mission societies and voluntary assistance. The large majority of volunteers in Africa are trained teachers, doctors, nurses, agricultural and technical specialists who have committed themselves to work with mainstream aid organisations like VSO and Skillshare Africa for at least two years. However openings for unskilled volunteers do exist through smaller charities and indigenous NGOs. It may be possible to offer your services on a voluntary basis to any hospital, school or mission you come across in your travels, though success is not guaranteed. If you have a useful skill and a letter of introduction from a church or family friend, your way will be made smoother. After leaving school, **Benjamin Fry** travelled to the Jiropa Hospital in the Upper Region of Ghana and persuaded the head of the mission hospital who was an acquaintance of his parents to keep him on for a while. He did odd jobs around the hospital such as cleaning the pharmacy and wards, assembling an incubator imported from Uganda and helping in the orphanage in exchange for his keep.

Till Bruckner is a veteran world traveller who has developed a strong preference for fixing up teaching and voluntary placements independently after arrival rather than with the help of an agency:

> My advice to anyone who wants to volunteer in Africa (or anywhere else) is to go first and volunteer second. That way you can travel until you've found a place you genuinely like and where you think you might be able to make a difference. You can also check out the work and accommodation for yourself before you settle down. If you're willing to work for free, you don't need a nanny to tell you where to go. Just go.

However for those who find this prospect daunting (and unless you are a mature and seasoned traveller you probably will), you might like to pursue the middle way which is to make contact with small local organisations in Africa which actively welcome volunteers from abroad, though be prepared for problems in communication. The following are listed in alphabetical order by country. Ghana probably has the most highly developed network of projects:

ICEYOM/Cameroon Vision Trust, PO Box 1075, Limbe, Cameroon (see entry in 'Directory of Volunteering Abroad').

CYTOFWEA, Charity Youth Travel & Working Experiences Abroad, PO Box CO55, Tema, Ghana (cytofwea2001@yahoo.com). Self-funding international volunteers placed in range of development projects in Ghana, e.g. schools, wildlife rehabilitation centres and eco-tourist projects, for varying periods.

RUSO (Rural Upgrade Support Organisation), c/o University of Ghana, PMB L21, Legon, Accra, Ghana (513149; www.interconnection.org/ruso). International volunteers join tree planting, AIDS awareness education, fish farming and other projects especially in the Kome area of Ghana. The cost to volunteers is a $300 registration fee plus $25 per week for stays of 1-3 months or $15 a week if staying 3-6 months.

Save the Earth Network (STEN), PO Box CT 3635, Cantonments-Accra, Ghana; +233-27-7743139; ebensten@yahoo.com). Ebeh Mensah, the Director, is currently developing a new volunteer programme and website.

Volunteer in Africa, 10 Tackie Tawiah Avenue Road, Adabraka, Accra, Ghana (+233-27-7346419; www.volunteeringinafrica.org). See entry in 'Directory of Volunteering Abroad'.

Future in our Hands (FIOH) Kenya, PO Box 4037, Kisumu, Kenya (03-40522; fiohk@hotmail.com). Volunteers needed for 5 weeks to 6 months. Branches also in Cameroon, Sierra Leone, Liberia and South Africa. UK link office is FIOH, 48 Churchward Avenue, Swindon, Wilts. SN2 1NH (www.fiohnetwork.org). The movement supports small charities in Africa with funding and volunteers.

Sénévolu, Dakar (550 4885; fax 855 7172; www.senevolu.mypage.org). Involves foreign young people in local community projects and schools while living with a local family and spending weekends in cultural workshops in drumming, batik, etc. Minimum stay 3 weeks; fee €625/$750.

AJVPE – Association des Jeunes Volontaire pour le Protection de l'Environment, B.P. 4568, Lomé, Togo (901 2506; enquiries@ajvpe-togo.org; www.ajvpe-togo.org). Summer workcamps last 21 days carrying out projects like tree planting and building a municipal garden in the small town of Agbodrafo.

WWOOF Uganda, PO Box 2001, Kampala, Uganda (+256-346856; bob_kasule@yahoo.com). Membership fee of £10/$15 (bank drafts only).

SOUTHERN AFRICA

Undaunted by the frightening levels of violent urban crime, many year out and volunteer agencies have programmes in South Africa, the majority of which involve placing volunteers in orphanages or special schools. *BUNAC* is unusual in offering a Work South Africa programme run in partnership with the South African Student Travel Services (11 Bree St, Cape Town 8000; 021 418 3794; www.sasts.org.za). The 12-month special work permit is available to full-time university students under 30 of any nationality or those who have graduated in the past six months. The programme fee is £350 plus flights, work permit and insurance. Participants are allowed to take any job they can find. BUNAC warns that finding a job can be tough, though easier in the high season between October and March. BUNAC also runs an eight-week summer volunteer programme in South Africa; the current fee is £795 excluding visa and flights to Cape Town. Departures are monthly between February and November.

One of the advantages of being attached to a school is that most gap year volunteers are free to travel during school holidays. Many in South Africa choose to do the Garden Route or explore the Cedarberg mountain range. Post-placement travel destinations include Victoria Falls in Zimbabwe, Botswana (with its Okavango Swamps) and Namibia.

African Conservation Experience (PO Box 206, Faversham, Kent, ME13 8WZ; 0870 241 5816; www.ConservationAfrica.net) sends people to game and nature reserves in southern Africa where they do conservation work with rangers and conservationists and get first-hand experience of animal and plant conservation. The total cost is about £4000 for 12 weeks (see 'Directory of Specialist Gap Year Programmes').

Wilderness Foundation, 47-49 Main Road, Broomfield, Chelmsford, Essex CM1 7BU; 01245 443073; www.wildernessfoundation.org.uk. Conservation volunteers help with the running of a small game reserve and a larger developmental mega-reserve programme in South Africa (as well as a community-based programme in Kenya). The average cost is £1500 for 3 months excluding flights.

Worldwide Experience (Guardian House, Borough Road, Godalming, Surrey GU7 2AE; 01483 860560; www.WorldwideExperience.com) is another specialist gap year programme available on South Africa's game reserves and in other community volunteer projects. Over the course of the placements, which last between a fortnight and three months, volunteers participate in a range of conservation activities to support the ongoing work being carried out to protect wildlife (see entry for *EcoAfrica Experience*). The price of £3900 for a 12-week placement includes flights from London.

Willing Workers in South Africa (WWISA) is a community service volunteer organisation based in The Crags, near Plettenberg Bay. Whatever their age and skills, volunteers work on projects alongside local villagers according to their interests, options and available dates, in the areas for example of schooling and education, youth development, business development, health care and environmental research. Programmes are geared to the social and economic enhancement of the local rural community of Kurland Village. Prices should be checked on the website www.wwisa.co.za, though as a rough guide participants pay £550 per month, £585 from 2006.

Volunteer sports coaches, recreation leaders and sports organisers over 20 are placed in rural or urban communities for 6-12 months from January or July. Further details of this programme are available from *SCORE/Sports Coaches' OutReach* (PO Box 4989, Cape Town 8000; info@score.org.za; www.score.org.za) or from the European office in Amsterdam (score.europe@planet.nl). Suitable candidates must be interested in hands-on development work and willing to live with a host family. Participants receive a nominal monthly stipend but pay an administrative fee of €2500 for six months, €3500 for 12 months, which covers living expenses and in-country travel. (See entry in 'Directory of Volunteering Abroad'.)

After starting his course in Sports, Exercise and Leisure Studies at the University Of Ulster, twenty-one year old Niall Johnson joined the SCORE programme in South Africa and found it fulfilling on various fronts:
The term of service for volunteers begins with a General Orientation in Paarl, Western Cape which aims to equip the group of mostly European volunteers with the skills to cope with the traumatic transition of moving from a relatively secure Dutch, Norwegian, Finnish lifestyle to the insecurities of Cape Town or

a rural African setting...Soon these people from all over Europe and Southern Africa became my best friends and adequately took the place of all those I had left at home. My firm friends from this programme have promised me places to stay for free in their own countries, one of the many benefits to arise from this year.

Professionally, the benefits have been immense... I have been not only teaching PE in three primary schools for up to six hours a day, but I have been teaching teachers how to teach and evaluating their progress together. I have had event management of a kind that cannot be found at home; the major event of my first three months was the Provincial Tournament which was hosted in my own village of Ga-Nchabeleng, Northern Province about 100kms south of Pietersburg. All these experiences are so different in an African setting. These are rural communities with little money around to spare for transport, expensive materials, equipment and manpower. It's a different mindset, the most important facet of which is 'African Time.'

Tourism

Cape Town is the tourist capital of South Africa including for backpackers, though jobs are harder to find here than elsewhere. Furthermore the job hunt is made much harder by the competition from a large number of Zimbabwean exiles who are willing to accept low wages.

Although himself at the upper end of 'youth', **Roger Blake** made extensive use of South Africa's youth hostels and several times was able to extend his stay by working for his keep:

There are more than 100 hostels in South Africa, many of which 'employ' backpackers on a casual basis. Within two weeks of arrival I was at a hostel in George on a work-for-keep basis. Through contacts made here I also sold T-shirts at the beach for a small profit and I did a few days at a pizza place for tips only. Then I was offered a job at a hostel in Oudtshoorn (Backpackers Oasis). They gave me free accommodation and 150 rand a week to run the bar and help prepare the ostrich braai (BBQ) that they have every evening. Also I did breakfasts for fellow travellers which was like being self-employed as I bought all the ingredients and kept all the profit. It was a small but worthwhile fortune after six weeks here.

Although Johannesburg is often maligned as a big, bad, city, it is the earning capital of South Africa with better job possibilities than many other places. Unfortunately some of the inner city areas where backpackers used to congregate and find jobs (Yeoville, Brixton) have succumbed to the crime and grime for which the city is known. Now the areas to head for restaurant and pub work are Sandton and Rosebank. Many travellers now prefer the northern suburbs to which hostels like the Ritz now in Dunkeld West (1A North Road, ritz@iafrica.com) and Rockey's have moved. Rockey's of Fourways (22 Campbell Road, Craigavon A.H., Sandton; 011-465 4219; www.backinafrica.com) is in an area where within a 5km radius there are more than 60 restaurants & bars, five huge night clubs, the new Montecasino complex and other backpackers' lodges. Travellers can often get jobs waiting tables, working on the bar, etc. as the owners of Rockey's of Fourways confirmed in 2005.

Conservation and Wildlife

An increasing number of companies and eco-tourism operations are marketing the South African wilderness to gap year students (and others) as a place to learn skills and see big game. The *African Conservation Trust,* PO Box 310, 3652 Link Hills (tel/fax +27 31-2016180; info@projectafrica.com/ www.projectafrica.com) is a South African based trust that recruits self-funding volunteers to staff environmental research projects in Botswana and KwaZulu Natal; the contribution expected is at least £450 per month.

A company in Cape Town called Bio-Experience (tel/fax +27 21-557 4942; www.bioexperience.org) aims to help South African nature reserves and wildlife rehabilitation centres by arranging for fee-paying international and local volunteers to spend a working holiday assisting them. International volunteers assist with various projects otherwise unaffordable to reserve owners due to a lack of funding. Volunteers can get involved in wildlife feeding and cage cleaning at wildlife centres and invader plant control and game counts at nature reserves. The inclusive participation fee differs but an example of two weeks monitoring baboons costs 3000 Rand and four weeks rehabilitating marine birds (mainly penguins) is R6,200.

One of the projects to which Bio-Experience sends foreign volunteers is the seabird conservation organisation, the South African National Foundation for the Conservation of Coastal Birds. SANCCOB requires volunteers to help with the cleaning and rehabilitation of oil-soaked birds since oil pollution is a major problem in the coastal waters of South Africa. Volunteers must pay a joining fee of R800 and fund their own living expenses for at least six weeks. Details are available from SANCCOB, PO Box 11116, Bloubergrant 7443, Cape Town (021-557 6155; www.sanccob.co.za).

Wild at Heart in Kwazulu Natal (see entry in 'Directory of Volunteering Abroad') offers hands-on opportunities to work with species such as lions, cheetah and elephants at wildlife rehabilitation centres in Africa. Approximately 2500 students visit these projects in Africa each year with Wild at Heart. See also the entry for the umbrella company *GoXPLOR* (www.goxploreafrica.com) which also has openings in community volunteering.

Kwa Madwala Private Game Reserve has a three-month gap year programme in the Kruger National Park (see entry in 'Directory of Specialist Gap Year Programmes'). Also Track Africa based in KwaZulu Natal (+27 33 330 2182; www.trackafrica.com) places volunteers aged 17 and above for 1-3 months on its 1000 sq km reserve in the North West Cape province of South Africa. It offers a specialised programme called 'Take the Gap' inviting gap year students to serve as wildlife custodians in a programme that includes wildlife and fishing safaris.

Another volunteer placement company is AVIVA (Africa Volunteering & Ventures Abroad, PO Box 60573, Flamingo Square, Table View, Cape Town 7439; 021-557 5996; www.aviva-sa.com). Their range of placements includes working with street children (fee of £1176/$2116 for 12 weeks) and working in a wildlife sanctuary (£873/$1613 for 4 weeks).

In Kenya, the Tsavo Conservation Trust (PO Box 48019, Nairobi, Kenya; 02-331191; www.originsafaris.info/community-volunteer.htm) runs a community volunteer programme which can make use of competent, but not necessarily qualified, volunteers in a variety of conservation and community projects in rural Kenya. The minimum stay is one month at a cost of $920. The Trust runs the Taita Discovery Centre in the wilds of Kenya where a number of gap year students are placed on organised schemes.

Willing Workers in South Africa places international volunteers in projects related to eco-tourism, skills transfer and social services. WWISA tries to match volunteer requests with projects which are all located along the Garden Route and in the Eastern Cape. Participants pay $380 for the first month, $350 thereafter and, in exchange for working six hours a day, are given free room and board. Details are available from WWISA, PO Box 2413, Plettenberg Bay 6600 (fax 044-534 8958; wwisaafrica@telkomsa.net; www.wwisa.co.za).

The US charity IDA Africa (In Defense of Animals), 700 SW 126th Ave., Beaverton, OR 97005 (503-643-8302; www.ida-africa.org/volunteer.html) sends volunteers who are able to communicate in French (rather than monkey language) to a chimpanzee sanctuary in Yaounde, Cameroon, for a minimum of six months. Very few opportunities present themselves in the vast nation of Congo, but it is possible to join a project to release orphaned chimps into the wild. H.E.L.P. Congo (BP 335, Pointe Noire, Republic of Congo) accepts volunteers with field experience in the tropical forest and with primates. Volunteers should send a CV and letter of motivation to carole.tisserand@free.fr or help.

congo@cg.celtelplus.com and, if accepted, contribute €400 per month for their keep and transport, for a minimum of three months.

EXPEDITIONS

The African continent hosts a huge variety of scientific and conservation expeditions and most interests can be accommodated, from measuring the height of waterfalls in Lesotho to tracking warthogs in a Ghanaian national park. If by any chance you know someone doing a PhD on a relevant African subject, you might be able to persuade him or her of your usefulness. But most gap year students will join a more formal expedition, either one organised through a university or the Royal Geographical Society or one set up by an expedition society like BSES or one of the following (most of which have entries in the *Directory of Specialist Gap Year Programmes)*:

Frontier, 50-52 Rivington St, London EC2A 3QP (020-7613 2422; www.frontier.ac.uk). Volunteers spend 4, 8, 10 or 20 weeks helping in wildlife and environmental research and conservation expeditions in the forests, savanna and marine habitats of Madagascar and Tanzania. Volunteers must make a contribution from £2000 for 10 weeks or £3500 for 20 weeks, excluding flights and insurance. Participants can choose to qualify for a BTEC Level 3 Advanced Diploma in Tropical Habitat Conservation.

Greenforce, 11-15 Betterton Street, Covent Garden, London WC2H 9BP (020-7470 8888; www.greenforce.org). Recruits volunteer researchers to join wildlife surveys in Tanzania to study threatened species and habitats. No previous experience needed as training is provided. The cost for 10 weeks is £2300 plus flight.

Raleigh International, 27 Parsons Green Lane, London SW6 4HZ (020-7371 8585; www.raleighinternational.org). Leading youth development charity that offers people aged 17-25 the chance to take part in challenging environmental, community and adventure projects as part of 4, 7 or 10-week programmes in Namibia. Community projects could involve installing sports facilities or adventure playgrounds in partnership with the Ministry for Basic Education Sports & Culture. On a sample environmental project, participants work in Khaudom National Park with the Ministry of Environment & Tourism to construct game-viewing hides or protection walls in rural areas so villages can collect water without fear of desert-dwelling elephants. Costs from about £1500-£3000 depending on duration (excluding travel).

Wind, Sand & Stars, 6 Tyndale Terrace, London N1 2AT (020-7359 7551; www.wind-sandstars.co.uk). Annual summer expedition for 16-23 year olds (and the young-at-heart) to the mountains or desert areas of the Sinai Peninsula of Egypt, combining local project work with the semi-nomadic Bedouin tribes and developing leadership and remote survival skills. Opportunities for camel trekking. The 4-week trip costs £1450 excluding flights.

Several years ago **Andrew Roland-Price** joined a *BSES* expedition to the Sinai. The expedition divided into six groups carrying out various scientific tasks and he felt himself fortunate that his group had the most variety. After studying water supplies in the granite desert of west Sinai for two weeks and then in the sandstone desert of east Sinai for two weeks, they carried out an historical and archaeological survey of various sites and a marine biology study of the Red Sea:

> For me the highlight of each day was lying around the camp fire, worn out but with a full stomach, chatting to the Bedouin guides and looking up at the stars. Away from the ambient light, the Milky Way was visible, and we saw countless shooting stars and satellites each evening…The highlight came with the viewing of sunrise from the top of Mt. Sinai.

Tom Watkins joined a *BSES* expedition at the other end of the African continent. In the summer before his A-level year, he went to Lesotho and found the experience satisfying in every respect. His group was studying an endangered species of plant, the spiral aloe, which is a national symbol and grows only on steep and remote mountain slopes in that country. In fact there was scope for pursuing non-botanical interests. For example Tom became interested in the history and politics of Lesotho and explored these topics with the help of Libe the local man who was their guide and interpreter and also by getting to know the expatriate Englishman who ran the local museum in Morija and who had written books about the region. By contrast, the assistant leader, who was just finishing an art degree, was more interested in the rock art and the architecture of Lesotho. The expedition benefited the scientists, the locals and the Young Explorers.

Richard Jenson enjoyed his time in Tanzania with Frontier tremendously:
Having narrowed down all the options, I chose to go to East Africa with Frontier, studying the savannah grasslands out there. Like a lot of people, I love the wildlife programmes on TV and the chance to go and track elephants on the African plains was mind-blowing. Of course there was the little matter of raising £2000…I can't imagine a better feeling than when I realised I had reached my target. Having worked so hard, I was determined to have the time of my life. It wasn't difficult. The area we were working in was right next to the Selous Game Reserve, the largest game reserve in the world and it was absolutely incredible. Elephants, giraffes, buffaloes, hippos, you name them, we saw them. It was like our very own mini-safari but without all the other tourists. My personal favourites though are zebras. It was only seeing them in real life that made me realise just how strange a black and white striped horse really is.
I spent a lot of time with the local traditional healers. Many of their children are attracted by the bright lights of the big cities and the healers have no one to pass their knowledge on to. My job was to make a note of all the plants and herbs they use. It was absolutely fascinating, hearing how they deal with rheumatism, headache and malaria. And as for the cure for male impotence involving a razor blade, that is definitely not something to be tried at home. I have so many great memories of Africa that my friends have nicknamed me 'Wiwia' because everything I say starts with 'When I was in Africa'. I have definitely caught the African bug and can't wait to go back. I just wish I could have my gap year all over again.

ADVENTURE TRAVEL

Anyone with a diver's certificate might be able to find work at Red Sea resorts like Sharm el Sheikh and Hurghada. If you aren't sufficiently qualified but want to gain the appropriate certificates, the Red Sea is a good place to train. Emperor Scuba Schools (www.emperordivers.com) have five schools on the Red Sea at Hurghada, Sharm El Sheikh, Nuweiba, Dahab and Port Sudan. Once you are qualified as an instructor, they might hire you or help you make contact with diving schools worldwide. At local dive centres, you can sometimes get free lessons in exchange for filling air tanks for a sub-aqua club. It is possible to be taken on by an Egyptian operator (especially in the high season November to January); however the norm is to be paid no wage and just earn a percentage of the take. You could also check out http://jobs.red-sea.com.

Overland tour operators make it possible for young travellers to visit remote parts of Africa in relative safety. Many companies are listed at www.go-overland.com. Some African specialists are:

Absolute Africa, 41 Swanscombe Road, Chiswick, London W4 2HL (020-8742 0226; www.absoluteafrica.com).

Acacia Expeditions, Lower Ground Floor, 23A Craven Terrace, London W2 3QH (020-7706 4700; www.acacia-africa.com).

Bukima Africa, PO Box 43963, London NW2 5WD (08707572230; www.bukima.com).

Economic Expeditions, 22 Craven Terrace, London W2 3QH (207 262 0177; www.

economicexpeditions.com).

Oasis Overland, The Marsh, Henstridge, Somerset BA8 0TF (01963 363400; www. oasisoverland.co.uk). Medium length trips in Africa cost around £100 a week plus about £40 a week local payment.

Overland Club, Salters House, Salters Lane, Sedgefield, Stockton-on-Tees TS21 3EE (0845 658 0036; www.africa-overland.com).

Phoenix Expeditions, College Farm, Far St, Wymeswold, Leicestershire LE12 6TZ (01509 881818; www.phoenixexpeditions.co.uk).

Truck Africa - www.truckafrica.com.

Young people interested in working as drivers, guides or couriers for an overland company should be aware that couriers are required to have first-hand knowledge of travel in Africa or must be willing to train for three months with no guarantee of work. Requirements vary but normally expedition leaders must be at least 23 and be trained diesel mechanics.

Once again travellers' hostels are a magnet for young travellers, and even in some cases provide opportunities for longer stays by offering a work-for-keep arrangement. It is something that many independent trans-Africa travellers do for the odd week, from the Red Sea to the suburbs of Johannesburg, and is a way to have a break without having to pay for it. Bear in mind that the Tourism Concern report published a few years ago, which lambasted gap year travellers for their insensitivity to other cultures, was largely based on research carried out in the backpackers' diving resort of Dahab in Egypt. If your aim is to experience an alien culture, it may be preferable not to move from one backpackers' enclave to the next.

If exploring the African bush always take the necessary precautions proffered by rangers and other old hands, to avoid what happened to a 19 year old gap year student a couple of years ago. When David Pleydell-Bouverie was working at the remote Matusadona National Park in Zimbabwe, he was killed by a pride of lions after he failed to zip up his tent.

While travelling throughout Africa, be prepared for contradictions and aggravations. One trick which might help at border crossings is to carry an official-looking list of addresses, for example of voluntary organisations, to show to suspicious immigration authorities.

Asia

Lumping together places as different as Java and Japan, Hong Kong and Ho Chi Minh City is a dangerous business. The gap year experiences of the student who spends six months in Singapore because her uncle can arrange a job for her in his export business may have almost nothing in common with those of the gap year volunteer who teaches at a village school in Nepal. Different corners of the vast continent of Asia beguile individuals for personal and possibly inexplicable reasons. Perhaps a childhood book, acquaintance or memory has bequeathed a longing to visit a faraway and mysterious place. This may not be the kind of reason which cuts much ice with college admissions tutors but it can be what sparks incredible and memorable experiences.

There are dangers in spending time at a young age in a seriously alien country. This is true of Bolivia, Zambia or even Romania but somehow the culture shock which gap year travellers experience in the Indian subcontinent or in a small industrial Chinese town is especially acute. A novelty-seeking foreigner is not really what a struggling village in Bengal or Borneo most needs. Preconceptions about what benefits you will be able to bring are often proved misguided in the first week. **Andy Green** spent some time with a long-established voluntary organisation in India and came to some rather negative conclusions about volunteering in India:

> I did two weeks' worth of workcamps and I feel that I was of no help to Indian society whatsoever. Due to differences in climate, food and culture, it is difficult to be productive. I could have paid an Indian a few pounds to do what I did in two weeks. It was however an experience I'll never forget.

In other words, the experience is bound to benefit you, the gap year traveller, but its value to local people may be questionable. That is not to say that a six-month attachment to a school or orphanage will not be valuable for the local community, but its value might lie in unexpected places.

The climate is not a trivial concern. Although Robert Abblett had carefully planned his trip to India and had the addresses of organic farms where he intended to work, he had not counted on the debilitating heat and decided to enjoy a holiday instead. This is an alternative worth considering, i.e. to make your fortune at home or in a western country, whether as an accountancy trainee in England, chambermaid in Switzerland or tomato picker in Australia, in order to finance months of leisurely travel in the developing countries of Asia.

Of course this may not apply to the countries of Asia with developed or rapidly developing economies, principally Japan, Taiwan, Korea, China, the Hong Kong Special Administrative Region and Singapore. Special schemes permit pre- and post-university students to work in some of these countries, mainly as teachers of the English language.

SENDING AGENCIES

Most of the key gap organisations make placements in a number of Asian countries including *GAP Activity Projects, Global Adventures Project, VentureCo's Himalaya Venture, Africa & Asia Venture, Project Trust, Students Partnership Worldwide, Travellers* and *Teaching & Projects Abroad*. India and Thailand are probably the most popular destinations, though opportunities exist throughout the continent.

> **Although he was born long after Simon and Garfunkel's song was a hit, Mike Jarvis was most struck by the sound of silence when he spent four months in the Indian subcontinent in 2005 with VentureCo Worldwide. His description captures some of the exotic magic of India:**
>
> India is hectic; full on. You are never on your own. That's the biggest difference between home and here: the sheer presence of humanity. But that is also India's biggest attraction, the culture, how people tick to Indian rhythms.
>
> The first part of our 4-month venture was to learn about our host community, the Vishnois, who are desert dwellers, eking out an existence on the edge of the Rajasthan desert. They are the original conservationists and have lived in harmony with their environment for centuries. As we first walked onto their lands I noticed a Blackbuck, which is a kind of deer. We walked within 20 yards of it before it wandered off, unconcerned, to find something else to eat. The Vishnois are vegetarian and hold all animal life sacred and the wild animals seem to know this and are really at home on Vishnois land.
>
> Our project with the Vishnois was to refurbish a local school and to put bearings into quern stones. Quern stones are used by the Vishnois women to mill their corn; by the time the women are about 40, they have permanently damaged their elbows because of the repeated action of pushing the heavy granite stones. So VentureCo organise this project to take the bearing from the back wheel of a bike and insert it between the quern stones, allowing the stones to turn with a fingertip. It takes 4 hours, and a local mason does the stone cutting: total cost? 47p! Such a neat solution!

> *After 4 weeks we left the Vishnois on camel back and set out across the Rajasthan desert. The first camp was close to some sand dunes so we went for a walk to watch the sun set, which was an incredible view, as well as watching huge dung beetles do what they do best! We headed back to our camp for dinner just before dark. And then the stars came out! We were so far from any town that there was zero light pollution; I never knew there were so many stars! The star-scape was so big that it felt as if you were beneath a dome. It was so quiet, I swear you could hear the silence. No light pollution; no sound pollution! A unique experience: an oasis of peace, far from the teeming masses. Then the moon came out and was amazingly bright and the air was still, with the silence broken only by the grunt of a camel or the gentle sound of a camel breaking wind - which happened very frequently. The final leg of this trip goes to Everest Base Camp. Can't wait!*

If you want to spend time in a less well-travelled country of Asia, it will be necessary to sift through the literature of all the relevant organisations to find which ones (if any) offer what you are looking for, for example the *Daneford Trust* has placements in Bangladesh, *Coral Cay Conservation* has projects in the Philippines, Fiji and Malaysia, *Travellers* in Brunei and Borneo (as well as China, Malaysia and Sri Lanka), *Raleigh International* in Sabah-Borneo, *GAP* in Vanuatu and Fiji, *Outreach International* sends people to Cambodia to teach English, computing, art, etc., *i-to-i* has sizeable programmes in Sri Lanka and Mongolia, and so on.

EXPEDITIONS & CONSERVATION

The mainstream London-based conservation expedition organisers all run projects in Asia. These expeditions are normally open to anyone reasonably fit who can raise the cost of joining (typically £2500-£3000; see *Directory of Specialist Gap Year Programmes* for further details):

Coral Cay Conservation, The Tower, 13th Floor, 125 High Street, Colliers Wood, London SW19 2JG (0870 750 0668; info@coralcay.org). Volunteers are needed to assist with reef and tropical forest surveys in the Philippines and Malaysia to help protect some of the world's most diverse tropical environments. Full training in marine and terrestrial ecology is provided. Marine expeditions cost about £1800 for 6 weeks, forest expeditions £1150 (excluding flights and insurance).

Frontier, 50-52 Rivington St, London EC2A 3QP (020-7613 2422; info@frontier.ac.uk/ www.frontier.ac.uk). Volunteers can spend 4, 8, 10 or 20 weeks in Fiji (10 weeks for £2400) or in Cambodia (10 weeks for £2000) helping in environmental research and conservation expeditions. Participants can choose to qualify for a BTEC Level 3 Advanced Diploma in Tropical Habitat Conservation.

Although **Joanne Roberts** from Newbury wanted to study law not ecology, she hugely enjoyed her six months with Frontier when it was active in Vietnam:

> *It took us three days to get from Hanoi to our work-site right up in the north. We started off in a Bedford truck, then swapped to a 4 wheel-drive once the road deteriorated. The final ten kilometres were covered on the back of ponies as we went up into the mountains. We really felt like we were going to the end of the world. Everything else seemed a lifetime away. Our six months in the mountains were amazing. The work we were doing really made a difference. We weren't building fences or other physical stuff but carrying out proper environmental research work, looking at the different species that lived in the forest and talking to the local people to find out what problems they faced. The people were incredible; they were so friendly, giving us food when they clearly didn't have enough for themselves and offering help. And they were curious. We were the first westerners they had seen in 20 years. Now I'm at university those six months in Vietnam don't seem real.*

Global Vision International (GVI), Amwell Farmhouse, Nomansland, Wheathampstead, St. Albans, Herts. AL4 8EJ (0870 608 8898; info@gvi.co.uk/ www.gvi.co.uk). Placements from 3 weeks to 1 year. Wildlife and community work in Thailand, Nepal and Sri Lanka, and work with orangutans in Sumatra. Prices from £735 to £1100.

Greenforce, 11-15 Betterton St, Covent Garden, London WC2H 9BP (020-7470 8888/ fax 020-379 0801; info@greenforce.org/ www.greenforce.org). Volunteer researchers are needed to join coral reef survey projects in Fiji and Indonesian Borneo. Training is given in the UK and in the host country. Projects involve studying endangered species and habitats. The cost is £2300 for 10 weeks plus PADI training at £200 if needed. Greenforce now also works in Nepal's Chitwan National Park assisting local people with reforestation, etc. Instruction in Nepali language is given.

Operation Wallacea, Hope House, Old Bolingbroke, Nr Spilsby, Lincolnshire PE23 4EX (01790 763194; www.opwall.com). Volunteer students, divers and naturalists assist with surveys of marine and rainforest habitats on remote islands of Southwest Sulawesi in Indonesia. Dive training can be given. Land surveys for studying birds and mammals also organised. Volunteers stay 2, 4, 6 or 8 weeks. Costs from £950 for 2 weeks to £2800 for 8 weeks, excluding flights.

Orangutan Foundation, 7 Kent Terrace, London, NW1 4RP (020-7724 2912/fax 020-7706 2613; info@orangutan.org.uk/ www.orangutan.org.uk). Volunteers are based in Kalimantan, Indonesian Borneo and participate in hands-on conservation fieldwork. Volunteers must note that there is no direct work with orangutans, although wild and/or rehabilitated orangutans will be in the vicinity where volunteers work. The 6-week programme costs £500 (excluding international flights and internal travel).

> **Despite the rigours, past volunteers have greatly enjoyed the Orangutan Foundation programme. The majority of the work undertaken is physical, for example constructing patrol posts, general infrastructure repairs or developing facilities for conservation education and wildlife appreciation. However, sometimes plans can change as volunteer Anna Fooks recounts:**
> *Prior to our arrival, Mike (the project manager) thought that we would be building a post and jetty in Beguruh. However, priorities changed at short notice when chainsaws (as I understood it) had been heard in another part of the park close to the research area. It was therefore decided that a patrol of assistants and 30 police be assembled to pinpoint illegal logging sites and nine volunteers were fortunate enough to accompany them on a 15-day patrol camping out in the forest. From a socio-economic and political standpoint, the experience was invaluable as we got to see logging activity, its subsequent forest destruction and some of the critical problems/dilemmas facing the OFI firsthand. We pinpointed two groups of loggers and Gambor workers and helped to break up one of the logging tracks. I was lucky enough to accompany Togu and a team of assistants when they unearthed the second logging camp and a network of logging tracks which ran for several miles. Visits were made to the second loggers' camp (by this time the 30 police had bailed). We also assisted with 'trail clearing', parangs in hand.*

Raleigh International, Raleigh House, 27 Parsons Green Lane, London SW6 4HZ (020-7371 8585; www.raleighinternational.org). Leading youth development charity which offers people aged 17-25 the chance to take part in challenging environmental, community and adventure projects as part of 4, 7 or 10-week programmes. Volunteers work with local and international scientists in some of the most remote areas of the world on the Island of Borneo in the Malaysian state of Sabah. One of these is called the Maliau Basin, accessible only since the 1970s. Participants also have the chance to go diving and to climb Mt Kinabalu.

Trekforce Expeditions, Naldred Farm Offices, Borde Hill Lane, Haywards Heath, West Sussex RH16 1XR (01444 474123; info@trekforce.org.uk/ www.trekforce.org.uk). Registered charity that organises conservation, scientific and community projects in the rainforests of Sarawak and Sabah, East Malaysia. The expeditions last one to four months and offer a week of jungle training followed by conservation teamwork on a challenging project and trekking in unexplored jungle. The longer programmes involve expedition work and then a second phase of teaching in remote jungle villages, for a further two months. Each expedition's project varies and in the past has included work at an orangutan rehabilitation centre, biodiversity studies and construction of wardens' posts in national parks. Help and advice on fundraising are given at introduction sessions, and initial training is given in the UK prior to departure.

Venture Co, The Ironyard, 64-66 The Market Place, Warwick CV34 4SD (01926 411122/fax 01926 411133; mail@ventureco-worldwide.com/ www.ventureco-worldwide. com). Their Himalayan Venture incorporates a nine-week expedition to Everest Base Camp as well as participating in community and conservation projects after undergoing cultural orientation in Delhi. Total cost of £4500 including flights and insurance. Indochina Venture includes working on an aid project with Cambodian children and trekking along the Great Wall of China.

Himalayas

Few gap travellers to Nepal can resist joining a trek in the Himalayas or a river rafting trip. *World Challenge Expeditions* run a number of trips in Nepal and elsewhere in Asia. Of course it is not necessary to book such a trip ahead with a UK agency. Many indigenous companies in Kathmandu can provide the support for expeditions at much less cost. The average cost for a trekking expedition is US$40 a day which includes permits, porters, food and lodging.

It may be possible to volunteer to work for one of the local companies running rafting trips, according to Rebecca Barber:

> When I went on a rafting trip (which are fantastic but expensive by Nepali standards – minimum $200 for ten days), I met a guy who had just done two free trips as 'safety kayaker'. No qualifications were needed apart from being confident of your ability to paddle the river. When in Kathmandu, simply walk into every agency you see and offer to work. You would be unlikely to get full-time or long-term work but as a way of getting a few free trips, living at no expense and getting some great paddling experience, not to mention the chance of future employment, it's ideal.

An American company called *Passage Project* organises semester-long and shorter experiential trips to Nepal and Tibet as well as Darjeeling, Ladakh and Kerala in India. These student trips include homestay, language study, interning and trekking. Prices start at $3255 for a 6-week summer stay in Ladakh and go up to $5175 for a 12-week semester in Nepal. Details are available from Passage Project, 2440 North 56th St, Phoenix, Arizona 85008 (tel/fax 1-602-840-9197; www.passageproject.org).

Caution

So many gap year travellers and other backpackers are wandering around India, Nepal and Thailand that it can be a challenge to get away from them (assuming that is your ambition). Although it is a good idea to try to step off the well-worn path between Goa, Kathmandu and Kho Samui, it may be unwise to stray too far from the beaten track. During his year out, Joel Emond from Bristol was travelling alone in northeast China. Unwittingly he wandered out of a national park mentioned in his guidebook and into North Korea where he was instantly arrested and put in jail. The Korean authorities contacted the British Embassy in Beijing to confirm that Joel was not a spy. Unfortunately, they got his name wrong and requested information about Joe Lemond. After several weeks, someone in Beijing twigged and the problem was resolved but not before Joel had gone on hunger strike in protest at the vile diet of rotten cabbages.

One way of exploring Asia in a protected environment is to join an overland tour such as those offered by *Exodus* (0870 240 5550) or *Encounter Overland* (0870 499 4478) which runs shorter and longer adventure trips in Asia.

TEACHING

Throughout Asia thousands of people of all ages are eager for tuition in English. Native English speakers, whatever their background, are wanted to meet that demand and school leavers can find voluntary placements in a range of countries. It can be a daunting prospect standing in front of a class of eager learners when you are just 18. Most teaching will be of conversational English rather than grammar. Several of the sending agencies insist that you do a short TEFL training course beforehand, for example *i-to-i* offers its own weekend course and *GAP Activity Projects* makes a 5-day course compulsory. **Emma Wolfson**, who went to teach in Vietnam, enjoyed GAP's preparatory course:

> The TEFL course I attended was the first chance I had to meet all the other people going to Vietnam and, in a way, that was the best part about it. However, we had a great teacher, who started our first class by talking at us in Czech, and making us learn the words for hello and goodbye without uttering a word of English. That I can remember this (although sadly not the Czech) makes me realise how important a good teacher is, and therefore how vital it was for us 18 year olds to learn at least the basics in teaching skills. We learnt a little of everything - how to get up in front of a class and not be afraid to open your mouth, ice-breaking games and other lesson fillers, how to plan a lesson and so on.

In the end Emma didn't have much chance to use what she had learned since she found herself teaching trainee cabin attendants for Vietnam Airlines, all older than her. They were chiefly interested in learning phrases like 'Would you like chicken or beef?' and 'the emergency exits are located to the rear'; and they wanted drills in saying 'rice' not 'rye'.

Paid teaching work is available primarily to people who have a university degree. Most commercial language school directors are looking for teachers who are older than 18 and who have finished university. In the case of Korea and Japan, a BA or BSc is virtually essential for obtaining the appropriate visa. Teaching English in Japan is one of the classic jobs for people filling a gap in their lives, but almost all are post-university.

The situation is different on the Indian sub-continent where very few private English language schools exist. Many gap students find themselves attached to schools, sometimes with a rather indeterminate role. The intention may simply be to enrich the lives of children by exposing them to a foreigner as much as to teach them English or anything concrete. **Suzanne Duffin's** placement in India involved teaching very basic English and maths, singing and playing games with the children and mainly giving the children lots of love and affection. She got to know each one very well and really enjoyed helping each child achieve the smallest things like writing his or her name. **Steven Stuart** found himself (under the auspices of *GAP Activity Projects*) teaching in a primary school in the jungles of Sarawak in Borneo. He taught only about two hours of lessons a day but enjoyed leading extracurricular activities like football and badminton clubs and learned a valuable lesson that 'improvisations are all part of the job'. He was pleased to feel he was trusted by the head of the school and never felt anyone peering over his shoulder:

> Helping children learn gave a crazy sense of achievement, and having to earn the respect of the village was such a great feeling.

Many other gap year students have found their placements thoroughly rewarding and worthwhile. But some have found themselves attached to schools for privileged children and wonder why they are there. **Rachel Sedley's** main complaint about her placement in Nepal was that she was teaching in a private school for privileged children when she had been led to believe that she would be contributing her time and labour to more needy children. She suspected that she was there partly to boost the prestige of the school and its head. Similarly **Tim Palmer** ended up teaching everything from English literature to Indian history at a very old traditional public school in Darjeeling which he imagined is run along the lines of Eton. So anyone with strong views about the kind of school in which they want to work should find out as many details as possible beforehand.

The agency *i-to-i* based in Leeds can place large numbers of graduates willing to spend six or 12 months in China, Thailand or South Korea teaching their native tongue; the cost of the placement is from £495 which includes return flights (paid at end of contract) and a job with furnished accommodation and a competitive monthly salary. It also sends hundreds of volunteers to teach in state schools and orphanages across Asia, with placements in China, Mongolia, Nepal, India, Sri Lanka, Thailand and Vietnam. A TEFL course is included with all i-to-i teaching placements.

There follows brief descriptions of the situation in the main countries of Asia, together with contact addresses. More detailed information on teaching English in the countries of Asia is contained in the 2005 edition of *Teaching English Abroad* by Susan Griffith (Vacation-Work Publications, £12.95).

Japan

Japan is an ideal destination for a post-university gap year or two. Thousands of English schools in Tokyo, Osaka and many other Japanese cities are eager to hire *gaijins* (foreigners) to teach. A great many of these are willing to hire native speakers of English with no teaching qualification as long as they have a university degree and preferably some teaching experience. Apart from a few schools which advertise and conduct interviews abroad, most schools recruit their teachers within Japan.

Britons, Canadians, Australians and New Zealanders are eligible to apply for a working holiday visa for Japan. British citizens must be aged 18-25 (or up to 30 in restricted circumstances). The working holiday visa allows 400 single young Britons to accept paid work in Japan for up to 12 months. Applicants must show that they have sufficient financial backing, i.e. savings of £2500. Note that applications are accepted from April and once the allocation of 400 has been filled, no more visas will be granted until April of the following year. So gap year students interested in spending a year in Japan should submit their applications around Easter of their A2 year. Further details are available by ringing 020-7465 6565 or on the embassy website at www.uk.emb-japan.go.jp. Recently a Volunteer Visa for Japan was launched which permits British nationals to work for a charitable organisation for up to one year.

The services of the Japan Association for Working-Holiday Makers (www.jawhm.or.jp) with offices in Tokyo, Osaka and Kyushu, are very helpful to people on working holiday visas. Jobs registered with JAWHM are normally in ski resorts, hotels or English schools.

Those who want to work in Japan but do not succeed in obtaining a working holiday visa must acquire a Japanese sponsor. This can be a private citizen but most teachers are sponsored by their employers. Graduates should investigate the government's flourishing *JET (Japan Exchange & Teaching) Programme*. Anyone with a Bachelor's degree in any discipline who is under 39 and from the UK, US, Ireland, Canada, Australia or New Zealand (plus a number of other countries) is eligible to apply. For British applicants details may be obtained from the JET Desk at the Japanese Embassy, 101-104 Piccadilly, London W1J 7JT (020-7465 6668/6670; info@jet-uk.org). Last year more than 400 Britons joined the programme. Other nationalities should contact the Japanese Embassy in their country of origin for information and application forms. Applications in Britain are due by the last Friday in November for one-year placements beginning late July. The annual salary is 3,600,000 yen (equivalent to about £18,000-£19,000) in addition to a free return air ticket if you complete your contract.

A number of the largest language training organisations recruit graduates abroad as well as in Japan. Among the main employers are:

ECC Foreign Language Institute, Kanto District Head Office: 5th Floor, San Yamate Building, 7-11-10 Nishi-Shinjuku, Shinjuku-ku, Tokyo 160-0023 (03-5330 1585; www. ecc.co.jp though the website for job applicants is www.japanbound.com). 600 teachers for 150 schools throughout Japan.

GEOS Corporation, GEOS Recruiting Office, St. Martin's House, St. Martin's Le Grand, London EC1A 4EN (020-7397 8405; london@geos.demon.co.uk). North American office: Simpson Tower 2424, 401 Bay Street, Toronto, Ontario M5H 2Y4, Canada (416-777-0109; geos@istar.ca; www.geoscareer.com). One of Japan's largest English language institutions employing 2000 teachers for 500 schools, all of whom are hired outside Japan. Recruitment campaigns held in UK, Australia, New Zealand and North America.

Interac Co Ltd. Fujibo Building 2F, 2-10-28 Fujimi, Chiyoda-ku, Tokyo 102-0071 (03-3234 7857; www.interac.co.jp/recruit). 600 Assistant Language Teachers in branches throughout Japan.

Nova Group, Carrington House, 126/130 Regent Street, London W1B 5SE (020-7734 2727; www.teachinjapan.com). Employ more than 6000 in 640 Nova schools throughout Japan. Recruitment in North America via Interact Nova Group, 2 Oliver St, Suite 7, Boston, MA 02109, USA (617-542-5027); and 1881 Yonge St, Suite 700, Toronto, Ontario M4S 3C4, Canada (416-481-6000).

China

Teaching opportunities continue to mushroom throughout the People's Republic of China and many schools and institutes are turning to the internet to fill teaching vacancies. Although many posts are open only to university graduates, younger people are also being accepted (albeit at a much lower wage) because of the acute shortage and some agencies and schools accept gap year students. For example GAP Activity Projects places gap year students in some fairly remote institutes which can cause a degree of culture shock. Ben Spencer visited a friend from his sixth form college who was doing her GAP placement in a middle school (for 13-16 year olds) in Jiangxi, a province considered something of a backwater, but which Rachel was mostly enjoying. Crime was so rare in this city of 300,000 that they were still talking about a bicycle that had been stolen five years before. The only aspect of life she minded was the authorities' attempt to curtail her freedoms, e.g. the supervisor/mentor tried (without success) to prevent her from joining an aerobics class and from eating at restaurants rather than at the school canteen.

University graduates will find it extremely easy to find a job at a school, college or private institute in China for example on the Teaching in China programme of IST Plus. Language Link (21 Harrington Road, London SW7 3EU; 020-7225 1065; www.languagelink. co.uk) is a TEFL training and recruitment agency that can place graduates of its CELTA course in London into its network of affiliated schools in China (and elsewhere).

With the explosion in opportunities, the job hunt is far more straightforward than it was a few years ago when most teacher applications were for state-run institutes of higher education and had to go through the Chinese Education Association for International Exchange (CEAIE; www.ceaie.edu.cn) or one of its 37 provincial offices. Nowadays there are many private recruiters, foundations or China-linked companies, on and off the internet, eager to sign up native speakers (with or without relevant experience) for an academic year. Many English teaching posts in the Chinese provinces remain unfilled, though aid agencies like VSO do their utmost to fill vacancies. The requirements for these two-year posts are not stringent and, in return, teachers get free airfares, a local salary and other perks.

Some of the tried and tested old schemes are still in place and still work. The British Council in co-operation with the Chinese Education authorities refers anyone who has done two years of higher education to schools and universities across China. The normal pay range is 2500-3500 Renminbi yuan (RMB) (£170-£240) per month. Details of the scheme are on line at www.britishcouncil.org/languageassistants-china.htm or can be obtained from the Chinese Links Officer at the British Council (10 Spring Gardens, London SW1A 2BN; 020-7389 4228; assistants@britishcouncil.org).

> **Although sheltering under the umbrella of a UK or US-based agency may make some things easier, it is also possible to arrange a teaching post independently, as William Hawke did in his last year at university:**
> *In my final year at Cambridge, I was unsure of what to do next. I did not take a gap year between school and university and by then I was desperate to really get to know a country, learn the language, meet the people, make friends, lead a normal life somewhere interesting without M & S, the Bill, kebabs and Heineken. At that time, my current hot country was China. I spotted an advertisement in the university job opportunities circular for a meeting with officials from the Chinese Embassy about English teaching. I liked what I heard (i.e. working in China sounded stable and foreign teachers were obviously established and familiar there) and after a quick interview to prove that I could speak English, I was handed a long list of universities and colleges which were looking for teachers. I sent faxes to the ten most suitable-looking ones with a letter and CV, and in time received five job offers. I quickly narrowed the choice to two, both offering a good salary in Chinese terms, and chose the Qingdao Chemical Institute in northern China because Mandarin would be prevalent but mostly because a friend of mind had taught there and strongly recommended it.*

For the most part having no protective agency caused no problems. The Institute looked after all the red tape and working conditions were favourable - 20 hours a week, the equivalent of £300 a month. Typically a gap year teacher would earn less. William Hawke spent his time very constructively and achieved all that he hoped, learned fluent Mandarin, made friends and got to know China well. His gap year experience put him in a strong position when he applied for a job as an International Officer with the Hong Kong Shanghai Bank, which he got soon after his return.

IST Plus in the UK runs 'Teach in China' for graduates from the UK while CIEE in the USA places Americans in the same programme. Placements are in secondary and tertiary institutions mainly in the developed eastern provinces of Jiangsu, Zheijang, Shandong and Hubei. Contracts last five or ten months and start in February and August. A local salary is paid and free accommodation is provided. The programme fee starts at £995 with the possibility of reimbursement for travel costs at the end of a ten-month contract. The fee also includes full insurance, comprehensive pre-departure information and advice, a week-long residential orientation in Shanghai and support from the local partner agency.

The Buckland International Education Group based in Guilin (buckland@china.com; www.bucklandgroup.org) advertises on the internet for native speaker teachers, preferably with a degree or TESOL certificate, to teach in a range of places for 3-12 months. The organisation even makes a contribution to airfares on completion of a contract and provides work visas and accommodation.

Some US-based placement programmes to consider are:

Amity Foundation, 71 Han Kou Road, Nanjing, Jiangsu 210008 (25-8331-4118; www.amityfoundation.org). Christian organisation that sends 60-80 graduates to teach English in China.

Appalachians Abroad Teach in China Program, Center for International Programs, Marshall University, One John Marshall Drive, Huntingdon, WV 2755, USA (304-696-6265; gochina@marshall.edu). Up to 60 graduates placed mainly in Beijing and Shanghai schools. Placement fee $950.

Colorado China Council, 4556 Apple Way, Boulder, CO 80301 (303-443-1108; www.asiacouncil.org). 20-35 teachers per year placed at institutes throughout China.

American International Education Foundation (AIEF), 18605 E Gale Avenue, Suite

230, City of Industry, CA 91748 (626-965-1995; www.aief-usa.org). Recruits mainly Americans with a BA to spend 12 months (occasionally six) teaching English to junior high and high-school aged students in many Chinese cities (and also Taiwan).

WorldTeach, Centre for International Development, 79 John F Kennedy St, Cambridge, MA 02138 (617-495-5527; www.worldteach.org). Non-profit organisation sends volunteers to teach adults for six months in Yantai and runs Shanghai Summer Teaching Program. Volunteers teach small classes of high school students at a language camp in Shanghai. Volunteers pay about $4000 for airfares, orientation, health insurance, living expenses and field support.

With an invitation letter or fax from an official Chinese organisation, you should be able to obtain a long term work visa from the Embassy of the PRC in your country. It is also possible to enter China on a tourist (L) visa and then the Foreign Affairs Office at your institute or equivalent at a private company offering employment will arrange for an Alien Residence Permit (Z visa). Make sure this happens before your visitor visa expires; otherwise you will be liable to a fine and will have to leave the country to change status.

Travellers in China have been approached and invited to teach English, as Ben Spencer discovered on his gap year travels in China. After visiting a friend teaching on a placement with GAP Activity Projects, Ben was attracted to the idea of teaching English and came across various possibilities as he travelled. For example in picturesque Yangshuo south of Guilin, Ben became friendly with a language school owner whom he paid for a week of Chinese lessons (two hours a day) and who offered him a job. For an insight into the complexities of modern China, look at the novel *The Drink and Dream Teahouse* by Justin Hill who did a stint in the provincial town of Yuncheng with VSO straight out of university (and wrote about that in *A Bend in the Yellow River*).

The classroom is not always the best place to draw out the students. Extracurricular activities can present a better opportunity for imparting the English language, as **Richard Vincent** found when he spent a year as a Project Trust volunteer in Southern China:

Most of the positive aspects of my year were achieved outside the classroom. The good students will always work all the hours god sends. However the less motivated can become motivated to try and learn. In my case, playing football gave lots of students who had been labelled 'dossers' the chance to speak English, and many of them became the best contributors in class. The emphasis should always be on fun and trying to get them to use the English they know.

Taiwan

The country remains a magnet for English teachers of all backgrounds. Hundreds of private language institutes or *buhsibans* continue to teach young children, cram high school students for university entrance examinations and generally service the seemingly insatiable demand for English conversation and English tuition.

Many well-established language schools are prepared to sponsor foreign teachers for a resident visa, provided the teacher has a university degree and is willing to work for at least a year. On arrival check the Positions Vacant column of the English language *China Post* though work tends to result from personal referrals more than from advertising.

The following language schools hire on a large scale:

Hess Educational Organization, No. 419, Chung Shan Rd, Sec 2, Chung Ho City, Taipei County 235 (02-3234 6188 ext 1053; hesswork@hess.com.tw; www.hess.com.tw). Specialise in teaching children including kindergarten age. 400 Native Speaking Teachers (NSTs) in more than 150 branches. Very structured teaching programme and curriculum. Quarterly intake of teachers in September, December, March and June.

International Avenue Consulting Company, 16F-1 No 499 Chung Ming South Road, Taichung City (04-2375 9800; www.iacc.com.tw). Recruitment agency with links to Canada who hire about 100 teachers who must be graduates.

Kid Castle Language Schools, Min Chuan Road No. 98, 8F, Hsin Tien City 231, Taipei (02-

2218 5996; personnel@kidcastle.com). 160 franchise branches throughout Taiwan.
Kojen ELS, 6F, No 9, Lane 90, Sung Chiang Road, Taipei (02-2581 8511; www.kojenenglish.
com). Employs 200-300 teachers at 21 schools, mostly in Taipei but also Kaohsiung
and Taichung. Starting wage is NT$540 per hour.

Korea

Although Korea does not immediately come to mind as a likely destination for British
TEFLers, it has been long known in North America as a country which can absorb an
enormous number of native speaker teachers, including fresh graduates with no TEFL
training or experience. Hundreds of language institutes *(hogwons)* in Seoul the capital,
Pusan (Korea's second city, five hours south of Seoul) and in smaller cities employ native
speaker teachers of English. The majority of these are run as businesses, so that making a
profit seems to be what motivates many bosses rather than educating people. Certificates
and even degrees are in many cases superfluous.

The English Program in Korea (EPIK) is a scheme run by the Ministry of Education,
and administered through Korean embassies in the west to place about 2000 foreign graduates in schools and education offices throughout the country. The annual salary (2005)
is 1.7, 1.9 or 2.2 million won per month (depending on qualifications) plus accommodation, round trip airfare, visa sponsorship and medical insurance. Work starting dates are
staggered over the summer with application deadlines falling between January and April.
Current information should be obtained from the Education Director, Korean Embassy, 60
Buckingham Gate, London SW1E 6AJ (020-7227 5547/fax 020-7227 5503; http://epik.
knue.ac.kr). Note that EPIK does not attract the praise that the JET Programme does;
check Dave Sperling's ESL Café website for details (www.eslcafe.com).

ELS International/YBM SISA employs 400-600 native English teachers for English
Conversation Centers and other kinds of institute throughout Korea. The central contact
address is 55-1 Chongno 2ga, Chongno Gu, 3rd Floor, Seoul 110 122 (2-2264 7472; www.
ybmhr.com).

Thailand

Thailand is one of the most popular destinations for gap year travellers but, until recently,
not many of the specialist placement agencies sent young volunteers to this country.
However, *i-to-i* and *GAP Activity Projects* have a TEFL programme in Thailand and
AFS has a flourishing counterpart which runs a year long educational and homestay
programme which is undersubscribed. *IST Plus* runs a Teach in Thailand programme for
graduates. Placements are in secondary institutions throughout Thailand for five or ten
months starting in August or February.

Any university graduate can pre-arrange a teaching job in Thailand through *IST Plus
Ltd* (address above) or CIEE in the US. Several hundred native English speakers with
university degrees are sent to schools in Thailand. Five or ten-month renewable contracts
start in May or October. The minimum salary is 12,000 baht per month plus free accommodation. The programme fee starts at £995 and includes full insurance, comprehensive pre-
departure information and advice, and a week-long residential orientation in Bangkok.

EIL (287 Worcester Road, Malvern, Worcs. WR14 1AB; 0800 018 4015; www.eiluk.
org) arranges volunteer work in Thailand from 6 to 29 weeks in a range of social, environmental and health projects. *Go Differently* is a programme run by a British travel company
for sending short-term volunteers to Thailand (see entry in 'Directory of Voluntary Work')
including to carry out Tsunami relief. Global Quest (One Longfellow Square, Suite 201,
Portland, ME 04101, USA; www.gquest.org) specialises in sending American gap year
students to study Thai language and culture, environmental issues, etc. for 12 weeks (fees
from $13,800).

Independent-minded gap year travellers can occasionally pick up casual teaching work in Bangkok but most respectable schools now want their native speaker teachers to have a university degree. Elsewhere wages are low (or non-existent) and working conditions not very satisfactory. The noisy Khao San Road is lined with expat pubs and budget accommodation, many with notice boards offering teaching work and populated with other foreigners (known as *farangs*) well acquainted with the possibilities. They will also be able to warn you of the dubious schools which are known to exploit their teachers.

Finding a list of language schools to approach on arrival will present few difficulties. The best place to start is around Siam Square where numerous schools and the British Council are located or the Yellow Pages which lists dozens of language school addresses. One of the best all-round sources of information about teaching in Thailand with an emphasis on Bangkok and on inside information about the main hiring companies is the website www.ajarn.com with stories and tips as well as many job vacancies (www.ajarn.com/Jobs/jobs_offered.htm). Another possible source of job vacancies is the English language press, viz. the *Bangkok Post* (with at least five adverts every day) and to a lesser extent the *Nation*. Teaching opportunities crop up in branches of the big companies like ECC (Thailand), 430/17-24 Chula Soi 64, Siam Square, Bangkok 10330 (2-253 3312; jobs@ecc.ac.th/ www.eccthai.com) with 25 branches in Greater Bangkok and about the same number elsewhere in Thailand. Teachers must have a Bachelor's degree with TEFL qualification or a minimum of six months teaching experience.

Tourist destinations like Chiang Mai are attractive to job-hunting teachers. According to Annette Kunigagon, the Irish woman married to a Thai whose Eagle Guest House is a great place to find out about the teaching scene in Chiang Mai (www.eaglehouse.com), there are lots of new so-called bilingual programmes opening up in local schools such as Anubaan Chiang Mai School, Wattano Payap School, Waree School and Fatih School. Native-speaking English people with a genuine interest can visit these schools, speak to the English-speaking teacher (who may be a little difficult to locate) and express an interest in helping to teach English, art, math, science, etc. through the medium of English. The Thai school year ends in mid-March and restarts the second week of May. Annette's general advice for the job hunt is to dress conservatively and cultivate a reserved manner: 'too many gesticulations and guffawing are not considered polite'. She has developed a volunteer programme called 'Helping Hands Social Projects' by which volunteers join projects in northern Thailand to teach at a centre for disabled people, school for the blind, refugee camps, etc.

Fee-paying volunteers are sent to a number of schools to teach English by a Thai company called *Thai Experience* (www.Thai-Experience.org); see 'Directory of Volunteering' entry. The idea is not to teach grammar but to overcome the children's reluctance to practise speaking English. Volunteers of all ages and levels of ability are welcome but they must pay €250-€400 a month to cover homestay accommodation, administration and orientation.

Unless you are a volunteer, the official line is that you need a work permit for Thailand; however the authorities normally turn a blind eye to trespassers. You will have to leave the country every three months to renew your visa; most choose Penang Malaysia for this purpose and many have done it four or five times. There is a fine of B200 for every day you overstay your tourist visa. With a letter from your school, you can apply for a non-immigrant visa, which is better for teaching than a tourist visa. It too must be renewed by leaving the country every 90 days for a fee of B500.

Thailand is one country where you might like to take a course instead of teach one. Gap travellers have been known to sign up for courses in massage and meditation as well as many in Thai cookery. For example the government-accredited International Training Massage School in Chiang Mai offers one- to-six-week courses in basic and advanced Thai massage and foot massage (17/6-7 Hah Yak Santitham, Chiang Mai; 053-218 632; www.itmthaimassage.com).

Diving is another option that may appeal. PJ Scuba is allied to an internship programme called Learn in Asia Dive Internships Co. Ltd. (Mermaids Group, 75/124 Moo 12, Jomtien Beach Road Nongprue, Banglamung, Chonburi 20260; www.learn-in-asia.com).

Other diving centres in the region offer PADI Divemaster training including EcoSea Dive & Adventure Cambodia, Ekareach St, Town Center, Sihanoukville, Cambodia (+855 12 654 104; Dive@EcoSea.com).

Vietnam & Cambodia

The largest growth area in English teaching has been in those countries which were cut off from the West for many years, viz. Vietnam, Cambodia and Laos, where a number of joint venture language schools have been opened employing native speaker teachers. In the quiet Cambodian town of Siem Reap, new schools and colleges have been set up with names like Build Bright and Future Bright, employing some foreign teachers.

Outreach International (Bartletts Farm, Hayes Road, Compton Dundon, Somerset TA11 6PF; tel/fax 01458 274957; www.outreachinternational.co.uk) is one of the few organisations with a programme in Cambodia, a country that is under-represented in the brochures of the main agencies. It sends volunteers aged 18-30 to work for three or more months with local NGOs, for instance to teach English (which can open a range of employment opportunities for local people), computing or art to landmine victims or to work in a small orphanage or art and craft centre. These placements are suitable for volunteers wishing to pursue a career in overseas development or aid work or genuinely help a damaged and vulnerable section of society. Physiotherapists and older volunteers are needed for some of the projects but others are ideal for younger people.

Nepal

Once one of the most promising destinations for gap year volunteers, Nepal's appeal has been severely harmed by Maoist insurgency. Since the king dismissed the government in early 2005, the Foreign Office has been warning of a high threat of terrorism in Nepal with a number of incidences of Maoist rebels carrying out attacks in areas frequented by tourists including the main trekking routes. A number of sending agencies have dropped Nepal entirely (as in the case of GAP Activity Projects and the UK-based Global Action Nepal; www.gannepal.org) or now limit their placements to the Kathmandu Valley, the second town of Pokhara and Chitwan in the south which have been considered safe.

The volunteer placement organisation *MondoChallenge* (see 'Directory of Specialist Gap Year Programmes') started in the village of Sermathang where the school was forcibly closed down by the Maoists and the 150 pupils thrown out overnight. Fortunately a certain number were moved to a school in Kathmandu where 30 MondoChallenge volunteers continue to work, as well as around Dhulikhel.

Travelling in western Nepal is not recommended. So far the rebels have not harmed foreigners though they do sometimes ask tourists (especially trekkers to Everest base camp) for a 'donation' of say $20. The situation may well be disintegrating; for example at the time of writing (June 2005) a passenger bus was exploded by a landmine not far from Chitwan killing more than 50 people, so it is essential to take expert advice if planning to incorporate Nepal into your gap year. Shrijana Rayamajhi of KEEP Nepal (listed below) summarised the situation for this book:

Nepal is going through a difficult phase. But, this is a political conflict and up until now tourists / foreigners have not been targetted. However, it has been a common practice for travellers to be asked for a 'donation'. KEEP has continued its volunteer programme with utmost caution. Prior to placement of any volunteers, we take every measure to understand the security situation in the region for the safety of our volunteers. In addition, right now our placements have been focused on areas where we have conducted previous programmes and we have a good rapport with the local community.

An impressive range of non-governmental organisations makes it possible for people to teach in a voluntary capacity including some in the 'Directory of Volunteering Abroad' (see entries for *RCDP Nepal* and *Volunteer Nepal National Group*). No indigenous organisations can afford to bestow largesse on foreigners joining their projects, so westerners who come to teach in a school or a village must be willing to fund themselves. None of the programme fees below includes airfares to Nepal. Of course living expenses are very low by western standards, prompting some young people to bypass the fees charged by many of the gap year agencies. Organising a school placement directly or with a Nepali-based agency is invariably cheaper. If you want to avoid an agency fee you can make direct contact with schools on arrival.

Relevant organisations include:

Cultural Destination Nepal, PO Box 11535, Dhapasi, Kathmandu (01-437 7623; cdnnepal@wlink.com.np; www.volunteernepal.org.np). Volunteer service work programme. Application fee €50 plus €650 fee includes 2-week pre-service orientation and homestay throughout. Placements last 2-4 months starting February, April, June, August and October.

Insight Nepal, PO Box 489, Pokhara, Kaski, Nepal (insight@fewanet.com.np; www.insightnepal.org.np). Volunteer placements for 6 weeks and 3 months in schools and community development projects mainly in the Pokhara Valley. Must be A-level or high-school graduate. Programme fee $840 for 3 months and $480 for 6 weeks includes pre-orientation training, a trekking excursion plus (on the 3-month programme) 3 days in Chitwan National Park.

Kathmandu Environmental Education Project (KEEP), PO Box 9178, Tridevi Marg, Thamel, Kathmandu (01-4412944; fax 01-4413018; www.keepnepal.org). KEEP sends volunteers to different trekking villages in Nepal to teach the English language to lodge owners, trekking guides and porters and also as teachers in government schools, for a minimum of 2 months. KEEP also sends volunteers to NGOs in the field of conservation or health and community development according to the interest and experience of the volunteers. Volunteers must be totally self-funding. Accommodation with mountain families. Application fee $50.

VSP/Nepal (Volunteer and Support Program Nepal), PO Box 11969, Kathmandu (fax 1-416144; vwop2000@hotmail.com). Willing volunteers looking for a cultural experience can be placed in variety of voluntary posts including teaching English in schools, in both urban and remote areas of Nepal. No special qualifications are needed. Volunteers stay with a local family and contribute $50 a month towards their expenses. Registration fee of $20 plus placement fee of $400 must be paid.

Eighteen year old **Giles Freeman** from Australia spent three months with Insight Nepal:

I would advise that applicants do have some teaching practice before coming. Classes easily reach 60 or 80 in many schools, making it necessary for the patient teacher to know what they are doing. With no teaching experience, this proved a little hard, but it's a great challenge. All in all it was extremely rewarding.

Nepal is so welcoming to foreigners that it is quite possible to arrange your own voluntary post simply by becoming known in a village and asking local teachers if you can help out, possibly in exchange for simple accommodation. This is a country to which many travellers flock for rest and relaxation, for eating, drinking and socialising. Tim Palmer is one such gap year traveller who enjoyed Nepal for five weeks (including trekking and rafting) but found it all too easy and soon hankered again for the 'hassle that is India' where he travelled until the last day of his six-month visa.

India

Volunteering in India sometimes takes the form of teaching but more often it involves social projects. Among the many projects supported by the UK-based *Development in Action* (entry in 'Directory of Volunteering Abroad'), teaching assignments and social welfare placements are most common. These last for a summer or five months from September.

Peter Hill returned from India from a successful placement though *Changing Worlds*:

Whether remembering my first attempts at eating rice with my fingers, watching the iron-flat plains stretch beneath me as I climbed a sacred hill barefoot with thousands of pilgrims during a Hindu festival or the exhilaration of my first successful hour as an English teacher, my six months in India remain unforgettable. Changing Worlds found me a voluntary placement in Southern India working with the People's Craft Training Centre, an organisation aiming to instil 'collective self-reliance' among the poor and disabled of their local area. One aspect of the centre's work lies in educating and monitoring the development of children affected by cerebral palsy. Although my time was mainly spent helping in this special school, my role was not strictly defined at all and it was more like working in partnership with a group of friends than being given a list of instructions. I think the clash of cultures was as novel for many locals as it was for me. The welcome I received and the friendships I made reflect the warmth of Indian hospitality; you will rarely be on your own for long. Changing Worlds fully briefed me on India and what to expect at their two-day pre-departure course. I felt welcomed by Krish, the local rep, on arrival in Chennai and felt well looked after during my entire stay in this wonderful country.

An Indian organisation which places graduates on a voluntary basis in Christian educational institutes in South India is the *Jaffe Punnoose Foundation* (Kunnuparambil Buildings, Kurichy, Kottayam 686549, India; fax 0481 430470; jaffeint@sify.com). Volunteers teach for a minimum of four weeks in English medium high schools, hotel management colleges, teacher training centres, vocational institutes and language schools in Kerala State and also at summer schools in various locations in India. As with all projects in India, no wage is paid but you are billeted with a family. Volunteers must have a relevant degree or diploma in the subject (e.g. beauty therapy, gardening, photography).

Several organisations in the UK send volunteers to teach English or undertake other voluntary work in India. For example *Teaching & Projects Abroad* arranges short-term teaching and other workplace assignments in Kerala and Tamil Nadu, South India costing £895 for 1 month and £1245 for three months excluding flights. *Travellers* (7 Mulberry Close, Ferring, West Sussex BN12 5HY; 01903 502595; www.travellersworldwide.com) organises teaching (Brunei, China, India, Sri Lanka, Malaysia), conservation (Brunei, Malaysia, Sri Lanka) and work experience (India, Sri Lanka). Teaching placements concentrate mainly on conversational English. Conservation programme includes working with orangutans, elephants, lions, monkeys, marine creatures and others. Work experience includes law and journalism. Asian placements start at £925 for three months teaching in China (excluding flights). *Cross-Cultural Solutions* with offices in the US and UK (www.crossculturalsolutions.org) places volunteers in grassroots projects in the Himalayas and Delhi (as well as Thailand and China).

Few opportunities of any kind exist in the restricted Himalayan state of Sikkim. One exception is a programme run by the *Muyal Liang Trust* at the Demajong Cheoling Academy located near Pemayangtse Monastery. Information about placements as volunteers to teach English or other subjects for up to 60 days is available in the UK from Jules Stewart, 53 Blenheim Crescent, London W11 2EG (020-7229 4774; JJulesstewart@aol.com). There is the possibility of teaching for longer periods in neighbouring Darjeeling. *MondoChallenge* offers 30 Indian placements mainly in the Kalimpong region near Darjeeling in the Himalayan foothills.

For information about teaching Tibetan refugees in Himalayan India, contact the

Dharamsala Earthville Institute (www.earthville.org/devi) who are especially keen to attract computer teachers and people with fund-raising skills for a minimum of six months. The website www.tibetweb.org/help/asia_service.html has links to several other voluntary organisations active in Tibet and with Tibetans in exile.

Sri Lanka

Volunteers for English in Sri Lanka or *VESL* (www.vesl.org; see entry in 'Directory of Volunteering Abroad') is a relatively new British charity that provides rural Sri Lankan schools with exposure to enthusiastic and creative native English speakers. VESL sent ten volunteers in the summer of 2004 and has plans to expand the programme in five rural communities in the North, East and Central Provinces, enabling projects to run within Sinhala, Tamil and Muslim communities. The cost inclusive of airfares is £970 for a four-week summer experience. The charity is also developing ways of involving volunteers in the rebuilding of communities devastated by the Tsunami.

Richard New was placed by VESL in a school in Nelliady on the Jaffna Peninsula (in the Tamil north of the country) and appreciated the insights he gained that mere travellers never could:
The north of Sri Lanka is probably the most fascinating place I have ever visited. Having emerged from twenty years of civil war, there is much evidence of the scars of battle. As we drove to our project, we saw numerous mine-fields peppering the countryside; many bombed-out buildings and stories of displacement and bloodshed made it clear that this area had suffered great hardship. Yet the people were some of the most hospitable and positive that I have ever met. Their welcome was as warm as their climate. From the first day, Dan and I were made to feel part of the community.

Our school was well equipped compared to others on the island, yet resources were still scarce. My classroom consisted of long benches, one of which snapped in the third week - no other seating was available for the rest of the month, so some of my pupils had to stand. Regardless of such problems, the students were enthusiastic and keen to learn. If I could stop them talking about cricket, developing their spoken English was both challenging and rewarding. I think we made good headway in improving their listening skills especially and even the younger students became better at understanding complex instructions. On the last day I was genuinely moved to see my pupils recite poetry by William Wordsworth at a full school assembly. They were also keen to tell me about their lives and country, so I think that overall they taught me as much as I taught them.

Our home life was equally interesting. Dan and I lived with a family who welcomed us into their lives. We took to calling our host 'Ama', which is Tamil for 'mother' - I was made to feel like part of the family. The food was different, varied and very tasty. Our neighbours were keen to meet us and we spent many evenings playing cards with our pupils. However, due to the lack of electricity our nightlife tended to end promptly at 8.30. This was in no way detrimental and I soon settled into a routine. Yet life was not tedious. I had many exciting and varied experiences I would not otherwise have gained. Dan and I went to a Hindu temple for their annual festival where we were welcomed, fed and blessed. We were special guests at a local football match, and experienced the thrill of a Karavedy local derby. Most interesting was a tour around an Arrack factory (distillery of the local tipple). It showed us the harsh working environment many Sri Lankan labourers must face. Such experiences would be impossible for most travellers to the area. VESL gave me a unique opportunity to understand the culture and people of northern Sri Lanka.

As mentioned above, *i-to-i* has volunteer travel placements in Sri Lanka (as well as in China, Mongolia, India, Nepal, Thailand, and Vietnam). To join, you must have a TEFL qualification; i-to-i provide an intensive weekend course which is included in the training and placement fee from £1395 for eight weeks (excluding travel costs).

MondoChallenge (Milton House, Gayton Rd, Milton Malsor, Northampton NN7 3AB; 01604 858225; www.mondochallenge.org) has expanded from its origins at one small village school in Nepal to arrange mainly three-month teaching placements in a number of other countries including Sri Lanka. The teaching takes place in Buddhist temple communities near Kandy (placement fee is £1000). When **Satya Byock** taught with MondoChallenge at a temple in Sri Lanka, she was dreading leaving but concluded that the temple near Kandy had given her peace of mind that she could carry with her for the rest of her life.

VOLUNTARY WORK

Many young people who have travelled in Asia are dissatisfied with the role of tourist and would like to find a way of making a contribution. It must be stressed that Westerners almost invariably have to make a financial contribution to cover food and accommodation as well as their travel and insurance.

If you have never travelled widely in the Third World you may not be prepared for the scruffiness and level of disorganisation to be found in some places. Not many 18 year olds would be capable of contributing or benefitting much from a long attachment to a grass-roots charity in developing regions. A further difficulty with participating in local voluntary projects (of which there are many) is in fixing anything up ahead of time. Occasionally Asian charities have a representative abroad (usually a committed former volunteer) who can send information about voluntary possibilities but this is unusual.

Indian Subcontinent

Here is a small selection of organisations which can sometimes use paying volunteers. It is possible to become a part-time volunteer at Mother Theresa's children's home in Calcutta (Shishu Bhavan, 78 A.J.C. Bose Road), in the Home for Dying Destitutes at Kalighat and other Homes run by the *Missionaries of Charity* in other Indian cities, but no accommodation can be offered. The work may consist of feeding and caring for orphaned children or the elderly. To register, visit the administrative office at 54A A.J.C. Bose Road, Calcutta 700016. Further information is also available from their London office at 177 Bravington Road, London W9 3AR (020-8960 2644; www.tisv.be/mt/en/vol.htm). Another organisation with a UK base is *Development in Action* (info@developmentinaction.org) which can arrange attachments to various Indian NGOs for volunteers to spend the summer or five months from September (see 'Directory of Volunteering Abroad').

Indian Volunteers for Community Service (12 Eastleigh Avenue, South Harrow, Middlesex HA2 0UF; www.ivcs.org.uk) sends willing volunteers over 18 on its DRIVE programme (Discover Rural India for a Valuable Experience). Volunteers start with three weeks at Amarpurkashi Polytechnic in Uttar Pradesh learning about development and then join a hands-on project in the region between September and March. The placement fee which includes orientation and training is only £175 while living expenses will be £3 a day. The India Development Group (IDG, 68 Downlands Road, Purley, Surrey CR8 4JF; 020-8668 3161; www.idguk.org) runs a similar six-month programme in Lucknow for 5-10 volunteers over 21, concentrating on appropriate technology to support village life.

Dakshinayan (c/o Siddharth Sanyal, F-1169 Ground Floor, Chittarangan Park, New Delhi 110019; /fax 011-262 76645; www.dakshinayan.org) works with tribal peoples in the hills of Rajmahal and nearby plains. Volunteers join grassroots development projects every month and contribute $300 per month.

A community organisation in the Himalayan foothills with the charming acronym *ROSE* (Rural Organization for Social Elevation, Sonargaon P.O., Kanda, Bageshwar, Uttaranchal

263631; www.rosekanda.info) can assist volunteers wishing to work with poor villagers, teaching children, doing office work, carrying out environmental work and organic farming in this village in the Himalayan foothills. Volunteers pay 350 rupees (about £4.50) per day for board and lodging. Originally from London, Heather Joiner wrote to say how much she was enjoying her time with ROSE:

> I am a volunteer who is currently here working in the tiny school. I am also here at ROSE in order to improve my basic Hindi. In the morning we join the primary school children learning basic reading, writing and counting.

During his year out before attending Bristol University, **Laurence Koe** followed up a lead he'd been given and visited a Catholic monastery in a suburb of Bombay where foreigners were a real oddity. The monks generously gave him their 'deluxe suite' and full board. He tried to repay their hospitality by offering to work but all they wanted was for him to discuss the western way of life with the trainee monks whenever he felt so inclined.

The *Bangladesh Workcamps Association* (289/2 Work Camp Road, North Shahjah-anpur, 1217 Dhaka, Bangladesh; fax 02-956 5506; www.mybwca.org) will try to place you on 10-15 day community development camps between October and February. The camp registration fee is $150 which includes food and accommodation. They publish detailed camp information in English on their website. BWCA can also accommodate foreign volunteers on a medium-term basis (minimum three months). In addition to the registration fee of $150, volunteers must pay $2 a day for their food.

In Sri Lanka short-term and long-term volunteers and interns can be accommodated at *Lanka Jatika Sarvodaya Shramadana Sangamaya* (98 Rawatawatte Road, Moratuwa, Colombo, Sri Lanka; 11-264 7159/ 265 5255; ssmplan@sri.lanka.net; www.sarvodaya.org) to engage in social, economic and technical development activities in villages; and planning, monitoring and evaluation work at the head office in Colombo.

Samasevaya Sri Lanka (Anuradhapura Road, Talawa N.C.P., Sri Lanka; 025-227 6266; samasev@sltnet.lk) invites volunteers to their rural locations. Volunteers can be used rather loosely for their educational and development programmes, though it is more akin to a cultural exchange. If the volunteer wants to stay past the initial month of their tourist visa, it is sometimes possible to arrange a renewal. The organisation provides simple accommodation in their office complex in Talawa or with local families. They expect a contribution of $90 a month for meals.

Southeast Asia and the Far East

Starfish Ventures (www.starfishventures.co.uk) is a relatively new British company that places volunteers of all nationalities in development projects in Thailand including teaching, dog rescue, school garden construction and turtle conservation. Fees are from £995 for a month to £1495 for three months which include homestay accommodation, in-country supervision and (if appropriate) preparatory TEFL training weekend.

Volunteers including gap year students are sent out to northern Thailand each year to work in communities of Karen tribespeople. Details of the programme are available from the *Karen Hill Tribes Trust*, Midgley House, Heslington, Yorks. YO10 5DX (see entry in 'Directory of Volunteering Abroad').

The Wild Animal Rescue Foundation of Thailand (65/1 3rd Floor, Pridi Banomyong Building, Sukhumvit Soi 55, Bangkok 10110; 2-712 9515; www.warthai.org) offers the chance to high-paying volunteers to work with animals including gibbons, ideally to people with an appropriate background. Mangrove forests along tropical coasts are among the most threatened habitats in the world. The Mangrove Action Project (MAP, PO Box 1854, Port Angeles, WA 98362-0279; tel/fax 360-452-5866; www.earthisland.org/map/map.html)

organises community-based mangrove replanting and eco-study work tours in Thailand as well as Malaysia, Sri Lanka and Ecuador. The cost of the two-week trip to Thailand in 2005 was $800 excluding airfares and meals.

Japan is a famously expensive country in which to travel. One way around it is to join a workcamp. The Japanese workcamp organisation has a reassuring name and acronym NICE: *Never-ending International Work Camps Exchange*. It is probably not worth writing directly to NICE unless you are already in Japan (2-4-2-701 Shinjuku, Shinjuku-ku, Tokyo 160-0022; http://nice1.gr.jp/wc-nicee.htm) but via one of their corresponding agents such as *Concordia* or *UNA Exchange*.

Japan and Korea have nascent WWOOF organisations, both of them web-based. It costs $40 to join WWOOF Japan (Honcho 2-jo, 3-chome 6-7, Higashi-ku, Sapporo 065-0042 Japan; www.wwoofjapan.com) whose list of member farms numbers about 50 and $50 for the Korean list from WWOOF Korea (No. 1008, Seoul B/D, 45 Jongno-1Ga, Jongno-Gu, Seoul 110-121; wwoof@wwoofkorea.com).

> **Just as his year's working holiday visa was about to expire, Joseph Tame went to a family-run pension called Milky Way in southwestern Hokkaido, as listed by WWOOF.**
>
> *WWOOF Japan have relaunched themselves with a new detailed list and other services. Members can log in and then download details of the 33 hosts (one of which is a community organisation made up of 80 organic farms). I would thoroughly recommend Country Inn Milky House. The pay is average for Hokkaido (800 yen per hour) which meant that most months I was able to save about £700 for future travels. In addition to working an average of 7 or 8 hours a day, I spent three hours studying this funny language and my Japanese really improved. The various tasks I was given by the pension owner included putting up fences around tennis courts, acting as secretary for foreign guests, chain-sawing, erecting a big canopy on the veranda, shovelling snow, avoiding the phone when it rings, accidentally driving over big stones with the ride-on mower, cutting telephone lines with a bush cutter, operating the mini-digger, painting walls and planting flowers. For a few weeks I taught groups of visiting schoolchildren how to perform a traditional English Country Dance. It's been a great experience.*

Perhaps if Joseph returns some day, he will be able to answer the phone since he is now studying Japanese at Sheffield University.

The *Korean International Volunteer Association* organises voluntary placements throughout Korea. Projects include teaching English at an orphanage for at least a month and working in sheltered communities. Details are available from KIVA, 11th Floor Sekwang B/D, 202 Sejong-ro, Chongro-gu, Seoul 110-050 (02-723 6225; info@kiva.or.kr). More and more workcamps organisations in exotic places are coming to light, most recently the Mongolian Workcamp Exchange (+967 9973 1777; mce-mn@magicnet.mn). An NGO in Ulaanbaatar that places volunteers is the New Choice Mongolian Volunteer Organization, Ikh toiruu, Building-15, Room-405, Ulaanbaatar, Mongolia (PO Box 159, Ulaanbaatar 210646; +967 9911 8767; www.volunteer.org.mn/new/index.html).

PAID WORK & WORK EXPERIENCE

Few paid jobs are available to gap year students unless they have a contact in Beijing or Singapore, for example, who is able to arrange a business internship. The booming Chinese economy and seeming whole-hearted embracing of Western business means that some Chinese companies do take on American and European staff. A couple of the gap agencies have capitalised on this and are able to make placements in Chinese offices (see next section).

Internships for people 18-25 are arranged by a company in Colombo Sri Lanka called

Volunteer International Projects (148/1B Kynsey Road, Colombo 7; 74-720658; www.volunteerinternational.com). They offer a structured programme in the hospitality industry, business, conservation, teaching and so on. Participants pay between £1495 for three months and £2395 for six months (plus travel). Some internship placements are available in the Maldive Islands for people fluent in French.

Global Adventures Project (38 Queen's Gate, London SW7 5HR; 0800 085 4197; www.globaladventures.co.uk) offer 6 month internship opportunities in India for anyone over the age of 20. A stipend of 18,000 Rupees is paid per month, with accommodation included. The internship involves working for a training company, which has offices around India, and training young Indian graduates for their first job in call centres. The work revolves around role plays, with classes being interactive and learning about the cultural differences with the UK. This internship allows for complete immersion on the Indian subcontinent with opportunities to travel. Prices start from £945 which includes orientation, 3 weeks training, accommodation and medical insurance. Note that voluntary placements can also be arranged in and around Delhi or in the lower reaches of the Himalayas (prices from £1745).

During Naomi Lisney's gap year business placement in Shanghai, arranged through Teaching & Projects Abroad, she was catapulted into an adult world, a long way from the average Chinese teenager who, when not studying hard, might be going to teahouses or KTV (karaoke bars) with friends:

I worked for the Chinese department of a Shanghai law firm. It was always tricky deciding what to answer when asked what I was doing in Shanghai. If I mentioned volunteer work and said I was working for a law firm, people would, at best, be confused, at worst, simply laugh at me. Why should this company be getting people to work for them for free? Usually, I got away with telling people I was doing an internship. It took me a long time to reconcile the harmonious, integrated image of the part-foreign, part-Chinese owned company that the new brochures depicted, with my experience of two tangibly separate 'departments' in that office!

Yet I have no doubt that I was some help to my boss and colleagues. I had applied for a 'PR/Marketing' placement with TPA, thinking that as a gap year student I would be shadowing someone and running errands. Instead, I was expected to provide them with ways to get new foreign clients. The week I arrived, I was asked to write a marketing report, with practical suggestions on how to expand their client base. I had only just turned 18, and had just passed my (scientific) baccalaureate - I hadn't even done any kind of business studies! Thankfully, the Americans seem to be very big on 'lawyer marketing,' so I found a lot of material on the internet, and transmitted this to my boss. Then I was asked to take steps to implement the cheaper ideas I'd put forward. For the next six months, I was more or less left to myself to do just that, my boss only once in a while summoning me to his office to ask about my progress.

I had very little contact with the lawyers, until the boss organised a trip to the 'Thousand Island Lake' for everyone to celebrate winning a tricky case. At the dinner, these smartly-dressed lawyers loosened up for the first time, some of them even attempting to speak to me in English to my great surprise, as I'd been told that none of them spoke any English. They were really friendly, and had just been too shy to approach me before. Like most Chinese who have learnt English at school, they found both speaking and understanding very difficult, having had no practice at all. After that outing, I was glad to let them practise their English on me. Sometimes, they would ask me for advice on how to act or react in certain situations with foreigners they met. They wanted to know how I would interpret what one drunken foreign potential client had said, for instance, and how seriously it was to be taken! Colleagues are generally delighted to find you curious about China, and in return, will have many questions to ask you about 'The West'. Remember, all they know is gleaned from books, sitcoms and Chinese propaganda! In the end, I think prob-

> ably I learnt just as much about my own culture from looking at it through 'foreign' eyes, as I did about China.
>
> Most of my socialising was with other TPA volunteers in foreign-owned bars and clubs on Maoming Nan Lu. I still felt that I was getting experience of life in China, maybe more so than most Western businessmen, living in their cosy foreign compounds in their centrally-heated accommodation. I loved living amongst the hustle and bustle of Puxi. I especially used to love taking a stroll on a Saturday morning to a bustling, colourful world, eons from the westernised Nanjing Road where my office was. The narrow streets were lined with stalls overflowing with different sweets, fruit and baskets full of steamed buns. People sat around tables, playing cards or chequers, with others stood around making comments about the game, while less than a foot away, someone was having his hair cut at a makeshift barber's stall. Peeking down the unique little alleys, you could watch little old ladies wielding bamboo poles between facing windows from which to hang their laundry. I could wander around these streets near the Yuyuan for hours on end. I actually took to walking home from the office, although it took me two hours!

In fact there can be a fine line between unpaid volunteer and 'intern'. To take one example a training institute in South Sulawesi in Indonesia indicated to this book that they operate an 'Internships With Adventure' programme, which includes a month's tuition in Bahasa Indonesian following by a month's vocational training and then an internship in an Indonesian company, e.g. in Business Admin, Management, Engineering, Human Resources or Technology. They also invite volunteers willing to practise English conversation with their students to come from overseas; details are available from LPTM, Jalan Tepi Kanal Baraya 9, Makassar, South Sulawesi 90153, Indonesia (+62 411-324203; lptm-mks@indo.net.id).

An Indian travel company called Timeless Excursions advertises gap year placements on the website www.gapyearinindia.com (see entry in 'Directory of Volunteering Abroad' and 'Directory of Work Experience Abroad'). It operates a programme called People Tree Gap Year Placements which includes work experience placements lasting between four weeks and six months in Delhi, Mumbai, Kolkatta, Chennai, Bangalore or Cochin. Sample costs are £950 for 4 weeks, £1550 for 13 weeks. It also offers other voluntary and training programmes throughout India.

Courses and Homestays

Young people interested in spending their gap year studying at a Japanese high school should investigate *Youth for Understanding* (see 'Directory of Specialist Gap Year Programmes'). The Japanese government subsidises this programme but it does not include student spending money or insurance costs.

> **Private Japanese language courses will be expensive, but very worthwhile according to CESA client Kathryn Lydon who spent 24 weeks studying Japanese in the small town of Okazaki during her gap year:**
> I had expected something similar to the French lessons I used to receive at school, which meant that my linguistic expectations were not particularly high. I did not expect to be able to read or write Japanese to any practical degree by the time I left. To be honest I spent most of my pre-trip time worrying about navigating the airport system, having never travelled alone before, rather than wondering what the course itself would be like. (Having said that, CESA were fantastic, particularly in calming my fears before the trip.)
>
> The experience has left me not only with an understanding of Japanese culture, but an ability to chat to Japanese people confidently. Arriving in the country with almost zero knowledge of the language, I surprised myself by reaching a stage where I could actually enjoy Japanese conversations. The lessons were

> *quite intensive and we did a lot of exercises involving real life interaction (i.e. post office trips, telephone calls, etc.)*
>
> *I became close to around six of my classmates, and we formed a private study group at Starbucks after school. We discovered that Japanese people actually went to Starbucks in the hope of meeting foreigners and we built up some great contacts this way. As a result of my gap year experience I am now taking Japanese Studies at Sheffield University. I would not have had the motivation to stick with it had I not had the experience of living in Japan.*

Partly because of the high cost of accommodation and the fascination of the cultures, staying with a Japanese or Korean family is worth considering. The Korean National Tourism Organization in London publishes a free booklet on the subject; ring 020-7321 2535 (http://english.tour2korea.com). It lists a few homestay agencies including Labo Korea (+82 2-736 0521; www.labostay.or.kr) which charges 35,000 won a night for B&B (about £20).

The Japan Homestay Service in Chiba-city (43-266-1926; http://home.att.ne.jp/orange/star/homestay) places foreigners with Japanese families for varying charges; the only requirements is 'not to hate Japanese food'. You can combine homestay with language study through programmes such as 'Experience Osaka' marketed by Nelson Research & Consultants for Study Abroad (9-2-8 Tanimachi 603, Chuo-ku, Osaka 542-0012; tel/fax 6-6762-8858; http://homepage2.nifty.com/ex-osaka). Try also the Hokkaido International Foundation (14-1 Motomachi, Hakodate, Hokkaido 040-0054; www.hif.or.jp/eng) which arranges a two-week homestay for 25,000 yen and also an intensive eight-week Japanese language and culture programme in the summer which costs $4250.

Budding writers under 25 might like to enter the Goi Peace Foundation International Essay Competition for a chance to win a prize of 100,000 yen and a free trip to Japan for the prize ceremony in November; the essay must be no more than 800 words and submitted by the end of June (details on the website www.goipeace.or.jp).

Turkey

Turkey is a wonderful country to travel in with a wealth of important historic sites which you will certainly have heard of like Troy and Ephesus. Its economy has shown signs of recovery and on January 1st 2005, the Turkish lira lost six zeros against the dollar. A loaf of bread went from costing 350,000 lire to .35 new lire (or 35 kurus). The government was able to do this because for the first time in many years, the rate of inflation dropped to single figures (i.e. 9%). Still your savings will go a long way in Turkey. Turkey is also a good choice of destination for fledgling English teachers though few opportunities are available to pre-university gap year students with no TEFL training or experience. Although Istanbul is not the capital, it is the commercial, financial and cultural centre of Turkey, so this is where most of the EFL teaching goes on.

For short-term opportunities, the Education Department of the youth travel and exchange organisation *Genctur* (Istiklal Cad. Zambak Sok. 15/5, 34435 Istanbul (212-249 2515; www.genctur.com) organises summer camps for children where English, German and French are taught by native speakers who work for seven hours a day in exchange for free board and lodging. Pocket money of $100-$350 is also given according to experience and skills. Applicants must have some experience of working with children. Genctur also runs 30 international workcamps.

On most camps you will have to work reasonably hard in the hot sun (and wear long sleeves and jeans in deference to Muslim customs). Mary Jelliffe recounts her experiences in Turkey:

I applied to UNA (Wales) quite late (in May/June) and heard from Turkey just one week before my camp commenced in August. My workcamp, which consisted of digging an irrigation canal from the nearby hills to the village, took place in Central Anatolia. I was told that our camp was the most easterly, since the majority are in Western Turkey.

Conditions in this remote village were fairly primitive. We lived in a half-built school-room sleeping on the floor and sharing the daily duties of collecting water and sweeping out the scorpions from under the sleeping bags. The Turkish volunteers were a great asset to the camp: through them we could have far more contact with the villagers and learn more about Turkish culture in general. In fact I later stayed in Istanbul and Izmir with two of the women volunteers I'd met on the camp.

An impressive new WWOOF exchange called Tatuta has started up in Turkey under the auspices of the (inauspiciously-named) Bugday Association at Luleci Hendek Caddesi No 120/2, Kuledibi-Beyoglu, Istanbul (212-252 5255; www.bugday.org/tatuta). TaTuTa is a Turkish acronym for Agro Tourism and Voluntary Exchange. At present there are just 25 member farms but this is predicted to increase.

Au pair jobs in Turkey normally involve more tutoring of English than domestic chores. The following agencies make placements in Turkey:

Anglo Pair Agency, 40 Wavertree Road, Streatham Hill, London SW2 3SP (020-8674 3605; anglo.pair@btinternet.com). Nannies and au pairs (approximately 100) for summer or academic year. Au pairs earn £50-£65 a week. Agency has office in Istanbul.

ICEP (International Cultural Exchange Programs), Yüksel Cad. 9/10, Kizilay, Ankara (312-418 4460) with office in Istanbul as well (www.icep.org.tr/english/aupairturkey.asp). Au pair in Turkey programme for 3-12 months. Minimum pocket money €200 a month. Internships and teaching positions also arranged. UK representative is Language Studies Network Ltd, 37 Great Russell St, London WC1B 3PP (020-7580 4460; info@ languagestudiesnetwork.com).

One persistent problem is that it is generally not acceptable for young women to go out alone in the evenings. But Turkish families are normally very generous and allow their live-in child-carers to share in family life on equal terms, even in their free time and on holidays.

The main Aegean resorts of Marmaris, Kusadasi and Bodrum absorb a large number of foreign travellers as workers. Other places firmly on the travellers' trail like Antalya on the south coast and Goreme in Cappadocia are also promising. The best time to look is March or early April. Major Turkish yachting resorts are excellent places to look for work, not just related to boats but in hotels, bars, shops and excursions. A good time to check harbourside notice boards and to ask captains if they need anyone to clean or repair their boats is in the lead-up to the summer season and the Marmaris Boat Show in May.

A Turkish company USEH International Training & Education Services arranges internships mainly in the hospitality industry in Istanbul and the Turkish Republic of Northern Cyprus open to college students of business, marketing, finance, hotel administration, etc.; details from USEH, Bagdat Cad. 217/14, Ciftehavuzlar, Kadiköy, Istanbul; 216-478-3444 (www.useh.org is in English).

The Middle East

Few gap year students are likely to be seriously considering the Middle East at a time when the region is so troubled. With heightened tension between Israelis and Palestinians and an escalation of anti-Western sentiment throughout the region, the taste for travel and employment in the Middle East has been soured and many prospective travellers have (understandably) been put off by fear for their personal security. The Iraq War has undoubtedly destabilised the area and fanned the flames of Islamic distrust of the West. Perhaps young intrepid travellers can play a small part in diminishing the distrust and tension between the two cultures, bringing people together, allowing individuals on both sides to gain some understanding of the complexity of the world's problems.

Many parts of the Middle East remain reasonably calm and untroubled. For example Yemen has a large and interesting expat community and is a good place to consider studying Arabic (see entry for *CALES* in the Directory of Courses). The CALES website (www. y.net.ye/cales) carries some first-hand accounts, including the following by Isabel Dietrich from Germany:

> *I studied at CALES for one month. Although it is only a short time, I have learnt a lot there. I want to tell everybody, this is a good school. The teachers are well experienced and the atmosphere is excellent… If you want or need to learn Arabic grammar, you will do so. If you prefer to have more practice of the speaking language they will give you the opportunity to speak a lot to practise the language.*
>
> *It is a good choice to study in Yemen. Here you can experience the real Arabic life, more than in the Arabic countries on the Mediterranean Sea where the western influence is greater. Yemeni people are really friendly and very open to western people. The school is situated in an authentic building in the old centre of Sana'a and this city is marvellous, a real wonder of architecture. In the souq, close to the school, you can practice the Arabic language all the time.*

Australia & New Zealand

AUSTRALIA

In response to its phenomenal popularity as a destination for so many young Europeans, Australia has developed a magnificent industry to cater specifically for backpackers. Hostels, both official and private, are full of gap-year travellers and working holidaymakers who will advise newcomers on the best travel deals and adventures, and the places to go to find jobs. Specialist travel offices, employment agencies and even outback farms specifically target the backpacking community, which in Australia includes everybody from people fresh from school to professionals in their 30s.

Picking up casual work to cover all your travelling expenses may not be achievable in the Australia of 2005/6. Partly because of the overwhelming numbers of young foreigners on working holiday visas, it is an employer's rather than a job-seeker's market. The job hunt can be a struggle and optimism needs to be tempered with realism. An article appeared in *Rough News* in the autumn of 2004 entitled 'Working Holiday Hell' written by a disgruntled traveller, though the following issue carried some spirited rebuttals (www. roughguides.com; click on 'Spotlight Archive'). **Roger Blake** is someone who is willing to turn his hand to anything and has successfully 'blagged' (talked) his way into all manner of jobs around the world. Yet he recently found Australia an uphill struggle, certainly compared to New Zealand. Although he managed to survive on his occasional earnings, he warns to expect a 'rough ride': *'I have met SO many travellers who are leaving Australia after just 3 months or less of their WHV, thoroughly disgusted with the attitude of employers towards backpackers and the associated struggles of finding an (often lousy) job in the first place. …. But it is not all doom and gloom and I've had fun between troublesome times.'*

On a more positive note first-time visitors to Australia are often surprised by the degree to which that far-off continent is an imitation of Britain. Despite their reputation as 'pommybashers', most Australians take for granted a strong link with the UK, and this may be one reason why British travellers are so often welcomed as prospective employees especially off the beaten tourist track. On the other hand, in the areas that backpackers have colonised, like certain suburbs of Sydney and certain Queensland islands, they are not at all popular since they have a reputation for 'Ibiza' type behaviour.

Red Tape

Since 2001, the compulsory tourist visa for Australia has not been available free of charge. The paperless visa, the ETA (Electronic Travel Authority), must be obtained via a private agency like Visas Australia or the Australian Immigration Department's website (www.eta. immi.gov.au) which will incur a fee of A\$20. The dispensing of visitor visas has in essence been privatised and specialist visa providers can charge a fee of their choice (none of which is passed on to the Australian government). Among the cheaper providers are www. fastozvisa.com (0800 096 4749) which charges US\$12/£7.50 and www.australiavisas. com which charges US\$15.

The number of working holiday visas has risen steadily from 33,000 in 1995 to 88,750 now. The visa is for people intending to use any money they earn in Australia to supplement their holiday funds. Working full-time for more than three months is not permitted, though you are now permitted to engage in up to three months of studies or training. Applicants must be between the ages of 18 and 30 and without children. You are eligible for a working holiday visa only once. The working holiday visa is valid for 12 months after entry, which must be within 12 months of issue, and is non-renewable.

Assuming you are using the traditional paper method of applying for a Working Holiday Visa, the first step is to get the information sheet and applications form 1150 (WHM) from the Department of Immigration (DIMIA) website www.immi.gov.au, from a specialist agent like Visas Australia (01270 626626; www.visas-australia.com) or Consyl Publishing (3 Buckhurst Road, Bexhill-on-Sea, East Sussex TN40 1QF; 01424 223111) enclosing an A4 stamped addressed envelope (66p stamp). The non-refundable processing fee in the UK is currently A\$170 (£70). Specialist agents like Visas Australia or Travellers Contact Point (www.travellers.com.au) will add a premium of about £15.

The second step is to get as much money in the bank as possible. Each application is assessed on its own merits, but the most important requirement is a healthy bank balance. You must have enough money for your return fare, although it is not essential to have a return ticket at the time of entry. You must show evidence of having saved a minimum of A\$5000/£2100. If your bank statements do not show steady saving, you may have to submit documents showing where the money came from (e.g. sale of a car, gift from a relative).

Now that ticketless flights are well established, paperless WH visas are now a possibility. For an e-WHM visa there is no need to provide proof of funds nor do you send in your passport. Your passport isn't physically inspected until you arrive in Australia when you must take it along to an office of the Department of Immigration. Applying online via www.immi.gov.au is normally straightforward and hassle-free and should result in an emailed confirmation inside 48 hours. To obtain the visa label in your passport, you must visit a DIMIA office in Australia in person, preferably not the busy downtown Sydney or Melbourne offices where queues can be horrific. Elsewhere it should be easier as Roger Blake found in Brisbane where he was 'in and out of the office within half an hour' with no request to show sufficient funds and no fee charged.

Placement Agencies & Special Schemes

Naturally, Australia is not included as a destination by those gap year organisations that focus on developing countries. However the following do make placements downunder, often in boarding schools, doing conservation work or working on outback properties: *GAP*

Activity Projects, Changing Worlds and *i-to-i*. For example i-to-i can arrange conservation packages through Conservation Volunteers Australia (see below). GAP Activity Projects has a big programme in Australia with a contingent of about 100 volunteers, most of whom work in schools. A number of fee-paying schools in Australia have country campuses where pupils spend one year (typically at age 14/15) and where the emphasis is on outdoor activity and developing team spirit. This can become an ideal setting for a year-out student away from home for the first time. Furthermore, some get paid a wage on top of free room and board, usually in the vicinity of $100 a week.

But even similar sounding school placements can be utterly different. For example GAP participant **Ben Hartley** was assigned to the country campus of a girls' school, 3½ hours drive north of Melbourne. He was a little surprised to learn that he would be assisting with sports like rock climbing and skiing which he had never done, but wasn't too worried about keeping the girls (aged 13-14) in line. In fact, late in his 10-month attachment, four of the girls for whom he was responsible perpetrated the heinous crime of smuggling in a bottle of Bacardi and were caught swigging, for which they were nearly expelled. The high points for Ben, on the other hand, came with the long periods of holiday and travel, which allowed him to spend Christmas in New Zealand, visit Perth, Sydney, the Northern Territory and then Queensland when his family flew out from England in the spring.

At the other end of the country, another GAP volunteer Matt Applewhite spent five months at a progressive school outside Darwin called Kormilda attended by white Australian and Aboriginal children from all over the Northern Territory. When Matt chose Australia, he was not bothered by the fact that Australia was considered a soft option by some of his contemporaries. It didn't always feel like a soft option when he looked at his very full timetable of teaching and supervising.

Matt Applewhite ended up having not only a fascinating but a fulfilling year:
As I walked around Kormilda College for the last time, it seemed that every room, every corner had a memory associated with it. A glimpse of the college canoes awakened the vivid memories of Year 8 Outback camps when by day under the blazing sun we noisily splashed around the leafy billabongs and bushwalked through Crocodile Dundee's back yard. A traditional Aboriginal drawing in the library allowed me to reminisce about my trip to the remote community of Peppimenarti and the way in which the welcoming community allowed me to observe the elders silently weaving traditional baskets, watch the village children learn English in the community school and appreciate their cultural traditions, dignity and warmth. I reflected on all the experiences I'd relished and how lucky I'd been to spend time in this place.
All these priceless memories, all for £1500 which was his total outlay for eight months.

BUNAC (16 Bowling Green Lane, London EC1R 0QH; 020-7251 3472) features Australia as one of its destination countries. Anyone who is eligible for the working holiday visa may choose to join the BUNAC Work Australia package which costs from £1750 depending on flight routing. This includes the round-the-world flight, visa, orientation on arrival and back-up services. Enquiries about this programme may be made by e-mail to downunder@bunac.org.uk.

CCUSA, Camp Counsellors USA, 1st Floor North, Devon House, 171/177 Great Portland St, London W1W 5PQ (020-7637 0779/ fax 020-7580 6209; www.ccusa.com) has a 12-month Work Experience Downunder programme that costs £230 plus insurance and visas. US applicants should contact CCUSA at 2330 Marinship Way, Suite 250, Sausalito, CA 94965 (800-449-3872; downunder@ccusa.com) for a 4-month programme.

Changing Worlds, Hodore Farm, Hartfield, East Sussex TN7 4AR (01892 770000/ fax 0870 990 9665; welcome@changingworlds.co.uk/ www.changingworlds.co.uk). Paid placements in hotels in tourist hotspots and on farms throughout Queensland including ones where there are riding opportunities. Voluntary placements in a zoo and on conservation projects. Placements last from three to six months starting in September, March and July.

Global Adventures Project, 38 Queen's Gate, London SW7 5HR (0800 085 4197; www.globaladventures.co.uk) offer a job service on arrival that provides collection from the airport, accommodation for the first four nights, assistance in setting up a bank account and obtaining a Tax ID number, assistance in compiling relevant CV's, and access to the latest job offers around Australia. This service can be included with one other work/volunteering/study placements that Global Adventures Project offer. Prices start from £3145 which includes a round the world ticket and a second 3-month placement.

Involvement Volunteers Association Inc (PO Box 218, Port Melbourne, VIC 3207; 03-9646 9392/ www.volunteering.org.au) arranges short-term (2-6 weeks) or long-term (up to 1 year) volunteer placements for individuals worldwide. Placements possible in all the states of Australia (and worldwide). Projects are concerned with conservation, the environment, animal welfare, social and community service, education and childcare. Programme fees start at A$710.

IST Plus Ltd, Rosedale House, Rosedale Road, Richmond, Surrey TW9 2SZ (020-8939 9057; info@istplus.com; www.istplus.com) offers the Work and Travel Australia programme in conjunction with AIFS. Fees start at £320 to include insurance, initial accommodation and a post-arrival orientation at the partner office in Sydney: AIFS Australia Pty Ltd, 91 York St, Sydney, NSW 2000 (02-9235 7000; www.workinaustralia.net). US young people may apply for the four-month working visa to CIEE, 7 Custom House Street, 3rd Floor, Portland, ME 04101 (800-407-8839; www.ciee.org). For a fee of US$425 (plus A$170 for the visa), participants receive work documentation and access to job-finding assistance.

Overseas Working Holidays (OWH), Level 1, 51 Fife Rd, Kingston, Surrey KT1 1SF (0845 344 0366; www.overseasworkingholidays.co.uk). Guaranteed hospitality work in Melbourne at major sporting events such as the Australian Grand Prix and Spring Racing Carnival, as well as ongoing corporate work. Programme fees from £189.

VisitOz Scheme, Springbrook Farm, MS188, Goomeri, 4601 Queensland (fax 07-4168 6106; www.visitoz.org) sends participants with the working holiday visa to a station on the Queensland/NSW border for a 5-day crash course in outback working techniques (or in hospitality industry skills if preferred) and then guarantees paid employment for 3 months on outback properties as tractor drivers, stock and horse workers, hospitality assistants on cattle and sheep stations and mothers' helps. The cost is A$1680. The UK contact can be reached on 07966 528664; will@visitoz.org.

In addition to the gap year specialists, an increasing number of backpacker travel and youth exchange agencies are offering packages that may be of special interest to first-time travellers in their gap year. Some are all-inclusive; others simply give back-up on arrival. Typically, the fee will include airport pick-up, hostel accommodation for the first few nights and a post-arrival orientation which advises on how to obtain a tax-file card, suggestions of employers and so on. Some even guarantee a job. Various perks are thrown in like a telephone calling card and maps.

For example Travellers Contact Point (2-6 Inverness Terrace, Bayswater, London W2 3HX; 020-7243 7887; www.travellers.com.au) operates a free job search centre in connection with recruitment agencies in six offices around Australia and New Zealand. Membership for £25 includes services such as mail forwarding, e-mail and word processing access. They sell an arrivals package for £75 which includes your first two nights in Sydney and a working holiday information kit, among other things. In Sydney the TCP office is at Level 7, Dymocks Building, 428 George St, Sydney 2000 (02-9221 8744/fax 9221 3746).

Working Holiday Starter Packs lasting two, four or seven days, starting from A$119, are also offered by the new company Launchpad Australia In Melbourne (PO Box 2525, Fitzroy, VIC 306, Australia; 1300 851 826 or 03-9419 9147; www.launchpadaustralia.com). The Backpacker's Resource Centre will help people with the working holiday visa to set up work as well as providing a range of other back-up services for a fee of A$330. Send for an information pack from Hotel Bakpak Group (167 Franklin St, Melbourne 3000; 03-9329 7525; info@bakpakgroup.com).

The international hostel group Nomads (www.nomadsworld.com) sells a Travel Guide & Adventure Card for £16 (A$39) through specialist travel agents abroad and in Australia. Nomads operate a number of working hostels (for example in Bundaberg) and sell a Job Package to new arrivals for A$199 (Sydney and Adelaide) or A$159 (Melbourne). They also maintain a database of job vacancies updated weekly, accessible by members via telephone.

Worldwide Workers (www.worldwideworkers.com) is a dedicated recruitment service for travellers and backpackers coming to Australia and New Zealand, located at 234 Sussex Street in Sydney's Central Business District (02-8268 6001). They specialise in placing working holiday visa holders in jobs lasting anything from one shift up to three months. Jobs are mainly in hospitality, labour/factory/warehouse, call centre and white collar. They offer a 'JobText' service whereby registered members are sent text messages of suitable jobs as soon as they come in.

Work Experience

Increasingly, Australian recruitment agencies are actively looking for people in the UK to fill their clients' temporary vacancies in Australia and are geared up to advise people with working holiday visas. Private employment agencies are very widespread and can be a good potential source of jobs for travellers, especially those with office skills, computer, data processing or financial experience. A surprising number positively encourage UK people on working holidays, often by circulating their details to hostel managers. This is more common in Sydney and Melbourne than in Perth where most recruitment agencies are just not interested in working holidaymakers. The offered wages are good too: from $12 an hour for clerical work, $14 for secretarial and $15 for computer work. This might be an ideal route for a student who has done a secretarial or business skills course at the beginning of their year out. Note that in some cases lower youth wages may apply to those under 20.

Cultural Cube Ltd. in Devon (www.culturalcube.co.uk; see entry in 'Directory of Volunteering Abroad') arranges internships in multinational or medium to big Australian companies. These can be in any field and last from 1 week to 12 months, starting year round. The vast majority are unpaid, however some companies may make a small contribution towards living expenses. Participants usually enter Australia on a student, working holiday or even tourist visa. The fee for arranging this is £440 for a 6-week placement, £1000 for a year; accommodation and airfares are of course extra.

An Australian company that claims to be Australia's biggest internship provider is the International Student Placement Centre which places international students in unpaid work experience placements with more than 1000 companies in Australia. The fee for an internship lasting 13-26 weeks is A$1650; details from ISPC, Level 8, 32 York St, Sydney, NSW 2000 (02-9279 0100; internships@ispc.com.au).

Anyone with experience of the horse industry could contact Stablemate, PO Box 1206, Windsor, NSW 2756 (+61-2-4587 9770; info@stablemate.net.au). They deal exclusively with placing equestrian and thoroughbred staff but are sometimes able to assist people (including those on working holiday visas) with limited experience of horses if they want to work as a nanny or general farm assistant.

Interesting research projects take place throughout Australia and some may be willing to include unpaid staff looking for work experience. For example a research station in northern Queensland operated by the Australian Tropical Research Foundation (PMB 5, Cape Tribulation, Qld 4873; 07-4098 0063; www.austrop.org.au) welcomes 50 volunteers a year to carry out all sorts of tasks to conserve the rainforest. Volunteers are asked to pay at least $15 a day to cover their food and accommodation. It might be worth trying the Heron Island Research Station (Great Barrier Reef, via Gladstone, Qld 4680; www.

marine.uq.edu.au/hirs) which has been known to offer free accommodation in exchange for about four hours of work a day.

The Australian Institute of Marine Science (AIMS) at Cape Ferguson near Townsville (07-4753 4240; visitor_coord@aims.gov.au/ www.aims.gov.au) runs a Prospective Visitors Scheme which encompasses volunteers; applicants with their own research projects or a scuba diving certificate are especially welcome. Application must be done online.

Often the state conservation organisation runs a voluntary programme, as is the case in Western Australia with the Conservation & Land Management Department of CALM (www.calm.wa.gov.au). The programme is open to anyone, though it can't provide accommodation in remote places; write to the Volunteer Co-ordinator at CALM for details (Locked Bag 104, Bentley Delivery Centre, WA 6983; 08-9334 0333). For people with a conservation background or relevant skills, CALM also runs an Educational Work Experience Programme, though none of the positions involves working with wildlife.

Anyone under 19 looking to spend a year attending an Australian secondary school should make enquiries of Southern Cross Cultural Exchange (Locked Bag 1200, Mt. Eliza, VIC 3930; +61 3 9775 4711; scceaust@scce.com.au).

The Job Hunt

If you decide not to organise a placement through an agency, you will be on your own looking for work, along with a huge number of other working holiday makers competing for the same jobs. The glut of travelling workers is especially bad in Sydney and on the Queensland 'Route' between Sydney and Cairns, whereas Melbourne and Adelaide offer better prospects. In addition to asking potential employers directly (which is the method used by most successful job-seekers in Australia), the main ways of finding work are via private employment agencies, newspaper advertisements and notice boards (especially at travellers' hostels).

Either before you leave Britain or once you are in one of the major cities, get hold of the 212-page booklet *Australia & New Zealand Travel Guide* published by the London-based travel magazine*TNT* (14-15 Child's Place, London SW5 9RX; www.tntmagazine.com/uk); the guide can be ordered online but postage is charged at £2.95. It includes a section on work and some relevant advertisements as well as travel advice. The same company publishes monthly magazines for Sydney/NSW, Queensland/Northern Territory and Victoria/Tasmania/South Australia/West Australia, available free in Australia at backpackers' hostels, bus and train stations, etc. Many of these job adverts can be consulted online at www.tntmagazine.com/au.

Some charities are perennial advertisers for paid fund-raisers. The most amusing account of earning money this way comes from **Chris Miksovsky**, who earned $12 an hour (but only for four to six hours a week) as a street collector in Brisbane:

My year in Australia ended with a rather fitting and hilarious job, collecting for the Wilderness Society, a sort of Australian Greenpeace, wearing a koala costume. After a brief interview with the Koala Coordinator ('So, Chris, do you have any experience walking around as a big furry animal?'), I found myself in a busy square wearing a full-body fluffy grey koala suit complete with fake felt claws and droopy oversize ears. Actually it works. Takings per hour were about $25 on average. For me, probably the best thing was that you learned to not take yourself so seriously.

If interested contact the Wilderness Society which in Sydney is on Level 2, 64-76 Kippax St, Surry Hills, NSW 2010 (02-9282 9553; wd.recruitment@wilderness.org.au); hourly earnings average $15-$20. Another charity that employs travellers as fundraisers is Sydney Spinal Cord Injuries Australia (PO Box 397, Matraville, NSW 2036; 02-9281 8214; fundraising@spinalcordinjuries.com.au which pays its collectors a quarter of donations collected, which can work out to be $50-$100 a day.

As mentioned, the dense network of hostels is a goldmine of information. Gappers find employment in the hostels themselves too. **Stephen Psallidas** describes the proliferation of work:

> I've met loads of people working in backpackers' hostels. Typically you work two hours a day in exchange for your bed and a meal. Work may be cleaning, driving the minibus, reception, etc. and is always on an informal basis. I will be jumping on the bandwagon myself soon. I'll be completely shattered from picking tomatoes so I'm going to 'work' in a hostel in Mission Beach, where the owners invited me to work when I stayed there earlier. I'm going to rest up in a beautiful place before continuing my travels, and not spend any of my hard-earned dollars.

One of the most successful groups of non-YHA hostels is VIP Backpackers Resorts of Australia which is especially strong in New South Wales and Queensland. A booklet listing their 146 Australian hostels is distributed far and wide or can be obtained from overseas by purchasing their VIP kit for A$41 (£16 in the UK) which gives $1 off each hostel stay among other discounts; contact VIP Backpackers in the UK: Riverbank House, 1 Putney Bridge Approach, London SW6 3JD; 020-7736 4200; www.vipbackpackers.com). Almost all VIP hostels have notice boards advertising jobs, flats, car shares, etc. and most charge about $20 a night for a dorm bed.

The Outback

Most of Australia's area is sparsely populated, scorched land which is known loosely as the outback. Beyond the rich farming and grazing land surrounding the largest cities, there are immense properties supporting thousands of animals and acres of crops. Many of these stations (farms) are so remote that flying is the only practical means of access, though having a vehicle can be a great help in an outback job search. **Sandra Gray** describes the drawbacks of spending time on a station:

> Be warned! Station life can be severely boring after a while. I managed to land myself on one in the Northern Territory with very little else to do but watch the grass grow. If you have to save a lot of money quickly station work is the way to do it since there's nothing to spend it on. But make sure the place is within reasonable distance of a town or at least a roadhouse, so you have somewhere to go to let off steam occasionally.

Your chances of getting a job as a station assistant (jackaroo or jillaroo) will be improved if you have had experience with sheep, riding or any farming or mechanical experience. Several farmers are in the business of giving you that experience before helping you to find outback work, like the one mentioned above in the Visitoz Scheme.

Shaun Armstrong thoroughly enjoyed an outback course in Queensland:
Should any traveller wish to discover an introduction to authentic rural Australia, no better window of opportunity exists than Pat and Pete Worsley's Rocky Creek Station. I braved the five-day jackaroo course with three other travellers. Horsecraft, cattle mustering, ute driving, trail biking (the 'ings' were numerous) and other tasks occupied our days: wonderful hospitality ended each evening. Memorable days. Station placement was arranged afterwards as was transport if needed. I was sorry to leave really. I'd say the course did prepare me for most experiences encountered in the job. For example I was able to muster cattle on horseback with four experienced riders having spent only 15 hours in the saddle. It wasn't easy, but I did it.

The course fee is $484 including job placement afterwards with one of more than 300 employers, plus ongoing back-up. Rocky Creek is located inland from Bundaberg (Isis Highway MS 698, Biggenden, Qld 4621; 07-4127 1377; www.isisol.com.au/rockycrkfarmstay).

Other farms offer such courses, for example the Leconfield Jackaroo and Jillaroo School in Kootingal NSW 2352 not far from Tamworth/Armidale (tel/fax 02-6769 1230; www.leconfieldjackaroo.com/info.html). On completion of the group course lasting 11 days and costing $850, successful participants will be guided in the direction of paying jobs.

Conservation Volunteering

Several organisations give visitors a chance to experience the Australian countryside or bush. The main not-for-profit conservation organisation in Australia is called, predictably enough, Conservation Volunteers Australia (CVA) and it places volunteers from overseas in its 'Conservation Experience' projects, though the charges are quite steep. Sample projects include tree planting, erosion and salinity control, seed collection from indigenous plants, building and maintaining bush walking tracks, etc. Overseas volunteers are welcome to become involved by booking a four-week or six-week package which include food and accommodation and some transport at a cost of A$815 and $1200 respectively (which works out at less than $30 a day for accommodation, food and transport). Further details are available from the National Head Office, Box 423, Ballarat, Vic 3353 (03-5333 2600; www.conservationvolunteers.com.au). There are volunteer offices in all the states.

Nicky Stead was forced to take a gap year at the last minute and hurriedly enquired about placements through i-to-i. The project that caught her eye was doing conservation work with ATCV (now CVA) in Australia and soon she was saving money for the placement and the flight (£2000+). She had done a few conservation projects in the Lake District so knew what she was letting herself in for, and this appealed more than teaching. So she signed up for eight weeks based in Adelaide and had a marvellous time:

> *Going to Australia was the best thing I ever did. Everything worked out as it was meant to. I had no problems at all. We lived in Adelaide but travelled all over South Australia on different projects. We planted trees by a flooded mine shaft, built a fence on the coast of the Great Australian Bight, and weeded on the banks of the huge River Murray. We were well looked after by the managers and team leaders of ATCV; although I never felt I needed their support, it was good to know it was there. They made us work from 8am to 4pm which was not unreasonable, and with a break mid-morning and an hour for lunch it wasn't too strenuous. The fee I'd paid (£1200) covered food, accommodation (which was often very very basic), transport and training. At the end the estate manager wrote me a great reference.*
>
> *The other volunteers were all English, doing six months through GAP Activity Projects. My new friends made it for me. We all got on really well and I hope they will be lasting friendships. Leaving them at the end of the two months was definitely the low point of the year. I had to leave a lovely holiday romance with the knowledge that he'd quickly forget me (he didn't) and suddenly I was alone again preparing to travel on to New Zealand, the US and Canada to visit friends.*

More ad hoc opportunities may present themselves and cost considerably less:

> **Daniele Arena from Italy stumbled across a project on the coast of Queensland that appealed to him:**
> *One of the most amazing experiences I had in Oz was the time I was volunteering at the Turtle Rookery in Mon Repos Beach. We could pitch our tent for free, and gave a small contribution of $5 a day for food. The work was to patrol the beach waiting for nesting turtles and, when they come in, to tag and measure them and the nest. This goes on between November and March. I was fortunate enough to*

> get this by chance but normally there's quite a few people who want to do it, so you
> should probably contact the Queensland Parks & Wildlife Service for info.

World Wide Opportunities on Organic Farms (WWOOF) is very active in Australia and their publicity is distributed by many hostels. WWOOF Australia (2166 Gelantipy Rd, W Tree, Via Buchan, Vic 3885; 03-5155 0218; www.wwoof.com.au) publish the *Australian WWOOF Book* with about 1500 addresses throughout Australia of organic farmers looking for short or long term voluntary help. The list is sold with basic accident insurance at a cost of A$50 within Australia, A$60 outside ($55 and $65 respectively for a double membership).

A free internet-based exchange of work-for-keep volunteers can be found at www.helpx.net where about 200 hosts in Australia are listed.

Fruit Picking

Many gap year students fund their travels around Australia by migrating between fruit and vegetable harvests. OzJobs publicises harvest vacancies online and via the telephone; contact the Go Harvest hotline on 1300 720126 or check www.goharvest.com or www.oz-jobs.com.au/harvest/destinationsDB.cfm. Also contact the National Harvest Labour Information Service based in Victoria (PO Box 5055, Mildura, Vic 3502; 1800 062 332; nhlis@madec.edu.au/ www.jobsearch.gov.au/harvesttrail). Australia's first specialist harvesting recruitment agency is flourishing: the unflinchingly named Grunt Labour Services has offices in Darwin, Katherine, Kununurra, Broome, Childers, Cairns, Bundaberg and Brisbane (www.gruntlabour.com).

In some regions demand for pickers is so strong that farmers publicise vacancies outside their region, as in the case of the Northern Victoria Fruitgrowers' Association Ltd, PO Box 612, Mooroopna, (2 Rumbalara Rd, Mooroopna, VIC 3629; 03-5825 3700; www.nvfa.com.au) and the Victorian Peach and Apricot Growers' Association (vpaga@cnl.com.au). Several large Australian orchard employers are listed in the 'Directory of Paid Seasonal Jobs' (see *Cornish* in Victoria and *Torrens Valley Orchards* in South Australia). For detailed information about harvest dates, locations, wages, etc. throughout Australia, see *Work Your Way Around the World* by Susan Griffith (Vacation Work, £12.95).

Although harvesting work is often not hard to *get*, some find it hard to make any money. The apple/pear/grape crates may look quite small at the outset but will soon seem unfillable with mysterious false bottoms. Many eager first-timers do not realise how hard the work will be physically, and give up before their bodies acclimatise. But you should have faith that your speed will increase fairly rapidly and with it your earnings.

The Tourist Industry

Casual catering wages both in the cities and in remote areas are reasonably good, for example the award rate for waiting staff in New South Wales is about $12.50 an hour, with weekend loadings of time and a half on Saturdays and time and three-quarters on Sundays and holidays. Although tipping was traditionally not practised in Australia, it is gradually becoming more common and waiting staff in trendy city establishments can expect to augment their basic wage to some extent.

Standards tend to be fairly high especially in popular tourist haunts, so inexperienced gap year students have little chance of being hired to work in a restaurant or pub. A common practice among restaurant bosses in popular places from Bondi Beach to the Sunshine Coast is to give a job-seeker an hour's trial or a trial shift and decide at the end whether or not to employ them. Stephen Psallidas was taken aback when he approached a hospitality employment agency in Cairns:

> *I was in Cairns in April and thought I'd have little trouble getting work. But though I
> had a visa and experience I had no references, having worked as a waiter in Greece,
> where they wouldn't know a reference if one walked up and said 'Hi, I'm a reference',*

so I was doomed from the start. The agency told me that if I'd had references they could have given me work immediately. Curses.

Anyone with experience as a cook or chef will probably find her/himself in demand. One tourist area which is not normally inundated with backpacking job-seekers is the stretch of Victorian coast between Dromana and Portsea on the Mornington Peninsula near Melbourne. Although most jobs don't start until after Christmas, the best time to look is late November/early December.

If exploring Australia is your target rather than earning high wages, it is worth trying to exchange your labour for the chance to join an otherwise unaffordable tour. For example camping tour operators in Kakadu and Litchfield Park have been known to do this; try for example Billy Can Tours (www.billycan.com.au).

Diving and Watersports

One of the larger employers is the dive industry. Although not many visitors would have the qualifications which got **Ian Mudge** a job as Dive Master on *Nimrod III* operating out of Cookstown (i.e. qualified mechanical engineer, diver and student of Japanese), his assessment of opportunities for mere mortals is heartening:

Anyone wishing to try their luck as a hostess could do no worse than to approach all the dive operators with live-aboard boats such as Mike Ball Dive Expeditions, Down Under Dive, etc. 'Hosties' make beds, clean cabins and generally tidy up. Culinary skills and an ability to speak Japanese would be definite pluses. A non-diver would almost certainly be able to fix up some free dive lessons and thus obtain their basic Open Water Diver qualification while being paid to do so. Normally females only are considered for hostie jobs.

Year-out students who have a sailing qualification might find temporary work instructing. To take just one example Northside Sailing School at Spit Bridge in the Sydney suburb of Mosman (02-9969 3972; www.northsidesailing.com.au) offers casual instructing work during school holidays to travellers who have experience in teaching dinghy sailing.

Flying Fish runs a structured watersports training and recruitment programme in Australia. After yacht, dive, surf and windsurf training, graduates can take advantage of the free careers advice and recruitment service to help find work in the industry for the rest of their gap year. Many trainees who have completed Professional Dive Training with Flying Fish at the Pro Dive Academy in Sydney go on to work at Pro Dive's network of resorts in Australia and the South Pacific. (See entry for Flying Fish in 'Directory of Specialist Gap Year Programmes'.)

> **Ed Fry spent the first half of his gap year (up till January 2005) doing a *Flying Fish* Yachtmaster course in Australia:**
> *I loved my time with FF and it was worth every penny. It has given me huge opportunities to sail anywhere in the world and I met some great people (of whom only a few were on post-school gap years). The rest of the time after the course was spent trying (with reasonable success) to get a job on a yacht in Australia. I found it hard to find work after sailing, particularly because with a working holiday visa one can only work for three months and many employers are looking for more commitment. I could have worked in a bar but I was loath to do so after spending so much time learning to sail properly. Eventually I did find work teaching a bit and doing odd jobs on boats which gave me work about four days a week, but much of this was just cash-in-hand.*
> *   All in all I have very few regrets about the time I have spent over the last 12 months. In retrospect I wish I had spent more time sailing but I did not have the money at the time. I think a year out is an unrivalled experience and one that almost every school leaver should take if they are lucky enough to have the opportunity.*

Ski Resorts

Another holiday area to consider is the Australian Alps where ski resorts are expanding and gaining in popularity. Jindabyne (NSW) on the edge of Kosciuszko National Park and Thredbo are the ski job capitals, though Mount Buller, Falls Creek, Baw Baw and Hotham in the state of Victoria are relatively developed ski centres too. The best time to look is a couple of weeks before the season opens, which is usually around the middle of June. Most successful job-seekers use the walk-in-and-ask method, though as everywhere the internet is playing an increasing role. Check out www.ski.com.au/jobs/jobs.html which has a Jobs Database and links to the resorts and pertinent email addresses like jobs@perisher.com.au or recruitment@thredbo.com.au.

Travelling Fairs

Travelling fairs such as the Melbourne Show are very popular and have frequent vacancies. Although it is partly a case of being in the right place at the right time, you can research likely times and locations. To get a job you need to go to the site and walk around asking for work. Some jobs are paid hourly while others pay a percentage of takings; the latter should be accepted only by those with very outgoing personalities who can draw in the punters. Even if you don't land a job before the show opens, it is worth hanging in there in case of last minute cancellations. You can also get a job dismantling the rides at the end which is very physically demanding work.

Geertje Korf, on a gap year between studying archaeology and taking up a career, was at first thrilled to land a job with a travelling fair but it wasn't all as exciting as she had hoped:

> The work itself was good enough, helping to build up the stalls and working on the Laughing Clowns game. But the family I got to work for were not extremely sociable company. As a result, when we left a place and headed for the next I would spend time (about a week) until the next show day wandering lonely around incredibly hot and dusty little country towns where there was absolutely nothing to do while the showmen sat in a little circle drinking beer and not even talking to me. Also, the public toilets on the showgrounds were not usually open until showday, never cleaned since the last showday and usually provided some company (at last!) such as frogs, flies and redback spiders. I got paid $200 a week plus the use of a little caravan and evening meals which was not bad.

> **Loneliness was not a problem for Sam Martell from the Orkneys when he spent a year going round the world after university - and he earned a fair whack for a short burst:**
> A girl I met on a tour at Byron Bay got me a job in Brisbane at the Queensland State Fair in the second week of August. I was paid $10 cash-in-hand working on a bouncy castle rescuing scared kids from the slide and chatting to the mums – it was great. In seven days I clocked up 73½ hours and took home $735 which meant I could afford the Whitsundays sailing trip.

Au Pairing

The demand for live-in and live-out childcare is enormous in Australia. Applicants are often interviewed a day or two after registering with an agency and start work immediately. Nanny and au pair agencies are very interested in hearing from young women and men with working holiday visas. A number of au pair agencies place European and Asian women with working holiday visas in live-in positions, normally for a minimum of three months. Not all placements require childcare experience. Try any of the following:

AAA Nannies, PO Box 157, Sanctuary Cove, Queensland 4212 (head office 07-5530 1123; www.nanny.net.au). Charges placement fee of $400 for international applicants.

Australian Nanny & Au Pair Connection, 404 Glenferrie Road, Kooyong, Melbourne, Vic 3144 (tel/fax 03-9824 8857; www.australiannannies.info).

Dial-an-Angel, PO Box 543, Edgecliff, NSW 2027 (02-9362 4225; www.dial-an-angel. com.au). Long established agency with branches throughout Australia. Wages offered $250-$500 per week.

Family Match Au Pairs & Nannies, PO Box 6406, Kincumber, NSW 2251 (tel/fax 02-4363 2500; www.familymatch.com.au). Online service for live-in positions including for working holidaymakers. 20-30 hours per week for pocket money of $150-$180 plus all live-in expenses.

People for People, PO Box W271, Warringah Mall, Brookvale, NSW 2100 (02-9972 0488; www.peopleforpeople.com.au). Welcome working holidaymakers for three-month summer positions.

Most agencies will expect to interview applicants and check their references before placement. As in America, a driving licence is a valuable asset. As well as long term posts, holiday positions for the summer (December-February) and for the ski season (July-September) are available.

Travel

The Australian Tourist Commission's *Traveller's Guide* contains quite a bit of hard information and useful telephone numbers as well as all the usual advertising; request a copy by ringing 0906 863 3235 (60p a minute). Your transport problems are by no means over when you land in Perth or Sydney. The distances in Australia may be much greater than you are accustomed to and so you will have to give some thought to how you intend to get around. The no-frills domestic airline Jetstar (131538; www.jetstar.com.au) has very good promotional fares (e.g. $69 one way Melbourne to Hobart or Adelaide) and is worth comparing to Richard Branson's Virgin Blue (136789; www.virginblue.com.au). Substantial discounts are offered on Qantas domestic flights to overseas visitors who buy domestic flights in conjunction with their international flight.

If you plan a major tour of the country you might consider purchasing a Greyhound coach pass along a pre-set route (131499/+61-7-4690 9950; www.greyhound.com.au). Sample prices are A$280 for the nearly 3000km trip between Sydney and Cairns and the all-Australia pass costing $2458 valid for 12 months; people with YHA or other cards should be entitled to a 10% discount. If you just want to get from one coast to another as quickly as possible and qualify for the very cheapest deals, you will pay around A$460 one way on the coach or train (excluding berth and meals). Students and backpackers are eligible for a very good deal on the railways: unlimited travel on the great transcontinental routes for six months costs $450 (www.railaustralia.com.au/rail_passes.htm). A multiplicity of private operators has sprung up to serve the backpacking market such as Oz Experience and Wayward Bus.

Having your own transport is a great advantage when job-hunting in Australia. Some places have second-hand cars and camper vans for sale which they will buy back at the end of your stay, for example Boomerang Cars in Adelaide (261 Currie St, 0414-882559; www.boomerangcars.com.au) or Travellers Auto Barn in Sydney, Melbourne, Brisbane and Cairns (www.travellers-autobarn.com). Expect to pay $2000+ for an old car (like a gas-guzzling Ford Falcon) and more for a camper van; the more you spend the better your chance of its lasting the distance and being saleable at the end of your stay.

Although, arguably behind New Zealand, Australia prides itself on being the land of adventurous activities. For example diving courses are widely available, ranging for a one-day introduction for less than $200 tor a basic PADI Open Water Diver four-day course starting at around $325. Any number of agencies, especially in Sydney and Brisbane, offer attractive adventure breaks, e.g. Wanderers Travel at 810 George St in Sydney (www. wanderers-travel.com) organises surf and scuba safaris for backpackers.

It is the rare gap year traveller who comes home from Australia disappointed. The Aussies are a fantastically friendly, good-natured and helpful bunch and very easy to socialise with. Many student visitors are struck by what a good standard of living can be enjoyed for not very much money.

NEW ZEALAND

Mothers of prospective gap year students have been known to tell their daughters that the only countries they will be allowed to visit are Canada and New Zealand. Mothers always know which countries are safe and friendly, and they don't come any safer or friendlier than New Zealand. These same mothers probably also have a list of expatriate cousins and old school friends who could be relied on in a crisis. New Zealand may be about as far away from Britain as it is possible to get, yet it makes things very easy for young travellers on a budget.

Most year-out students simply travel around New Zealand rather than work or study. Typically, students earn money in Australia to fund a holiday in NZ which includes the obligatory bungy jump or other adrenalin sport in Queenstown. Other enterprising gap year students get a working holiday visa for New Zealand (see below) and hunt out their own jobs.

If you are combining Australia with New Zealand, you should investigate the trans-Tasman airfares available from Pacific Blue or Freedom Air (www.freedomair.co.nz) which flies into the smaller North Island cities of Palmerston North and Hamilton.

Placement Organisations

A new company launched its online services in September 2005 to help young people plan and organise a gap year in New Zealand; see the entry for *Gap Year NZ* in the 'Directory of Specialist Gap Year Programmes'. Its sister company at the same address provides work experience placements in New Zealand for British students who need to find a placement as part of their course (see entry for *PlaceMe NZ* in the 'Directory of Work Experience).

GAP Activity Projects has been sending year-out students to boarding schools for many years. Because New Zealanders are so fanatical about sport, schools place a strong emphasis on outdoor activities, and GAPpers make ideal helpers. Most of these placements last for a whole year from the end of August, though a few eight-month placements start half-way through the year.

BUNAC (downunder@bunac.org.uk) has a Work New Zealand programme which provides the usual range of services to students and non-students: flights, stopovers, initial hostel accommodation, orientation on arrival and ongoing support. The package is available for an inclusive fee from £1900.

CCUSA, 1st Floor North, Devon House, 171/177 Great Portland St, London W1W 5PQ (020-7637 0779; www.ccusa.com) operates to New Zealand as well as Australia. The application and programme fees come to £230 plus insurance, travel and visas.

Changing Worlds (Hodore Farm, Hartfield, East Sussex TN7 4AR (01892 77000; www. changingworlds.co.uk) offer paid placements in hotels in the Bay of Islands, Rotorua and Queenstown and also on farms throughout the North Island. Unpaid opportunities exist to work on a tall ship. Changing World's New Zealand placements last three to six months starting in September, January and June.

IST Plus, Rosedale House, Rosedale Road, Richmond, Surrey TW9 2SZ (020-8939 9057; info@istplus.com). Work and Travel New Zealand programme fees start at £320 to include insurance, initial accommodation and a post-arrival orientation at the partner office in Auckland (Backpackers World).

Red Tape

Visitors from the UK need no visa to stay for up to six months. Young travellers entering the country may be asked to show an onward ticket and about NZ$1000 per month of their proposed stay (unless they have pre-paid accommodation or a New Zealand backer who has pledged support in a crisis). In practice, respectable-looking travellers are unlikely to be quizzed at entry.

The UK Citizens' Working Holiday Scheme has been deemed such a success in addressing severe labour shortages in seasonal work that as of July 2005 the maximum duration has been extended from one year to two years, and the quota of 9,000 removed. The scheme allows any eligible Briton aged 18-30 to obtain a working holiday visa, allowing him or her to do temporary or full-time jobs in New Zealand. Information can be obtained from the New Zealand Immigration Service, Mezzanine Floor, New Zealand House, 80 Haymarket, London SW1Y 4TE (fax 020-7973 0370) in person, by phone on 09069 100100 (charged at £1 per minute) or via the internet at www.immigration.govt.nz. This is an admirably clear and thoroughly up-to-date website, which is just as well since from 2005, applications for all working holiday schemes will have to be made online. The fee (currently NZ$120/£50) will be payable by credit card at the time of application.

Casual Work

New Zealand is a country where it may be better to take enough money to enjoy travelling, and perhaps supplement your travel fund with some cash-in-hand work, odd jobs or work-for-keep arrangements. Camping on beaches, fields and in woodlands is generally permitted. Hitch-hiking is rewarding. Hire cars can even be free. So many hirers leave their hire cars in Wellington before catching the ferry to the South Island and then in Christchurch, that the major outlets need people to deliver these cars north again to Auckland.

Because New Zealand has a limited industrial base, most temporary work is in agriculture and tourism. As in Australia, hostels and campsites are the best sources of information on harvesting jobs (and there is a wealth of budget accommodation throughout New Zealand). Often local farmers co-operate with hostel wardens who collate information about job vacancies or they may circulate notices around youth hostels, for example, 'Orchard Work Available January to March; apply Tauranga Hostel' so always check the hostel board (bearing in mind that some hostels entice job-seekers with a vague promise of local work simply to fill beds). **Ian Fleming** soon realised how valuable hostels could be in his job hunt:

> During our travels around the North and South Islands, the opportunity to work presented itself on several occasions. While staying in the Kerikeri Youth Hostel, we discovered that the local farmers would regularly come into the hostel to seek employees for the day or longer. (This was in July, which is out-of-season.) My advice to any person looking for farm work would be to get up early as the farmers are often in the hostel by 8.30am.

A website maintained by the Budget Backpackers Hostels group includes job information (www.bbhnet.co.nz/billboard_home.asp). At the time of writing there were 19 vacancies for hostel jobs listed plus 14 other vacancies. The main BBH site (www.backpack.co.nz) links to its 350 member hostels.

Private agencies are also involved in the working holiday market. New Zealand Job Search (www.nzjs.co.nz) is located in Auckland Central Backpackers (Level 3, 229 Queen St; 09-357 3996; jobs@nzjs.co.nz) and operates as a job agency for backpackers. Registered members have access to vacancy information in the hospitality, construction and temp industries; a six-month registration costs $50, 12 months $75. NZJS also sells a starter pack which includes 12 months registration with Job Search, airport pick-up, four nights accommodation on arrival, etc. for $245.

Similarly Travellers Contact Point has an office in Auckland at 87 Queen St (09-300 7197; info@travellersnz.com). Their arrival package costs £60 in the UK from TCP, 2-6 Inverness Terrace, Bayswater, London W2 3HX (020-7243 7887; www.travellers.com.au) and includes a free job search facility in connection with recruitment agencies in New Zealand plus your first two nights in Auckland, airport pick-up, membership, a working holiday information kit, etc. A stand-alone TCP membership for £21 includes 12 months mail forwarding, e-mail and word processing access.

Try also Seasonal Work NZ (www.seasonalwork.co.nz) based in Rotorua, which provides splendidly full details on employers, and www.gumtree.co.nz with links to Jobs as well as Accommodation, etc.

Rural & Conservation Volunteering

World Wide Opportunities on Organic Farms or WWOOF NZ is popular and active, with 780 farms and smallholdings on its fix-it-yourself list that welcome volunteers in exchange for food and accommodation. The list can be obtained from Jane and Andrew Strange, PO Box 1172, Nelson (tel/fax 03-544 9890; www.wwoof.co.nz) for a fee of £16/US$30/NZ$40.

Another organisation matches working visitors with about 190 farmers throughout New Zealand. Farmstays can last from three days to several months. *Farm Helpers in New Zealand* (FHiNZ, 16 Aspen Way, Palmerston North; tel/fax 06-355 0448; www.fhinz.co.nz) charges NZ$25 for their membership booklet containing all the addresses. No experience is necessary and between four and six hours of work a day are requested. The co-ordinator advises that hosts in the Auckland area tend to be oversubscribed, so that it is best to head into the countryside.

A free internet-based exchange of work-for-keep volunteers can be found at www.helpx.net where about 250 hosts in New Zealand are listed.

The New Zealand Department of Conservation (DOC) carries out habitat and wildlife management projects throughout New Zealand and publishes a detailed Calendar of Volunteer Opportunities (see their website www.doc.govt.nz) which lists all sorts of interesting sounding projects from counting bats to cleaning up remote beaches. Most require a good level of fitness and a contribution to expenses, often quite small. The DOC also needs volunteer hut wardens at a variety of locations. Details are available from any office of the Department of Conservation (all addresses are listed on website).

Paul Bagshaw from Kent spent a thoroughly enjoyable week on an uninhabited island in Marlborough Sound monitoring kiwis, the flightless bird whose numbers have been seriously depleted. An ongoing programme removes them from the mainland to small islands where there are no predators:

> *The object of the exercise was to estimate the number of kiwis on Long Island north of Picton. As the kiwi is noctural, we had to work in the small hours. As it's dark, it's impossible to count them so we had to spread out and walk up a long slope listening for their high-pitched whistling call. During the day they hide in burrows and foliage so it is very rare to see one. One night, when we heard one rustling around our camp, my girlfriend went outside with a torch and actually managed to see it. She was so excited that she couldn't speak and resorted to wild gesticulations to describe its big feet and long beak.*
>
> *The island has no water source except rainwater which collects in tanks, all very basic. We lived in tents and prepared our own meals from supplies brought over from the mainland. Our one luxury was a portaloo.*

The New Zealand Trust for Conservation Volunteers was set up in 1999 to match both local and international volunteers with conservation projects of all kinds, to counteract the loss of native bush and wildlife. Whereas DOC projects take place only on DOC lands, NZTCV registers projects run by many local and national organisations as well as DOC projects. Details are available on their website www.conservationvolunteers.org.nz (tel/fax 09-415 9336; conservol@clear.net.nz).

Ski Resorts

The last couple of years have seen a sizeable number of New Zealand ski schools beginning to offer instructor training to people from the northern hemisphere. Skiers and riders from all over the world congregate in New Zealand during the northern summer (beginning of July to October). The four New Zealand ski schools listed in the 'Directory of Ski Training Courses' operate in different ski centres in the South Island: Craigieburn, Queensland, Methven and Wanaka. Many of New Zealand's ski fields are wonderfully uncrowded compared to Europe. Most courses lead to the NZSIA (New Zealand Ski Instructors Alliance) Stage 1 Exam, a qualification which is recognised around the world; every year graduates from New Zealand's ski schools go on to work in the USA, Canada, Switzerland, Andorra, Italy, Korea, Japan, etc. All the schools profess to be ideally suited to gap year students since they provide a safe and friendly English-speaking environment, while being on the other side of the world.

Canada

Canada is one of those countries your mum probably won't mind you visiting for part of your gap year (New Zealand is another). It has what mums like in abundance: low crime rate, prosperity, orderliness, polite and friendly natives and an excellent communication system. On the down side, it is expensive (especially compared to Nepal and Bolivia and the countries of which she doesn't approve) and bureaucratic (as you will soon discover when you look into obtaining a student Employment Authorization). It is also the country which inspired the writer Saki to say 'Canada is all right, really, but not for the whole weekend'. However most gap students who choose to work or travel in Canada end up disagreeing strenuously with Saki.

Special Schemes

The *British Universities North America Club* provides the easiest route to spending all or part of a gap year in Canada. BUNAC (16 Bowling Green Lane, London EC1R 0QH; 020-7251 3472) offers three programmes: for students, gap year students and non-students. Work Canada is for both full-time tertiary level students aged 18-30 (departures mostly in summer) and for non-students aged 18-35, and Gap Canada is for candidates with a confirmed place at university who depart between October and December. Altogether about 1500 students obtain Employment Authorizations through BUNAC, including finalists with proof that they will return to the UK. Early application is advised because of the quotas set by the Canadian government. The great majority of participants go to Canada without a pre-arranged job and spend their first week or two job-hunting.

The BUNAC programme fee is £156, and insurance from £152 for four months. Participants can choose to travel on a BUNAC group flight (costing approximately £470 return to Toronto, £570 to the west coast) or independently which would be cheaper. Places are allocated on a first come, first served basis so early application is advantageous (from December). Departure for Canada can be anytime between the beginning of February and the end of the calendar year. Note that Gap Canada application forms are not available until May and the visa cannot be issued until after A level results are known and university offers accepted in August.

BUNAC distributes to Work Canada participants a free guide called *The Vital Info Handbook* which includes contact details for companies that have employed foreign students in the past. The majority of jobs are in hotels and tourist attractions in the Rockies, a beautiful part of the world in which to spend a summer. British university students have an edge over their North American counterparts in this sphere of employment since they don't have to return to their studies until mid to late September rather than the beginning of September.

Changing Worlds arranges paid hotel jobs for students in the two main Canadian ski resorts of Banff and Whistler. The six-month jobs start in November or March and cost £1975 or £2075 including airfares. Hotel staff are paid on average $9 an hour and will have $12 a day deducted for room and board. British students between school and university can be placed in resort jobs in the Rockies both summer and winter. As with BUNAC, school leavers must have unconditional acceptance from a college or university. Note that when time is short, it is sometimes possible to obtain an Employment Authorization in person by queuing all day at the Canadian High Commission. *Overseas Working Holidays* offers a working holiday package for the summer. The programme fee of £349 includes access to scheduled job interviews in London in March for summer jobs lasting from May/June to October. Their partner tourist industry employers are located mainly in the Muskoka holiday region of Ontario, i.e. Deerhurst Resort, Clevelands House and Delawana Inn plus hotels in the Fairmont hotel group.

IST Plus operates an Internship Canada programme on which British, Irish, Swedish and Finnish students can work in Canada for up to one year. Participants must be enrolled in full-time further or higher education, including gap students with a confirmed place at college and those due to graduate. Interns must find their own work placements in their field of study, often with advice from their tutors.

Several schemes designed for gap year students who want to ski or train to be ski instructors in Canada are described below under the heading Skiing.

Red Tape

To work legally in Canada, you must obtain an Employment Authorization from a Canadian High Commission or Embassy before you leave your home country. The Canadian government offers in the neighbourhood of 13,000-15,000 temporary authorisations each year. The General Working Holiday Programme allows any UK national under 35 including non-students to apply for a 12-month Employment Authorization via BUNAC. Participants of programmes via BUNAC do not require a definite job offer but must show sufficient funds. It is also possible for students and those who have graduated within the past 12 months to apply for a temporary authorisation directly to the Canadian High Commission but in this case they must show proof of a job offer from a Canadian employer and be prepared to work only for that named employer for the duration of their visa.

Interested students should check the website www.canada.org.uk/visa-info or obtain the general leaflet 'Student Temporary Employment in Canada' by sending a large s.a.e. with a 50p stamp and marked 'SGWHP' in the top left-hand corner to the Canadian High Commission (Immigration Section, 38 Grosvenor St, London W1K 4AA); the visa Info number is 020-7258 6699. Processing of work authorisations normally takes ten working days and is free of charge.

All participants of approved student schemes benefit from orientations and back-up from the Canadian Federation of Students' SWAP (Student Work Abroad Program) offices in Toronto and Vancouver. They even organise occasional pub outings and excursions for participants, as well as advising on nitty-gritty issues like tax.

To illustrate the stringency of immigration regulations, even work-for-keep arrangements are difficult to find, as described by the Jericho Beach Youth Hostel in Vancouver (1515 Discovery St, Vancouver, BC V6R 4K5; 604-224-3208):

*Unfortunately, due to Canadian employment regulations, we are unable to have for-
eign nationals participate in our work exchange programme at the hostel (two hours
work in exchange for a free overnight). We do have an employment board at the
hostel where we post notices from local companies and individuals offering employment. In addition, the front desk staff are a valuable resource for finding employment
in the city.*

However students with a work authorisation should be able to stay long-term at a hostel in
exchange for some work. For example Global Village Backpackers in Toronto, Vancouver
and Banff have in the past willingly hired gap year students with permission to work; their
website has a section about working visas (www.globalbackpackers.com/work.html). One
useful exception is to stay for less than three months on a visitor visa on a work-for-keep
basis on an organic farm (see WWOOF below) or as a family helper.

THE JOB HUNT

Those students without a pre-arranged job might encounter some difficulty finding work
since the job hunt is tougher in Canada than most places. On average BUNACers take
at least six or seven days to find a job in Canada. Even Canadian students find it hard
to get summer jobs and there will be stiff competition for most kinds of seasonal work. It
will be necessary to look presentable, eager to please, positive and cheerful, even if the
responses are negative or the employers unhelpful.

Jobs for sales staff are advertised wherever you go in Canada. **Tanufa Kotecha** joined
BUNAC's Work Canada programme and quickly learned that Canadian selling techniques
are just as aggressive as American ones:

*I landed a job within a week in Toronto working in a French Canadian clothing
store. In my store as soon as a customer walked in, they had to be greeted by a
'sales associate' within 15 seconds! The North American way of selling is pushy and
upfront, but it does get results. One must have confidence to sell.*

Almost all shop jobs of this kind pay the minimum wage. Wages are fairly good in Canada
with statutory minimum wages, e.g. $7.45 per hour in Ontario (from February 2005) and
$5-$7 in most of the other provinces except British Columbia where it is $8. Most working
holiday makers (like most Canadian students) earn the minimum wage, with an average
weekly wage of $300 and average accommodation costs of $115-$170 per week.

Skiing

The past few years have seen a mini-explosion in companies offering programmes to
young skiers and snowboarders from the UK taking a year out partly to improve their form
or even train as instructors.

**Alice Mundy decided to include a snowboard instructor's course in her gap
year in 2005:**
*I went with a company called Nonstopski after researching (mainly on the internet)
a lot of companies that ran the same sort of courses. I chose Nonstopski mainly
because, even though it has grown massively over the last few years, it still had
that caring, family-run feel to it. Their course seemed a lot more flexible and laid-
back than most other companies and the fact that it included extra courses such
as Winter Camping, Mountain Photography and Avalanche Training made their
brochure stand out.*

*As Canada is an English speaking country, language wasn't a problem. Once
you realised that 'shropping the narr' was actually a positive term used by Cana-*

> *dians for riding powder and not some horrific torture method as it sounds, things were fine! Without a doubt, the highlight of my gap year was passing my Canadian Association of Snowboard Instructors (CASI) Level 2 exam on the same day as my 19th birthday in Fernie British Columbia, on a perfect April's day. I remember not being able to talk properly from smiling and feeling like the world was at my feet (or should I say snowboard boots?) Overall, my experiences of the past year have given me both a new enthusiasm towards education and learning…as well as the bug for exploring all countries and cultures of the globe, for which I now have a qualification that will help on my adventures in the future!*

Nonstop Ski & Snowboard run programmes in Fernie and Red Mountain, BC plus Banff in Alberta. Experienced snowboarders who want to qualify as an instructor in Canada should check entries in the 'Directory of Ski Training Courses' for example with *International Academy* at Whistler and Lake Louise in the Rockies or Mont Tremblant in Quebec.

Ski Le Gap (see 'Directory of Sports Courses') in Québec runs one- and three-month programmes during the ski season in the resort of Mont Tremblant. The course combines ski/snowboard instruction with French conversation lessons plus other activities such as igloo-building, dogsledding and extreme snowshoeing. The programme is geared to British students and prices are in sterling: £6525 (2006) which includes London-Montréal airfares.

Also see the directory for the new ski/snowboard instructor and adventure training programmes in Mont Tremblant offered by *Gap Snowsports* (www.gapski.com) lasting six or ten weeks, as well as *Pro-Ride Snowboard Camps* at Whistler. Similarly *Ski-Exp-Air* offers an intensive training programme aimed at British skiers at a resort near Québec City, Mont Ste. Anne. *Peak Leaders'* gap year programmes in Canada takes place in Banff and Whistler. Their website (www.peakleaders.com) gives full details of the 11-week programmes of ski/snowboard instructor/leader training (see 'Directory of Ski Training Courses'). The all-in price is £5850.

Evan Bailey aged 18 travelled to Lake Louise in the Canadian Rockies with *Peak Leaders* for the 2004 season:

> *I decided to train as a snowboard Instructor when I first went to the snow in Victoria, Australia in 1998. I had an amazing time riding with my friends and, although the conditions were average, I knew snowboarding was for me. Since then I've been hooked and having a chance to work doing something you love is fantastic. I didn't see it as a job at all, just a great lifestyle and a ticket to travel.*
>
> *Riding with mates while improving my skills with awesome instructors and riders provided amazing training. Canada was magic, and everyday seemed better than the last. Memories that will last forever. Personally I learnt to set achievable goals to work towards - not only Instructor qualifications but physically being fitter and more flexible. These 9 weeks were my most memorable ever, not only through riding perfect champagne powder or improving 100%, but riding with mates you keep for life sharing the same passion as you.*

Another company providing 11-week instructor courses is PowderTrip Ltd (Mayfair House, 14-18 Heddon St, London W1B 4DA; 08454 900 480; www.powder-trip.com) held at the Kicking Horse Mountain Resort in the Rockies. The cost is £4999.

A more flexible arrangement can be made through companies like *Mountain Life* (see entry in the Directory) or Alpine Elements (Lyon House, 160-166 Borough High St, London SE1 1JR; 08700 111360; info@alpineelements.co.uk). The latter specialises in renting out affordable accommodation to young skiers and snowboarders for the whole season, some of whom take lessons, others work and others just ski. Through this company you can book a bed in a multi-bedded chalet in Whistler starting at £100 a week if you stay for the whole season. Whole season chalet accommodation costs from £2500.

To offset this expense, it is possible to pick up work in Whistler/Blackcomb and the other main resorts like Banff/Lake Louise, provided you have a work permit from BUNAC. Ski resorts throughout Canada create a great number of seasonal employment vacancies which can't be filled by Canadian students since they're all studying. The contact address for the Whistler/Blackcomb Resort is 4545 Blackcomb Way, Whistler, B.C. V0N 1B4 (604-938-7366). Intrawest is the company that runs the ski operations at Whistler (as well as many other North American ski resorts). The website www.whistlerblackcomb.com/employment also gives dates of the annual recruiting fair and allows you to apply online; alternatively you can ring the jobline on 604-938-7367.

James Gillespie spent the winter and summer of his gap year working in Whistler. After taking the beautiful train ride from Vancouver, it soon became clear that getting a place to stay would be a major problem. But soon he had a job as a ticket validator which came with a free ski pass and subsidised accommodation:

It was an excellent job and, although sometimes mundane, it was often livened up by violent and abusive skiers trying to get on the lift for free. Going there was the best thing I've ever done and I hope to be living there permanently eventually. I came home with a diary full of experiences, a face full of smiles, a bag full of dirty washing and pockets full of… well nothing actually. I was in debt, but it was worth it.

VOLUNTARY WORK

Some interesting practical community projects are organised by Frontiers Foundation (419 Coxwell Ave, Toronto M4L 3B9; 416-690-3930; www.frontiersfoundation.ca) in low-income communities in Canada, including native communities in isolated northern areas. Some of the Operation Beaver projects consist of helping aboriginal people to build low-cost well-heated houses or community centres. Others take place on wilderness camps for Native children. More recently volunteers have been working in schools in the three northern territories (Yukon, Northwest Territory and Nunavut) tutoring in maths, science, English, music and drama. The accepted volunteer must commit to stay for at least five months from September or January and then only needs to obtain a medical certificate of fitness, fund a return flight to Toronto and get the appropriate volunteer visa. The Frontiers Foundation will pay all food, accommodation, travel and insurance expenses within Canada plus a modest allowance of $50 a week.

The work itself does not occupy all of your time and energies. According to **Sarah King**, there was time left over to participate in some quintessentially Canadian backwoods activities:

One of the great benefits about being a guest worker was that our activities became a focal point for the community. We played volleyball, helped break in wild horses, watched bears, made wild berry pies and rose-hip jelly, went camping, hunting, fishing and swimming, baked porcupine packed in clay, ate a delicacy of sweet and sour beaver tail, and all took up jogging around a local basketball park.

If you are interested in working your way from farm to farm and want to meet Canadians, you might consider volunteering for WWOOF-Canada (World Wide Opportunities on Organic Farms). You can find the WWOOF Canada application form on the website www.wwoof.ca; membership costs C$35 (cash) plus $5 postage which should be sent to John Vanden Heuvel, 4429 Carlson Road, Nelson, B.C. V1L 6X3; wwoofcan@shaw.ca. You will then be sent a booklet that lists more than 500 farms across Canada including descriptions of the farms. All volunteers must have valid tourist visas. Obbe Verwer used his farm visits as a springboard to further travels in western Canada:

After enjoying my visits to a couple of farms listed by WWOOF, I went on by myself to Vancouver Island. I set off to hike through the rainforest along the Clayoquot Valley

Witness Trail. When I came to the trailhead, I met the trail boss who was working with a group of volunteers to build boardwalks at both ends of the trails. This was to enable more people to walk part of the trail which is important because this valley has to be saved from clearcut logging. I decided to join them. Actually you are supposed to go through the organising committee to become a volunteer worker but I just pitched my tent and joined on the spot. All the wood to build the boardwalk had to be carried into the trail, steps, stringers, nails and tools. We worked till 4pm, but it was not strict at all. Sometimes it was pretty hard, but it was fun. The forest impressed me more and more. The big trees, the berries, the mushrooms and the silence in the mist. It was just amazing. It was very satisfying to be helping to save this forest.

The *Western Canada Wilderness Committee* can be visited at 341 Water St, Vancouver, BC V6B 2K7; 604-683-8220; www.wildernesscommittee.org). Volunteers should bear in mind that while building trails in the rainforests of the Pacific coast one is bound to get wet. The WCWC also needs people to work in roadside kiosks, selling T-shirts, etc. for fund-raising.

COURSES

Although culturally hard to distinguish from the USA in some respects, Canada's French language and culture guarantee its distinctiveness. Few gap year students think of Canada when considering places to improve their French, but the French-speaking province of Québec has lots of language schools (mostly for English-speaking North Americans). For example the Point3 Language Centre in Montréal (404 rue St-Pierre, Bureau 201, Montréal, Québec H2Y 2M2; www.point-3.com) and College Platon (4521 Park Ave, Montréal, Québec H2V 4E4; 514-281-1016; www.platocollege.com) offer short intensive courses with homestays at reasonable prices, e.g. 22 hours of tuition a week for four weeks costs C$925. The Surrey-based language agency Vis-à-Vis can place students of French in Canada as well as in France and Belgium. Bear in mind that the Québecois accent is very different from Parisian French and incorporates many more loan words from English.

The *English-Speaking Union* offers scholarships to young people to spend six or 12 months in a private Canadian high school during their gap year. The scholarship covers free board and tuition; all other expenses must be met by the exchange participant. (See entry in 'Directory of Specialist Gap Year Programmes'.)

TRAVEL

For accommodation in North America (mainly Canada), get hold of the list of hostels from Backpackers Hostels Canada (Longhouse Village, RR 13, Thunder Bay, Ontario P7B 5E4; www.backpackers.ca). The list can be downloaded for free or sent by post in exchange for $5 or four IRCs.

The network of 60 student travel offices on or near Canadian university or college campuses is Travel CUTS (www.travelcuts.com). They also administer an outgoing work abroad programme for Canadian students, known as SWAP (www.swap.ca).

The system of Allo-Stop (ride-sharing) is well developed in the province of Quebec but has been ruled illegal in Ontario after complaints were received from coach operators; check www.allostop.com for up-to-date information.

Israel

Israel is not a happy country. The conflict between the Israelis and Palestinians often seems beyond resolution. Predictably, as the Peace Process has unravelled, Israel has lost much of its appeal for student travellers, and the number of young people choosing to head for what has been a favourite travellers' destination is drastically down. At present few if any opportunities exist in the Palestinian-governed Territories and many projects such as archaeological digs have been curtailed or cancelled because of the current situation in Israel.

But behind all the shocking violence and retaliation in the headlines, thousands of individuals and groups do not consider the situation hopeless and are working patiently towards peace and reconciliation. Spending time in Israel will enable people from outside the region to gain more insight into one of the world's most bedevilling trouble spots. Personal security is bound to be a consideration but the statistics should be reassuring, that tourists and volunteers are rarely if ever the targets of violence. If entering the country under the auspices of for example a kibbutz placement organisation, you should seek up-to-the-minute advice about where it is considered safe to go, and of course always consult the Foreign & Commonwealth Office advice (www.fco.gov.uk/travel).

Most students associate working in Israel with staying on a kibbutz or a moshav. Although there are other working opportunities, these are by far the most common ways of having a prolonged visit in Israel, and one of which many thousands of gap year students of all nationalities have taken advantage over the past decades. The popularity of kibbutz stays is no doubt partly due to the low cost of fixing up a placement and the reasonable cost of getting to Israel, typically £300-£400 altogether. Even if most of the work assigned to volunteers is not very stimulating, most participants agree that Israel is a good country in which to meet young people of different nationalities and to see something of the Middle East.

For work outside kibbutzim, the situation has become much more difficult because of visa changes implemented quite recently by the Israeli government. The Immigration Authority now prohibits all foreigners working without a work permit and tourists are not permitted to stay more than three months. To illustrate the serious impact this has had, the owner of a long-established au pair agency in Rishon-le-Zion south of Tel Aviv reported in November 2004 that she had been forced to close her agency (Hilma's Intermediary) due to the ferocity of the clampdown on all foreigners working in the country:

Due to government regulations and severe actions against foreigners working here, there is NO WAY for any agency or individual to work in Israel as an au pair, mother's helper, etc. Basically it comes down to the fact that no one should even try to work on a tourist visa, because many people are just sent back at the airport. If they do receive a tourist visa, they may be able to stay for only two weeks or at most three months. No family wants a mother's helper for that short a period. Besides this, there is now a special police force that goes after anyone working that does not have a working permit and many people are being stopped in the streets or sometimes picked up from their homes (when a neighbour gives information!). Israel is at the moment a no-go country for those who want to work as nannies, au pairs, housekeepers or in a moshav. It is sad to see a foreigner getting into trouble and many Israelis are against this situation. But for the time being at least, I advise no one to come.

Some gap year students, especially those from Jewish backgrounds, decide to spend a year in Israel learning Hebrew. A number of kibbutzim operate ulpan courses in conjunction with the Jewish Agency for Israel; the ulpan programme is designed for young people who want to gain a working knowledge of Hebrew and an understanding of the Jewish way of life and history with a view to settling in Israel. Finally, paid casual work is readily available in resorts and other tourist-related businesses, though wages are almost universally low.

Specialised Gap Year Programmes

The *Friends of Israel Educational Foundation* (PO Box 7545, London NW2 2QZ; fax 020-7794 0291; info@foi-asg.org) has long run a gap year programme called the Bridge Programme for 12 candidates a year who are sent to Israel on a structured programme which includes a kibbutz stay, community service, English teaching and other projects for six months from January. After being chosen at interview in July, participants' expenses are covered, apart from spending money; £600 is recommended (see entry in 'Directory of Specialist Gap Year Placements').

Elizabeth Petchey appreciated the Bridge Programme as a way of getting to know individuals from many backgrounds and being given the chance to confront the complexities of the Middle East situation:
For me membership of the Bridge group was a license to become Israeli for six months. I have spent the year since my return trying to make sense of those experiences in relation to the debates and opinions that have flooded the political scene. My reflections on Israel are profoundly influenced by encounters with the people I met, like Mohammed, a Christian in Jerusalem (no mistake there), Orthodox Jews in Galilee, secular Jews in Kibbutz Yahel, a Palestinian who felt trapped in Bethlehem, an Egyptian hotel owner who wanted to know details of my Israeli connections, youths telling me of their eagerness or reluctance to serve in the army, a young Russian Christian Israeli, Arab children in Peki'in, Jews motivated by Zionism and Holocaust survivors. My understanding and appreciation of the country came to be based on contact with these individuals and they served to mould any political opinions I have developed.

On her return to Europe, she felt impatient with some of the anti-Israeli positions she heard expressed so strongly:

I found myself on the defensive because so much of the hostility seemed irra-tionally to attack individuals I felt I actually knew. Perhaps in my naivety I could not connect Israeli soldiers on demonstrators' placards with the eighteen year olds whom I had taught English, or the Palestinian children on television to the Arab children with whom I had put on a fashion show. Later I returned to Israel to work on a summer camp for Arab and Israeli children. I could not help but feel nervous as I travelled on a bus around Tel Aviv the day after a suicide bomb attack. Yet most of all I was overwhelmed by the sheer number of people who came up to me, the majority of whom I did not know, and expressed their gratitude for my returning to help work with the children. Some said they felt they had been cut off from the world and felt I was reaching out to them.

The Association of Jewish Sixth Formers (AJ6, Hillel House, 1/2 Endsleigh St, London WC1H 0DS; 020-8846 2277; office@aj6.org/ www.aj6.org) runs a year-out scheme in Israel for school leavers combining study and volunteer work. Participants on the Machon (Leadership) Year Out must be supported by their sponsoring youth movement. AJ6 also has more flexible volunteering schemes like the Israel Experience on which Jewish young people arrange voluntary work that suits them for 3-12 months.

KIBBUTZIM and MOSHAVIM

Everyone has some idea of what a kibbutz is: it is a communal society in which all the means of production are owned and shared by the community as a whole. For more than two generations, this idea has appealed to young people from around the world who have flocked to the 250 kibbutzim of Israel to volunteer their services and participate in this utopian community based on equality.

But recent headlines such as 'Kibbutz Kiss of Death' and 'Israel to Privatise Kibbutzim' have alerted the outside world to something that Israelis have known for some time, that the kibbutz movement is in decline or at least changing almost out of recognition. As further evidence of the decline, only one-fifth of the number of foreign volunteers who came in the 1970s arrive in Israel now, i.e. 10,000 instead of 50,000. It is symptomatic that after 33 years of placing volunteers on kibbutzim, the London and Tel Aviv-based company Project 67 has ceased trading.

Having said that, foreign volunteers are still welcome to join some kibbutzim for two to six months and many continue to enjoy the experience. In return for their labour, volunteers receive free room and board and about £50 a month in pocket money. Many kibbutzim make considerable efforts to welcome volunteers, for example by providing organised sightseeing tours every so often. The majority of kibbutzim still accept volunteers and some recruit online e.g. Kibbutz Ketura (www.ketura.org.il). The unofficial site www.kibbutzvolunteer.com has links to about 25 kibbutzim with their own websites.

If the kibbutz is broadly based on a socialist model, the moshav is on a capitalist model, with members owning their own machinery and houses, though the produce is marketed co-operatively. The kind of experience the volunteer has on a moshav is very different and usually more demanding. Although the term 'volunteer' is used of moshavim, a wage is paid (normally the shekel equivalent of $350-$500/£250-£350 a month) which allows a frugal person to save enough to fund further travels (often in Egypt) especially if an end-of-season bonus is paid.

Kibbutz and moshav placements can be fixed up either inside or outside Israel. There is no doubt that registering in advance will give you peace of mind. In Britain the main kibbutz placement organisation is Kibbutz Representatives at 16 Accommodation Road, London NW11 8EP (020-8458 9235/ fax 020-8455 7930; enquiries@kibbutz.org.uk/ www.kibbutz.org.il). To register with them you must be between the ages of 18 and 40 (sometimes 50), be able to stay for a minimum of eight weeks, attend an informal interview in London, and provide a signed medical declaration of fitness. Processing takes two or three weeks. The kibbutz package (which costs about £410) guarantees placement and the B4 visa, and includes flights and transport to the kibbutz. Insurance is compulsory. You can either arrange your travel independently and present yourself at the kibbutz office in Tel Aviv, or you can book flights through KR, as an individual or as part of a group. Group participants are met at the airport.

A number of offices in Tel Aviv are able to place volunteers who simply show up, particularly between October and May. The official Kibbutz Program Center has an active Volunteer Department (18 Frishman St, Cnr. 90 Ben Yehuda St, Tel Aviv 61030; 03-527 8874/ fax 03-523 9966; kpc@volunteer.co.il; www.kibbutz.org.il/eng/welcome.htm). The office is situated in apartment 6 on the third floor, and the opening hours are Sunday to Thursday 8am-2pm. Bear in mind that if you arrive during religious holidays such as the week of Passover in the spring, working hours may be reduced or offices closed. The buses needed to reach the office are: number 222 from the airport, 10 from the railway station and 4 from the Central Bus Station. To register you will need your passport, medical certificate, insurance policy (which must show that your insurer has an Israeli representative), an airline ticket out of Israel, two passport photos and registration fee of $60. They may also want to see proof of funds ($250). Comprehensive insurance cover is compulsory, so if your policy is not sufficient, you can buy a suitable kibbutz policy at the KPC for $120 which provides cover for up to 12 months. A returnable deposit is payable to guarantee that you stay for the minimum period of eight weeks.

Kibbutzim are not the version of holiday camps they once were. The average working week has increased from 36 to 48 hours in recent years, though hours may be reduced in the hot summer and extended at busy times. Most of the necessities of life are provided by the kibbutz including stationery, tea, coffee, basic toiletries and cigarettes, though perks differ and have been generally shrinking as pocket money has risen. New volunteers are often assigned the undesirable jobs though most volunteer organisers are willing to transfer a dissatisfied volunteer to a different job. **Catherine Revell** claims that if you are assertive and show willingness to work hard, you can find yourself doing more interesting work; among the jobs she did on three different kibbutzim were kitchen manager, shepherdess and a sculptor's assistant.

Meeting people is the central theme of kibbutz volunteer life according to many volunteers including **Bela Lal** who decided to take a gap year to work and travel after university and before trying to break into publishing:

The wonderful benefits of being a volunteer on a kibbutz remain with you: the knowledge that such a shared/communal lifestyle can work, the feeling of complete relaxation and inner harmony and some excellent friends with whom I will definitely stay in touch. I would recommend the kibbutz experience to anyone who is open-minded, not too proud to undertake often fairly menial work, operating on a budget and most importantly wants to live in a community of people about their own age and experience something entirely unique.

Life is very different on a moshav where workers regularly get up at 5am and put in 75 hour weeks for £250-£350 a month. Often the social life is less appealing than on a kibbutz though this varies. The high season for most moshavim is November to April, so spring is when you are most likely to receive a bonus of up to two months' wages. Information about specific kibbutzim is provided in the book *Kibbutz Volunteer* published by Vacation-Work Publications (£10.99).

OTHER OPPORTUNITIES FOR GAP TRAVELLERS

Most gap year students will start their time in Israel with a spell on a kibbutz or a moshav which is an excellent way to meet other travellers and make friends. Once their stay is over, many move on to less formal arrangements.

Tourism

The current situation in Israel and the Middle East generally has crippled the tourist industry, so much of the kind of casual work that used to be so plentiful will have to wait until more peaceful times return. When that happens the most likely places for finding work in tourism are Eilat, Tel Aviv, Herzliya (a wealthy resort north of Tel Aviv) and, to a lesser extent, Haifa and Jerusalem. There is a plethora of cheap hostels around Israel, almost all of which employ two or three travellers to spend a few hours a day cleaning or manning the desk in exchange for a free bed and some meals. If you prove yourself a hard worker, you may be moved to a better job or even paid some pocket money.

The Youth Hostel Association of Israel (1 Shezer St, PO Box 6001, Jerusalem 91060; 02-655 8400; www.youth-hostels.org.il) can provide a list of their 32 member hostels around the country which may be in a position to offer free accommodation, meals and pocket money in exchange for six hours of work a day. The hostels along Hayarkon Street in Tel Aviv were once valuable sources of job information or jobs themselves, though the employment situation is much tighter now and in fact many of the hostels have closed such as the Gordon Hostel and No. 1 Hostel which used to maintain Work Lists. At last report this system was still being used at Momo's Hostel at 28 Ben Yehuda St (03-528

7471; www.angelfire.com/il/momos). Another Tel Aviv hostel worth trying is the Mugraby Hostel at 30 Allenby St (03-510 2443; www.mugraby-hostel.com) which is reputed to have among the cheapest dorm beds in Tel Aviv (NIS35/$8) as well as some doubles and an internet café. The Kibbutz Program Center recommends several hostels on its website including The Hayarkon 48 Hostel at 48 Hayarkon St (03-516 8989; info@hayarkon48.com) and Dizengoff Square Hostel at 13 Ben Ami St, Dizengoff Square (03-522 5184; www.dizengoffhostel.com).

Eilat is an important yachting and diving centre. Vacancies are sometimes posted on the gates to the Marina or on the Marina notice board, but work as crew or kitchen staff, cleaners or au pairs is usually found by asking boat to boat. **Sarah Jane Smith** had the best time of her life in Eilat after she landed a job as a deckhand and hostess on a private charter yacht for scuba divers:

I was taken on cruises lasting between a week and a month to the Red Sea, Gulf of Suez, etc. to some of the best diving spots in the world. I was taught how to scuba dive and also did lots of snorkelling. I saw some of the most amazing sights of my life – the sun rising over Saudi Arabia as the moon sank into Egypt, coral reefs, sharks, dolphins, and so on.

The social life on the marina was better than the kibbutz with hundreds of other travellers working on boats or in Eilat. Every night was a party and I hardly know how I survived it. The only bad thing is the low wages (if you get paid at all) and the hard work. But the harder you work and longer you stay, the better the wages and perks become.

VOLUNTARY WORK

Connect Youth International at the British Council (10 Spring Gardens, London SW1A 2BN; 020-7389 4030/ www.britishcouncil.org/connectyouth-programmes-european-voluntary-service.htm) has in the past run a programme for British volunteers aged 18-25 in northern Israel, working with groups of young people aged 9-15 at summer language clubs. However due to 'instability in the Middle East and other current circumstances', this programme is not available at present.

The Jewish/Arab village of Neve Shalom/Wahat al-Salaam (which means Oasis of Peace in Hebrew and Arabic) between Tel Aviv and Jerusalem accepts a few volunteers to work in the guest house, school or gardens attached to the community's School for Peace. The minimum stay is six months. In addition to board and lodging, volunteers receive $50-$70 a month pocket money. Details are available from the Volunteer Co-ordinator, 99761 Doar Na Shimshon (02-991 2222; www.nswas.com).

Several organisations can use voluntary assistance for Palestinian projects. The *Universities' Trust for Educational Exchange with Palestinians* or UNIPAL (BCM UNIPAL, London EC1N 3XX; www.unipal.org.uk) sends volunteers over the age of 20 to work on short-term summer projects with Palestinian teenagers living in refugee camps. In theory these projects take place in the West Bank, Gaza and Lebanon; however because of concerns about security, volunteers over the past few summers have gone only to Lebanon, mainly in and around Sidon. Most projects involve teaching English or activities with children. Applications should be in by the end of February in time for interviews in late March. Candidates must raise about £400 to contribute to expenses including airfares.

Friends of Birzeit University has assisted the Palestinian Birzeit University near Ramallah in the Occupied West Bank to recruit international volunteers for summer work camps since the 1970s. In previous years volunteers, working alongside Palestinian students, built the area's first park and planted trees in the refugee camps. Further details and an application form are available from Friends of Birzeit University, 1 Gough Square, London EC4A 3DE (020-7373 1340; admin@fobzu.org; www.fobzu.org).

In Nablus, the Zajel Youth Exchange Programme was established in 2001 to encourage interested young people from the west to spend time in Nablus and participate in short, medium or longer-term volunteer projects. Accommodation is provided free in university flats belonging to An-Najah National University. Further information is available from Zajel Programs Office in the university's Public Relations Department (9-238 1113/7; youthexchange@najah.edu/ www.najah.edu).

Christian organisations are active in Israel. To find out about voluntary opportunities. The Christian Information Centre in Jerusalem (PO Box 14308, 91142 Jerusalem; 02-627 2692; cicinfo@cicts.org) keeps a list of schools and institutes, mainly for people with disabilities, that take on volunteers; from their website www.cicts.org follow the links to Social Service. Try for example the Sisters of Charity in Ain Karem; contact Sister Susan Sheehan, PO Box 9209, Jerusalem 91190 (02-641 3280).

Archaeology

Volunteers are needed to do the mundane work of digging and sifting on a range of archaeological digs. In the majority of cases, volunteers must pay a daily fee of $35-$40 to cover food and accommodation and sometimes considerably more, plus a registration fee (typically $50-$75). Most camps take place during university holidays between May and September when temperatures soar. Volunteers must be in good physical condition and able to work long hours in hot weather. Valid health insurance is required.

Archaeology Abroad's bulletins contain a sprinkling of digs in Israel. Information on volunteering at archaeological digs in Israel is available on the website of the Israel Ministry of Foreign Affairs: www.israel-mfa.gov.il/MFA/History/Early+History+-+Archaeology. An example of an ongoing dig that accepts volunteers is the excavation of the ancient port of Yavneh Yam run by the Department of Classical Studies at Tel Aviv University (69978 Ramat-Aviv; fax 03-640 9457; yavneyam@post.tau.ac.il) where the charge is a hefty $700 for two weeks. A dig at ancient Tiberias has an ongoing need for paying volunteers for spring and autumn sessions (details on http://archaeology.huji.ac.il/tiberias).

Jennifer McKibben, who worked on a kibbutz, in an Eilat hotel and on a dig in the Negev desert, waxed most enthusiastic about the latter experience:

> *Actually the work was often enjoyable but not usually before the sun had risen (it gets incredibly cold at nights in the desert). It did seem madness at times when a Land Rover would take a team of us out to an unremarkable spot in the desert marked only by a wooden peg, and we were told to start digging. I think the romance of excavations quickly fades once the blisters begin to appear and that long term camps are suitable only for the initiated or fanatic.*
>
> *However despite the difficulties I really enjoyed the camp. Group relations were good – there were people of all nationalities – and there was normally a camp fire going with a couple of musicians. It was wonderful just to spend time in such a beautiful desert, to go off wandering over footprintless dunes, over great red hills to look and see no sign of civilisation. More practically, it was a cheap way to eat well for a couple of weeks, see another area and extend one's all-too-short stay in Israel.*

COURSES

Many of the archaeological projects mentioned above plus others listed by *Archaeology Abroad* include lectures and seminars on the history of the period of the site being excavated and on archaeological techniques. These provide an excellent practical introduction to the field for anyone planning to study ancient history, archaeology or anthropology at university. It would also be a useful addition to the CV of those hoping to get into museum work after graduation.

The Israeli Ministry of Foreign Affairs is offering scholarships to students and researchers from many countries. For information about these scholarships, check the website www.mfa.gov.il/mfa/mfaarchive/2000_2009/2003/8/scholarships+offered+by+the+isra eli+government+to.htm or contact the Scholarship section at the MFA in Jerusalem at scholarship@mfa.gov.il.

As mentioned earlier, ulpan courses are offered alongside kibbutz stays. These normally last 5½ months and include instruction in conversational Hebrew, lectures on Israel and Judaism, seminars on contemporary events and educational tours. Ulpan students usually live in a part of the kibbutz set aside for them, sometimes in a complex with classrooms and study areas. The programme is designed for Jewish students, and is open both to temporary visitors to Israel and prospective settlers. Non-Jewish students can enrol in the three-month Working Hebrew Scheme which is aimed at total beginners in the language. Places are limited and acceptance competitive. Enquiries should be addressed to Kibbutz Representatives (address above).

Many dive schools are centred on Eilat offering a range of scuba courses in the Red Sea including the basic qualification, the five-day PADI Open Water Diving course which starts from about £200 including equipment hire. The largest dive centre in Israel is the Red Sea Sports Club (Ambassador Hotel, Coral Beach, Eilat 88000; 08-637 6569; www. redseasports.co.il). One independent tour operator offering diving instruction in the Red Sea is Regal Dive (58 Lancaster Way, Ely, Cambs. CB6 3NW; 0870 220 1777; info@regal-diving.co.uk).

Latin America

Two or three decades ago, when everybody was flocking east, few adventurous young travellers from Britain considered South or Central America. Possibly because Britain has few colonial ties with that part of the world, it was less well known than India or Southeast Asia or Africa. With the recent decline in airfares to the Americas, the situation has changed and thousands of gap year students now head to that great Spanish-speaking continent (including Portuguese-speaking Brazil). They travel independently, go on adventure tours, join a grassroots voluntary organisation or sign up with one of the specialist gap year programmes which combine volunteering in community service or scientific research, language study and active travel.

PLACEMENT AGENCIES

The project and expedition organisation *Quest Overseas* (The North West Stables, Borde Hill Estate, Balcombe Road, Haywards Heath, West Sussex RH16 1XP; 01444 474744; www.questoverseas.com) operates a 13-week package from January to April split into three phases: an intensive Spanish language course in Quito or Sucre or Portuguese course in Brazil followed by a month-long attachment to a voluntary project (either working with deprived urban children in Peru, conserving Ecuador's rainforest or working in animal rehabilitation in Bolivia) and finally the longest stint is an expedition in the Andes. Their website gives a good flavour of their trips as does their photo-filled brochure. The current cost excluding flights and insurance is £1560-£4880.

Gap year specialist *Venture Co* (The Ironyard, 64-66 The Market Place, Warwick CV34 4SD (01926 411122; www.ventureco-worldwide.com) combines language course, local aid projects and expeditions on 3 programmes lasting 4 months in Latin America. *Inca Venture:* Ecuador, Peru, Chile and Bolivia; *Patagonia Venture:* Peru, Bolivia, Chile, Argentina and Tierra del Fuego; and *Maya Venture:* Mexico, Guatemala, Belize, Honduras, Nicaragua, Costa Rica and Cuba. Programmes start with 3-week intensive Spanish course given in Quito (Ecuador), Cusco (Peru) and Oaxaca (Mexico). Participants then spend 4 weeks on a local aid project before embarking on an 8 or 9 week expedition through the Andes.

Madventurer, The Old Casino, 1-4 Forth Lane, Newcastle-upon-Tyne NE1 5HX (0845 121 1996; www.madventurer.com) arranges expeditions from 2 to 15 weeks to Peru, Bolivia, Chile, Argentina, Uruguay and Brazil (as well as Africa and the South Pacific) combining voluntary work and adventure travel. The summer fee for 8 weeks is from £2460.

Outreach International has been sending volunteers overseas since 1997 (Bartletts Farm, Hayes Road, Compton Dundon, Somerset TA11 6PF; tel/fax: 01458 274957; www. outreachinternational.co.uk) and offers gap year programmes in Ecuador (including the Galapagos) and Mexico. All the projects encourage volunteers to learn the local language and offer good language training. The placements include helping in orphanages, running a Feed the Children programme, organising sea turtle and whale conservation, arts and crafts project with the Huicholi Indians and English teaching in coastal primary schools. There are also projects working with dolphins and volunteering at the premier dance school in Mexico. In Ecuador compassionate volunteers are needed to help run a project for street children and to work at an orphanage. Opportunities are also available to work in the Amazon rainforest. Volunteers live together in an Outreach International house but work in pairs on their project.

A recent addition to the companies sending gap year students to the Spanish-speaking Americas is *Echo Communities* (56 Ridgeway Road, Bristol BS16 3EA; 07971 853927; www.echocommunities.org.uk/gap-year-projects-mexico/gap-year-projects.html)　who send out young volunteers to Mexico on three-month placements in community projects in Oaxaca; the fee is £2700.

The main gap year organisations have links with the following countries: *GAP Activity Projects* send volunteers to Argentina, Brazil, Chile, Ecuador, Mexico, Paraguay and the Falkland Islands; *Project Trust* offer possibilities in Brazil, Bolivia, Chile, Peru, Guyana, Honduras and the Dominican Republic; *i-to-i* arranges supported placements in teaching, building, conservation, community work and media in Bolivia, Brazil, Costa Rica, the Dominican Republic, Ecuador, Guatemala, Honduras, Mexico, Peru and Venezuela; full training is included. Projects start at £695 (excluding flights) for two weeks. *Teaching & Projects Abroad* send volunteers including English teachers to Bolivia, Chile, Peru and Mexico. *The Leap Overseas Ltd* has 6, 10 or 12-week conservation and community placements in the field of eco-tourism in Argentina (including riding and polo), Guyana, Ecuador and Costa Rica. See entries in the 'Directory of Specialist Gap Year Programmes' for dates, fees, etc. See section below on Expeditions for information on *Raleigh International* and other expedition organisers.

Frances Pountain wanted to make a quick getaway after A-levels:

I left for Costa Rica a week after finishing my A-levels, which meant that none of my friends had gone away and I had none of their experience to back me up, so it felt like a true adventure. I chose to do a two-month teaching placement (with i-to-i) because one of my main objectives was to improve on the language and get to know people and the culture (living in a family really helped achieve this) before going on to do languages at university. Interestingly, among our group of volunteers, the 'teachers' had all studied Spanish to at least GCSE whereas the 'conservation' people mainly hadn't. As it was a voluntary placement it wasn't very pressurising. I was living with the teacher whom I helped and her family so we became quite close. Going to live in Costa Rica helped my Spanish no end.

Placements generally fall into one of three categories: community service, teaching or conservation; the former tend to be in cities while the latter take place in remote areas. *Trekforce Expeditions* offer an ambitious five-month programme in Central America (Belize and Guatemala), which combines conservation work with teaching in rural communities, as well as a language course (current fee £3900; shorter programmes also available). The full experience appealed to **Damien Rickwood** before he went on to study French and Spanish at Sheffield University:

> *I chose to do a Trekforce placement because it offered a combination of activities. I spent two months on a project building a ranger station in the jungle, one month learning Spanish in Guatemala and two months teaching in a community school. I wanted to spend a significant amount of time away in order to get a real feel for the culture of the country and 5 months seemed just right. To raise the money I had a full-time job but I also held a barbeque, a raffle and received sponsorship from my school. I raised £1500 through fundraising. I found the fundraising really difficult but if I did it again I would definitely try to fundraise more of the money.*
>
> *From doing my gap year with Trekforce I learnt that an organised expedition is possibly the best way to see it all and you get opportunities that individual travellers miss out on. I also learnt so much about the cultures of Belize and Guatemala without really realising it, instead I lived it! The best moment of my project was the ceremony to open the ranger station we had built because it gave us such a massive sense of achievement. It was opened by the directors of a local conservation charity and they had big plans to continue developing the site for research and eco-tourism, etc. It was brilliant to know that what we had slaved on for 2 months was just the beginning of bigger things. Other high points were reaching the destination of our 5-day trek through the Cockscomb Basin Jaguar Reserve and simple things such as gazing up at the stars on a full belly of Spam and noodles and making some brilliant friends.*
>
> *The teaching phase was really challenging, mainly because of the cultural differences. My teaching partner and I were placed in a remote Maya village in the south of Belize. One of the most difficult things was to have people staring at you wherever you go. But eventually you feel like you really belong. This was what I feel was my biggest achievement whilst teaching, becoming part of the family I was living with.*
>
> *There were a few bad moments on project, mostly to do with the really hard work we did! Now I look back and think it was just character building. The jungle trek I did was the hardest thing I have done in my life, but also the biggest adventure.*

Note that Trekforce also offer a programme in Guyana and Peru which offers a combination of project-based expeditions, trekking, teaching in Amerindian communities and a Spanish course in Peru.

Non-Specialist Placement Organisations in the UK

The following accept gap year students for Latin American projects if they fulfil the requirements (which in several cases include strong Christian commitment) but they do not specialise in placing year-out students:

AFS Intercultural Programmes UK, Leeming House, Vicar Lane, Leeds LS2 7JF (0113-242 6136; info-unitedkingdom@afs.org/ www.afsuk.org). AFS is very active in South and Central America with community service programmes lasting 6 months in Bolivia, Brazil, Costa Rica, Ecuador, Guatemala, Honduras, Mexico, Panama, Paraguay, Peru and Venezuela, for volunteers generally aged 18-29. Older applicants are also welcomed. Accommodation is arranged with host families. The cost for participating is £3300. The Schools Programme for 15-18 year olds can be requested for a Latin American destination at a cost of £3950. Fundraising support is offered to all participants.

Cactus Language, 4 Clarence House, 30-31 North St, Brighton BN1 1EB 0845 130 4775/ fax 01273 775868; enquiry@cactuslanguage.com; www.cactuslanguage.com). Spanish and Portuguese language courses followed by voluntary placements. Short and long-term work in a wide range of social, healthcare, educational, conservation, customised and student service placements in Guatemala, Costa Rica, Peru, Ecuador, Bolivia, Argentina and Brazil. Examples include working at a hatchery for Leatherback turtles on

Costa Rica's Pacific Coast, helping in an orphanage for girls in Cusco, Peru and a professional internship in Buenos Aires, Argentina.

Caledonia Languages Abroad, The Clockhouse, 72 Newhaven Road, Edinburgh EH6 5QG (0131-621 7721; www.caledonialanguages.co.uk). Language courses for all levels and voluntary work projects starting throughout the year from 3 weeks upwards in Brazil, Costa Rica, Cuba, Mexico, Chile, Argentina, Bolivia, Ecuador and Peru.

Challenges Worldwide, 13 Hamilton Place, Edinburgh EH3 5BA (0131-332 7372; www.challengesworldwide.com). Volunteer placements in Belize, Ecuador and several Caribbean Islands, in projects run by local governments, NGOs or community groups to address issues such as environmental/conservation challenges, human rights, rural development, poverty alleviation and social development.

EIL, 287 Worcester Road, Malvern, Worcs. WR14 1AB (0800 018 4015; www.eiluk. org) provides community service opportunities in Mexico and longer-term community service programme in Ecuador (3, 6, 9 or 11 months). The month-long project in Mexico involves re-forestation projects and food distribution to 'cardboard cities'. Ecuadorian projects are in civic projects or in a social environment (e.g. orphanage, cerebral palsy centre). Community service projects also available in Argentina, Brazil, Chile and Guatemala.

Global Adventures Project, 38 Queen's Gate, London SW7 5HR (0800 085 4197; www.globaladventures.co.uk). Three month placements for over 18's teaching English to primary and secondary aged street children and working in care centres. With projects in different areas throughout Brazil, a basic understanding or a willingness to learn some Portuguese is recommended. Environmental projects are available to participants who can speak and understand Portuguese. Prices start from £1745 and include internal flight, orientation, homestay accommodation and meals.

Global Vision International (GVI), Amwell Farmhouse, Nomansland, Wheathampstead, St. Albans, Herts. AL4 8EJ (0870 608 8898; info@gvi.co.uk/ www.gvi.co.uk). Placements from 2-20 weeks. Marine conservation and TEFL community expeditions in Mexico, work with children in Guatemala and Ecuador, wildlife research expeditions to the Amazon and Costa Rica, turtle conservation in Panama and exploration in Patagonia. Prices from £825 to £2945.

ICYE: Inter-Cultural Youth Exchange, Latin American House, Kingsgate Place, London NW6 4TA (tel/fax 020-7681 0983; info@icye.org.uk/ www.icye.org.uk). International exchange organisation that sends volunteers to spend a year abroad with a host family and undertake voluntary work placements, for example in drug rehabilitation, protection of street children and ecological projects. Placements available in Bolivia, Brazil, Costa Rica, Honduras, Colombia and Mexico.

Latin Link STEP Programme, 175 Tower Bridge Road, London SE1 2AB (020-7939 9014; step.uk@latinlink.org). Self-funded team-based building projects in Argentina, Bolivia, Brazil, Ecuador, Mexico, Cuba and Peru, for committed Christians only. Spring programme runs March to July; summer programme for 7 weeks from July.

MondoChallenge, Milton House, Gayton Rd, Milton Malsor, Northampton NN7 3AB (01604 858225; info@mondochallenge.org). Volunteer placement in the Monte Grande region north of Santiago close to La Serena. Teaching in several small mountain village schools.

Liga Millers thought that the mountain location in Northern Chile was beautiful:
The Elqui Valley is a perfect place with a stunning climate and I think it is a great location for MondoChallenge. I am having a fantastic time here and it is a shame that this is my last week. I will have lots of fond memories of singing in a choir, climbing in the mountains and seeing condors and chinchillas, enjoying various fiestas and barbecues, playing football and dominoes with the locals and looking at Jupiter from an observatory and jointly confirming the toxic effects of Pisco Sours.

Oasis Trust, 115 Southwark Bridge Road, London SE1 0AX (020-7450 9000; globalaction@oasistrust.org). Short and long-term practical projects in slum areas run alongside local Christian groups and churches in Brazil and Peru. Applicants should be committed Christians.

SAMS (South American Mission Society), Allen Gardiner Cottage, Pembury Rd., Tunbridge Wells, Kent TN2 3QU (01892 538647; persec@samsgb.org/ www.samsgb.org). Committed Christians work as self-funding volunteers, particularly in English teaching and work with underprivileged children in Peru, Bolivia, Brazil, Paraguay, Uruguay, Argentina and Chile.

TASK Brasil (Trust for Abandoned Street Kids), PO Box 4901, London SE16 3PP (020-7737 5545; www.taskbrasil.org.uk). Volunteers over 21 work on the streets of Rio. Placements cost £1200-£2500.

Youth with a Mission, Highfield Oval, Harpenden, Herts AL5 4BX (01582 463216; www.ywam.uk.com). Projects working with street children followed by discipleship training in Brazil and Bolivia for committed Christians.

Organisations in the US

American Friends Service Committee, 1501 Cherry St, Philadelphia, Pennsylvania 19102-1479, USA (215-241-7295; mexicosummer@afsc.org). Quaker organisation which recruits Spanish-speaking volunteers aged 18-26 to participate in long-established scheme with Mexican partner organisation SEDEPAC. Summer scheme lasts seven weeks; volunteers mostly work on building or teaching projects (programme fee $1250 plus travel expenses). Application deadline mid-March.

AmeriSpan Unlimited, PO Box 58129, Philadelphia, PA 19102 (800-879-6640; info@amerispan.com). Specialist Spanish language travel organisation with expertise in arranging language immersion courses, voluntary placements and internships throughout South and Central America.

Amigos de las Americas, 5618 Star Lane, Houston, TX 77057 (800-231-7796; www.amigoslink.org). Summer training programme for 700+ high school and college student volunteers (minimum age 16) mostly in community health projects in Central America (Mexico, Costa Rica, the Dominican Republic, Honduras, Nicaragua, Panama) and Paraguay. Participation fee is $3650 including travel from the US. All volunteers must have studied Spanish at school or university and undergone training.

Adelante LLC, 601 Taper Dr., Seal Beach, CA 90740 (562-799-9133; www.adelante-abroad.com). Internships, volunteer placements, teaching abroad and semester/summer study opportunities from 1-12 months in Costa Rica (San José), Mexico (Oaxaca) and Chile (Vina del Mar/Valparaiso). Prices range from $1600 for 1 month in Chile and Mexico to include language classes, various housing options and work assignment placement.

Alliances Abroad Group, 1221 South Mopac Expressway, Suite 250, Austin, Texas 78746 (512-457-8062; www.allianceabroad.com). Sends mainly Americans to Ecuador, Brazil, Argentina, Peru and Costa Rica (8 weeks to a year) to live with local families, learn Spanish or do some voluntary work as an English teacher, to work or intern with various industries, etc. Fees are normally about $1200-$1600 for three months plus homestay fees (e.g. $12 a day in Peru).

Amizade Volunteer Vacations, PO Box 110107, Pittsburgh, PA 15232 (888-973-4443; www.amizade.org). Projects lasting 2-4 weeks in Bolivia, 1-12 months in Jamaica and 2 weeks in Brazil. Varying fees.

Casa Alianza, c/o Jim Harnett, SJO 1039, PO Box 025216, Miami, FL 33102-5216 (volunteer@casa-alianza.org; www.casa-alianza.org). Volunteers work with street children in Mexico City, Guatemala City, Tegucigalpa and Managua for 6-12 months. Accommodation varies according to country e.g. $70 a month in Nicaragua but up to $200 in Honduras.

Foundation for Sustainable Development, 870 Market St, Suite 32, San Francisco,

California 94102 (tel/fax 415-283-4873; www.fsdinternational.org). Summer and longer term internships in all areas of development in Bolivia, Peru, Ecuador, Argentina and Nicaragua (as well as Tanzania, Uganda, Kenya and India). Sample fees are $2000 for 8 weeks (June/July) in Nicaragua and $2650 for 9 weeks in Peru.

ICADS, Apartado 300-2050 San Pedro Montes de Oca, San José, Costa Rica (506-225-0508; info@icads.org; www.icadscr.com). The well regarded programmes of the Institute for Central American Development Studies combine study of the Spanish language and development issues with structured internships in Costa Rica and Nicaragua lasting a semester ($8500) or a summer ($3800).

WorldTeach, Center for International Development, Harvard University, 79 John F Kennedy St, Cambridge MA 02138 (617-495-5527; www.worldteach.org). Sends fee-paying college graduates to teach English for nine months in Costa Rica, Ecuador and Honduras.

Youth Challenge International, 20 Maud St, Suite 305, Toronto, Ontario M5V 2M5, Canada (416-504-3370; www.yci.org). Teams of volunteers carry out community development projects lasting from 5 weeks to 3 months in Costa Rica and Guyana.

EXPEDITIONS

Raleigh International, 27 Parsons Green Lane, London SW6 4HZ (020-7371 8585; www.raleighinternational.org). Chile is the longest running expedition country for Raleigh International. Environmental research projects take place in Patagonia (region Aysen). Additionally Raleigh also work in Costa Rica and in Nicaragua near the Cosiguina Volcano, site of the largest volcanic eruption in the history of the Americas and nowadays of a number of communities living in extreme poverty. Volunteers stay in these communities while working with local people to build latrines and repair water sources such as wells.

Tom Saunders had no difficulty describing his Raleigh expedition to Costa Rica in glowing terms:
> One of the most enjoyable moments was climbing Cerro Dragõn, the main summit of the trek. It was amazing as not many tourists go there. We had to walk through virgin rainforest, along a tiny path that obviously had not been walked for years. At the same time one of the biggest challenges I faced was on the trekking phase. Trekking in the heat is hard work, but with the staff, venturers and the team spirit you were able to get through it. It was such a good feeling getting to the top. Another favourite time was having fires on the beach; everyone was in a good mood – times like that make Raleigh amazing, especially with no alcohol. It is so good to see the Ticos' love for their country. They were all so friendly and hospitable.
>
> I think 99% of my time on Raleigh will remain in my memory. One memory I shall take away with me was walking down the beach with the project manager and a Welsh venturer at high tide in Corcovado at sunset – just amazing. The expedition has changed the way I see people. It has also inspired me to get out and see the rest of the world and now one of my ambitions is to climb Kilimanjaro. After expedition I am travelling around Central America with the friends I have met here. I shall go surfing in Tamarindo, see the volcanoes, go diving in Honduras and see the Mayan ruins in Guatemala. Then it is back to start a geology course at Birmingham University.

Coral Cay Conservation, The Tower, 13th Floor, 125 High Street, Colliers Wood, London SW19 2JG (0870 750 0668; www.coralcay.org) runs expeditions in Honduras to survey the coral reefs and establish a database for coastal zone management. This part of the Caribbean is known for its diverse coral reefs, whale sharks and spectacular marine life. A sample 6-week marine project would cost £1800 (£1900 for dive trainees). Prices exclude flights and insurance.

Greenforce, 11-15 Betterton Street, London WC2H 9BP (020-7470 8888/ fax 020-379

0801; info@greenforce.org/ www.greenforce.org) is looking for volunteers to join wildlife survey projects in the Ecuadorian Amazon. Projects involve studying endangered species and habitats. No previous experience is necessary as training is given in the UK and in Peru. The cost is £2300 for 10 weeks plus flights.

Operation Wallacea, Hope House, Old Bolingbroke, Nr Spilsby, Lincolnshire PE23 4EX (01790 763194; info@opwall.com). Volunteer students, divers and naturalists assist with surveys of marine and forest habitats in Honduras and (from 2006) in Cuba.

Trekforce Expeditions, Naldred Farm Offices, Borde Hill Lane, Haywards Heath, West Sussex RH16 1XR (01444 474123; www.trekforce.org.uk). Registered UK charity organises and runs conservation projects in the rainforests of Central America and in the Amazon jungles of South America. Expeditions last from one to five months and offer a week of comprehensive jungle training followed by conservation teamwork on a challenging project. There is also the opportunity to trek into different areas of the country. The longer programmes involve expedition work followed by a phase of learning Spanish in a second country for a month and then teaching in rural communities for a further two months. Each expedition's project is unique and in the past has included building a research centre in a jaguar reserve, or working in support of scientific research with the Natural History Museum. Help and advice on fundraising are given at introduction sessions and initial training is also given in the UK prior to departure.

Expeditions form the final part of the programmes in South America run by *Quest Overseas,* as a reward for taking Spanish classes and helping on a voluntary project. For many, like **Ronan O'Kelly** who travelled with Quest Overseas, the expedition proved a fitting end to an exhilarating gap year experience:

> *The Quito phase was an absolute blast (though surprisingly we actually learned some Spanish!) as were the weekends off. The Yachana Project, though challenging at times (chicken feet soup took some getting used to), was a hugely fulfilling and fantastic experience. And the final phase, the expedition, really was the culmination of all the great things of the previous months. It should be taken as a compliment that the only real criticism I could find was that we did too much. I've never been so tired in my life; but likewise, never before have I fulfilled so much.*

A similar scheme is run by Venture Co.

COURSES

As mentioned earlier in this book, trends show that increasing numbers of people are learning Spanish. Whereas most prospective learners think of developing their language skills in Spain, more and more are looking to the many Spanish-speaking countries of South and Central America, particularly Ecuador, Peru, Mexico and Costa Rica. A number of schools have been working very hard to bring their courses, whether in travellers' survival Spanish or in advanced Spanish, to the attention of potential clients in Europe and North America. Not only are the prices very competitive when compared to courses in Spanish cities, but you are likely to receive a warmer welcome if staying with a family.

Many cultural exchange organisations and Spanish language course providers can advise or even place their 'graduates' in voluntary positions and internships where they will have a chance to immerse themselves in the Spanish language. Both *Caledonia Languages Abroad* and *Cactus Language* mentioned above can send detailed information about their courses and voluntary programmes in South and Central America. Caledonia Languages Abroad mentioned above have a website with full details of their courses and voluntary programmes in South and Central America. For example Caledonia offer a combined language study and volunteering programme, e.g. three weeks Spanish tuition in Peru followed by three weeks of voluntary work at a community project in Cusco (fees are

£1100 including 6 weeks accommodation). **Keri Craig's** successful time in Costa Rica arranged by Caledonia makes it clear why Costa Rica is another favourite destination for people who want to learn Spanish:

> *Everyone at the school was friendly and so helpful, whether it was organising extra classes or booking hotels at the weekend. My teacher Gaby was wonderful and my Spanish improved no end having endless gossips with Gaby each afternoon. Considering my Spanish was very basic, I was very pleased with the way it developed so quickly. It was certainly an advantage being so immersed in the culture. The dance classes after school were my particular favourite. Frank and Victor were amazing teachers and soon had us salsa-ing like the locals. My only complaint would be the Thursday night dance class outing – European boys just can't dance like the Latin men!*

Gala Spanish in Spain offers intensive language courses and optional cultural programmes in various locations in South America. *CESA* is also expanding its operations in South America (see entry). **Lucy Jackson**, one of CESA's satisfied customers who studied Spanish in Ecuador after finishing university, describes how her apprehensions about travelling so far from home were soon dispelled:

> *I was very tired and very nervous. I was on the other side of the world from home and didn't know a soul. My fears had been fuelled by my dad who, prior to the flight, had been posting me every report on attacks on foreigners in South America. I was entirely ignorant of the continent, let alone Ecuador and had no idea what to expect from the language course in Cuenca or the two months I had set aside to travel around Ecuador and Peru with a friend. I went to refresh my very rusty Spanish and to explore a part of the world friends told me was amazing.*
>
> *The most memorable aspect of my experience has to be the openness of the Ecuadorian people. During my degree I spent a year in France and it took a good three months before the French opened up enough to go out with me. Yet in Cuenca it took no more than a week and I'm still in touch with most of them now. People always wanted to help and rarely did I feel unsafe, despite my father's dire warnings.*
>
> *Lessons were intensive and concentrated on grammar, oral work and consolidating lessons. We also had homework every night, which was a novelty for a uni graduate. At the end of the course I had improved way beyond my lapsed A-level ability. The combination of teacher enthusiasm, small classes (up to five) and the range of student nationalities ensured good progress. The fact that I had to speak Spanish with my host family every day was the icing on the cake. I loved the school. I was impressed by the organisation, the standard of the teachers and the extracurricular activities, e.g. cooking classes, regional and Latin American dance classes and excursions to craft villages, national parks and jungles.*

Individual language schools often have links with local projects and can arrange for students of Spanish to attach themselves to projects that interest them. Typically Carisa Fey started her big trip round South America with a short language course in Quito which led to some voluntary work afterwards teaching knitting to street kids. For example the Equinoccial Spanish School in Quito (Reina Victoria 1325 y Lizardo Garcia; tel/fax 02-2564 488; www.ecuadorspanish.com) arranges volunteer positions throughout Ecuador (for ESS language school clients) in a variety of fields from ecological studies to community work. Similarly APF Languages in Quito (www.apf-languages.com) combine a programme of Spanish tuition at $5 an hour with homestays ($14 per day) and ecological or humanitarian volunteering. For candidates with advanced Spanish and a keen interest in the Amazon, APF can fix up minimum six-month jungle-guiding jobs. Mundo Verde Spanish School, Nueva Alta, 432-A Cusco, Peru; (+51-84 221287; www.mundoverdespanish.com) has links with a development project in the rainforest and with many other voluntary projects to which students can be assigned for no fee. In Guatemala, *Eco-Escuela de Espanol,* c/o Tikal, Calle 15 de Septiembre, Ciudad Flores, Petén 17001, Guatemala (tel/fax 502-7926-4981; www.tikalcnx.com) arranges for language students to assist local conservation projects (see entry).

Almost any Spanish language school in Guatemala can help arrange a volunteer position. To find links to many of these language schools, visit www.xelapages.com/schools. htm. Casa Xelaju, Apartado Postal 302, Quetzaltenango, Guatemala (502-761-5954; www. casaxelaju.com) runs Spanish courses and refers clients to internships and voluntary work in Guatamala. The city of Quetzaltenango offers many opportunities to do volunteer work in the community. In exchange for a fee of $25 the language school Casa Xelaju (Postal 302, Quetzaltenango, Guatemala; 502-761-5954; www.casaxelaju.com) will search for a suitable position.

Of course many websites link to Spanish course providers; for example www.yo-hablo.com has a useful facility allowing you to search Latin America by topic (e.g. Spanish with voluntary work, or Spanish with scuba) and by country. For other Spanish language courses, check entries for the following in the 'Directory of Language Courses': *Via Hispana* in Buenos Aires and *Sin Fronteras* in Bariloche (Argentina); *Bridge-Linguatec International* with schools in Santiago, Rio de Janeiro and Buenos Aires at which you might be able to teach English while learning Spanish; *Ruta del Sol* in Quito; *La Escuela de Idiomas d'Amore* in Costa Rica; *La Union Language School* in Guatemala; *CIS* and *El Salvador Spanish Schools* in El Salvador; *Ixbalanque Spanish School* in Honduras; and *Academia Hispano Americana, IMAC* and *Instituto Chac-Mool* in Mexico as well as the *Dunham Institute* in Chiapas which allows you to obtain TEFL training while learning Spanish.

> **Even if you do not have a chance to brush up your Spanish (or start from scratch) ahead of time, you may well thrive, as Katherine Shirtcliffe did in Urubamba Peru with *Teaching & Projects Abroad*:**
> *For my placement I assisted in a kindergarten school. Because I didn't speak Spanish I was worried about how I was going to communicate with the children, but their enthusiasm, interest and persistence to get to know me made me ditch my fears and gave me the confidence I needed to interact with them. Knowing just a few key Spanish words and phrases can go a long way and what you can't say can be overcome by actions, games and songs. Learning to speak Spanish was the biggest challenge, yet it was one that I thrived on. In school I was always bad at languages, but living in an environment where I needed to learn another language in order to be able to communicate, and driven by the frustration of not being able to say what I wanted, encouraged me to learn the lingo. I came to love the language, the people and their attitude towards life. It was an amazing experience in which I had many adventures that I long to relive.*

PAID WORK

It will not be easy for a school leaver to find paid work or work experience opportunities in South or Central America. Although demand is ubiquitous for English teachers, from dusty towns on the Yucatan Peninsula of Mexico to Punta Arenas at the southern extremity of the continent, south of the Falkland Islands, most of the customers are business people looking for something more professional than what most gap year students can offer in the way of conversation practice. Furthermore, in a land where baseball is a passion and US television enormously popular, American (and also Canadian) job-seekers have an advantage. More detailed information about teaching in Latin America can be found in the 2005 edition of *Teaching English Abroad* (£12.95 from bookshops and Vacation Work Publications).

But there are always exceptions. **Eleanor Padfield** from Cambridge was determined to work abroad after finishing her A-levels but without going through an agency where she would be with lots of other British students. After spending the first half of her year in Salamanca, Spain, she sent e-mails all over the world to fix up something to do, preferably in Latin America. Of the many schools and language schools she contacted, one of the few to reply was the Redland School in Chile (Camino El Alba 11357, Las Condes, Santiago), an upmarket private school. Although they told her that they didn't normally accept gap year students (since so many previous gappers had left prematurely to travel), they made an exception for Eleanor when she promised to stick it out till the end of the term beginning in March and ending in August. By June she was tempted to leave early but her conscience (or her mother's exhortations) persuaded her to keep her promise, though she was availing herself of any available free time to see some of Chile.

Leaving England for the first time, Linda Harrison travelled on a one-way ticket straight from the picturesque Yorkshire town of Kirkbymoorside to the picturesque state of Michoacàn, and suffered severe culture shock. She and a Spanish-speaking friend had pre-arranged jobs at the *Culturlingua Language Center* (Plaza Jardinadas, Local 24 y 25, Zamora, Michoacàn). Although it provided accommodation, it offered no pre-service training:

> *The director told me that I might as well start teaching the day after I arrived. I stumbled into my first class with no experience, qualifications or books. Twelve expectant faces watched while I nervously talked about England. Twelve faces went blank when I mentioned soap operas.*

The *British Council* (assistants@britishcouncil.org) arranges for language assistants to work in local secondary schools and higher education institutions in a number of Latin American countries for a year. Applicants must be aged 20-30 with at least A-level Spanish and preferably a degree in modern languages. Application forms are available from October for a 1st December deadline.

In Buenos Aires, *Colonias de Inmersion* places native speakers of English as language facilitators in positions in Argentina and Chile (see 'Directory of Work Experience').

English is of course not the only thing that can be taught. The flourishing skiing industry of Chile and Argentina creates some openings for ski instructors. A Scottish firm called *Peak Leaders UK Ltd* (see entry) runs snowboard and ski instructor courses in the popular resort of Bariloche in Argentine Patagonia with trips to Chile and Buenos Aires, specifically for gap year and timeout students. The nine-week course (July-September) costs £6500.

Work experience placements in a number of fields can be arranged by several agencies in Ecuador; see entries for *EcuEVP* and *ELEP* in the 'Directory of Work Experience.

Argentina is among the most Europeanised countries in Latin America. A cultural exchange organisation, Grupo de Intercambio Cultural Argentino, invites paying volunteers from abroad to work in various sectors including hospitality and national parks. Participants will be assigned to work within the Los Glaciares and Nahuel Huapi National Parks (both in Patagonia) and Iguaçu Falls National Park in northwest Argentina. Assignments last at least eight weeks and range from helping park rangers, to conducting guided visits, generally for four or five hours a day. Spanish language abilities are not required though make it easier to communicate with your host family. Accommodation is provided for a fee of US$485 or US$515 a month. Details are available from GIC Argentina, Lavalle 397, 1st Floor, Suite 1, Buenos Aires, C1047AAG, Argentina (+54-11-6311 3373; info@gicarg.org/ www.gicarg.org).

Work experience placements in Brazil are arranged by several mediating agencies, viz. *CCUSA (Camp Counsellors USA)* and *Gwendalyne*. CCUSA offers a choice of office work, sports jobs, hotel/tourism placements or working with children mainly in Sao Paulo but also in Florianópolis and Vitória (both islands) plus Rio de Janeiro.

Unusual opportunities may crop up in the vast empty spaces of South America. For example Ramón David Jorajuría has a ranch in Carmelo in Uruguay which welcomes people who want to improve their Spanish while working on the farm. Participants live in a traditional farmhouse in the midst of nature, have opportunities to go riding and learn how to carry out ranching chores. Details are available from David Jorafuría (C.C. 40160 C.P. 70100, Carmelo, Uruguay; +598-540-2028; migranja1@yahoo.com.

VOLUNTEERING

Short-term voluntary work projects are scattered over this vast continent, and many of the opportunities are for Spanish-speakers. If you happen to have any contacts with a charity operating in South America, there is every chance you will be invited to spend time. For example during Eleanor Padfield's campaign to fill her gap year, she heard from her aunt about a Methodist mission in southern Bolivia (in a town the *Rough Guide* labels the 'armpit of the universe') who told her she was welcome to come and help. She helped generally with the chores and found the experience fascinating.

The internet has made it much easier to unearth opportunities for volunteering, whether from one of the mainstream databases like *WorkingAbroad.com* or from indigenous organisations. A specialist advisory service based in Brighton will tailor-make a list of voluntary projects in Latin America to which clients can apply directly; see *www. volunteerlatinamerica.com* (prices from £22). The excellent online guide to Ecuador *www. EcuadorExplorer.com* has listings and links to teaching and voluntary projects as well as what to do. Another good source of opportunities is on *www.volunteeringecuador.org*. In some cases a centralised placement service makes choosing a project much easier, though you will have to pay for the service as in the case of *Volunteer Bolivia* (www.volunteerbolivia.org) located in Cochabamba. They encourage their clients to sign up for a month of Spanish tuition while staying with a local family before becoming a volunteer; a combined language course, homestay and volunteer placement programme costs $1150 for one month.

The student service organisation ProWorld Service Corps (264 East 10th St, No.5, New York, NY 10009; 877-733-7378; www.proworldsc.org) offers a range of internships lasting one to six months with aid agencies in Peru and Belize. The fee of $1950/£1150 includes Spanish tuition followed by placement with an NGO and lodgings for the first four weeks. In fact combining a Spanish language course, homestay and voluntary placement over two to six months is a route favoured by many.

Nikki D'Arcy from Watford signed up with *Cross-Cultural Solutions* on their Lima, Peru programme for four weeks to volunteer at Los Martincitos, a home for the elderly, and experienced the same culture shock that many gap year students have also experienced:

> *Despite considering myself an independent, confident person, the thought of completely immersing myself in another culture was still slightly daunting. That's why I chose Cross-Cultural Solutions. The programmes seemed so well organised and the idea of a safe home-base to return to was appealing. All of the UK staff I spoke with were so helpful and helped me to decide on the Lima programme for four weeks. It all happened so quickly, which was probably a good thing, because I worried so much about daft things, like what clothes to take, whether there would be hot water (there was!), if the people in the house would like me, you name it, I worried about it! As soon as I arrived at the house in Lima, I wondered why I had bothered getting so stressed. I felt instantly comfortable and at home.*
>
> *After a weekend of getting to know my fellow volunteers and the area where the house is based, the working week at Martincitos began. The centre provides food, basic medical care and social activities three days of the week, and staff and volunteers visit their homes on the other two days. I won't lie, during my time there, I saw some things that saddened and shocked me, I didn't realise that people could live in such poverty. But I also got to know those people and saw such amazing strength*

in them. They were so happy to invite me into their lives, to share their stories and were so full of life, it put me to shame for moaning about the tiny problems we have. Even after a few days, I felt my attitudes and perceptions changing. I began to really understand what is important in life. Not the material things that so many of us seem to become obsessed with, but family and friends and enjoying life. Don't get me wrong, I already knew that, but I don't think you can fully understand it until you see people who have nothing, and I mean literally nothing, sometimes not even a roof, but yet they meet up with their friends and dance and sing and laugh like they don't have a care in the world. They are truly inspirational.

Grassroots Voluntary Organisations

There are hundreds of such organisations throughout Latin America, not all of whom can attract Western volunteers through sending agencies. As you travel throughout the region you are bound to come across various charitable and voluntary organisations running orphanages, environmental projects and so on, some of which may be able to make temporary use of a willing volunteer. The Quaker-run service centre in Mexico City, *Casa de los Amigos*, has information on volunteering opportunities throughout Mexico and Central America for Spanish speakers able to commit for at least three months. The initial fee is $50 plus $25 per month to cover admin expenses. The Casa is at Ignacio Mariscal 132, 06030 Mexico, D.F., Mexico (055-5705-0521; amigos@casadelosamigos.org) and provides simple accommodation for 70 pesos ($6) per night to people involved in volunteer projects.

Many worthwhile social projects rely on volunteers. One of the most famous and long-established is *Casa Guatemala*, an orphanage and attached backpackers' hostel which relies on travellers to carry out maintenance, cooking, building, organic gardening, teaching the children English, etc. They can use as many as 100 volunteers a year preferably for a minimum of three months. The orphanage office in Guatemala City is at 14th Calle 10-63, Zona 1, 01001 Guatemala (Apdo. Postal 5-75-A; 502-232-5517; casaguatemal@guate.net; www.casa-guatemala.org), while the orphanage itself is about five hours north of Guatemala City, a short boat ride from the town of Fronteras on the road to the Petén region. The director is Angelina de Galdamez who warns that volunteers should expect a certain amount of hardship. Volunteers must pay a non-refundable fee of $180 however long they intend to stay.

Genesis Volunteer Program, Malecon 1312 y Ascazubi St, Bahía, Ecuador (05-692400; www.bahiacity.com/volunteer). Foreign travellers to Ecuador are invited to teach for a couple of hours a day in one of four schools in the coastal town of Bahía de Caráquez. Volunteers must stay at least four weeks between April and January. The programme fee is $300 plus homestay accommodation costs $85 a week. An English teaching programme in Peru can be accessed via *Eco Trek Peru* (see entry in 'Directory of Volunteering').

One of the most acute problems in many South American cities is the number of street children. Working with one of the many charities that are tackling this problem can be both discouraging and rewarding by turns, as recounted by a volunteer in Quito for *CENIT* (Spanish acronym for Centre for the Working Girl) with an entry in the 'Directory of Volunteering Abroad':

My name is Heidi and I am 20 years old. It is almost two months since I got to know CENIT, and I am so glad I started working here! What made me interested in this job is that we get in direct contact with the children in the street. There are five different sectors where the volunteers do outreach work. I work from 9.30am to 12.30pm, which is when we do most of the outreach work in the street. I have worked mostly in three sectors: the Camal Marketplace, the Villaflora (an urban neighborhood) and the local trolley station. When we walk through the big Camal market to gather the kids (aged 2-10) to play, there are usually some shy kids and parents, while other kids run towards us and their parents are happy to see us. I feel that the work in the Camal is very rewarding because you see the benefits then and there: the kids are happy to get a break from working with their parents, and the parents are happy to have a little while free from their kids.

At one of the other sectors where we work (Villaflora), we have gotten to know kids, mostly boys, between the ages of 11 and 17. These kids are true street kids since they sleep and eat on the street. Most of the volunteers love hanging out with these kids, but it is hard as well since these kids use drugs (they sniff glue).

The hard thing about this work, I think, is that sometimes I feel really useless. Often in the mornings we can sit for sometimes half an hour without any kids wanting to play with us. It happens as well occasionally that the kids don t want to talk to us at all. What is important to always keep in mind, though, is that these kids are living hard lives with a lot of abuse and abandonment. Our job is to show them there are responsible, caring adults in this world. We have to build up trust with them. Just the fact that the kids want to play with us and even come to CENIT to eat with us is a big step. Establishing this trust is not easy – it takes loads of time and many volunteers to get that far. Most of the days I have a wonderful time playing with the kids, though, and the thought that maybe one of these kids will go back to school one day makes everything worthwhile.

Conservation

An increasing number of organisations, both indigenous and foreign-sponsored, is involved in environmental projects throughout the continent. For opportunities in Ecuador investigate the Ecotrackers Network (www.ecotrackers.com) which charges $50 to register plus $2 a day while you're on a project, in addition to the daily average charge of $8 paid to the project organisers to cover board and lodging. For further leads try www.my-quito.com/eco-tourism.html.

Many placements can be pre-arranged in exchange for a fee which may be equivalent to the price of a holiday. For example the Volunteer Galapagos programme (on which volunteers teach English, environmental sciences) costs about $50 a day for the first month, half as much thereafter. Nurses and biologists are also needed. Details are available in the UK from House of Ecuador, 94 Roman Way, London N7 8UN (0845 124 9338; www.volunteergalapagos.org). A cheaper way of spending time in those famous islands is to become an International Volunteer with the Darwin Foundation (External Relations Unit, Charles Darwin Research Station, Casilla Postal 17-01-3891, Quito, Ecuador; 011-593-552-6146/147; volunteer@darwinfoundation.org). Volunteers without relevant scientific skills have to pay their way with a contribution of $11 a day for food and dormitory accommodation and must stay for a minimum of six months.

For ecological projects in Ecuador that need volunteer input, see the entries for *FBU* and the *Fundacion Jatun Sachu* in the 'Directory of Volunteering Abroad'. The highest concentration of projects is probably in Costa Rica where the National Parks & Communities Authority runs a voluntary programme *Asociacion de Voluntarios para el Servicio en las Areas Protegidas* (ASVO). To be eligible you must be willing to work for at least one or two months, be able to speak Spanish and provide a copy of your passport and a photo. The work may consist of trail maintenance and construction, greeting and informing visitors, research or generally assisting rangers. There is also a possibility of joining a sea turtle conservation project. Details are available from the Volunteer Co-ordinator (alopez@asvocr.com), International Volunteer Program, Servicio de Parques Nacionales, Apdo. 11384-1000, San José 10104-1000 (506-233-4989; www.asvocr.com). Food and accommodation cost about $14 a day. The AVSO website is currently only in Spanish though there is a link to www.tropicjoes.com about short volunteer vacations planting trees.

BUNAC now has volunteering programmes in Costa Rica and Peru under the auspices of partner student organisations which provide back-up during the two to six month placement. Students (including gap year students) and recent graduates can participate if they have GCSE level Spanish. The Costa Rica programme fee for 2005 is £490 plus volunteers will need funds to cover their living expenses. The Peru programme costs £695 for two months and £895 for three.

Foreign guides are occasionally hired by expatriate or even local tour operators. For example the Tambopata Jungle Lodge (PO Box 454, Cusco, Peru; tel/fax 084-245695; www.tambopatalodge.com) takes on guides for a minimum of six months who must have formal training in the natural sciences and (preferably) speak Spanish, all of which should be indicated on a CV. Information about the resident naturalist programme and research opportunities in the same area can be sought in the UK from TreeS, the Tambopata Reserve Society, c/o John Forrest, PO Box 33153, London NW3 4DR). Guides for the naturalist programme must be graduate biologists, environmental scientists or geographers over the age of 20. They receive free room and board throughout their stay.

Andrew James was there in his gap year (before they began insisting on a background in biology):

We lived in a jungle camp consisting of wooden lodges a four-hour boat trip up the Tambopata River from Puerto Maldonado. I was one of three English guides who took visitors of all nationalities in groups of about five on dawn walks to explore the rainforest and see the amazing plant life and the occasional animal. I was there for three months and was paid $150 a month for working 20 days a month with the other ten days free to do research or live it up in Puerto Maldonado (a town straight out of the Wild West).

The organisation *Rainforest Concern* (27 Lansdowne Crescent, London W11 2NS; 020-7229 2093; info@rainforestconcern.org/ www.rainforestconcern.org) has rainforest conservation projects in Central and South America (as well as Asia). Volunteers and students who are prepared to work for part of the day can stay at a cloud forest lodge in Ecuador or help with turtle protection projects in Panama and Costa Rica. *Quest Overseas* works with Rainforest Concern by sending volunteers to conservation projects in Ecuador, Bolivia and Chile. Partnerships with other sending agencies like i-to-i are also in operation.

Travel

Journey Latin America, South American Experience and *South America Explorers* have already been recommended in the introductory chapter on 'Travel'. Independent travellers should exercise a reasonable amount of caution when travelling in some parts of the continent. It is not uncommon for bandits to hold up buses between Quito and Lima. The Foreign Office advises people not to travel on public transport late at night, though for some journeys this is unavoidable; the Quito-Lima trip takes the better part of two days and two nights.

Many gap years in Peru centre on the classic Inca Trail to Machu Picchu. This is a fairly strenuous high altitude hike which takes four days comfortably (three days minimum). In order to control numbers in order to preserve the fragile environment, the authorities now insist that hikers travel together in groups with an authorised trek agent and camp only in designated areas. Only 500 permits are issued per day which means that it is necessary to book in advance to guarantee a place, as much as eight weeks in advance of the high season (July, August, Christmas). The fee will be around $300. Good information is available at www.andeantravelweb.com.

The Caribbean

The islands of the Caribbean are far too expensive to explore unless you do more than sip rum punch by the beach. Few agencies make placements in the Caribbean.

One exception is *Challenges Worldwide* which sends volunteers to several islands including Antigua, which is where Lucy Bale spent a fantastic three months at the beginning of her gap year:
Antigua was paradise compared to the rat-race I had been running four months earlier in England, work, exams, stress... It was peaceful, hot and friendly and my decision to volunteer with Challenges Worldwide was a good one. Being placed at a refuge for victims of domestic violence was a bonus I could have only dreamed of.

There was never a dull moment. My duties included teaching at The Learning Centre pre-school, where I had responsibility for the 4+ age group, preparing them for primary school and teaching the basics in Maths, Reading, Writing and Science. The 'little darlings' were noisy, boisterous and naughty, much tougher than their UK counterparts but with their wide smiles, innocent eyes and broken dialect it was hard not to be amused by these colourful characters. I was also charged with teaching teachers of the Youth Skills Training Programme, a local vocational college, a task I found daunting at the start. They were educated and eager to learn; I, on the other hand, am young, inexperienced and with no formal qualifications. What could I possibly teach them? I needn't have worried, since they were very appreciative of my time and skills. Our work in Antigua was useful and good fun. The staff looked after us with true Caribbean hospitality and we were spoilt rotten!

It was definitely not all work and no play during my three-month placement. Famed for its cricket, rum, beaches and laid-back atmosphere, Antigua certainly doesn't disappoint. A short 20-minute walk from the project is Fort James beach, a gorgeous stretch of white sand, palm trees and clear blue sea – the perfect Caribbean image. And there are plenty like it. Well, 365 according to the locals, though we failed to find them all.

If you're preparing for Antigua, pack a mossie net, bikini, sun lotion and a good sense of humour. Prepare for hard work, lots of rice and male attention ('hey white girl, sexy one' being the common greeting from male passers-by). Make the most of it, time flies by and before you know it, you'll be where I am, working in an office by day, pulling pints by night scraping money together for university. I had a fantastic three months, made loads of good friends and would jump at the chance to do it again. My only regret: missing Carnival! Well there's always next year.

A number of gap year students have managed to spend time in this exotic part of the world by working for their keep, mostly on yachts.

Research opportunities exist as well. The Bermuda Biological Station for Research Inc. (Ferry Reach, St. George's, GE01 Bermuda; www.bbsr.edu) accepts students throughout the year to help scientists carry out their research and to do various jobs around the station in exchange for room and board. Volunteer interns from around the world are chosen on the basis of their academic and technical backgrounds. Summer is the peak period (applications must be in by February); otherwise apply at least four months in advance. Applicants should make personal contact with the faculty member(s) for whom they wish to work and applications should be sent direct to those faculty members. The section 'Graduate/Undergraduate Opportunities' on the website provides a list of faculty members who are looking for volunteer interns.

Cuba's economy is suffering badly from its position in world politics, but its music and vibrant culture attract some prospective year-out students. **Nick Mulvey** from Cambridge arranged to spend several months studying guitar with a Cuban musician before starting his university course in World Music at SOAS. But the infrastructure continues to disintegrate and one of two gap year placement organisations like the Project Trust and Coral Cay have dropped Cuba from their list of destinations. *Caledonia Languages Abroad* arranges Spanish and salsa courses in Cuba.

The *Cuba Solidarity Campaign* (c/o Red Rose Club, 129 Seven Sisters Road, London N7 7QG; 020-7263 6452; tours@cuba-solidarity.org.uk) runs a work/study scheme (called brigades) twice a year in which volunteers undertake agricultural and construction work for three weeks either in July or December/January. No specific skills or qualifications are required but applicants must be sympathetic to the revolution and be able to demonstrate a commitment to solidarity work. The cost of the brigade is approximately £800, which includes flight, accommodation, food and basic travel insurance. For further information contact the Brigade Co-ordinator.

Greenforce (11-15 Betterton Street, Covent Garden, London WC2H 9BP; 020-7470 8888; info@greenforce.org/ www.greenforce.org) is looking for volunteers to join a coral reef survey project in the Bahamas. Projects involve studying endangered species and habitats. The aim is to establish three new marine protected zones for the Bahamas National Trust. No previous experience is necessary as diving instruction and scientific training are provided. The cost is £2300 for 10 weeks plus flight.

United States

The spirit of Jack Kerouac is far from dead even though not many gap year students are familiar with his *On the Road* these days. Dubious foreign policy notwithstanding, the lure of America continues strong among young Britons and Europeans. The home of so many heroes and of ideas which have shaped the thinking of most people in the west, the USA attracts a wide range of people, including school leavers, who want to experience the reality for themselves. Extended travel around the United States is expensive but various schemes and travel bargains can bring that vast country within reach of gap year students and older travellers. It is possible for students to qualify for an Exchange Visitor Programme visa which permits them to enter the US and work legally. If you end up looking for a job after arrival, you will find the task infinitely easier if you have a car and a conservative appearance.

Red Tape

Despite the wide open spaces and warm hospitality so often associated with America, their official policies are discouraging for those who want to earn money while in the US. Most British citizens (and those of 27 other countries) do not need to apply for a tourist visa in advance. Tourists can wait until arrival to obtain a visa-waiver which is valid for one entry to the US for a maximum of 90 days. Individuals entering visa-free or with a visitor visa for business or tourism are prohibited from engaging in paid or unpaid employment in the US. Those planning trips of more than 90 days, including those who wish to work or study, must obtain a visa in advance from the Embassy. This has become much more complicated than it once was and requires a face-to-face interview and a £60 fee (even if the visa is denied) as well as completing a long and detailed form.

British travellers and tourists arriving in the US on the visa waiver programme face increasingly rigorous restrictions. Upon arrival you will have a digital photograph and an inkless fingerprint taken, before being given permission to enter for three months. Since October 2004, the US authorities have insisted that all incoming visa-less visitors have a machine-readable passport (which most European passports are). In the near future everyone will need a 'smart' passport, i.e. one that has a chip containing your biometric data including facial recognition. At first the US authorities were insisting that passports issued after 26 October 2005 would have be 'smart' to qualify for visa-free entry; however because the UK Passport Agency has not managed to put the technology in place in time, the American government has extended this deadline. Check the Embassy website (www. usembassy.org.uk) or dial the premium line 09055 444546 for full visa information and application forms or request an outline of non-immigrant visas from the Visa Branch of the US Embassy (5 Upper Grosvenor St, London W1A 2JB).

The visa of most interest to the readers of this book is the J-1 which is available to participants of government-authorised programmes, known as Exchange Visitor Programmes (EVPs). The J-1 visa entitles the holder to take legal paid employment. You cannot apply for the J-1 without going through a recognised Exchange Visitor Programme like the British Universities North America Club (BUNAC), IST Plus or Camp America. Only they can issue the document DS2019 necessary for obtaining a J-1 visa.

Numerous opportunities are available on summer camps and as au pairs (both described in detail below). These programmes are allowed to exist because of their educational value and many are open only to full-time students. Some will accept those between school and university, provided they have a confirmed place at a tertiary institution, and summer camp programmes are open to non-students with specific skills.

Apart from the J-1 visa available to people on approved EVPs, other possible visa categories to consider include the Q visa which is the 'International Cultural Exchange Visa' which must be applied for by the prospective employer in the US (e.g. the Disney Corporation) and approved in advance by an office of the Immigration and Naturalization Service (INS). Another possibility is the B-1 'Voluntary Service' visa. Applications must be sponsored by a charitable or religious organisation which undertakes not to pay you but may reimburse you for incidental expenses. Applicants must do work of a traditional charitable nature.

By law, all employers must physically examine documents of prospective employees within three working days, proving that they are authorised to work. Employers who are discovered by the Immigration and Naturalization Service to be hiring illegal aliens are subject to huge fines and those caught working illegally run the risk of being deported, prohibited from travelling to the US for five years and in some cases for good.

WORK AND STUDY PROGRAMMES

BUNAC (16 Bowling Green Lane, London EC1R 0QH; 020-7251 3472) administers three basic work programmes in the US: one is the 'Work America Programme' which allows full-time university students to do any summer job they are able to find before or after arrival; the second is 'Summer Camp USA' which is open to anyone over 19 interested in working on a summer camp as a counsellor; the third is 'KAMP' (Kitchen & Maintenance Programme) which is open to students who want to work at a summer camp in a catering and maintenance capacity. All participants must join the BUNAC Club (£5), travel between June and October and purchase compulsory insurance (about £130). BUNAC runs its own loan scheme.

As part of the application for student-only programmes, you must submit a letter from your principal, registrar or tutor on college headed paper showing that you are a full-time student in the year of travel. Gap year students should submit evidence of an unconditional offer for the September/October after they have returned from the US. You are also required to take at least $400 in travellers cheques (or $800 for certain jobs).

To assist Work America Programme applicants in finding work, BUNAC publishes an annual Job Directory with thousands of job listings in the US from hundreds of employers, many of whom have taken on BUNAC participants in the past. The Directory is available to all potential applicants and is free of charge. To widen your scope, you might look at job search web-sites such as www.seasonalemployment.com which lists summer jobs mainly in resorts and parks. Further contacts can be found in the annually revised book *Summer Jobs for Students in the USA* distributed in Britain by Vacation Work at £14.99.

BUNAC is also one of the biggest summer camp placement organisations, sending between 3000 and 4000 people aged between 19 (occasionally 18) and 35 to participate in the Summer Camp USA programme. The registration fee of £67 includes camp placement, return flight and land transport to camp and pocket money of $820-$880 (depending on age) for the whole nine-week period. The fact that you do not have to raise the money for the flight is a great attraction for many. Interviews, which are compulsory for all first-time applicants, are held in university towns throughout Britain between November and May.

BUNAC's other summer camp programme is called KAMP, the Kitchen and Maintenance Programme. KAMP is open only to full-time students (including those at the end of their gap year) who are given ancillary jobs in the kitchen, laundry or maintenance department, for which they will be advanced their airfare and in some cases paid more than the counsellors, i.e. at least $1225 for the eight or nine-week period of work.

The other major camp recruitment organisation is *Camp America* (37a Queen's Gate, Dept. WW, London SW7 5HR; 020-7581 7333; brochure@campamerica.co.uk/ www.campamerica.co.uk) which each summer arranges for a massive 9,000 people aged 18 or over, from around the world, to work on children's camps in the USA. The work is for nine weeks between June and August where you could be teaching activities such as tennis, swimming and arts and crafts. Camp America provides a free return flight from London to New York and guidance on applying for a J-1 visa. The camp provides free board and lodging plus pocket money. At the end of your contract, you will be given a lump sum of pocket money which will range from $600 to $1100 depending on your age (as of June 1st), experience, qualifications and whether you've been on Camp

America before. Upfront charges include the registration fee of £299 (which rises for later applicants) and the visa fee.

One way to avoid last-minute uncertainty is to try to attend one of Camp America's recruitment fairs in London, Manchester, Birmingham, Edinburgh or Belfast in February and March, which is what **Colin Rothwell** did:

> *At the recruitment fair at Manchester Metropolitan, you could actually meet the camp directors from all over the States and find out more about particular camps. If you are lucky, like me and a thousand others, you can sign a contract on the spot. Then you leave all the 'dirty work' to Camp America and wait until they call you to the airport in June sometime.*

Camp America also offers two other summer programmes: Campower for students who would like to work in the kitchen/maintenance areas at camp and the Resort America programme (www.resortamerica.co.uk) whereby people work in holiday resorts and are paid $1400 for the minimum 12-week summer period.

Summer Camps

Summer camps are uniquely American in atmosphere, even if the idea has spread to Europe. An estimated 8-10 million American children are sent to 10,000 summer camps each year for a week or more to participate in outdoor activities and sports, arts and crafts and generally have a wholesome experience. The type of camp varies from plush sports camps for the very rich to more or less charitable camps for the handicapped or underprivileged. Thousands of 'counsellors' are needed each summer to be in charge of a cabinful of youngsters and to instruct or supervise some activity, from the ordinary (swimming and boating) to the esoteric (puppet-making and ham radio).

After camp finishes, counsellors have up to six weeks' free time and normally return on organised flights between late August and the end of September. Camp counselling regularly wins enthusiastic fans and is worth considering if you enjoy children and don't mind hard work. Some camps are staffed almost entirely by young people from overseas, which can be useful if you are looking for a post-camp travelling companion. In the opinion of most gap year travellers who have worked on summer camps, the amazing travel opportunities after camp justify all the hard work.

After the first year of her software engineering course at Birmingham University, Victoria Jossel spent a wonderful summer in the US with Camp America which she felt really enhanced her CV:

On June 9th, I apprehensively boarded my flight to Blue Star camp in North Carolina. Not only did I have the privilege of bonding with the children in my cabin from whom you receive constant love, caring and attention, but I also met new people from all over the world and received amazing references for my future career. I learned how to organise, motivate and lead people as well as negotiate positive outcomes to conflicts. From a normal 19 year old girl, I became a responsible, motivated, adaptable and independent person with 14 children who were my responsibility. I had never been camping and had never wanted to go camping. Yet it was the most amazing experience: I learned to start a fire on my own, cook food for all 14 girls and organise it so the kids all got EXACTLY the same amount of Hershey's chocolate.

In addition to BUNAC and Camp America, *Camp Counselors USA (CCUSA)* places young people aged 18-30 and recruits from over 60 countries. CCUSA's programme includes return flight to the US, one night's accommodation in New York City, visas and insurance, full board and lodging during placement as well as the chance to earn $675-$875 as a first year counsellor depending on your age (as of 1st June), experience, qualifications and whether you've been a camp counsellor in the US before. Enquiries should be made as early as possible to Camp Counselors (CCUSA), Devon House, 171/177 Great Portland St, London W1W 5PQ (020-7637 0779; info@ccusa.co.uk). Early applicants pay a lower registration fee than later ones. The deadline for applications is April 1st.

Other Work Programmes

The other principal work and travel programmes (as distinct from career-oriented internship programmes described in the next section) are those of *IST Plus* (Rosedale House, Rosedale Road, Richmond, Surrey TW9 2SZ; 020-8939 9057; info@istplus.com) and *Camp Counselors USA* (Devon House, 171/177 Great Portland St, London, W1W 5PQ (0207-637 0779; info@ccusa.co.uk; www.ccusa.com) which are broadly comparable. CCUSA's *Work Experience USA* or WEUSA programme and IST Plus's *Work and Travel USA* programme provide students aged 18 to 30 with the opportunity to live and work in the US during the summer. Students in their year out are eligible provided they can prove that they are returning to full-time education. Participants on Work and Travel USA are free to find their own summer jobs before departure and are required to show minimum back-up funds. The fee starts at £390 excluding travel.

The CCUSA programme works with up to 100 employers in resort and vacation centres throughout the United States to find placements for participants. The 'security' programme guarantees a job to those who are accepted and costs £515 whereas to undertake the job hunt independently costs £335. The total package includes a Directory of Employers, four months insurance and visa sponsorship. Most recruitment takes place before April 1st. The company has a network of interviewers around the UK and organises various open houses and recruitment fairs.

Gwendalyne in London (020-8297 3251; www.gwendalyne.com) co-operates with Intrax in San Francisco (www.intraxinc.com) to run a Work/Travel Programme as well as the International Career Training Program (mentioned below).

INTERNSHIPS and WORK EXPERIENCE

Internship is the American term for traineeship, normally unpaid, providing a chance to get some experience in your career interest as part of your academic course. These are typically available to undergraduates and recent graduates rather than to school leavers.

Several organisations in the UK arrange for students and graduates to undertake internships in the US. These agencies help students, graduates and young professionals to arrange career-related work placements in the US lasting from 3 to 18 months. The placement can take place at any time during studies, during a sandwich year or after graduating. Although you are responsible for finding your own placement, the sponsoring organisation usually assists in the job search as part of the programme by offering a searchable database of internships/work placements, job advice, CV writing feedback and so on. Those who qualify get a J-1 visa allowing them to work in the USA for up to 18 months. Typical programme fees start at £300 for a stay of up to two months.

The following organisations may be of interest:

Alliance Abroad Group (1221 South Mopac Expressway, Suite 250, Austin, Texas 78746; 512-457-8062/ 1-888-6-ABROAD; www.allianceabroad.com) is accredited to grant J-1 visas to European candidates. Internships in Denver, San Francisco and Washington DC.

CDS International (871 United Nations Plaza, 15th floor, New York, NY 10017-1814; 212-497-3500; www.cdsintl.org) offers practical training placements in the US in a variety of fields including business, engineering and technology. The opportunities for internships are open to young professionals, aged 21-35.

Cultural Cube (16 Acland Rd, Ivybridge, Devon PO21 9UR; www.culturalcube.co.uk)

runs internship programmes for the hospitality industry and in business. Internships are available for 12 or 18 months, usually based in and around Atlanta. Approximate 12-month inclusive programme fee is £2000; monthly stipend $400 or $750 with accommodation included.

Cultural Homestay International (104 Butterfield Road, San Anselmo, CA 94960; 415-459-5397; chimain@chinet.org/ www.chinet.org) manages a Work and Travel Programme for full-time university students and two Internship Trainee programmes for qualifying candidates; the short-term one called 'STEP' (1, 2 or 3 months) is for any students or recent graduates aged 20-30 and the intensive one lasting 6-18 months is for graduates and young professionals aged 22-35 (fee $3000+). CHI also operates Academic High School, Au Pair and Summer Camp Counselor programmes. CHI was founded in 1980 and handles about 15,000 participants per year from 42 countries.

Gwendalyne (c/o Twin Training and Travel Ltd, 2nd Floor, 67-71 Lewisham High St, Lewisham, London SE13 5JX; 020-8297 3251; www.gwendalyne.com). Newly launched Outbound department of Twin Training & Travel offering 'Work & Travel USA' and 'Career Training USA' programmes.

InterExchange (161 Sixth Avenue, New York, NY 10013; www.interexchange.org).

International Employment Training, a division of the Work & Travel Company, assists anyone with a degree from a recognised UK university and some work experience in a chosen field to find a placement with a US company for 3-18 months; details from IET, 45 High St, Tunbridge Wells, Kent TN1 1XL (www.jobsamerica.co.uk). Fees vary from free (for arborists) to £1178 for 18 months of a self-arranged placement, for example in the hotels industry. Wages are paid on a par with US co-workers.

IST Plus (Rosedale House, Rosedale Road, Richmond, Surrey TW9 2SZ; 020-8939 9057; info@istplus.com). Helps full-time students and recent graduates to arrange course-related placements in the US lasting 3 to 18 months. The placement can take place at any time during your studies, during the summer, as a sandwich year or up to 12 months after graduating. Although you are responsible for finding your own course-related position, CIEE through its partner agency, IST Plus supplies practical advice on applying for work and a searchable database of internships/work placements. Those who qualify get a J-1 visa. The programme fees start at £405.

Kingsbrook USA Inc, PMB 117, 303 B Anastasia Boulevard, St Augustine, FL 32080 (904-46-429; Kbamericainc@aol.com/ www.kingsbrookusa.com). Various incoming programmes including paid internships in the American hospitality industry for 12-18 months and also summer hotel jobs in USA for enrolled university students only (3-5 months). Can organise H-2B visas for seasonal work in ski resorts (the H-2B is for temporary or seasonal vacancies that employers have trouble filling with US citizens).

Mountbatten Internship Programme (Abbey House, 74-76 St John St, 5th Floor, London EC1M 4DZ; 020-7253 7759; www.mountbatten.org). Work experience in New York City for about 120 people aged 21-28 with business training and in the majority of cases a university degree. Placements last one year and provide free accommodation as well as a monthly allowance of about $900. Interns pay a participation fee of £1955 (from September 2005).

UK/US Career Development Programme is administered by the Association for International Practical Training (AIPT) in Maryland (www.aipt.org). This programme is for people aged 18-35 with relevant qualifications and/or at least one year of work experience in their career field. A separate section of the programme is for full-time students in Hospitality & Tourism or Equine Studies.

Young people with an aptitude for working in agriculture or horticulture may be eligible for the International Agricultural Exchange Association (IAEA) exchange (see entry for *Agriventure* in the 'Directory of Work Experience Abroad'). With at least one year's practical agricultural experience you may be able to apply for an equine traineeship through *IEPUK (see entry*

Young people with an aptitude for working in agriculture or horticulture may be eligible for the International Agricultural Exchange Association (IAEA) exchange (see entry for

Agriventure in the 'Directory of Work Experience Abroad'). With at least one year's practical agricultural experience you may be eligible for an equine traineeship through *IEPUK* (see entry in 'Directory of Work Experience').

The 764-page book *Internships* published by Peterson's Guides lists intern positions which are paid or unpaid, can last for the summer, for a semester or for a year. The book offers general advice (including a section called 'Foreign Applicants for US Internships') and specific listings organised according to field of interest, e.g. Advertising, Museums, Radio, Social Services, Law, etc. This annually revised book is available in the UK from Vacation-Work for £19.99 plus £3 postage.

After a consultation with 'Taking Off', a consultancy near Boston, **Elisabeth Weiskittel** fixed up a short internship at the Ocean Mammal Institute (www.oceanmammalinst.com) on the island of Maui in Hawaii in the middle of her gap year. Every January, the woman in charge of the Institute takes some of her students and a few interns (often people taking a year off) to Hawaii for three weeks; the 2006 fee is $2000:

> *The purpose of the Institute was to study humpbacked whales and the effects of nearby boats on their behaviour. Our data was intended to support a pending law restricting the use of speedboats and other craft in these small bays where the whales and calves were swimming. One group watched and recorded the whales' behaviour in the morning and had the afternoon off, and the other group watched in the afternoon and had the morning off. I had no problem adjusting to life in Hawaii. Most people were there to get a tan and go to bars, but even if that's not your scene it's still lots of fun in Hawaii. During our last week there was a large conference on environmental issues, which all the interns were invited to attend. Some of the speakers were well-known, and one or two spoke to our group, such as the founder of Greenpeace. When the internship ended, I flew back home to New York for a few days to do my laundry and repack, and then continued my gap year in Italy.*

HOMESTAYS & COURSES

Secondary school students who want to spend up to a year living with an American family and attending high school in the US should consider the programmes offered by the following:

Aspect Foundation, 350 Sansome St, Suite 740, San Francisco, CA 94104 (415-228-8050/toll-free 800-879-6884/fax 415-228-8051; exchange@aspectworld.com/ www.aspectfoundation.org). Inbound homestay programme for 15-18½ year olds and a college programme for those aged 18-21 who have finished secondary school in their country. Most participants are from non-English speaking countries.

Cultural Homestay International, 104 Butterfield Road, San Anselmo, CA 94960, USA (415-459-5397; chimain@chinet.org/ www.chinet.org).

Educational Resource Development Trust (ERDT), 475 Washington Blvd, Suite 220, Marina del Rey, CA 90292 (310-821-9977; rriske@erdtshare.org). Short-term homestays and farm or ranch stays for ages 15-18.

EIL, 287 Worcester Rd, Malvern, Worcs. WR14 1AB (0800 018 4015; www.eiluk.org). Runs an Academic Year Programme for students aged 16-19. Programme fees depend on length of placement.

English-Speaking Union, Dartmouth House, 37 Charles Street, London W1J 5ED (020-7529 1550/fax 020-7495 6108; www.esu.org). 30 British gap year students are offered two or three term scholarships to a private school in the USA (or Canada).

WISE (Worldwide International Student Exchange), PO Box 1332, Dyersburg, TN 38025 (731-287-9948; wise@wisefoundation.com). 5 or 10 month academic stays in the USA for 15-18 year olds.

Childcare

The au pair placement programme allows thousands of young Europeans with childcare references to work for American families for exactly one year on a J-1 visa. They apply through a small number of sponsoring organisations which must follow the guidelines which govern the programme, so there is not much difference between them. The arrangement differs from au pairing in Europe since the hours are much longer and, if the au pair comes from the UK, there is no language to learn.

The basic requirements are that you be between 18 and 26, speak English, show two childcare references, have a clean driving licence plus at least 50 hours of driving experience and provide a criminal record check. The childcare experience can consist of regular babysitting, helping at a local crèche or school, etc. Anyone wanting to care for a child under two must have 200 hours of experience looking after children under two and must expect the programme interviewers to delve into the experience you claim to have. The majority of candidates are young women though men with relevant experience (e.g. sole care of children under five) may be placed. (It is still not unusual to have just a handful of blokes out of hundreds of au pairs.)

The job entails working up to 45 hours a week (including babysitting) with at least one and a half days off per week plus one complete weekend off a month. Successful applicants receive free return flights from one of many European cities, four-day orientation in New York which covers child safety and development, and support from a community counsellor. The counsellor's role is to advise on any problems and organise meetings with other au pairs in your area. Applicants are required to pay a good faith deposit of $400 which is returned to them at the end of 12 months but which is forfeit if the terms of the programme are broken. Some programmes charge an additional fee.

The fixed amount of pocket money for au pairs is $139.05 a week which, although it hasn't gone up for seven years, is not an unreasonable wage on top of room, board and perks. An additional $500 is paid by the host family to cover the cost of educational courses (three hours a week during term-time) which must be attended as a condition of the visa. Au pairs are at liberty to travel for a month after their contract is over but no visa extension is available beyond that.

As in all au pair-host family relationships, problems do occur and it is not unusual for au pairs to chafe against rules, curfews and expectations in housework, etc. When speaking to your family on the telephone during the application period, ask as many day-to-day questions as possible, and try to establish exactly what will be expected of you, how many nights babysitting at weekends, restrictions on social life, use of the car, how private are the living arrangements, etc. The counsellors and advisers provided by the sending organisations should be able to sort out problems and in extreme cases can find alternative families. Consider carefully the pros and cons of the city you will be going to. **Emma Purcell** was not altogether happy to be sent to Memphis Tennesee which she describes as the 'most backward and redneck city in the USA':

> I was a very naïve 18 year old applying to be an au pair for a deferred year before university. During my eight months so far, I have experienced highs and lows. I have been very lucky with my host family who have made me feel one of the family. I have travelled the USA and Mexico frequently staying in suites and being treated as royalty since my host dad is president of Holiday Inn. On the bad side, I have lost numerous friends who have not had such good luck. One was working 60 hours a week (for no extra pay) with the brattiest children, so she left. Another girl from Australia lasted six months with her neurotic family who yelled at her for not cleaning the toaster daily and for folding the socks wrong. Finally she plucked up the courage to talk to her host parents and their immediate response was to throw her out. A very strong personality is required to be an au pair for a year in the States.

About half a dozen agencies in the UK send au pairs to the US, and it is worth comparing their literature. The *Au Pair in America* programme (see 'Directory of Specialist Gap Year Programmes') is the largest organisation placing in excess of 4500 young people in au pair and nanny placements throughout the country. Brochures and application forms can be requested on 020-7581 7322 or online at www.aupairinamerica.co.uk. It has representatives in Europe, South Africa, Australia, etc. and agent/interviewers throughout the UK and worldwide. The programme operates under the auspices of the American Institute for Foreign Study or AIFS (37 Queens Gate, London SW7 5HR) though some of the selection has been devolved to independent au pair agencies such as Childcare International Ltd, Trafalgar House, Grenville Place, London NW7 3SA (020-8906 3116; www.childint.co.uk). Au Pair in America also has representatives in more than 50 countries and agent/interviewers throughout the UK.

Other active au pair Exchange Visitor Programmes are smaller but may be able to offer a more personal service and more choice in the destination and family you work for:

Au Pair Care, 600 California Street, Floor 10, San Francisco, CA 94108 (415-434-8788; www.aupaircare.com).

EurAupair, 238 North Coast Highway, Laguna Beach, CA 92651 (949-494-7355; www. euraupair.com). Plus three other regional offices in US. UK partner is EurAupair UK, 17 Wheatfield Drive, Shifnal, Shropshire TF11 8HL (01952 460733/ maureen@asseuk. freeserve.co.uk).

Global Choices, Barkat House, 116-118 Finchley Road, London NW3 5HT (020-7433 2501; info@globalchoices.co.uk).

goAUPAIR, 111 East 12300 South, Draper, UT 84020 (1-888-287-2471; 2baupair@goaupair. com; www.goaupair.com).

InterExchange, 13th Floor, 161 Sixth Avenue, New York, NY 10013 (212-926-0446; www. interexchange.org).

TRAVEL

If you intend to travel widely in the States check out air passes from any branch of STA Travel. Bus passes have already been mentioned in the 'Travel' chapter. College notice boards and student common rooms often carry notices posted by people looking for or offering rides, particularly at weekends. A contribution to the petrol will be expected, but this is vastly preferable to hitch-hiking which is decidedly dodgy in the US.

Escorted trips aimed at young people might appeal, for example those offered by Trekamerica (www.trekamerica.com) or Green Tortoise (494 Broadway, San Francisco, CA 94133; 800-867-8647; www.greentortoise.com) which uses vehicles converted to sleep about 35 people and which make interesting detours and stopovers.

Drive-Aways

The term 'drive-away' applies to the widespread practice of delivering private cars within North America. Prosperous Americans and Canadians and also companies are prepared to pay several hundred dollars to delivery firms who agree to arrange delivery of private vehicles to a different city, usually because the car-owner wants his or her car available at their holiday destination but doesn't want to drive it personally. The companies find drivers (an estimated three-quarters of whom are not American), arrange insurance and arbitrate in the event of mishaps. You get free use of a car (subject to mileage and time restrictions) and pay for all gas after the first tankful and tolls on the interstates. Usually a time deadline and mileage limit are fixed, though these are often flexible and checks lax. A good time to be travelling east to west or north to south (e.g. Chicago to Phoenix) is September/October when a lot of older people head to a warmer climate. On the other hand, when there is a shortage of vehicles (e.g. leaving New York in the summer), you will be lucky to get a car on any terms.

Unfortunately most companies are looking for drivers over the age of 21, so year-out students aren't eligible. If you (or an older friend) are interested in pursuing this, look up 'Automobile Transporters and Driveaway Companies' in the *Yellow Pages* of any big city. Companies to try are:

Auto Driveaway Company – www.autodriveaway.com; 800-621-4155. Available cars are listed on the website (updated daily) and it is possible to sign up online. In some cases fuel costs are covered. Website gives numbers of branch offices from Salt Lake City to Syracuse, Tucson to Toronto.

Across America Driveaway – www.transportautos.com/driveaway.htm; 800-677-6686.

SEASONAL JOBS

Labour demands in summer resorts sometimes reach crisis proportions especially along the eastern seaboard. Time can productively be spent searching the internet. Dozens of sites may prove useful, though www.coolworks.com and www.jobmonkey.com are especially recommended for seasonal jobs in the tourist industry.

The majority of catering staff are paid the minimum wage, and some are paid less. Because tipping is so generous, employers can get away with offering derisory wages, e.g. $10 for an evening shift. In fact the legal minimum hourly wage for tipped employees is less than half of the standard minimum. The standard minimum wage is $5.15 an hour, though some states have legislated a higher wage, e.g. $6.75 in California, $7.10 in Connecticut, and so on. However workers aged under 20 may be paid the youth minimum of $4.25 for the first 90 days of their employment. These can be checked on the Department of Labor's website (www.dol.gov/esa/minwage/america.htm).

Live-in jobs are probably preferable, and are often available to British students whose terms allow them to stay beyond Labor Day, the first Monday in September, when most American students resume their studies. After working a season at a large resort in Wisconsin, **Timothy Payne** concluded:

> *Without doubt the best jobs in the USA are to be found in the resorts, simply because they pay a reasonable wage as well as providing free food and accommodation. Since many resorts are located in remote spots, it is possible to save most of your wages and tips, and also enjoy free use of the resort's facilities. Whatever job you end up with you should have a good time due to the large number of students working there.*

Popular resorts are often a sure bet, especially if you arrive in mid-August (when American students begin to leave jobs), or in April/May (before they arrive). **Katherine Smith**, who got her J-1 visa through BUNAC, describes the range of jobs she found in Ocean City, a popular seaside resort in Maryland which absorbs a large number of Britons:

> *I decided to spend my summer in Ocean Beach because I knew the job scene would be favourable. I found a job as a waitress in a steak restaurant and another full-time job as a reservations clerk in a hotel by approaching employers on an informal basis and enquiring about possible job vacancies. In my case this was very fruitful and I found two relatively well-paid jobs which I enjoyed very much. Other jobs available included fairground attendant, fast food sales assistant, lifeguard, kitchen assistant, chambermaid and every other possible type of work associated with a busy oceanside town. Ocean City was packed with foreign workers. As far as I know, none had any trouble finding work; anyone could have obtained half a dozen jobs. Obviously the employers are used to a high turnover of workers, especially if the job is boring. So it's not difficult to walk out of a job on a day's notice and into another one. It really was a great place to spend the summer. I would recommend a holiday resort to anyone wishing to work hard and have a really wild time.*

Other resorts to try are Wildwood (New Jersey), Virginia Beach (Virginia), Myrtle Beach (South Carolina) and Atlantic Beach (North Carolina).

The International Casting Department of Walt Disney's EPCOT Center (PO Box 10090, Lake Buena Vista, Florida 32830-0090; fax 407-828-3330; http://disney.go.com/disneycareers/wdwcareers/international/index.html) prefers to rely on the word-of-mouth network rather than to publicise their six-month or one-year vacancies for young people to work as 'cultural representatives'. People aged 18-28 from the UK and about a dozen other countries are hired to represent the culture and customs of their countries; in the case of the UK this means *olde worlde* pubs, Scotch eggs and Royal Doulton china. Anyone applying will have to wait until a Disney recruiter comes to your country. Contact details are provided on the above website. In the UK, the annual recruiting presentations normally take place in March and October; for details contact Yummy Jobs (The Georgian Village, Unit 5, 100 Wood Street, London, E17 3HX; 020-8521 9615; www.yummyjobs.com). Any job which involves tips is usually more lucrative than others; wages can be swelled by more than $100 in a five-hour shift. The staff facilities are attractive with pools, jacuzzis, tennis courts and subsidised rent.

Paul Binfield from Kent describes the process of being hired by Disney as 'a long and patient' one:

> I initially wrote to Disney in October and started my contract in January, 15 months later. It was the most enjoyable year of my life, experiencing so many excellent things and making the best friends from all over the world. The pros far outweigh the cons, though some people did hate the work. Disney are a strict company with many rules which are vigorously enforced. The work in merchandising or the pub/restaurant is taken extremely seriously and sometimes it can be hard to manufacture a big cheesy Disney smile. There are dress codes (for example men have to be clean shaven every day), and verbal and written warnings for matters which would be considered very trivial in Britain, and indeed terminations (which is a very nasty word for being fired). If you go with the right attitude it can be great fun.

Advertisements for sales positions proliferate. You may find telesales less off-putting than door-to-door salesmanship, but it will also be less lucrative. On the other hand, some gap year students do not shy away from the hard edge of selling and tackle commission-only jobs. The Southwestern Company with its headquarters in Nashville markets educational books and software door-to-door throughout the US and has a recruitment office in the UK (Unit 4, Bakers Park, Cater Rd, Bishopworth, Bristol BS13 7TT; 0117-978 2121) which targets gap year students. Its website (www.southwestern.com) contains glowing reports from past students whose earnings have been impressive. They claim that the average seller earns more than $100 a day. Their statistics possibly exclude all the students who give up in disgust after a few weeks of failure.

An offbeat suggestion has been proffered by Mark Kinder who wrote from rural Maryland:

> After spending the summer on the Camp America programme, a friend and I decided to do a parachute jump. Once you have made about ten jumps, the instructors expect you to learn how to pack parachutes, which takes about five hours to learn. Once you have learnt how to pack you get paid $5 per chute cash and with a bit of practice can pack three or four chutes an hour which is good money. I would say that 90% of parachute centres in the US pay people cash for packing the chutes but you generally have to be a skydiver to do the job. It is definitely a fun way of earning money. Skydivers are very friendly people and are thrilled to meet foreigners, so they will often offer a place to stay. If not, you can always camp at the parachute centre.

A list of the 275 parachute centres in the US can be obtained from the national association USPA, 1440 Duke St, Alexandria, VA 22314 or via the Drop Zone Directory section of their website www.uspa.org/dz.

Soccer Coaching

Soccer is fast gaining popularity in North America, and demand is strong for young British coaches to work on summer coaching schemes. A number of companies recruit players to work regionally or throughout the country including Hawaii:

Britannia Soccer, 10281 Frosty Court, Suite 100, Manassas, VA 20109, USA (703-330-2532; www.britanniasoccerusa.com). See entry in 'Directory of Paid Seasonal Jobs'.
Goal-Line Soccer Clinics, PO Box 1642, Corvallis, OR 97339 (541-753-5833; info@goal-line.com; www.goal-line.com). Minimum age 21. Mostly in Oregon and Washington. Recruits through BUNAC for July and early August only.
Major League Soccer Camps, 47 Water St, Mystic, CT 06355, USA. UK corporate office: MLS Camps, Malmarc House, 116 Dewsbury Rd, Leeds LS11 6XD (0113 272 0616/ 0113 270 4200; employment@mlscamps.com. The largest and best known. Registration fee of £310 includes flights from UK, rental car and gas expenses plus at least $150 per week. MLSC assists with processing of H-2B visas.
Soccer Academy Inc, PO Box 3046, Manassas, VA 20108, USA (fax 703-393-1361; pellis@soccer-academy.com/ www.soccer-academy.com).
Others advertise in the specialist press. It is more important to be good at working with kids than to be a great football player, though of course it is easier to command the respect of the kids if you can show them good skills and a few tricks.

> **Among the many things Theo West did in his gap year before going to Liverpool University, he coached soccer and describes the application process and the job itself:**
> *The procedure involved in getting a place is time-consuming and difficult but well worth the effort. It includes an interview to see if you have the right personality and experience in coaching followed by a couple of coaching days where you are evaluated at close quarters by senior coaches (which proved a slight problem for me since my home is in Inverness and the nearest coaching day was in Newcastle). Finally you accept a contract, list preferred working locations, pay a membership (which covers flights to the US), apply for a J-1 visa through BUNAC and attend an induction.*
> *On arrival in America we were briefed on where our first week-long assignment was to be and given our coaching equipment. The next day we headed off in hire cars for Monroe Woodbury, a rich area in upstate New York where we were introduced to the families which were to put us up for a week. In terms of pay it was not great but the benefits generally come from the families that house you, feed you and entertain you. The benefits of an English accent in America are still many. I spent five weeks coaching in New York, Connecticut and finally worked with under-privileged kids in New Jersey. It was an amazing and draining experience as I got to meet many great people, saw some wonderful sights and negotiated myself with some difficulty into a number of bars (the strictness of the adherence to the 21 age limit for drinking proved annoying).*

VOLUNTARY WORK

The three main workcamp organisations in the USA (see chapter 'A Year Off for North Americans') have incoming programmes as well as outgoing, though prospective volunteers should register through a workcamp organisation in their own country. For example *Volunteers for Peace* (www.vfp.org) place about 500 foreign volunteers on 40-50 workcamps in the US. *CIEE* accepts around 200 individuals from abroad over the age of 18 to participate in its international voluntary service projects. In the past, volunteers have been placed on environmental projects in Yosemite National Park, the Golden Gate

National Seashore and northern Idaho's Kaniksu National Forest, assisted with urban renovation and preservation of historic landmarks in New York and New Jersey, and worked with disabled children and adults on their summer holidays.

Voluntary opportunities in the US range from the intensely urban to the decidedly rural. In the former category, you can build houses in deprived areas throughout the US with *Habitat for Humanity* (Global Village, 121 Habitat St, Americus, GA 31709; www.habitat. org) or work with inner city youth, the homeless, etc. in New York City with the *Winant Clayton Volunteers*; send an s.a.e. for an application pack to WCVA, St. Margaret's House, 21 Old Ford Road, Bethnal Green, London E2 9PL; 020-8983 3834; wcva@dircon.co.uk). Volunteers with a British passport are recruited to work for eight weeks from mid or late June followed by two or three weeks of travel.

Camphill Special School Beaver Run offers volunteers an opportunity to experience a unique method of living, learning and working together with developmentally delayed children and youth in a beautiful community setting in Pennsylvania. Volunteers are encouraged to come for at least six months, preferably one year. They offer room and board, a monthly stipend, health insurance and car use. Details are available from www.beaverrun. org or contact Anne Sproll at Bvolunteer@aol.com (610-469-6993).

The General Convention of Sioux YMCAs in South Dakota offers summer camp and longer positions (February-October). Volunteers live in rural Native American communities in order to help run the local YMCA Youth Center, working with Lakota children, families and schools. The Y provides housing, a small living stipend and cultural training. Contact the YMCA for application details: PO Box 218, Dupree, South Dakota 57623 (605-365-5232; www.siouxymca.org/volunteers.htm). International applications are accepted via the YMCA International Camp Counselor Program (ICCP, 5 West 63 St, New York, NY 10023-9197; www.ymcaiccp.org).

The American Hiking Society collates volunteer opportunities from around the United States to build, maintain and restore foot trails in America's backcountry. No prior trail work experience is necessary, but volunteers should be able to hike at least five miles a day, supply their own backpacking equipment (including tent), pay a $120 registration fee and arrange transport to and from the work site. Food is provided on some projects. For a schedule of projects, go to www.AmericanHiking.org or send an s.a.e. to AHS, Volunteer Vacations, 1422 Fenwick Lane, Silver Spring, MD 20910 (301-565-6704).

The Student Conservation Association Inc. (SCA, 689 River Road, PO Box 550, Charlestown, NH 03603-0550; 603-543-1700; www.thesca.org) places anyone 18 or older in conservation and environmental internships in national parks and forests nationwide. Position lengths vary from 12 weeks to 12 months and travel expenses, housing, training and a weekly stipend are provided. The SCA website includes a searchable database of open positions as well as an application form.

Part IV

Appendices

Currency Conversion Chart

Embassies/Consulates in London

Address List of Organisations

Appendix I

Currency Conversion Chart

COUNTRY	£1	US$1
Eurozone	1.51 Euro	0.83 Euro
Argentina	5.2 peso	2.9 peso
Australia	A$2.36	A$1.30
Brazil	4.4 real	2.4 real
Canada	C$2.24	C$1.23
Chile	1,057 peso	581 peso
China	15 renminbi	8.3 renminbi
Costa Rica	870 colon	478 colon
Czech Republic	45 koruna	25 koruna
Denmark	11.2 kroner	6.2 kroner
Ecuador	1.82 US dollar	1 US dollar
Egypt	10.5 Egyptian pound	5.8 Egyptian pound
Hong Kong	14 HK dollar	7.8 HK dollar
Hungary	373 forint	205 forint
India	79 rupee	44 rupee
Israel	8.3 new shekel	4.5 new shekel
Japan	199 yen	109 yen
Korea	1,845 won	1,012 won
Malta	0.65 Maltese lira	0.36 Maltese lira
Mexico	19.6 peso	10.8 peso
Morocco	16.5 dirham	9.1 dirham
Nepal	129 rupee	71 rupee
New Zealand	NZ$2.57	NZ$1.42
Norway	12 krone	6.6 krone
Poland	6.1 zloty	3.3 zloty
Russia	52 rouble	28.6 rouble
Slovakia	58 koruna	32 koruna
South Africa	12.2 rand	6.7 rand
Sweden	14.2 krona	7.8 krona
Switzerland	2.33 franc	1.28 franc
Thailand	75 baht	41 baht
Turkey	2.47 new lira	1.35 new lira
USA	1.82 dollar	–
UK	–	0.55 pence

Current exchange rates are available on the internet, for example at www.oanda.com or the Universal Currency Converter at www.xe.net/ucc.

Appendix II

Embassies/Consulates in London

AUSTRALIA: Australia House, The Strand, London WC2B 4LA ; www.australia.org.uk.

AUSTRIA: 18 Belgrave Mews West, London SW1X 8HU. Tel: 020-7235 3731; www.austria. org.uk.

BELGIUM: 103-105 Eaton Square, London SW1W 9AB. Tel: 020-7470 3700; www.belgium-embassy.co.uk.

BRAZIL: Consular Section, 6 St. Alban's St, London SW1Y 4SG. Tel: 020-7930 9055; www. brazil.org.uk.

CANADA: 38 Grosvenor St, London W1X 0AA. Tel: 020-7258 6600; www.dfait-maeci.gc.ca/london.

CHILE: 12 Devonshire St, London W1G 2DS. Tel: 020-7580 1023; e-mail: cglonduk@congechileuk. demon.co.uk; www.echileuk.demon.co.uk.

CHINA: Visa Section, 31 Portland Place, London W1N 3AG. Tel: 020-7631 1430; www.chinese-embassy.org.uk.

COSTA RICA: Flat 1, 14 Lancaster Gate, London W2 3LH. Tel: 020-7706 8844; embcrlon.demon. co.uk.

CZECH REPUBLIC: 26-30 Kensington Palace Gardens, London W8 4QY. Tel: 020-7243 1115.

DENMARK: 55 Sloane St, London SW1X 9SR. Tel: 020-7333 0200; www.denmark.org.uk.

ECUADOR: Flat 3, 3 Hans Crescent, Knightsbridge, London SW1X 0LS. Tel: 020-7584 2648.

EGYPT: 2 Lowndes St, London SW1X 9ET. Tel: 020-7235 9777; www.egypt-embassy.org.uk.

FINLAND: 38 Chesham Place, London SW1X 8HW. Tel: 020-7838 6200; www.finemb.org.uk.

FRANCE: 21 Cromwell Road, London SW7 2EN. Tel: 020-7838 2000; www.ambafrance-uk.org.

GERMANY: 23 Belgrave Square, London SW1X 8PZ. Tel: 020-7824 1300/0906-833 1166; www.german-embassy.org.uk.

GREECE: 1A Holland Park, London W11 3TP. Tel: 020-7221 6467; www.greekembassy.org. uk.

HUNGARY: 35b Eaton Place, London SW1X 8BY. Tel: 020-7235 2664; http://dspace.dial.pipex. com/huemblon.

INDIA: India House, Aldwych, London WC2B 4NA. Tel: 020-7836 8484; www.hcilondon.net.

ISRAEL: Consular Section, 15a Old Court Place, London W8 4QB. Tel: 020-7957 9516; info@israel-embassy.org.uk.

ITALY: 38 Eaton Place, London SW1X 8AN. Tel: 020-7235 9371; www.embitaly.org.uk/uk.

JAPAN: 101-104 Piccadilly, London W1V 9FN. Tel: 020-7465 6500; www.embjapan. org.uk.

MALTA: Malta House, 36-38 Piccadilly, London W1V 0PQ. Tel: 020-7292 4800/0870 005 6958.

MEXICO: 8 Halkin St, London SW1X 7DW. Tel: 020-7235 6393; www.mexicanconsulate.org.uk.

NEPAL: 12a Kensington Palace Gardens, London W8 4QU. Tel: 020-7229 1594; www. nepembassy.org.uk.

NETHERLANDS: 38 Hyde Park Gate, London SW7 5DP. Tel: 020-7590 3200/09001-171 217; www.netherlands-embassy.org.uk.

NEW ZEALAND: New Zealand House, Haymarket, London SW1Y 4TE. Tel: 0906 9100 100 (£1 a minute); www.nzembassy.com.

NORWAY: 25 Belgrave Square, London SW1X 8QD. Tel: 020-7591 5500; www.norway.org.uk.

PERU: 52 Sloane St, London SW1X 9SP. Tel: 020-7838 9223; www.peruembassy-uk.com.

POLAND: 73 New Cavendish St, London W1N 4HQ. Tel: 020-7580 0476; www.poland-embassy. org.uk.

PORTUGAL: Silver City House, 62 Brompton Road, London SW3 1BJ. Tel: 020-7581 8722; www.portembassy.gla.ac.uk.

RUSSIAN FEDERATION: 5 Kensington Palace Gardens, London W8 4QS. Tel: 020-7229 8027; www.russialink.org.uk.

SLOVAK REPUBLIC: 25 Kensington Palace Gardens, London W8 4QY. Tel: 020-7243 0803; www.slovakembassy.co.uk.

SOUTH AFRICA: South Africa House, Trafalgar Square, London WC2N 5DP. Tel: 020-7451 7299; general@southafricahouse.com.

SPAIN: 20 Draycott Place, London SW3 2RZ. Tel: 020-7917 6400.

SWEDEN: 11 Montagu Place, London W1H 2AL. Tel: 020-7917 6400; www.swedenabroad.

SWITZERLAND: 16/18 Montagu Place, London W1H 2BQ. Tel: 020-7616 6000; www.swissembassy.org.uk.

THAILAND: 29/30 Queen's Gate, London SW7 5JB. Tel: 020-7589 2944.

TURKEY: Rutland Lodge, Rutland Gardens, London SW7 1BW. Tel: 020-7591 6900; www.turkconsulate-london.com.

USA: 5 Upper Grosvenor St, London W1A 2JB. Tel: 09055 444546 (premium line); www.usembassy.org.uk.

Address List

Accenture Horizons School Sponsorship Scheme, 60 Queen Victoria St, London EC4N 4TW (0500 100189; ukgraduates@accenture.com/ www.accenture.com/ukgraduates

Adventure Alternative, 31 Myrtledene Road, Belfast BT8 6GQ (tel/fax 02890 701476; office@adventurealternative.com/ www.adventurealternative.com)

Africa and Asia Venture, 10 Market Place, Devizes, Wiltshire SN10 1HT (01380 729009/ fax 01380 720060; av@aventure.co.uk/ www.aventure.co.uk)

African Conservation Experience, PO Box 206, Faversham, Kent, ME13 8WZ (0870 241 5816; info@ConservationAfrica.net/ www.ConservationAfrica.net)

AfricaTrust Networks, Africatrust Chambers, PO Box 551, Portsmouth, Hants. PO5 1ZN (01873 812453; info@africatrust.gi/ www.africatrust.gi)

AFS Intercultural Programmes UK, Leeming House, Vicar Lane, Leeds LS2 7JF (0113 242 6136/ fax 0113 243 0631; info-unitedkingdom@afs.org/ www.afsuk.org or www. afs.org)

Agriventure, International Agricultural Exchange Association (IAEA), Speedwell Farm Bungalow, Nettle Bank, Wisbech, Cambridgeshire PE14 0SA (tel/fax 01945 450999; uk@agriventure.com/ www.agriventure.com)

AIESEC International Association for Students of Economics and Management, 29-31 Cowper St, 2nd Floor, London EC2A 4AP (020-7549 1700; national@uk.aiesec.org/ www.workabroad.org.uk)

AmeriSpan, PO Box 58129, Philadelphia, PA 19102 or 117 S 17th St, Suite 1401, Philadelphia, PA 19103 (800-879-6640/ fax 215-751-1986; info@amerispan.com/ www.amerispan.com)

Anglo-Polish Universities Association (APASS), 93 Victoria Road, Leeds LS6 1DR (fax 020-7498 7608)

Archaeology Abroad, 31-34 Gordon Square, London WC1H 0PY (020-8537 0849/fax 020-7383 2572; arch.abroad@ucl.ac.uk/ www.britarch.ac.uk/archabroad)

The Army Gap Year Commission, HQ Recruiting Group, ATRA, Bldg 165, Trenchard Lines, Upavon, Wiltshire SN9 6BE (08457 300111/ www.armyofficer.co.uk)

Art History Abroad, 179C New Kings Road, Fulham, London, SW6 4SW (020-7731 2231/ fax 020-7731 2456; info@arthistoryabroad.com/ www.arthistoryabroad.com)

Atlantis Youth Exchange, Rådhusgt 4, 0151 Oslo, Norway (tel/fax 22 47 71 79; atlantis@atlantis.no/ www.atlantis.no)

Au Pair in America, 37 Queen's Gate, London SW7 5HR (020-7581 7322/ fax 020-7581 7355; info@aupairamerica.co.uk/ www.aupairamerica.co.uk)

Azafady, Studio 7, 1A Beethoven St, London W10 4LG (020-8960 6629/ fax 020-8962 0126; mark@azafady.org/ www.madagascar.co.uk)

Base Camp Group, Unit 30, Baseline Business Studios, Whitchurch Road, London W11 4AT (020-7243 6222; contact@basecampgroup.com/ www.basecampgroup.com)

BBC, Work Experience Placements – www.bbc.co.uk/workexperience

Biosphere Expeditions, Sprat's Water, Nr Carlton Colville, The Broads National Park, Suffolk NR33 8BP (01502 583085/ fax 01502 587414; info@biosphere-expeditions. org/ www.biosphere-expeditions.org)

Blue Ventures, 52 Avenue Road, London, N6 5DR (020-8341 9819/ fax 020-8341 4821; enquiries@blueventures.org/ www.blueventures.org)

Brathay Exploration Group, Brathay Hall, Ambleside, Cumbria LA22 0HP (tel/fax 01539 433942; admin@brathayexploration.org.uk/ www.brathayexploration.org.uk)

British Council, 10 Spring Gardens, London SW1A 2BN (Education & Training Group 020-

7389 4596; www.britishcouncil.org).

The British Institute of Florence, Piazza Strozzi 2, 50123, Florence Italy (+39 055-2677 8200/ fax +39 055-2677 8222; info@britishinstitute.it/ www.britishinstitute.it)

British Trust for Conservation Volunteers, BTCV Conservation Centre, Balby Road, Doncaster DN4 0RH (01302 572244/fax 01302 310167; information@btcv.org.uk/ http://shop.btcv.org.uk)

BSES Expeditions, Royal Geographical Society, 1 Kensington Gore, London SW7 2AR (020-7591 3141/ fax 020-7591 3140; info@bses.org.uk/ www.bses.org.uk)

BUNAC, 16 Bowling Green Lane, London EC1R 0QH (020-7251 3472/ fax 020-7251 0215; enquiries@bunac.org.uk/ www.bunac.org)

Cactus Language, 4 Clarence House, 30-31 North St, Brighton BN1 1EB 0845 130 4775/ fax 01273 775868; enquiry@cactuslanguage.com/ www.cactuslanguage.com)

Caledonia Languages Abroad, The Clockhouse, 72 Newhaven Road, Edinburgh EH6 5QG (0131-621 7721/2; courses@caledonialanguages.co.uk/ www.caledonialanguages.co.uk)

Camp America, 37a Queen's Gate, London SW7 5HR (020-7581 7333; brochure@campamerica.co.uk/ www.campamerica.co.uk)

Camp Counselors USA (CCUSA), Devon House, 171/177 Great Portland St, London W1W 5PQ (020-7637 0779/ fax 020-7580 6209; info@ccusa.co.uk/ www.ccusa.com). Northern office: 27 Woodside Gardens, Musselburgh, Scotland EH21 7LJ (0131-665 5843; 101355.257@compuserve.com).

Camps International Ltd, Unit 1, Kingfisher Park, Headlands Business Park, Salisbury Road, Blashford, Ringwood, Hants. BH24 3NX (01425 485390/ fax 01425 485398; info@campsinternational.com/ www.campsinternational.com)

Canvas Holidays, VRG Camping Recruitment, East Port House, 12 East Port, Dunfermline, Fife KY12 7JG (01383 629012; recruitment@vrgcampingrecruitment.com/ www.vrgcampingrecruitment.com)

CESA Languages Abroad, CESA House, Pennance Road, Lanner, Cornwall TR16 5TQ. (01209 211800/ fax 01209 211830; info@cesalanguages.com/ www.cesalanguages.com)

Challenges Worldwide, 13 Hamilton Place, Edinburgh EH3 5BA (tel/fax 0131-332 7372; elizabeth@challengesworldwide.com; www.challengesworldwide.com)

Changing Worlds, Hodore Farm, Hartfield, East Sussex TN7 4AR (01892 770000/ fax 0870 990 9665; welcome@changingworlds.co.uk/ www.changingworlds.co.uk)

CIMO (Centre for International Mobility), PO Box 343, 00531 Helsinki, Finland (+358 1080 6767; http://finland.cimo.fi)

Community Service Volunteers – see CSV

Concordia, 2nd Floor, Heversham House, 20-22 Boundary Road, Hove, East Sussex BN3 4ET (tel/fax 01273 422218; info@concordia-iye.org.uk/ www.concordia-iye.org.uk)

Connect Youth, British Council, 10 Spring Gardens, London SW1A 2BN (020 7389-4030/ fax 020-7389 4033; connectyouth.enquiries@britishcouncil.org/ www.connectyouthinternational.com)

Conservation Volunteers Australia (CVA), National Head Office, Box 423, Ballarat, Vic 3353 (03-5333 2600; www.conservationvolunteers.com.au)

Coral Cay Conservation, The Tower, 13th Floor, 125 High Street, Colliers Wood, London SW19 2JG (0870 750 0668/ fax 0870 750 0667; info@coralcay.org/ www.coralcay.org)

Council for British Archaeology, St Mary's House, 66 Bootham, York YO30 7BZ (01904 671417/ fax 01904 671384; info@britarch.ac.uk/ www.britarch.ac.uk)

Cross-Cultural Solutions, UK Office: Tower Point 44, North Road, Brighton BN1 1YR (0845 458 2781/2; infouk@crossculturalsolutions.org/ www.crossculturalsolutions.org)

CSV – Community Service Volunteers, 5th Floor, Scala House, 36 Holloway Circus, Queensway, Birmingham B1 1EQ (0800 374991; volunteer@csv.org.uk/ www.csv.org.uk)

Cultural Cube Ltd, 16 Acland Road, Ivybridge, Devon PL21 9UR (0870 742 6932/ fax 0870 742 6935; info@culturalcube.co.uk/ www.culturalcube.co.uk)

Daneford Trust, 45-47 Blythe Street, London E2 6LN (tel/fax 020-7729 1928; info@danefordtrust.org/ www.danefordtrust.org)

Deloitte, Stonecutter Court, 1 Stonecutter Street, London EC4A 4TR (020-7303 7019/ fax 020-7007 3465; hmanthorpe@deloitte.co.uk/ www.deloitte.co.uk/scholars)

Development in Action, Voluntary Services Unit, UCL Union, 25 Gordon St, London WC1H 0AY (07813 395957; info@developmentinaction.org/ www.developmentinaction.org)

Disneyland Paris, Service du Recrutement-Casting, BP 110, 77777 Marne-la-Vallée Cedex 4, France (www.disneylandparis.com/uk/employment)

Disney World, EPCOT Center, PO Box 10090, Lake Buena Vista, Florida 32830-0090, USA (fax 407-828-3330; http://disney.go.com/disneycareers/wdwcareers/international/index.html)

Don Quijote, 2-4 Stoneleigh Park Road, Epsom, Surrey KT19 0QT (020-8786 8081/ fax 020-8786 8086; uk@donquijote.org/ www.donquijote.org)

Earthwatch Institute (Europe), 267 Banbury Road, Oxford OX2 7HT (01865 318838/ fax 01865 311383; info@earthwatch.org.uk/ www.earthwatch.org/europe)

Eco Africa Experience/Worldwide Experience, Guardian House, Borough Road, Godalming, Surrey GU7 2AE (01483 860560/ fax 01483 860391; info@WorldwideExperience.com/ www.WorldwideExperience.com)

Ecologia Trust, The Park, Forres, Moray, Scotland IV36 3TZ (tel/fax 01309 690995; gap@ecologia.org.uk/ www.ecologia.org.uk)

Edinburgh School of Food & Wine, The Coach House, Newliston, Edinburgh EH29 9EB (0131-333 5001; info@esfw.com/ www.esfw.com)

EF Gap Year, Dudley House, 36-38 Southampton St, London WC2E 7HF (freephone 0800 0683385/ fax 020-7836 7334; eflanguages@ef.com/ www.ef.com)

EIL: Experiment in International Living, 287 Worcester Road, Malvern, Worcs. WR14 1AB (0800 018 4015/ 01684 562577/ fax 01684 562212; info@eiluk.org/ www.eiluk.org)

English Speaking Union, Dartmouth House, 37 Charles Street, London W1J 5ED (020-7529 1550/ fax 020-7495 6108; education@esu.org/ www.esu.org)

Euro-Academy Ltd, 67-71 Lewisham High St, London SE13 5JX (020-8297 0505/ fax 020-8297 0984; euroacademy@twinuk.com/ www.euroacademy.co.uk)

Eurocamp Holidays, (Ref TGY/05), Hartford Manor, Greenbank Lane, Northwich, Cheshire CW8 1HW (01606 787525; www.holidaybreakjobs.com)

Eurolingua, 61 Bollin Drive, Altrincham WA14 5QW (tel/fax 0161-972 0225; info@eurolingua.com/ www.eurolingua.com/Work_Experience.htm)

European Commission, Bureau des Stages, 200 Rue de la Loi, 1049 Brussels, Belgium (02-299 23 39/ fax 02-299 23 40; eac-stages@cec.eu.int/ www.cec.org.uk/work/stage.htm)

European Voluntary Service, see Connect Youth above.

Flying Fish, 25 Union Road, Cowes, Isle of Wight PO31 7TW (0871 250 2500/ fax 01983 281821; mail@flyingfishonline.com/ www.flyingfishonline.com)

French Encounters, 63 Fordhouse Road, Bromsgrove, Worcestershire B60 2LU (01527 873645/ fax 01527 832794; admin@frenchencounters.com/ www.frenchencounters.com)

Friends of Israel Educational Foundation, Bridge Programme, PO Box 7545, London NW2 2QZ (020-7435 6803/ fax 020-7794 0291; info@foi-asg.org/ www.foi-asg.org)

Frontier, 50-52 Rivington St, London EC2A 3QP (020-7613 2422; info@frontier.ac.uk/ www.frontier.ac.uk)

Gala Spanish in Spain, 8 Leigh Lane, Farnham, Surrey GU9 8HP (tel/fax 01252 715319)

GAP Activity Projects, 44 Queen's Road, Reading, RG1 4BB (0118 959 4914/ fax 0118 957 6634; Volunteer@gap.org.uk/ www.gap.org.uk)

Gap Enterprise Consultants, East Manor Barn, Fringford, Oxfordshire OX27 8DG (01869 278346; johnvessey@gapenterprise.co.uk/ www.gapenterprise.co.uk)

Gap Guru, Futuresense Ltd. 6 Forest Hill, Great Bedwyn, Marlborough, Wilts. SN8 3LP (0870 609 1796; info@gapguru.com/ www.gapguru.com)

GAP SPORTS, Willow Bank House, 84 Station Road, Marlow, Bucks. SL7 1NX (0870 837

9797; info@gapsports.com/ www.gapsports.com)

gapwork.com – 0113-274 0252; info@gapwork.com/ www.gapwork.com)

Gap Year NZ and *PlaceMe NZ,* Leeds Innovation Centre, 103 Clarendon Rd, Leeds LS2 9DF (0870 4020 606/ fax 0870 4020 607; info@gapyear-newzealand.co.uk/ www. gapyear-newzealand.co.uk)

Global Choices, Barkat House, 116-118 Finchley Road, London NW3 5HT (020-7433 2501; info@globalchoices.co.uk/ www.globalchoices.co.uk)

Global Experiences, 1010 Pendleton St, Alexandria, VA 22314 (1-877-432-2762/ fax 703-519-0650; admin@globalexperiences.com/ www.globalexperiences.com)

Global Crew Network, 23 Old Mill Gardens, Berkhamsted, Herts. HP4 2NZ (07773 361959 or 01442 389153; info@globalcrewnetwork.com/ www.www.globalcrewnetwork.com)

Global Vision International (GVI), Amwell Farmhouse, Nomansland, Wheathampstead, St. Albans, Herts. AL4 8EJ (0870 608 8898; www.gvi.co.uk). Also in USA: PO Box 8124, Delray Beach, FL 33482-8124 (1-888-653-6028; www.gviusa.com)

Goethe Institut, 50 Princes Gate, London SW7 2PH (020-7596 4000; german@london. goethe.org)

GoXPLOR, 47 Old Main Road; Suite 7a Cowell Park; Hillcrest, 3610; Kwa Zulu Natal; South Africa (+27 31 765 1818/ fax +27 31 765 4781; wildlife@goxploreafrica.com/ www.goxploreafrica.com)

Greenforce, 11-15 Betterton St, Covent Garden, London WC2H 9BP (020-7470 8888/ fax 020-379 0801; info@greenforce.org/ www.greenforce.org)

Gwendalyne, c/o Twin Training and Travel Ltd, 2nd Floor, 67-71 Lewisham High St, Lewisham, London SE13 5JX (020-8297 3251/ fax 020-8297 0984; info@gwendalyne. com/ www.gwendalyne.com)

Holidaybreak, Overseas Recruitment Department (Ref TGY/05) – (01606 787525; www. holidaybreakjobs.com)

IAESTE UK, International Association for the Exchange of Students for Technical Experience, Education & Training Group, British Council, 10 Spring Gardens, London SW1A 2BN (020-7389 4774/4771/ fax 020-7389 4426; iaeste@britishcouncil.org/ www.iaeste.org.uk)

IALC (International Association of Language Centres), Lombard House, 12/17 Upper Bridge St, Canterbury CT1 2NF (01227 769007/ fax 01227 769014; info@ialc.org/ www.ialc.org)

IBM UK, PO Box 41, North Harbour, Portsmouth PO6 3AU (023 92 564104 – Student Recruitment Hotline) or 023 92 283777; student_pgms@uk.ibm.com/ www-5.ibm. com/employment/uk)

ICYE: Inter-Cultural Youth Exchange, Latin American House, Kingsgate Place, London NW6 4TA (tel/fax 020-7681 0983; info@icye.org.uk/ www.icye.org.uk)

IEPUK Ltd, The Old Rectory, Belton-in-Rutland, Oakham, Rutland LE15 9LE (01572 717381/ fax 01572 717343; info@iepuk.com/ www.iepuk.com)

InterExchange Inc, 161 Sixth Avenue, New York, NY 10013 (212-924-0446; info@interexchange.org/ www.interexchange.org)

International Academy, St Hilary Court, Copthorne Way, Culverhouse Cross, Cardiff CF5 6ES (02920 672500/ fax 02920 672510; info@theinternationalacademy.com/ www. theinternationalacademy.com)

International Exchange Center (IEC), 89 Fleet St, London EC4Y 1DH (020-7583 9116/ fax 020-7583 9117; isecinfo@btconnect.com/ www.isecworld.co.uk)

International Student Placement Centre (ISPC), Level 8, 32 York Street, Sydney, NSW, 2000 (02-9279 0100/ fax 02-9279 1028; info@ispc.com.au/ www.ispc.com.au)

Interspeak Placements and Homestays, Stretton Lower Hall, Stretton, Malpas, Cheshire SY14 7HS (01829 250641; enquiries@interspeak.co.uk/ www.interspeak.co.uk)

Involvement Volunteers, PO Box 218, Port Melbourne, Victoria 3207, Australia (03-9646 9392/ fax 03-9646 5504; ivworldwide@volunteering.org.au/ www.volunteering.org. au). German office: IVDE, Volksdorfer Strasse 32, 22081 Hamburg (+49 41269450; ivgermany@volunteering.org.au)

IST Plus Ltd, Rosedale House, Rosedale Road, Richmond, Surrey TW9 2SZ (020-8939 9057; info@istplus.com/ www.istplus.com)

i-to-i, Woodside House, 261 Low Lane, Horsforth, Leeds LS18 5NY (0870 333 2332/ fax 0113-205 4619; info@i-to-i.com/ www.i-to-i.com). Also in USA: 190 E 9th Avenue, Suite 350, Denver, CO 80203 (800-985-4864/ fax 303-765 5327; usca@i-to-i.com)

IVS - International Voluntary Service, www.ivs-gb.org.uk. *IVS South,* Old Hall, East Bergholt, Colchester CO7 6TQ (01206 298215; ivssouth@ivs-gb.org.uk); *IVS North,* Oxford Place Centre, Oxford Place, Leeds LS1 3AX (0113-246 9900/ fax 0113-246 9910; ivsnorth@ivs-gb.org.uk); *IVS Scotland,* 7 Upper Bow, Edinburgh EH1 2JN (0131-226 6722/ fax 0131-226 6723; scotland@ivs-gb.org.uk)

JET (Japan Exchange &Teaching) Programme, c/o JET Desk, Japanese Embassy, 101-104 Piccadilly, London W1J 7JT (020-7465 6668/6670; info@jet-uk.org/ www.jet-uk.org). 85, 363

Jobs in the Alps, 17 High Street, Gretton, Northants NN17 3DE (01536 771150/ fax 01536 771914; info@jobs-in-the-alps.com/ www.jobs-in-the-alps.com)

John Hall Pre-University Course, 12 Gainsborough Road, Ipswich, Suffolk IP4 2UR (01473 251223/ fax 01473 288009; info@johnhallpre-university.com/www.johnhallvenice.co.uk)

JST Youth Leadership @ Sea Scheme, Jubilee Sailing Trust, Hazel Road, Woolston, Southampton SO19 7GB (023-8044 9108/ fax 023-8044 9145; info@jst.org.uk/ www.jst.org.uk)

Keycamp Holidays, Overseas Recruitment Department (Ref TGY/05), Hartford Manor, Greenbank Lane, Northwich, CW8 1HW (01606 787525; www.holidaybreakjobs.com)

Kibbutz Representatives, 16 Accommodation Road, London NW11 8EP (020-8458 9235/ fax 020-8455 7930; enquiries@kibbutz.org.uk/ www.kibbutz.org.il)

Kibbutz Program Center, Volunteer Department, 18 Frishman St, Cnr. 90 Ben Yehuda St, Tel Aviv 61030, Israel (03-527 8874/524 6156; fax 03-523 9966; kpc@volunteer.co.il/ www.kibbutz.org.il)

Kwa Madwala, PO Box 192, Hectorspruit 1330, South Africa (+27 13-792 4219/ fax +27 13-792 4534; info@kwamadwala.co.uk/ www.kwamadwala.co.za/gap_year.htm)

Lanacos, 64 London Road, Dunton Green, Sevenoaks, Kent TN13 2UG (01732 462309; languages@lanacos.com/ www.lanacos.com)

Landdienst-Zentralstelle/Service Agricole, Central Office for Voluntary Farm Work, Mühlegasse 13 (Postfach 728), 8025 Zürich, Switzerland (1-261 44 88/ fax 1-261 44 32; admin@landdienst.ch)

Language Courses Abroad Ltd, 67 Ashby Road, Loughborough, Leicestershire LE11 3AA (01509 211612/ fax 01509 260037; info@languagesabroad.co.uk/ www.languagesabroad.co.uk)

Launchpad Australia, PO Box 2525, Fitzroy, VIC 306, Australia (1300 851 826 or +61 3 9419 9147/ fax +61 3-9445 9375; workingholiday@launchpadaustralia.com/ www.launchpadaustralia.com)

The Leap Overseas Ltd, 121 High St, Marlborough, Wilts. SN8 1LZ (01672 519922/ fax 01672 519944: info@theleap.co.uk/ www.theleap.co.uk).

Leiths School of Food and Wine, 21 St. Albans Grove, London W8 5BP (020-7229 0177/ fax 020-7937 5257; info@leiths.com/ www.leiths.com)

Leonardo da Vinci Programme, British Council, 10 Spring Gardens, London SW1A 2BN; 020-7389 4174/ fax 020-7389 4627; leonardo@britishcouncil.org/ www.leonardo.org.uk)

Madventurer, The Old Casino, 1-4 Forth Lane, Newcastle-upon-Tyne NE1 5HX (0845 121 1996/ fax 0191-269 9490; tribe@madventurer.com/ www.madventurer.com)

Malaca Instituto, Calle Cortada 6, Cerrado de Calderón, 29018 Málaga, Spain (+34 952-29 3242/ fax +34 952-29 6316; gapyear@malacainstituto.com/ www.MalacaInstituto.com)

Mark Warner, 0870 033 0750 (www.markwarner-recruitment.co.uk)

Millennium Volunteers, Youth Volunteering Team, Room E4C, Department for Education and Skills, Moorfoot, Sheffield S1 4PQ (0800 917 8185; millennium.volunteers@dfes. gsi.gov.uk/ www.millenniumvolunteers.gov.uk)

MondoChallenge, Milton House, Gayton Rd, Milton Malsor, Northampton NN7 3AB (01604 858225/ fax 01604 859323; info@mondochallenge.org/ www.mondochallenge.org)

Mountbatten Internship Programme, Abbey House, 74-76 St John St, 5th Floor, London EC1M 4DZ (020-7253 7759/ fax 020-7831 7018; www.mountbatten.org)

natives.co.uk, 39-40 Putney High St, London SW15 1FP (08700 463355/ fax 08700 62636; info@natives.co.uk/ www.natives.co.uk)

New York Film Academy, 100 E 17th St, New York, NY 10003 (212-674-4300/ fax 212-477-1414; film@nyfa.com/ www.nyfa.com)

Nonstop Ski & Snowboard, Shakespeare House, 168 Lavender Hill, SW11 5TF (0870 241 8070/fax 020-7801 6201; info@nonstopski.com/ www.nonstopski.com).

Oasis Overland, The Marsh, Henstridge, Somerset BA8 0TF (01963 363400/ fax 01963 363200; info@oasisoverland.co.uk/ www.oasisoverland.co.uk)

Oasis Trust, 115 Southwark Bridge Road, London SE1 0AX (020-7450 9000/ fax 020-7450 9001; enquiries@oasistrust.org/ www.oasistrust.org)

Objective Travel Safely Ltd, Bragborough Lodge Farm, Braunston, Daventry, Northants NN11 7HA (01788 899029/ fax 01788 891259; office@objectiveteam.com/ www. objectivegapsafety.com)

Ocean Youth Trust South, Spur House, 1, The Spur, Alverstoke, Gosport, Hampshire PO12 2NA (0870 241 2252/ fax 0870 909 0230; office@oytsouth.org/ www.oytsouth.org)

Operation Wallacea, Hope House, Old Bolingbroke, Nr Spilsby, Lincolnshire PE23 4EX (01790 763194/ fax 01790 763825; info@opwall.com/ www.opwall.com)

Orangutan Foundation, 7 Kent Terrace, London, NW1 4RP (020-7724 2912/ fax 020-7706 2613; info@orangutan.org.uk/ www.orangutan.org.uk)

Outreach International, Bartletts Farm, Hayes Road, Compton Dundon, Somerset TA11 6PF (tel/fax 01458 274957; gap@Outreachinternational.co.uk/ www.outreachinternational. co.uk)

Overseas Working Holidays, Level 1, 51 Fife Road, Kingston, Surrey KT1 1SF (0845 344 0366 or 020-8547 3664/ fax 0870 460 4578; info@owh.co.uk/ www.owh.co.uk)

Oxford Media and Business School, Rose Place, Oxford OX1 1SB (01865 240963/ fax 01865 242783; courses@oxfordbusiness.co.uk/ www.oxfordbusiness.co.uk)

Peak Leaders UK Ltd, Mansfield, Strathmiglo, Fife KY14 7QE, Scotland (01337 860079/ fax 01337 868176; info@peakleaders.com/ www.peakleaders.com)

People Tree Gap Year Placement, 215, 2nd floor, Somdutt Chambers II, 9 Bhikaji Cama Place, 110 066 New Delhi, India (011-26174206/ 26193247/ 26163098; peopletree@ gapyearinindia.com or timeless@vsnl.com/ www.gapyearinindia.com). London office: Flat 8, 105 Westbourne Terrace, London W2 6QT (020-7402 5576; fax 020-7262 7561)

Piccola Università Italiana, Largo Antonio Pandullo 6, 89861 Tropea, Italy (0963-603284/ fax 0963-61786; info@piccolauniversitaitaliana.com/ www.piccolauniversitaitaliana. com)

Planet Wise, 10 Swan St, Eynsham, Oxfordshire, OX29 4HU (0870 200 0220; info@PlanetWise.net; www.PlanetWise.net)

PricewaterhouseCoopers, Southwark Towers, 32 London Bridge Street, London SE1 9SY (0808 100 1500 – Student Information Line); schoolsteam@uk.pwc.com/ www.pwc. com/uk/careers)

Projects Abroad – see Teaching & Projects Abroad

Project Trust, Hebridean Centre, Ballyhough, Isle of Coll, Argyll PA78 6TE (01879 230444/ fax 01879 230357; info@projecttrust.org.uk/ www.projecttrust.org.uk). Also: 12 East Passage, London EC1A 7LP (020-7796 1170/ fax 020-7796 1172)

Queen's Business & Secretarial College, 24 Queensberry Place, London SW7 2DS (020-7589 8583; info@qbsc.ac.uk/ www.qbsc.ac.uk)

Quest Overseas, The North West Stables, Borde Hill Estate, Balcombe Road, Haywards Heath, West Sussex RH16 1XP (01444 474744/ fax 020-8637 7623;

emailus@questoverseas.com/ www.questoverseas.com).

Raleigh International, Raleigh House, 27 Parsons Green Lane, London SW6 4HZ (020-7371 8585/ fax 020-7371 5116; info@raleigh.org.uk/ www.raleighinternational.org)

Rank Foundation Gap Award Scheme, 28 Bridgegate, Hebden Bridge, West Yorks. HX7 8EX (01422 845172/ fax 01422 844329; charles.harris@rankfoundation.com/ www.rankfoundation.com)

Royal Society for the Protection of Birds (RSPB), The Lodge, Sandy, Bedfordshire SG19 2DL (01767 680551/ fax 01767 692365; volunteers@rspb.org.uk/ www.rspb.org.uk/ volunteering/residential)

Safetrek, East Culme, Cullompton, Devon EX15 1NX (tel/fax 01884 839704; info@safetrek. co.uk/ www.safetrek.co.uk)

SCORE/Sports Coaches' OutReach, 2nd Floor, Satbel Centre, 2 de Smit St, Greenpoint (PO Box 4989, Cape Town, 8000), South Africa; 21-418 3140/ fax 21-4181549; info@score.org.za/ www.score.org.za)

S.I.B.S. Ltd, Beech House, Commercial Road, Uffculme, Devon EX15 3EB (01884 841330/ fax 01884 841377; trish@sibs.co.uk/ www.sibs.co.uk)

Ski-Exp-Air, 770 Colonel Jones, Ste. Foy, Québec GIX 3K9, Canada (418-654-9071/ mobile 418-520-6669; info@ski-exp-air.com/ www.ski-exp-air.com)

Ski Le Gap, 220 Wheeler St, Mont Tremblant, Quebec J8E 1V3, Canada (+001-819-429-6599 or freephone from England 0800 328 0345/ fax +001-819-425-7074; info@skilegap.com/ www.skilegap.com)

Specialist Holidays Group, Kings Place, 12-42 Wood St, Kingston upon Thames, Surrey KT1 1SH (0845 055 0258; overseasrecruitment@s-h-g.co.uk/ www.shgjobs.co.uk.)

Sport Lived Ltd, The Innovation Centre, 103 Clarendon Road, Leeds LS2 9DF (0870 9503837; info@sportlived.co.uk/ www.sportlived.co.uk)

SPW – Students Partnership Worldwide, 2nd Floor, Faith House, 7 Tufton St, London SW1P 3QB (020-7222 0138/ fax 020-7233 0008; spwuk@gn.apc.org/ www.spw.org)

STA Travel – 0870 160 6070; www.statravel.co.uk

STEP (Shell Technology Enterprise Programme), 11-13 Goldsmith Street, Nottingham NG1 5JS (0115 941 5900/ fax 0115 950 8321; enquiries@step.org.uk/ www.step.org.uk)

Sudan Volunteer Programme, 34 Estelle Road, London NW3 2JY (tel/fax 020-7485 8619; davidsvp@blueyonder.co.uk)

Swiss Hotel Association, Monbijoustrasse 130, 3001 Bern, Switzerland (+41 31-370 43 33/ fax 031-370 43 34; hoteljob.be@swisshotels.ch / www.hoteljob.ch)

Tall Ships Youth Trust, 2A The Hard, Portsmouth, Hants. PO1 3PT (023-9832 2055/ fax 023-9281 5769; info@tallships.org/ www.tallships.org)

Tante Marie School of Cookery, Woodham House, Carlton Road, Woking, Surrey GU21 4HF (01483 726957/ fax 01483 724173; info@tantemarie.co.uk/ www.tantemarie.co.uk)

TANZED, 80 Edleston Road, Crewe, Cheshire CW2 7HD (01270 509994; enquiries@tanzed.org/ www.tanzed.org)

Teaching & Projects Abroad, Aldsworth Parade, Goring, West Sussex BN12 4TX (01903 708300/ fax 01903 501026; info@teaching-abroad.co.uk/ www.teaching-abroad.co.uk)

Tearfund, 100 Church Road, Teddington, Middlesex TW11 8QE (020-8943 7777; transform@tearfund.org/ http://youth.tearfund.org/transform)

Tema Theatre Company Ltd, A1 Value Office, 225-229 Church Street, Blackpool, Lancashire, FY1 3PB (01253 299988 or in Ghana +233 24 310 6066/ fax in Ghana +233 22 413 822; Clare@tematema.com/ www.tematema.com)

Travellers, 7 Mulberry Close, Ferring, West Sussex BN12 5HY (01903 502595/ fax 01903 500364; info@travellersworldwide.com/ www.travellersworldwide.com)

TravelPharm – www.travelpharm.com

Trekforce Expeditions, Naldred Farm Offices, Borde Hill Lane, Haywards Heath, West Sussex RH16 1XR (01444 474123; info@trekforce.org.uk/ www.trekforce.org.uk)

UCAS, Rosehill, New Barn Lane, Cheltenham, Glos. GL52 3LZ (01242 222444; Enquiries line 0870 1122211; enquiries@ucas.ac.uk/ www.ucas.com)

UK Sailing Academy, West Cowes, Isle of Wight PO31 7PQ (01983 294941/ fax 01983 295938; info@uksa.org/ www.uksa.org)

Ultimate Gap Year, 5 Beaumont Crescent, London W14 9LX (020-7386 9101; info@ultimategapyear.co.uk/ www.ultimategapyear.co.uk)

UNA Exchange, United Nations Association, Temple of Peace, Cathays Park, Cardiff CF10 3AP, Wales (029-2022 3088/ fax 029-2022 2540; info@unaexchange.org/ www.unaexchange.org)

UNIPAL (Universities' Trust for Educational Exchange with Palestinians (UNIPAL), BCM UNIPAL, London EC1N 3XX (www.unipal.org.uk)

Vacation Work Publications, 9 Park End St, Oxford OX1 1HJ (01865 241978/ fax 01865 790885/ www.vacationwork.co.uk)

VAE Teachers Kenya, Bell Lane Cottage, Pudleston, Nr. Leominster, Herefordshire HR6 0RE (01568 750329/ fax 01568 750636; vaekenya@hotmail.com/ www.vaekenya.co.uk)

Venture Co Worldwide, The Ironyard, 64-66 The Market Place, Warwick CV34 4SD (01926 411122/ fax 01926 411133; mail@ventureco-worldwide.com/ www.ventureco-worldwide.com)

Venue Holidays, 1 Norwood St, Ashford, Kent TN23 1QU (01233 649950/ fax 01233 634494; jobs@venueholidays.co.uk/ www.venueholidays.co.uk)

Village Camps, rue de la Morache, 1260 Nyon, Switzerland (022-990 9450/ fax 022-990 9494; personnel@villagecamps.ch/ www.villagecamps.com)

Vis à Vis, 2-4 Stoneleigh Park Road, Epsom KT19 0QT (020-8786 8021/ fax 020-8786 8086; info@visavis.org/ www.visavis.org)

VisitOz Scheme, Springbrook Farm, MS 188, Goomeri, 4601 Queensland, Australia (07-4168 6106/ fax 07-4168 6155; info@visitoz.org/ www.visitoz.org). UK Contacts: Will and Julia Taunton-Burnet, Visitoz UK, 49 Hurst Lane, Oxford OX2 9PR (01865 861516; Mobiles 07966 528644 or 07771 992352; will@visitoz.org)

Volunteers for Peace, 1034 Tiffany Road, Belmont, Vermont 05730 (802-259-2759; vfp@vfp.org/ www.vfp.org)

Wild at Heart, 47 Old Main Rd, Suite 7a, Cowell Park, Hillcrest, Kwa-Zulu Natal, 3610 South Africa (31-765 2947/ fax 31-765 7245; billy@wah.co.za/ www.wah.co.za)

Wind, Sand & Stars, 6 Tyndale Terrace, London N1 2AT (020-7359 7551/ fax 020-7359 4936; office@windsandstars.co.uk/ www.windsandstars.co.uk)

Winston Churchill Memorial Trust, 15 Queen's Gate Terrace, London SW7 5PR (www.wcmt.org.uk)

World Challenge Expeditions, Black Arrow House, 2 Chandos Road, London NW10 6NF (020-8728 7200; welcome@world-challenge.co.uk/ www.world-challenge.co.uk)

World Exchange, St Colm's International House, 23 Inverleith Terrace, Edinburgh EH3 5NS (0131-315 4444/ fax 0131-315 2222; we@stcolms.org)

Worldwide Volunteering for Young People, 7 North Street Workshops, Stoke sub Hamdon, Somerset TA14 6QR (01935 825588/ fax 01935 825775; worldvol@worldvol.co.uk/ www.wvv.org.uk)

WWOOF (World Wide Opportunities on Organic Farms), PO Box 2675, Lewes, East Sussex BN7 1RB (01273 476286; hello@wwoof.org/ www.wwoof.com)

Year for God, Holmsted Manor, Staplefield Road, Cuckfield, West Sussex RH17 5JF (01444 440229/fax 01444 450770; YWAM@holmsted.org.uk/ www.holmsted.org.uk)

Year in Industry, The University of Southampton, Southampton SO17 1BJ (02380 597061; enquiries@yini.org.uk/ www.yini.org.uk)

Year Out Drama Company, Stratford-upon-Avon College, Alcester Road, Stratford-upon-Avon, Warks. CV37 9QR (01789 266245/ fax 01789 267524; yearoutdrama@stratford.ac.uk)

Year Out Group, Queensfield, 28 Kings Road, Easterton, Wilts. SN10 4PX (07980 395789; info@yearoutgroup.org/ www.yearoutgroup.org)

Young Explorers' Trust, c/o YET Secretary, Stretton Cottage, Wellow Road, Ollerton, Newark, Notts. NG22 9AX (tel/fax 01623 861027; ted@theyet.org/ www.theyet.org)

Youth Action for Peace UK (YAPUK), PO Box 43670, London, SE22 0XX (08701 657927; action@yap-uk.org/ www.yap-uk.org)

Youth for Development, 317 Putney Bridge Road, London SW15 2PN (020-8780 7500/ fax 020-8780 7300; yfd@vso.org.uk/ www.vso.org.uk/volunteering/youth)

Youth for Understanding UK, 15 Hawthorn Road, Erskine, Renfrewshire PA8 7BT (tel/fax 0141-812 5561; yfu@holliday123.freeserve.co.uk/ www.yfu.org)

Youth Hostels Association, Recruitment Department, PO Box 6030, Matlock, Derbyshire DE4 3XA (01629 592650; jobopportunities@yha.org.uk/ www.yha.org.uk). YHA HQ: Trevelyan House, Dimple Road, Matlock, Derbyshire DE4 3YH (0870 770 8868)

Youth with a Mission, Highfield Oval, Harpenden, Herts AL5 4BX (01582 463216/ fax 01582 463213; enquiries@oval.com/ www.ywam-england.com)

Vacation Work Publications

Vacation Work Publications, 9 Park End Street, Oxford OX1 1HJ
Tel 01865-241978 Fax 01865-790885

Visit us online for more information on our unrivalled range of titles for work,
travel and gap years, readers' feedback and regular updates:

www.vacationwork.co.uk

Books are available in the USA from
The Globe Pequot Press, Guilford, Connecticut
www.globepequot.com